IN DEFENSE OF FREEDOM

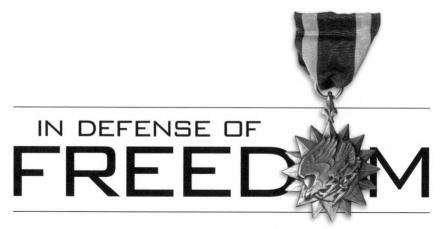

IN DEFENSE OF
FREED M

Stories of Courage and Sacrifice of World War II Army Air Forces Flyers

*To Michael with
best wishes —
Wolfgang E Samuel
2/04/2016*

WOLFGANG W. E. SAMUEL

COLONEL, UNITED STATES AIR FORCE (RETIRED)

FOREWORD BY JAMES F. TENT

UNIVERSITY PRESS OF MISSISSIPPI / JACKSON

www.upress.state.ms.us

The University Press of Mississippi is a member
of the Association of American University Presses.

Copyright © 2015 by University Press of Mississippi
All rights reserved
Manufactured in the United States of America

First printing 2015
∞
Library of Congress Cataloging-in-Publication Data

Samuel, Wolfgang W. E.
In defense of freedom : stories of courage and sacrifice of World War II Army Air Forces
flyers / Wolfgang W.E. Samuel, Colonel, United States Air Force (Retired) ; foreword by
James F. Tent.
pages cm
Includes bibliographical references and index.
ISBN 978-1-62846-217-3 (cloth : alk. paper) — ISBN 978-1-62674-594-0 (ebook) 1. World
War, 1939–1945—Personal narratives, American. 2. World War, 1939–1945—Aerial opera-
tions, American. 3. United States. Army Air Forces—Biography. 4. Air pilots, Military—
United States—Biography. 5. World War, 1939–1945—Campaigns. I. Title.
D790.2.S26 2015

940.54'49730922—dc23   2014045127

British Library Cataloging-in-Publication Data available

*Dedicated to the young men of the
United States Army Air Forces who flew into
the face of fear to free our world from tyranny.*

*When they finished their work, in spite
of horrific losses, the Empire of the Rising Sun
was history, as was Hitler's Germany and
Mussolini's Italy.*

*Their courage and sacrifice helped make possible
the world we now live in.*

*We owe them great thanks for what they
accomplished and the sacrifices they made
for you and me.*

CONTENTS

Contents

Contents

TERMS AND ABBREVIATIONS

AAA	Antiaircraft artillery
AAF	Army Air Forces
AFB	Air Force Base
AGL	Above ground level
Aileron	Moveable wing control surface to bank airplane
Bf	Bayrische Flugzeugwerke (builder of the Bf 109 and Bf 110), renamed Messerschmitt A.G. in 1938. All subsequent Messerschmitt aircraft designs received the Me instead of the Bf prefix.
CG	Center of gravity
CIA	Central Intelligence Agency
CPMB	Captured Personnel and Materiel Branch (AAF)
DFC	Distinguished Flying Cross
DulagLuft	Durchgangslager at Oberursel—the initial POW processing center for Allied airmen shot down over Germany or occupied countries
ECM	Electronic countermeasures
EGT	Exhaust gas temperature
ETO	European Theater of Operations
EW	Electronic warfare
FAA	Federal Aviation Administration
Flak	German antiaircraft gun (Fliegerabwehrkanone)
Flap	Moveable winglet at inboard trailing edge of wing to provide increased lift at reduced airspeed
GCA	Ground Control Approach radar
Gestapo	German—Geheime Staatspolizei (secret police under the Nazis)
ILS	Instrument Landing System
IP	Initial Point (entering a bomb run against a target)
IR	Infrared

Luftwaffe	German Air Force
MiG	Russian aircraft designed by the Mikoyan and Gurovich design bureau such as the MiG 15/17/19 and 21
MP	Military police
MTO	Mediterranean Theater of Operations
NCO	Noncommissioned officer
OSS	Office of Special Services (predecessor organization to the CIA)
POW	Prisoner of war
PSP	Perforated steel planking
RAF	Royal Air Force (United Kingdom)
Rally Point	Where the formation of bombers reassembles after the bomb run
RCAF	Royal Canadian Air Force
RLM	Reichsluftfahrtministerium, the Nazi German air staff
ROK	Republic of Korea (South Korea)
RPM	Revolutions per minute (measure of combustion engine efficiency)
R&R	Rest & Recreation
RTU	Replacement training unit
SAC	Strategic Air Command
SAM	Surface to air missile
SEA	Southeast Asia
SHAEF	Supreme Headquarters Allied Expeditionary Force (WW II Europe)
SRS	Strategic Reconnaissance Squadron
SRW	Strategic Reconnaissance Wing
StalagLuft	POW camp administered by the German air force—Standard Lager Luftwaffe—followed by a Roman numeral to designate the camp number
Stall	The point at which a wing no longer produces lift
TDY	Temporary duty
TEWS	Tactical Electronic Warfare Squadron
TRS	Tactical Reconnaissance Squadron
TRW	Tactical Reconnaissance Wing
USAAF	United States Army Air Forces
USAF	United States Air Force
USAFE	United States Air Forces Europe (the former USSTAF)
USSTAF	United States Strategic Air Forces (WW II Europe)
Volkssturm	German home guard equivalent of WW II (old men/young boys)
ZI	Zone of Interior (WW II term for US)

ACKNOWLEDGMENTS

I want to express my thanks, gratitude, and appreciation to those very special members of a fast-vanishing generation who over the years consented to be interviewed and shared with me their often very personal experiences in war. It doesn't matter how noble a war may have been, how justified it was—those who were directly involved in combat emerge from the experience as changed men, never again to see the world quite the way it was before it all started, before they saw comrades and friends die, before they saw the incredible agony, destruction, and brutality that only war can produce. Many of them have gone "west" and I want to express my appreciation to their families as well, who provided original documents, pictures, and insights so I could complete this tribute to the flyers whom I so greatly admire. I have a personal preference for portraying history through the eyes of those who shaped and made it, and therefore, whenever possible, I used their words to describe events they were directly involved in. I edited interviews only for clarity and brevity, and at times added factual background to give their experiences the proper contexts.

My thanks goes to Yvonne Kinkaid from the Air Force Office of History, who generously assisted me in locating critical information on Operation Market Garden and the associated air effort, as well as on unique, and at the time highly classified, air operations against the Third Reich. Paul Andrews and Axel Kornfuehrer reviewed aspects of this book, and I am grateful for their candid comments and suggestions. As she has for past books I've written, my wife, Joan, went over every page of this book editing for punctuation, spelling, and clarity of text. I also want to especially thank Dr. James F. Tent, a historian of the first order and recognized expert on aspects of the Third Reich, for consenting to write a concise and meaningful foreword, putting the brutality of the air war over Europe in perspective. The accompanying pictures in this book are especially important, giving life to each story told. Obviously, many of the pictures came from those I interviewed but as the book evolved,

I received pictorial contributions from as far away as Germany—such as from Herr Martin Frauenheimer, a pilot and historian, who resides near the former World War II Me 262 air base of Achmer. It was Samuel "Sam" Whitt II who presented me with a booklet of World War II poetry written by the men who fought the war in the ETO. The poems provided me with a unique perspective on the brutality of war. Finally, I want to thank Mr. Craig Gill, editor-in-chief at the University Press of Mississippi, and the entire staff, for their continued support. This is the fifth book of mine they have shepherded through a complex publication process—and I am really pleased that they have chosen to do this book. I totally enjoy working with them—a dedicated, competent, and approachable group of men and women whose aim is to help an author produce the best book possible. It was a pleasure to write and assemble *In Defense of Freedom: Stories of Courage and Sacrifice of World War II Army Air Forces Flyers*. I hope it will be an equally enjoyable experience for readers.

—Wolfgang W. E. Samuel
Colonel, US Air Force (Retired)
Fairfax Station, Virginia

FOREWORD

Many successful Americans come from stable, middle-class families. They are educated in American public schools and universities, then enter professions wherein they use their talents to pursue successful careers. Admittedly, this idyllic profile does not fit all distinguished Americans. There are many exceptions. One of those exceptions is Wolfgang Samuel, the author of this memorable book. Wolf has led at least three lives, or rather, it can be said that his long, productive life has fallen into three distinct phases: a horrific, deprived childhood and youth in World War II Germany, an extraordinary career as a professional soldier/airman in the US Air Force, and finally, as an accomplished author of autobiographies, vivid biographical sketches, and fascinating accounts of aviation history. However, if a reader were to ask Wolf to identify his greatest accomplishment in life, he most likely would reply: I became an American.

In *In Defense of Freedom: Stories of Courage and Sacrifice of World War II Army Air Forces Flyers*, Wolfgang ties it all together: autobiography, biography, and a refreshing examination of aviation history from World War II through both the jet age and the crucial phases of the Cold War. He ties it all together with his compelling prose. His love and admiration for the heroes of his childhood and youth shine through as he connects their lives to his own: one dedicated to public service as an avid aviator who, like them, defended his chosen country, serving alongside many of them in succeeding wars, be they hot or cold. What about those American airmen who first came into Wolfgang's life in World War II and who became his heroes during the Berlin airlift of 1948/49? This book is a graphic reminder of how heroic and totally necessary they were to Allied victory over Hitler, Mussolini, and the Empire of Japan. A few salient facts prove how deadly the peril was they faced. From the onset of USAAF operations against Germany in the summer of 1942 until late February 1944 (Big Week), American bomber crews suffered the highest casualties (KIA, wounded, MIA, and POW) of all American armed services in World War II. The premise that heavy bombers could fight their way alone to and from targets and endure acceptable losses proved devastatingly wrong. For example, the raids on Schweinfurt and its crucial ball-bearing plants in August and October 1943 saw the loss of sixty heavy bombers and their ten-man crews on each of the two raids, with scores of other aircraft so badly damaged that they were simply written off. Those losses exceeded 30 percent of the attacking force. The chances of a bomber crew surviving twenty-five missions and a rotation home—as finally happened with the crew of the *Memphis Belle*—were, statistically speaking, nearly impossible. A member of a heavy bomber crew in the Eighth Air Force in the period from mid-1942 to spring 1944 was less likely to survive than a US Marine fighting on Iwo Jima or Okinawa.

USAAF leadership echelons were chastened by those daunting losses. They learned to flood airfields with replacements by the day after such heavy losses so that crews entering mess halls did not find dining facilities half empty. Medical support was revolutionized to allow food services to provide diets compatible with high-altitude environments, extremely low temperatures and very high stress levels. They learned to provide periodic leaves for airmen, rest facilities, and festive occasions and became more open-minded in conferring decorations for valor and exemplary service. They also mobilized psychiatrists and other specialists to treat airmen who had to confront dangers on a regular basis that no ordinary human being would ever have to. Of course, all of the above were palliatives which might help to soften the blows. The raw courage of most of those young flyers not to let their buddies down kept them flying (their comrades on the ground and on the high seas were not much different).

What saved the American strategic bombing effort from failure? It was the advent of long-range, high-performance escort fighters, most notably the P-51 Mustang (plus the lowly drop tank) that changed the game, blasting the Luftwaffe out of the skies. Together, the heavy bombers and their new escorts achieved air supremacy in the skies over Europe by the time the Normandy invasion began. Within five months preceding the invasion they had killed or incapacitated 2,262 of the Luftwaffe's single-engine fighter pilots out of a total force of 2,395, an attrition rate of nearly 95 percent. Their replacements were youngsters with little training and no experience. General Eisenhower and his staff had been well aware that it was air power that would make the Normandy invasion a viable operation, knowing that Allied land and sea forces were not by themselves sufficient. Aerial operations over Normandy all the way up to the breakthrough into the crucial second front in August 1944 proved Ike right. Fighter-bombers blasted German tanks behind hedgerows. Heavy bombers helped blast a hole in German defenses at St. Lo, leading to that crucial breakout into a genuine second front.

Aerial warfare of 1939–45 exacted heavy costs. The Americans and British, in round numbers, lost 55,000 airmen for each nation in the ETO. Looking at the air losses for both sides shows that well over 200,000 young airmen in thin aluminum cocoons died in the skies over Europe during six years of total war. Flyer POWs present an interesting discrepancy. Britain's Royal Air Force Bomber Command registered over 55,000 KIA, but fewer than 10,000 POWs in the ETO. The USAAF also registered over 55,000 KIA/MIA, but nearly 30,000 POWs. Why were there so many more American survivors? The answer is straightforward: the escape hatches for British bombers were simply too narrow. Also, the British fought mostly at night. Thus, British aircrews had little or no warning when their aircraft were fatally struck by night fighters or flak, and the narrow hatches did the rest. Today, visitors to British military cemeteries (such as the one in Berlin) will see a beautiful cemetery's stunning centerpiece set among a long column of headstones seven ranks deep. The headstones mark the grave sites of entire seven-man crews of airmen who had manned the Lancaster, Halifax, and Stirling bombers deployed by Britain's RAF Bomber Command.

Looking forward from Normandy to ultimate victory on May 8, 1945, one sees that American and British air forces continued to play a vital role in defeating Axis forces. In the context of a remorseless total war, the Germans had accelerated their efforts on a nationwide scale to achieve victory after the defeat of the Sixth Army at Stalingrad by February 3, 1943. Thus, German scientists and technicians and the entire military-industrial complex went into high gear. The results were startling. Germany ended World War II in possession of a most impressive array of advanced weapons systems (except for two—the atomic bomb and the proximity fuse) that the Allies could not match. The Luftwaffe was flying the most advanced jet fighter/interceptor, the Me 262, which could exceed 550 mph and was 100 mph faster than the American P-51. It had a lethal sting against Allied bombers with its new air to air rockets and four 30mm cannons. Those same German scientists and engineers deployed the world's only jet reconnaissance bomber, the Arado 234, which at 540 mph was also nearly untouchable and could conduct aerial reconnaissance and bombing raids over Allied territory with impunity. The Kriegsmarine, the German navy, had also benefitted. Aerial intelligence would have been invaluable to Germany's new high performance submarines such as the Mark XXI or the shorter-range Mark XXIII with revolutionary propulsion systems that promised to renew the Battle of the Atlantic. The Wehrmacht had continued to benefit from Germany's superior tanks such as the Mark V Panther and Mark VI Tiger which were fully a generation ahead of American and British tanks. Some units carried advanced infrared night fighting scopes that no other army deployed until the 1960s. The 88mm antiaircraft guns with excellent radar guidance and Carl Zeiss optics continued to pummel Allied flyers to the very last day of the war. The Germans had the only cruise missile, the V-1, and the only ballistic missile, the V-2. What actually was it that slowed down all of these advanced weapons systems? It was identification of Germany's most vulnerable target, oil. Starting on May 12, 1944, the USAAF struck its first massive blow on German oil targets. The results for Germany's war economy were simply devastating. All of the German advanced weapons systems listed above depended on petroleum products. By May 1945, all of them had failed to save the Third Reich—but, as always, at a heavy price for the Anglo-American airmen.

The Americans had sought specific industrial bottlenecks, such as ball bearings in order to destroy crucial production of combat vehicles, versus Bomber Command's focus on burning down the cities which housed Germany's workers. Hence the raids on Schweinfurt in 1943. It was a good idea, but it failed because, once warned, German planners could and did diversify production including placing factories underground (with slave labor), as well as purchasing from the neutral industrial centers of Sweden and Switzerland. By contrast, Germany's highly complex above-ground, petrochemical refineries proved to be the true Achilles heel for the German war effort. Yet, the aircrews of the Eighth and Fifteenth Air Forces continued to pay a high price as they attacked distant, heavily defended targets such as the oil fields of Ploesti in Romania and the complex of refineries in eastern Germany. Losses to Luftwaffe fighters/interceptors decreased starting in the spring of 1944, but German AAA continued to exact a heavy toll on all Allied aircraft and their crews all the way up to VE Day. American aerial attacks on aircraft industries, air bases, railroad systems, canals, and the entire transportation system, plus the electrical grid, also played an important role in destroying German defenses, Nazi fanaticism notwithstanding. Coal piled up at mine entrances in the Ruhr, but could no longer be transported to power-generating plants and factories. Entire industries shut down in the spring of 1945, and the Rhine River ran clean for the first time in hundreds of years although no one perceived that development as an environmental victory.

The US tactical air forces played a crucial role as well. They pioneered in the development of air-ground cooperation in the ETO, led foremost by Major General Elwood "Pete" Quesada. Big burly fighter bombers, such as the Republic P-47 Thunderbolt, began evening the odds on the battlefield by strafing German armor in coordination with Allied armored columns on the ground. Quesada placed experienced tactical pilots in lead American tanks, who talked in real time by direct radio link to fellow pilots in the air to form deadly one-two punches against their German armored foes. As in nature, where agile aerial predators can ambush prey from on high, so too could

P-47s and British Typhoons render German Panthers and Tigers helpless with cannons and rockets penetrating ventilators and radiators from on high. The same tactical air forces, using the same heavy fighter bombers and fast medium bombers, engaged in far-ranging strafing runs, destroying innumerable locomotives, rolling stock, parked aircraft, trucks, river traffic, bridges, viaducts, and other targets that helped bring Nazi Germany to its knees. These victories came at a high cost in pilots' and aircrews' lives. Ground support meant strafing heavily defended targets in proximity to the ground with little chance to bail out if such was required—part of the price the airmen of the USAAF paid for final victory.

A glimpse at the aerial operations in the Pacific and East Asia is warranted. It is true that Japan achieved astounding victories in the first year of the war. Then, Japan's air forces began to atrophy with the deaths of most of its first cohort of superb flyers, and the unalterable fact that its training programs and technological infrastructure simply could not keep pace in producing skilled pilots and more advanced aircraft as the war continued. Nevertheless, there remained constant, unyielding dangers for Allied airmen from first to last as they fought in the skies over the vast Pacific and Asia. The sheer size of those theaters of operation was foremost. Airmen had to reckon with long-range missions of many hundreds of miles over open seas against targets on remote islands. Their navigation skills had to be more than just good. They had to be precise. There were few if any radio beacons or other navigational devices to aid them. There were few emergency landing strips on which to abort a mission or make an emergency landing, and all flyers feared falling into Japanese captivity. The complex piston-driven aircraft engines of the 1940s with thousands of moving parts failed frequently, a kind of sword of Damocles that hung over every crewman's head as they overflew the Pacific, often in turbulent, changeable weather. It was just such scarcities of assets, inherent mechanical weaknesses, and unpredictable weather conditions that compelled the Americans to seize formidable Iwo Jima and its invaluable air fields in 1945. Iwo Jima was simply indispensable as an emergency landing zone for crippled B-29 Super Fortresses and their escorts. At a cost of nearly 7,000 US Marines killed and another 21,000 wounded and missing, out of a total force of 75,000 troops, the Americans wrested that island from Japan's most skillful defenders in a month-long battle. Iwo Jima was worth the sacrifices. That godforsaken island played a crucial role in what proved to be the last strategic aerial campaign of World War II.

In the final strategic drives in the Pacific in 1945, the American public was made aware of the strenuous efforts mounted for air-sea rescue of American flyers in the Pacific realm. They were assured that scores of surface vessels, many more amphibious rescue aircraft, destroyer pickets, and submarines were standing by. They did the best they could. What was not admitted to the American public during the war, and has scarcely been acknowledged since, is the fact that only half of all of those American airmen who ditched in the Pacific Ocean and in the seas adjoining East Asia were rescued. The other half suffered lonely watery sometimes lingering deaths.

In spite of, and actually because of, these grim realities, it is important that the American flyers' (and Allied flyers' as well) efforts continue to be recorded for succeeding generations. Knowledgeable German specialists, like Armaments Minister Albert Speer, had known as early as the autumn of 1944 that the game was up because of ever-increasing Allied air power. Goering laughed in contempt in 1941 when President Roosevelt called for an annual production of 50,000 war planes. Fatso Goering thought that the sybaritic Americans could build refrigerators, but certainly not warplanes, nor in the quantity FDR sought. Goering was somewhat right in a sense, but not in the way he predicted. In 1944 the United States did not produce 50,000 war planes, but nearly 100,000 instead! This unique American half of the Anglo-American aerial onslaught emptied out Germany's industrial pipeline by late winter/ early spring of 1945. Allied boots on the ground did the rest. Speer had been dead right in his predictions.

In this, his latest book, Wolfgang Samuel has chosen his American heroes well. The chapters that follow prove that point in stark detail. Those flyers of World War II remain an inspiration for all of us. Wolf's book is, in a singular way, an eloquent plea to all readers not only to honor, but also to emulate his boyhood heroes of World War II. He has every right to issue that plea. After all, Wolf joined the ranks and shared their dangers when German Boy became an American Boy, and in manhood developed his own distinguished flying career, one dedicated to his beloved adoptive nation.

—**James F. Tent**
Professor and University Scholar Emeritus
Chair (Retired) Department of History
University of Alabama at Birmingham

IN DEFENSE OF FREEDOM

INTRODUCTION

I am a child of war—born in 1935 in a poverty-stricken village north of Berlin. My father, Willie, served in the 100,000-man post–World War I German army in a cavalry unit garrisoned in the town of Pasewalk, near the village of my birth. In 1936, Willie transferred to the newly created Luftwaffe. By the time World War II broke out, on September 1, 1939, my small family lived in government housing in the town of Sagan, in the province of Lower Silesia, now part of Poland. My father was briefly stationed at Sagan's *Kuepper Fliegerhorst*, one of Hitler's many newly created air bases. Our housing development was close enough to the airfield for him to be able to walk to work. After the war broke out, he soon was transferred. My mother, sister, and I remained behind until January 1945 when we fled approaching Russian tanks. I recall as a very young boy—I was probably four years old—playing in a sandbox outside our apartment house when a Junkers 52 transport from the nearby air base passed overhead. I saw the pilot looking down at me from a side window. I waved at him. And I believe he waved back. I never forgot that magic moment. From that day hence I fantasized about flying my own airplane.

I was four years old when World War II broke out in Europe. I knew nothing of it. Sagan, about ninety miles southeast of Berlin, with a population of less than twenty-five thousand, was a bucolic backwater of no interest to Allied aerial target planners. The town remained untouched by war until its very end. Spring of 1944 was sunny and bright. I turned nine that February—after a very cold winter. All the winters I can recall were very cold and snowy then. My friends and I built snow forts and we sledded and skied the nearby hills outside the air base. When the sun finally made its appearance, we had tired of snow and were happy to see the snow and ice turn to water and run into the nearby Bober river. It was April, I recall, the 11th of April to be precise, when the air raid sirens wailed for the first time—a scary sound I was to hear many, many times in days to come, and it was a sound that would haunt me for much of my life. Women air raid wardens donned their helmets and

3

attempted to round up all of us children and get us to go into the basements of our apartment houses—which according to them had been built to withstand air attack. A claim that even we children doubted. We asked ourselves, how did they know there was going to be a war when they built our houses? Maybe they did—just we children didn't know that. At the time the sound of the wailing sirens was exciting and I wanted to see what happened next. I hid behind some bushes in front of our apartment house. There was utter silence where only minutes before my friends and I had screamed at each other in playful ardor. What could the Americans possibly want to bomb in our little town, I thought? Probably the air base. But then I knew the base had a prisoner-of-war camp for British and American flyers shot down over Germany. So why would they want to bomb their own people? I knew it was American planes the warning was about, because I had heard that the British only attacked at night. I hid in the bushes and waited, and waited.

Then I heard a sound I had never heard before. It sounded like a huge swarm of bees was heading straight for me, although I knew it wasn't bees, but that's what it sounded like. Then, in the distance, up in the clear blue sky far above me, I saw a dark cloud approaching. The cloud had a faintly shimmering quality to it. It grew larger, and the sound grew louder. Minutes passed. I was sure the ominous sound came from that dark cloud up high in the blue sky above. Then I recognized that it wasn't a cloud at all, but a huge formation of bombers, the sun reflecting brightly off their canopies and their many whirling propellers. The sound made by hundreds of aircraft engines churning through a cloudless spring sky was a deep, penetrating hummmmm, hummmmm, hummmmm. . . . With every minute the bombers came closer and the sound grew stronger. Windows in our apartment house began to vibrate. I could feel the vibrations in the ground below my feet penetrating my body. The huge bomber formation came closer and closer—heading straight for me. They were nearly overhead when I began to make out individual aircraft—it looked like maybe two hundred airplanes, maybe more. I had never seen so many airplanes together at one time in my life, and I lived near an air base and had seen many German war planes over the years. I knew they were B-17 bombers. I thought I knew every airplane there was—German, English, American. I was fascinated by the spectacle of the huge formation of American bombers overhead. Strangely, I wanted to be one of the unknown men high up in the sky, forgetting that they had come to bomb my country. I felt no hatred toward them, rather admiration and a deep sense of kinship. For me, a nine-year-old, it was all about the magic of flying. Then the formation made a slow, ponderous turn to the north, passing over the nearby town of Sorau. I couldn't see the bombs fall and it was too far away to hear the explosions, but after the bombers passed out of sight, a huge black mushroom-like cloud rose into the blue spring sky, and since there was no or little wind, the black cloud hung over the wounded town of Sorau for the rest of the day, until it slowly drifted away to the northeast.[1]

Years later I learned that the 303rd, 379th, and 384th Bomb Groups from the 1st Air Division of the 8th Air Force in England had fielded that force of over a hundred B-17 bombers. They were flying at an unusually low altitude of eleven thousand feet, dropping one-hundred-pound general purpose and five-hundred-pound incendiary bombs on the Focke Wulf 190 aircraft assembly plant at Sorau. As they passed, and before turning toward Sorau, they also photographed StalagLuft III, the prisoner-of-war camp at Sagan, where around eleven thousand Allied airmen, nearly all officers, were imprisoned.[2] Although living nearby at the time, I didn't know any of that. All I knew as a nine-year-old boy was that there was a POW camp over the hills from us, and on occasion at night I could see the camp lights—that was all. Nor were we boys curious about the camp until that same year when seventy-six British officers escaped and we children were forced to help look for them. It happened in March, prior to the Sorau raid. Snow still covered the ground. The trees were without leaves, the days were short and the nights long. Nearly every day the skies were grey and overcast with a never-ending drizzle chilling us children and keeping us inside. But when the news of the escape from StalagLuft III became public, Hitler Youths came looking for us children and forced us down to the Bober river to help look for the escapees. We didn't know who we were looking for, what they might look like if we ran into them or what they might do to us. We assumed the worst and were scared, and didn't look very hard. We just wanted to go home to our mothers. The movie *The Great Escape* depicts part of my life as a young child: trying to grow up, learning to read and write, playing, and, like it or not, being forced to deal with war even if none of us children understood what it was all about, nor what war was really like—bloody, brutal, and unforgiving. I would learn all that soon enough.

On January 24, 1945, war caught up with my family when Russian tanks approached within ten miles of our housing area. My mother, Hedy, little sister, Ingrid, and I, loaded down with three suitcases, trekked to the Sagan train station where we waited in the bitter cold on the exposed platform for a promised train to Berlin—which didn't arrive for another yweny-four hours. When the train did arrive, it was already full. Hedy and Ingrid managed to get on. I didn't. When the train began to move out of the station, I knew I would never see them again, and I wanted to die rather than be left behind amongst an uncaring crowd of strangers. At the last possible moment, as I was running beside the train, unseen hands yanked me off the platform and onto the train. The nightmare of that experience, told in my earlier book *German Boy*, stayed with me well into my early forties, when the nightmares of my wartime experiences, too horrendous for a little boy to cope with, finally vanished from my sleep. Only three days later, on the 27th of January, the eleven thousand or so American and British prisoners of war at StalagLuft III began their brutal march to Moosburg, Bavaria, where they were finally liberated by a unit of Patton's Third Army on April 29, 1945. The war ended on May 8, as beautiful a spring day as anyone could wish for. For the former prisoners of StalagLuft III an ordeal ended—mine was just beginning.[3]

Once the train delivered us to Berlin, bombings became a daily constant, something which each of us, young and old, dealt with in our own way. I recall turning ten in February 1945. My birthday turned out to be a dreary overcast day. There were no air raids. But the following day was a beautiful blue-sky day, and it was the day General Spaatz, the commander of the United States Strategic Air Forces in Europe, USSTAF, launched his first thousand-bomber raid against Berlin. As we sat in a basement shelter, feeling the carpet of bombs coming closer and closer, the terror of the situation hushed us all, young and old, huddled together in silence, pressing handkerchiefs, scarfs, whatever we could find, over mouths and noses to keep out the whitewash falling off the walls as the bombs burst. We survived that raid, but all of us—there were only women, children and old men in the basement shelter—knew that we would die soon, if not today, then tomorrow, or the day or night thereafter. I could not deal with the terror of those raids, and from then on, when entering the basement shelter, I forced my mind to escape into the ethereal world of the Leatherstocking series, including *The Last of the Mohicans*, books about America's early years written by James Fenimore Cooper, or one of the many Karl May books I had read about the American West and its brave Apache and Sioux Indians. I may have been physically sitting in that basement shelter during an air raid, but my mind was somewhere else, and I never again mentally experienced another raid. When it was all over, my mother, thinking I was asleep, would tap me on the shoulder and say, "Wolfgang, wake up, it's over. Time to go up." She thought I was asleep, and in a way I was. I blanked out every air raid, and for all practical purposes my mind left my body and went somewhere else. The terror of a bombing raid is not something easily put into words, even this many years later.

The last days of the war were beyond anything my young mind could have imagined. Death was all around me. We three—Hedy, Ingrid, and I—survived Russian tanks, artillery, rockets, and strafing attacks by dive-bombers, not because of anything we did, but by the grace of God. The years passed and we survived life in the Russian Zone of Occupation, eventually fleeing to the British Zone, ending up in a wretched refugee camp off one end of the Fassberg air base runway, a former German bomber base put to use by the Royal

Air Force. Life for us was all about surviving one day at a time, and focused on the very basics that sustain life—food of whatever kind, water, shelter and warmth. The winter of 1947 to 1948 was brutally cold. I would wake in the mornings with wind-driven snow covering my blanket, or whatever I was using to stay warm. The former German army barracks we lived in leaked when it rained, and the wind driven snow would find its way inside through a myriad of cracks and crevices. The bucket with our drinking water, after a cold night, would have a thin layer of ice on its surface. At age thirteen I began to lose all hope for a better life and it became my unspoken wish not to awake in the morning—just to die in my sleep. That's what I, a thirteen-year-old boy, wished for. Then I grew angry with myself for being so selfish. Wasn't I alive? So many of my young friends had died in the past three years. They no longer could feel hunger, cold, and pain. I could. How fortunate I was to still be able to experience life, no matter how difficult it seemed at times. Just as I had dealt with the terror of the bombing raids in Berlin, I found ways to create hope for myself, and once warmer spring days arrived everything began to look better—at least I wasn't so cold anymore.

I recall the fear that gripped me when in early spring of 1948 I heard about the Russians blockading the city of Berlin. The men in our camp, nearly all unemployed, predicted that if the Americans didn't stop the Russians, they would soon take over the rest of Europe. There was no one else who could stop their armies, they said. I was horrified at the thought. I had lived over two dreadful years in the Russian-occupied zone of Germany, and swore to myself that I would rather die than ever again live under a communist regime, regardless of its nationality. Then something truly wonderful happened—the first uplifting event I could recall since learning that my mother, Hedy, had not died from a Russian officer's gunshot in the summer of 1945. Euphoria overtook me that morning on my way to school in Fassberg when I saw at the airfield my first American aircraft. I felt personally saved, rescued from a terrible fate. I believed in my childish innocence that *the Americans had come to save me*—a scared and hungry young German boy. The streets of Fassberg soon filled with American uniforms—men without guns, with smiles on their faces, always ready to share a piece of chewing gum or a candy bar with a German kid. Their huge four-engine C-54 transport planes turned over my wretched camp after takeoff on their way to Berlin. They flew so low, at times I thought I could touch them. They flew day and night, rain or shine, ice or snow. I would go to sleep at night to the comforting sound of aircraft engines droning overhead—the sound of freedom for me. One December night one of them crashed just beyond our camp as it was making its usual turn to the east. I went out to the crash site three days later, a site darkened with scattered coal, spilled engine oil and fuel. Aircraft parts and engines protruded from the soft, marshy ground. I nearly cried when I saw the terrible sight where three American airmen died. Standing at that crash site deeply affected me. I wondered, as only a young boy could wonder, "Who are these Americans?" Three years earlier, when I lived in Berlin, they bombed me in massive thousand-bomber raids. Now they were here saving that same city from hunger and cold—even dying to do so. I had no heroes in my world of death and darkness. But if I wanted to be like anyone, I wanted to be like these men in their brown, often rumpled uniforms, wearing their crushed "25 mission" garrison hats, men who seemed not to know the meaning of hate. I didn't know what made these Americans do what they did, but I wanted to be just like them, maybe wear their uniform, and if such miracles were possible, better yet, fly with them. Of course, being a child of war and a total realist, I understood that such musings were the dreams of people like me, the losers of the world, and such dreams would remain just that, and would never come to pass.

Well, I was wrong—my strange fantasy became a reality. In my air force career of thirty years I not only flew with some of the men of the Berlin airlift of 1948–1949, which set the limit to Soviet expansionism in Europe; I also flew and worked with many men who spent time in StalagLuft III, who survived the brutal march in January 1945 to Moosburg, and even some who bombed me while I was still a child in Berlin. None of these men I met and served with ever personalized their war experiences. A good friend of mine who "went west" only recently had three B-17 bombers shot out from under him—he landed them, but they never flew again— and was awarded the Silver Star and several Distinguished Flying Crosses. Carl Ousley never had an easy mission, he recalled for me. I used to joke with Carl that the only reason I was still around was because he told his bombardier on a Berlin mission to offset his target by a hundred yards: "There is a German kid down there I intend to meet some years from now. I want him to stick around." We always got a good laugh out of that story. I miss Carl—my friend. I miss all of those men whose bravery gave me my freedom and a future that in my wildest dreams I could never have imagined. Most of them have gone "west" as we airmen describe the passing of our friends, but I feel a kinship with them, as if I'd been with them in their darkest hours over Germany when their machines faltered and they fell out of the sky into uncertainty. I understand their pain and marvel at the generosity toward their former enemy when it was all over.

I also know the sacrifices they made. In a little over three years of air war the 8th Air Force lost over 6,500 heavy bombers in combat and due to accidents. The latter case is frequently ignored in statistics of World War II. It didn't really matter if one died as a result of enemy action or flying into each other while assembling over one's air base—you were just as dead. Including the 3,214 B-17 and B-24 bombers lost in the Mediterranean Theater of

Operations (MTO), the total loss of heavy bombers in the ETO/MTO due to enemy action and accident came to 9,714. A total of 94,565 men were killed, wounded, became POWs, or went missing in action by the 8th, 9th, 12th, 15th, and 1st Tactical Air Forces, according to the AAF's Statistical Digest.[4] The air war over Germany was as bloody as any ground battle one might choose to compare it to fought by Americans in World War II. In this book I will share with you the life stories of some of the many men I had the privilege to call my friends—men who flew B-17s and B-24s, P-47s and P-38s, Mosquitos and B-25s. They didn't stop flying when World War II ended in 1945. Many of them went right on flying the Berlin airlift in 1948 to 1949, then found themselves involved in the Korean War, referred to at the time as a "police action," which turned as bloody as anything airmen had experienced in World War II. It was the bravery of F-51 and B-26 flyers who saved the 8th US Army in the summer of 1950 from being thrown into the Sea of Japan by the North Korean invaders. They paid a very high price for their courage, losing over 350 F-51 fighters alone, but saving the men of the 8th Army.[5] Some of them continued flying right into the early days of the Vietnam War. All said and done, it is an incredible testament to a generation of airmen who never quit their country when they were needed. They were always there, always willing to go one more time—regardless of the cost to themselves. And we, who flew combat over North Vietnam, stood on their shoulders and remembered that there was no such thing as turning back—such was and is our heritage. We all owe them a debt of gratitude for their courage and self-sacrifice, and for the example they set for every American airman of today and tomorrow. Clearly Tom Brokaw got it right when he called those who served in World War II "the greatest generation"; at least in my lifetime they were just that.

All of the men whose stories appear in this book in one way or another shaped and affected my life. Some I knew personally and flew with during my air force career, such as Joe Gyulavics, Bob Walker, and Sam Pizzo. Others were my commanders, such as "Hack" Mixson and David Jones. Some were incarcerated near where I lived in StalagLuft III, such as Art Exon, Chat Bowen, and Robert Slane, while so many others flew the Berlin airlift, which truly changed my life—among them Hal Austin, Dave Taylor, Barney Dobbs, Moe Hamill, and many others. I owe each one a debt of gratitude. When you have read their stories of commitment and sacrifice, of near death and imprisonment, of survival and "just doing my job," as they tend to refer to even the most difficult situations, then you will understand the true legacy they left behind for us all. I wished I could shake the hand of each and every one I've written about in this book—unfortunately time has taken its toll. Yet we can honor them by recalling their deeds and passing them on to the next generation—the future leaders of America.

During the Berlin airlift, Captain Robert Walker flew coal from RAF Fassberg to Berlin. Shown is a Fassberg C-54 before the delivery of the final ton of coal to Berlin.

ROBERT P. WALKER

Mosquito/C-54/B-66/Test Pilot

Advice at Dawn

Soldier, put that picture down, the time is past for dreaming.
Those soft blue eyes and a silken gown won't halt our battle scheming.
What if others win her grace—don't look back or waver.
Someone home might take your place (no one truer, braver).
No use now to ask me why the fates sent you away.
Keep your eyes and carbine dry, there's work to do today.
Regrets will get no battle won; let's heed that bugle call.
You'll come home a hero, son, or you won't come home at all.
—Lieutenant Charles J. Hackett, WWII ETO

In the days of the Berlin airlift from 1948 to 1949, in a desolate refugee camp, I lay in my bed of straw every night listening to the reassuring sounds of C-54 engines droning overhead on their way to the beleaguered city of Berlin. One of those C-54 Skymaster pilots was a young captain by the name of Robert Patrick Walker. He knew not of me down below, nor I of him flying above. But as fate would have it, many years later, in a far-off land, in a war no one yet could foresee, Bob Walker and I would be comrades in arms, wearing the same flight suits, flying the same airplanes into combat. The war we shared was called the Vietnam War.

Robert Walker went by many names in his life. His younger sister, Silvia, called him Bud; the Canadians and the English would refer to him as either Pat or Paddy, and his fellow Americans called him Bob. Whatever name anyone chose to address him by, Robert Walker was a driven young man who—like so many of his generation—always wanted to fly. By the time Bob turned ten, on March 17, 1933, the sound of an airplane overhead made him turn his head skyward. Like most youngsters of his generation, he surely was fascinated by the exploits of daring "barnstormers" like Roscoe Turner. And everyone's hero of heroes was, of course, the incredible and dashing Charles Lindbergh, the conqueror of the Atlantic in a flimsy single-engine aircraft named *The Spirit of St. Louis*, now prominently displayed in the National Air and Space Museum in Washington, DC. Flying was a seemingly impossible dream for most, but it was to come true for many youngsters in a strange way—war. Bob graduated from high school in 1941 and had followed the war in Europe with great interest, especially the exploits of the German Luftwaffe and England's desperate struggle for survival against high odds in the Battle of Britain. Bob's country, America, appeared to be sitting on the sidelines. So, like many young Americans his age, he decided to do something about it. One day, without telling anyone of what he was about to do, Bob took a train from Austin, Texas, to Detroit, crossed over to Windsor, Ontario, and joined the Royal Canadian Air Force (RCAF). By the winter of 1942 Bob was a sergeant pilot and sailed from Halifax, Nova Scotia, for England aboard the *Queen Elizabeth*, along with eight thousand Canadian troops. Bob surely had no idea what challenges lay ahead. But he was a good pilot, a natural, as they say, and he would do all right.

Once in England, RCAF Sergeant Pilot Robert Walker, along with other American volunteers, was assigned to augment a British Mosquito squadron. The Mosquito, a very fast airplane for its day and mostly built of plywood, was affectionately known to its flyers as "Mossie." Mossie bedeviled the German night skies throughout the war. With the United States entering the war against Germany in December 1941 after a seemingly delusional Adolf Hitler declared war on the United States soon after the Japanese attack on Pearl Harbor, pilots suddenly were in great demand. Men who had joined the RAF Eagle squadron or its Canadian equivalent, such as Walker, were given the option by the United States government to either "come home" or lose their citizenship. Bob shed his RCAF uniform and put on American "pinks and greens" as a first lieutenant in the Army Air Forces. Bob, however, never returned to the ZI, the Zone of Interior, as the United States was commonly referred to, for any formal officer or flight training. All Bob did was change his uniform. He continued to wear his English leather flying helmet and a dashing mustache he had become quite fond of. What surely was a downer for a Mosquito pilot like Bob was his initial assignment to the 27th Air Transport Group which had the task of ferrying newly arrived aircraft to Army Air Forces combat units in the United Kingdom.

Lieutenant General Carl A. "Tooey" Spaatz, the commander of the United States Strategic Air Forces in Europe—redesignated USAFE in 1947 with its headquarters in Wiesbaden, Germany, where I served from 1969 to 1973—was a great believer in reconnaissance operations. When first assigned to Europe by General Henry H. "Hap" Arnold in late 1942 as commanding general of the 12th Air Force in North Africa, Spaatz had Colonel Elliot Roosevelt build him a photo reconnaissance group, knowing the importance of having accurate and current battlefield information. Once Spaatz assumed command of USSTAF in January 1944, he had Elliot Roosevelt, recently promoted to brigadier general, do the same thing with the 8th Air Force as what he had done for him earlier when assigned to the 12th, form the 325th Photographic Wing, which included the 25th Bomb Group. The 25th formed at RAF Watton, County Norfolk, in February 1944. It was anything but a bomb group, its name a convenient wartime cover. The group's three squadrons specialized in all types of reconnaissance operations including weather, day and night photographic and electronic reconnaissance. In addition, the wing flew pathfinder missions for bombing operations against the Third Reich. One of the more important tasks of the 25th Bomb Group, highly classified and seldom talked about, was to provide support to the Office of Strategic Services, the OSS, the predecessor organization to the present day Central Intelligence Agency, CIA, by flying agents into and out of German-occupied territories.

Of the three squadrons assigned to the 25th Bomb Group, the 652nd Bombardment Squadron (Heavy) flew B-17 and B-24 bombers equipped, however, with appropriate meteorological equipment, flying long-range weather reconnaissance missions over the North and South Atlantic. The 653rd Bomb Squadron (Light) flew the British DeHavilland Mosquito Mark III and Mark XVI also on weather reconnaissance missions, but over German-occupied territory. In addition, aircraft of the 653rd were used to drop chaff, aluminum strips cut to the radio frequencies of German radars, in support of the 8th Air Force and RAF Bomber Command operations. Along with the 654th Bomb Squadron, the 653rd flew a limited number of Frantic missions with its Mosquitos. *Frantic* was the code name for B-17 bombing missions launched from England, landing in Russia. Then, after refueling and rearming, they were to proceed to Italy, and finally return to their bases in England. It was a concept that enjoyed only limited success, principally due to a lack of support provided by a suspicious Russian ally. It was the 654th Bombardment Squadron (Heavy Special), however, which flew the most hazardous missions assigned to the 25th Bomb Group—night photography Joker missions, day photography PRU missions, and the missions no one talked about in support of the OSS. Because of the variety of missions assigned to this squadron, it not only flew the Mosquito Mark III and Mark XVI, like its sister squadron, the 653rd, but in addition had a collection of B-25, A-26, AT-23, VC-64, and P-38 aircraft assigned. The Mosquito and the A-26, painted black, flew a total of thirty-two of these very demanding and dangerous deep-penetration missions over enemy-held territory. If you were an "airman's airman," and Paddy Walker certainly was that, then that was the kind of flying you gave an arm and a leg for. Paddy, to the British, Bob, to his American fellow flyers, was thrilled with his reassignment to the 654th Squadron of the 25th Bomb Group, having been selected personally by General Roosevelt based on his extensive flying experience in the Mosquito.[6]

Bob's early missions were relatively easy—weather reconnaissance over the Atlantic and shallow penetration photo reconnaissance missions over occupied France. By the time Operation Market Garden got itself into trouble in September 1944, the pace picked up for Walker and his navigator, Major Roy C. Conyers. Market Garden, an operation reluctantly agreed to by General Eisenhower, was an armored and airborne thrust through Holland aimed at the industrial Ruhr Valley of Germany. It was Field Marshal Sir Bernard Montgomery's brainchild. Holland was not tank country and the entire operation bogged down quickly, resulting in heavy Allied losses without showing any noteworthy gains. SHAEF, Supreme Headquarters Allied Expeditionary Force, did not know who controlled a particular bridge in Nijmegen, of *A Bridge Too Far* fame, and Walker and Conyers were to visually ascertain who held it—the Germans or the British. On September 22, Walker approached the bridge at five hundred feet above ground level (AGL), then went down to treetop level. As his Mossie passed over the bridge, he was fired on by German guns from both ends of the bridge—the bridge was in German hands. Walker recalled, "The first hit was a direct strike by 20mm- or .50-caliber rounds that disintegrated the left drop tank. I immediately punched off both tanks. The right engine was soon in flames. I feathered it and shut off fuel to that engine. We then made for the coast flying on-the-deck, but soon ran into antiaircraft fire from the German coastal batteries. We were trying to get out of range of their guns while staying near water level. I remember the water spouts from rounds hitting the sea around us. When out of range of the shore batteries I climbed into the weather, still on only one engine, to establish radio contact. All England was socked in. There was no way to reach Manston, our emergency RAF base near Dover." Nearly out of fuel, Bob and Roy finally made it into Tangmere. It took about a week to fix the aircraft before Walker could fly it back to Watton. Sadly, upon returning from this flight Roy Conyers learned that his brother-in-law, Willard Hesketh, was killed during Operation Market Garden. Hesketh was flying a C-47 pulling a glider loaded with troopers from the 101st Airborne when hit by German antiaircraft fire.[7]

Walker and Conyers, and a second navigator, Lieutenant William G. Miskho, flew together every opportunity they got. Most of their missions were night photography in the Mossie, referred to as Joker missions. Daylight photo missions were nicknamed PRU. Grey Pea missions involved chaff drops ahead of the bombers, while Red Tail Missions required them to serve as the lead aircraft for RAF Bomber Command night raids to designate their targets. Sky Wave missions involved experimental flights over occupied France testing a long-range radar system called Loran, and Mickey missions involved radar photography of bomb-run approaches to important targets. There was no dearth of action for the men of the 25th Bomb Group, and Walker, Conyers, and Miskho flew every mission there was. While most returned from their combat missions with perhaps a few holes in their aircraft or a lost engine, over a period of less than two years, twenty-seven 25th Bomb Group aircraft did not make it home. Another five aircraft were lost to nonoperational causes. Some of the losses were especially tragic. On August 12, 1944, a Mosquito flying as a weather scout ahead of a bomber formation, returning from a Frantic mission, was misidentified by a P-51 and shot down. Fortunately, the crew of two survived. Another Mosquito was downed by a P-47 on March 24, 1945. That time the Mosquito pilot was killed. The navigator ended up in StalagLuft I, near Barth, Germany. And finally, just before war's end in Europe, on April 4, 1945, a Mosquito was downed by the guns of a B-24 bomber which the Mosquito was escorting. It was not unusual for the Mosquito to be identified as an enemy aircraft, leading to many unfortunate losses. A total of eighty-four 25 Bomb Group flyers perished, and eleven more became prisoners of war.[8]

War always requires sacrifice, but it is doubtful that Paddy, or Bill, or Roy—his two navigators—dwelled on that fact of life. On November 25, 1944, Walker and Conyers departed RAF Watton on a night weather reconnaissance mission over central Germany, a Blue Stocking mission. It should have been "a piece of cake" as airmen refer to missions they consider especially easy and of low risk; but then one never knows. They took off at 01:53 hours for eastern Germany. While at flight level 270 their oxygen system failed. They dropped down to ten thousand feet, checked the equipment and thought they could chance it again. Back to altitude they went and Conyers promptly passed out. Walker came close to losing consciousness. Walker dropped down to ten thousand feet again and Conyers revived. Climbing back up to flight level 280, twenty-eight thousand feet, on emergency oxygen, they completed their mission and returned home. Of course, when they got to RAF Watton the base was weathered in, nothing unusual for England, and they diverted to another base. In war there are many ways of dying—and not always from enemy bullets.

In December of 1944 Walker began flying missions for the OSS as part of the Joan-Eleanor project (J-E). No flight plans were filed for these highly classified missions. No briefings or debriefings were recorded. There was no paper trail. For all practical purposes these missions never happened. When researching files at headquarters USAF, I found no record of any of the OSS missions flown by Robert Walker, or anyone else for that matter. The lone exception was a terse sentence in a Red Stocking post-mission navigation report of a routine mission flown on March 1, 1945, inadvertently giving an indication that maybe some missions flown by the 25th Bomb Group were at best unusual, if not very different. Noted Captain Lionel Prouly, the Assistant 25th Group navigator, in his report, "Lt Walker as pilot and Major Walch and Lt Miskho as navigators were alerted for a special meteorological operation in A-26, 740." Why Captain Prouly included that sentence in an operational report must remain a mystery.[9] The two A-26 aircraft assigned to the 654th squadron were exclusively used for deep-cover OSS missions, not special meteorological missions, if there even was such a thing.

Joan-Eleanor missions, those involving dropping agents behind enemy lines, were by definition dangerous. Others, involving listening to and recording the radio broadcasts of the inserted agents, were less so. But there was always the chance that they could be picked off by a German night fighter, a not uncommon occurrence. The Joan-Eleanor project was run by Lieutenant Commander Stephen H. Simpson, United States Navy, who was also the principal engineer and designer for the radio systems used by the agents. Steve Simpson started out as a lieutenant in the US Army Signal Corps, but since OSS support fell under the purview of the US Navy, Steve was transferred and in a flash became a naval officer with the rank of lieutenant commander—receiving a nice promotion in the bargain. The UHF broadcasts used by the J-E system, at 260MHZ, were short range and difficult, if not impossible, for the Germans to intercept. So the agents could speak in plain English, Dutch, or German without compromising themselves, and the aircraft would record their transmissions on a wire recorder. Since no encryption was required, and if an intelligence officer was on board the aircraft, the agents could even be questioned for clarification, if that became necessary. It was a responsive way to gather critical intelligence. Walker flew several Red Stocking missions, as they were later referred to, in support of an agent named Bobby, in Holland. Bobby had parachuted into Holland on November 22, 1944. These were all night missions of course, and flown at around thirty thousand feet over a designated area. In January and February 1945 Walker and Miskho flew several Red Stocking missions in support of an agent named Troy near Stuttgart, as well as several resupply missions to both agents in one of the two Douglas A-26 Invader aircraft assigned to the Group.[10]

On March 2, 1945, a very special mission came their way. Commander Simpson wanted Walker, Walch, and Miskho to take one of their A-26 Invaders and drop two agents within the Berlin city limits. Major John Walch, the 654th Bomb Squadron's senior navigator who had been working on this project for some time, thought it chancy. He refused to guarantee the drop, and the drop zone was moved ten miles outside Berlin. The mission was to be flown at an altitude of five hundred feet or less to Berlin and back. Walch and Miskho carefully studied known flak sites and possible locations for aerial balloons and fighter bases. They evolved a zigzag route to avoid the danger areas. Joseph E. Persico, in *Piercing the Reich*, describes this mission in great detail: "Major Walch spent two weeks plotting a detailed flight plan. He shaped the course along large bodies of water, the only reference points which would be visible on the night selected for the Hammer mission. The two native Berliners chosen for the Hammer mission were Paul Land and Toni Ruh, both Communists living in English exile.... The complex flight plan was rehearsed on four practice runs to Berlin, during which the navigator recorded each checkpoint with a stopwatch and compass. On March 1, the night set for the agents' departure, a special precaution had been taken. They would not leave until a weather plane returned and declared conditions for the drop favorable over Berlin.... Ten minutes before midnight the weather aircraft returned. A light rain was falling at Watton, but over Berlin the weathermen reported the night clear and moonlit. Commander Simpson gave the order for the team to depart. A-26 #524 pulled up to within fifty feet of the operations hut. A fuel truck pulled up to the aircraft. The engine warm-up had consumed seventy-five to one hundred gallons of fuel, and the tanks were being filled again just before takeoff. The trip to Berlin and back was expected virtually to dry the tanks. Fuel was their biggest problem, again topping off their tanks at the end of the Watton runway to give them every chance to make it home."

The Hammer team of two agents sat in the rear behind the lead navigator, Major Walch. Once "Sergeant Derr, the radio operator, tapped their helmets," writes Persico, "they and their containers had eight seconds to clear the plane if they were to land close to the pinpoint." After they penetrated Holland, Walker went down to one hundred feet, hedgehopping across the countryside. From the air, Germany at night appeared like an endless crossword puzzle. Miskho lay in the nose of the aircraft peering at the countryside below looking for landmarks to determine their exact position. He called out checkpoints to Major John Walch, who plotted their position, also using Gee and Loran as navigation aides whenever that was possible. They located the drop zone, a near miracle, opened the bomb bay doors and dropped supplies and the two agents. On the way back Walker flew the shortest route, made a straight-in approach to Watton, and landed with less than a hundred gallons of fuel remaining. Talk about a hair-raising mission—this was it. But it paid off. By March 12 a Mosquito sat over Berlin at thirty thousand feet altitude and recorded the findings of the Hammer team.[11]

Not all such missions were crowned by success, especially when they were not thoroughly planned and executed on a whim. As fate would have it, Major

John W. Walch, who flew on that very successful March 2, 1945, mission with Paddy Walker, was assigned as the lead navigator on a similar mission after Walker returned to the United States. Walch's pilot that time was a young and inexperienced lieutenant named Oliver Emmel. Their mission was to drop an OSS agent near Hamm, Germany. The squadron and their Mosquito and A-26 aircraft, for unknown reasons, had been reassigned from RAF Watton to RAF Harrington, a B-24 bomber base. The new hosts provided little support to the newcomers, and seemed to have little understanding of their unique mission requirements, nor cared to get involved. "The A-26 scheduled to fly the mission," according to Joseph Persico, "was #524, the same aircraft that had deposited the Hammer team in Berlin. Its navigation gear badly needed calibrating. The engines were overdue for their hundred hour check. The weather on the day of the mission began ugly and overcast. The crew assigned to the Chisel mission had never flown together; Lieutenant Emmel had not yet completed A-26 training. The weather report showed a heavy front moving across Harrington and foul conditions on the Continent as well. Flak was said to be heavy along their route." Simpson objected strenuously; he didn't want to fly the mission. Things just weren't right for this mission to succeed. He was overruled. At ten-thirty that evening the aircraft departed from RAF Harrington. "Stiff winds drove sheets of rain across her black fuselage. Simpson watched the plane disappear into the blackness. The aircraft never returned." When they arrived north of Osnabrueck, skirting the German Me 262 fighter base of Achmer, something went tragically wrong—for whatever reason, the A-26 crashed, killing all four of its occupants. This mission should never have been flown.[12]

Dropping the Hammer team near Berlin was Robert Walker's last mission with the 25th Bomb Group. He had flown a total of twenty-one OSS-related missions by the time his combat tour ended. He received orders to report to Westover Field in Massachusetts to fly C-54s, the principal AAF transport at the time. What a comedown for a man like Walker who had flown nothing but hair-raising combat since joining the RCAF. He was to fly C-54s for years to come, including the Berlin airlift of 1948 to 1949, as a member of the 11th Troop Carrier Squadron, flying coal out of RAF Fassberg to Gatow airfield in Berlin. The airlift missions were important, but none incorporated the type of danger, nor required the daring, that was Bob's bread and butter during the war years. After liftoff and gaining a couple of hundred feet of altitude Bob would initiate his turn to the east over a small refugee camp adjacent to a pine forest. He never noticed the camp below and never knew that his flights and those of his fellow airmen, brought hope for a better life to me, a young German boy, down below. Bob Walker continued to fly C-54s during the Korean War, his efforts to get reassigned to fighters proving unsuccessful. So, Bob decided to apply for test pilot school at famed Muroc Field in southern California—later renamed Edwards Air Force Base after Glen W. Edwards, one of the pilots who perished flight-testing the YB-49 flying wing. To his great delight Bob was accepted, graduating in Class 54C. The B-66 program was just getting under way and Bob was assigned to the nearby Douglas facility as acceptance test pilot. Cliff Parrott, Douglas program manager for the B-66 reconnaissance program, in later years earning the moniker of "B-66 doctor of Shaw Air Force Base," recalls: "Bob was the first jet qualified air force officer to be assigned to Douglas–Long Beach as acceptance test pilot, and he was a breath of fresh air to the B-66 program. Bob looked like the proverbial fighter pilot—cocky, with a let's go fly something attitude. He never talked much about his World War II experience. In 1955 Bob was reassigned to our Tucson facility from where all but the RB-66C models were delivered to their respective squadrons."[13]

While I was writing my book *Glory Days*, the only book written about the B-66 and the men who flew it, Bob Walker wrote me to let me know that they used JATO/RATO when delivering aircraft from the Douglas plant in California to Tucson, Arizona, where he and Fred Borman flew the final acceptance tests before releasing aircraft to crews from receiving squadrons at Shaw AFB in South Carolina. Bob had no idea, while serving as acceptance test pilot, that he was in fact married to the B-66 for the remainder of his flying career. After the last B-66 aircraft came off the Douglas production line, Bob was assigned to the 10th Tactical Reconnaissance Squadron at Spangdahlem Air Base, Germany. Later on he transferred to the 30th TRS at RAF Alconbury in England. Lieutenant General George D. Miller, for whom I worked as an action officer at one time while assigned to the Pentagon, and who flew the RB-66B photo-reconnaissance aircraft with the 30th TRS in the early '60s, recalled that Bob Walker was his squadron operations officer—the man who was responsible for all that involved flying in a squadron. "I always considered Bob a very fair and decent man. It was an honor to have known and worked for him," recalled General Miller. Neither General Miller nor I, nor any of the men Bob flew with, knew of his World War II flying record. For one thing, much of it was highly classified; for another, Bob was not a man to talk much about himself.

His time in Europe over, Bob transferred to Shaw AFB, then the home of USAF tactical reconnaissance. It was flying reconnaissance of every stripe that truly defined Bob's flying career. He was getting on in years and had more experience in B-66 operations than nearly anyone else around. It was natural for him to be appointed the chief of B-66 maintenance at Shaw. That was Bob's position when the 363rd Tactical Reconnaissance Wing began deploying its aircraft to Southeast Asia (SEA)—RB-66s and RF-101s. The first to leave Shaw AFB for Tan Son Nhut Air Base, South Vietnam, were four infrared-equipped RB-66Bs. The B-models were nuclear bombers reconfigured as electronic warfare aircraft with the job of jamming enemy radars. Their IR equipment was used to locate Viet Cong campfires in the nearby jungle when they were preparing their evening meals. Once located, the B-66s would direct artillery fire against those locations. Bob went along as their maintenance officer. As RB-66 deployments to SEA increased, Major Walker was assigned as chief of B-66 maintenance at Clark Air Base, near Manila in the Philippines. Clark was where the heavy maintenance was done that could not be accomplished at Tan Son Nhut, South Vietnam, or Takhli, Thailand, where the bulk of the B-66 force was based. Bob was a flyer, and he wanted to fly, not be relegated to a desk and aircraft maintenance. Bob, of course, had lots of contacts in the B-66 community and before one could say "pack your bags" Bob was out of Clark and headed for the 6460th TRS, later redesignated the 42nd Tactical Electronic Warfare Squadron (TEWS) at Takhli Royal Thai Air Force Base, Thailand, about a hundred miles north of Bangkok, flying what he liked most—combat. I later on flew with the 41st TEWS, also equipped with the EB-66 and based at Takhli.

On February 25, 1966, Major Walker and his crew were assigned RB-66C 54-0457—an electronic reconnaissance aircraft with a crew of six: pilot, navigator, and four electronic warfare officers. They were tasked to fly a surveillance mission over the Gulf of Tonkin, crossing over to the water side near Vinh, North Vietnam, an area that was designated as Route Pack 3. Bob's navigator was Captain John Kodlick. Lieutenant Beatty flew as Raven 1, with the principal task of picking up the BG06 missile guidance signal for the Soviet designed and built SA-2 surface to air missile system, should a missile be launched against them. Captain Wayne Smith flew as Raven 2; Captain Jim Thomson was the Raven 3, and Captain John Causey was Raven crew commander and flew in position 4. The Ravens, as the electronic warfare officers were referred to, sat in what used to be the bomb bay of the aircraft which had been reequipped with appropriate reconnaissance gear and downward ejection seats. The weather was lousy, it being the monsoon season. Smith was the first to hear the faint sound of an SA-2 Fansong tracking radar as they passed Vinh, and he alerted the crew leader, Captain Causey. Captain Causey looked, but couldn't locate the radar on his scope. "After our return down the coast, I heard the Fansong radar come up again," Smith recalled, "and I called Causey's attention to it. When he intercepted the signal, it was very strong and he told the pilot to turn. Then the Raven 1 intercepted the BG06, and Captain Causey, the chief Raven, told the pilot to start a steep SAM break." SAM breaks were flown to cause the missile to exceed its turning capability and lose track. "I heard a loud pop. When Major Walker was finally able to level off, he discovered that he had little control over the aircraft."

Walker recalled that the plane wanted to pitch up. He had no rudder, but seemed to have enough aileron to keep the wings level. "Both engines were still operating. The aircraft began going nose up, as though about to start a loop. By chopping off the power, the plane began to free-fall, nose down. Then as it fell through the horizon, keeping the wings level, I applied power to bring the nose up. Throttles on, throttles off—the only way I could fly the plane." When the SA-2 missile exploded near the rear of the aircraft, it damaged the stabilizer to the point that it was either locked in place, or became a floating slab, accounting for the pitching of the aircraft. The yoke, the control column, remained locked in the extreme pitch up position and Walker, as much as he tried, could not move the column forward and stow it when he needed to. Walker had no intention of ejecting his crew over land while the airplane was still flying, and, using all the skills a pilot acquires over years of flying, he nursed the broken EB-66 for 130 miles out over Gulf waters. Then, and only then, fearing the aircraft was about to break up, he gave the order to eject. He motioned to his navigator to go—the intercom was inoperable—then jettisoned both escape hatches. Kodlick was the first to go. The crew in the rear compartment, without communication with the front end, heard Kodlick eject, the aft compartment depressurized, and the four Ravens prepared to follow suit—Raven 1, then 2, then 3, then 4, in that order. Ravens 1, 2, and 3 ejected. Captain Causey did not. Walker was having problems in the cockpit—as he pulled the preejection handles the control column did not stow forward and his seat did not move aft. He moved the seat aft manually, then squeezed the ejection trigger—nothing happened. He squeezed the trigger again—still nothing happened. Bob contemplated a manual egress, which surely would have killed him had he done so. Then he decided to give the seat one more chance—strapped down, squeezed the trigger, and that time the system worked. He broke both ankles and a kneecap on egress. Cliff Parrott, the Douglas Aircraft Company B-66 expert, believes that Walker's and Causey's seats were misrigged, that there was too much slack in the cable of the handles and trigger mechanisms. Causey, being number four in the ejection sequence, had the least time to get out of the stricken aircraft and just couldn't make it.

The navigator, Captain Kodlick, had made a Mayday call over the radio before ejecting, not knowing if anyone heard him. Someone did. Seventh Air Force, headquartered in Saigon, launched a recovery effort, but the precise location of the crash site was unknown. A US Navy A-1H Skyraider from the USS *Ranger* was participating in a practice search and rescue exercise when its pilot picked up several emergency beepers from an area where none were supposed to be. He established voice contact with one of the EB-66 crew members and vectored two navy helicopters to the pickup. Walker's efforts surely saved his crew from a terrible fate had they ejected over land. Becoming a prisoner of war of the North Vietnamese was something every flyer wanted to avoid, their methods of torture being well known and reminiscent of the

L–R: Robert Walker, Sergeant Scott, combat artist for *Yank Magazine*, and Roy Conyers, Walker's navigator, in front of Walker's Mosquito at RAF Watton, June 1944.

Walker at the controls of his Mosquito aircraft. Even after transfer from the RCAF to the AAF Bob continued to wear his British leather flying helmet, and never shaved off his mustache.

middle ages. For saving his crew Major Walker was awarded the Silver Star. Walker's crew could not know that the Vinh SAM site was staffed by Russian missile experts, there to train North Vietnamese missile crews. The Russians were highly skilled operators and most likely used data derived from their Flat Face or Spoonrest acquisition radars to track Gull 1, the call sign of Walker's aircraft, and launch two SA-2 Guideline missiles when the opportunity offered itself, only turning on the Fansong tracking radar and BG06 missile guidance transmitter when the missiles were already in midflight. Although Captain Causey's warning allowed Walker to initiate a SAM break, Walker didn't have enough time to get far enough away from the first missile, which

A B-66B bomber using JATO on takeoff on March 18, 1957, flown by either Bob Walker or Fred Borman, both of whom acted as acceptance test pilots from the Douglas plant at Long Beach, California, for all but the C-model of the B-66, which was produced in Tulsa, Oklahoma.

exploded near the aft section of the aircraft and ultimately brought it down. And of course Major Walker had no chance to observe the missile launches because of layered cloud decks—ideal conditions for the SA-2 SAM system to succeed. Seventh Air Force chose not to publicize the loss of Gull 1. Few knew of its loss at the time, other than those involved.

Robert Walker was transferred to Letterman Hospital in California for recuperation. Upon his discharge from the hospital, he had six months remaining before retiring. Bob went back to test piloting, as acceptance test pilot for the Northrop T-38 Talon and the F-5 Freedom Fighter programs, testing each aircraft as it came off the production line. After retiring in the rank of lieutenant colonel, Bob flew a number of years for Delta Airlines, and come age sixty he had to hang up his flying suit for the last time. He then moved to Merritt Island, Florida, where he died on January 7, 2010, at age eighty-six. "I believe Bob could fly any aircraft, even if he had never seen it before," says his friend and admirer Cliff Parrott. "He would have it all figured out on the take-off roll. There was only one like him."[14] Walker's and my paths crossed many times without either of us knowing about the other. He dropped OSS agents near Berlin when I lived there as a ten-year-old, and flew only feet above the wretched refugee camp I called home during the days of the Berlin airlift. And I flew many missions in the EB-66C reconnaissance aircraft out of Takhli RTAFB, Thailand, from where Bob flew his last combat mission. We talked and corresponded in later years after his retirement from the air force—but we never met in person. Robert Walker was the kind of pilot one wanted to fly with—a superb airman, and a great American patriot. Robert Patrick Walker served his country from age eighteen to his last breath. We flyers are honored to have flown in such great company. An airman's airman—that was my friend Robert Paddy Walker.

DAVID M. TAYLOR

B-17/C-54/C-47

When a Soldier Dies

Does he hear the sound of bugles, does he hear the high-toned fife?
Is there a muffled drum-beat, as a soldier gives his life?
I'll not ask you for an answer, I'll not ask you if you care;
But I'll tell you, if you listen, and I'll ask you for a prayer.
There is no sound of bugles, there is no high-toned fife,
And there is not a drum-beat, as a soldier gives his life.
The sound he hears is gunfire, or a bomb from out the skies,
These mark the ebbing hours as slow the soldier dies.
The flag he sees is bloody, his shirt, mud-stained and red.
With his own blood it's colored, and now the soldier's dead.
He meets his death in honor, not to a hero be.
But that life and freedom might be left to you and me.
—P.B. Holmes, WWII ETO

In May 1998 I received a call from the Eisenhower Center for American Studies inquiring if I would be willing to participate in a symposium on Berlin and the Cold War, a symposium commemorating the fiftieth anniversary of the start of the Berlin airlift. I was willing to participate, of course, since no other event changed my life more profoundly than did the Berlin airlift of 1948–49. But I questioned the caller's judgement and asked her what I could possibly contribute to such a forum when at that time, fifty years ago, I was just a young German refugee boy living in a rotting former Wehrmacht barrack at the north end of the Fassberg runway, one of four American airlift bases—the other three being Wiesbaden, Frankfurt, and Celle—and had nothing to do with what was the first confrontation of the emerging Cold War. "I was not a pilot flying day and night in all kinds of weather to keep the people of Berlin from starving and freezing to death," I told her. "I was not a maintenance man who kept the planes flying, nor an air police man, not even a lowly German cargo loader. I was just a boy wanting to be a boy who was constantly hungry, cold, and poorly clothed, hoping that some day for me and my family that war that had brought us to this desolate camp from the east of Germany would finally end." I related to the caller that I still remembered the euphoria I experienced when I saw my first American plane in April 1948 flying out of Fassberg. I knew then, or I thought I knew, that I would be safe if the Americans came to help, to stop the Russians from taking Berlin, then the rest of Germany, as many of us believed would be the case if the Russians prevailed. The American flyers didn't know about starving German kids watching their planes, or about the hope they brought to us youngsters just by being there. Hope—for a better future.

"Yes, we want you to be part of our forum," the caller insisted. "Your experience is exactly what we want." And so, on the 11th of June 1998 I showed up at the National Archives where I was informed that I would be part of a round-table discussion with several Berlin airlift veterans. One of those veterans was Colonel David M. Taylor. As I held his hand in greeting late that afternoon, looking into his calm, steady eyes, I could see the man of fifty years ago. The man who compartmented his fears somewhere in his heart and brain where they could not interfere with the task at hand. I could visualize Dave Taylor flying his food-laden C-54 Skymaster into fog-shrouded Berlin, down a narrow radar beam, seeing nothing before him but fog, totally trusting in the disciplined voice on his radio giving him directions to the Tempelhof runway below. Once he was on the ground, the fog was often so thick that Dave Taylor could barely see the Follow-Me jeep guiding him to his parking place. Flying like that took courage and trust in the competence of others. Now, this man stood before me. As I looked into Dave Taylor's steady eyes, I saw that he, the man, had conquered his fears years ago. "I was in Berlin in early 1945," I said to Dave, still holding his hand. "So was I," he responded, an open smile crossing his face, "but twenty-five thousand feet above you." And his smile deepened. "Maybe you bombed me?" I said, knowing the answer.

"Maybe I did," he replied, in a voice dusted with pride. It was all in his voice. Steady, with a touch of irony. There was no animosity, no glee, no scorn. Just the steady voice of a soldier who served his country to the best of his ability. I liked Dave instantly. That evening I lost track of him. Then I saw Dave Taylor again in July 1998, at another function honoring veterans of the Berlin airlift at the National Air and Space Museum in downtown Washington, DC. He was one of the honorees. I was one of the evening's guest speakers.

I went around the tables shaking the hands of the aging airlift veterans, and finally, at the last table, there sat Dave Taylor. This time I got his home address and we promised each other to get together and talk. One Monday in early August 1998 I picked up the phone and called Dave at his farm on the south side of Charlottesville, Virginia, located right back of where Thomas Jefferson and James Monroe once looked from their mountaintop homes and contemplated the future of their fledgling nation—the United States of America. Two days later I left my home in Fairfax Station at eight in the morning, following narrow and winding country lanes through the cool oak forests of northern Virginia. Skirting Manassas, I finally got to historic Route 29, which would take me straight to Charlottesville. When passing Culpeper I could envision the mass of Union and Confederate cavalry facing each other in the largest and only cavalry battle of the Civil War. A little over two hours later I skirted Charlottesville, turned onto Route 20. Just past the turnoff to Ash Lawn, Monticello, and Michie Tavern I saw the sign on the left side of the road—Cedar Hill Farm. Dave's place. I jumped on my brakes, made a sharp left turn onto a dirt road. Finally a house on the side of a hill overlooking a broad valley and a large pond seemingly teeming with fish came into view. As I drove up the incline, I could see the fish breaking the surface, snatching insects which had tempted them. I pulled up to the house in the shade of a broad-beamed oak. As I stepped out of my car, I was captivated by the sound of silence—total silence. No man-made sounds, only the chirping of insects, the echoing cry of a red-tailed hawk—it was a beautiful moment in a beautiful valley, the home of Dave Taylor—a true American hero.

Dave came around the house to greet me. He was a thin man, tall and straight, belying his two heart attacks some years ago which forced him to give up his cattle and horses. "I love your spread," I complimented Dave. "An incredible setting in one of the most beautiful and historic parts of our great country." Dave smiled. We talked about the pond and the bass, about his famous neighbors and how a road once led from his spread straight down to Michie Tavern below Jefferson's Monticello. We sat down in his comfortable family room, across from the TV, and I spent the rest of the day listening to a man who had spent his life serving his country in its many conflicts with the tyrants of our world. Dave Taylor was born in 1921 and grew up in the small Mississippi town of Grenada. He occasionally played with his younger cousin, Trent Lott, who would one day become majority leader of the US Senate. Young Dave's horizons were not limited by the surrounding cotton fields. He soon became enamored with flying while helping fuel Ford Trimotors at a nearby airfield in exchange for an occasional ride. Flying got into his blood, although there appeared to be little chance he would be able to follow his dream. Then in 1941, with a war raging in Europe, he joined the Army Air

Corps. He remained a private until 1942 when he was assigned to flight training as an aviation cadet. He completed basic training at what is now Lackland Air Force Base in San Antonio, Texas, where I, many years later, would go through basic training as well. Then he went in quick succession through primary, basic, and advanced flight training. On May 24, 1943, at Ellington Field near Houston, Texas, Aviation Cadet David M. Taylor received his pilot wings and the brown bars of a second lieutenant in the United States Army Air Forces—bars which his proud mother pinned on her young son's shoulders.

Intensive B-17 crew training followed at a succession of airfields from Washington State to Florida. Twice Dave's crew and the units they trained with were certified combat ready. Twice his combat ready squadron was designated a replacement training unit, RTU, to train others for combat in the skies over Europe. At times Dave wondered if the war he wanted to fight would be over by the time he got his chance. Dave was promoted to first lieutenant and progressed to instructor pilot. He was very good at flying the B-17. Dave Taylor's crew finally received its long-awaited orders to proceed as a replacement crew to England. The meaning of the term *replacement* didn't really sink in until he got there. Replacement for what? For those who had died, gone missing or, if lucky, become POWs. Dave had handpicked his crew of nine—copilot, bombardier, navigator, radio operator, and four gunners, all well trained in their respective specialties. On October 9, 1944, the men took a brand-new B-17 bomber from Hunter Field in Savannah, Georgia, and flew it along the northern Atlantic route via Goose Bay, Labrador, and Scotland to England. "After first being part of a replacement pool, we were eventually assigned to the 336th Bomb Squadron, 95th Bombardment Group, Heavy, part of the 13th Combat Wing of the 3rd Bombardment Division commanded by Major General Earl Partridge," Dave recalled. "General Partridge replaced Major General Curtis E. LeMay that spring, who had gone on to organize the B-29s in the Pacific. Our combat wing consisted of the 95th Bomb Group at Horham, the 100th at Thorpe Abbot, and the 390th at Framlingham. I flew a B-17G out of Horham, one of many air bases located in rural Suffolk and adjacent Norfolk counties, halfway between Norwich to the north and Ipswich to the south."

By the time Dave Taylor and his crew joined the 95th, the group had experienced some of the heaviest aerial combat of the war in Europe, and suffered some of the worst losses of any bombardment group. On June 13, 1943, the 95th launched twenty-six aircraft to lead a raid on Kiel. Two aircraft aborted, leaving twenty-four. The wing was led by Brigadier General Nathan Bedford Forrest, a descendant of the famed Civil War hero. Forrest's was the first of the wing's aircraft to go down. That day the 95th Bomb Group lost ten of its twenty-four aircraft and 103 men. Only fourteen damaged aircraft returned to base, many of which fell into the nonrepairable category. On March 4, 1944, the 95th participated in the first American raid on Berlin. This time four of its aircraft did not return and nine were damaged. And on the 6th of March, only two days later, the 95th lost another eight aircraft over Berlin. Eighty men dead or prisoners of war. The air war over Europe was brutal and the 95th was paying a terrible price.[15]

"The winter of '44 was bitter cold," Taylor recalled. "Our Nissen huts, heated only by a potbellied stove, provided little comfort. The real problem was getting enough coal to keep the stove going. The Brits controlled the coal. My buddy and I figured out a little scheme. He would approach the English guard at the coal yard, make small talk, and offer the guard a much-prized American cigarette. While they were chatting, I jumped into the coal bin from the opposite side and threw chunks of coal over the wall. The guard never caught on. Or maybe he didn't want to. We had lots of coal all winter long and a cozy hut. We were not assigned living quarters by crews but rather by rank. Officers and enlisted men were housed in separate huts, which had a dubious advantage: when a crew was lost in combat, an entire hut was not emptied at once. Near each bed was an oxygen container. Early in the mornings, those chosen to go on a mission were awakened. We usually took an oxygen mask and did some pre-breathing before washing up, eating, and going to the briefing. Those not selected, at least in our hut, took a swig of wine from a large, twenty-five-liter, straw-wrapped wine flask mounted on the ceiling. We had run surgical tubes from the flask to each bed. After fortifying ourselves that way, we rolled over and went back to sleep. We tried hard to give our barren existence some touches of congeniality. We were just kids, ranging in age from the late teens to mid-twenties.

"Not only was the place cold, the food was lousy too. There were two mess halls at Horham—one for the air crews, and another for the permanent party. The permanent party consisted of staff and other nonflyers who remained at the base while air crews moved on—some died, some went home after thirty-five missions, some became 'guests' of the Germans. The mess for the permanent party served good food both in quality and method of preparation. The aircrew mess was lousy in both respects. We couldn't do much about that. I became the best chicken procurer in England. I quietly entered nearby henhouses, tucked an obliging chicken under my blouse, and soon we had fried chicken to supplement our diet of Spam and powdered eggs prepared by a disinterested kitchen staff. Another opportunity to improve our food situation offered itself when the group staff wanted to fly on my crew. One day the group commander announced that he was going to fly with me as my copilot. He was a lieutenant colonel. 'You're not flying with us,' I told him in my capacity as pilot in command, 'unless you eat like us.' The group commander was unaware how bad the food was for his aircrews, and after entering our chow line and seeing what was offered, he took us over to the other mess. After that the food situation in the aircrew mess improved for a while. But it soon reverted to its former deplorable state. Eating a good meal before a combat mission was important. Our missions were six to eight hours in duration, under extremely difficult conditions. If we were shot down, we knew we probably wouldn't eat again for at least three days. That's what experience had taught us.

"Our first missions after arriving at Horham were training missions to familiarize ourselves with local procedures and the area. We did some practice bombing. I remember during this time we came under V-1 rocket attack. The 95th Bomb Group and our next-door sister group at Thorpe Abbotts, the 'bloody' 100th, received special attention from the Luftwaffe. Our group had flown the first daylight raid against Berlin on March 4, 1944, and had been in the thick of things ever since. It was no surprise that the Germans took a special disliking to us. I was disdainful of the V-1s, and when the alarm was given, everyone else raced for the nearest shelter. I stayed in my bunk. I heard an ominous 'put-put-put-roar' and then smelled the exhaust from the V-1 as it passed the open window of my hut. Silence followed. Then I heard a loud explosion beyond a nearby hill. I catapulted out of bed, dove through an open window, and leapt into the nearest trench—which was filled with water. More V-1s followed with the same result. They exploded harmlessly on that hillside, doing no damage. The next day, Dirty Gerty, as we called the German woman broadcasting to us over the radio, announced that the 95th Bomb Group had been wiped out. We had a good laugh.

"Before my first combat mission I received several visits from old-timers, pilots who had nearly finished their thirty-five combat missions and were looking forward to going home. (The number of combat missions required of heavy bomber crews before going home varied from twenty-five in early 1943 to thirty-five starting in May 1944.) They just wanted to give me a heads-up. As the newest replacement, I would have to fly in what was referred to as Purple Heart corner. My crew would be the most exposed and vulnerable aircraft in the lowest squadron, flying the low echelon, on the right wing of the element leader. We would have the least defensive support from any of the other aircraft in the formation. 'Watch out for the new German missiles,' the old-timers said, frowning. 'They leave telltale smoke trails as they streak toward your aircraft. You'll see the smoke, but never the missiles. They're too fast.'

"Flying the Purple Heart corner on our first combat mission was enough stress without also having to worry about German missiles. Our target was the rail yard at Giessen. As we got into the area, I saw the dreaded smoke trails. By that time I was too busy flying a tight formation and holding our assigned altitude to worry much about missiles. Our group lost one aircraft that day.

On the way home I discovered I wasn't really that afraid. I completely forgot about the German antiaircraft rockets. At the intelligence debriefing, when I reported the smoke trails, I learned that there really weren't any new German missiles. It was a story the old-timers nurtured and told to replacement pilots. Rather, the smoke trails I saw were our own marker bombs dropped by the lead aircraft, on which the following aircraft immediately behind the lead would release their bombs. The rest of us just dropped our bombs into the cauldron down below. The marker bombs emitted trails of smoke on their way down which looked much like missile trails coming up. At least that's what I thought. Never having seen an antiaircraft missile before, how would I know?

"A typical combat mission started with the wake-up call for those designated to fly. From the time they woke us until we landed was a long day. Only part of it was the seven to nine hours of flying time. After washing up, we got dressed and donned our bulky flying gear and headed for the mess. After eating, we assembled in the briefing room, where we learned for the first time where we were going. Our group of three squadrons, twelve B-17s per squadron, was dispersed on hardstands along the perimeter road which ran around the field touching each end of the three crisscrossing runways. Regardless of weather conditions, the engine start and takeoff procedure was followed in complete radio silence. At engine start, we warmed up our engines and ran through the pretakeoff checklist. The control tower then fired a yellow flare to start the taxi sequence. At our assigned time, and watching the aircraft ahead of us move out, we taxied toward our takeoff position. I knew who came ahead of me. When he started to move, I got ready to go next. When the tower fired a green flare, the group started the takeoff sequence. It was an intricate process and not without its problems.

"On fourteen of my twenty-seven combat missions, mine was the lead aircraft. On three of those fourteen I led the entire Eighth Air Force. Being lead meant that as we approached the target, I had to keep the aircraft at our assigned altitude, usually around twenty-five thousand feet, at an airspeed of 170 knots from the IP, the Initial Point, to the target. From the IP to the target, the bombardier flew the aircraft while I worked the throttles to control our airspeed and watched the altimeter to maintain our assigned altitude. As lead aircraft, our bombs were smoke bombs to mark the target for the others. On April 3, 1945, we flew a mission against submarine pens at Kiel. I was lead. Just before the IP I had to shut down one engine because of flak damage. On only three engines, I was barely able to maintain the formation's airspeed. The aileron was shot up, too, with a large hole, making the entire aircraft shake. On top of that the bombardier was jerking the aircraft around. He had a hard time locating the target. The Germans had constructed a dummy target, and only at the last moment did our bombardier identify the real target. He jerked the aircraft onto the new heading, and we released the smokers. We hit the right target that day, judging from the fireballs we saw on our way out. When I was hit, I should have relinquished my position as formation leader to the deputy lead and headed to Sweden. In Sweden, I knew, we would have been interned for a time and subsequently released when a C-87 (the transport version of the B-24 bomber) came over from England to pick us up. The C-87 came to pick up ball bearings to be sent back to the States, where they were in critical supply. Air crews were incidental cargo for this nighttime run." The Germans did the same thing, and at times American and German aircraft would sit on the same tarmac. War does strange things.

Dave Taylor flew missions against Kiel on April 3 and 4, 1945. The submarine pens in Kiel were the preferred target for both Bomber Command and the 8th Air Force late in the war, but the damage to the heavily fortified pens was minimal. The city, however, was practically leveled in the process. Detlef Boelk was a wounded World War I veteran living in Kiel who kept a detailed diary from the first air raid against the city on July 2, 1940, to the last raid on May 4, 1945. He writes about the April 3 and 4 raids: "Today, April 3, 1945, we experienced a severe bombing raid in beautiful weather. At first several enemy aircraft circled the town [probably Mosquito fighters which accompanied the bombers and marked the targets] then waves of heavy bombers followed dropping high explosive and fire bombs. After the last aircraft left, the town was a shambles. It is impossible to list the damage individually; it was too wide spread. Several warships in the harbor were severely damaged, including the heavy cruiser *Admiral Hipper* and the cruiser *Emden*. Streetcars are no longer able to run—gas, water and light are no longer available. 230 people died in the Moltke mineshaft used as an air raid shelter when the entrance was covered by debris, and another 20 people died in another shelter when hit by a bomb." About the April 4 raid Herr Boelk wrote: "We experienced a heavy raid yesterday afternoon, and early this morning another. A terrible air raid. Several waves of enemy aircraft brought death and destruction dropping high explosive and fire bombs. We had thunderstorms, lightning and thunder competed with the sounds of exploding bombs—a gruesome spectacle. All three of the shipyards were severely damaged, as were adjacent sections of the city. Kiel is turning into a town of pure rubble. A bread wagon, pulled by a horse, was hit by a bomb in the Gaarden army barracks, leaving behind nothing. Twenty-six lives were lost."[16]

Dave Taylor remarked, "I never thought of turning over lead to anyone else as long as my aircraft could fly and I could stay with the formation. At the Rally Point, our mission complete, I throttled back on the three good engines so as not to lose another, and dropped out of formation. I headed for a lower altitude and denser air to stabilize the aircraft. Upon reaching the North Sea,

I leveled off at ten thousand feet, continuing to head for England. Soon, an American P-51 fighter came swooping down and flew alongside us. Through hand signals, the fighter pilot gave me to understand that he was going to stay around. That was a great relief. He climbed back to altitude and circled above us as we lumbered slowly toward England. We were joined by a second B-17. I thought the aircraft looked strange, not quite like our own. It had no familiar group markings. Flying abeam of us, the stranger kept edging closer and closer. Suddenly the P-51 showed up behind him and shot him down. It turned out to be a reconditioned B-17 used by the Germans to shoot down stragglers and to call out altitudes to their flak. With the help of that P-51 pilot we made it home on three engines." Kampfgeschwader 200 was a German special missions unit that flew reconditioned DC-3, B-24, and B-17 bombers in one of its three squadrons. The greatest fear of Luftwaffe aircrew flying captured American aircraft was being shot down by their own antiaircraft guns—which happened on several occasions.[17]

"On my 15th mission against Nuernberg, on February 21, 1945, I was lead again. Before reaching the IP, my engineer put my flak suit on me. He was to fasten the flies on my left shoulder to leave my right arm free to adjust the autopilot while the bombardier was guiding the airplane to the target with the Norden bombsight. The flak was intense and things didn't go as planned. The engineer had fastened the flies of my flak jacket on the right instead of the left side, causing the jacket to continually slide off, hitting my right arm when I tried to adjust the autopilot. When the jacket hit my arm, it also caused my helmet to drop over my eyes. This happened over and over again—I adjusted my equipment, the flak jacket slid down as I moved my right arm, my helmet slid over my eyes. When I could see, I saw flak. The Germans were firing salvos in boxes at 25,000 feet, then changing altitude and firing at 24,500 feet, and so on. The effect was a massive blanket of flak. We were taking a lot of hits. The little black puffs of smoke were so numerous that they looked like a blanket, the kind of stuff some people said they could walk on. When I could see the fireball within a puff of smoke, I could expect to be showered with shrapnel. It was no place to bail out and hope to reach the ground alive.

"Our group commander was flying as command pilot in the right seat. I was working with the bombardier when he called, 'Bombs away!' The cockpit was instantly engulfed in smoke so thick I couldn't see the command pilot to my right. He thought the plane was on fire and hit the bailout button. The tail gunner jettisoned the exit door and the rest of the crew got ready to jump. The scene below us was flak hell. I got on the mike and yelled to the crew, 'Do not bail out! Do not bail out!' I could see all four engines were still turning. The bailout lights continued flashing. I saw the command pilot rise in his seat to head toward the bomb bay to bail out. I punched his lights out, adjusted the autopilot into a gradual turn, and pushed the button to open the bomb bay doors. As the bomb bay doors opened, the smoke was instantaneously sucked out of the cockpit. The cause of the smoke turned out to be a damaged smoke bomb which had gone off just as we called for the doors to open. The bomb probably got hit by shrapnel. I jumped out of my seat and headed for the bomb bay, leaving my chute behind. There wasn't enough room to take my chute along. I gave the faulty bomb a kick and watched it drop away. I balanced on a narrow ledge of the open bomb bay. Below me was twenty-five thousand feet of empty space, a blanket of flak, and the raging fires we had started in Nuernberg. I got back to the cockpit and found to my delight that the airplane was still flying without any major problems. The command pilot had come to again. The Germans had missed our altitude and we had only scattered flak damage. I turned at the Rally Point and headed for home. Two of my men told me later they were ready to jump when they heard my command not to bail out. A second later would have been too late for them. We returned to Horham a happy crew. As for my command pilot and group commander? I wrote him up for a decoration."

Dave Taylor recalled his worst mission. "We had a radio operator on board who spoke German. We usually referred to them as Mickey operators. His job was to listen to the German fighters and disrupt their attacks by inserting himself into the stream of shouted warnings, sightings, and commentary by giving out false information in German as if he was one of them. The flak was really heavy that day, ripping numerous holes into our aircraft. A large piece of shrapnel hit below the Mickey operator, tearing a large hole into the fuselage under his legs, knocking out the central oxygen supply, and severing electrical cables. More shrapnel forced me to shut down an engine. I had my hands full flying the airplane and analyzing what I had lost and what still worked. The Mickey operator was terrified, looking down at the gaping hole below his legs, ice-cold air rushing up at him. His electric suit had failed and he wasn't getting any oxygen. He thought he was dying—and he was. He started screaming over and over again on the intercom, 'I'm dead. I'm dead. I'm dead . . .' totally blocking the intercom so I couldn't talk to the rest of the crew. I had to make a choice. I went first to check on Jones, the ball-turret gunner. He didn't have portable oxygen because of a lack of space in the turret; the Mickey operator did. I donned a portable oxygen mask and rushed to the rear of the plane to see if Jones was all right. It was the job of the waist gunner to get oxygen to the ball-turret gunner. The waist gunner had pulled Jones out of the turret and given him oxygen. Except for exposure to the cold and a bad headache, Jones suffered no lasting effects. After I got back to my seat, I dropped the plane down from twenty-five thousand to ten thousand feet so we could breathe. I had to leave the formation and returned to England alone. The Mickey operator survived.

"We could always tell when the assigned target was a bad one. Outside the briefing room would be a large number of military police and ambulances. As we sat in the room, the briefing officer would pull the curtain slowly from left to right past Cologne, Hamburg, Berlin, and sometimes as far as Koenigsberg. The farther he pulled the curtain to the right, the more distraught many of the aircrew became. Even late in the war, German antiaircraft defenses were deadly. A man could take only so much stress, and on difficult missions some would break. The military police and medical orderlies were there to put them into straitjackets and take them away. I saw firsthand what fear could do to a man on one of my missions. He was my copilot. I asked him to take the controls. Looking over, I saw him raise his hands. And then he froze. He tried to force his hands down onto the controls, but he couldn't do it. I could see him trying. His face bathed in sweat, muscles rippling, he couldn't get his hands to move. He was frozen stiff with fright.

"I remember one particularly bad mission. I was looking at my best friend flying next to me, off my right wing, and he was looking over at me. I still remember the look on his face. Then he took a direct hit. His aircraft exploded. There was nothing left for me to see. On many of our missions, the killing started before we got going. On bad-weather days—and there were many of those in England—we called them crash and burn days—after takeoff we were to assemble over a radio beacon near our base. In theory it was a good procedure. In practice, it left a lot to be desired and we never fixed the problem throughout the war. As we took off, the lead aircraft made a spiraling left turn until breaking out of the overcast and then waited for his squadron mates to join up. Unfortunately, there were numerous bases nearby. As we spiraled up to altitude, our turns got wider and wider, like an inverted cone, and in time our cone would overlap with the cone of another base. The aircraft crashing into each other never knew what happened. On takeoff I frequently could see the bodies of my friends strewn across meadows, hanging over fences. Others burned to death in the inferno of a crashing aircraft. Do you know what a human body looks like after it has burned in an air crash? A little black ball which you can hold in your hands. That's all that's left of a man." Dave paused, the recollections of tragedies flitting past his inner eye as if they happened yesterday. He frowned. His eyes shone brightly. The *Mighty Eighth War Diary*, by Roger A. Freeman, notes that between June 1942 and May 1945, more than 6,500 B-17 and B-24 heavy bombers were lost over Europe. One in six, more than a thousand aircraft, were lost to accidents rather than to enemy action. The Eighth Air Force heavy bomber force in England was maintained at a strength of two thousand aircraft.

"Once our group assembled," Dave continued, "or whatever was left of it, we'd join up with other groups. We flew tight formations, the tighter the better, until our wingtips nearly touched. It provided the best defense against German fighters. Our targets varied from industrial to military. On a mission to Fulda I wrote in my log book, 'The target is women and children.' I simply saw things differently then." A faded, frequently folded piece of paper issued by the 95th Bombardment Group, Heavy, certifies that David M. Taylor flew the following missions on dates indicated against targets shown:

1. Hamm 11-20-44
2. Giessen 11-21-44
3. T.S. #25/Hamm 11-26-44
4. Abandoned/WX 12-02-44
5. Friedberg 12-04-44
6. Berlin 12-05-44
7. Giessen 12-11-44
8. Darmstadt 12-12-44
9. Biblis Air Field 12-24-44
10. Fulda 01-03-45
11. Kaiserslautern 01-06-45
12. Cologne 01-07-45
13. Cologne 01-10-45
14. Osnabrueck 02-19-45
15. Nuernberg 02-21-45
16. Munich 02-25-45
17. Leipzig 02-27-45
18. Datteln 03-07-45
19. Frankfurt 03-09-45
20. Swinemuende 03-12-45
21. Steenwijk/Holland 03-24-45
22. Hamburg 03-30-45
23. Kiel 04-03-45
24. Kiel 04-04-45
25. Burg 04-10-45
26. Point De Grave/France 04-16-45
27. Straubing 04-18-45

"Toward the very end of the war, in late April and early May 1945, I flew some low-level relief missions into Holland dropping food and medical supplies to the starving Dutch people. There was an agreement with the Germans that we wouldn't drop bombs and they wouldn't shoot at us. I recall on one of those relief missions on the way in, overflying very low, about five hundred feet or so, a German submarine lying at anchor in the harbor, I think it was Amsterdam. The crew was on deck watching us, shaking their fists at us. We shook our fists right back at them. But nobody fired at anybody. On the way out we lost one aircraft—it caught fire, a real tragedy." Notes the 95th Bomb Group history: "In the closing days of the campaign, the planes flew mercy missions to Holland, dropping containers of rations to avert a critical food crisis. They were designated 'Chowhound' missions to feed the starving Dutch people. Ground men clambered excitedly on these ships for a look at the picturesque Dutch countryside. And the grateful people clustered at every village square. It was a picnic and a pleasant ride. One returning ship however developed a fire in an engine. It threatened to spread and the pilot ditched into the sea while men bailed out. A wrong swell hit the plane a terrific blow as the pilot tried to slide it in. Two out of seventeen men were picked up by Air-Sea Rescue. One survived. Before returning to the United States the 95th Bomb Group flew several 'Revival' missions—returning prisoners of war from StalagLuft I at Barth to France for eventual processing at Camp Lucky Strike, near Le Havre, and home."[18]

When the war in Europe ended in May 1945, Dave Taylor was out of a job. The 95th Bomb Group headed home that June and was inactivated in August. But for the men who flew its missions, there was no such thing as inactivation. Their experiences stayed with them for the remainder of their lives. In combat since May 1943 to the bitter end, 359 B-17 Flying Fortresses became part of the group, 157 of them lost in combat, another 95 lost to other causes. In that brief period of two years 575 men lost their lives, 31 went missing in action, fate unknown, and 865 men served part of their lives as prisoners of war. The 95th Bomb Group had put the first B-17s over Berlin on March 4, 1944, and received a total of three Presidential Unit Citations, one of which was for that Berlin raid, the other two for raids on Regensburg and Muenster. War is hell, as the saying goes, and the 95th went through it and survived—but at a price. Dave Taylor was not the same man in May 1945 as the man who first reported for duty at Horham in late 1944. He, like most soldiers, sailors, and airmen, got out of the service and went back home to Mississippi. He found that it wasn't what it used to be. "I did some crop dusting after the war. Planes were cheap then. Five hundred dollars or so. I wanted to keep on flying after I got out of the Army Air Forces, and crop dusting seemed a good way to make a living. Things were going all right until this particular day when I was dusting a watermelon field. I had completed my first swath and was heading for the tree line when I remembered that a power line ran right behind the trees. I yanked back on the wheel. Too late. I hit the top of the pole with one of my wheels as I was climbing out. Sparks flashed before my face. As I came out of my inside loop which I had involuntarily gotten myself into, I had no altitude left and struck the ground. I lay there stunned for a moment. Then I slowly extricated myself from the aircraft. Once outside, I saw that the power lines were down, as well as three poles. Usually the power company made us pay for the line, but this time they said it was on them—but I had to pay for the poles.

"I looked a mess after I got out of the aircraft. I was wet all over, had white crop dust all over me, blood smeared across my face, and I wore a leather flying cap. I must have looked like a creature from outer space. I walked to a sharecropper's shack. His thirteen kids were sitting out on the porch. When they saw me, without making a sound, they all disappeared inside the house. After much coaxing I got the man to come out and take me into town to a doctor. He dropped me in front of the doctor's office and took off. The doctor sewed up my cuts with regular sewing thread. I came home that evening and my wife said, 'Honey, you're early. You must have had a good day,' never noticing anything."

By 1948 the downsized and one-time Army Air Forces, which had come into its own as the United States Air Force in September 1947, was ready to take on a new crop of flyers. Dave Taylor couldn't get back in fast enough—this was the life he knew, and that's really all he ever wanted to do—fly. The Berlin airlift required all the transport resources of the fledgling USAF, and more. Dave went to Montana to check out in the C-54, flying a course similar to what he would have to fly in Germany. "I flew out of Frankfurt to Berlin, Tempelhof, starting in January of 1949. I didn't have my family along like many others did. So I just wanted to fly as much as possible. I flew a total of 132 airlift missions; probably more. What do I remember the most about the airlift? Brigadier General Smith did a really great job organizing the lift. Major General Tunner subsequently took command, but General Smith laid the groundwork, continued to work for Tunner, and implemented the nuts and bolts that made the Berlin airlift work.

"The weather was lousy much of the time, but since we flew strictly instruments at all times, had good GCA and ILS, it didn't really interfere too much with our operations. I remember on one particular foggy day sitting at the end of the runway at Tempelhof waiting for clearance to take off. A C-54 broke out of the fog just before touchdown. He didn't flare properly and touched down hard. As the gear collapsed and the aircraft hit the runway, the wings came off. The fuselage, totally uncontrolled now, continued to shoot down the runway aiming directly for the GCA shack. The GCA crew immediately abandoned their now perilous position and watched as the body of the C-54 stopped just before impacting the shack. No one on board the aircraft was hurt, except the flight engineer who scraped his right knee." Dave Taylor had his 8mm movie camera handy the day of this crash. As the C-54 approached at too steep an angle, he knew it wasn't going to make it. Dave whipped out his camera and filmed what happened next. He turned on the TV during our interview and showed me his 8mm film sequence of the crash, now on videotape. I had never in my years of air force flying heard of an aircraft losing its wings, but here it was. The C-54 fuselage hurtling down the runway, the wings falling off to the sides. It was a strange sight indeed. Shortly after the crash Dave Taylor took off from Tempelhof for Rhein-Main airport in Frankfurt. The airlift didn't stop for anything. "On another occasion I was asked on my departure to fly as close as possible to a building near the end of the Tempelhof runway. Someone was taking movies of the airlift operation and wanted a really close-up shot of a departing aircraft. I said, OK, I'll do my best. On takeoff, I aimed for that building, just topping it, blowing the camera off the roof with my prop wash. The photographer was nowhere in sight. My copilot and I had a good laugh. I came as close as I could to that building without crashing into it. That's what they asked for. That's what they got."

The Berlin airlift, as important as it was, lasted but a year. It was a way station for Dave Taylor, who soon found himself in Special Operations flying C-46, C-47, and B-26 aircraft out of Kimpo airfield near Seoul. It was his kind of flying, mostly at night and dangerous. At that point in his air force career, danger was a normal part of Dave's life and he didn't let it influence him too much, although he was not a foolhardy pilot—those rarely lived long enough to tell their stories. Dave knew his limits; he took his chances and counted on the odds being in his favor. On May 24, 1953, two months before the Korean armistice, Dave flew one of his most dangerous missions, in a flying career filled with danger, a mission which nearly cost him and his crew their lives. As reported by the Associated Press, and reprinted in the *Santa Fe New Mexican* in the December 29, 1997, issue, a South Korean agent operating behind North Korean lines had liberated from the back of a North Korean army truck the five survivors of a downed B-29 bomber. The agent probably had previously been inserted by Dave or by another member of his flight, euphemistically called B-Flight, which stood for Base-Flight. In the case of Kimpo Air Base, B-flight included special missions, a clandestine organization, using the B-Flight designation as cover, which normally only provided routine air base flying support.

The South Korean agent was most likely a double agent, like so many of them. Using his radio, the agent informed his American contacts of the opportunity to rescue the downed aircrew, commanded by its pilot, a first lieutenant, whose name I am not including in this story. Dave Taylor received the go-ahead to extricate the crew with his specially modified C-47 transport. The rescue aircraft was a forerunner of more sophisticated, but similar, rescue systems employed years later in the Vietnam War using C-130 aircraft. The system used a combination of harness and cabling extended between upright poles to allow an aircraft with a hooking device to come over low and pull a downed airman off the ground to safety. Dave made several flights to locate the downed B-29 crew. Once he found them and thoroughly reconnoitered the area from the air, he dropped the ground portion of the rescue equipment, which included two tall poles to allow the suspension of rescue lines. To confirm their authenticity, and to assure himself that this was not a trap, Dave dropped a camera and a homing pigeon, asking the agent to take pictures of the crew and return the film via the pigeon. The pigeon returned, but the film only showed pictures of the Korean agent, not of any of the aircrew. On the day before the rescue was to take place, Dave returned to the area and spoke over the radio to the lieutenant, asking him to authenticate himself by revealing private information that only he knew. The lieutenant did so and assured Major Taylor that everything was all right.

In the early morning hours of May 24, 1953, Major David Taylor took off in his slow C-47 to effect the rescue. As he approached the pickup site, he made contact on the radio and proceeded to approach the clearing at treetop level. Dave remained suspicious, and his senses were alert. Again, something didn't seem the way it should be. He wasn't quite sure what it was, but he felt that he was flying his crew into a trap. He had the lieutenant go through several authentications before committing himself and his crew. He saw the two poles, and his tail hook was extended. As he flew between the poles, the trap was sprung. The rescue poles turned out to house .50-caliber machine guns. "The bullets were coming straight up between the two engines and the cockpit. They ripped into our belly. I punched the throttles forward, climbed, and by constantly changing heading penetrated a wall of small-arms fire as we escaped the trap. I believe to this day that I was deliberately betrayed for reasons I cannot fathom. I consider the lieutenant a traitor," referring to the B-29 pilot. "He could have warned me off, and didn't. I wanted to napalm the whole area, that's how mad I was." Instead, Dave returned to the area several days later in a B-26 bomber rigged with a voice recording system. He circled over the mountain hideout and spoke briefly with each of the five B-29 crew members to verify that they were alive. To his surprise, the men spoke as if nothing unusual had transpired. "They gave me no hint whatsoever of distress. That was the last contact I had with them. After the armistice, the B-29 crew was not returned by the North Koreans, and they were eventually declared dead by the air force. I wonder to this day why an American officer allowed me to be ambushed."[19]

"When I made that rescue attempt, I had a formation of F-84s flying overhead to give me support the instant I got into trouble. They did nothing as they watched the sky erupt around me with tracers flying in all directions. I practically stood my airplane on its wing and made it fly sideways to get out of there. I got my crew out alive, but it was close. I was mad as hell. After landing

I got that 84-lead together with our colonel. I wanted the same bunch of guys to go back and bomb and strafe that valley the next day. I wanted to know they had the balls to do it. The colonel agreed, provided I could assure him that the prisoners were no longer there. I was never able to provide the colonel that assurance. Why didn't the 84s support me? Because they thought there was too much flak down there. That's what their lead told me.

"A similar incident happened to me earlier in the year. I was flying a night flare mission for some 84s. There I sat, at low level, punching flares out of my unarmed, slow-moving C-47, an easy target for the North Korean flak. Down below I could see a long line of trucks. I couldn't get the 84s to come down and hit them. The flak was too heavy, they told me later. Yeah, didn't I know that? I was down there. In anticipation of similar responses, my crew and I removed the chutes from a number of flares and added dynamite and scrap metal. On the next flare mission when the 84s were reluctant to come down low because of flak, I had my *presentos* ready. We punched them out of the flare tubes and without chutes the flares dropped quickly. Flares burn very hot and with the added dynamite they blew the assembled trucks right off the highway. We did that several times until someone blew the whistle on us. In a way I understood the F-84s' attitude. They didn't have wet suits and the waters around Korea were cold. A man would die in only minutes if he had to punch out over water. Of course, that's what you did, because no one wanted to bail out over land if he could help it and become a prisoner of the Chinese. Once the F-84 guys were provided the necessary suits—and I helped get the suits for them from navy stocks—they were much more willing to take risks. Their success against ground targets improved greatly."

One of Dave Taylor's more hush-hush missions was to insert Korean agents into the North Korean hinterlands. On one of those missions he took his C-47 way up north. "It was night, and in the distance I could see the lights of Vladivostok twinkling. After I made my drop, I had to keep on doing something else in the area, or anyone who saw me would know where to look and quickly pick up our agents. I kept flying up and down snowy ridges until, when topping one ridge, I saw a long line of trucks moving below me. The trucks were difficult to spot in the dark because they had snow on top of their tarps and were driving without lights. What to do? Such a fat target and no guns. No *presentos* either. Then I had an idea. I slid behind the ridge, turned, and as I crested the ridge again, I pushed my aircraft's nose down, facing the trucks, and turned my bright landing lights on. Trucks slid in every direction down the mountainside, exploding in bright flashes as they hit something in the valley below. My crew had a good laugh. We turned and disappeared behind the ridge. I decided to give it one more try. But the next time around, they were waiting for us. I had to do a max power climb to get out of range of their guns.

"One frequent problem I experienced with our South Korean agents was that they often refused to jump. Usually there were two of them, and if one wouldn't go, the other wouldn't either. When I flew a C-47, it wasn't that much of a problem. When the bell rang and the green light came on and the agent froze in the door, my jump master would cut him loose and push him out. Most of the time we used a modified B-26. We fashioned two seats in the bomb bay for the agents. When it was time to go, I would open the bomb bay doors, the jump master signaled to them, and all they had to do was roll forward—that is, if they wanted to jump. If they didn't want to jump, the jump master couldn't do a thing because he couldn't get to them. His threats and scowls couldn't get those guys to move once one of them froze. The word got around quickly among the Korean agents, and soon more and more of them played this 'I don't want to jump' game with us. I fixed that problem quickly. I had one of my maintenance people insert a pin in the bottom of each seat. The pins had cables attached to them which led to the jump master. Then, when the agents didn't want to jump, he pulled the pins. The seats dropped, and so did the agents. The word soon got out among the agents, and the problem went away.

"Of course we had our fair share of double agents. On a mission deep over North Korea, I was flying a C-47, and one of the agents had two bandoliers of hand grenades slung across his chest. As he was preparing to jump—jump masters standing to his left and right—he yanked a grenade off one of the bandoliers, pulled the pin, and threw the grenade back into the aircraft. The jump master, who had made three jumps in World War II behind enemy lines, cut the agent's throat with his knife as he was falling away from the aircraft. The assistant jump master grabbed the live grenade and threw it on top of the falling agent, who exploded in a violent flash. I saw the explosion, looking out the window, but had no idea what had transpired.

"In April 1953, just weeks before the armistice was signed on July 27, I attempted one final rescue mission on the spur of the moment—something you should never do. I was walking into base operations when a navy captain I knew spotted me and hollered, 'I have a pilot down. Will you go and get him?' Without hesitation I responded, 'I'm gone.' Off we went, just north of Panmunjom. When I got into the area, I could see the wreckage of the fighter still burning fiercely, emitting black swaths of smoke. No sign of the pilot. I dropped the nose of the C-47 until I got down to treetop level, clipping the tops of the trees with my propellers. The ground fire was intense. I tried several times but it was no good. I couldn't locate the pilot and had to abandon the mission. When I landed at Kimpo, the navy captain met me at the flight line. He walked around my aircraft and exclaimed, 'I've never seen an aircraft with so many holes.'"

42

It was late afternoon of my interview with Colonel David Taylor, but there was one more story he insisted he had to share with me. "The Chinese had noise-activated searchlights. They were almost impossible to get away from once they had a track on you. I figured there had to be a solution to that problem. What I did was to fly really tight turns, flying one engine at max power while powering down the other, slamming in opposite rudder. While the maximum sound traveled in one direction, I traveled in another. I repeated that trick several times until I had the searchlights going all over the place, unable to track me. Then I let them have several of my *presentos*, and that was the end of the Chinese sound-tracking searchlights."

Dave Taylor went on to serve in the early days of the Vietnam War, assigned to the 51st Fighter Interceptor Wing flying F-102 Delta Daggers at Naha Air Base, Okinawa. In 1964, as a result of the Gulf of Tonkin incident, it was Dave's job to move a squadron of F-102 fighters and another squadron of C-130s from Naha into South Vietnam. He bedded them down without a mobility plan or any kind of preplanned support. Quite a feat for one air force colonel. "I told my sergeants, if I get there and run out of anything, I'll come back and hunt you down and kill you. I didn't run out of anything." The 51st Fighter Interceptor Wing became host to the famed 555th Triple Nickel fighter squadron, equipped with F-4Cs in December 1964. And yes, Colonel David M. Taylor checked out in the F-4C—what else would you expect of him? Taylor served his country with every breath of his body. He was recognized for valor and heroism with the award of the Silver Star, Distinguished Flying Cross, Bronze Star, and Air Medal, to name only his combat-related decorations. His first Distinguished Flying Cross was awarded while he was flying B-17s against Germany with the 8th Air Force. The Silver Star was awarded for "gallantry in action against an armed enemy of the United Nations" for action "on 23 April 1953. On that date, Major Taylor flew an unarmed, unescorted C-47 cargo-type aircraft on a search mission behind enemy lines. In the vicinity of Yulli, North Korea, near which an F-84 had been shot down, Major Taylor flew his aircraft at tree-top level for approximately one hour to search for the downed airman. In making the search, eight or ten passes were made over the same spot, each pass under fire from enemy troops. With no thought of his own safety, Major Taylor disregarded the intense light arms and automatic weapons fire which resulted in hits and damage to the aircraft and continued the search until directed to leave by the controller. By his high personal courage in the face of the enemy and outstanding devotion to duty, Major Taylor reflected great credit upon himself, the Far East Air Forces, and the United States of America," so reads his citation.

On the occasion of Colonel David M. Taylor's retirement from the United States Air Force on June 1, 1972, the Air Force Chief of Staff, General John

Smoke marker bombs dropped by Taylor's B-17 on March 24, 1945, over Steenwijk, Holland.

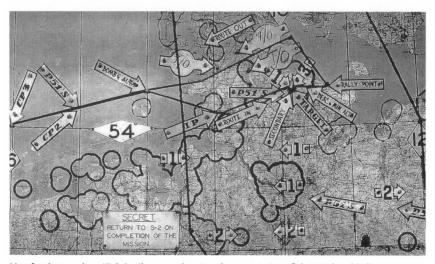

Map for the attack on Kiel, April 3, 1945, showing the route in/out, flak, Initial and Rally points.

D. Ryan, sent Dave a personal letter. In part the general wrote, "As you recall the events of your military career, you should derive deep satisfaction from your many contributions to the success of the Air Force. After completion of pilot training you were assigned to the Europan Theater where you flew 27 combat missions in the B-17 and earned the Distinguished Flying Cross and the Air Medal. You were again called upon to perform in a combat role in Korea where you flew 83 combat missions in C-46, B-26, and C-47 aircraft. During this period you were awarded the Second Oak Leaf Cluster to the Distinguished Flying Cross, the Bronze Star, the Silver Star, and the Eighth Oak Leaf Cluster to the Air Medal. Your combat role continued in Viet Nam where

Colonel Taylor in front of an F-4C Phantom II fighter in Vietnam. Dave went from flying B-17s at 170 knots to the F-4C jet fighter with a demonstrated speed of up to Mach 2.

you flew 32 combat missions in TF-102A and C-130 aircraft. . . . The Air Staff joins me in extending best wishes for many years of happiness and success. Sincerely, John D. Ryan, General, USAF, Chief of Staff."[20]

Colonel David M. Taylor retired to his farm on the other side of Charlottesville, Virginia. When I first met Dave at age eighty, he stood tall and straight, and his brown eyes were true and steady like those of a man who had seen more danger than he cares to remember. The boy from Mississippi never knew what awaited him when he helped gas up those Ford Trimotors in 1935. Dave is no longer with us—a member of that great generation of American fighting men who for me will always be my heroes—and their deeds will never die as long as we talk and write about them.

CHARLES P. JOHNSON

B-17

POW StalagLuft I, Barth, Germany

Sentiment of an Ally

Will you miss me when I've gone, London town?
You've been home to me for months, London town.
Though you've had your share of "Blitz,"
And the fly-bombs gave one fits.
Will you not forget me when your bright lights are lit again?
No matter, I'll still love you, London town.

—W. T. Manning, WWII ETO

By 1944 the German fighter threat to the American air armadas that launched their near-daily attacks from bases in England and Italy against the crumbling Reich had greatly diminished. The Luftwaffe had suffered grievous losses in experienced pilots which couldn't be replaced. American fighters—P-38s, P-47, and the new P-51—accompanied nearly every air strike, at times outnumbering the bombers they were escorting. By late 1944 the 8th and 9th Air Forces routinely put up 400 to 500 fighters at a time—something the Luftwaffe could only dream of. On February 3, 1945, when General Spaatz launched his first 1,000 bomber raid against the city of Berlin—a raid that I as a young boy, cowering in a cellar of a Berlin apartment house, remember all too well—over 600 P-51s accompanied the B-17 bombers of the 1st and 3rd Air Divisions. Twenty-three bombers and fewer than ten fighters were lost in that raid, not to German fighters, but to flak. The German antiaircraft artillery continued to take its toll, damaging another 339 of the attacking bombers to varying degrees.[21]

In spite of the Luftwaffe's diminished potency in the air, in July of 1944 it began to modernize and added the remarkable Me 262 jet interceptor and the Arado 234 reconnaissance bomber to its inventory. Most American airmen never became targets of an Me 262 attack. Most never even caught sight of one of the sleek, very fast jets which the fighter boys referred to as "blow jobs." But if you were a bomber and became the target of an Me 262, your .50-caliber machine guns did little good, especially if the German jet was armed with RLM 4 air-to-air rockets. While the fighter boys had a fair chance of coping with an attacking Me 262 by either taking evasive action or ganging up on the enemy and overwhelming him with sheer numbers, the bombers had no such options. They flew straight and level in their ponderous formations designed to maximize their defensive fire power against conventional fighters. They stood little chance of surviving a determined attack by a swift-moving German jet. A young lieutenant by the name of Charles P. Johnson barely survived such an attack by an Me 262, his B-17 going down in flames, taking three of his crew to their death.

The staggered formation of nearly three hundred 8th Air Force B-17 bombers of the 1st and 3rd Air Divisions had crossed the English Channel after their ponderous assembly over the East Anglia countryside. The individual bombardment groups were still climbing to their assigned altitudes which they would not reach until well over central France. So far they had suffered no incidents. Although it was rare to encounter a German aircraft in this area that late in the war, just the process of getting hundreds of bombers airborne from fields located all too close together and then assembling in a small piece of English sky was a hazardous operation in itself. Midair collisions happened all too frequently. The old timers spoke of crash and burn days, when the cloud cover was thick and multilayered, and aircraft from different airfields slammed into each other on climb out. It all happened so swiftly, the crews never knew what ended their lives. No one aboard any of the three hundred heavily laden bombers on this sunny afternoon on March 20, 1945, relaxed until after the formation was well on its way heading east, toward France and then Germany.

The gunners tested their guns over the English Channel, firing rounds downward, into the water, or outward and away from other aircraft, careful not to damage one another. Yet, it did happen. Some of the gunners playfully pointed their .50-calibers at their P-51 escorts flying circles overhead. Those same guns were nearly useless against an attacking Me 262 which moved much too fast for the gunners to properly aim and fire. The bombers were flying at less than half the airspeed of the sleek P-51s, for whom escort duty that late in the war was pretty boring stuff. Over France the bombers finally reached their assigned altitudes and leveled off between twenty-four thousand and twenty-six thousand feet. Everyone was on oxygen. The crews, even those in their bulky, electrically heated flying suits, were shivering in the cold, thin air. Charlie Johnson, a second lieutenant navigator, flew on a brand-new 303rd Bomb Group B-17G with the tail number 42-39160. It wasn't one of the squadron's aircraft. He flew with the 358th Bomb Squadron. This airplane came from the 360th, one of their three sister squadrons at RAF Station Molesworth, near Kettering. He couldn't believe his eyes earlier that morning when he pulled himself up through the hatch of 39160 and saw that the plane was carpeted throughout the cockpit area. Charlie looked into the pilot's compartment—carpet; past the bomb racks to the gunners' stations—carpet. He climbed down to his position to the front and below the two pilots—carpet again. Quite a contrast to what he usually flew—old, nearly worn-out bombers, with too many patches covering holes made by shrapnel from German flak. Those beasts shook and rattled and the wind whistled through loose joints and cracks. As Charlie tried to make himself comfortable at his position, he noticed that this aircraft also featured state-of-the-art heaters. What would they think of next, he thought. His enthusiasm for the airplane quickly waned. He hoped it wasn't a bad omen for this mission—a new, strange bomber with carpet throughout and heaters for the crew. It struck him that he wasn't supposed to be comfortable fighting a war. It just didn't feel right. He wished he was on one of those worn "battle horses" instead—at least they had always come home.

Charlie Johnson hailed from Mount Rainier, Maryland, and was drafted on April 28, 1943, along with a slew of his high school buddies. While being processed by a gruff army sergeant he asked about flight training, and to his surprise the sergeant obligingly got him the application forms which would send him on his way to the Army Air Forces. "That's a good idea, young fella," the sergeant had said to Charlie, smiling when he handed Charlie the application forms. "That's a really good idea you have there. I do hope it works out for you, kid," and there was that enigmatic smile on the sergeant's face again. Greensboro, North Carolina; Spartanburg, South Carolina; Nashville, Tennessee; Montgomery, Alabama; Fort Myers, Florida; Valdosta, Georgia; San Marcos, Texas; and Lincoln, Nebraska, were the many way stations Charlie passed through before he found himself at an overseas replacement center in Dyersburg, Tennessee. It was in Dyersburg where Charlie met a bombardier at the bar of the officers' club by the name of Winfield Wiegelt. Charlie and Winnie, his newfound friend, made small talk. Winnie cried into his drink, "If we'd just find a good navigator, then our crew would be complete and we could get on with things. The war is going to be over before we get there." Charlie thought he didn't hear right. The crew he had been assigned to just didn't want to jell. "I'm a nav," Charlie revealed to Winnie. "A good nav too." A little bragging couldn't hurt, he figured. "Do you think I could get on your crew?" It turned out to be a perfect match.

Wiegelt introduced Charlie to the pilot and copilot later on that evening at the officers' club. "My first impression," Charlie recalled, "of the pilot was very positive. He was slightly larger than I, very good looking, with features that made him appear both competent and tough. A real no-nonsense-looking kind of guy. He hailed from St. Louis and was a second-generation German. He didn't talk a lot, but when he did speak people were inclined to listen. His name was Francis Taub; everyone called him Taub. The copilot was John Cooper. Cooper had a soft Memphis drawl and an appearance that did little to instill confidence in his ability to perform. I soon learned how wrong my initial impression was. He turned out to be a competent pilot, and both friendly and likeable, although somewhat distant. The next day I met the rest of the crew. Warren Chrisman was our flight engineer and top gunner; Mike Dugan served as armorer and waist gunner; Jim Hollowell, a little guy, was the ball turret gunner; Chester Maluchnik served as radio operator; Elmer McWilliams was the waist gunner; and Jim Spencer served as tail gunner."

It was an all-American crew Charlie Johnson joined up with, their individual heritage as diverse as their last names. After a few training missions with his new crew Charlie got a break and he and a friend took a milk train to Memphis. "The train stopped at every little town along the way, a milk train. In Memphis we had lunch and then started making the rounds of the department stores searching for women's silk gloves to wear when flying at high altitudes where the temperatures were near zero or less. We met a lot of nice salesladies, but got nowhere with the nice ladies—nor did we find any gloves. We returned to our hotel, the Peabody, hoping for some action at the hotel's nightclub. We retired to our rooms unaccompanied that night. Back at Dyersburg I complained to Wiegelt, who had sung the praises of the Memphis girls. He explained that we had gone to the wrong hotel. 'The Claridge is where the action is,' Winnie said. 'The next time you come with me.' I did. Winnie was well known at the Claridge and we got an above-average room, with sitting room, for five dollars a night. Now that we had our lodgings, our next priority was to purchase some whiskey, since the hotel's nightclub only served beer. We went to a nearby liquor store where they sold name-brand whiskey, but only if you also bought a bottle of rum. I thought it an odd arrangement, so we bought both. Winnie had a steady girlfriend. I soon found one too. On our return to Dyersburg, Winnie and I marveled about how beautiful life was in the air corps."

On January 2, 1945, Taub and his crew set off for the war in Europe in a brand-new B-17 that was configured with all the latest innovations, including cabin heaters. "Our route took us over the snow-covered plains states, across Pennsylvania, New York, and into New England, where we landed at Manchester Army Airfield, New Hampshire. It wasn't until January 6 that we received departure clearance for Goose Bay, Labrador. We landed at Goose Bay in the evening darkness with the surface temperature twenty degrees below zero and a forty-mile-per-hour wind. Mike Dugan got frostbite while he tried to cover the engines with specially designed canvas engine covers. He lost part of one of his ears, but was again ready to go just in time to rejoin the crew for our trip to England. Thankfully the barracks at Goose Bay were warm and quite comfortable, and the officers' club was cozy, its only shortcoming being that it served no alcohol because crews had to be ready to fly on short notice. Goose Bay was boring. There was little to do but sleep and eat. Frigid weather conditions prevailed over the North Atlantic and had all the airplanes sitting on the ground. Some unlucky crews had been there for two weeks waiting for the weather to improve. Finally, on January 17, the weather eased and we were cleared for a night departure. We sat in our position in the dispersal area with the engines running from 7 p.m. to ten minutes past midnight when we were finally cleared to start taxiing. At the takeoff runway the ground crew refilled our depleted gas tanks. Then we took off for Reykjavik, Iceland, where we landed after fourteen anxious hours in the air. The next afternoon we departed for Prestwick, Scotland, and arrived that same evening safely and without incident." Taub, Cooper, and Chrisman flew the aircraft to a depot for assignment to a combat unit. The rest of the crew took the train to Stone, where Charlie and his crew were "stored" for the time being at a combat crew assignment center until someone needed replacements.

"We were billeted in a large, old concrete building," Charlie Johnson recalled, "which at some previous time probably served as factory workers' quarters. The building had numerous small rooms and a huge communal bathroom with big stone bathtubs, and a magnificent great room, which served as the officers' club. Bomber crews coming to or leaving England passed through this assignment center. There were a fair number of happy warriors—those going home. Poker was the game to pass the time. I watched. The good players soon won all the money from the not-so-good players. The good players walked around with large bundles of money stuffed into every pocket of their uniforms. It was not uncommon for five or six players to be playing with fifty-pound note bundles, each pound worth about four dollars, wagering one to ten bundles at a time. It's the most money I had ever seen in my life. They were exciting games, but way out of my league.

"While waiting for our assignment I spent my time sleeping late, eating lunch, watching high-stakes poker games, writing letters, and listening to the radio. I soon got bored with my routine and went to a local pub where I promptly met a pretty English girl, Lorna Holland. I could see that she was cold, especially her feet. So I let her wear my warm fur-lined flight boots. Thus began a memorable romance. We spent every night together until my crew received its assignment to the 358th Bomb Squadron of the 303rd Bombardment Group at Molesworth, England, which was part of the 41st Air Wing, 1st Air Division. The 1st and 3rd Air Divisions principally flew the B-17; the 2nd Air Division flew the B-24. On February 14, I flew my first combat mission against Dresden. We were flying within sight of a B-24 formation which had a different target than ours. The B-24s came under heavy attack by flak. In a matter of only a few minutes, nearly half of the B-24s had fallen out of their formations—some severely damaged, struggling to regain contact with the main body. Others spun away into the mist or exploded in a bright flash. Parachutes appeared on the horizon, but not enough to account for all the flight crews whose planes had been hit and were going down. No training film had prepared me for such an awful sight. This frightening scene put me in a cold sweat. I was shaking. I felt I was getting a preview of what would happen to us over Dresden. But the opposition over Dresden was light. Only one plane in our formation was seriously damaged. This mission was later described as the Valentine's Day Massacre because so many civilians were killed, reportedly thirty thousand or more. As we headed back home, my stomach and all my joints began to ache. I felt like I was frozen and could hardly move. The only thing I could do to try to relieve the excruciating pain was to curl up on the plane's deck in a fetal position. I remained in that position until letdown. I wondered, was my condition caused by fear? The last thing any airman wanted to say was that he was not brave. My concerns were relieved when the doctor told me that I had contracted a slight case of the bends brought on by the extreme cold and the protracted time of flying at over twenty-five thousand feet. 'Dress warmer,' the doctor told me, and 'start breathing 100 percent oxygen sooner.' I got a pat on the back and was back on flying status.

"On my second mission against an oil refinery on February 16 my plane sustained major damage. Two engines had to be shut down, the props feathered to prevent them from running away and shearing off into the crew compartment. Then a third engine quit on us—we were flying with only one good engine over Germany, losing altitude rapidly. Our immediate problem was to get through our own formation without a midair collision. Once Taub and Cooper had accomplished that feat, they managed to get a second engine running again. Then Taub and Cooper nursed our ailing craft back home, steadily losing altitude as we went. But we got home without having to ditch or a German fighter picking us off. Our escort was nowhere in sight. We flew another mission the following day in a different aircraft. Clouds were solid up to twenty thousand feet. For nearly an hour we slowly circled above our control point, climbing at a steady but slow rate, sweating like crazy, fearing that midair collision which could happen in a split second. When we finally broke through the clouds, bathed in brilliant sunshine, the crew let out a collective cheer of relief. With three missions under our belts we felt we were seasoned combat veterans, even though we really weren't when compared to many of the other crews in our group. To our surprise, we were given a two-day pass. Taub, Cooper, and I decided to head for London. In London we went to the officers' mess on Grosvenor Square. We had a couple of drinks and a delicious steak dinner costing all of twenty-five cents. After dinner we walked around town and then found us some rooms for the night. After freshening up a bit we headed for Piccadilly Circus. Legend had it that you were not a real airman until you had been to Piccadilly. Piccadilly was the answer to an airman's dreams—there were more beautiful girls there than I could have ever imagined. Some of them were there to find dates, others to find relief from their otherwise boring lives. Most were there to supplement their meager income. Whatever their reasons for being there, they were a delightful sight to young airmen away from home for the first time.

"With our mini-leave over, on February 22 we became part of a two-thousand-plane raid against the rail system of the Third Reich. Bombers and fighters from the 8th, 9th, and 15th Air Forces and the 1st Tactical Air Force participated in this mass raid. This was the initial attack of a sustained five-day air offensive code-named Operation Rail Smash. Our assigned target was the marshalling yard at Uelzen, an easy target. Although we flew only at twelve thousand feet, our bombing was mediocre. The next day we attacked Kitzingen. Neither fighters nor flak were encountered and our bomb drop was good. But because of the flight's deep penetration and our position on the outside wing, in heavy prop wash, we realized very early on that we would not have enough gas to make it back to Molesworth. We discussed the situation and decided we would remain with the squadron until we were out of enemy territory and then strike out on our own and find a place to land. We located a fighter base in northern France and made contact with the control tower advising them of our fuel situation. We were well received by the fighter pilots who treated us royally. The food and accommodations were great and the officers' club was superb—partly because of the whiskey, rarely available at Molesworth. But mostly because of the outstanding pilots we met who made us feel very comfortable as their guests. After a good night's sleep and a leisurely breakfast we prepared for what normally would be a routine and uneventful flight back to Molesworth. But Taub had a surprise in store for us. Since this was not a mission with a bomb load nor full gas tanks, the crew did not follow the normal procedure of sitting in the radio compartment for takeoff, but rather at our flight stations, which gave the engineer, the bomb toggler, and me an excellent view of what was to happen next. Everything seemed to be routine on takeoff.

Taub made a 180-degree turn as if to head for England. We were no more than ten feet above the runway, but instead of climbing, Taub aimed for the control tower. We came so close that I could see the controllers dive to the floor of the tower. At the last instant Taub raised the right wing just enough to clear the tower, dipping the left wing to only a few feet off the runway. After I regained my composure, I called Taub on the intercom. 'What are you trying to do? Get us killed?' 'Na,' came back Taub's laconic reply, 'just showing them that bomber pilots can fly just as good as fighter pilots.'

"Because we had not returned the previous day to Molesworth, we were not on the schedule, which was fine with us. Especially since this was the day of our squadron party. There were some Red Cross girls, nurses, and English girls from the adjoining villages, and plenty of food and drink. Everyone had a good time. Getting together informally like this also gave us the opportunity to meet some of the other aircrews whom we seldom got to meet. One memorable character was a first pilot named Werner Goering, a nephew of German Reichsmarschall Hermann Goering—the chief of the German Luftwaffe. Our Goering's claim to fame was that he had volunteered for a second tour and had a standing offer to fly any time another pilot did not want to fly a mission, no questions asked. The aftermath of the party wasn't so wonderful. Everyone likes to sleep in after a good party, but that was not to be. We were awakened after little more than two hours sleep and ordered to get ready for another mission. With bleary eyes and unclear heads we were hearing that we were to bomb Friedrichshafen. A rather disgruntled and motley looking group of flying officers left the briefing room to fly this mission. I put on my oxygen mask and set it to 100 percent. That had always worked wonders for a hangover in the past. Because of intense cloud cover we didn't bomb our primary target. And hit our secondary target instead, the marshalling yards at Ulm. On our return I hit the sack early to catch up on much-needed sleep.

"The following day, the twenty-sixth of February, we did the Big B—Berlin. The shock came in the briefing room when the briefing officer informed us that we were to bomb from east to west, something we had never done before. We flew east past Berlin, then made a 180-degree turn, heading west, into the wind. The winds at twenty-five thousand feet were ferocious, giving us a ground speed of only thirty-five knots. We were sitting ducks, but didn't encounter anything but ineffective flak. At least now we could say we had bombed Berlin." While Charlie Johnson was flying over Berlin at twenty-six thousand feet, I, a ten-year-old boy, was sitting down below in a cellar trying my best to cope with the fear and terror induced by exploding bombs. Berlin, of course, was a large city and a huge target which could absorb the bomb loads of hundreds of aircraft. Not every attack came close. But in time I knew, my mother knew, and even my six-year-old sister knew, we would all die sitting in this cellar not built to survive the power of high explosives, or even worse, the terrifying phosphorus bombs dropped at night by the Royal Air Force.

"Mission after mission followed—Leipzig, Hagen, Bruchsal, then Chemnitz. We were becoming rather confident as a crew to survive thirty-five missions. The Chemnitz mission was our deepest penetration so far and was scheduled for nine hours and thirty minutes. It turned out we wouldn't make it back to home base. As we approached the English Channel, we were running low on gas and left the formation. Cooper, usually the calmer of our two pilots, called me to find the closest airfield for an emergency landing. There was one just five miles straight ahead of us, just beyond the White Cliffs of Dover. When I gave Cooper the azimuth, he replied, 'I hope we can make it over the cliffs.' Suddenly we went from a feeling of relative security to one of fright. Once we made it over the cliffs, everyone breathed easier. Taub and Cooper managed to get the plane on the ground on our first try. It turned out to be a life-saving event. As we were taxiing, one of the engines quit—out of gas. Before we got to the end of the field, a second engine sputtered and quit. Only then did we realize how close we had come to disaster. Had this happened several minutes earlier, we probably would have crashed into the cliffs at Dover, or at best had to ditch in the channel. There are so many ways to die in war. We later learned that eight other planes in our group had to land at other bases, running short of gas, before returning to Molesworth. We wondered why B-24s, with their greater range, hadn't been sent on this deep penetration mission instead of us. On March 7 we flew a mission against Dortmund. After debriefing we went to dinner, where all the talk was about a bridge at a place called Remagen. Someone explained that now the US Army was on the other side of the Rhine River. The best news of the day, however, was that we were issued a two-day pass starting the next day.

"Taub, Cooper, and I headed for London. We immediately went to the Red Cross hostel between Piccadilly Circus and Oxford Circus and reserved rooms. Then we set out to enjoy the sights and pubs of London. We worked our way up to Bond Street, where we ordered Eisenhower jackets at a tailor shop for each of us. We would pick them up on our next visit to London. We had to pay in advance, because many jackets were never picked up by people who had been shot down. After a few drinks and supper we headed for Piccadilly Circus and the girls which were always there in great numbers. On March 13 we bombed a marshalling yard at Betzdorf, a railway bridge at Minden the following day. This time we were at the tail end of 1,200 planes ahead of us. The dense cloud cover required the bomb drop to be made from twenty thousand feet using radio beams as a targeting aid. I suppose the planners believed that with this many planes some would be lucky enough to hit the bridge. Reconnaissance later revealed that the bridge was still standing, but we caused a great deal of damage to the city. We encountered no flak or enemy aircraft and reported the mission as another milk run. On our return leg, while over France, Taub decided to leave the formation to conserve fuel. It was a good decision. But it delayed our arrival at Molesworth until after 7 p.m., which was when clouds often socked in the field. As we approached Molesworth, we could see that the clouds had indeed gotten there before us. The tower informed us that all of England was socked in and for us to return to France. Great advice, except we didn't have enough fuel to do so. Taub contacted the tower again and they informed us that the clouds were at about one thousand feet. If we wanted to give it a try, they would turn on the landing lights for us. We had no choice. To our delight, once we broke out of the clouds we were no more than two hundred feet to the right of the runway. The landing was one of the smoothest Taub ever made. Because we had survived so many narrow escapes, we were getting pretty confident as a crew that we would make it through our thirty-five missions. We were not only good, we thought, but also lucky.

"By March 20 I had flown seventeen of my required thirty-five combat missions. Things were looking good; the war should be over soon. As the ground crew closed the hatch on our brand-new B-17G serial number 42-39160, I remember the crew chief yelling up at us, 'Bring her back in the same condition you got her.' The ship was so new it didn't yet have a name, and it had only flown five missions so far. I studied my maps as we made our way across France. Our formation was following the lead ship. There wasn't much for me to do. Our position was on the extreme right flank of our squadron of twelve aircraft. We were the high group. Over France, we finally reached our cruising altitude of twenty-six thousand feet. Neither Taub nor I had been told where or what our target was before we crossed into Germany. We would release our bombs when the lead ship released its bombs. After crossing the Rhine River, we set course for Hamburg. From the Initial Point of our bomb run onward, Taub and I saw several German planes pacing us, just out of range of our guns. Obviously they were passing our altitude to flak controllers on the ground. I don't know what had happened to our P-51 escort. As we neared Hamburg, the flak grew in intensity. I watched for the lead plane to drop its bombs. And when it did, Mike Dugan, the waist gunner who also served as our bomb toggler, dropped ours and we began the race for home. Our group initiated a sharp left turn, heading for the North Sea. About halfway through our turn all hell broke loose. I felt a tremendous jolt shaking the entire plane. My first thought was that we had a midair collision. As I turned my head to the right, I glimpsed a Messerschmitt Me 262 jet fighter streaking past my window—a plane I had heard about but never seen before. I switched my radio from the group channel to intercom just in time to hear Spencer, our tail gunner, reporting extensive damage to the tail section. Taub then came on the intercom and warned that he had trouble controlling the aircraft and that we should prepare to bail out. I hollered at Taub, 'Don't you do that. We are still over Hamburg. If we bail out now, we're gonna be captured by the people we just bombed. Our chances of remaining alive will be slim to zero! Stay on a northerly heading, and try to make Sweden, or at least Denmark.'

"'I'll try,' Taub replied. The aircraft was shaking badly. I started to plot an alternate course when I felt two near-simultaneous explosions. I looked out and saw that two of our four engines were burning fiercely. The wings were shredded. Taub yelled, 'Bail out, bail out.' This was the end of my war. Maybe the end of my life. We were at twenty-six thousand feet. I couldn't believe what was happening. I tightened the straps of my parachute. At the escape hatch, Chrisman, the flight engineer, struggled to get it open. He could only open it a crack, not large enough for him to get through. He started to squeeze out, feet first. He got stuck. I stepped on the escape hatch handle and pushed him out. Then I squeezed through the hatch opening, plunging away from the plane, which exploded in a fiery flash. The nose section separated from the fuselage at the escape hatch from which I had just exited. Mike Dugan, still in the plunging nose section, climbed out as the nose dove toward the ground and parachuted to safety. Cooper and Taub had kept on trying to control the airplane until it exploded. Those two never had a chance. I think about them every day, every day of my life. If I hadn't tried to talk Taub into going on, maybe. . . .'"

A post-mission report prepared from interviews with aircrew upon their return to Molesworth notes that Lieutenant Taub was flying on the right wing of the flight leader of the high 360th Bomb Squadron formation—the most vulnerable position in the formation. Three Me 262 jet fighters attacked, shooting off the vertical stabilizer of Taub's aircraft on their first pass. On a second pass one of the Me 262s hit the number 3 engine and set the right wing of Taub's aircraft on fire. The B-17 formation was attacked by a total of six Me 262s. Taub's B-17 was about a thousand feet below the formation and three-fourths of a mile behind when the aircraft exploded. Three B-17s were lost on March 20, 1945, in the raid on Hamburg. Another aircraft was so heavily damaged it never flew again. Another 54 B-17s were damaged to varying degrees. The loss of 3 aircraft out of a total force of 146 B-17s, 2 percent, was considered light, unless it happened to be one of the aircraft you were flying in. Second Lieutenant Francis R. Taub flew a total of nineteen combat missions, Lieutenant Johnson was Taub's navigator on eighteen of those missions.[22]

"After clearing the plane," Johnson recalls, "I think I blacked out for a short time. When I gained consciousness, I instinctively pulled the ripcord, but held on to the smaller pilot chute until I was at a lower altitude, then let it blossom

MARCH 20TH 1945
HAMBERG

2NDLT	FRANCIS R. TAUB	P	*
2NDLT	JOHN T. COOPER. JR.	CP	*
2NDLT	CHARLES P. JOHNSON	N	●
S/SGT	CHESTER S. MALUCHNIC	R	●
SGT	WARREN. F. CHRISTMAN	E	●
SGT	MICHAEL A. DUGAN. JR.	T	●
SGT	JAMES L. HOLLOWELL	BG	●
SGT	JAMES P. SPENCER	TG	●
SGT	ELMER D. MCWILLIAMS	WG	*
SGT	ROBERT GILBERT		●

KIA *   POW ●

A stone tablet on display in the memorial garden of the 8th Air Force Museum in Pooler, Georgia, showing the names of Charlie Johnson's crew the day his aircraft was shot down by an Me 262 fighter over Hamburg, Germany. Hamburg is misspelled on the tablet.

to deploy the main chute. Rather than watch the horizon, as I had been taught, I looked down at the ground. I saw a farm house with a woman standing near it who no doubt had been observing my descent. Thinking I still had a distance to go, I hit the ground hard, severely spraining my right arm and leg. I was bleeding from the back of my head as well, the blood running down my neck onto my flight jacket. I ignored it. I tried to spill the chute as I had been taught, but a gust of wind filled it and dragged me across an open field. I eventually managed to catch up with the chute, fell on it, collapsed the chute, then unbuckled the harness. The chute and harness became airborne again when caught by a sudden gust of wind and blew away. I let it go. I knew I had been seen anyway and I was too exhausted and traumatized to chase after it. Instead, I headed toward a grove of trees and hid as well as I could. Once it was dark, using the North Star as a guide, I headed north, toward Denmark, if I could pull it off. I didn't really know where I was, but felt the further I could get away from Hamburg the better off I would be should I be captured. Fatigue, shock, fear, hunger, and exposure were taking their toll on me, and before light came I huddled in a furrow of an open field. I fell asleep, and was abruptly awakened after daylight by guttural voices. Ten elderly men armed with shotguns and pitchforks had surrounded me. I instantly knew that for me the war was indeed over. They took my gun, knife, money, and survival kit and marched me to their village where they turned me over to an elderly, uniformed man. He spoke a little English and gave me to understand that I would soon be transferred. To where I could not understand. When he tried to take my flight jacket, I pushed him away shouting loudly, 'Take your hands off of me. I am an officer!' My forceful reaction worked. He stepped back from me and didn't try to take my jacket again. I was then escorted to the back of an old truck, with two farmers seated opposite me pointing their shotguns at me. We bounced away over rural dirt roads, me fearing that one of those guns would discharge and blow my head off. At my request, and pointing at the guns, they finally complied and held the guns upright. After about fifteen minutes we reached a small town where I was incarcerated in the local jail. That evening a young pregnant girl brought me dinner and spoke to me in broken English about the war, apparently resigned to the fact that they were not going to win. After she left, I threw out some of the food even though I had not eaten for two days. A few days hence I wished I had even a small portion of the food I had so thoughtlessly thrown away.

"In the morning two elderly soldiers escorted me to an interrogation center. The younger guard, about fifty-five, spoke fluent English, and I learned from him that I was in the town of Bad Segeberg. He ran off when I heard a commotion outside, returning with a dozen soldiers, who immediately fixed bayonets onto their rifles and formed a cordon around the building I was in. A group of Hitler Youths, led and incited by a fat old man, apparently intended to abduct and punish me. Whenever one of the young boys came close, a soldier would jab at him with his bayonet, so they kept their distance. The German soldiers got me safely aboard a train accompanied by my two guards. We stood in the back of a passenger car where I chatted in English with two German naval officers who, like the farm girl earlier, also seemed resigned to the fact that they were losing the war. We arrived in Neumuenster and were forced to walk across town, because the day before, the 8th Air Force had nearly leveled the place. Older women and children were in the process of piling bricks into neat stacks of what used to be the walls of their houses. When they realized who I was, a captured American *Terrorflieger*, they grabbed whatever they could lay their hands on and tried to attack me. My English-speaking guard said to me, 'Let's make a run for it.' After about twenty or thirty harried minutes we reached another train station where I was placed under guard by several teen soldiers who appeared delighted to see me. In broken English they wanted to talk about Babe Ruth, Joe Lewis, Benny Goodman, Chicago, and New York City. I was put on another train which would take me to Hamburg, leaving behind my teen guards who hated to see me go.

"Once I got to Hamburg, the word soon spread that an American pilot was being held in the station. The stationmaster approached some German soldiers, who quickly dropped their packs, fixed bayonets, and surrounded the building I was in. There were about thirty soldiers holding off hundreds of enraged civilians. Having seen the utter destruction of their city, I could find no reason to blame them for wanting to take revenge on me. As far as they were concerned, I had devastated their homeland. My two guards finally delivered me safely to an interrogation center. With their job done, the youngest, in parting, asked me for my Army Air Forces wing emblems off my shirt collar. I gladly gave them to him. He had been my savior. At any time he could have abandoned me to the mob and let revenge take its course. He did what he thought was right, at considerable risk to himself. I never saw him again and have no idea of his fate, but I will never forget this German soldier and what he did for me.

"It was eight days since I was shot down. I feared the interrogation, but nothing untoward happened. The German officer spent most of his time talking about the war's coming end, which he expected would be in four weeks or so. He was solicitous about my head wound, which by now had largely healed, although the dried blood was still in my hair and on my shirt and jacket. He had a doctor take a look at me who assured me that I had nothing to worry about. The following day, I and twenty-five other scruffy-looking Americans were addressed by an English-speaking major. He informed us that we were to be transported to a permanent POW camp, and advised us that he only had six guards available for our march to the train station to defend us against any enraged citizens. He advised us not to respond to anything that might happen on the way: 'Endure the insults, taunts, and spitting' he requested. We did, and arrived safely at the station where we immediately boarded a train. The safest place for us to be. Soon after we pulled out, we were diverted onto a siding, from where we could watch German soldiers boarding a train headed east—probably to fight the Russians. I was astonished to see that with the exception of a few officers, they were just kids, twelve to fifteen years old. The flower of Germany's next generation being sent to slaughter for a cause long lost. Seeing these young boys is the saddest memory of my wartime experiences.

"Twenty-four hours later we arrived at StalagLuft I near the former resort town of Barth on the Baltic Sea. Barth lies equidistant between Rostock to the west and Stralsund to the east. It was a sprawling, ugly POW camp of about fifty acres, holding nine thousand British and American flying officers. The camp was divided into four compounds—South I held British and Commonwealth officers, and North I, II, and III was for Americans. I was assigned to the North III compound, where I was the twenty-fourth man in one room of a ten-room barrack. Colonel Hubert 'Hub' Zemke was the senior allied camp officer, and Lieutenant Colonel Francis 'Gaby' Gabreski was the senior officer of my compound. Zemke was of German heritage, Gabreski Polish. What a strange war it was. Although guarded by old men, Volkssturm, the camp was quite secure with its double-barbed-wire fences, machine gun towers and searchlights. We newcomers were ordered by American officers to leave our leather flight jackets with them to have the jackets painted with the letters POW. This seemed like a reasonable thing to do, but the jackets were never returned to us by our fellow American officers. Who knows what favors they traded those jackets for. Losing our leather jackets left us colder in the weeks that followed, and with deep resentment toward some of our fellow officers.

"I was warmly welcomed by my twenty-three fellow prisoners in the room to which I was assigned. However, my reception by the committee assigned to interrogate and verify new arrivals was less than cordial. Their task was to make sure that I wasn't a German plant, but the real thing. Fortunately, a few days later Captain Robert Johnson arrived, acting commander of the 358th Bomb Squadron, who had been shot down a few days after me. He remembered seeing me in the officers' club at Molesworth, satisfying the security committee. Through the grapevine I learned that other members of my crew were held in the North II compound. Talking through the fence separating our compounds I learned of the fate of Taub, Cooper, our pilots, and McWilliams, one of our waist gunners. The other survivors of my crew had traumatic experiences similar to mine. However, they all had pulled their rip cords immediately after clearing the plane and were carried by strong winds to the vicinity of Luebeck, about thirty miles east of where I had landed.

"The room to which I was assigned was approximately fifteen feet square and contained eight tiers of shelves on which we slept, three shelves to a tier— very cramped. As the new man I got a middle shelf, the only one vacant. The room had one door opening onto a middle corridor which led to doors exiting to crude latrines and trough urinals at either end of the building. Russian prisoners had the job of emptying the human waste tanks every morning. Each barracks room had two windows with shutters that had to be closed at night. In one corner of our room was a pot-bellied stove, primarily used for cooking, not heating, since we only had enough fuel for cooking our meals— when we had something to cook. The barracks were constructed about three feet off the ground, resting on wood pilings driven into the sandy soil, which enabled the guards with their German shepherd dogs to search beneath the buildings. Each compound contained about twelve barracks, a central latrine facility, and an open area in the center of the compound where each morning we lined up to be counted—what the Germans called *Appell*. Although all three American compounds were similarly laid out and constructed, ours, being the newest addition, did not have a water distribution system. As a result we in Compound III, twice daily, sent men to Compound II to get our drinking water.

"Our daily schedule never varied and focused around our three meals of the day, a near-continuous softball game and walking the fence line. We were always hungry. Each week every prisoner received one Red Cross parcel weighing eleven pounds which was immediately turned over to our kitchen personnel. Cigarettes, candy bars, and other sweets were returned to us. Everything else was used to prepare our meals. Only the three officers from our room designated as cooks could touch the boxes, and only when all three were present—a very exacting ritual was adhered to dividing our food into twenty-four equal shares. The content of those Red Cross boxes was not always the same. But they usually contained Spam, canned or dried fruit, cheese, meat spreads, powdered milk, and other foods that did not easily spoil. Not only was every morsel of food consumed, but each container was saved and put to good use. Eating was our principal obsession; fantasizing about food we wanted to eat once we got home was the other. Breakfast usually consisted of one thin slice of black bread, an even thinner covering of whatever kind of preserves had been included in the Red Cross parcels, and one cup of ersatz coffee, made from roasted barley. The bread and coffee were compliments of the Germans. Lunch was pretty much the same, except instead of jelly or preserves there was cheese on the bread. On rare occasions the Germans furnished some vegetables. And on even rarer occasions, real meat was served from horses or cows killed by American or British fighter planes.

"In our room only three were less than model flight crew officers, the first of whom had been in captivity the longest of anyone, shot down and captured in 1943. He had emotional problems, had difficulty comprehending what was going on, and seemed to barely exist. A second one had been blown out of his plane without a parachute, fell through a large tree and landed in a haystack. He awoke from his trauma six weeks later in a German hospital. He suffered severe head injuries, causing him to go in and out of reality. We did our best to care for him. The third was a 'schmuck' from New York City who didn't seem to get along with anybody. He was belligerent and constantly created problems and stirred up trouble. Fortunately, the rest were great guys—brave, honest, all-American boys. The Kriegie organization (Kriegie being an abbreviation for the German word for POW—*Kriegsgefangener*) that was doing its best to ensure some semblance of internal order and control was the responsibility of Colonel Hubert Zemke, an 8th Air Force fighter group commander and the senior allied officer of the camp. Our Compound III senior officer was Lieutenant Colonel Francis J. Gabreski, an ace in Hub Zemke's 56th Fighter Group. Zemke and Gabreski and others involved in various committees provided us with information about what was going on in the camp and in the war, and they dealt with a lot of gossip and rumors. The escape committee planned and carried out breakouts, supervised tunnel construction, and procured appropriate clothing, identification cards, money, maps, and train schedules that might prove useful to escapees. The information committee built radios and monitored the BBC news broadcasts. Only a few senior officers knew the location of the radios and were the only ones to have access to them. The security committee focused on warnings of unannounced searches, and the barter committee traded with the Germans for whatever was needed, including firearms.

"During the last days of April, artillery fire could be heard coming from the east. From our clandestine radios we learned that the Russian army was moving west and that a great battle along a wide front was in progress. For several days the sounds of battle increased in intensity and volume. On April 30, 1945, we were informed that the Russians were close and we began digging slit trenches and foxholes in anticipation of a fire fight. The guards ignored what we were doing." Unbeknownst to Charlie Johnson, Colonel Hubert Zemke, who spoke fluent German, had made arrangements with the camp's senior German officers allowing the trenches to be dug and for the German guards to leave their posts quietly one night as the Russians approached, avoiding unnecessary casualties.[23] "On the first of May the rumor mill had it that the guards, which were all old men, *Volkssturm*, were preparing to abandon the camp before the Russian army arrived. The following morning some of us climbed out the windows of our barracks. When there was no response from the guard towers, we knew that the guards had left. Prisoners from throughout the compound followed our example. Doors were ripped off their hinges, fires were lit, the gates of the interior fences were broken down, and within a short time all the camp inmates were outside shouting, laughing, crying, and hugging one another—free at last.

"After breakfast we had our Red Cross rations. Five of us decided to explore the outside world. We headed for the main gate which stood wide open. What happened that afternoon is difficult to relate in a manner believable to anyone not experiencing it firsthand, but I swear that the following account is the truth without exaggeration, exactly as it occurred: as we approached the town of Barth we heard automatic weapons fire. Our first reaction was to head for cover. But before we could decide where to go or what to do the firing stopped. We soon discovered the source of the firing. What we saw we could not believe, but it was happening right before our eyes. There was a magnificent coach drawn by two dappled-gray horses, driven by a small, young Russian soldier wearing the most outlandish uniform. He periodically fired short bursts into the air from his submachine gun. He was flanked by two pretty German girls who appeared to be enjoying the experience. As the carriage passed, someone who could read German explained that it was a funeral carriage. The young Russian officer in the outlandish outfit was blindly drunk, leading a Mongol horde of unkempt and equally drunk scavengers and pillagers. This strange army passing before us was composed of both men and women, the women looking as scraggly and tough as the men. They rode in captured old cars they scarcely knew how to drive, or in horse-drawn wagons piled high with loot. The rest of the mob staggered along on foot. All seemed to be carrying bottles, presumably vodka or schnapps. When they looked over at us, some of them pointed at the gas tanks of the cars, then to their bottles, then lifted their bottles to their lips, laughing hysterically. I could not be sure if they meant they were drinking gasoline and using vodka for fuel, or vice versa. We just stood there watching in amazement, which shortly gave way to concern. These people were wild and totally uncontrolled. The only Caucasian of the three hundred or so of this motley group was the young officer driving the funeral carriage, all others were Asians. We were not about to go near them, and quickly returned to the relative safety of our camp. Upon return to the camp it was explained to us that the soldiers we saw were not regular army, but rather terror troops to subdue the German population. They certainly were accomplishing that.

"Most of us ex-Kriegies, as we referred to ourselves, wandered around the camp to see what was happening in other compounds. In Compound II I met Bill Kaplan, a high school classmate, whose B-17 had been shot down over Germany. Our tail gunner Spencer was one of many who left the camp on his own, too impatient to wait for the arrival of American planes to return us home. Spencer eventually made it to the British lines; many others who chose to strike out on their own didn't make it, never to be heard from again. It was a beautiful May and some of us spent the time on the nearby beaches sunbathing, eating from our Red Cross parcels and speculating about our future. Through the efforts of Hub Zemke and Gaby Gabreski, an agreement was finally negotiated with the Russians which allowed the Army Air Corps to fly us out. On the eighth of May we marched down the road through the town of Barth to a nearby military airfield. It was an exhilarating experience. Eighth Air Force B-17s landed at the field and flew us to a military airfield in France. There we boarded trucks which drove us to a railroad station where we were to board a train to Camp Lucky Strike, near Le Havre. While we waited for the train to arrive, we noticed a tank car on a siding. According to the sign on its side it contained *vin*. One of our guys spoke French and asked the stationmaster if he would allow us to tap the contents of the tank car. Without hesitation the Frenchman proclaimed, 'As allies and liberators of France you are entitled to have as much wine as you want.' He broke the seal and opened the valve and we filed by filling our canteens with red wine. The wine was not very good. But who cared. This was the happiest and drunkest bunch of passengers a train had ever carried. The French conductors joined the merriment and in the end they were as drunk as the rest of us. Camp Lucky Strike was a huge tent-city, one of several, from which ex-Kriegies were processed for their return home."

In his book *Zemke's Stalag: The Final Days of World War II*, Hub Zemke writes about the evacuation from Barth. "Just before 1400 hours on the 12th of May 1945 a familiar sound was heard and a cheer went up from the camp. For there, sweeping low, with landing gear extended, was a B-17—a wonderful sight." The B-17 was piloted by Brigadier General William Gross, commander of the 1st Air Division. "Two other B-17s and a C-46 had followed Gross's aircraft into the field. The B-17 carried radio operators who set up their equipment to establish a control link with England and 36 more B-17s expected to land later in the afternoon. . . . Next day the greater proportion of the former inmates of StalagLuft I departed, a total of 6,250. Out of the west came a stream of B-17s sweeping down one after the other, some not even cutting all engines while 25 to 30 ex-POWs piled on board." Forty-six C-46 transports arrived midmorning and were loaded with sick and wounded and took off for France or England. By the morning of the 14th the remaining ex-POWs were flown out on B-17 bombers and C-46 transports. Hub Zemke was the last to leave. "I have never," he wrote, "been a man to carry sentiments for places that have featured large in my life. Yet I will never forget the last view of what was StalagLuft I: the gate wide open, the weather-beaten wood buildings gaunt and silent, no wisps of smoke, no kriegies pounding round the inner boundary wire. That said, of all my wartime haunts, it is the one I never wish to see again."[24] The B-17s that evacuated the POWs from StalagLuft I at Barth were from the 95th Bombardment Group at Horham. One of the B-17 pilots was David Taylor.

"From Camp Lucky Strike," Johnson recalls, "I was moved to England and during the following three months, May to July, I visited familiar places. One day I walked down Bond Street, to the tailor shop where I had ordered my Eisenhower jacket along with Taub and Cooper. The jacket was waiting for me. I could not get myself to ask about Taub's or Cooper's jackets—I was haunted by my memories. Why was I the lucky one? Why did they have to die and I survive? I knew I needed more time to sort things out and I also knew that I wasn't emotionally ready to become a civilian quite yet. In late July, at Bristol, England, I boarded the *Pierre L'Enfant*, a Liberty ship that had been converted to a troop transport. I arrived two weeks later in Boston. From Boston's Camp Miles Standish it was only a one-day train ride to Fort George G. Meade, in Laurel, Maryland. I was home again. It took a long time to push the memories of war into a remote recess of my being—and to transition into civilian life. One vision never left me—the picture of an Me 262 fighter flashing past my window. Then I think of Taub and Cooper. If only I had not. . . . The war goes on for me, it never ends."

First Lieutenant Charles P. Johnson was awarded the Purple Heart and the Air Medal with two oak leaf clusters upon his discharge from the Army Air

Charlie Johnson at age twenty in 1944 after graduating from navigator training at San Marcos, Texas.

Johnson's crew. L–R back: Taub, Cooper, Johnson. L–R front: Christman, Dugan, Hollowell, Maluchnik, McWilliams, Spencer.

Forces in 1945. Charlie settled in Rockville, Maryland, took advantage of the GI Bill of Rights, and obtained a degree in civil engineering. He then formed his own company which specialized in land development in a growing America. Johnson's company prospered over the years with offices in Maryland and Virginia. Like so many of his generation Charlie Johnson helped build postwar America. As for StalagLuft I near the town of Barth—it was one of several POW camps administered by the Luftwaffe. At the time of its liberation on April 30, 1945, the camp held nearly 9,000 American, British, and Canadian airmen, nearly all of them officers. The majority of the captives, 7,725 of the 9,000, were Americans, including Gaby Gabreski, the leading American fighter ace in Europe, and Hub Zemke, the commander of the 56th Fighter Group—Zemke's Wolf Pack.[25] StalagLuft III near Sagan, Germany, now in Poland, where I grew up as a young boy, was the other prominent Luftwaffe-administered POW camp, holding around 11,000 American, British, and Commonwealth airmen, again nearly all officers. In March 1944, seventy-six British POWs managed to escape the camp, memorialized in the film *The Great Escape*. All but three of the escapees were recaptured, and fifty were shot by the Gestapo, the German secret police, on Hitler's orders. In the air war over Germany over 95,000 American airmen became casualties. The air war over Europe was a bloody affair, but without the sacrifices made by American and British airmen it is difficult to imagine a successful landing on the beaches of Normandy on June 6, 1944.

BYRON A. DOBBS JR.

P-38/F-5/B-26

POW Korea

Korean Solitary

As I sit here and dream of home
and ones I love so dear.
I pray to God that some day soon
their voices I will hear.
But if God wills that I remain
to die on foreign soil,
Then comfort bring to those I love
through all of life's turmoil.
—Major Byron Dobbs, POW Korea

Byron Dobbs, Barney to his friends, slowly taxied his heavily laden Douglas B-26 Invader toward the end of the runway at K-8, a desolate airstrip near Kunsan, on the west coast of South Korea's midsection. Barney flew with the 8th Squadron of the 3rd Bombardment Wing, one of two B-26 wings dedicated to interdicting North Korean supply lines during the hours of darkness. It was the early morning hours of February 19, 1952. Only four weeks earlier Barney had turned thirty-two. He applied the left brake to his swaying aircraft. Slowly the Invader turned to face down the runway. There were no lights. He didn't need lights. Barney would steer down the center of the strip and when he reached 120 knots pull back on the yoke and lift off. He intended to hit his target hard and get out of the area quickly. To linger was a sure invitation to a "Chinese rest camp"—or worse.

"I always flew alone at night. You don't have to worry about a wingman while moving 240 knots at 250 feet above the ground. Neither in World War II in the Pacific nor in Korea did I ever fly in a formation larger than two aircraft. Mostly I flew alone; I liked it that way. I made a quick final check of the instruments dimly bathed in red light to preserve my night vision. Everything looked good. RPM and manifold pressures were in the green. The engines sounded smooth, my crew chief had seen to that. I carried fourteen forward firing .50-caliber machine guns, eight in the nose and three in each wing. At times when I fired, trucks just blew apart when they were hit by that many guns at once. On each wing I carried four five-hundred-pound bombs. I intended to use every round of ordnance and every bomb I carried. We knew the Chinese were building up for a big push, but without ammo and supplies they couldn't get far. My crew chief sat to my right. The top turret gunner sat behind and above us. It was our twenty-second mission in twenty-eight days, or nights, because I never flew during daylight hours. I had talked to the pilots who bombed my target in daylight. I knew approximately where the antiaircraft guns would be. I moved the throttles forward to full takeoff power. The engines responded smoothly. I released the brakes. Then I concentrated on the dark runway ahead, our liftoff, and my first heading. There were landmarks, dimly outlined against the night sky, which served as my reference points. There was no need to worry about the good guys shooting at us as they had in World War II. The bad guys didn't have airplanes which came down low to bother the troops on the ground."

Captain Byron Alexis Dobbs Jr. was born in Phoebus, Virginia, on January 14, 1920, under the muzzles of the quiet guns of Fort Monroe. His father was a carpenter. When the depression hit, his family barely managed to stay alive, moving from one relative to another, always chasing the next dollar or the next meal. "One summer we stayed on my grandmother's forty-acre farm. My dad got a contract from the Heinz company to grow pickles. I recall riding the pickup loaded with cucumbers down to their plant. The job only lasted for the summer but that gave us enough money to make it through the winter. Eventually we settled in Birch Run, a small village in Michigan. Both of my parents were from Michigan. I graduated from high school in 1937. I tried to enlist in the navy. They wouldn't take me because the doctor said I had hammertoes. I tried again in 1939, but that time I went to the army recruiting office. The doctor who examined me asked, 'Is there anything else I should know about your health, Barney?' Well, I always tried to be honest, so I told him the navy had turned me down in '37 because I had hammertoes. 'I don't care which way your toes point,' the doctor said, 'as long as there are five on each foot.'

"I was assigned to Selfridge Field. They had P-35s there. At night I would go and sit in the cockpit of a plane and think about flying. I dreamed of being a pilot. When I sat in one of those planes, I was on top of the world. The officers were gods to me. They treated us real well, and I did everything they told me to do. By 1941 I made corporal and my pay was increased to forty-two dollars a month. A year later I was promoted to staff sergeant, and I applied for enlisted pilot training. I was accepted. Late that year I got my wings and was promoted to flight officer. I ended up at Peterson Field in Colorado Springs, where I checked out in the P-38. What a beautiful airplane! After only forty hours in the P-38 we were considered combat ready by our instructors. At Peterson I met Allen H. Blum. He hailed from Omaha, Nebraska, a Cornhusker. Our friendship would last a lifetime, bonded by the year that lay ahead of us. Allen was good at keeping a daily log so I'll let him tell part of his and my story."

"I was getting a little sack time at Peterson Field," writes Al Blum. "It was Sunday, July 25, 1943, when the phone rang. The terse command to report to the orderly room immediately gave us a clue of what was coming. Our orders were to board a Transcontinental Airlines flight the next morning for San Francisco. Half of our guys could not be located. After all, it was Sunday. The rest of us bitched over the short notice. That night was a hustle and bustle for Jo [his wife] and me to get my junk packed. What to take and what not. The next morning we loaded into Flight Officer Barney Dobbs's car, who lived right across the street from us, and drove out to the field. There we learned that our plane didn't leave until 1500 hours that afternoon, so we had plenty of time to get our base clearances. I said goodbye to my swell little wife. We had just been married on June 5, not knowing if I'd get to see her for a long time or not. Dobbs and I planned to meet our wives at Hamilton Field, near San Francisco, just in case we had a few days to spend there. We arrived at Hamilton Field the next noon and found that our whole group was short on shots. They gave us the first series and we had to wait five days for the second series. I called Jo and Kay [Dobbs] right away and had them get on the next train westward bound. In the meantime we were busy getting our supplies—jungle kits and life rafts attached to parachutes, impregnated gas proof clothing, and more. It made us realize we were going to war. The good news was that we were to fly to our destination rather than going in a convoy, as we had supposed. After two days Kay Dobbs and Jo arrived. From then on until the morning we left we spent every minute together. The girls stayed at the Field with us during the day until 1600 hours, at which time we were free to go into Frisco. We took in Fisherman's Wharf for seafood, the International Settlement for entertainment, and stayed at the Sir Francis Drake Hotel. Sunday [August 1, 1943] came and at about 1100 we went to the swimming pool at Hamilton Field. When we checked in with the orderly room, we learned that we were scheduled to leave sometime that night. It wasn't until the next morning that we actually left. We said goodbye to our wives and boarded a big B-24 cargo ship, also known as a C-87."

"On Monday morning," Dobbs continues, "August 2, 1943, our group loaded on a B-24 with secret orders and instructions not to open them until two hours into our flight. My close friend Al Blum and I speculated where we were going. When we ripped open the envelopes, we found our destination was Amberly Field, Brisbane, Australia. We landed at Hickam Field, Honolulu, Hawaii. The island was blacked out at night, but we could still see some of the destruction from the Japanese raid. The next morning, August 3, we headed for Canton, a tiny island in the Phoenix Group. Once we arrived, we were surprised to see that all it was was a tiny coral reef, so small that one could take in the whole island standing in one place. We stayed there for eight hours. Then took off at midnight for Nandi in the Fijis. There we had breakfast—eggs and wieners. Al consumed seven eggs and I don't know how many wieners. We barely finished eating when we loaded up again, this time heading for New Caledonia, which we made in time for dinner. In the meantime we crossed the equator, the international date line, and jumped ahead a day. Once we arrived in Brisbane, we were told our final destination—the 8th Photo Reconnaissance Squadron at Port Moresby, New Guinea—The Eight Ballers: Eyes of the Fifth Air Force was our somewhat lengthy but appropriate handle. Al and I stayed in Brisbane two nights and thought they were crazy when they issued us six blankets each. But after the sun went down we discovered the reason—though it was August, it was midwinter downunder.

"In Moresby they were glad to see us. Their numbers were pretty well depleted. We lived in tents, and our comfort depended entirely on how hard we worked at it. Lumber was nearly impossible to get, but Al and I managed by hook and by crook to build us a little hut with a tent for a roof. At least we had a clean place to put our feet in the morning. The air was so humid our B-4 bags began molding after only a few days. Cigarettes absorbed so much moisture they were barely smokeable. There were five or six landing strips in the area identified by their distance from Port Moresby—three-mile strip, five-mile strip, seven-mile strip, and so on. We were to fly the F-5, the photo version of the P-38 fighter. Al Blum and I stayed together as much as we could throughout our tour, flying missions all over that part of the world. I spent thirteen months flying eighty-eight combat missions from Australia and New Guinea, fighting mosquitoes, malaria, jungle rot, and Japanese. Al flew one hundred combat missions. Al kept a diary of our day-to-day experiences in the Pacific. Years later, he sent a copy to me, and on the cover page he wrote, 'I occasionally reread it, Barney. I can still feel the anxieties, fears, frustrations, satisfactions, joys, memories of friends and comrades, sadness when someone didn't return, and the many other emotions of a shavetail involved in the greatest transition of his life—from farm boy to combat pilot.' I sure loved Al's diary, and I'm glad he kept it and sent me a copy. It brought back those bittersweet memories of when we were young and thought of ourselves as being indestructible." Al Blum kept a daily log of his experiences in the Pacific until his return to the United States a year later. Wrote Al Blum:

21 August 1943—In a few days I went on my first combat mission with Flight Officer Ludtke—one of the old pilots—and of course I was plenty nervous. We always fly in pairs—one to watch for the enemy, while the other does the photo work. Sent three of the old and three new pilots to Charters Towers, Australia, for fighter training. Our new policy was to have pursuit ships in our own squadron to escort photo ships.

28 August 1943—My second mission was to Wewak with Captain Foster, our squadron commander. I didn't see the Zeros coming up after us, although they were only 3,000 feet below us. Captain Foster said he could see the red spots on their wings, and he didn't like it when I told him I didn't see them. Can't blame him, since I was his cover. Several nights later I got orders to get ready to leave for Marilinian, about 35 miles from the nearest Jap base at Lae. Found that I was to be quartered with the 44th Fighter Squadron. Our planes arrived that evening.

1 September 1943—I flew my third mission with Lieutenant Sykes to Wewak. Clouds covered the target. Didn't get any pix. Came back to Alexishafen and Madang which were clear and then on to Moresby to deliver the film and reload. We had no facilities for processing film at Marilinian.

2 September 1943—Lieutenant Duke and I ran a recce over the Markham Valley. I took pictures of the valley; Duke did the coastline from Lae to Hopoi. This was in preparation for a big Aussie and American landing at Lae. 15,000 Aussie troops landed and were covered by P-39s, P-47s and P-38s. The operation was a success, even though they were opposed by 13,000 Japs.

4 September 1943—I was at 17,000 feet when I began feeling woozy. I checked my oxygen hose and everything seemed to be OK. In another minute or so I was really feeling weird. Then I found a hole in my mask. I called my escort and he went on while I peeled off to get some air at a lower level.

5 September 1943—The Aussies landed 1,500 paratroops in the Markham Valley at Nadzab. It was a beautiful sight to see the transports covered by P-47s and P-38s. B-25s went in first to strafe ground positions and lay smoke screens.

6 September 1943—Major Hocutt gave me the Hollandia mission. I had one escort along. We got there, but the target was covered with a thin layer of clouds. I was ready to turn back, but changed my mind. Right over the airfield was a hole in the clouds. I got the pictures, then headed home. I was the first one to fly this mission successfully. Our operations officer, Captain Guerry, put me in for the Distinguished Flying Cross.

7 September 1943—Had three red alerts last night. The first was the only one when bombs were dropped. We suffered no damage—bombs missed the strip and the camp.

8 September 1943—Lieutenant Haigler and I were washing up in the creek when we heard shots, just below the first bend in the river. That afternoon we learned that several engineers were bathing just below us when a Japanese soldier rose up out of the weeds and fired at them, hitting one of them in the shoulder. Of course they started running, went to the military police, who wouldn't believe them. They borrowed guns and went back. They got him with automatic fire. He evidently was a pilot who had bailed out near there and had been wandering around. They found his bed. There was also a second one. So there must be one more wandering around somewhere.

10 September 1943—Rained all night. Our dirt runways are fair, which is to say they are about a foot deep in mud.

13 September 1943—My baptism of fire. Duke flew to Moresby yesterday and I was down at Ops awaiting his return. About 10:30 I looked out and saw the linemen running for cover. I then looked over my shoulder and saw a beautiful formation of eleven bombers and thirty Zeros directly overhead. We headed for the slit trenches just as the bombs began bursting. I am now a strong believer in slit trenches and will no longer just lay in bed at night when a red alert is sounded.

14 September 1943—We got orders to return to Moresby, which made everyone plenty happy. Got to Moresby and the first thing I heard was that Taylor was missing. This was a real shock. He was en route to Moresby from Dobodura and ran into bad weather. This evening I had to help sort and pack his personal belongings to be sent home.

16 September 1943—Went on another mission to Wewak to cover this morning's strike. On yesterday's raid on Wewak B-24s shot down 38 Nip fighters and 16 probables. P-38s shot down nine with six probables.

19 September 1943—Mission to Dumpu to get low obliques of an old landing strip. Japanese dropped a few bombs here at Moresby last night but scored no hits.

21 September 1943—Started out with Dobbs to new Britain but just as we got there the diaphragm on my oxygen regulator busted and I had to come back.

29 September 1943—Farmer and I started to make the circuit—Ramu Valley, Madang and Cape Glouster, but had to return due to weather, as did all the other ships that started out today.

8 October 1943—Ludtke with Holton and Bateson as escorts went to Madang to check up on some convoy activity. Just out of Madang they were jumped by Zeros. Bateson failed to return. They didn't see him get hit, so he may be safe in the Markham Valley. My orders came through today awarding me the DFC.

10 October 1943—My 16th mission. Walt Langdon and I took off for Madang. At 18,000 feet started through a cloud deck on instruments. I hadn't turned on boost pumps yet and was flying close to the lead ship so as to keep it in sight. About that time my left engine gave out. I immediately turned on the boost pumps, but lost sight of Walt. I came out beneath the cloud deck while he continued on until he got on top. Tried to call him on the radio, received him OK, but couldn't transmit. We got the pix of Madang and Alexishafen and started for Finschafen. Over Finschafen, at 24,000 feet, I saw two planes approximately half a mile away. They peeled off toward me. I immediately dropped my tanks and pushed the throttles to full RPM in a slow climb toward home. Was able to outdistance them. Love that high altitude foxhole!

13 October 1943—Ran into a front about 20 minutes out of Rabaul. Had to return with no pix. My hydraulics went out, so I had to hand pump my landing gear down—talk about sweat!!

14 October 1943—My first combat leave to Sydney. How one does appreciate hot showers, soft beds, thick steaks. It all costs a lot of money, but it is worth it.

30 October 1943—Took two fighters for escort from the 39th Fighter Squadron and started for Kavieng in New Ireland. My first try at this particular target. On our way up landed at Lae for gas. Two short months ago we wouldn't fly over here under 30,000 feet, now we are landing here. You should see the destroyed Japanese planes—fighters, bombers. Dozens of bullet holes through them all. One bunch of rising suns which have definitely set.

2 November 1943—My 19th mission. Murphy and I took off for Madang, Alexishafen and Nubia. Got pix of all the airdromes and returned to base.

8 November 1943—Two fighters from the 39th flew as my escort. One had to return for some reason. We got there OK and did all the airfields but two, the harbor and the town. Antiaircraft fire was at our altitude but about 100 yards behind us.

13 November 1943—My 22nd mission. Picked up my fighter escort at Nadzab—P-47s. And if anyone says anything about a 47 out flying an F-5, they're wrong. Got to Wewak but was clouded over.

15 November 1943—Loos and I did Cape Gloucester, New Britain, then Finschafen. We were jumped by two Zeros at Finschafen. Wasted no time in getting out of there—leaving them in the dust so to speak.

17 November 1943—Flew to Sydney as copilot on a B-26. Picked up furniture and food for the club. Right brake locked on landing blowing out the tire, wrecking the wheel and ruining the nose strut. Took about a week to get repairs. Had lots of fun—flew under the Sydney bridge and got back to Moresby just in time for Thanksgiving dinner. General [George C.] Kenney had been at the squadron in the morning to award medals, but I missed mine. [General Kenney was the commander of the Far East Air Forces including the 5th, 7th, and 13th Air Forces.]

6 December 1943—Orders came through promoting me to first lieutenant.

26 December 1943—Colonel Hutchinson with Colonel Arnell as copilot started out from our airdrome in our B-17 this morning to cover the allied landing on New Britain. It wasn't daylight yet, and there was heavy ground fog. The ship crashed off the end of the strip killing two. There were 17 men aboard of which four were war correspondents. It was a terrible mess. The smell of burning flesh is a very unpleasant experience. Two more men died later in the hospital. I flew a mission to Hansa Bay, but no pix due to weather.

29 December 1943—Today I am 24 years old and flew my 29th mission.

31 December 1943—We lost another pilot. The last seen of Lieutenant Erb—yesterday morning—his plane was on fire, and he was turning back, but didn't make it. I spent an hour and a half this morning searching for him. His little daughter had just been born a couple of weeks ago. Lt Fairbanks and Colonel Darnell were released from the hospital this morning. They were survivors of the B-17 crash.

5 January 1944—Rigsby, Clark and I started for Kavieng, but just as we got over the range we saw weather building up, so we turned back.

23 January 1944—Gailfus and I went to Manus Island. Got the pix but Gailfus's left engine quit. He landed at Finschafen. I went on to Garove Island and New Britain. Flew a total of 6:45; of which 5 hours was at one sitting for my longest mission so far.

5 February 1944—Lt Shipway and I started out to cover a big strike at Kavieng. Weather stopped the whole show.

12 February 1944—Colonel Darnell as my escort and I started for Kavieng, but returned due to weather. Two days ago Flight Officer Davis was lost in weather.

15 February 1944—Went to Townsville to ferry up a fighter. Had to wait a week before it was ready.

9 March 1944—Captain Counselman and I started for Hollandia, by going around Finschafen we got as far as Bagbag Island at about 50 feet over the water. Counselman got lost and I had to bring him back. It sure tickles me to have one of the big dogs get lost. One does learn from experience.

19 March 1944—With eight fighters for escort took pix of Wewak at 15,000 feet. Saw 14 Japanese planes airborne but they didn't bother us. Intelligence reported from Manus Island that the Japanese intended to lead a life of ease and luxury. Quantities of beer and liquor were found and Geisha girls with their throats slit rather than let the Yanks capture them.

25 March 1944—Holton and I started to Wewak but a 20,000 foot ceiling made it no go for pix.

29 March 1944—44th mission. Holton and I went to Hollandia to cover a strike. They really left a trail of damage. Using 20 pound fragmentation bombs they knocked out 112 planes on the ground and shot down ten more. Got pix at Wewak, Tadji and Nubia.

4 to 22 April 1944—Combat leave to Sydney.

30 April 1944—48th mission. To Wakde Island. Couldn't get mapping on account of clouds. Got Wakde airdrome and several small dromes. This gives me 152 combat hours—halfway home!

6 May 1944—Today ended in tragedy. Lieutenant Walt Langdon, a good friend, was killed in a crash on takeoff. I took off first, made my turn, and saw that he was off the ground and turning. When he didn't join me I looked back and saw the black smoke from a fire. He was killed instantly. He leaves a wife and 6 months old son. The second crash in a week. Who's next?

7 May 1944—50th mission. Captain Shipway as pilot, me as copilot in a B-25 to Biak Island to obtain oblique pix of 20 miles of coastline at 500 feet. We were accompanied by another B-25 and had fifteen P-40s for escort. Got the pix and on our return sighted a merchant vessel approximately 200 feet long. We both went down and strafed it. Fourteen .50-caliber guns shoot a lot of lead. The ship blew up.

23 May 1944—Monroe and I started out for Baboa but couldn't get pictures due to weather. We are doing our cooking over an outside fire, using 100 octane gas. Had lots of good bacon for a change. Everyone sleeps with their .45 under their pillow. The Japanese out in the hills are pretty hungry and sneak into camp trying to find food.

28 May 1944—Our detachment moved to Wakde Island, 200 miles west. I didn't go. Had to stay so that I could test-hop a ship that was in the process of having its engines changed. Found that my chute had gone with our detachment to Wakde, so I had to fly without one. You sure feel naked when you don't have your chute. Probably would have been court-martialed in the States for doing that. Flew the test-hop and then went on to Wakde to get my chute, bedroll and other personal equipment. Have to take this bird back to Nadzab tomorrow.

29 May 1944—58th mission. Took off and delivered the ship to Nadzab where I learned that the squadron is moving to Biak Island—our next home. A jump of 800 miles into Japanese territory. The Allied landings were only made two days ago. On Wake Island they have been bombed heavily and one night even strafed with landing lights on. A small group of Japs made a suicide attack on an Air Corps unit but their own end was all they accomplished. They had bombs tied to themselves as well as machine guns and rifles with fixed bayonets. We'll have plenty of use for a good slit trench when we get to Biak. Two American nurses, presumably from the Phillippines, were found in a Japanese brothel at Hollandia. They were nearly crazy from drugs and dope.

1 June 1944—61st mission. Holton and I each got full K-18s of mapping the Wewak area. We saw P-47s dive bombing at Hansa Bay, so we entered their bombing pattern and followed them in even though they were only dry runs for us. Some fun.

23 June to 23 July 1944—Flew nearly every day, and on July 23 ended up with 303 combat hours and 100 missions. In one three day period I had to return twice on single engine. The last time was for four hours which is quite a while with only one fan. Our detachment moved back to Hollandia because Wake was too small for our planes. One night on landing I ran over some shrapnel and cut up a tire. Had to leave the bird on the taxiway. During the night we had a raid. Bombs destroyed six planes and a gasoline storage area filled with 50 gallon drums of aviation gas. My plane survived because it wasn't parked where the others were.

26 July 1944—Six of us went to Brisbane to pick up six new F-5Es and bring them back.

3 August 1944—My promotion to captain finally came through.

31 August 1944—Just eating dinner at Nadzab when Dobbs and Holton got in from Hollandia and Biak. They brought with them our going home orders.

1 September–2 September 1944—Found we were scheduled to leave on a C-54, a beautiful thing. I wasn't feeling too well, came down with Malaria on the way to Guadalcanal—chills, fever. From there we flew to Canton Island. The flight engineer took pity on me and let me lay down in one of the crew bunks. Took off from Canton for Hawaii, crossed the international date line and once more it was 1 September. Arrived at Hickam Field. A nurse came around with thermometers. I saw her first and ducked into a latrine until she was gone. I wasn't about to be stuck into a hospital this close to home. Took off on the last leg and after 14 hours landed in Frisco. It was about 1600 when we stepped off the plane. Right then and there started the red tape, paperwork and "shoot the bull, pass the buck and make seven copies of everything," which is the identifying characteristic of the Army. Pulled a fast one on the medic who examined me for fever. He stepped out for a minute. I looked at my thermometer which was too high, so I shook it down to normal. Got a good shower, hot water, then a big steak. Dobbs, Holton and I were home again.

Barney Dobbs and Al Blum survived a bloody war; many of their fellow pilots didn't. They were not the same men that had left San Francisco for Australia a year earlier. They changed in ways they had yet to understand for themselves. It was only 1944 and the war in Europe and the Pacific still had a year to go before it was finally over.

"In 1946 my wife and I left for our new assignment in Germany," Barney recalled wistfully, an assignment he and his wife thoroughly enjoyed. "I flew the P-61 Black Widow night fighter out of Schweinfurt until the Black Widow was phased out of the Army Air Forces inventory. In 1948 I found myself at Oberpfaffenhofen where I prepared fighter aircraft for turnover to allied nations. I was quickly drafted into the evolving Berlin airlift. I was sent to Wiesbaden to fly as a copilot in C-47s. I had always flown fighters, and I knew nothing about the C-47 transport. It makes my hair stand up in back of my neck when I think of that time in the C-47. They put us fighter jocks in the right seat. I knew enough to keep the thing right side up. I flew into Tempelhof, landing between five-story apartment houses. It was awful. But the GCA radar controllers were superb. I was awfully glad when the airlift was over and I went back to the used-aircraft business. From Germany I was reassigned to the Military Air Transport Service, MATS, at Westover Air Force Base in Massachusetts. While there I flew C-97 Stratocruisers, the military version of the Pan American double-decker airliner. I hated every minute of it. One day while flying a huge four-engine C-97, I surreptitiously joined up with a formation of fighters coming in for a landing. I think they would have court-martialed me for what I did, but a war had broken out in Korea, and I volunteered to be an F-51 replacement pilot. That saved me. Once in Korea I was assigned to K-8, 'Kunsan by the Sea,' as we referred to it, flying the twin-engine B-26 Invader. The B-26 was no fighter plane but the closest thing to it. I soon fell in love with the airplane.

"In the dark early morning hours of February 19, 1952, I skimmed across the craggy Korean countryside at five hundred feet above the ground, intending to be at no more than two hundred feet above the terrain in our target area. My crew and I had been to this target before, and we were good at identifying trucks moving on dark roads with their lights out. If there wasn't anything happening at the location, we had plans for two other sites. I saw the telltale shadows of slow-moving trucks thrown up against the side of the road by residual fires from the daylight raids. I pointed the nose of the Invader down the valley and made my first pass. I dropped my bombs to bottle up the trucks. The eight bombs slammed into the lead trucks, blowing two off the road. Explosions lit up a string of trucks reaching back into a tunnel. As I emerged from the valley, banking to my left, I heard a call from a C-47 flare ship asking me if I wanted flares dropped. 'Roger, no flares,' I told the flare ship pilot. I had no time to chat with the fellow. I was busy concentrating on flying my airplane down a dark mountain valley adjacent to the one I had passed through.

"'I can't go home until I drop my flares,' the flare ship pilot continued to badger me. I ignored him. I was lining up for my second pass. I knew I had surprised the antiaircraft gunners on my first pass, but this time they would be ready for me. I figured they'd expect me to reenter the valley the way I exited. I made a shallow wide turn instead, flying down the adjacent valley, planning to reenter the way I came in on my first pass but from the opposite side. I was concentrating on my approach to the target with no further thought of the flare ship. I could clearly see the trucks on the winding mountain road. I was lined up, ready to fire my guns, when a bright flare lit up the valley, blinding me, destroying my night vision. To the North Korean gunners I must have looked like a target at their gunnery school. I pulled the aircraft up, cursing the flare ship. I was going to get that pilot's ass when I got home. But first I had to get out of here. Then the flak hit. I felt the impact of the shells as they ripped into the left engine. Fire was everywhere. Get out, I yelled and jettisoned the hatches. The crew chief exited over the right wing. I couldn't see the gunner exit, but I thought he was out when I abandoned the aircraft. My chute opened. I swung once or twice and then I was in the trees, on the ground. I was dazed, it happened so fast. The damn flare ship, I thought. I remember unbuckling my chute and how quiet it was. I was alone. I looked around for my crew. Only silence. I knew exactly where I was and prepared to make my way back to friendly lines. A river ran below and I toyed with the idea of crossing over to the other side to throw off any search parties which I knew were going to come looking for me. I discarded that idea and decided to move inland and south. There was a slight moon to aid my travel. I felt the cold. The snow reminded me that escape was going to be difficult. Someone surely would pick up my tracks. I could hear dogs barking in a village below me. I decided to hide and wait until daylight. I was dressed for the weather and thought I'd be able to stay fairly comfortable if I found a good hiding place. But by morning the dogs had tracked me down, and three villagers escorted me down the mountain, where they turned me over to soldiers. I didn't know if they were Korean or Chinese. My crew chief was there too. No sign of our gunner. We were kept for several days in a back room of a simple cottage. One day a Russian officer showed up. The Russian was friendly and spoke English well. He loaded me into the back of a truck and to my amazement drove me out to my aircraft. The damn aircraft hadn't crashed. It made a smooth belly landing and was barely damaged. The Russian was a ground pounder and didn't know what questions to ask. What he seemed to want to know from me was what we had in our aircraft that allowed it to belly land, nearly undamaged, without a pilot. Of course we had no such thing. I don't know how that airplane landed in a mountain valley without tearing itself to pieces."

For nearly nineteen months Barney Dobbs endured torture and degradation as a prisoner of war of the Chinese People's Army. He was interrogated repeatedly. Barney recalled seven different interrogators who tried to convince him to admit that he was using germ warfare. He was deprived of sleep, food, and water to make him compliant. He didn't break. He was repeatedly put in solitary confinement, including imprisonment in a three-by-six-foot hole in the ground for six months. Finally, his interrogators gave up and put him in an unheated shack with twelve other uncooperative American prisoners. When Barney lay in the hole in the ground, he sought something to hold onto, to keep his sanity, to be able to endure and survive. He tried to recall every hymn he ever sang in church, and in time he composed his own hymn in his mind, writing it down on paper once he was released:

Korean Solitary

The accusation, it was made: of course it was denied.
They said of them germ bombs I'd dropped, and about it I had lied.
A bomb that's filled with flies and fleas, dear Lord, I've never seen;
but men for propaganda's sake can sure be mighty mean.

Interrogators came and went, their lies were all the same.
"Confess," they said, "and you'll go free, or here you will remain.
God can't help you, he's not real, you're living in a dream."
"Not so," said I, "He's real to me, so go to your extreme."

"An execution is your fate, since you've made up your mind
not to confess and tell the truth about your heinous crime."
So they threw me in a hole, never to return.
And I'm afraid their souls will rest in Hell and burn, burn, burn.

The hole was deep, not very long, and only three feet wide.
The sun and air through a window came, six inches on each side.
The roosters woke us up at four, the guards came round at five;
they brought us food, 'twas just enough to keep a man alive.

Fish heads and rice were all we had, sometimes a piece of bread,
but we ate it with God's blessing, who watched from overhead.
Soap they gave us, but water none, tobacco but no fire.
They called it "lenient treatment," but only aroused our ire.

I've seen men come and I've seen men go, but some men stayed forever.
They paid the price for that plot of ground up on the Yalu River.
I've seen 'em beg and scream and yell for a doctor and some pills,
to stop the dysentery, and drive away their ills.

As I sit here and dream of home and ones I love so dear,
I pray to God that some day soon their voices I will hear.

Byron A. Dobbs Jr.

But if God wills that I remain to die on foreign soil,
then comfort bring to those I love through all of life's turmoil.

As I look 'round me at the foe who's never heard His name,
I wonder where their souls will go when they're through life's earthly game;
never to have heard His word, nor felt His saving grace,
nor seen the love of Jesus Christ for the human race.

For they are children under God, the same as you and I,
but I wonder where their souls go when their earthly bodies die.
In this land of Commie rule, church bells are never heard,
and folks don't go to Sunday School to study Jesus's word.

Four thousand years they've gotten by with oxen and with hoe,
seems to me that without God, they're progressing mighty slow.

"Humbly dedicated to those who didn't make it."
—Byron Dobbs

Major Barney A. Dobbs was shot down on his twenty-second night combat mission. On September 15, 1953, the last day of the POW exchange, Barney Dobbs was released. "As they were getting ready to release us, they assembled us in a large camp, gave us decent food for several days and clean clothes. Then they put us on a train to our final camp. On the last day of the prisoner release, I was put on the last truck. I thought I was going to be left behind. Prior to my release, my wife, Kay, had no idea if I was alive or dead. All she knew was that I had been declared missing in action. As the POWs were released throughout September 1953, each day the names of the latest batch of prisoners to be released were announced on TV. It went on for days, and finally she saw my name. In a cruel hoax, Kay had been told by an early released POW that her husband was killed in an escape attempt. That POW, using a false name, then demanded money for more details. Kay turned him down. I still have the prison suit in which I returned home. My life as a prisoner, although much of it taken up by interrogation and by nine months of solitary confinement, included being harnessed to a cart like an ox and pulling it through the village. Fish heads, barley, and occasionally rice was the food I was fed. I lost fifty pounds. I constantly thought about meat and vowed that when I got home I would open a barbecue restaurant, Barney's Barbecue, to ensure I had a guaranteed supply of barbecued ribs for the rest of my life. Of course that didn't happen. Three months after my release, I was back flying airplanes. I retired from the US Air Force in 1965, after twenty-six years of military service, at

Lieutenant Barney Dobbs, second from right, and fellow pilots in front of one of their F-5 aircraft in 1943, at Nadzab, New Guinea.

Barney Dobbs was the last American POW released by the North Koreans in 1953. The picture was taken soon after Barney's release. He is wearing his prisoner garb, freshly issued by the Chinese just before his release.

Barney Dobbs at Air Force Village West near March Air Reserve Base, Riverside, California, 2001. Barney was an avid hunter and is wearing his German *Jaegerhut*.

Hamilton AFB, near San Francisco, where it all had started for me years earlier when my friend Al Blum and I left to fight World War II in the Pacific."

For his service in two wars Barney Dobbs was awarded the Silver Star, the Distinguished Flying Cross, and the Purple Heart, each medal twice, for heroism and wounds suffered in combat. He settled in Riverside, California, near March Air Force Base, never far from the smell of kerosene and the comforting sound of aircraft engines. Barney's two sons followed in their father's footsteps and joined the air force as well. Mark, a pilot, was killed in a plane crash in 1982. As much as Barney tried to let it go, the past stayed with him—dreams of being tortured by his interrogators, dreams that never faded.

EDGAR E. McELROY

B-25

An Airman's Prayer

God guard and guide us as we fly through the great spaces of the sky.
Be with us as we take to air in morning light and sunshine fair.
Eternal Father, strong and brave, give us courage and make us brave.
Protect us where so'er we go from shell and flak and fire and foe.
Most loved member of our crew, ride with us up into the blue.
Direct our bombs upon the foe, but shelter those whom thou dost know.
Keep us together on our way, grant our work success today.
Deliver us from hate and sin and bring us safely down again.
Oh God protect us as we fly through lonely ways across the sky.
—Copied from "Hand Written Prayer"—no author given.

In February 1955, only days after I celebrated my twentieth birthday, I, Wolfgang Samuel, was notified of my pending assignment to England, my final destination to be determined once I got there. I was a young one-striper, an airman-third-class, assigned to the 7th Bomb Wing at Carswell Air Force Base, Fort Worth, Texas. My job as payroll clerk was to pay the enlisted gunners and crew chiefs their flying pay each month, after they showed me a form signed by their B-36 aircraft commanders certifying that they had in fact flown the minimum of four hours qualifying them for this extra pay. At the time I was willing to go anywhere the air force wanted to send me, anywhere. I wanted to see the world. Being in the air force was exciting. It was the first time in my turbulent life that I felt I belonged to something worthwhile, felt secure, not threatened, and was very proud to be wearing the uniform of the United States Air Force. I had arrived in this country only four years earlier from Germany, finished high school in Denver, Colorado, two years later, then joined the air force when an initial attempt at college proved that I wasn't ready for that experience, nor had the financial resources to pay for it. I was excited when I received my orders to report to Camp Kilmer, New Jersey. It rained a lot while I was there. The red mud was ankle deep, and the kitchen duty, scrubbing pots and pans and peeling potatoes, was dirty and mind numbing. So I was very happy when my name showed up on the bulletin board directing me and a hundred other airmen to "be transported by railroad or bus on 30 April for further movement outside the continental US via USNS *General S Buckner*." The *General Buckner* was a troop ship that shuttled airmen and soldiers between the east coast of the United States and Southampton, England, and Bremerhaven, Germany. I was assigned a top bunk in the forward section of the ship, where I felt every wave the ship plowed through. A steam pipe ran two inches above my face when I lay in my bunk, and there wasn't a night when I didn't bang my head against that pipe. I spent most of my time topside, regardless of the wind and cold. Down below it stank from the "puke" of seasick airmen who relieved their agony over open barrels placed throughout the ship. This was a voyage the end of which I very much anticipated.

Once we arrived in Southampton, we were bussed to a distribution center. I soon found myself in Bushy Park, London, the former site of General Eisenhower's headquarters where he planned the D-Day landings of June 6, 1944. My assignment turned out to be the 28th Weather Squadron, which had detachments at every air force base in England. I was assigned to Detachment 2, at RAF Station Sculthorpe, the home of the 47th Bomb Wing, three squadrons of which were equipped with the B-45 bomber, America's first all-jet bomber. A fourth squadron, the 19th Tactical Reconnaissance Squadron, was equipped with the RB-45C, the reconnaissance version of the B-45. The on-base weather detachment provided the daily weather briefings for crews scheduled to fly that day. My detachment was located in the Shooting Box in South Creek, a small village several miles outside the main base. The Shooting Box was a former hunting lodge, leased by the air force and converted into the 47th Bomb Wing's remote command post. One of my detachment's functions, located in the Shooting Box, was to support reconnaissance flights over the Soviet Union and its satellites by aircraft of the 19th TRS. RAF Sculthorpe, and its RB-45C aircraft, played a significant role in the early days of the Cold War, a phrase yet to be coined. Deep penetrations of the Soviet Union had been flown by RB-45C reconnaissance aircraft from this remote air base in East Anglia in 1952 and 1954—using British aircrews. The last flight into the Soviet heartland, however, was flown by crews of the 19th Tactical Reconnaissance Squadron, only a month before my arrival at Sculthorpe, led by their intrepid

A B-45 bomber of the 47th Bomb Wing's 86th Bomb Squadron lined up on the ramp at RAF Sculthorpe, Norfolk, England, with other aircraft at an armed forces day open house, May 1954. Sunny days were the exception in this part of England, rain being the rule.

squadron commander, Major John B. Anderson. The 47th Bomb Wing was commanded by Brigadier General David M. Jones.

I knew nothing about the brave men who flew these dangerous reconnaissance missions deep into the Soviet Union, about General Jones or Major Anderson, yet I met and worked with them on a daily basis. The Shooting Box was where they came during exercises and on other special occasions. At the time it was deemed a secure facility. The weather detachment I worked at was at the lower level of the two-story building; communications and briefing rooms were upstairs. Our weather forecasters supported the overflights of the Russian Zone of Occupation, flights which served as training missions for the deeper penetrations into the Soviet Union itself. I had no knowledge at the time that General Jones had been one of sixteen American pilots who flew their B-25 bombers on April 18, 1942, off an aircraft carrier in the Pacific to bomb the Japanese mainland. Nor did I know that upon return to the United States, then Major Jones was given command of the 319th Bombardment Group in North Africa, flying Martin B-26 Marauders. He was shot down over Bizerte on December 4, 1942, less than eight months after launching off the USS *Hornet*. He was imprisoned at StalagLuft III in Sagan, Germany, my former hometown. I lived in government housing in Sagan, so close to the POW camp that at night I could see its camp lights. But I had no idea at the time, as an eight-year-old boy, what the lights represented.

General Jones was reassigned soon after my arrival at RAF Sculthorpe in the spring of 1955, and was replaced by General Joseph R. Holzapple, under whom I would serve again at headquarters USAFE in 1969 in Wiesbaden, Germany, after completing a combat tour at Takhli RTAFB, Thailand, during the height of the Vietnam War. It was Holzapple who took over the reins of the 319th Bomb Group in North Africa after Jones was shot down and captured. General Holzapple's deputy at Sculthorpe was Colonel John G. Glover, holder of the Distinguished Service Cross, the second-highest military decoration after the Medal of Honor. Seven years later, during the Cuban Missile Crisis of October 1962, Colonel Glover would be my wing commander at Forbes AFB, Topeka, Kansas, from where we flew RB-47H electronic reconnaissance aircraft around the island of Cuba, twenty-four hours a day, looking for Russian-manned SA-2 surface to air missile radars. Looking back on my own life, I am unfailingly amazed at the men I met over the years whose paths crossed mine. How could I have known as a young boy that some of my future commanders were imprisoned only a few miles from where I grew up as a youngster? In 1944 I marveled at a the sight of a large formation of B-17 bombers which bombed a nearby aircraft plant. I wanted to be one of them. Fly up high in the sky like they did—and in time I would do just that.

The first air raid on Japan's mainland was led by Lieutenant Colonel James H. Doolittle, who flew the first B-25 off the aircraft carrier USS *Hornet*. Captain David M. Jones, who thirteen years later would serve as my wing commander at RAF Sculthorpe, was number five to lift off the *Hornet*, with Tokyo as his target. First Lieutenant Edgar E. McElroy was number thirteen. His target, and the target of the two aircraft preceding him, was Yokosuka. Nagoya and Kobe were the targets of the last three B-25s to lift off the *Hornet*. The spirit of the men, who were all volunteers, is reflected in the names they chose to give their assigned aircraft—*Whiskey Pete, The Green Hornet, The Ruptured Duck, Whirling Dervish, Hari Kari-er, Fickle Finger of Fate, TNT, The Avenger,* and *Bat Out of Hell*. These truly brave flyers would become the "bats out of hell" for the Empire of the Rising Sun, sowing terror and foreshadowing the empire's demise. The story of *The Avenger*, as told by its pilot, Edgar "Mac" McElroy is one story out of eighty: the number of men who manned the sixteen B-25 bombers that day—the pilots, bombardiers, navigators, gunners, and flight engineers. McElroy's crew, besides himself as the pilot, included Lieutenant Richard A. Knobloch as copilot. Lieutenant Clayton J. Campbell served as the navigator. Sergeant Robert C. Bourgeois was the bombardier. Sergeant Adam R. Williams was the lone gunner and crew chief on McElroy's aircraft. This is McElroy's gripping story as told by him.

"My friends call me Mac," retired air force Lieutenant Colonel Edgar E. McElroy begins his story. "I was born and raised in Ennis, Texas, the youngest of five children of Harry and Jennie McElroy. Folks say that I was the quiet one. My dad had an auto mechanic's shop downtown, close to the main fire station, and I was expected to work at Dad's garage after school and on Saturdays. I grew up in an atmosphere of machinery, oil, and grease. Occasionally I would hear a lone plane fly over and would run out in the street and strain my eyes against the sun to watch it. Someday, I thought, that would be me up there. I really liked cars. I was always busy on some project and it wasn't long before I decided to build my own Model-T from spare parts. I got an engine from over here, a frame from over there, and wheels from someplace else—using only the good parts from old cars. It wasn't pretty, but it was all mine. I enjoyed driving my Model-T on the dirt roads around town and the feeling of freedom and speed. In high school, I played football and tennis, and was good enough in football to receive an athletic scholarship from Trinity University in Waxahachie. In class I often thought about flying my own airplane and being up there in the clouds. So I decided to take a correspondence course on aircraft engines.

"With what was going on in Europe and Asia, I figured that our country would be drawn into war someday. So I decided to join the Army Air Corps in November 1940—to follow my dream. Training was rigorous and frustrating at times. We trained at airfields all over California. It was tough going, and many of the guys washed out. When I finally saw that I was going to make it, I wrote my girl back in Longview, Texas, Agnes Gill, and asked her to come to California for my graduation, and by the way, also marry me. I graduated on July 11, 1941. Two days later I married 'Aggie' in Reno, Nevada. I received orders to report to the 17th Bomb Group based at Pendleton, Oregon. Neither Aggie nor I had traveled much before and the drive north through the Cascade Mountains of the Sierra Nevada was interesting and beautiful. It was an exciting time for us. My group was the first to receive the new B-25 medium bomber. When I saw it for the first time, I was awed. It looked huge to me, sleek and powerful. The guys started calling it the 'rocket plane.' I could hardly wait to get my hands on it. It reminded me of a big scorpion, ready to sting. We were transferred to another airfield in Washington where we spent a lot of time flying practice missions and attacking imaginary targets. We participated in maneuvers and more practice in Mississippi and Georgia. On our way home on December 7, 1941, we got word of a Japanese attack on Pearl Harbor. We listened with mixed emotions to the announcements on the radio, and to the declaration of war the next day. What the president said just rang over and over in my head: 'With confidence in our armed forces, with the unbounding determination of our people, we will gain the inevitable triumph. So help us God.' By gosh, I felt as though he was talking straight to me.

"The first weeks of the war we were back in Oregon flying patrols at sea looking for possible Japanese submarines. We had to be up at 3:30 in the morning to warm up the engines of our planes. There were eighteen inches of snow on the ground, and it was so cold that our engine oil congealed overnight. We placed big tarps over the engines that reached down to the ground. Inside these tents we used plumbers' blow torches to thaw out the engines. I figured my dad would be proud of me if he could see me inside the tent with all this machinery, oil, and grease. After about an hour of this, the engines were warm enough to start. We flew patrols over the coast of Oregon and Washington from dawn to dusk. Once I thought I spotted a submarine and started my bomb run—even had my bomb bay doors open—but pulled out of it when I realized it was just a big whale, not a submarine. In early February we were ordered to Columbus, South Carolina. Little did I know what was coming next. Once Aggie and I settled in, my squadron commander called us all together. He talked of an awfully hazardous mission being planned and was looking for volunteers. I stepped forward. My copilot was shocked. 'You can't volunteer, Mac,' he said. 'You are married, and you and Aggie are expecting a baby soon. Don't do it.' I told him that I got into the air corps to do what I can and Aggie understands how I feel. The war won't be easy for any of us, I reminded him.

"In late February, those of us who had volunteered were transferred to Eglin Field, Florida. There were about 140 of us and we were told that we were now part of a special B-25 project. We began our training but none of us knew what it was we were training for. We were told not to talk, not even to our wives. In early March we were called together for a briefing. In walks Lieutenant Colonel Jimmy Doolittle. Doolittle was already an aviation legend, and there he stood right before us. Colonel Doolittle explained that this mission would be extremely dangerous, that only volunteers could participate, that he couldn't tell us where we were going, but he could say that some of us would not be coming back from this mission. There was silence following his presentation. You could have heard a pin drop. Then Doolittle announced that anyone could withdraw from the project now and no one would be criticized. No one backed out. We worked from the early morning hours to after sunset to get ready. All excess weight was stripped from the planes and extra gas tanks were added. The lower gun turret was removed, as well as the heavy liaison radio and the tail guns. More gas tanks were added, extending our range from 1,000 miles to 2,500 miles.

"Then it was time for us to be assigned our crews. They were all a bunch of swell guys, regular all-American boys. We got a few ideas from our training as to what type of mission we had signed on for. A navy pilot had joined our group to coach us on short takeoffs and also on shipboard etiquette. We began our short takeoff practice, taking off first with a light load, then a normal load, and finally with a load of thirty-one thousand pounds. The shortest possible takeoff was obtained with flaps full down, stabilizer set three-fourth, tail heavy, full power against the brakes, and releasing the brakes simultaneously with the engines at maximum power. It was a very unnatural and scary way to get airborne. The first time I took off with a full gas load and dummy bombs in seven hundred feet in a near stall condition, I could hardly believe it. We were for all practical purposes a slow flying gasoline bomb. In addition to takeoff, we refined our skills in day and night navigation, gunnery, bombing, and low-level flying. After we began the short-field takeoff routine, we had some pretty spirited competition between crews. I think one crew got down to about three hundred feet takeoff distance on a hot day. Then we were told that only the best crews would be selected to go on this mission, and the rest would be held in reserve. One crew stalled their aircraft on takeoff, slipped back to the ground, damaging the landing gear. The crew was eliminated. Doolittle emphasized again and again the extreme danger of this operation, and made it clear that anyone who desired to drop out could do so without any questions asked. No one did.

"We were abruptly told to pack our things. After three weeks of practice we were on our way. It was the middle of March and I was thirty years old. Our orders were to fly singly to McClellan Field near Sacramento, California, at the lowest possible flight level. We went out west, scraping the treetops at 160 miles per hour, skimming along just 50 feet above plowed fields. We crossed north Texas, then the panhandle, scaring livestock, buzzing farm houses and many a barn along the way. Once we arrived in Sacramento, the mechanics went over our planes with a fine-toothed comb. Of the twenty-two planes that made it to Sacramento, only those whose pilots reported no mechanical problems were allowed to go on. After having our plane serviced we flew on to Alameda Naval Air Station in Oakland. As I came in for my final approach, I saw it. I excitedly called my crew to take a look. There below us was a huge aircraft carrier, the USS *Hornet*. There were already two B-25s parked on the flight deck. Now we knew. As soon as we landed and taxied off the runway, a jeep pulled in front of me with a big FOLLOW ME sign on its back. We followed the jeep straight up to the wharf alongside the towering *Hornet*. As we left the plane, there was already a navy work crew swarming around our plane, attaching cables to the lifting rings on top of the wings and the fuselage. As we were walking toward our quarters, I looked back and saw them lift our plane into the air and swing it over the carrier's deck.

"Later that afternoon all crews met with Colonel Doolittle who gave us last-minute assignments. He told me to go to the Presidio and pick up 200 C-rations. I saluted smartly, turned, and left, having no idea where the Presidio was or exactly what a C-ration was. I got a navy staff car to take me to the Presidio. I walked into the army supply depot and made my request. The supply officer asked, 'What's your authorization?' I told him that I could not give him one. 'What is the destination?' The aircraft carrier *Hornet* docked in Alameda, I responded. 'Can you tell me who ordered the rations?' I smiled and responded, 'No, I cannot.' The supply officers talked things over, then assured me that the rations would be delivered that afternoon. The next morning we boarded the ship. Our task force of ships—two cruisers, four destroyers, and a fleet oiler—moved slowly with us under the Golden Gate bridge. Thousands of people looked on.

"Once at sea Doolittle called us together. 'Gentlemen, your target is Japan.' A sudden cheer exploded out of us crews. 'Specifically Yokohama, Tokyo, Nagoya, Kobe, Nagasaki, and Osaka. The navy task force will get us as close as possible. We will hit our targets, then proceed to airfields in China.' One last time Doolittle asked if anyone wanted to back out. No one did. We finally knew where we were going. It was a relief. I set up quarters with two navy pilots. They were part of Torpedo Squadron 8. There were sixteen B-25s tied down on the flight deck. I was flying number 13. The carrier's planes were stored away on the lower hangar deck. Our army mechanics were all on board, as well as our munitions loaders and several backup crews, in case any of us got sick or backed out. Day after day we met with the intelligence officer and studied our mission folders. We went over our approach routes and our escape route to China. Every day at dawn and dusk the ship was called to general quarters and we practiced finding the quickest way to our planes. Were we discovered by the Japanese fleet we were to launch our bombers immediately so the *Hornet* could bring up its fighters. We put some tail guns in place of the ones taken out at Eglin to save weight—not exactly functional, two broomsticks painted black.

"On Sunday, April 14, we met with Admiral 'Bull' Halsey's task force just out of Hawaii and joined into one big force. The carrier *Enterprise* was now with us, another two heavy cruisers, four more destroyers and an oiler. Our designation was Task Force 16. It was quite an impressive sight and represented the bulk of the United States Navy after Pearl Harbor. As we steamed further west, tensions rose. Colonel Doolittle called us together on the flight deck. He pulled out some medals and told us how these Friendship medals from the Japanese government had been given to some navy officers several years back. 'And now the Secretary of the Navy has requested us to return them.' With that Doolittle wired the medals to a bomb while we posed for pictures. I began packing my things for our flight, scheduled for the 19th. I settled my mess bill; it only came to five dollars a day. By then my two navy roommates were ready to get rid of me. They were all right. I later learned that both were killed in the Battle of Midway. They were good men, very good men.

"Colonel Doolittle let each crew pick its target—we chose Yokosuka naval base, about twenty miles from Tokyo. We loaded 1,450 rounds of ammunition and four five-hundred-pound bombs. We checked and rechecked our plane several times. Everything was ready. I felt relaxed, yet tensed up at the same time. Day after tomorrow we will launch when we are four hundred miles out. I lay in my cot that night and rehearsed the mission over and over in my head. It was hard to go to sleep as I listened to the sounds of the ship. Early the next morning I was enjoying a leisurely breakfast, expecting another full day on board, when I noticed that the ship was pitching and rolling quite a bit, more than usual. All of a sudden the intercom blared, 'General quarters. General quarters. All hands man your battle stations. Army pilots, man your planes.' Food trays went crashing to the floor. I ran down to my room jumping through the hatches along the way, grabbed my bag and ran as fast as I could go to the flight deck. I met my crew at the plane, my heart pounding. The word was that the *Enterprise* had been spotted by an enemy trawler. It had been sunk, but before sinking had managed to transmit some radio messages. We had been found out. The weather was crummy, the seas ran heavy, and the ship was pitching up and down like I had never seen it do before. Great waves crashed against the bow, washing over the front of the deck. This wasn't going to be easy. Last-minute instructions were given. We were reminded to avoid nonmilitary targets, especially the emperor's palace. Do not fly to Russia! Fly as far west as possible, land on the water, and launch your rubber raft. This was going to be a one-way trip. We were still much too far out and we all knew that our chances of making land were somewhere between slim and none. At the last minute, each plane loaded an extra ten five-gallon cans of gas to give us a fighting chance of reaching China. We all climbed aboard, started engines and warmed them up, just feet away from the plane in front of us. Williams, our gunner, was in the back, separated from the rest of us by a big rubber gas tank. I called back to Williams on the intercom and told him to look sharp and don't take a nap. He replied dryly, 'Don't worry about me, lieutenant. If they jump us, I'll just use my little black broomsticks to keep them off our tail.' The ship headed into the wind and picked up speed. There was now a near gale-force wind and water spray coming straight over the deck. I looked down at my instruments as my engines revved up, my mind racing. I went over my mental checklist—and said a prayer. 'God, please help us.'

"Past the twelve planes in front of us I strained to see the flight deck officer as he leaned into the wind and signaled with his arms for Colonel Doolittle to come to full power. I looked over at Knobby, my copilot, and we looked each other in the eye. With the deck heaving up and down, the deck officer had to time this just right. Then I saw him wave Doolittle to go, and we watched breathlessly to see what happened. When his plane pulled up above the deck, Knobby just let out with, 'Yes! Yes!' The second plane piloted by Lieutenant Hoover appeared to stall with its nose up and began falling toward the waves.

We groaned and called out, 'Up! Up! Pull it up!' And up he came, staggering into the air, much to our relief. One by one the planes in front of us took off. The deck pitching wildly, sixty feet or more, that's what it looked like. One plane seemed to drop down into the drink and disappeared from sight for a moment and then pulled back up into sight. There was a sense of relief with each one that made it. Then it was our turn. We gunned our engines and started to roll forward. Off to the right I saw the men on deck cheering and waving their covers. We continued to inch forward, careful to keep my left main wheel and my nose wheel on the white guidelines that had been painted on the deck for us. Get off a little bit too far left and we go off the edge of the deck. A little too far right and our wing-tip will smack the island of the ship. We watched Lieutenant Bower take off in plane number 12, and I taxied up to the starting line, put on the brakes and looked down to my left—my main wheel was right on the line. I applied more power to the engines and then turned my complete attention to the deck officer on my left who was circling his paddles. My adrenaline was really pumping. I went to full power, he circled the paddles furiously, then dropped them, and I said, 'Here we go.' I released the brakes and started rolling forward. We slowly gained speed and the deck gradually began to pitch back up. I pulled up and our plane slowly strained up and away. There was a big cheer from the crew. I just felt relieved.

We made a wide circle above our ships to check our compass heading and get our bearings. When I looked down passing over one of our cruisers, I could see the men on deck waving to us. I dropped down low, so low we could see the whitecaps breaking. It was just after nine o'clock in the morning. There were broken clouds at five thousand feet and the visibility was about thirty miles. Up ahead and barely in sight I could see Captain Greening, our flight leader, with Lieutenant Bower on his right wing. Flying 170 miles per hour I was able to catch up to them in about thirty minutes. We were to stay in formation until making landfall, then go on our separate ways. We settled in for the five-hour flight—Tokyo, here we come. Williams was in the back emptying the extra gas cans into the gas tank as fast as we burned off fuel. He then punched holes into the tin cans and pushed them out the hatch against the wind. Some of the crew ate sandwiches that the navy had put aboard for us. I wasn't hungry. I held on to the controls firmly as we raced along westward just fifty feet above the cold rolling ocean, as low as I dared to fly. Being so close to the choppy waves gave you a true sense of speed. I felt as though the spirit of our whole country was pushing us along. I didn't feel too scared, just anxious. As we began to near land, we saw an occasional ship here and there. At one-thirty in the afternoon we sighted land, the eastern shore of Honshu. With Williams now at his guns in the top turret and Campbell on the nose gun, we came ashore still flying as low as possible and were surprised to see people on the ground waving at us. Campbell, our navigator, said, 'Mac, I think we are going to be about sixty miles too far north. I'm not positive, but pretty sure.' I decided he was right and turned left ninety degrees, just off shore, and followed the coast line south. When I thought we had gone far enough, I climbed to two thousand feet to find out exactly where we were. We started getting antiaircraft fire. When we spotted Tokyo Bay, we turned west and put our nose down diving toward the water. Once over the bay I could see our target—Yokusuka Naval Base. Off to our right there was already smoke visible over Tokyo. I increased speed to two hundred miles per hour and told everyone to get ready. Approaching our target I pulled up to 1,300 feet and opened the bomb-bay doors. There were black bursts of antiaircraft fire all around us. I flew straight ahead, spotting our target—the torpedo works and drydocks. I saw a big ship in the drydock just as we flew over it. The flak was really getting close, bouncing us around, when I heard Bourgeois shout, 'Bombs away.'

"I couldn't see anything, but Williams had a bird's-eye view from the back and shouted jubilantly, 'We got an aircraft carrier. The whole dock is burning.' I turned to the south and strained my neck to look back. At that moment I saw a large crane blow up and fall over. There was loud yelling and slapping each other on the back. We were ecstatic—and still alive. But there wasn't much time to celebrate. We had to get out of here fast. Some thirty miles out to sea we took one last look back at our target, seeing huge billows of black smoke. Until then we had been flying for Uncle Sam—now we were flying for ourselves. We flew south over open ocean, parallel to the Japanese coast. By late afternoon Campbell calculated that it was time to turn and make for China. The weather out ahead of us looked bad. We had not had time to think about our gasoline supply. It didn't look good for us to make it. Each man took turns cranking our little hand radio to see if we could pick up the promised radio beacon. There was no signal. It was getting dark, so we climbed. I was now flying on instruments through dark, misty rain. Just when it looked hopeless of us ever reaching land we picked up a strong tailwind. It was an answer to our prayers. Maybe, just maybe, we could make it. At nine o'clock in the evening, in total darkness, we figured we must be crossing the coast into China. I began a slow climb to be sure of not hitting any high ground. We were getting real low on gas. The guys were still working the radio—no radio beacon. Then the red light started blinking. We had twenty minutes of fuel left. We started to get ready to bail out. I turned the controls over to Knobby and crawled to the back of the plane, past the collapsed rubber gas tank. I dumped everything out of my bag and repacked just what I really needed—my .45 pistol, ammunition, flashlight, compass, medical kit, fishing tackle, chocolate bars, peanut butter, and crackers. I told Williams to come forward so we could all be together. At ten-thirty that night we were at 6,500 feet, still over Japanese-occupied China. We couldn't see the stars, so Campbell couldn't get a fix on our position. We were flying on fumes, and I didn't want to run out of gas before we were ready to jump. Each man filled his canteen, put on his Mae West life jacket and parachute and filled his bag with C-rations from the Presidio. I put her on autopilot and we all gathered in the navigator's compartment, around the hatch in the floor. We checked each other's chutes and harnesses. Everyone was scared, without a doubt. None of us had ever done this before. I said, 'Williams first, Bourgeois second, Campbell third, Knobloch fourth, and I'll follow you guys. Go fast, two seconds apart. Then count three seconds off and pull your ripcord.'

"We kicked open the hatch and gathered around the hole looking down into the blackness. It did not look inviting. I looked up at Williams and said, 'Jump.' Within seconds they were all gone. I turned and reached for the autopilot, but couldn't reach it. So I pulled the throttles back, then turned and jumped. The chute opened with a terrific jolt. At first I thought I was caught up on the airplane, but after a few agonizing seconds that seemed like hours I realized I was drifting down. I looked down through the black mist to see what was coming up. I was in a thick fog and the silence was so eerie after nearly thirteen hours inside that noisy plane. Then I heard a loud explosion—my plane. Looking for my flashlight I groped through my bag with my right hand, finally pulled it out and shone it down toward the ground. I picked up a glimmer of water and thought I was landing in a lake. I relaxed my legs a little, thinking I was about to splash into water and would have to swim out. Then—bang. I crashed over onto my side, lying there in just a few inches of water. I raised my head and put my hands down into thick mud—it was a rice paddy. There was a burning pain, as if someone had stuck a knife in my stomach. I must have torn a muscle or broke something. I lay there dazed for a few minutes. After a while I struggled to my feet, dug a hole and buried my parachute in the mud. It was a cold dark night. At one o'clock in the morning I saw a single light off to the east. I flashed my light in that direction briefly. It had to be Knobby. I waited, then called out softly, 'Knobby?' A voice replied, 'Mac, is that you?' What a relief. Separated by a wide stream, we sat on opposite banks communicating in low voices. After daybreak Knobby found a small rowboat and came across. We started walking east, toward the rest of the crew. Knobby had cut his hip as he went through the hatch. But it wasn't too bad. We walked together toward a small village. Several Chinese came out to meet us. They seemed friendly enough. I said, 'Luchu hoo megwa fugi,' meaning I am an American. We found the others later that morning. Williams had wrenched his knee when he landed in a tree, but he was limping along just fine. There were hugs all around. I have never been so happy to see four guys in all my life.

"Well, the five of us eventually made it out of China with the help of the local Chinese people and the Catholic missions along the way. They were all very good to us. We learned later that they were made to pay a terrible price for helping us. For a couple of weeks we traveled across country. We were strafed by enemy planes, but kept on moving by foot, by car, by train, and by airplane until we made it to India. I stayed on in the China-Burma-India Theater of Operations for the next several months flying a C-47 Gooney Bird. I flew supplies over the Himalayas, or as we called it—the Hump. When B-25s finally arrived in India, I flew combat missions over Burma, and then later in the war, I flew a B-29 out of the Mariana Islands to bomb Japan again and again. After the war I remained in the air force until 1962 when I retired as a lieutenant colonel. Then I came back to my beautiful Texas, first moving to Abilene, then Lubbock, where Aggie taught school at MacKenzie Junior High School. I worked at the S&R Auto Supply store, once again in an atmosphere of machinery, oil, and grease. I lived a good life and raised two wonderful sons that I am very proud of. I feel blessed in many ways. We have a great country, better than most folks know. It is worth fighting for. Some people call me a hero, but I have never thought of myself that way. No. But I did serve in the company of heroes. What we did will never leave me. It will always be there in my fondest memories. I will always think of the fine and brave men I was privileged to serve with—'Remember us, for we were soldiers once and young.' With the loss of all aircraft, Doolittle believed that the raid had been a failure, and that he would be court-martialed upon returning to the United States. Quite to the contrary, the raid proved to be a tremendous boost to American morale which had plunged following the Pearl Harbor attack. It also caused serious doubts in the minds of Japanese war planners."[26]

Instead of being court-martialed, as Lieutenant Colonel Doolittle had expected after losing sixteen airplanes and inflicting in his own estimation minor damage on the Japanese, President Roosevelt awarded him the Medal of Honor and promoted him to brigadier general, skipping the rank of colonel all together. Corporal David J. Thatcher, a member of aircraft number 7, and First Lieutenant Thomas R. White, flight surgeon/gunner on plane number 15, received the Silver Star. All others received the Distinguished Flying Cross. Those wounded or injured were awarded the Purple Heart. Nineteen of Doo-little's Raiders flew combat in North Africa after first returning to the United States. Four of the nineteen were killed in action, another four became prisoners of war. One of those four POWs was David M. Jones, the pilot of airplane number 5, who was imprisoned in StalagLuft III, a few miles from where I lived and played as a young boy in Sagan, Germany. Jones, like McElroy, had bailed out of his aircraft over China when he ran out of fuel. Once he returned to the United States, he was assigned to the 319th Bombardment Group to develop low-level bombing tactics. His luck ran out on December 4, 1942, over Bizerte, when his B-26 Marauder was struck by antiaircraft fire. At StalagLuft III it was

Lieutenant Colonel Jimmy Doolittle put the versatile B-25 medium bomber into the history books with his daring and totally unexpected raid on the Japanese homeland on April 18, 1942.

Lieutenant Colonel Edgar McElroy just before his retirement from the US Air Force.

David Jones who led digging of a tunnel named "Harry" (three escape tunnels were dug named Tom, Dick, and Harry) which was used in the great escape on March 24, 1944, by seventy-six British airmen held as prisoners of war at StalagLuft III. Three made good their escape. The remainder were recaptured and fifty of those were executed by the Gestapo on Hitler's orders. The escape was made into a movie in 1963, appropriately entitled *The Great Escape*, with Steve McQueen playing the leading role. David Jones retired from the air force as a major general. He was one of five Doolittle Raiders promoted to the rank of general. Of course there was James H. Doolittle himself. John A. Hilger, Everett W. Holstrom, and Richard A. Knobloch were the others selected in subsequent years. Doolittle flew aircraft number 1, Holstrom was the pilot of number 4, Jones piloted aircraft number 5, Hilger was the pilot of number 14, and Knobloch served as copilot on Edgar E. McElroy's aircraft, number 13.

Of the eighty airmen who participated in the Doolittle raid, sixty-seven managed to make good their escape after bailing out over China or ditching at sea and returned to either the United States for reassignment or remained in the Pacific Theater of Operations, as did McElroy. Three crew members were executed by the Japanese. One died as a Japanese prisoner of war as a result of a starvation diet. Four were imprisoned and survived until freed by American troops in August 1945. One crewman died during bailout over China. Two drowned after their aircraft ditched off the coast of China. The crew of Captain Edward York, number 8, landed their aircraft in Siberia, beyond Vladivostok. The aircraft was confiscated by the Russians and the crew interned. Edgar "Mac" McElroy, Lieutenant Colonel, United States Air Force, passed away at his residence in Lubbock, Texas, early on the morning of Friday, April 4, 2003. We are a nation blessed to call men like Mac McElroy, and others like him, our own. General Doolittle, like General Jones, would find himself assigned to North Africa in 1942 as commander of the 12th Air Force. That November, he pinned on his second star, taking command of the 15th Air Force in June of 1943. On June 10, Major General Doolittle, with Jack Sims as his copilot, a fellow Tokyo Raider, flew a B-26 Marauder assigned to the 320th Bomb Group against the Italian island of Pantelleria, off Sicily. The Italian garrison surrendered on June 11 after an intense aerial bombardment. It didn't happen all that often for men of Doolittle's rank to fly combat, and he did whenever he could get away with it. He then assumed command of the 8th Air Force, pinning on a third star in March of 1944, and led the 8th until the end of hostilities in Europe. Doolittle was an American icon if ever there was one. On April 10, 1985, sixteen years after his retirement, a grateful nation promoted him to full general. President Ronald Reagan and Senator Barry Goldwater pinned the fourth star onto his shoulders. Jimmy Doolittle died at age ninety-six, on September 27, 1993.[27]

ROBERT S. HAMILL

B-25/C-54/KC-97

Mom

Hi ya mom. Gosh you're grand!
I wish I were near you holding your hand.
I miss you a lot, and miss pop a lot too,
But you both realize we have jobs to do!
So keep up your chins, and I'll do the same!
And we'll prove that we're "Nordbaks" in more than name.
We aren't the cause of this war, but we are on the beam,
And we know we'll beat Hitler at his own little scheme.
I'll close with a smile! And you do the same.
And pray for the end of this rotten war game.
—Private Tom G. Nordbak, WWII

"I was born in 1918 in Hamill, South Dakota. My father, Gail Madison Hamill, after whom the small community was named, ran a trading post on the Rosebud Sioux Indian Reservation. In 1925 my family moved to southern California. I had a talent for football and qualified for the San Jose football team under Coach Dudley DeGroot, who later coached the Washington Redskins. By 1941 my coach was Glenn S. Warner, better known as 'Pop' to us players. I didn't come from a wealthy family. To be able to attend college, I had to cash in on my football skills. In addition, I served as campus policeman, male model (with my clothes on), cleaned the stadium after games, and had my own Coke machines in fraternity, sorority, and other campus houses. There wasn't anything I wouldn't do to earn an extra nickel to stay in school as long as it was legal. My mother taught me the value of education and never let me forget it.

"In 1939 San Jose was the highest-scoring college football team in the nation. I was a sophomore. By 1941 I was a two-way lineman and cocaptained the team. I was voted Little All-American. On December 3, 1941, accompanied by our coach, Pop Warner, I led the San Jose Spartans to Honolulu, Hawaii, to participate in a series of charity games against the University of Hawaii. Ben Winkleman was officially listed as our coach, but Pop Warner did all the coaching. We were having breakfast in the Moana Hotel on Waikiki Beach, the morning of December 7, when we saw a lot of stuff happening in the water. The Filipino waiters were yelling: 'Whales! Whales!' That's what they thought it was. It must have been bombs or antiaircraft fire. We kept on eating. The night before we had been told the army would be conducting maneuvers off the beaches and we would see tow targets. We kept looking for tow targets. It took a while to realize what was going on. Once we knew that Japan had attacked Pearl Harbor, our entire team went to the Honolulu police department to volunteer for whatever it was they needed. They made us security guards. We were issued guns and ordered to secure a section of beach and our hotel. We never got a chance to play football.

"Three weeks later we returned to the mainland aboard the *President Coolidge*. During the voyage, two players each were assigned a stateroom to tend to the wounded. It was horrible. They were burned all over their bodies and stank from the burned flesh and disinfectant. Every night bodies were taken on deck to the fantail and buried at sea. I never thought about going into the military before that, but as soon as we landed in San Francisco I led my football team to the navy recruiting office. They had a program which let you finish college before you went into flight training, and we all wanted to fly. I was the first in line. A dentist looked at my teeth and told me that I couldn't fly for the navy. I had an underbite, and that wouldn't do. I sat dejectedly on a bench, watching my teammates go through their exams. One finally came over and asked, 'What's the matter, Moe? You look down.' I told him. Within five minutes my team walked out of the navy recruiting office and we went next door to the Army Air Corps office, where we signed up. The navy lost a hell of a good pilot," Moe Hamill noted in our interview, a broad grin crossing his face. "When I returned to the Varsity House, my home at the time, I found eight draft notices waiting for me. One notice was from the Chicago Bears offering me $150 a game. That was a fortune then. Another notice informed me that I had made Little All-American. The last notice I opened was from Uncle Sam. It was the most important.

"In early 1942 I reported for active duty and started aircrew training. I was sluiced through a number of bases—Santa Ana was full, so they sent us to Bakersfield for basic training. There they issued us mechanics' coveralls, no uniforms. At Merced Field I went through primary training, then ended up at

Williams Field in Arizona for advanced pilot training. I got to the point of my check ride. The commander of the squadron was Captain Glen Edwards, he gave me my ride." (After completing a combat tour flying the A-20 in Europe in 1944, Glen Edwards became a test pilot at Wright Field, and died, along with the entire flight test crew, on June 5, 1948, at what was then called Muroc Field, testing the YB-49, flying wing. Muroc Field was renamed Edwards Air Force Base in his honor on January 27, 1950.) "After we landed, Captain Edwards got out and looked up at me and said, 'Where did you learn to play football?' I started telling him my whole life story. He walked away. I found out later that I was so rough on the controls that he thought I must have been a football player. He was trying to tell me how much I over-controlled the airplane when he asked that question. He had no idea I ever played football. He made his point, and walked away. At Williams Field in Arizona, in advanced twin-engine training, I flew plywood AT-10s. The Arizona heat made the AT-10s fall apart, and the planes were grounded. It was decided that anyone with over one hundred hours flying time would graduate. I graduated without a check ride and was appointed a second lieutenant. B-25 training followed at Columbia, South Carolina. I got checked out ahead of my class. My first solo mission was at night. I tried to be an eager pilot, being the first one checked out. At the end of the runway my instrument lights didn't come on. I was not about to abort my first solo mission and get the stigma pilots get for aborting. I was going to be a hotshot pilot. I had the engineer run his flashlight across the instrument panel, and we did the run up. As I started down the runway, I had runway lights, so I had no problem. When we got to the end of the runway, I pulled back on the stick and it turned pitch black in the cockpit. I couldn't see the instruments. I told the engineer to give me some light. He did, and that blinded me. Now I had no night vision. From the seat of my pants I kept flying. Pretty soon I felt a slap on my face. The flight engineer was shaking a pine branch at me. 'Sir,' he said, 'I think you went through the trees.'

"The plane was pretty badly beaten up. The bombardier's hatch was torn off, and the wind was rushing through the airplane. As I am making my approach to land, I yelled to my copilot, 'Flaps.' He either didn't hear me or was too scared to move, but I didn't have flaps, I realized, as I was going down the runway like a son of a bitch. I went around, got the flaps down, and made the landing. Two days later I met a flying evaluation board headed by the group commander. He read me the riot act. Then he grounded me. They made me a second lieutenant squadron commander of a processing squadron of active duty people who had been accepted for pilot training. I didn't even know how to set up a morning report, but the sergeants took care of me and made me look good. One Sunday the local Columbia paper did a story on my squadron. The group commander read about this second lieutenant and his great squadron and promptly called me into his office. He gave me two choices—be a permanent ground pounder squadron commander, or go overseas flying B-25s. I went back to flying.

"I was at Walterboro, South Carolina, for advanced training. One morning we were going on the range for bomb training. We had to go to Myrtle Beach to pick up the bombs first, real early in the morning. There had been a party at the officers' club the night before, and my bombardier was a happy drunk. I couldn't take him, but I wasn't going to abort the mission. I took my bombardier to his room and told him to stay there. He went right to sleep. Six of us were flying formation up to Myrtle Beach to get the bombs. One by one the guys dropped out, buzzing people in the cotton fields below. Finally, there was only lead and me. I wanted to go down and buzz like the rest of them. Then I saw a fairly big river. It was wider than a B-25, with steep banks. In those days the epitome of being the greatest pilot was to fly close enough over the water to get water in the lower turret. Here I went. The guys in back were yelling, 'We're getting water, we're getting water.' I didn't realize two things. First, the river wasn't going to stay straight forever. Second, the migration of ducks in February. There was a major turn in the river, and thousands of ducks were on the near side, out of the wind, where I couldn't see them. I thought, 'Do I pull up, or shall I carefully turn and not hit my wing in the water?' The banks looked pretty high to pull up, so I decided to turn. Well, the ducks heard the roar of that noisy B-25, and thousands of them came up right through me. The bombardier's hatch was completely busted in. The rocker boxes were broken and dangling. The leading edges of the wings were dented. I didn't land at Myrtle Beach. I knew that airplane wasn't going to fly again.

"I was the only one landing at Walterboro. Everyone was there to meet me. We dropped the hatch and four of us got out. It was a five-man crew. They looked into the bombardier's compartment, and all they could see was blood and guts and feathers. The compartment was full of dead ducks. They thought the bombardier had been killed and was lying under that bunch of dead ducks. Well, the Lord was looking out for me that day and for my bombardier, Frank Snow, for if he had been along he would have been killed for sure. There went my flying career again, I thought. The only thing that saved me, I believe, was that at this period of the war in 1943 they desperately needed pilots. I completed the remainder of my training, and my crew and I went by train up to Kellogg Field, Michigan, where we picked up a new B-25 at the factory. Then we flew the long circuitous route from Michigan to Florida to South America to Ascension Island and on to North Africa.

"At a rear base near Cairo, Egypt, we were assigned to the 12th Bomb Group. We went into town to look around. Only the copilot stayed behind. Soon a half-track came after us, picked us up, and took us directly to our aircraft.

The engines were running. The operations officer said to me, 'The copilot has been briefed. Just don't fly above four hundred feet.' I taxied out into an open spot to take off—I didn't know where the runway was—when all at once they flagged me down. I had taxied into a minefield at the forward base. Then, carefully, they led us out of there, and I took off. The following day I checked the mission board in front of the operations tent and found that I was on the schedule to fly a night mission. I confronted the operations officer and said to him, 'There must be some mistake. I just got here, and I am listed on the mission board to fly at night. I am not checked out yet.' The operations officer turned to me and said, 'Are you the pilot?'

"I responded, 'Yes, Major. I haven't been checked out day or night.'

"'Didn't you fly yesterday?'

"'Yes, sir.'

"'Was it daylight when you took off?'

"'Yes, sir.'

"'Did you land after dark?'

"'Yes, sir.'

"'You are checked out, Lieutenant.' And with that comment I was dismissed.

"I remember that first mission against the Afrika Korps. The flak—it sounded like gravel hitting the aircraft. A couple weeks later, on May 6, 1943, just before the Germans surrendered in Tunisia, I was flying my sixth mission. The aircraft in front of me received a direct hit. It was the new group commander on his first mission. The aircraft disintegrated. I was busy dodging debris. When I got back to base, I was pretty well shot up. We couldn't get the gear down. I gave the crew the opportunity to bail out, but they opted to stay with me. I was going to belly in. The procedure was for the copilot to back up his seat and get out, then the pilot. Then there is room for the bombardier to exit, and so on. I was still sliding down the desert, props throwing up dust, when I felt a foot on my ear. My bombardier was standing on my shoulders, trying to get out. I don't remember who got out first. Later on we tried to get out the way he did, but without that adrenaline we couldn't do it. I popped three disks in my back. Otherwise, no one was hurt. After my muscle spasms died down, I went back to flying.

"The next day the army captured Cape Bon. In the German hospital tent, they found two of the crew of the plane that had blown up in front of me the day before. I had told them that no one could have survived. The pilot's leg had been amputated. The medical records were there. Everything the German doctors had done was perfectly recorded. The other survivor was the bombardier. I asked him how he got out. He didn't know. As the weeks passed, I worked my way up to Sicily. I was bombing on the other side of Mount Aetna when an 88mm shell went through my right wing and exploded above the aircraft, killing the gunner in the upper turret, knocking out the intercom. I finished the bomb run before returning to base. After we landed, we counted over five hundred holes in the plane. We junked the aircraft. The dead man got the Purple Heart. The rest of us got nothing. When I returned to the US in December 1943, I had flown forty-two combat missions in the B-25. I had contracted malaria and yellow jaundice while in North Africa. After I recuperated, I was assigned to the 1st Air Force at Mitchell Field, New York, as a B-25 and B-26 instructor. Once they learned that I had played football in college, I found myself on the 1st Air Force football team. My back began bothering me again and I was operated on at Letterman Hospital in San Francisco. They took out three discs, which ended my football career for good.

"I got out of the air force in 1947 with the rank of major. I opened a little fast-food restaurant in Santa Ana, California. One day an air force major came into the restaurant and asked, 'How would you like to fly airplanes again? I can get you an airplane so you can go anywhere you want. I can check you out right here in Long Beach. All you have to do is sign up in the reserve.' I signed up. I was bored. This was in 1948. I had not even checked out yet when I got a letter: 'Welcome to the air force,' it read. 'We need you for the Berlin airlift.' That's how I got back in. I went to Montana for C-54 training. They checked us out, and then they sent us over to Germany. I ended up in the 29th Squadron at Fassberg. My first flight was on April 13, 1949. On June 16, 1949, I flew my 100th mission and was awarded the Air Medal. My last flight was on August 24, 1949. I flew a total of 205 missions in seventeen weeks. I flew more than what my records show. On Tunner's Easter Parade I flew five missions which are not recorded in my records, but I know I flew them. I flew whenever I could.

"Most of the flying was boring, boring, boring, with the exception of one mission. We landed at the French base of Tegel. We carried coal, and the British carried fuel. We'd sit there waiting to take off and watch the Brits land. The fuel baffles weren't too good on the Brit airplanes. When they'd land, the fuel went one way, and they bounced. Then the fuel went the other way, and they bounced again. Of course we were supposed to observe radio silence, but every Yank out there said 'One, two, three.' The Brits called back, 'OK, Yanks, shut up.' Every once in a while they'd have an accident landing. One mission I remember well was when Tegel was closed because one of the British fuel tankers had crashed. They diverted us to Tempelhof. On this mission I flew through my first really big thunderstorm. I remember going from two thousand feet to eight thousand, and back down again. We put on the lights in the cockpit, and the copilot worked the throttles. All I could do was keep the airplane level. First it was solid black in the cockpit, then with the lightning around us it would turn brighter than daylight. By the time I got to my GCA run into Tempelhof, I probably lost ten pounds. Well, we were coming out of the clouds on final approach. I had never been to Tempelhof before. We were breaking out of the overcast. I looked to my left and saw that I was right in between these apartment houses. The windows were lit up. I became really frightened, because I just knew I was going to crash. I added power. I was ready to pull up and go back. Then I saw the runway. I had already added power. Now I was trying to get the power off. I landed so fast. I recall yelling for the copilot to help me on the brakes—we didn't have reverse props in those days. I used up the entire runway. It was that approach in between those apartment houses that frightened me to death. That thunderstorm made me forget everything. Fassberg was a good base. We never missed a mission, and I never aborted. Everything I remember was 'Mach schnell. Mach schnell,' hurry up, hurry up. I would get out there with the German crews and help them unload the coal from their trucks. That's how I got my exercise. Then we'd go down to the wagon and get a coffee and donut. All I did was fly and sleep. Three days off, ten days flying. Some days off I flew for guys who wanted time off to play poker."

All was not work for the Berlin airlift flyers. The spring and summer of 1949 were beautiful. Off-duty American airmen strolled through the streets of Fassberg, a town untouched by war, looking for something to do. They crowded the few bars, sitting outside on sunny days, drinking German beer, smoking, and whistling at German girls passing by. Master Sergeant Chester J. "Jim" Vaughn is probably representative of many of the young single men who served in Germany at the time. Jim was an Indiana boy, born in 1927, growing up in the depression years. "Those were tough times for us," Jim recalled. "I learned firsthand what sacrifice was all about, so when I arrived in Germany in 1948 I could empathize with the plight of the German people. As a twenty-one-year-old airman, I did the job I was required to do as an aircraft mechanic." Jim was stationed at Fassberg with Moe Hamill—Moe flew the planes Jim fixed. According to Jim, "When I was not on the job, I took the time to explore the local sights, keeping on the lookout for beautiful German girls. I found one, a lovely young lady, Ursula, who lived in the town of Lueneburg. After a fast and furious courtship, we were married in the Fassberg base chapel on August 17, 1949, and then spent our short honeymoon on the island of Sylt in the North Sea. In late September 1949 I brought my new German bride to the United States."

Jim's and Ursula's marriage must have been one of the very first airlift weddings, but many more airmen were to marry German girls in the weeks to follow—including Technical Sergeant Leo Ferguson who married my mother, Hedy, in 1951—that's how I came to the United States. Other relationships were more casual. Prostitutes drifted to American military bases making easy money. The problems that soon surfaced became a headache for squadron commanders. The commander of the 29th Troop Carrier Squadron, Moe Hamill's squadron, Lieutenant Colonel Elmer E. McTaggart, was faced with the age-old problem of what to do about venereal disease, which began to affect his operations. Not really knowing what to do about it, Colonel McTaggart wrote the following letter to his men, appealing for them to mend their ways:

Subject: Letter of Commendation   30 June 1949

To: All Officers and Airmen 29th TC Sq

1. Again during the month of June, the 29th Squadron proved it was the best unit on the station. As we did in May, we carried more coal to Berlin in the greatest number of flights. We had the greatest number of aircraft in commission, and the least amount of turn-around maintenance.

2. As a matter of interest, let me enumerate what the 29th Squadron was leading in for the month of June:
  a. Greatest number of flights to Berlin.
  b. Greatest amount of coal to Berlin.
  c. Largest number of aircraft in commission.
  d. Greatest number of discrepancy reports.
  e. Greatest number of VD cases.

3. There can be no doubt from the above that we are the workingest, fightingest, -------- outfit on the field. It is a real pleasure to commend each individual in the fighting 29th for his part in the record we have achieved. It is a wonderful outfit and I am proud to be a member of the team.

4. It is nice to deal in superlatives when speaking of our squadron. However, I wonder if it is possible to eliminate discrepancy reports and VD rate from our list? Each one of you is certainly entitled to a "well done." Let's keep up the good work.

Elmer E. McTaggart
Lt Colonel, USAF, Commanding

I have no idea how successful Colonel McTaggart was in his appeal to his men, but three months later the airlift ended and RAF Fassberg reverted to its former quiet self. I myself was still there, still living in that wretched refugee camp off the north end of the Fassberg runway. After the Berlin airlift ended, Moe Hamill piloted Boeing KC-97 Stratotankers for the Strategic Air

Major Hamill received the Purple Heart in 1948 at Malmstrom AFB, Montana, while he was undergoing training for the Berlin airlift, for wounds he suffered five years earlier on a bombing run in 1943 flying a B-25 bomber over Sicily.

A crashed British fuel tanker at Berlin Tegel airport, 1949.

During the Berlin airlift of 1948–49 Moe Hamill flew coal out of Fassberg Air Base, near Hannover. He frequently joined the German workers heaving sacks of coal onto his C-54.

MOM'S PLACE   FASSBERG

The Regina Bar in Fassberg was opened by an enterprising German woman to cater to American GIs. The place quickly became known as Mom's Place—Mom was the bar's owner. My school was located on the same street near the bar and I would see the GIs sitting at their tables smoking, drinking beer, and whistling at passing German girls. The end of the Berlin airlift in 1949 also meant the end for the Regina Bar, as the base reverted to its former standby status.

Command, and commanded a KC-97 squadron before transferring to SAC headquarters at Omaha, Nebraska. Moe retired after thirty years of air force service in the rank of colonel to pursue a successful career as a financial securities broker in Newport Beach, California. Master Sergeant Jim Vaughn retired from the air force in 1966 and went to work for United Airlines as an aircraft mechanic. As for myself, a young German boy? I was so inspired by the flyers of the Berlin airlift that all I ever wanted to do was fly with those brave men. I did eventually come to America and in July 1960 my proud mother pinned the gold bars of a second lieutenant in the United States Air Force on my shoulders just before I left for flight training. I did get to fly with men of the Berlin airlift after all, and I even got to meet Colonel Gail Halvorsen, who for me embodied the spirit of what America was and is all about. Gail Halvorsen began dropping small bundles of chocolates and gum when making his final approach to Tempelhof to young girls and boys standing on heaps of rubble. Soon others followed his example and tons of candy were dropped to the children of war-torn Berlin. With that simple gesture Colonel Gail Halvorsen changed the world I grew up in and made it a better place for us all.

RUSSELL B. WITTE JR.

B-25/Test Pilot

Soldier's Poem

If I go to the great beyond, among the martial shadows there;
If I should fall against the foe, and if my fortune others share,
What will we leave to those we love that can be measured with the cost?
And will the living reap the harvest or the victory be lost?
When we change the fate of nations will we change the hearts of men?
If we chain the conquered savage will he break his bonds again?
Yes—for chains are to be broken as are prison walls to scale,
For a nation knows no bondage and, attempting it, we fail.
—Corporal Robert L. Jewell, WWII ETO

"I have vivid memories of the dust, the noise, the thrill and excitement of flying a tight formation, the fear and terror that came with near misses by attacking German fighters and bursting flak, and the grief you feel when you see a friend, flying near you, shot down."

Russell B. Witte was born in 1916 in Cincinnati, Ohio, and very early in life knew that he was going to follow in his father's footsteps. Russell Witte Senior had a successful construction business and was so pleased when his firstborn was a boy, he promptly changed the name of his construction company to R. B. Witte & Son. Russell attended the University of Cincinnati and in 1939 graduated with a degree in civil engineering, an education that perfectly fit into the business he was destined to run one day in the distant future. Russell was also a patriotic American; he joined the Reserve Officer Training Corps while in college and upon graduation was commissioned a second lieutenant in the Anti-Aircraft Coast Artillery Reserves. Soon after his graduation, war broke out in Europe, when Hitler's armies invaded Poland on September 1, 1939. A little over a year later, in early 1941, Russell was called to active duty and assigned as personnel officer of the 5th School Squadron at Chanute Field, Illinois—something that had little or nothing to do with his background as an engineer, nor with his own aspirations. That August, Russell noticed flyers posted on bulletin boards asking men to become pilots in the Army Air Corps. Army officers from any branch were given permission to apply for pilot training without having to first resign their commissions, provided they had excellent proficiency reports, weighed less than 215 pounds, were under six foot three inches tall, and could pass an aviator's physical examination. Russell applied, and on January 5, 1942, reported to Maxwell Field in Alabama for processing. Assigned to pilot training class 42H he reported on February 24 to his primary training flying school in Orangeburg, South Carolina. At the Hawthorne Flying School Russell's budding flying career nearly met its end the first time he got up in the air.

"I had a civilian pilot as an instructor. All of our instructors were civilians, and this guy had been a barnstormer before he settled down. He was a very good pilot. The PT-17 Stearman was a single engine, open cockpit, fixed propeller, and fixed landing gear biplane with the instructor in front, the student sitting behind the instructor. It was kind of an odd arrangement I thought, as was the fact that the instructor could talk to me, the student, but I couldn't talk to him over the rudimentary interphone installed on this aircraft. The instruments available to me, the student, were not much more inclusive. I had an altimeter to allow me to gauge my altitude, a magnetic compass for direction, a tachometer indicating engine performance, and a 'ball and needle' to allow me to monitor my attitude. But I had no airspeed indicator to allow me to gauge how fast I was moving, nor a stall indicator to warn me that I was about to crash. Our instructors explained the lack of instrumentation by saying, 'We want you to learn to fly by the seat of your pants.' Oh well. On our first flight, leveling off at a thousand feet, my instructor turned around, looked at me and said, 'You don't look very good, Witte. Are you about to get sick?'

"I shouted, he couldn't hear me of course, 'I am sick as hell.' He gave me another look and said, 'You look kind of green. I am going to land at an auxiliary field we have over here, and I want you to get out and get rid of your lunch—then we'll finish the flight.' Before we took off again, he said to me, 'Maybe you'll get over this. But you'll get washed out if you get sick three days in a row.' So on the next day we went up and I got sick again. On the third day we practiced taxiing. I got sick again on the fourth day and on the fifth. On the sixth day we did some more stuff that didn't make me sick. If it hadn't been for that understanding instructor, I'd have washed out of pilot training. My roommate's instructor was not that understanding. He got sick three days in a row and he was gone. Once I completed primary training at the Hawthorne Flying School, I transferred to Greenville, Mississippi, for basic training in the BT-13 Vultee, which was a great improvement over the Stearman. It had an enclosed cockpit, still featured a fixed landing gear, but was a monoplane with variable pitch propellers, flaps, and, believe it or not, a radio. Everyone called it the 'Vultee Vibrator' for good reason. By the time I got into advanced pilot training in Columbus, Mississippi, we were flying a pretty hot airplane, the North American AT-6 Texan, which had a retractable landing gear and all the instrumentation and features you would expect of a modern aircraft. The AT-6 was a fun airplane to fly. I wasn't going to go into fighters, so I finished my training in the twin engine Cessna A-17. After primary training I managed to control my airsickness problem. And I graduated and received my silver pilot wings on September 6, 1942.

"Immediately after receiving my wings I was assigned to Greenville Army Air Field in South Carolina to the 334th Bombardment Group for B-25 training. We had three training squadrons. What we referred to as the First Squadron trained aircrews for combat to go overseas; the Second Squadron's mission was to teach airmen to fly the B-25 Mitchell bomber, and in the Third Squadron, to which I was assigned, we learned all about the B-25 sitting behind a desk listening to instructors telling us about the aircraft's characteristics, electrical and hydraulic systems, armament, and so on. Then we would sit blindfolded in a cockpit and the instructor would call out a control or instrument and you were to put your hand on or point at whatever the instructor called for. Once you went through the Third Squadron, you really knew the airplane inside out and were ready to move into the Second Squadron for actual flying training. When I moved into the Second Squadron, I received about three hours of flying time in two weeks. There weren't enough airplanes to go around, and the First Squadron had priority. Since we were doing so little flying, I asked my squadron commander to allow me to go home on leave for a couple of weeks. To my surprise my squadron commander actually gave me a week of leave time. That wasn't considering that it took a day and a half by train to go from Columbus, South Carolina, to Cincinnati, Ohio. No sooner had I arrived home I received a telegram ordering me to return to base immediately. I called a friend to find out what was going on. This was in the days when you didn't make a long distance telephone call unless it was really important, like a death in the family.

"My friend laughed when he told me the story. 'You won't believe this,' he said. 'But, so-and-so, I can't recall his name, in the First Squadron, had his mother call their congressman. The mother told her congressman that her son was being sent overseas with inadequate training. She wanted the congressman to do something about the situation. Well, the congressman called the

War Department. That same afternoon the guy was put on a special flight to the West Coast where he was assigned to an outfit that was in the process of leaving for the war in the Pacific. Now they needed someone to replace this pilot in the First Squadron because, as you know, they are about to leave. What they did was to throw all of our names into a pot. Then someone came up with the idea to have Tom Harmon, who is in the squadron behind us, the famous football player from the University of Michigan at Ann Arbor, pull a name from the pot. Yours was the name Tom Harmon pulled.' I had three hours flying time in the B-25 and I was going overseas into combat.

"When we deployed, we were a squadron of eighteen brand-new B-25 Mitchell bombers flying from West Palm Beach, Florida, to San Juan, Puerto Rico; to Trinidad; to British Guiana; Belem, Brazil; the Ascension Islands in the middle of the South Atlantic; and then on to Accra, Africa. With two pilots in a plane we switched first pilot positions after each landing. By the time we had flown down to South America, across the Atlantic, into Africa, we were all well trained. We were a crew of five—two pilots, a navigator/bombardier, and two gunners, one of which also served as the radio operator. But on this deployment each aircraft carried an additional three maintenance and armament men, for a total of eight. We carried spare parts in the bomb bay—even torpedo sights—we had no idea what they were for. We were not allowed to take anything personal but our B-4 bags. Everything else, foot lockers and so on, were to follow on another airplane that would fly direct to our final destination, an APO number that no one knew where it actually was. Well, you always have some super sleuth in every outfit, and ours found out that the final destination for thirteen of our aircraft was to be Karachi, India [now Pakistan]; the remaining four were destined to go to Cairo, Egypt. We carried a packet of secret orders we were to turn in to the commanding officer in Khartoum, Sudan, which is at the split of the Nile, the White Nile and the Blue Nile. We were eighteen ships, eight guys in each ship, and that made for a big packet of individual secret orders. I think what happened was that a clerk opened the first envelopes and they were for the five ships to go to Cairo, Egypt. He probably took the names off all the rest of the envelopes and sent us all to Cairo. We didn't go to Karachi, India, but Cairo instead, where we were assigned to the 8th British Army commanded by General Montgomery. When we got there, we were only sixteen ships, not eighteen. We had lost a couple in transit. One airplane had a smoking engine and remained at Acra. We never heard from them again. Then, when we were flying across the Lake Chad area, there were a bunch of tremendous pinnacles rising up out of the sandy desert. A couple of them were fairly close together. One of our guys thought he'd bank through them. He caught a wing. We circled for half an hour, but never saw a sign of life. The aircraft was scattered all over the place.

"On January 3, 1943, we arrived at Ismailia, Egypt, at an army depot. They took possession of our airplanes and modified them for desert warfare by installing larger carburetors and air filters, among other things. Ten days later we headed west to Landing Ground 142 at Gambut, about thirty miles south of Tobruk, Libya, where officially we became members of the 12th Bombardment Group, which had arrived a couple of months earlier and flew its first missions during the Battle of El Alamein. When we arrived at LG 142, our crews were split up, and all the pilots were assigned as copilots on newly formed crews led by pilots with combat experience. I was assigned to a crew in the 82nd Bombardment Squadron of the 12th Bombardment Group, which consisted of four squadrons: the 81st, 82nd, 83rd, and 434th. We were officially assigned to the 9th Air Force, commanded by General Lewis Brereton, which included B-17 and B-24 groups flying strategic missions. But our 12th Bomb Group was attached to the Western Desert Air Force commanded by Air Vice Marshal Sir Arthur Coningham. We, along with South African, Australian, and British air groups flew tactical missions only in support of General Montgomery's 8th Army. I learned that Coningham and Montgomery maintained a joint headquarters in which air and ground elements worked together: a new and successful arrangement it proved to be.

"By the time we arrived there was little fighting going on. British airmen had the time to teach us how they did their flying in the desert:

-Line up six planes abreast, take off crosswind, so the wind will blow the dust to the side and the next six planes can take off immediately without having to eat the dust we generated.
-Land three planes abreast crosswind, for the same reason.
-Fly in boxes of six planes, using as many boxes as needed for a target.
-When over enemy territory fly at altitudes between 7,000 and 12,000 feet. Vary altitude and direction constantly.
-Maintain radio silence.
-Desynchronize engines.
-Disperse planes and personal tents.
-No lights at night.

"Being attached to the British army meant that we flew where they wanted us. We wore British flight suits with American insignia, ate British rations, and dropped British bombs. One of the less desirable things of this arrangement were the British rations—we ate mostly 'bully beef' and orange marmalade on white bread. In the desert we had no runways. They just bulldozed all the hummocks, smoothed things out, that was it. It was extremely dusty. When you got up in the morning, it was calm. The wind would come off the hot desert and then collide with colder air over the Mediterranean. Then the wind would pick up to twenty-five to thirty-five miles per hour in the afternoons. That's when it was tough taking off crosswind. When we made camp at a landing site, and we moved frequently, we put our tents about 50 yards apart, and parked the planes about 150 to 200 yards apart. So we were not a very good target for the Germans. Once, when we were close to the 'Americans'—those flying from western bases near Casablanca—they still lined up their planes one next to the other. They were based up the coast west of us, assigned to the 12th Air Force. They got bombed every night by the Germans, probably because they made better targets. The Germans never bombed us.

"We lived as one five-man crew—enlisted and officer—in a tent, slept on canvas cots, and were issued five blankets each, which wasn't enough to keep warm during the cold winter nights when the temperatures dropped below freezing. When we moved, each crew took down its own tent and loaded it along with all of its gear and sleeping cots into their airplane and flew to the next landing ground. We did all of our bombing visually. We did not have the Norden bombsight. We used a little Sperry bombsight which primarily involved lining up a couple of blips over the target. We did saturation bombing, carried 3,000 pounders, 500-pound, and 250-pound bombs. One of the things our armament men did was to weld a rod on the front of the bomb, in front of the fuse, with a little metal pad, so when the prod hit the ground it would push in the fuse and the bomb exploded above ground. It worked. We called them stick bombs. We flew most of our missions between seven and twelve thousand feet, usually between seven and ten—because we didn't have oxygen on board. One of our superiors once decided we should fly a mission at fourteen thousand feet. You are flying in formation in a box of six aircraft, flying up and down and all around so the Germans couldn't track you for their flak. It was physically hard flying. We flew this mission, and as soon as we were debriefed by our intelligence people, we headed for our tents and slept for twenty-four hours—after flying for three hours without oxygen at fourteen thousand feet, we were spent. Most of us had a mild case of the bends. I didn't sleep much because it felt like a thousand ants were crawling over my body.

"We took off six planes abreast, crosswind, so that the wind would blow all that dust away and then the next six guys would take off. You know what crosswind takeoffs and landings are like. They are not things you like to do. And taking off six planes abreast with a bomb load of twelve live bombs in each plane was a roll of the dice. We dropped British bombs. American bombs had an arming wire that went through a trigger in the fuse. The bomb on release slipped off that arming wire, and the bomb was now armed. A British bomb had a fuse screwed into its nose when it was loaded and it was a live bomb from then on. So you have a bomb bay full of live bombs taking off six planes abreast in a crosswind. We tried to be very careful.

"The German antiaircraft, their light flak, was always very heavy, but you could fly over it—it only came up to seven thousand feet. However, they were quite accurate with their heavier guns, especially if they caught you on your bombing run, when we had to fly straight and level. As soon as we dropped our bombs, we turned. If the turn was to the left, you hated to be the guy on the far right. One of my best friends was flying on my right side. I was leading the second element of three. So he was the guy on the far right of our little group when we initiated our turn to the left. I had two guys on my wings and was following the lead element. I had to go wherever he went. I glanced over to my right. I heard the flak popping. You only heard that pop when it was really close, and that instant my friend's plane was hit. That 88mm shell tore the fuselage right off behind where he was sitting. I knew he was gone. The next time I looked the ship had disappeared. My top turret gunner said that he saw two parachutes and one was on fire. This friend of mine who was killed on that mission was a very neat guy. For the rest of us, when we patted our flight suits, dust would fly out. Our hair was full of dust, our eyebrows, our eyelashes were dust covered. He didn't seem to pick up the dust like the rest of us. He was 'Mr. Clean.' We landed and debriefed. As soon as we finished debriefing, I ran over to my friend's tent and removed the knife and fork from his mess kit's handle. I had lost mine somehow and he didn't need his anymore. War does things to you. As for our losses—half the men I went over with didn't make it back. You really hated it when your guys got shot down. It hurt deep down. And you knew you were going to be next. Just a matter of time.

"When the Kasserine Pass debacle happened, we were tasked to fly support for 'the Americans.' The Germans had launched a surprise attack around Kasserine Pass in Tunisia and driven back American forces. I recall that particular mission because we had to come down through an overcast to bomb a rail and road intersection. A hole opened up in the clouds right over our target. There were German fighters underneath circling, but they didn't want to come up and get trapped by the clouds. We were able to bomb the target but then we had to get down below the clouds with the German fighters, because the Atlas Mountains were sticking up into that overcast. And of course we had no radar. We broke off individually and got back to base on our own. On one of those missions an American general flew with us. He wanted to see how we flew our missions. We usually had Spitfires flying cover for us. I believe they were New Zealanders. They did a great job. On this mission we were supposed to have American P-38s fly cover for us. We kept on looking for the P-38s but couldn't see them anywhere. Then someone said over the radio, 'Look down.' There they were, flying right close to the ground in a little tight group. We waggled our wings and they waggled theirs. We wondered why they didn't get above us. Actually, we never saw them again. They just disappeared. We got jumped by some Me 109s and got shot up pretty badly. The general flying with us nearly was hit. After we landed, we pilots got together with the general and told him, 'We want our Spitfires back.' We got them back.

"We were frequently attacked by German fighters. On one occasion, I was leading the second element, with two guys on my wings, when I happened to look up in the two o'clock position. There was a Fw 190 about to turn into us. He came straight down, his cannons and guns going. We were firing back at him but we didn't have a heck of a lot to work with. He just kept on coming, flying right between our two elements. I asked my top gunner if we got hit. He replied, 'It's sort of windy up here.' We had a lot of holes in our airplane but he didn't hit anything vital and we kept right on flying. I thought it was unbeliev-able. What was my hairiest mission? I had a number of them. One time I had a new copilot. I wanted him to get some formation flying experience, because we were always flying in formation. As the copilot he sat in the right seat. We were flying on the lead's wing to our left. So I slid my seat back so he could see across more easily. When we were getting ready to pass the bomb line, I thought it best for me to take over again. The bomb line was an imaginary line on the ground beyond which we could drop our bombs but not before we crossed that line. I slid my seat forward again, and hadn't even locked it in place, when 'blam' an 88mm shell came right up through the bottom of the fuselage, right through the pilot's compartment floor, right where I had been sitting a second earlier. And the shell went right out the canopy. It didn't go off. All it did was make these three holes in the aircraft. The pilot's compartment floor is filled with hydraulic lines, fuel lines, control lines—it didn't damage anything. The shell just made three holes. An experience like that makes you wonder about a lot of things. Some of the B-25s had a ball turret in their belly. That turret was totally useless. First, you had to let the thing down. Once the gunner got into the ball turret, he had a thirty-degree cone of vision through an eye piece. Imagine trying to track a fast-moving target that way. It was very difficult, quite impossible at times.

"B-25 number 33 was my favorite airplane. The number 33 was painted in large white letters across the vertical stabilizers and rudders. On one mission, it was shot up so badly that we were unable to lower the landing gear and I had to make a belly landing, which wiped out the 250-pound ball turret. When the maintenance crew patched up the plane, they sealed the hole with a piece of Plexiglas containing a ball socket with a .50-caliber machine gun mounted in it. This was a much lighter piece of armament and more effective than the ball turret. The plane was easier to fly as well. On some of our aircraft we installed a black painted broomstick in the tail to make the German fighter pilots think that we carried a tail gun. In some planes we did just that. We installed a .30-caliber machine gun mounted on a jeep spring, loaded with tracers. The top turret gunner couldn't aim the gun but he had an on/off switch which allowed him to fire it.

"We got over to Egypt in December 1942, right after the Battle of El Alamein. We didn't get any mail until April 1943. Our mail went to the APO number that we were to go to. But never did. All of our mail went to India. We never again saw our trunks and other baggage that was flown on a transport plane to India. When we first arrived, we were told that we would rotate back to the States after twenty-five combat missions. When twenty-five came around, we were told that we needed to fly five more. When we got to thirty-five missions, we all figured they'll keep us until we had flown at least fifty. Catch 22. So, we had that number in our minds. But when we got to fifty missions, we kept right on flying. I came home after flying fifty-five combat missions, never lost a plane, never lost a crewman. But we came awfully close to doing just that all too many times. I went over as a second lieutenant and returned as a first lieutenant. I was never anywhere where there was room to get promoted. We were all lieutenants. The replacement pilots always outranked everybody, so there were few promotions. Unless there was an opening you couldn't be promoted to a higher grade.

"One of the things we hated doing most was dropping leaflets—suggesting to the German soldiers to surrender. We dropped those leaflets while they were shooting at us. A friend of mine's plane got shot up terribly bad on one of those missions. He gave the order to bail out to the crew. He was the last to go. By the time it was his turn, he was so low he couldn't crawl out the bottom of the plane. He jettisoned the canopy. All of us hated to have to do that because of all the wires and stuff up there. He remembered clearly trying to pull the D-ring on his chute. Nothing happened. When he looked down, he saw that his right arm had been shot off below the elbow. So he pulled the ring with his left hand. He was so low by this time that when the chute opened he immediately hit the ground, breaking both legs and thigh bones. His arm was spurting blood. Luckily for him, he landed near a German ambulance crew which had watched him as he came down. Right away they put a tourniquet on his arm, loaded him into the ambulance, and took him to a field hospital in Tunis. Three days after this happened the Germans surrendered; they were boxed in at Cape Bon and couldn't get out. Friends of mine went into Tunis cruising around to see what they could see. I couldn't go along because I had sprained my ankle playing volleyball. They came across this German hospital and wondered if anyone was in there they might know. They stopped. And as you always did when you leave your jeep, they popped the hood and took the rotor off, pulled some ignition wires, and removed some spark plugs and put them in their pockets. You had to do this if you wanted to find your jeep when you returned where you left it. Even then it wasn't always there—the Arabs were very good at pilfering anything not nailed down. They went into the hospital, and as they walked around among the wounded, they saw a patient who had casts on both legs, the legs suspended in the air with a cable over a pulley mounted to the ceiling and a weight attached to it holding up his legs. He also had a bandaged arm. It turned out to be my friend who had received excellent service from the German medical staff and was in pretty good spirits."

Lieutenant Robert S. Hamill also flew with the 12th Bombardment Group, but he was in the 81st Bombardment Squadron, and Witte and Hamill never met, although they probably flew more than once in the same formations bombing the same target. Hamill, on his sixth mission, saw his lead aircraft get hit and explode. The B-25 was carrying the new 12th Group commander on his first combat mission. Hamill thought all had perished. Yet, when he went to the same hospital visited by Witte's friends in Tunis, near Cape Bon, after the Germans had surrendered, he found that two of the crew had survived. The pilot's leg had been amputated. The other survivor, the bombardier, didn't recall how he got out of his stricken aircraft. Once the Afrika Korps surrendered on May 12, the 12th Bombardment Group began flying missions against the islands of Pantelleria and Lampedusa, which quickly surrendered.

"We started bombing targets in Sicily," Witte recalls, "mostly as individual planes at night with one aircraft over the target every five minutes or so from dark until dawn. Our targets were German and Italian airfields and harbor installations. We received considerable attention from antiaircraft guns, searchlights, and night fighters. But our losses were light. We continued flying such missions until late August when we moved to Grabini, near Catania, Sicily, and began bombing targets on the Italian mainland. I was on a mission flying out of Sicily dropping bombs in Italy. The flak was really heavy over the target, but I didn't get hit until we were on our way back. Shells exploded just a little below and ahead of me, my left engine caught fire, stopped running, and I feathered the prop. The fire went out. Then I got hit in my right engine. It was struggling, it kept running, but there was no way for me to keep up with the formation, and I dropped out. Our base was to the south of Mount Aetna. We were coming in from the north and I had to fly all the way around Aetna. Looking at the ground I couldn't see a level spot anywhere where I could have landed. I spotted our field. You never want to turn into a dead engine, so I made all right turns, and as I was coming in, I realized I had no hydraulics. We cranked down the wheels manually. Just as I was flaring to make the landing the right engine stopped running. I had no flaps, no brakes. We finally came to a stop when we ran into something. On September 11, 1943, my target was a crossroads near Salerno in preparation for the upcoming landing. It was a night mission, my 55th combat mission, and my last.

"On October 16, 1943, twelve of us from the 12th Bombardment Group boarded the *Empress of Scotland*, formerly the *Empress of Japan*, a small Canadian Pacific ocean liner, for Newport News, Virginia. Its former staterooms were crowded with triple-deck bunks. On board were wounded, other soldiers and airmen returning home, some pregnant WACS, and Frenchmen going to the United States for pilot training. We pilots were asked by the ship's captain if we would be willing to stand submarine watch in the two crow's nests that were on tall masts at either end of the ship. We were on duty four hours at a time. Then off for twelve hours, for the duration of the voyage. Because our ship was relatively fast, we proceeded alone, without escort. After weathering a terrible storm, which had me wondering if we were going to survive, we anchored off Newport News on October 24, waiting for a pilot to take us through a protective mine field into the harbor. We were actually met by a GI band, and I boarded a train for Cincinnati—home after ten, at times hair-raising, months of combat. After a few weeks of leave at home, I reported to the Army Air Forces redistribution center in the Ritz Carlton Hotel in Atlantic City, New Jersey. I requested duty as a test pilot at Eglin Field, Florida. To my great surprise, that's where I went. At Eglin I was assigned to the Heavy Bomb Group flying tests in the B-17, B-24, B-29, and B-32 aircraft. The B-32 Dominator was similar to the B-29 with remotely controlled gun turrets and undergoing flight testing at Eglin along with the B-29 to determine which aircraft was to go into mass production first. Production problems dogged the B-32; its pressurization was deleted to hurry things along, but by the time the B-32 went into production the B-29 had already carried the air war to Japan. We loved flying the B-29 because the cabin was pressurized to eight thousand feet while you could go up to thirty thousand feet." Only one bombardment squadron was ever equipped with B-32s, the 386th on Okinawa. It garnered the dubious honor of having the last American killed in World War II on a reconnaissance mission over Tokyo on August 18, 1945—three days after the signing of the surrender on August 15.[28]

"Of all the aircraft I flew, the B-25 was by far the noisiest—it cost me my hearing. MGM came to Eglin Auxiliary #9 where the Doolittle Raiders trained for their epic mission against Japan. There they filmed the movie *Thirty Seconds over Tokyo*. We removed the tail turret from a B-24 and MGM installed a movie camera mounted on a tripod in its place. The cameraman stood back there in that open space with nothing to hold onto but the camera. Scary. I got to fly their cameraman when he made the air-to-air shots, met the actors, and upon completion of the movie they presented me with one of the flying suits they wore while filming the movie. I met all the principal actors and learned that Van Johnson and I were the same age. Although I was in bomber test at Eglin, I did get to fly our first jet, the P-59. It was amazingly different from

Shadows of 12th Bomb Group B-25s over the desert near Cape Bon. American air power forced the vaunted Afrika Korps to surrender. Russ Witte piloted one of the planes shown here.

Witte's crew getting ready to fly his fifty-fifth, and last, combat mission against a target in Italy, September 11, 1943.

S/Sgt. Kinny, radio gunner; Sgt Creed, top turret gunner; 2nd Lt. Jim Steinberg, navigator bombardier, 2nd Lt. Dick Sawyer, co-pilot; and 1st Lt. Russ Witte, pilot. Here were ready to climb into our plane for my 55th and last combat mission.

Russell Witte in 2012 at age ninety-six in front of a B-25 Mitchell bomber at the Tri-State Warbird Museum in Batavia, Ohio. He is wearing the same British flying suit issued to him in 1943 when he first arrived in Egypt.

anything I had flown before. When you are flying a single-engine conventional aircraft, you have a lot of torque to deal with, but not in that airplane. On the other hand, after flying around the field three times, I was out of kerosene. The P-59 had short legs.

"Come VJ Day, August 15, 1945, it was time to think of what I wanted to do in the future. The airlines were busy recruiting among Eglin test pilots, some of the best pilots around. Since I loved flying, this was very tempting. I chose instead to join my father at R. B. Witte & Son, who had written me and asked me to please get out of the army because he needed help. So, that's what I did." Russell Witte and his father ran a successful construction business in Cincinnati for many years. But he didn't give up flying, earning all possible civilian ratings. Russell retired in 1981 after thirty-one years in the construction business, turning the business over to his son, and instead he concentrated on playing a good game of golf and competing in swimming in the Senior Olympics, winning many gold medals.

CHARLES E. SCHREFFLER

P-38/F-51

And We Complain

Last week I happened to meet a couple of boys who were lacking their feet.
They've been over there, they've seen what it's like,
It left them with scars that they'll carry for life.
They lived in fox holes for days at a time,
Their food was K rations garnished in grime.
They fought and they sweated, some bled and some died,
The world calls them heroes, they're just men who tried.
They were given their orders, they were told what to do,
Sure they griped like the devil, but they still saw it through.
No, it isn't your brawn, and it isn't your size,
For war has no mercy, on smart or wise guys.
You listen to orders and then do your best.
And God being with you, you'll live through the test.
—Pvt. Bernard Tatz, WWII ETO

In the sunshine of southern California, where Charlie Schreffler settled after an eventful air force career, he recalled for me one particular June afternoon in 1950. "While sitting on the porch of my quarters at Clark Air Base in the Philippines, I saw innocent-looking puffs of smoke seeping out of the jungle foliage. It was an artillery duel between the communist Huks and the local constabulary, just beyond the Clark Air Base perimeter. A flight of four Philippine F-51 Mustangs passed overhead in echelon formation to join the fray. My unit, the 18th Fighter Bomber Group, had converted to the F-80 Shooting Star jet only recently, giving our World War II vintage Mustang fighters to the Philippine air force. Maybe one of those attacking planes was mine, *Sally Flat Foot*. I could see the Mustangs descending one at a time, strafing what they thought were guerilla positions. In the jungle it was hard to tell where anything was—I knew that from experience. The Mustangs pulled up sharply at the end of their high-angle strafing passes. I saw them reforming for a second run at the Huks. A feeling of nostalgia overcame me as I watched them. I missed flying the 'Stang' as we affectionately referred to the Mustang. But then I couldn't remember any plane I flew I didn't like.

"I remember one of my last flights in the F-51, a routine training flight just before I transitioned into the F-80 jet. My wingman and I were on our initial approach to Clark when without warning we were jumped by a couple of F-51s from our sister squadron, the 12th. I flew with the 67th squadron. We maintained our flying skills by engaging each other in mock air battles, but this wasn't quite the way it was supposed to happen, and the resulting mid-air collision bent *Sally Flat Foot*'s props and put a few dents in her nose. The other Mustang had its tail chewed up. We landed safely. It's trite to say that flying is hours of boredom and moments of stark terror, but it is true. That June of 1950 my wife was making arrangements for our move back to the States. I was reading the base paper and having a beer on our porch. I hated everything associated with moving. The packers were coming on Friday, June 24. Our household goods were to be picked up on Monday, the 27th. That day I intended to clear the base and stay out of the way, spend my time in the squadron or at the Officers' Club. After they picked up our stuff, we would spend a night in the base hotel and then embark on a boat at the nearby Subic Bay Navy Base for a leisurely trip back to San Francisco. I was looking forward to going home. I tried to go back to reading the paper, but I was still too distracted by idle thoughts as a result of the Philippine F-51s, who by then were on their second strafing run. I put down my paper and decided to watch them instead. My war was behind me, I thought smugly, and I was glad.

"I'll never forget December 10, 1941, three days after the Japanese attacked Pearl Harbor. My friends and I, in a patriotic fervor, went to the army recruiting office in Fort Wayne, Indiana, and signed up for the Army Air Corps. I was born in 1921 in Coshocton, Ohio. When I was still very young, my parents had moved to Indiana. I always wanted to fly, ever since the barnstormers came by when I was seven and gave me a five-minute ride. I passed my physical and became an aviation cadet. I went through preflight and primary training in the PT-13 Kaydet and the Vultee BT-13 Valiant 'Vibrator.' The BT had flaps and a sophisticated set of instruments, none of which the PT had. In advanced training I got to fly the fighter-like AT-6 Texan at Luke Field, Arizona. I graduated in December 1942, and that same day was put on a train to transition into P-38 fighters at Glendale, California. In March 1943 I crossed the country by train, processed through Fort Dix in New Jersey, and embarked on a ship which joined a large convoy across the Atlantic, bound for Oran, Algeria. From there I shipped to a dusty base outside Casablanca for P-38 refresher training. Finally, I got to fly my first combat mission. It was against a small harbor in Sardinia. I had never dropped a bomb before and felt a little foolish not knowing how to aim my bomb or even when I was to drop it. I watched my flight leader closely and did exactly what he did. When he released his bomb, I let go of mine. I don't know where the bomb went or if it hit anything other than water.

"On my next mission over Sicily, we ran into some German Me 109s. In the ensuing melee one of our own aircraft shot up my leader, and we both returned to base. Up until then everything seemed sort of unreal, even comical at times. After all, I was a fighter pilot, not a bomber pilot, and I didn't expect our own planes to fire on us. But then everything in combat is confusing. My perceptions of war changed drastically on my next mission, a long-range sweep by over two hundred P-38s against German and Italian air bases around Foggia on the Italian mainland. I finally got to use my guns. We came in from the Adriatic side, flying at fifty feet to avoid detection. We totally surprised the enemy and destroyed over one hundred of their aircraft on the ground. Soon after that mission, I learned about fear and how to fly through it. It was August 30, 1943. We were escorting a group of B-26 Marauders up the Italian boot when we were jumped by seventy-five to eighty Me 109s and Fw 190s. We got all the B-26s into the target and out without losing one, but we lost eleven of our own. I lost an engine in the melee. In the confusion of the air battle, a German Me 109 suddenly came into my sights, and I fired instinctively. The 109 burst into flames and exploded. I added one more probable enemy fighter destroyed that day before returning to my base." For his extraordinary performance on that mission First Lieutenant Charles E. Schreffler was awarded the Distinguished Flying Cross. Read the official orders awarding Charlie his first DFC:

Headquarters Twelfth Air Forces
APO #650

13 October 1943

Charles E. Schreffler, 0-734000, First Lieutenant, Anderson, Indiana. For extraordinary achievement while participating in aerial flight in the North African, Sicilian and Italian Theaters of Operations as a pilot of a P-38 aircraft. On 30 August 1943, while escorting a B-26 bombardment group over Lago di Patria, Italy, Lt. Schreffler's flight of 4 P-38s was attacked by thirty Me 109s. Observing a lagging comrade in grave danger he unhesitatingly led his flight in an aggressive assault on the threatening enemy aircraft, destroying one Me 109 and probably destroying another. Lt Schreffler so expertly maneuvered his small flight, despite one engine being disabled by hostile fire, that the flight safely rejoined his squadron. His outstanding ability as a flight leader and combat pilot has reflected great credit upon himself and the armed forces of the United States.

By Command of Major General Doolittle

"By September 1943 I had racked up fifty combat missions over Italy and was returned home to Bradley Field, near Hartford, Connecticut. There I stayed until April 1945 as a P-47 Thunderbolt instructor pilot. I liked flying and wanted to stay, but was discharged that October along with thousands of other pilots. I returned to Fort Wayne, Indiana, to my old job as a draftsman. I stayed in the air force reserve, and to my great surprise, in 1947, I was offered a regular air force commission. I accepted immediately and was assigned to Andrews Air Force Base, near Washington, DC, as a maintenance officer. In July 1948 I transferred to the 18th Fighter Group at Clark Air Base in the Philippines. World War II should have been my only war. I was wrong. In a few days I was involved in another equally brutal war. The 18th Fighter Bomber Group was quickly thrown into battle to stem the surging tide of the North Korean People's Army.

"Our household goods were picked up as scheduled. That evening my wife mentioned a curious thing to me. The household goods people had contacted her and asked if she wanted to change the destination of our shipment. When she asked them why she would want to do that, they told her that her husband wouldn't be accompanying her. 'Is that true?' she asked me. That's how I found out about the invasion of South Korea by the North. My wife took the ship home to San Francisco, while I left for Johnson Air Base, near Tokyo, Japan, to pick up an F-51. By the time her ship docked in San Francisco harbor, some of the returning wives learned that their husbands had died in South Korea, in a war of which they knew nothing."

General Matthew B. Ridgeway, who was appointed Supreme Commander, Far East, by President Truman on December 26, 1951, replacing General Douglas MacArthur, wrote when he learned of the attack on South Korea, "The outbreak of the war came to me as a complete surprise, as it did to all our military men—from Seoul to Washington."[29] The situation in South Korea was desperate. The US military in Japan was largely an occupational constabulary, poorly trained and not much better equipped. What remained of American military power was built around the jet fighter plane, just coming into the inventory, and the new super weapon, the atomic bomb. The atomic bomb couldn't save

Americans trapped in Seoul or, later on, in the tight Pusan perimeter. The available air bases in South Korea were so crude that the 18th Fighter Bomber Group's F-80 jets could not operate from them. The two-hundred-mile distance from Japan to targets in South Korea gave the F-80 almost no loiter time over the target. Air force commanders had to look for quick alternatives. The F-51 was not ideal for its intended mission of ground support, but it was rugged enough to operate from crude airfields, carried a lethal weapons load, and was still available in large numbers. The "indestructible" P-47 which did such a great job in Europe supporting ground troops unfortunately was no longer available in adequate numbers. It, like many other World War II aircraft, had been turned to scrap or been given to needy allies. The F-51 would have to do, and the decision was made to reequip the 18th Group with F-51 Mustangs.

"All 18th Group pilots were F-51 qualified. Many of us had extensive World War II experience. Our group had three squadrons—the 12th, the 44th, and the 67th." The pilots of the 12th Squadron, augmented by fliers from the other two squadrons, were the first to convert. They were flown to Johnson Air Base where they picked up thirty reconditioned F-51s that had been in storage. The "Dallas Provisional Squadron," as they were to be called, flew their Mustangs to Ashiya in southern Japan, then moved on to a dirt airstrip, K-2, near Taegu, South Korea, flying their first combat missions on July 14, 1950. In the meantime, 145 F-51s assigned to the air national guard were rounded up and loaded on the aircraft carrier USS *Boxer*, which left the port of Alameda on July 15 with its load of Mustangs and seventy pilots. After a maximum-speed voyage, the *Boxer* arrived in Japan on July 22. Pilots of the 67th Fighter Bomber Squadron from Clark picked up a batch of the newly arrived Mustangs and became part of the 51st Fighter Group (Provisional), joining their advanced party of the Dallas Squadron at K-2 to carry the war to the enemy. By August 4 the name game ended when the two squadrons regained their original designations as the 12th and 67th Fighter Bomber Squadrons of the 18th Fighter Bomber Group. They fought under this designation for the rest of the war and accumulated an outstanding combat record. The 12th Squadron "Blue Noses," the former Dallas Squadron, became known as the Flying Tigers of Korea, after South Korean President Syngman Rhee commented on their gallantry and compared them to the Flying Tigers of World War II fame. Their aircraft soon sported shark's teeth. The Red Noses belonged to the 67th Squadron, and Charlie Schreffler flew a red nose out of K-2 in July 1950.

"I remember leading a flight of two Mustangs on a road reconnaissance mission in the area of Hamhung, North Korea. As we turned south to return to base, the visibility began to deteriorate and our position was not completely clear to me. As we crossed over a coastline, all hell broke loose. We had flown over Wonsan harbor, which was loaded with North Korean ships. They let us know we were not welcome. From Taegu the 18th moved first to K-9, Pusan East; then to K-23, Pyongyang East; then to K-13, Suwon near Seoul; and finally to Chinhae, K-10, which became our main operating base for the remainder of the war. Conditions at Chinhae were basic—dirt, rocks, and tents defined the base. But we didn't lose our sense of humor, and we called Chinhae 'Dogpatch' and 'Lower Slobovia.' Al Capp, the guy who drew the *Li'l Abner* comic strip, somehow got wind of us and took us under his wing. He designed a patch for us. I still have mine. The patch shows Li'l Abner riding an F-51 Mustang firing its guns, with the inscription 'Dogpatchers.' That's how we got our name Dogpatchers.

"Major Louis J. 'Lou' Sebille was my squadron commander. On a routine close-air-support mission on 5 August, one of Lou's five-hundred-pound bombs didn't release. He tried to shake the bomb loose on his second firing pass, but by then the enemy had his range, and he took several hits. Again, the bomb didn't release. Lou should have returned to Chinhae, had the bomb removed, and the holes patched. Instead, he chose to continue his attack. On his next firing pass, getting hit all the way in, he never pulled out and flew directly into the enemy vehicles and exploded. For that action Lou received the Medal of Honor. I can't vouch for the exact number of firing passes Lou made, but the squadron's reaction on hearing of his loss was one of great sorrow. Lou was a fine pilot!

"My bunch, the 67th Squadron, launched its first missions in June 1950 from Ashiya, Japan. By the first week in August we were operating from K-2, at Taegu, within the Pusan defensive perimeter. It was a dusty, rock-strewn field with quick access to the bomb line, constantly moving south. One problem we soon discovered was differentiating between friend and foe. We were moving so fast and close to the ground it was difficult to determine who was who. The GIs were supposed to display colors of the day; they didn't always do so. Mistakes were made and sometimes there were the unavoidable friendly-fire losses." But there wasn't a GI whose heart didn't jump for joy when he heard the high-pitched whine of an F-51 engine bearing down on the enemy at thirty feet above the ground. The F-51's killing power became legendary. With six wing-mounted .50-caliber machine guns, three in each wing, and a load of nearly 1,900 rounds of ammunition, the "Stang" could put on a very impressive firepower display. Napalm was the weapon most feared by North Korean infantry, and their rockets were the most dreaded by the North Korean tanks. The two 18th Group squadrons quickly established a tank-killing unit of ready-to-go, rocket-armed aircraft. Whenever a call came in that enemy tanks had been sighted, this unit went after them. When the Pusan perimeter really got tight, pilots flew as many as five or six missions a day. Almost immediately after takeoff, they found themselves over enemy lines. For a

Ready to go at a moment's notice—scene at K-9 just behind the lines at Pusan. Rocket-armed F-51 with ambulance in the background to take care of wounded pilots as soon as they landed.

Captain Schreffler at K-9, Pusan, also known as Dogpatch to its crews, in 1950, in front of his antitank rocket-armed F-51 fighter. They went after the North Korean T-34 tanks as soon as they were spotted.

An armorer at K-9 listens to a pilot who just returned from a mission. The truck is carrying the armament load for the six .50-caliber guns carried by an F-51—nearly 1,900 rounds.

When the squadron moved to K-10, Chinhae, just a few miles down the coast from K-9, an enterprising Korean woman opened a laundry and tailor shop—"repair of every clothes," she promised.

Young South Korean orphan boys served as waiters at the makeshift Officers' Club at Chinhae. The flyers of the 18th Fighter Bomber Wing became their surrogate parents and took good care of them. One or two lucky ones may even have made it to the United States.

pilot to fly a hundred missions in two months wasn't difficult—if he lived that long. Losses were high, operating so close to the ground, where every enemy weapon could reach them. There was an aggregate loss of 351 F-51s in more than sixty thousand combat missions. Nearly fifty thousand of those missions were flown by the pilots of the 18th Wing, including a South African F-51-equipped squadron—the Flying, Fighting Cheetahs—which were under the control of and flew with the 18th Wing. The 18th's F-51s, along with the twin-engine B-26 Invaders of the 3rd and 452nd Bomb Wings, helped break the back of the initial North Korean invasion force and gave the US Army the time it needed to reconstitute itself.[30] Charlie Schreffler's "second" war in one lifetime was more intense than anything he had experienced in fifty combat missions over Europe. In time Colonel Charles E. Schreffler retired from the United States Air Force and settled in Air Force Village West, adjacent to the former March Air Force Base, at Riverside, California. The Village is a popular air force retirement community and became the home of a number of the men whose wartime stories I have been privileged to write about in this book. The Korean War, often referred to as the forgotten war, was fought largely by the men who had fought in World War II, using the weapons of that war. According to the official history of the United States Forces, Korea, between July 1, 1950, and July 27, 1953, the Far East Air Force lost a total of 1,838 aircraft on operational missions, 944 being lost due to enemy action. The majority of those 944 aircraft were F-51 fighter bombers and B-26 medium bombers.[31]

KENNETH O. CHILSTROM

A-36/Me 262/Test Pilot

Wright Field, 1944: The Ready Room

On the benches in this room were morning vacant spaces
for some that saw the sky turn dark, at noon, with youthful faces.
Too soon, too low, too high, too fast—they hurried on into the past.
The crashes often most were blamed on grievous pilot errors
but on the hill where the coffin was, six pilots were the bearers.
The feathering button that didn't work. The gear-down switch with the funny quirk.
Flinders and flames, flinders and flames, the names soon forgotten with the blames.
The echoes ring here yet, of engine test cells roaring.
Above drift the skies they touched and tried, alone, aloft, exploring.
The games of chess unfinished still—the rain, the line, the morning chill.
Farewell, once more, my vanished friends.
—Author Unknown, WWII AAF Flight Test Center

Wright Field had been testing captured German fighters and bombers since 1943 to determine their strengths and weaknesses. Whatever the Wright Field test pilots learned about those aircraft was passed on to the men fighting the Luftwaffe. One of many test pilots at Wright Field was Kenneth O. Chilstrom. Ken was assigned to the Fighter Section of the Flight Test Division of the Army Air Forces Technical Service Command. His assignment was a fighter pilot's dream—at least that's what he told me. Flight test was what every hotshot pilot aspired to, and Ken thought of himself as a hotshot pilot. Dick Johnson, a Wright Field test pilot, described this feeling of being the best of the best, of having arrived in fighter pilot heaven, this way: "We all knew that, for an aviator, Wright Field was the greatest place on earth.... At Wright

Field, one was privileged to fly seven days a week. . . . Aviator Heaven? It was indeed!"[32]

For young Chilstrom, flying was a dream that came true with the advent of World War II, as it did for so many young "boys" of his generation. Born in 1921 in Zumbrota, Minnesota, Ken started building model airplanes soon after entering grade school. One week out of high school, Ken and two friends went to the Army Air Corps recruiting office and enlisted. They wanted to become pilots. Their problem was that they didn't have the two years of college required to enter the aviation cadet program. So Ken and his friends enlisted and were sent to Chanute Field, Illinois, where they became aircraft mechanics. Ken attended night school to gain the needed college credits for pilot training. By 1941 the world situation had changed dramatically, and Ken was allowed to enter the aviation cadet program without the previously required two years of college. He graduated in Class 42I at Lake Charles, Louisiana, and as a freshly minted second lieutenant pilot was assigned to a squadron of the 58th Fighter Group at Bolling Field, Washington, DC, on the banks of the Potomac River. "We had three squadrons in the 58th," Ken recalled. "My squadron was assigned to Bolling Field, the other two were in Baltimore and Philadelphia. Each squadron had twenty-five pilots and an equal number of aircraft assigned. The mission of the 58th was to guard the nation's capital. But more important, since there was no real aerial threat to Washington, we also served as a replacement training unit to make up the losses experienced by squadrons in combat. In February 1943 all of my group's pilots took a train up to the Curtis Airplane Factory in Buffalo, New York, and we picked up brand-new P-40N Warhawks, painted in desert camouflage and flew them to Norfolk, Virginia. In Norfolk we embarked on the aircraft carrier USS *Ranger*." None of these young Army Air Forces pilots had ever been on an aircraft carrier before, much less flown off one. They were all second lieutenants, except for the squadron commanders, who were captains. They were soon to be seasoned combat pilots. Or die trying.

"It took us ten days to cross the Atlantic, and when we were about one hundred nautical miles off the North African coast, all seventy-five of us were told to strap on our P-40s and get ready to launch for an airfield near Casablanca, Morocco. I was number thirty-five when we launched off the *Ranger*. They had turned the carrier into the wind and got her up to maximum speed to get as much wind across the deck as they possibly could. As I sat there with the prop turning, I never saw anyone else fly off. Everyone went off to the left of the carrier and disappeared. The flight deck was about seventy-five to eighty feet above the water. I didn't know if they made it or not. We didn't lose anyone, I later learned, but I didn't know that as I sat there sweating in my P-40 cockpit wondering what awaited me. After I launched and dropped off the

Ken Chilstrom, right, as an enlisted aircraft mechanic at Chanute Field, Illinois, in 1940. When Ken became a test pilot, his maintenance training came in handy.

side of the carrier, I quickly discovered that as I got near the water I picked up additional lift from the ground effect and I flew on just above the wave tops as all the others had done.

"Something had happened to our airplanes at Norfolk which we pilots were not aware of until we launched off the *Ranger* toward Casablanca. When we landed in Norfolk, coming from the Curtiss factory in Buffalo, we had to taxi our new planes a couple of miles to get alongside the aircraft carrier to be loaded. In the process we wore down our brakes. None of us realized that until we sat on the deck of the *Ranger* getting ready to launch. The deck controller would give the wind-up signal with his hands. The pilot whose turn it was then applied power, the brakes wouldn't hold, and the plane began to eke forward. As soon as the controller saw him moving forward, he gave the signal to launch. Like all the others before me, when my turn came, all I could do when my P-40 began to slide forward because of the bad brakes was to move the throttle to full power and pray. The whole thing was a little disconcerting. Subsequent air groups also launched in this manner off a carrier and lost some planes, and the practice was discontinued.

"We got to North Africa soon after the disaster at Kasserine Pass. The 33rd Fighter Group, which had preceded us, lost most of its airplanes when General Erwin Rommel's troops overran their airfield in a night attack. The German tanks rolled over their aircraft and crushed them. Because their pilots had some combat experience and we had none, they took our planes and gave them to the 33rd Fighter Group, commanded by a Lieutenant Colonel William

Momyer, who in later years would become a four-star general and run the air war against North Vietnam. Having no airplanes, our group, the 58th, was disbanded. We sat around for a month or two until a batch of A-36A Apache attack aircraft was delivered. The Apache was the earliest version of the highly successful P-51 Mustang fighter, but without that Merlin engine that was to make the Mustang one of the premier aircraft of World War II. The A-36 was a better airplane than the P-40, at least I thought so. It carried two five-hundred-pound bombs and had six .50-caliber machine guns, two of which fired through the propellers. I dive-bombed and strafed myself through the North African campaign, into Sicily and up the boot of Italy as far as Naples.

"Newly equipped with A-36 aircraft we were redesignated the 27th Fighter Bomber Group. The 27th was actually a group destined for the South Pacific. The Japanese sank the ships that carried their airplanes, A-20 Bostons. The ground crews that survived the attack were returned to the US, and then shipped over to North Africa. They were the ones who got our newly arrived A-36s ready at the Casablanca depot. I was assigned to the 523rd Fighter Bomber Squadron. The other squadrons were the 522nd and the 524th. We got our initial checkout while taking the airplanes from Casablanca to Fez, halfway between Casablanca and Oran. Then we had a month of training at Fez. We, the pilots, liked the airplane a lot better than the P-40. It handled better and had a more spacious cockpit—a real improvement over the P-40. About June we deployed to Cape Bon. The Italians were still in the war with the Germans at the time and our first missions were against the airfield on the small island of Pantelleria, halfway between the North African coast and Sicily. Cape Bon was nothing but sand. The engineers put down PSP, pierced steel planking, on the field to allow us to taxi and takeoff and land. I was the element leader getting ready to fly a combat mission. The fellow on my wing and I taxied out for takeoff. The prop wash stirred up the sand to a degree that we just couldn't see anything ahead of us. I told my wing man to take the right side of the runway. I would take the left. This allowed us to stay together and proceed in the same direction—we just couldn't see a thing because of the blowing sand. I took off following the left side of the runway. My wing man was following on the right. Once I took off, I circled the field but couldn't see my wing man. He had followed the right side of the runway all right, when suddenly the wing of a C-47 transport appeared before him out of the blowing sand, sticking out over his side of the runway. The C-47 had blown a tire and just sat there. He couldn't see it. The C-47's wing took off his landing gear, and the two five-hundred-pound bombs he carried ripped off his aircraft and rolled around on the desert floor. My wing man survived, bellying in at the end of the runway. Flying under such conditions of very poor visibility was truly dangerous. We learned from experience.

"We then supported the invasion of Sicily. Lieutenant General George S. Patton was the US Army's ground commander and General Montgomery led the British forces. The Brits went up the eastern side of Sicily, and Patton took the other side of the island, both heading for the Messina Straits between the Italian mainland and Sicily. Mount Aetna was a prominent feature of the island in the northeast corner. We supported Patton's advance up the island. We hardly ever saw any German fighters. None ever opposed us. As soon as we could, we moved out of Cape Bon over to Sicily and flew out of a field by the name of Gela. In addition to our group, the 31st Fighter Group also supported Patton's operations. They flew British Spitfires. There was little to bomb in that campaign. Most of our missions were strafing. For that the A-36 was a very effective airplane, with its six .50-caliber machine guns. We shot at everything that moved beyond the 'bomb line' that was given to us on a daily basis. We denied the enemy the use of the highways in daylight. In the invasion of Sicily a great tragedy occurred. Paratroopers of the 82nd Airborne Division, commanded by Major General Matthew B. Ridgway, were to make a night landing near Gela, the base we were to use for our operations in support of General Patton's advance. Patton knew that without close air support he wouldn't go anywhere. On the night of July 11, an air armada of nearly 150 C-47 transports approached Sicily, loaded with paratroopers of the 82nd Airborne. Navy ships off shore opened fire and 23 out of 144 C-47s were shot down in flames, many others damaged. Some transports turned back when they saw the carnage; others pressed on and dropped their troopers. There are names for such disasters in war—fratricide, friendly fire, collateral damage. Whatever you call it—it is an immense tragedy when you are killing your own men. Those who managed to survive and land secured our base, and we arrived shortly thereafter.[33]

"When Palermo was taken, some of us flew there. We parked our airplanes and went into the city. Lo and behold, there was Bob Hope and his troop entertaining the troops. He had moved in the day after the town was taken, on 22 July. We had dinner with Bob Hope in downtown Palermo that night. While in Palermo I bought a couple of cases of champagne to take back to my squadron. A case of champagne fit precisely behind the pilot's seat of the A-36. My wing man and I returned to our base at Gela. It was July, and we had no refrigeration of any kind. No one wants to drink hot champagne. So we dug a deep hole and lowered the champagne into that hole and left it overnight. It worked. Once we left Gela, we moved to a field across the Straight of Messina, Merazo. The landing strip was bulldozed by the engineers right near the beach and we took off and landed on PSP. It worked well. From this strip we supported the Salerno beachhead. Another bloody battle. We were flying off the beach near Salerno on the second day of the invasion, on September 10, supporting the army. Our landing strip was so close to the enemy that when we were in the traffic pattern to land they were shooting at us. Our mission, as before, was mainly ground support—close air support of the troops and interdiction of German road and rail traffic. On September 20, 1943, I led a flight of A-36s to relieve the pressure on the Salerno beachhead. German tanks and infantry were massing north of Salerno in an olive grove, getting ready to launch their attack. My flight, and Lieutenant Santala's flight, dropped down to treetop level and strafed everything that came into sight—tanks, trucks, infantry. There was mayhem below when we left, so many explosions as to obscure our visibility. We totally destroyed that German unit in that olive grove, and what was left of them was forced to withdraw.

"But we had our own losses. Here is an example of a typical mission. I was leading a flight near Rome in early October. I went out with eight airplanes, two flights of four. And when I came home, myself and two others landed. I lost five men on that one mission. The Germans usually knew we were coming. They would fire an 88mm colored burst at eight to ten thousand feet to warn their troops up the road that we were coming. They had 20-millimeter quad antiaircraft guns which were very effective. We always flew at treetop level, never more than a hundred feet off the ground. They would see us coming and spray the air and let us fly into it. The weak part of our airplane was the cooling system. Being liquid cooled, once the radiator was hit you were done for. When you are flying at treetop level, everything happened very fast. You don't know if the guy who was hit was able to pull up and bail out, or if he went in with his plane. Three of the men on that particular mission were able to bail out and became POWs. Two died. When we debriefed after a mission, we didn't know much about those who went in. All you saw, if anything, was just a puff of black smoke.

"North of Rome there is a large lake. I was leading a flight of eight. Coming up on the lake I saw three SM 79s, Ju 52 transports on floats, taxiing for takeoff. As soon as I saw them, I slowed down my flight, trying to let the German aircraft get airborne so we could claim an airborne kill. It all took too long and we had to shoot them on the water. It was one of those unusual events which happens now and then in war. Our missions typically were just repeat performances supporting the army—mostly strafing, some bombing. Our bombing wasn't very accurate, but the eight .50-caliber machine guns each plane carried were. In November of 1943, my tent mate, Eugene Santala, had accumulated eighty-seven combat missions. I had eighty. We had heard something to the effect that fighter pilots could rotate after fifty missions, and bomber pilots after twenty-five. But nothing ever happened. We kept on flying. One day my group commander accompanied by the flight surgeon came over to our tent and said that the morale of the outfit was being affected by our losses—we had terrific losses as I already mentioned. Said the group commander, 'We would like to send you guys home. You are the first to leave the 27th Fighter Bomber Group, and that should boost morale.' Obviously Eugene and I didn't object. Then we received orders sending us back to the US, but without telling us how to get there. We hitchhiked our way back from Italy to North Africa to Casablanca and flew to the US on a B-24 bomber. I came home with a Distinguished Flying Cross and eight Air Medals, one Air Medal for each of ten combat missions.

"In the aircrew redistribution center near Miami they tried to send me to a P-40 RTU, a replacement training unit. That was the last thing I wanted to do. I went to see my commanding officer, a major, and told him that I wanted to go to Wright Field and be a test pilot. I didn't know anything about being a test pilot and what it involved, but that's what I wanted to be. My commanding officer ordered his adjutant to check with personnel if there were any openings in Flight Test at Wright Field. A couple of days later the answer came back—no. I said to the major, 'You let me go to Wright Field and I'll get a job.' To my surprise he issued the orders sending me to Wright Field. I took the train to Dayton, Ohio, and walked into the flight test section. Major Chris Petrie, the chief of Fighter Test (he was killed in an aircraft accident only a few months later on May 7, 1944), told me that he didn't have a job for me in Flight Test. But, he added, 'I need a maintenance officer. Can you do that?' I lied. 'I'm a good maintenance officer, sir,' I replied, looking him straight in the eyes. That's how I got my foot in the door. Flight Test was just in the process of expanding. A good time to be there. Industry was producing numerous prototypes, some good, some bad; all had to be tested at Wright Field. A lot of airplanes were built, one or two of a kind, and eventually I got to fly them all. Most never got into production. I wore a flight suit all day long going from one airplane to another. Out at Vandalia, now the Dayton airport, we opened a test pilot school and I went through the second class with Glenn Edwards. Glenn and I were roommates. Glenn crashed on June 5, 1948, testing the YB-49 flying wing, and perished along with four others from the Bomber Test section—Dan Forbes, Chuck LaFontaine, Claire Lesser, and Ed Swindell. Muroc Field in California was later renamed Edwards Air Force Base, and the one-time bomber and reconnaissance base near Topeka, Kansas, was named after Major Daniel Forbes.

"Being a test pilot in those heady days of aviation exacted a heavy price at times. I lost many friends," Ken added, sadness entering his voice. "But for a guy who wanted to fly everything with wings on it, Wright Field was beyond belief. The ramp was always filled to near overflowing with airplanes. I got to fly everything. And there was great camaraderie among all of us test pilots, regardless of what we were flying, and we shared each other's thrills." In 1943, as a result of the North African campaign and the Allies' advance into Italy, several captured German aircraft showed up at Wright Field. "Two Me 109Gs, two Fw 190s, and a Ju 88 twin-engine bomber were the first to arrive. The first two Me 262 jet fighters arrived in the spring of 1945, and by the time Colonel Harold 'Hal' Watson brought his German airplanes back to the United States as part of Operation Lusty, we already had twenty-four German and Japanese aircraft sitting on our ramp. I got to fly them all," said Chilstrom. "The fact that I got to know and fly many different types of airplanes forced me to keep the basics in mind. As a test pilot you quickly get familiar with what is critical on an airplane—the fuel system. You have to keep that engine running to have a long and happy life. And to keep it running you have to understand the fuel system of whatever airplane you are flying. Then you can learn about a plane's handling characteristics, and fly it conservatively in the beginning, until you become familiar enough to push the envelope.

"Another important thing to a test pilot's survival is to know an airplane's center of gravity. Watson brought in a couple examples of a new and unusual German aircraft, the Dornier 335, with a push-pull engine arrangement. It was in the fall of 1946 when the plane was supposedly ready for flight test over at Freeman Field in Indiana. Chuck Yeager was in my Fighter Test section then, and when I learned that the 335 was finally ready, I said to Yeager, 'Why don't you and I go and fly that airplane.' We took a B-25 and flew over to Freeman Field. The German airplane was absolutely huge for a fighter. I talked at length with the mechanics and engineers and they couldn't convince me that they knew where its center of gravity was. Well, the center of gravity is one of the key elements as far as control of an airplane is concerned, and in this particular airplane knowing the CG appeared to me to be especially critical. Yeager and I never did fly the Dornier 335. I don't believe anybody flew that airplane after Watson brought it over, except for Jack Woolams's brief and near catastrophic flight at Newark." Jack Woolams was a Bell Aircraft Corporation test pilot who participated in Operation Lusty and was subsequently killed in an aircraft accident.[34]

"We damn near lost Russ Schleeh due to a CG problem on the first Me 262 we got. Russ was a pilot in Bomber Test, one of the few bomber pilots I ever knew who loved to fly fighters. Schleeh took a year off to fly with us in Fighter Test, and while he was in the fighter section with me, we put together that first Me 262 over at Vandalia. I watched Russ make his first takeoff. He used the whole length of the runway because he didn't have enough elevator power to overcome a CG problem he encountered on takeoff. We hadn't installed the guns in its nose, and taking guns out of an airplane that is designed to have guns installed changes its CG aft. And its handling characteristics become very different. We hadn't given that fact sufficient consideration and nearly killed Russ as a result of our oversight. I remember standing there watching his takeoff roll and wondering, 'Boy, is he going to make it?' He finally got it off the ground and immediately headed for Wright Field and landed. He said to me when I got back to Wright Field, 'Ken, you can have this project.' That was the last time Schleeh flew the 262. I then gave the project to Walt McAuley. Walt bailed out of that Me 262—it did not have an ejection seat—near Springfield, Ohio, when one of its engines caught fire and exploded. It was a harrowing experience which gave Walt nightmares for years to come. You are willing to take a certain amount of risk in the flight test business, but you want to do it with understanding and for a good reason.[35]

"I spent much more time testing the Fw 190 fighter than any other. For one thing, it became available to us fairly early." Ken Chilstrom's Form 5, an airman's official flying record, revealed that the first time Ken flew the Fw 190 was on July 26, 1944. Between then and February 26, 1945, Ken flew the Fw 190 for a total of fourteen hours on eighteen separate occasions to determine the airplane's handling characteristics. "It was my tenth flight on February 24, 1945, that came close to being a disaster. I was performing a functional test flight after some adjustments had been made to the engine controls. That day I had been up to twenty thousand feet and was satisfied with the engine's operation, so I returned for a landing at Wright Field. It was the custom for all fighter pilots in those days to come down low, approximately fifty to a hundred feet over the end of the runway, and peel up in a tight, left-hand, 360-degree turn without any power. It was the mark of a good fighter pilot that once the peel-up started you would not use engine power before touchdown. This required skill in gauging distance, trading off speed by sideslipping, and the use of flaps while aiming for the end of the runway. I was comfortable in my approach to the runway and was heading north and parallel to the flight line. I had a good tight pattern and was down to maybe two hundred feet in a turn with the power off. When I adjusted the tail plane trim switch to relieve some of the forward stick pressure, the stick came back and the airplane pitched nose up. This is a bad situation to be in close to the ground and I immediately tried to get the nose down and added power for a climbing recovery. I went up to several thousand feet to experiment with the trim switch. Then I discovered that it was a runaway switch which went to either nose full up or full down. I chose the nose-down position, which I could manhandle for a landing. This experience didn't change my mind about the Fw 190 as one of the best fighters of World War II. But this particular airplane had an electrical problem in its trim switch and it nearly killed me."[36]

Many such problems were encountered in flight testing and a test pilot was expected to be able to deal with them. A runaway trim switch? Things happen—and it wasn't necessarily an occurrence passed on to others. Ken couldn't have known that he survived one of the Fw 190's fatal flaws, and it wouldn't be the last time that an American pilot would have to deal with such a situation. On September 12, 1945, Lieutenant Robert Anspach, one of Colonel Watson's Whizzer pilots, was flying an Fw 190 from Newark, New Jersey, to Freeman Field in Indiana. Bob was making a gradual descent over Pennsylvania heading for the Pittsburgh airport to refuel. He reached over to make a slight trim adjustment when the trim cycled to full-up and the Fw 190 pitched violently nose up and over. Bob had never heard that the Fw 190 may have had a systemic trim control problem, and he wasn't a test pilot like Ken Chilstrom. To make things worse, the trim setting could not be manually overridden. Bob adjusted the aircraft's power setting and was able to crash-land and walk away from the wreck. Lieutenant William Haynes wasn't that lucky. When he was demonstrating an Fw 190 at Freeman Field on September 22, 1945, the electrical trim on his aircraft failed just as he was preparing to land. The young officer, another of Watson's Whizzers and a World War II survivor, perished in the crash. Who knows how many German pilots suffered a similar fate as a result of that failure-prone electrical trim switch?[37]

By 1946 the P-80 Shooting Star began to appear in numbers and the Army Air Forces gave it maximum public exposure. "We put on air shows," Colonel Chilstrom wistfully recalled. "We tried to set all the speed records in the world with the P-80; we tried to break everyone else's record as well. Gus Lundquist, who was the most experienced test pilot at Wright Field in my opinion, Jack Sullivan, and I were off to fly the P-80 in the 1946 Cleveland Air Race. When the time came and we were walking out to our aircraft, Gus, who outranked me, pointed to my aircraft and casually said, 'I'll take that one.' I got to fly his airplane—and that little switcheroo would cost me the race. As we three raced down the track, we were wing tip to wing tip. Going into the third turn I was indicating about 515 miles per hour, right on the deck, full throttle at 101 and ½ percent, when the power boost goes out on me. I couldn't move the stick and I'm in a turn. All I could do was pull back and I was out of the race. The early P-80s had an electrically driven hydraulic pump and the pump shorted out on me. I could land the aircraft, but not much else. Gus won the race flying my airplane." Air races provided a great amount of publicity for the new jet aircraft. In September of 1947, the Army Air Forces became the United States Air Force and the P-80 became the F-80. As a result of accidents, the air races were moved from Cleveland to Reno, Nevada.

Flight testing was an extremely demanding profession and dangerous in the bargain. Yet the "best of the best" fighter pilots wanted to be just that—test pilots. They were a competitive bunch of men. Major Kenneth Chilstrom was the chief of Fighter Test at Wright Field in 1946. His crew included Majors Frank Everest and Richard Johnson, Captain Charles Yeager, and Lieutenants

Robert Hoover and Walter McAuley, among others. They eagerly participated in air races and attempted to beat every speed record there was. The
first jet speed record was set in the United Kingdom on November 7, 1945,
by RAF Group Captain H. J. Wilson in a Gloster Meteor, who was clocked
at 606.464 miles per hour. Colonel Albert Boyd, the chief of the flight test
division at Wright Field, tasked Major Kenneth Chilstrom to lay out a three
kilometer speed course at Muroc Field in California (later Edwards AFB) to
do one thing—break the Englishman's record. After Ken laid out the course
and had it certified by the US Coast and Geodetic Survey, Colonel Boyd gave
Ken the nod to be the first to attempt to break Group Captain Wilson's record.
Ken went for it in a standard Lockheed P-80 fighter. His supporting engineers were doubtful that he could break the record. And they were right. He
did 608 miles per hour, not sufficient differential to be recognized as a new
world speed record. Then Ken's boss, Colonel Boyd, decided to give it a try.
But he used a modified P-80R with a racing canopy and razor-sharp leading
edges, and it was powered by a water/alcohol injected engine that developed
5,097 pounds of static thrust, versus only 4,600 pounds of thrust for Ken's
engine. Colonel Boyd broke the record at 670.834 miles per hour. But the day
of the three kilometer speed record was waning, the last being set in an F-104
Starfighter on October 24, 1977, at Tonopah, Nevada.[38]

Over a lifetime of flying fighters, Colonel Chilstrom managed to acquire
a few firsts, but not in every case the kind of "firsts" that a hotshot test pilot
aims for. The YP-59A, one of which hangs in the vestibule of the National Air
and Space Museum, was America's first jet fighter, intended to tame the German Me 262. The Me 262 jet fighter first appeared in the skies over Europe in
July 1944—the P-59 never did make an appearance. The follow-on P-80 didn't
show up either for WWII, other than a few (four) feel-good demonstrators
shipped over to Europe—one of which crashed, killing its pilot, Major Frederick Borsodi. That America had difficulty getting into the jet age is probably
an understatement, and was the very reason for Operation Lusty. As for the
YP-59A, according to the Wright Field test community—it just didn't have it.
Nathan "Rosie" Rosengarten, a highly regarded flight test engineer at Wright
Field, summed up the P-59 in these words: "It could hardly be considered a
combat airplane—at best it was a good safe airplane, a training vehicle for
indoctrinating pilots into the Jet Age."[39] Ken Chilstrom's "first" flying this airplane involved having the first major accident of an American-built jet aircraft.
The NACA (National Advisory Committee for Aeronautics, the predecessor
of NASA) at Langley Field in Virginia desperately wanted one of the jets for
test purposes. On February 15, 1945, Ken took off from Wright Field for Langley Field. The weather deteriorated en route, then one of the engines flamed
out due to fuel starvation. The "pucker factor" was high, Ken recalls. "I saw

an airfield directly below me, Reidsville, North Carolina. It was a grass field. I contacted an accompanying C-47 and told them where I was going. They had JP1 jet fuel on board in fifty-gallon drums. Jet fuel was not readily available at most airports in those days and you had to plan ahead where you might land. I refueled, but since it was late in the day I stayed overnight. The next day the weather was good and I got an early start. I was just becoming airborne, ready to retract the landing gear, when I realized I was not accelerating, but sinking. Everything then happened very fast. I thought it was the end for me. I clipped some really big trees and ended up in a farmer's front yard. The nose and tail sections of the airplane had separated, and I was sitting in the midsection with the wings and engines and tanks filled with JP1. There was no fire, or I would have been a goner for sure. A quick call to Wright Field brought out a two-seater P-38 and by evening I was back at Wright Field enjoying a 'highball' and a steak in the Eight Ball Café. The other flight test pilots listened eagerly as I told 'what went wrong.'" But there was another more positive "first" for Ken flying the YP-59A. He delivered the first jet airmail in it to none other than Orville Wright, flying a letter from Wright Field to Chicago, where Ken was met personally by Orville Wright, to whom he handed the letter from the cockpit of the P-59.[40]

But among the many firsts for Colonel Kenneth Chilstrom, the one he is most proud of was, in fact, a test pilot's dream. "The ultimate aim and goal of a military test pilot is to be the first to fly a new aircraft. In the case of fighters, the initial flights (Phase I tests) are made by contractor test pilots, then followed by Phase II tests performed by the military to verify aircraft performance. In 1947, my boss, the chief of the flight test division at Wright Field, Al Boyd, decided that the air force would fly Phase II performance and stability tests as early as possible. As chief of Fighter Test I was assigned the XP-86 project by Colonel Boyd. I became familiar with the airplane in preparation for the flight tests. The early design of the XP-86 by North American Aviation had straight wings and tail planes. And the usual tricycle landing gear. Wind tunnel testing quickly confirmed that this configuration could not attain the six-hundred-mile-per-hour speed the air force called for, and as such was no great improvement over the straight wing P-84 design. To overcome this speed deficiency the engineers followed the B-47 example by using German design and wind tunnel test data and sweeping the wings back by thirty-five degrees. This wing sweep caused some undesirable stability problems at low airspeeds which, like in the German Me 262 fighter, were resolved by installing leading edge slats which operated automatically without any pilot input required.

"The General Electric J-47 engine wasn't ready so we used the J-35 General Motors Allison engine which powered the P-84, redesignated F-84 after the air force gained its independence in September 1947. The J-35 only had 4,900 pounds of thrust versus the 5,200 pounds of thrust the J-47 would provide once it was available. As a result, the XP-86 would not have the same performance of later versions of the F-86 fighter. In early December 1947 North American called Colonel Boyd recommending a delay in the start of Phase II flight testing because of weather and flooding at Muroc and other issues. Boyd turned to me and said, 'Ken, go out there and make things happen.' I did just that. Over the objections of North American's test pilot, George 'Wheaties' Welch, and with my boss's permission, I flew my first test flight on December 2, 1947, from the very short runway at North Field, rather than from the flooded Muroc lake bed. The airplane performed so well, I flew another test flight that same day. I was indeed impressed with the aircraft's performance using the same engine as the straight wing F-84. Within six days I had tested the aircraft up to forty-five thousand feet at a speed of up to Mach .9. My conclusion, supported by the demonstrated test data, was that this was the very best fighter produced to date for the air force. The following years confirmed the F-86 as the very best there was in the world and it kept that record for at least a decade.[41] With the start of the Korean War in 1950 it was the F-86 that kept the Soviet MiG 15 in check with a kill ratio of seven to one.[42] Flying the XP-86 was my dream come true as a military test pilot."

Ken Chilstrom was not untypical of his generation of flyers. He survived eighty combat missions in World War II and survived test-flying American, British, German, and Japanese aircraft, many of which tested his flying and survival skills to the limit. And he flew air races which were no less dangerous at exceedingly high speeds at very low altitudes. As if that wasn't enough, he volunteered to be an exchange pilot with the United States Navy and checked out and qualified as a carrier pilot on the USS *Leyte*—earning the US Navy's gold wings. It was 1948 when Ken was chided at the bar for the last time by a US Navy pilot, "Piece of cake landing on a ten-thousand-foot highway. Try landing on a postage stamp out on the water. Now that's real flying." Chilstrom trained with other Navy "interns" at Pensacola Naval Air Station in Florida, then moved on to Quonset Point Naval Station, Rhode Island, where he made eighty carrier-type landings on land. Then he was assigned to the USS *Leyte*, where he made fifty carrier landings in the F8F Bearcat.

After Ken's flying days were over, he worked at headquarters level on the F-100, F-105, and F-107 development programs. He became program manager for the F-108, an interceptor that came along too late and was canceled in 1959. He retired from the air force in January 1964 after twenty-five years of service, going to work for General Electric and several other aviation companies. Ken settled in Palm Springs Gardens, Florida. Upon the death of his wife, Mary Ruth, he moved to the Washington, DC, area where many of his pilot friends

Captain Chilstrom after completing eighty combat missions in the A-36 Apache in the Mediterranean Theater of Operations—time to go home.

Gus Lundquist, a fellow Wright Field test pilot, standing in front of Ken's P-80 at the Cleveland Air Races in 1946. Gus won the race flying Ken's aircraft; Ken lost aileron boost flying Gus's P-80 and was eliminated from the race.

had chosen to settle. In his many years of flying, Colonel Kenneth Chilstrom flew over two hundred different aircraft types and models, an astounding number, exceeded only by a few, all of whom were test pilots themselves, such as Admiral "Whitey" Feightner, US Navy. Whitey Feightner flew over three hundred different types and models, including the German Me 262, the Arado 234, and the Japanese Zero fighter that crashed early in the war in the Aleutian

Ken's favorite aircraft was the F-86 Sabre Jet—according to Ken, it was a test pilot's dream.

Islands, was recovered, and provided critical flight performance data for navy combat pilots in the Pacific war.

Wrote Dick Johnson, a Wright Field test pilot: "One might hunt fox in the middle of Wright Field with Jim Doolittle. At Wright Field one was privileged to fly seven days a week—with time off, if one chose, to shoot at clay pigeons for an hour or so on Sunday afternoon. When the day's work was done, we could hustle down to base flight to fly a P-51H and contest anyone or a group of like-minded dogfight enthusiasts. Aviator Heaven? It was indeed!"[43] Yet, the cost in lives, largely overlooked, unknown to the public, rarely remembered for long, was exceedingly high. Colonel Chilstrom, in his book *Test Flying at Old Wright Field*, lists the names of 114 pilots and engineers who gave their lives testing the limits of flight. Once flight test was moved to Muroc Field, later Edwards AFB, in California, many others would make the ultimate sacrifice living their dream. Aviator Heaven, for a test pilot, is never far away.

ROBERT M. SLANE

B-17/B-26/B-47E

POW StalagLuft III, Sagan, Germany

Hitch in Hell

I'm sitting here and thinking of things I left behind.
And it's hard to put on paper what's running through my mind.
I've flown in a batch of airplanes over a hell of a batch of ground.
A drearier place this side of hell is waiting to be found.
But there's one consolation, sit closer while I tell,
When I die I'll go to heaven, for I've done my hitch in hell.
The angels all will greet me, the harps will start to play.
It's then you'll hear St. Peter say loudly with a yell,
"Here take this soft front seat, Milt, you've done your hitch in hell."
—Author unknown, StalagLuft I, WWII ETO

"I remember the helpless feeling when flying through a barrage of dirty-looking puffs of flak and watching as a train of these black demons gets closer and closer until you can see the red glow of destruction and hear the muffled sound of the exploding shell. I can still see the red tracers of 20mm flak arcing overhead and fading into distant space. I can hear the shattering sound of guns within our aircraft as the gunners fought for our lives to deter an enemy determined to down our aircraft. I have vivid recollections of Room 4, Block 36, South Compound of StalagLuft III, at Sagan, Germany. My home for fourteen of the eighteen and a half months that I was a prisoner of war in Germany. Most of all I remember the feeling of despair as the days passed and freedom seemed so remote.

Robert Slane's B-17 bomber crew. L–R front: Foster-N; Slane-P; Johnson-CP; Runner-B. L–R back: Kuhlman-R; Groth-WG; Smith-TG; Sly-E/G; Brown-BTG; Soloman-WG.

"I left home on August 5, 1941, my eighteenth birthday, to enlist in the Army Air Corps. The recruiting office in Trinidad, Colorado, gave me a train ticket to Denver with my final destination the nearby Fort Logan army camp. I had a physical examination scheduled for the next morning. But I was so excited that it was three days before my heart rate slowed down enough to take the physical. That day, August 8, I was sworn in. I weighed 119 pounds. The quartermaster had no khaki trousers small enough to fit my waist. The temporary solution was a set of blue fatigues to be worn until I arrived at 'boot camp.' Off I went to Fort Sill, Oklahoma. That was a mistake. The army was not conducting boot camp at Fort Sill. Another train, still wearing my blue fatigues, this time to Ellington Field near Galveston, Texas. While in boot camp I learned that the army was accepting applications for enlisted pilot training—minimum age eighteen. Aviation cadet training required one to be twenty. I immediately applied for pilot training as an aviation student with the understanding that upon graduation I would be promoted to the rank of staff sergeant. Of course, nothing is ever made easy and my application was returned with the comment to resubmit once I arrived at my first assignment out of boot camp. Upon arrival at Lerdo Field near Bakersfield, California, I immediately resubmitted my application. By mid-October I was scheduled for a flight physical at March Field. Again, I was so excited, that it took three tries for my heart rate to settle down. My heart rate didn't bother the doctor, but what he called a 'deviated septum' did, and I needed to get corrective surgery. I returned to Lerdo, managed to get the recommended surgery two months later, but by the time I resubmitted my paperwork it was returned with the comment 'Time expired. Resubmit application.'

"I was disheartened, but didn't give up, and started all over again. In the meantime I worked as an aircraft mechanic on BT-13s, became a crew chief, and with the help of my boss was rescheduled for another flight physical. I graduated from pilot training in Class 43A in January 1943, but not as a staff sergeant as expected, but as a flight officer. At Gowen Field near Boise, Idaho, I entered B-17 training and was put as copilot on a newly formed crew. The first pilot developed a night vision problem and I became the first pilot. As first pilot I could not be a flight officer, but had to be a commissioned officer, and was given a reserve commission as second lieutenant in the Army Air Corps. Things were looking up. Crew training complete, we were assigned to a provisional group and sent to Grand Island, Nebraska, where we picked up a brand-new B-17G, heavier than our training aircraft, with additional fuel tanks and armor plating. It was August 26, 1943, when we took off for our first destination—Bangor, Maine. It was the flight 'from hell.'

"We ran into towering thunderstorms. The sound of hailstones striking the aircraft was deafening. At times we were flying in total darkness, and looking out I could see that the leading edge of the left wing was dented by hail. We entered updrafts and downdrafts. The airspeed varied as much as one hundred miles per hour. All I could do was to maintain our normal power setting and keep the wings level. There was a time during flight when everyone was hanging on to whatever they could reach. One crew member inadvertently grabbed onto a parachute hanging from a rib of the aircraft; it opened and spilled out into the fuselage. We landed at Bangor after an eight-hour flight with golf ball–size dents on the leading edges of the wings and the deicer boots torn to shreds. Repair crews got to work as soon as we shut down the engines. The next day, after a test flight, we continued on to Gander, Newfoundland. Then Prestwick, Scotland, where our aircraft was turned over to a depot. The ten of us were put on a train for London, then sent to a crew replacement center at RAF Bovington, where we stayed for a couple of weeks for additional survival training and theater indoctrination. I was assigned to the 401st Bombardment Squadron of the 91st Bomb Group at Bassingbourne. To my surprise, I was assigned quarters in a large brick building. I had expected to stay in a Quonset hut, or something like it. My roommate was Captain Harry Lay, a seasoned combat pilot. He had completed his twenty-five combat missions and had volunteered to fly an additional five. If he survived, he would be the first in the 91st Group to do so. I learned that the permanent quarters I was assigned to were only for first pilots, not other crew members or copilots. My navigator and bombardier were together in one building and the enlisted crew was in another.

"On our orientation flight I rode in the copilot's seat to get a feel for the area. Then we flew a simulated combat mission, including a formation join-up with other bomb groups—hundreds of aircraft filled the sky. Another training mission—then came the real thing on September 27, 1943. Our target was Emden, a seaport town in Germany. At the briefing we were told that P-47 fighters would escort us to the target and back—a first for the group I was told. Takeoff was uneventful and I had no problems in the join-up. I flew formation on the right wing of the lead aircraft in the middle element at twenty-three thousand feet. My gunners could see the P-47s in the distance. As we approached the target, I could see flames shooting from a B-17's right wing flying to the right and above me. The aircraft remained in formation as we turned at the IP (Initial Point for the bomb run). When the struggling B-17 opened its bomb doors, the flames were sucked into the bomb bay and I could see a raging fire developing. The aircraft drifted to the left, debris from its right wing striking my aircraft. I had to throttle back. Then the hatch from the ball turret came whistling past and the gunner followed, dropping out of sight. The struggling aircraft began to nose down, turn left, then upside down—and then there was nothing. It had exploded. All I could see were small pieces of debris floating by. Flying back I got a call from an aircraft behind us—they had not seen our bombs release when the lead released his. We checked, and sure enough, we still had our bombs. We dropped them over water. Another aircraft had experienced the same problem—the bombs not dropping when they should have. On this, our first mission, there was little flak, and the only damage we suffered was from the debris of the aircraft that exploded above and ahead of us. *Vagabond Lady*, as we had named our B-17G, was in good shape.

"On October 4, 1943, the target was Frankfurt. We were flying our assigned aircraft, number 742—*Vagabond Lady*. We came under enemy fighter attack soon after crossing the English Channel but didn't seem to lose any aircraft. We were flying at twenty-six thousand feet, before reaching the IP, when the crew stations aft of the bomb bay reported an oxygen problem. They had to use their emergency walk-around bottles, which needed frequent refilling. On the way back we began to run out of oxygen and I was forced to leave the formation. I began a steep descent, hoping to reach a lower cloud layer before enemy fighters spotted us. Too late. One of the waist gunners reported seeing two Me 109s above us, in a spiraling dive. At about seven thousand feet altitude a stream of 20mm shells streaked past the cockpit. Looking out the left window I could see holes where enemy gunfire hit the wing. Then suddenly I sighted another Me 109 off our left wing, going in the opposite direction. I turned into him so our guns could remain on him. We got down to three thousand feet and into the safety of a thick layer of clouds. We had been in the clouds about three minutes. When we broke out into a clear area, there was an Me 109 no more than a hundred feet ahead of us. The left gear was down and the pilot had the canopy open, totally unaware that we were right behind him. I called to the navigator and bombardier to open fire—the guns were frozen and wouldn't fire. We reentered the layer of clouds and made it back to England. We were the last aircraft to return to Bassingborne. *Vagabond Lady* was badly damaged. It was our last flight in *Vagabond Lady*. She was repaired, and went down on November 3 while being flown by another crew.

"During periods between combat missions crew members were scheduled for classes relative to their crew responsibilities. Both of my navigators received training in handling the .50-caliber twin guns in the nose turret. The gunners reported to a range where skeet shooting was used to teach them to lead their target and improve their accuracy. Our next mission was on October 10, 1943, against targets near Muenster. *Vagabond Lady* was still in the hangar for repairs, so we were assigned *Sir Baboon McGoon*. It was an older F-model, although it had been retrofitted with some of the improvements on the newer Gs. Takeoff was in near zero visibility and each aircraft followed instrument climb-out procedures. As we departed the English coast, I received a call from the navigator, a substitute since my assigned crew navigator had not returned in time from an authorized trip to London. This new navigator insisted I abort the mission because he was feeling ill and was about to throw up. This was his fifth mission and he informed me that he had become ill on all his previous missions and had never completed a single mission because the pilots had to abort due to his illness. His suggestion was totally unacceptable to me and we pressed on. Over the target Fw 190 fighters attacked head-on, flew directly into and through our formation. Vic Kuhlman, our radio operator, verified that the bomb racks were empty. And Bill Runner, our bombardier, reported that the navigator showed no signs of being sick, did not fire the turret guns, and did not follow the flight path. He just sat there, with his back against a bulkhead. There was little opposition on our return flight—but my fuel consumption was excessive. Due to the modifications made to this F-model it was considerably heavier than most Fs and required me to increase the engine power settings to stay in formation. The first low-fuel light illuminated when we were still over water. We were unable to get a fix of any kind, and the substitute navigator's inability to do his job made our problem worse. I finally found a small break in the clouds—confirming we were over land—and passed over an airstrip with B-24 bombers parked on a ramp. As I began a turn to line up parallel to the sighted runway, the fog closed in and the airfield disappeared from sight. I just completed my turn when the two engines on the right wing began to lose power. I had precious little time to get on the ground. We were too low to bail out and I had insufficient fuel to increase power to regain altitude. It was 'white knuckle' time for Joe Johnson, my copilot, and me. We got a glimpse through the fog of a plowed field to our right. I banked, the gear was up, the flaps just coming down when we made contact. For a brief moment after we came to a stop—there was dead silence. I looked over into Joe's ashen face, my adrenaline had peaked, and I was suddenly very tired.

"Four days later, on October 14, our target was Schweinfurt. I had my regular navigator back, no substitute this time. My flight position would be 'tail end Charlie' in our group, and the group leader was my roommate, Captain Harry Lay—this was to be Harry's last mission, his thirtieth. Our aircraft was from another squadron—the 323rd. A distraught crew chief informed me 'there has to be a mistake. This is an old aircraft, used only for training.' While we were talking, the bombs arrived and were being loaded. The weather was wet and foggy. But there was no cancellation. Instead, a green flare appeared and we were on our way. Enemy aircraft began their attack as soon as we crossed into France—Me 109s, Fw 190s, and Me 110s. Ju 88s and He 111s were pacing our formation just out of range of our gunners and reporting on us. Fw 190s lined up ahead of our formation and then made head-on attacks, split-essing after passing under our formation. At the IP the fighters let up and the German flak took over. Just after bomb release we took a direct hit and number four engine caught fire. We were able to feather the props, extinguish the fire, and remain in formation. About forty-five minutes after bomb release Fw 190s appeared dropping bombs into and through our formation.[44]

"I had turned over control of the aircraft to Joe Johnson and was helping Sherman Sly, the top turret gunner, locate fighters overhead, when we were hit. The right inboard engine was hit, the main oxygen tank in the passageway below the pilots exploded with a loud bang, and Joe let go of the wheel and slumped forward. The aircraft went into a steep dive. From my position next to him I was unable to move him. I got out of my seat, forced his body into an upright position, and regained control of the aircraft. Joe came to. Our aircraft was out of formation and severely crippled with two engines out. I descended to eighteen thousand feet where we could operate for a time without oxygen. There was no cloud cover to help us in our predicament. The last words I heard from our tail gunner, Claud Smith, were, 'Skipper, there are seven Me 109s trailing us with their gear down. They are making single passes, gear up, and attack.' I told Sergeant Smith to get one for me. Suddenly, the left outboard engine lost power. Smoke and flames were shooting out of the lower part of the engine. I couldn't feather the propellers. I pulled the bailout warning bell, opened the bomb bay doors and the crew began to bail out. Claud Smith lay unconscious in the rear. Lieutenant Foster, the navigator, and I were the only two left onboard. I sent him aft to take care of Smith when a Ju 88 struck. I turned into the Ju 88 and began a spiraling descent. I got the airspeed down to 150 miles per hour, saw a clearing, and went for it. The aircraft crashed through a wire fence and came to a stop. All this had taken place without me being strapped in. I scrambled through the aircraft calling out Foster's and Smith's names. No response. The aircraft appeared to be empty. I ran across the field to a hedgerow when the Ju 88 reappeared overhead at low altitude, then began a climbing turn away from my location. I returned to the aircraft intent on destroying it. I found the flares but couldn't find our flare pistol, and the canister designed to destroy an aircraft didn't work. I heard voices—'Halt.' I glanced over my shoulder and saw a man pointing a rifle at me. Two men had driven a 1936 Ford onto the field and arrived only ten minutes after I had landed my stricken aircraft. As I was being held, one of the men discovered Sergeant Smith's body aft of the main entrance. He had apparently crawled back into the aircraft from his tail gun position and was killed when the Ju 88 attacked."

Second Lieutenant Robert Slane was a prisoner of war now, something he had not really ever imagined being. He, like so many youngsters of his generation, entered the military at age eighteen, right after graduation from high school. Bob was twenty now. His nine fellow crew members were his age or younger—representative of the young men who flew these bloody raids against Nazi Germany. If aged twenty-four or somewhat older, a crew member would be referred to by his fellow aircrew as "old man." In the past two years, Bob had gone through pilot training and mastered to fly a B-17 bomber with a crew of ten. He and his crew was one of sixty B-17 bombers lost on that first Schweinfurt raid on October 14, 1943. Another seven aircraft were so heavily damaged that they would never fly again. And 138 aircraft received varying degrees of damage—out of a total of 229 B-17s who reached their assigned target. Over six hundred men were wounded, killed in action, or declared missing that day—most of the latter becoming POWs.[45] Bob and his fellow crew members had been too busy flying and surviving, and had no idea of any of this except for their own fate. For two days Slane was kept in a makeshift jail and was offered food that smelled so bad that he couldn't get it down without gagging, so he didn't eat. The interrogation was sporadic and unfocused. A German officer confirmed that Sergeant Smith had died from massive chest wounds. However, they would not let Bob see his body. On day two he was taken from his cell. "My cell door opened and a guard led me down the corridor. Outside the building was a line of ten or twelve armed soldiers. I thought it was a firing squad. The guard took me around the building and there was Joe Johnson, my copilot, and our top turret gunner, Sherman Sly. Along with four guards we were loaded into a truck and driven to 'where to, we didn't know.' It was getting dark when the truck stopped and three more members of my crew were put aboard—Vic Kuhlman, the radio operator, was badly injured when he struck the ground, shoulder first, after his chute got tangled.

He had received no medical attention and was in great pain. Lou Brown, our ball turret gunner, and Robert Solomon, waist gunner, were the other two. Three of my crew were still unaccounted for. As we drove on, I tried to read road signs—Metz and Nancy were familiar names. At a railroad station we were put into a waiting room. Kuhlman was in great pain. I tried to comfort him, when a guard rushed over shouting. Another guard finally calmed him down. Kuhlman said to me in a very low voice, 'You didn't ask permission to help me.' Until then I didn't know Kuhlman could speak German. After a two-hour wait we boarded a passenger train, the guards moving people out of their seats to make room for us. Kuhlman's low moans of pain brought looks of sympathy from some of the passengers. The next morning we arrived in Frankfurt and were taken to an interrogation center, DulagLuft, where officers and enlisted aircrew were separated. I was put in solitary confinement. I had eaten nothing since I was shot down except for a small piece of stale bread. I was very hungry. The small bowl of pea soup I was given seemed delicious. Breakfast was a slice of bread served with a substitute for coffee [Katreiner made from roasted barley and chicory]. The midday meal consisted of a cup of soup and a slice of bread. Supper was another slice of bread with margarine and a red jelly spread. It wasn't exactly a bread and water diet, but close to it.

"I found that by pushing my cot up to the rear wall I could look out the barred window and listen in on conversations of prisoners in adjacent cells. On my second day of imprisonment I overheard two men discuss their experiences. One said, 'I delayed opening my chute in order to lessen the chance of being captured. After I was on the ground, I waved at my pilot as our aircraft passed me before crashing. Then a low-flying German twin-engine plane fired at me. I didn't get hurt except for a shell fragment that found its way into one of my boots under my big toe.' Bill Runner, is that you? I called out. It was Bill Runner, my bombardier. On the fourth day of solitary confinement I finally faced my interrogator, a tall, distinguished-looking officer. He spoke in excellent English and laid out the facts for me—that I was flying an aircraft assigned to another squadron, and he wondered if perhaps the 401st had suffered such grievous losses on the previous mission against Anklam that the squadron could not fully support the Schweinfurt mission." Eighteen B-17s were lost during the Anklam raid, with five from the 91st Bomb Group.[46] "I didn't know the loss rate, but knew it was high. Probably why we were assigned an aircraft from another squadron which was not even considered combat ready by its crew chief. Standing behind his desk he opened a large book and noted that I graduated in pilot training class 43A on January 4, 1943. After running his finger down a column, he noted that many of my classmates already were 'guests of the Reich.' Then he asked about my health and treatment. I told him that my cell was infested with fleas. He had me raise my shirt and glanced at the swellings on my chest. He promised to help, but first needed a bit of information. 'What is the name of the new commander of the 401st?' I didn't respond and was then led to a cell in the interrogation building. This cell had a shower. A guard appeared with soap and a large towel, indicating for me to strip and to give him my clothing for delousing. I removed my wings and insignia and entered the shower carrying only my underwear and shoes. When the guard brought a cup of soup and bread late in the evening, I asked for the return of my clothing. He shrugged his shoulders and left without saying anything. I remained in the windowless cell in my underwear for the next two days.

"On the third day of my confinement the cell door suddenly opened and a grinning guard handed me a huge, heavy overcoat. 'Rooski, Rooski,' he exclaimed several times, grinning from ear to ear. I put on the coat and was led back into the interrogation room. I asked for my clothing back and was assured that I would get it back and be sent to a comfortable POW camp where I would receive proper clothing, have comfortable living conditions, letters from home, and no solitary confinement. My interrogator again asked for the name of the 401st Bomb Squadron commander's name. I once again stated that I would provide only my name, rank, and serial number. I was escorted back to my cell. Late that same afternoon I was handed an old blue heated undergarment, with a flap in the back, worn by waist gunners as protection from the freezing air at high altitudes. I had no choice but to put on that oversized monstrosity, and was led outside into a courtyard where several other prisoners were assembled. Most wore their flying clothing. Only I wore an open-flapped electric flying suit and an oversized coat that once belonged to some Russian giant. Bill Runner was part of the group and broke out in loud laughter when he saw me. We boarded a train at the Frankfurt rail station. I noted that the huge terminal had a glass ceiling and was surprised to see that there was not a single broken pane of glass. A mystery to me, since I knew that the rail terminal had been the primary target on one of our raids. For the first time since being captured we were provided food from Red Cross parcels. One of the guards distributing the food was friendly and told us that he had lived and worked in Chicago and asked if any of us were from Chicago. His friendly demeanor produced a change in mood amongst us prisoners. We learned that we were being taken to a POW camp at Sagan, a small town southeast of Berlin in the province of Lower Silesia. We arrived the following day, October 28, 1943, and were marched from the train station to StalagLuft III."

Sagan was my hometown. I was eight years old in 1943 when Bob Slane arrived at StalagLuft III. My days then were filled with school and playing games with friends involving a lot of running around until dark. Some of our school buildings had been converted into military hospitals. To accommodate additional students we attended classes from eight to twelve in the morning

or one to five in the afternoon, alternating each month. I lived in a government housing area, on the other side of a low chain of hills from StalagLuft III,
which was located adjacent to a military airfield where at one time my father
had been assigned, the reason for my family living in government housing.
At night I could see the dim lights of the camp on the other side of the hills,
but never really knew what it was I was looking at, and caring little. I was just
a little boy doing what little boys do. When not learning my numbers and
letters I was outside with my friends running around, playing the games of
childhood, a childhood that was to end all too soon in January of 1945. Sagan,
although it had an air base, was a backwater and largely untouched by war
until the arrival of the Russian army in January 1945. Young Lieutenant Slane
knew nothing of me, and I knew nothing of him, although we would share
similar experiences as time passed.

The winter of 1944 was brutally cold and snowy, as all the other winters had
been that I could remember. Both Bob Slane and I were to flee the advanc-
ing Russian army, but under very differing circumstances. I would become a
refugee that January of 1945, and would remain so for years to come until I
emigrated to the United States in January 1951. Bob, with thousands of other
POWs from StalagLuft III, was to go on a forced march heading west along
the Czechoslovak border, then southwest into Bavaria, for over six hundred
miles, in that bitterly cold winter. His ordeal finally ended that April in an
overcrowded POW camp near Moosburg, when the Nazi regime collapsed
and the war in Europe came to its end. That April my own ordeal was just
beginning. In years to come, long after World War II was over, Bob and I
would serve together in the United States Air Force flying B-47 jet bombers.
Our paths would not cross until long after both of us had retired from the
United States Air Force.

StalagLuft III was one of six large prisoner-of-war camps operated by the
German air force, the Luftwaffe. The camp began in 1942 with a few wooden
barracks buildings adjacent to an existing Russian POW camp. In time, the
camp was expanded to hold nearly eleven thousand prisoners, mostly American and British flying officers—enlisted men were kept in separate camps. The
numbers of imprisoned flyers provide an idea of the ferocity of the air war
over Germany and its cost. The barracks, with triple bunks, were cramped and
of the same type that I would live in between 1946 and 1950 when surviving
in a makeshift refugee camp adjacent to the Fassberg air base in the British
zone of occupation. The barracks were cold in winter, hot and stuffy in summer. Food at StalagLuft III was enough to keep men alive—thin potato or
cabbage soups being the norm, with little meat, if any. However, Red Cross
packages, containing a variety of canned fruits, meats, raisins, sweets, coffee,
and cigarettes augmented the prisoners' diet. The German air force, in general,

ran their camps in accordance with the provisions of the 1929 Geneva convention on the treatment of prisoners of war, refrained from torture, and insured that the coveted Red Cross packages went only to the POWs whom they were intended for. Harsh living conditions and boredom is what defined POW life. At StalagLuft III those conditions were the perfect setting for well-planned and occasionally successful escape attempts—the POWs' only way of continuing the war and to remain, so to speak, gainfully occupied. Tunnels were the preferred approach for escapes and in March 1944, seventy-six British airmen succeeded in escaping through a long and carefully constructed tunnel. The escape embarrassed the Nazi leadership. All but three of the escapees were recaptured, and fifty of them were subsequently shot by the Gestapo, the German secret police. The 1963 movie with Steve McQueen, *The Great Escape*, is a generally accurate portrayal of this courageous yet tragic attempt at freedom. I, as a young boy living nearby, remember being rounded up by Hitler Youths to help find escaped prisoners along the nearby Bober River with its heavily wooded banks. We, eight- and nine-year-old boys, were forced into something that we did not understand, participated reluctantly, and certainly didn't want to find anyone at all—which we didn't. Not until years later did I learn what really happened the weekend of March 24, 1944.

"On March 26, 1944, we awakened to news that there had been a mass breakout of British prisoners from the adjacent North Compound," Bob Slane recalled. "The news generated excitement and joy throughout the prison population. It wasn't until the first week in April that we were informed that the majority of escapees had been recaptured and that fifty men had been murdered. This unpredictable action by the Germans was devastating news and had a profound effect on the prison population." In spite of this terrible news, Bob continued to plan his own escape—it was what kept him sane and focused. He had planned to escape even before arriving at the camp but given up when fellow prisoners pointed out the flaws in his plans. Undaunted, he continued to develop his escape plans which he presented to the X-Committee for approval. His plans were deemed lacking a sufficient chance of success—and therefore turned down—especially after the fateful March 1944 escape by the seventy-six British airmen with its bloody aftermath. Then, in January 1945, the escape committee approved Bob's latest escape plan.

"It was late on the afternoon of January 17, 1945, when a light snow began to fall. I knew this was the night I had been waiting for. The plan was simple: cross the clearing from the barracks to the wooden warning rail. Crawl under the guardrail and continue on to the double rolls of barbed wire, cut through the wire, through more wire and fences, and then crawl across the perimeter road, past the guard tower at the main entrance to the south compound. The gate guards, I had observed, frequently took shelter in a small guardhouse in inclement weather and I hoped they would do so this time around. My friend Glenn Oster, who lived in a room adjacent to mine, and I set off on our odyssey. Glenn made the first cut at the perimeter fence, which sounded like a rifle shot. Oster made the mistake of not packing his cutters with snow to muffle sound. But we were not detected. We made it through the second fence by the road, when the guard at the gate suddenly started down the fence line in our direction. He turned back before he got to us and we were out of our compound and on schedule. Near the main gate the guard did not go into the gatehouse as we had expected him to. We lay in the snow shivering. Then a larger group of guards passed us, one trailing. He didn't notice Glenn and me. But then I saw a German shepherd coming up the road, lagging about thirty feet behind his master. He came up to me, spread his front feet in a playful gesture, then ran toward his master when he whistled for him. We couldn't believe our luck. We lay in the snow for two hours, waiting for the gate guard to enter his shelter—he never did. We continued on, dodging searchlights, trying to remain in shadow when available. Suddenly I became aware of a dog growling. I looked back and saw the blur of a dog leaping at my face. I put up my left arm and the dog grabbed it. I managed to get to my feet, with the dog hanging from my arm. I raised the other arm, begging the guard not to shoot. Glenn was on his feet as well. There was nowhere left to go. When captured we were stiff with cold. Late on the first afternoon of confinement I began to feel the effects of my long crawl in the snow. I couldn't raise my arms without experiencing severe muscular pain in my shoulders, stomach, and chest. Solitary confinement also meant that we, Glenn and I, would no longer have the benefit of food from the Red Cross packages.

"On January 27, 1945, the tenth day of confinement, we still had no idea of the length of our sentence, when I became aware of unusual activity. When a guard opened my cell door bringing our evening meal, I saw columns of prisoners marching down the road adjacent to the compound. For the next several hours Glenn and I nervously paced our adjacent cells. Then a guard yanked open our cell doors and directed us to join a column of prisoners passing nearby. We were not allowed to retrieve any of our personal belongings and had no gloves, hat, or any other warm clothing to face the freezing outside temperatures. We worked ourselves forward in the column and found men from our 'block—136.' They shared hats, gloves, scarves, and blankets. Everyone from Room 4 had on heavy woolen overcoats that had been issued to everyone upon arrival at the camp. We walked in twos and threes in a loose formation. Walking with us were German guards, some with dogs. Before departure from the camp there had been an additional issue of Red Cross food parcels. Some had accumulated several cartons of cigarettes and chocolate bars, the items most prized for trading with the guards." None of the

StalagLuft III POWs at the time knew where they were heading or how long this winter march was going to be. It would not end until that April in a camp near Moosburg, Bavaria. During the march Robert Slane would again escape, was recaptured, and before arriving at OfLag VIIB (Offizierslager), a ground forces POW camp, he would be strafed by passing P-47s which caused many casualties amongst the marching POWs—who probably looked like a column of German soldiers to the flyers above.

"New prisoners evacuated from other locations continued to arrive. The tents already in place when I arrived at the camp sheltered a mass of humanity. There were not enough beds in some of the many compounds and prisoners had to sleep on the ground. Most of the cooking was done outside the barracks and tents. The outside cooking stoves were generally constructed out of 'Klim' cans, the powdered milk containers from the Red Cross parcels. The faces and bodies of my friends had changed considerably since we left StalagLuft III. All had lost considerable weight. Their faces were sallow and their eyes seemed to have grown larger. Fortunately, none of my close friends had a serious illness, but it was quite obvious to me that we were slowly starving to death. On April 28, we became aware that American forces were in the area. The rumor had it that the Germans had agreed to declare the camp neutral territory. That evening someone called 'Attention' at the barracks entrance. Two German officers entered the building accompanied by an American colonel in khaki uniform and an American major with a .45 at his waist. I knew the major from when I was an apprentice aircraft mechanic. I went to pilot training; he was color-blind and didn't get to go. Now here he was. I called out to him, but in the dim light he didn't recognize me. They passed through the barracks exiting at the far end. I had difficulty sleeping that night seeing my friend Whitfield and the realization that soon we would be free. On Sunday, April 29, I awakened to the distant sound of gunfire. It went on for about two hours, then it ended. We were all milling about. I climbed to the roof of a barracks when I heard the sound of an approaching tank. The tank headed for the main gate of the camp. Then the turret opened and the most beautiful flag in the world appeared—the Stars and Stripes. The tank kept right on coming through the main gate into the center of the camp. It was the moment we all had hoped for and dreamed of. We were laughing, shouting with joy. Life was very good. Sometime later General Patton, 3rd Army Commander, arrived. His jeep looked factory fresh with flags attached to both sides of the windshield. The general stood tall and resplendent in his uniform, his two pearl-handled revolvers at his side. He wore jodhpur riding breeches and highly polished boots. I couldn't hear what he said, I was too far back, but his presence was an inspiration."

Bob Slane and thousands of inmates were liberated the 29th of April 1945 by the men of the 14th Armored Division led by Lieutenant Colonel Clark. They stayed where they were. The war wasn't over yet, and there were no means to transport all these men to Camp Lucky Strike in France, where they would eventually end up to receive proper medical attention before being shipped home. Bob just couldn't stand going back to the camp. He learned from the soldiers of a tank destroyer unit that the nearest American field hospital was located at Epinal, France, near the German border. He had a bad toothache that needed fixing. "Early in the morning of May 2, several friends and I just walked out of the camp and flagged down a passing army truck. The truck driver had a resupply schedule to meet and we drove for hours through a countryside that showed the horror and tragedy of war wherever we looked. We arrived in Epinal in the afternoon. The young truck driver knew exactly where the hospital was located and drove right to the main entrance. The first order of business was to take a delousing shower. With the exception of my A-2 leather flying jacket, all my clothing was taken away to be destroyed. I was to see a dentist the next morning. New clothing was to be issued after we received our physicals. In the meantime we were ambulatory patients with beds assigned. The added bonus for the day was to sleep in a bed with a mattress and a pillow and with vermin-free sheets and bedding. The physical was comprehensive. My weight had dropped from 148 pounds to 103. We were issued new clothing and introduced to the new Eisenhower jacket. The following day I learned that I was to be the troop commander for seventy-seven patients being discharged for processing to Camp Lucky Strike near Le Havre. It was an international group hailing from the British Isles, Canada, New Zealand, and Australia. We left on a train for Le Havre. No one missed that train."

When Bob Slane arrived home, the first order of business he tended to was to get married to his sweetheart, Mary Lee, a student nurse in Salem, Oregon. Then he reported to Hobbs Field in New Mexico for retraining in the B-17. "After the Japanese surrender, the retraining program at Hobbs was terminated and all the B-17 aircraft were flown to an airfield at Walnut Ridge, Arkansas, where they were destroyed. The base at Hobbs was closed and I was transferred to Midland, Texas. There it became my duty to participate in the cleaning of a bombing range. We were reminded daily that if we didn't like the work we could be discharged immediately. Demobilization was taking place so rapidly that military life was pure chaos for the next several years. Then Midland closed and I was transferred to Lowry Field in Denver, Colorado. I was on a discharge list at Lowry, but managed to get off the list. In 1951 I was at Sheppard Air Force Base, Wichita Falls, Texas, for B-47 training. I was thrilled to get into our newest jet bomber. Then my assignment was suddenly canceled and I was sent to the 3rd Bomb Wing in Korea instead to fly the B-26 Invader out of Kunsan Air Base, South Korea. I had never flown a B-26 before, but by flying day and night for ten days I was checked out and certified combat ready. I flew a total of forty combat missions, all but one at night, and many right up to the Manchurian border. I carried a .38-caliber Colt automatic pistol as well as the standard army issue .45-caliber automatic. One thing was certain—I was never going to be a prisoner of war again. Eighteen B-26 crews were lost over North Korea during the period that I was assigned to the 3rd Bomb Wing."

Barney Dobbs, whose story is in an earlier section of this book, was one of the eighteen aircrews lost over North Korea while Bob Slane was flying out of Kunsan. Barney's is an especially gruesome story of captivity, with periods when he was buried underground in a wooden box, barely able to breathe to sustain life. The combat missions flown by the B-26 crews were as dangerous as they come, not only because of enemy opposition, but also because of their nature: low-level flight at night over mountainous terrain. To make matters worse, when they fired their twelve to sixteen wing and nose mounted guns, the number of guns depending on the model of aircraft flown, the gunfire blinded the pilot who then flew into total darkness on a preplanned track until his eyes regained their night vision. Nothing was easy flying the B-26 bombers—but between them at night and the F-51s during the day, they decimated the North Korean army and saved the US 8th Army from being pushed off the Korean peninsula. But the flyers didn't lose their sense of humor. Bob Slane named his aircraft *Midnight Rendezvous*, which was all too real for most of his missions. Upon Bob's return to the United States he finally got back into the B-47 program, first as a copilot, then as aircraft commander. Bob had crashed a B-17 in England when he ran out of fuel on October 10, 1943. Four days later Bob's B-17 was shot down. The old adage of aircraft incidents always coming in threes applied to Bob Anspach, whose story is in a later section of this book, and it was to apply to Bob Slane as well.

On 30 November 1956 Bob took off from Barksdale Air Force Base, near Shreveport, Louisiana, on a four-ship night exercise. Lieutenant Richard Martin was his copilot, Lieutenant Donald Petty the navigator, and a second navigator instructor came along, Lieutenant Max Workman, who did not have an ejection seat, but sat in the aircraft aisle below the two pilots on takeoff and landing. It was to be a long thirteen-hour mission requiring two aerial refuelings with their flight path taking them to Greenland, then across Canada and eventually back to Barksdale Air Force Base. Bob's aircraft was scheduled to be an intruder and simulate bomb runs against select targets after he penetrated the US border. During the flight the aircraft experienced hydraulic problems with the controls to the ailerons. At worst, Bob figured, he and his copilot would have to hand-fly the aircraft without the boost provided by the hydraulic systems. They were at thirty-two thousand feet over Canada. The four-ship formation that Bob was a part of had just made a five-degree adjustment to the left, when the control wheel began a slow, steady turn to the right "despite the fact that I was exerting pressure to keep the wheel centered. Martin, my copilot, suddenly asked me, 'Why are we doing Mach .81?' The aileron control wheel was slowly and steadily turning to the right and I could not by brute force stop the wheel from turning. My reply to Martin was, 'Shut up and get ready to get out of this thing.' The only sound I heard over the intercom was a gasp of disbelief, or terror. I saw Petty, my navigator, point to the extra navigator to head for the exit in the aisle. I called for Martin to hold and turn the control wheel back to center. All of the aileron power control lights were red, indicating failure. I was applying full left rudder, pulled off the power on our six J47 engines—nothing helped. At this time the aircraft was in a left-wing high attitude at about sixty degrees. The nose of the aircraft was slightly below the horizon. I knew then that we were flying a doomed aircraft. A terrifying experience. I radioed the other aircraft that I was in trouble.

"I gave the ejection order just as the aircraft rolled violently to the right. After releasing the control column, my arms were forced against the side of my body with such force that I had great difficulty moving them. It took all my strength to slide my arms forward along my legs to grab the ejection seat handles. I grasped the left handle first, then the right—which activates the ejection sequence. I felt a sudden jolt as the seat bottomed and the control column stowed. As I looked to my left, I looked directly into the eyes of Max Workman, who had been immobilized by the G-forces exerted on the aircraft as it shot toward the ground below. I couldn't do a thing for him. I squeezed the trigger in the right handle and closed my eyes. The seat shot out of the aircraft and tumbled away. My chute opened much too high above the ground with a terrific jolt. I noticed a huge red glow beneath me as my B-47 impacted the ground. Then there was only darkness. I wondered if Petty and Martin, possibly Workman, might also be drifting down in their parachutes. When I finally broke through the overcast, I saw a snow-covered forest. I hit the ground feet first. For a while I did nothing. Then I thanked God for my life and prayed for my crew. Mostly I prayed for Workman. I knew that unless he was thrown out of the aircraft by some miracle he had little chance to survive. Martin and Petty I felt certain had ejected. I expected at any time to hear their voices. Despite some chest pain I carried my parachute and survival pack to a small level clearing. There I used the inflated life raft and the chute to fashion a bed for myself and I lay down to organize my thoughts. Later I unpacked my survival kit—radio, survival knife, socks, a parka, and a small .22-caliber rifle, which I assembled. When I picked up voice transmissions on my radio, I tried to transmit, but made no contact. I lit a fire from wrappings I saved as I unpacked the survival kit. I didn't have enough to keep the fire going for long."

The following day a helicopter located Bob Slane and pulled him out of his predicament, leaving behind his chute, raft, and survival gear. "My first words

Robert Slane was part of the famed 91st Bomb Group, which included Robert Morgan's *Memphis Belle*, the first B-17 to complete twenty-five combat missions—shown here while undergoing restoration at the Museum of the USAF in Dayton, Ohio.

A B-47E bomber, like the one flown by Colonel Slane, taking off for home from an air base in England after pulling six weeks of Reflex nuclear alert. The black smoke was caused by a water/alcohol mixture injected into engines on takeoff to gain an extra thousand pounds of thrust per engine. The B-47 nearly cost Bob Slane his life and caused the death of three of his crew.

Robert Slane in 2009, age eighty-six, flanked by Louisiana governor Bobby Jindal at a ceremony in the state capitol honoring Colonel Slane's military service. Bob died a year later.

were, how many others have you found? 'You are the only one,' was the reply. I was stunned. The helicopter flew directly to an airport, now named Thunderbay. Two days later, I was back home at Barksdale. The subsequent accident board went to the Boeing plant at Wichita and pulled an aircraft directly off the assembly line. Aileron failure, as I had described, was duplicated by both mechanical and electrical means and the ailerons 'locked' each time. The lock could not be broken by other than disconnecting the hydraulic line at the power control unit in the wing. One Boeing representative told me during the investigation that my testimony had provided information that could account for the loss of five other B-47 bombers. I gained some solace that I was able to describe the events and may have contributed to a solution that saved the lives of others. Subsequently all B-47 bombers were modified to preclude a recurrence of an accident of this type. The investigation board ascribed the most probable cause of the loss of my crew as excessive G-forces, estimated between three and four times the force of gravity, which completely incapacitated them. After the accident investigation was completed, I again flew the B-47 with a new crew."

When Bob Slane's B-47 aircraft went down over Canada on November 30, 1956, near Port Arthur, one B-47 from his flight of four circled overhead until search and rescue planes reached the area. Bob had enough time to unpack his survival gear, but was soon located, picked up by helicopter and flown out, leaving behind his parachute, survival kit, and loaded .22-caliber rifle. The equipment sat where he left it in the Canadian bush for sixteen years. In the summer of 1972 a Canadian hunter, Herbert Schaefer, from Thunderbay, came across Bob Slane's survival gear. Herb, as his friends call him, was hunting moose when he saw something in the leaves that caught his attention. "I started pulling at it," he said, "and it just kept on coming as if it was all connected together." It was Slane's parachute which the wind had wrapped around some trees. Nearby were Slane's survival rations, still in nearly perfect condition. "I didn't know what to think when I saw that stuff," Herb recalled. "I thought someone might have died out here." But after talking to an old friend, Herb learned of the B-47 crash and traced the pilot's address through old newspaper clippings from the Port Arthur *News Chronicle*. "I just thought he might want some of his stuff back. The next day I asked the telephone operator in Shreveport if there was anyone named Robert Slane there, and to my astonishment she gave me his number. The next thing I knew I was talking to Mary Lee Slane, his wife." Herb was lucky. Slane had just returned from a combat tour in Vietnam. When Slane's plane crashed, he was a major; now sixteen years later he was a full colonel and the commander of Barksdale Air Force Base. Herb Schaefer would call Bob Slane each year on the anniversary of Bob's crash near Port Arthur, renamed Thunderbay in 1970. After Bob retired from the air force, on a whim, he and Mary Lee drove up to Thunderbay. Bob, the World War II bomber pilot and former prisoner of war, and Herb, the German kid who emigrated to Canada after the war, finally met and became fast friends. "Our friendship is the kind of thing you just can't put into words," Schaefer explained.[47]

After the B-47 bomber was replaced by the B-52, "I checked out in and flew the B-52 for over three thousand hours as an aircraft commander, then served as vice commander of the B-52 wing at Plattsburgh AFB, New York." During the Vietnam War, Bob Slane served as commander of the 553rd Reconnaissance Wing at Korat Royal Thai Air Force Base, Thailand, and later as base commander at Bien Hoa air base near Saigon, South Vietnam. Colonel Robert Slane served his country for nearly thirty-three years in three wars—WW II, Korea, Vietnam—flying a total of 118 combat missions. He flew forty missions during the Korean War in the B-26 Invader, then another seventy-eight during the Vietnam War in EC-121, A-37, and OV-10 aircraft, in addition to the four B-17 missions he flew in World War II—the last of which was on Black Thursday against Schweinfurt when sixty B-17 bombers and their crews didn't come home. Robert Slane was a true American hero, a man I am proud to have known and to have served alongside. Bob died in March 2011 at age eighty-seven. Blue skies, fair winds—my dear friend. Our country's hero.

HAROLD R. AUSTIN

C-54/RB-45C/RB-47E

A Thought

For life was made for things like this:
A laugh, a smile, a woman's kiss!
—Lieutenant William H. Lancaster III, WWII ETO

Born on a farm near Sweetwater, Oklahoma, and raised in Brownfield, Texas, thirty-five miles south of Lubbock, Hal Austin was fascinated by airplanes as long as he could remember. On the rare occasions when an airplane passed overhead, he would run out of the house to watch until the plane passed from sight. On a warm summer day in 1934, at the age of ten, his uncle came by and drove him to the edge of town, where a group of barnstormers had landed their biplanes on a farmer's meadow. They were giving fifteen-minute rides to anyone who could come up with five dollars. "Five dollars was a lot of money then," Hal recalled. "I didn't have five dollars and was content to watch them perform their tight turns, dangerous-looking loops, and come skimming low and fast across the ground. I walked around each plane and touched it gently as if it had a soul. Then, totally unexpected, my uncle bought me a five-dollar ride. It was the most exciting thing that had ever happened to me. After that ride I dreamed of flying airplanes someday. It changed my life."

In 1943, when Hal was nineteen, the Eighth Air Force experienced terrible losses over Europe, and the aviation cadet program was opened to teens with only a high school education. When Hal learned of that opportunity, he immediately joined the Army Air Forces. In April 1945, after passing through a number of training bases, he received his pilot wings and a reserve commission as second lieutenant. By then, the war was nearly over in Europe, and after the Japanese surrendered later that year, Hal was declared surplus, along with many other young men, and released. "To make a living, I accepted a post office job in a small town in New Mexico, Deming. My mail route proved to be less of a challenge than I expected. I really missed flying. One day in January 1947 I stepped into the office of the local air force recruiter and volunteered to return to active duty in any capacity. I was offered a position at Luke Field in Arizona as a tower operator with the rank of master sergeant. As a tower operator I would control the takeoff and landing of aircraft. I took the job.

"It felt good to be back in uniform," Hal confessed, sitting in his comfortable home in Riverside, California, a popular retirement location for air force flyers. "Soon after reporting to Luke Field, I was assigned to attend communications school at Scott AFB in Illinois." After the air force became an independent service in September 1947, coequal with the army and navy, all former air-fields were redesignated air force bases, so Luke Field became Luke Air Force Base. "Once I graduated in January 1948, I regained my former rank of second lieutenant. As a trained communications officer I was assigned to McChord AFB in Washington State. There I was promptly put in the right seat of a C-87 transport [the transport version of the B-24 bomber] as copilot, flying support missions for the US Army. I never got a chance to work as a communicator. Six months later I received orders to report to Hamilton AFB, near San Francisco, to await shipment to somewhere in the Pacific. I sat around Hamilton for sev-eral days, waiting for my orders to arrive. When they finally did arrive, I didn't go to the Pacific; instead I was sent to Great Falls, Montana, to check out in the C-54 Skymaster to fly the Berlin airlift. On November 30 I arrived at Rhein-Main Air Base, near Frankfurt, Germany. On December 1 I flew my first mis-sion to Berlin in the right seat. After that it was fly, fly, fly—ease the power back, ease the nose up, touch down. Unload. Back to Rhein-Main for more coal.

"We flew Christmas and New Year's Eve. Of course, we acted up when we arrived at Tempelhof on Christmas Eve. We announced our arrival as Santa and his reindeers. We were promptly told to shut up. The C-54 was a fantastic airplane to fly. They only fixed the engines, things which we absolutely had to have to fly the airplane. Other malfunctions were ignored. I had a working autopilot on only one aircraft I flew, but that time I nearly got into big trouble. It was night and we were on our second run to Berlin, me and my copilot Dar-rel Lamb. We had taken off at two in the morning. Both of us were sleepy. We didn't call in over the Berlin beacon. When I awoke, I saw Darrel was sound asleep. The 'bird dog,' our radio compass, was pointing toward the tail. There were not many lights on the ground below—everything was pitch black. I really got scared. I awoke Darrel, who was as startled as I was. He cranked in Berlin radio. It was weak. We had no idea how long we had been asleep, but we promptly did a 180. It took us thirty minutes to get back to Berlin, about ninety miles or so. We were probably near Stettin, somewhere over the Baltic Sea, when we made our turn. The corridor wasn't always full of aircraft, so we waited until we heard someone call in over the Berlin beacon. Six minutes later, someone else called in his hardstand number. We waited three minutes and then called in our own number and rejoined the stream of aircraft into Berlin. We sweated blood for a couple of days, expecting the hammer to come down on us at any time. Nothing ever happened."

Fatigue was one of the greatest hazards during the Berlin airlift. Hal Austin's dangerous incursion into Poland, although rare, is an example of how quickly things can go wrong. Fatigue combined with a night, zero-visibility landing could be a deadly combination. Ice on wings, propellers, and on the runway also did not help. As a result of the frequent landings while loaded to maximum capacity, many of the aircraft badly needed maintenance before their scheduled two-hundred-hour inspections. In such an assembly-line flying environment, where crews flew day and night regardless of weather conditions, with marginally maintained aircraft, a price had to be paid: thirty-one Americans died carrying food and coal to a hungry and cold Berlin. In addition thirty-nine Royal Air Force personnel and British civilian employees performing airlift duties lost their lives, as did thirteen German workers.

I was a thirteen-year-old boy in 1948 living in a decrepit refugee camp off the north end of the Fassberg Air Base runway. The Americans flew coal from Fassberg to Berlin. At night, lying on my straw mattress, I went to sleep to the comforting sounds of C-54 transports turning northeast over my barracks. To me as a young boy it was the sound of freedom. Even when I knew rain clouds were nearly touching the tips of the tallest trees in the surrounding pine forest, I could hear the drone of the planes overhead. I thought about the pilots, those brave men sitting in their cramped cockpits holding on to their control columns, staring into what must have seemed to them impenetrable cloud. I wondered if they were ever afraid to fly, and how they found their way to Berlin, and why they didn't crash in weather like this. Then, on a clear December night, a C-54 turned over our barracks and fell out of the sky like a rock. I didn't see it happen or hear it crash because I was inside at the time. I heard the commotion outside. Some men had watched the plane turn and had seen it fall to its death. They heard the explosion when the plane crashed. "Not far from us," one of the men said to me, "probably on the Trauen Research Center," a former Nazi research and development center for the V-2 ballistic missile. Later I learned that the coal had shifted inside the aircraft as it made its turn. The plane crashed outside the fence line of the Trauen Research Center. The crew of three was killed. I visited the crash site after most of the debris had been removed. The site was black from oil and fuel that had seeped into the soft, marshy ground. One engine lay half buried, and another was underground, buried too deep ever to be seen again. The airplane had dug itself deep into the marsh. I felt deep sorrow for the American airmen who had died for us Germans. Only three years ago they were fighting against my country and bombing me in Berlin—and now they were dying flying coal to Berlin to give German people light and heat. The Americans were strange people to me. I didn't understand them. I wondered, as only a child can wonder, what made these people do the things they did. When I grow up, I mused, I would want to fly with these men, whom I began to admire.

While Hal Austin still looked over his shoulder after his inadvertent penetration into Poland, he was hatching another way to get himself into trouble. He had met Rosemary, the stepdaughter of an army warrant officer who was stationed near Frankfurt. Hal thought he could impress the young lady if he took her on a flight to Berlin. Rosemary agreed to go. "Hal told me I would have to come on short notice," Rosemary, who later became Hal's wife, said, "and it would be at night. He found a parka for me, with a hood that had a fur lining to hide my face, and a pair of men's overalls. When he called, I put that stuff on. 'Keep your hands in your pockets,' Hal said to me when he picked me up. 'Your hands will give you away, not being a man.' Well, to get into the GI truck, a weapons carrier, to take us out to the plane, I swear, the stairs into the truck were up to my waist. All the guys were yelling, 'Hurry up. Hurry up.' Hal whispered to me, 'Look down and go to the end of the truck and sit in a corner.' No way could I get on that truck on my own. The guy in front of me finally turned around and held out his hand. I had to take my hand out of my pocket and take his. He had this expression on his face, like, what am I holding? He pulled me up and kept watching me. He didn't say a word. But he kept watching me as I sat in the far corner of the truck. Hal in the meantime acted like I wasn't there. We got on the plane. It was supposed to be ready. And lo and behold, two GIs were working on something in the cockpit. Hal quickly grabbed me and shoved me into one of two bunks behind the cockpit and shut the curtains. 'How much longer?' I heard him say to the maintenance men. 'I have a window to make.' The maintenance men responded in their usual colorful language, followed by a 'Sir,' and suggested to Hal to take the blankety-blank spare on the next hardstand. Hal didn't want to do that because the plane was loaded and the rear door was already closed. He kept stalling. Finally, when he realized the maintenance men were not about to move, he opened the curtains and said, 'Come on, honey,' and reached in and grabbed me. Off we went out the door behind the copilot's seat. The two maintenance men stood there looking like, what have we got here?"

"That was the first time after three months of flying that I had an airplane that wasn't ready to take off," Hal interrupted Rosemary. "The next airplane we went to was ready."

"Some airplanes were crashing," Rosemary continued her story. "They didn't publicize it. But after his first plane wasn't ready, Hal thought it wise to give me a safety briefing. 'If anything happens, crawl away from the plane as far as you can,' he said." Rosemary laughed loudly, recalling the incident. "I would probably be dead by then. How could I crawl then? In Berlin they unloaded the plane. I stayed in the bunk behind the curtains. Once we got back to Rhein-Main, it was light by then, Hal worried that someone would see me and recognize I was a woman."

Hal Austin apparently was not a fast learner when it came to taking young women along for rides. Two weeks later he took not only Rosemary but also her friend to Berlin. "On the way back from Berlin the girlfriend sat between and behind us, in the flight engineer's position," Hal recalled. "It's night, and the weather is rough. Her eyes are as big as saucers. I tell her not to worry, but if she should get scared, please, not to scream. St. Elmo's fire was on the props and the wings, and number four engine suddenly began to cough, and I had to shut it down. Rosemary's girlfriend started to scream like a wounded banshee and wouldn't quit. She thought we were going to crash. That was the last time I took any of them along." Hal and Rosemary were married on July 2, 1949, in Frankfurt am Main, Germany. With the end of the airlift in September 1949, Hal and Rosemary Austin transferred to Barksdale AFB, Louisiana, near Shreveport, where Hal would learn to fly the new and fast RB-45C Tornado reconnaissance jet. Hal was assigned to the 324th Strategic Reconnaissance Squadron (SRS) of the 91st Strategic Reconnaissance Wing (SRW). The wing had two squadrons, the 322nd and the 323rd. In the summer of 1950, Hal was selected to transition into the RB-45C. He picked up a brand-new aircraft from the factory in Long Beach and began the task of learning to fly a jet. In those days they had no checklists, no technical data, and no company technical representative with pilot qualifications who could answer the many questions that arose among the aircrews. Everything they learned about this new airplane they learned by doing.

"Every one of us, of course, had to try to see how high we could get in the new airplane. We got to nearly 50,000 feet—49,500 feet is the highest I took it. It took forever. We were light, having burned off most of our fuel at the end of our mission, when we got to that altitude over our home base of Barksdale. In the early days, no one else was up there except for a few F-86 fighters. We flew cruise-climb for our departures. North American told us to do that. We would normally end up over Barksdale at 43,000 feet. The day I took it up to 49,500 feet, when I pulled the power back, the airplane hardly slowed down. It had no speed brakes, nothing to slow it down. I started pushing the airplane down, which put me in a high-speed buffet, and of course when I pulled back, I was in a stall, or right between buffet and stall—coffin corner. It took me thirty minutes to get back to 40,000 feet. To land, we flew a teardrop approach from over Barksdale. In a steady descent toward the Gulf of Mexico, I would eat up a third of the altitude. Then the second third was in the turn, and the final third would be coming into Barksdale. When I made my turn at the widest point, I was 120 miles southeast of Barksdale. There was no way to slow that aircraft down. We finally talked the FAA into letting us use a letdown coming straight in. Initially the FAA said, 'What do you mean, you want to let down en route? We've never heard of such a thing.' They finally let us do it. We fussed about the lack of braking from day one with the RB-45. You couldn't get the plane out of the sky.

"We also pushed it through Mach 1 more than once; at least we thought we did. Our group lost eight airplanes in that first year. One of the first we lost, we think the guy went through the Mach trying to get down, trying to see what the airplane would do. I went through the Mach with it—rough as hell going through, rougher coming back out. The one that crashed had the tail section come off. He was southeast of Barksdale at forty-three thousand feet when it happened. That's the altitude where I pushed mine through, the only time I ever pushed it through. We lost other aircraft going through the Mach before anyone survived to tell us what happened. An aeronautical engineer finally explained to us that the right wing passed the vibrations encountered going through Mach 1 to the tail section. Unfortunately, the airplane wasn't designed to handle such stress. It was basically a World War II airplane powered by jet engines."

All this experimentation by the RB-45C pilots occurred in 1950 and 1951. The first flight exceeding the speed of sound had been made only three years earlier, on October 14, 1947, by then Captain Chuck Yeager in the Bell X-1 experimental aircraft. In his autobiography Yeager wrote of his historic flight, "Suddenly the Mach needle began to fluctuate. It went up to .965 Mach—then tipped right off the scale. I thought I was seeing things! We were flying supersonic [at forty-two thousand feet]! And it was as smooth as a baby's bottom.... After all the anxiety, breaking the sound barrier turned out to be a perfectly paved speedway."[48] It wasn't that way for the RB-45, an airplane that lacked the smooth lines of the X-1. After many catastrophic incidents, the RB-45C was limited to speeds of less than Mach .85 (85 percent of the speed of sound).

"Another problem that took a couple of crashes to resolve," Hal Austin continued, "was the bomb bay fuel tanks. We had two thousand-gallon bomb bay tanks—that was before we went from gallons to pounds—hung on old B-17 bomb shackles. The shackles were not designed for such a continuous load and the stress of day-in, day-out flying pulling a lot of Gs. One instructor pilot, flying in the copilot's seat in the third or fourth plane that crashed, survived. He told us that all of a sudden the aircraft started twisting. He couldn't remember how he got out of the airplane, couldn't recall ejecting. When he became conscious of his situation, he found himself still sitting in his ejection seat, heading for the ground. When the wreckage was examined, the inspectors found the back-bay shackle had given way and hit the bomb bay doors. The doors flipped out and hit part of the empennage, the tail assembly of the airplane. Once that happened, the tail section twisted off, and the aircraft was out of control. North American redesigned the shackles, and that solved the problem. Every major problem we discovered cost one or two air crews their lives. We were, in fact, test pilots.

"The RB-45C was powered by the early model of the J-47 engine, which in later years proved to be quite reliable on the B-47 and F-86. But that engine wasn't reliable when we were flying it in early 1951. The engine had to be pulled every twenty-five hours of flying time for a complete overhaul. The number one and number three engines had the generators—today they're called alternators. The generators had a solid shaft. When the bearings wore, the shaft began to wobble, finally fail, and tear up the engine, sometimes resulting in an engine fire. When the second engine became disabled, the crew had to bail out. We lost two aircraft from this particular problem. Number two and number four engines powered the hydraulics. Number two operated the left aileron, and number four the right. There was no aileron crossover. If I lost number two, and it wasn't wind milling, then I lost my hydraulics on the left side and my aileron control. I was in deep trouble when that happened. If I had an engine problem and I needed to shut it down, I had to do it slowly. If I shut the engine down too quickly, the shroud ring in the hot section back of the engine could warp, and if that happened, the engine seized. If it was the number two or number four engine, I lost my ailerons. At high speed and with the ailerons not working, I had a hell of a control problem. The only alternative, and it was a difficult one, was to steer the aircraft with the rudder. We finally got the aileron crossover problem resolved. The hydraulics were redesigned so number two or number four engine could power both left and right ailerons. It was the only safety modification made to the airplane. It was a great aircraft to fly, except for the aileron crossover problem.

"I recall a landing in early 1951 at Goose Bay. I was on a flight to Sculthorpe, near Kings Lynn, on the east coast of England. Our usual route was from Barksdale to Goose Bay, Labrador, then on to Iceland, and finally Sculthorpe. With full tip tanks and bomb bay tanks, we could fly without refueling for five and one-half hours, about 2,500 miles. It was routine for us to cross the Atlantic without the use of a tanker. On this trip I landed first at Wright-Patterson AFB in Ohio, where I topped off my tanks. Coming into Goose Bay, I still had too much fuel and had to spend time burning it off. I flew around a bit since I had no way of dumping fuel. When I was light enough, I eased back on the power to make my letdown into Goose. I was right over the spot where a friend of mine had crashed only two weeks earlier and my number three engine seized. It flipped us over. I know we were past ninety degrees. It scared the hell out of me. I rammed the power back up and managed to roll it level. My navigator sitting in the nose of the aircraft not knowing what was happening, called over the intercom, 'You son of a bitch, what are you doing up there?' I got her down safely, but it was difficult. For a moment, when the aircraft went out of control, I thought we were going to join my friend. They never did find out what happened to his aircraft.

"We also had some comfort problems with the airplane. The canopy was welded shut. I guess they didn't know at that time how to hinge the canopy. In an emergency, the pilots punched through the canopy with their ejection seats. The navigator didn't have an ejection seat, though. He had to bail out of the access door on the left side of the aircraft, forward of the cockpit. In the summer it got pretty hot at Barksdale, and the crew-compartment temperature was unbearable. Every time the maintenance men put a meat thermometer in there to measure the temperature, the thermometer would blow up. Our maintenance people installed brackets alongside the canopy so we could carry a shade. Even with a shade, it was still hot as hell when we first got in. So it was our procedure to taxi out, push all four engines to 80 percent to cool down the cockpit and finally, the crew chief would take the shade off the cockpit."

Although the RB-45s tail guns did not contribute to any flight safety problems, they were not installed in SAC aircraft, for reasons unknown to me or to the pilots I interviewed. The USAFE assigned B-45B bombers, however, did have their tail guns. And once the RB-45Cs transferred from SAC to TAC, then to USAFE, the tail guns were reinstalled. There was one exception, however, to the no gun policy. Aircraft number 48042, assigned to the 91st Strategic Reconnaissance Wing, while operating out of Yokota Air Base, near Tokyo, Japan, as part of an RB-45C SAC detachment in 1952 and 1953, for some strange reason had a set of tail guns mounted in a fixed position. One gun pointed straight back, while the other was mounted in a thirty-degree downward slant. The guns could be remotely fired by the pilot using a simple on/off switch, according to Colonel Howard "Sam" Myers, who flew the aircraft on several occasions over Communist China. In April 1952 this same aircraft, tail number 48042, was used by the RAF in an overflight of the western Soviet Union. And on July 29, 1952, Major Louis H. Carrington made the first nonstop, transpacific flight in RB-45C 48042 from Elmendorf AFB, Alaska, to Yokota AB, Japan, with the help of two KB-29 in-flight refuelings, which earned him and his crew the Mackay Trophy for 1952. RB-45C 48042 undoubtedly had the most amazing history of any of the RB-45C reconnaissance aircraft.[49] "The visibility was excellent. The air-refueling receptacle was behind the canopy, so the airplane ended up right under the KB-29 tanker and didn't feel the prop wash as much as one did in the newer B-47, with its receptacle in front of the canopy. By 1952 we had resolved our engine problems. We didn't fix them, mind you, except for the crossover problem. We learned how to manage the engines. A great airplane," Hal Austin added wistfully. "I loved flying it."

Air force pilots fly whatever airplanes they are given. In a period of one year the 91st SRW lost eight of thirty-three aircraft, 24 percent of the force. Each aircraft carried a crew of three. In most cases all aboard the doomed aircraft perished. This was the sort of attrition flying units experienced in combat in Korea and later in Vietnam. But this was peacetime flying in the early 1950s. For Austin to say it was "a great pilot's airplane" when every flight was more or less a test flight was an understatement worthy of an Englishman, not a matter-of-fact American flyer. Austin coped with day-to-day stress by focusing on those aspects of the airplane that gave him pleasure, and the RB-45C was indeed a pleasure to fly when compared to most piston-engine powered aircraft. When it was put into service, the Korean War was going on. There was little time for extensive flight testing. The airplane was needed to complement the slow RB-29s and RB-50s, a fair number of which had already been shot down by Soviet fighters. The RB-45C was the airplane that could cope with such threats, although one aircraft was lost early on in the war, on December 4, 1950, just on the other side of the Yalu River.[50]

By 1949 Hal Austin had become a charter member of the newly formed and rapidly expanding Strategic Air Command, SAC, first flying the RB-45C out of Barksdale AFB, and later out of Lockbourne AFB, near Columbus, Ohio. Hal and his fellow 91st SRW flyers frequently deployed on TDYs to England and other European countries. "Flying was a thrill in the nearly empty skies of postwar Europe. I never made more than two or three radio calls on an entire mission. In between those two or three calls, I flew at whatever altitude I chose. One of my jobs was to photomap the Rhine River basin and Spain. This was an important prerequisite for the future stationing of ballistic missiles in Europe. What a way to see Europe." In 1953 Hal Austin transitioned from the RB-45C to the more advanced RB-47E. "The RB-47 was a sleek aircraft with swept wings, a raised cockpit which provided fighter-like visibility, and lots of speed. I loved flying the B-47. It was an aircraft of advanced design which eliminated many of the troublesome shortcomings of the RB-45." The B-47 soon became the SAC mainstay, with a total build of over two thousand bomber and reconnaissance versions. In April 1954 crew S-51 of the 91st SRW, consisting of Captain Harold Austin, his copilot Captain Carl Holt, and Major Vance Heavilin, the radar navigator, deployed with seven other RB-47E photo-reconnaissance aircraft from Lockbourne AFB to RAF Fairford.

Fairford, near the campus of Oxford University, was a Battle of Britain base, many of which were used by SAC aircraft during the Cold War years. Hal and his crew spent a couple of weeks familiarizing themselves with the area by flying short training flights and had enough time off to enjoy the nearby historic sights and the many offerings of London. In the early '60s, I would fly reconnaissance missions out of the same base against the Soviet Union, and from other bases in the United Kingdom. The Columbia Officers' Club in downtown London, a large mansion donated during the war by a patriotic and grateful Englishman, fronted Bayswater Road and sat across from Hyde Park. The club served as a hotel for visiting airmen and was frequented by Hal Austin and his crew. I also enjoyed the Columbia Club on many occasions while visiting London. There was no better and certainly no cheaper place to stay and it became a favorite for 55th SRW crews, the reconnaissance wing I was flying with in the early '60s.

Fairford's March weather was exceptionally bad while Austin was flying out of there, and the group of aircraft was recalled to Lockbourne after only two weeks in-country. During the two weeks, however, they flew two long-range reconnaissance training missions against the island group of Spitsbergen, high above the Arctic Circle. Once Hal and his crew returned to Fairford in April, they again were directed to plan a flight to Spitsbergen. On May 6, 1954, Austin and five other RB-47E photo-reconnaissance aircraft took off in the early morning hours for their distant target. The countryside reverberated from the throaty roar of powerful jet engines until all six B-47s faded into the morning mist. Slower KC-97 tankers had departed earlier that night to meet them at the prearranged rendezvous point off the coast of Norway. That evening at the local pub, some older Englishmen confessed over a glass of warm beer that they thought World War III had started when they heard those Yank airplanes taking off. The six RB-47Es, outfitted with the same camera suite as in the RB-45C, flew in a loose trail formation referred to as *station keeping* on a great circle route, north out of England. Past the Faroes, over open ocean, the bombers refueled from their waiting KC-97 tankers and continued northward between Jan Mayen and Bear Islands until reaching their target. When they turned their cameras on, the navigators noted in their logs that they were at eighty degrees north latitude, where the ice never melts. They were only miles from Soviet Franz Josef Land, just a few minutes' flying time east of Spitsbergen. The small crew of the lone Russian Kniferest early warning radar site on Franz Josef Land must have come to life when the American B-47s showed on their radar screen. But after momentary excitement, even alarm, and after reporting the Americans to Murmansk control, with the blips again fading off their radar screens, the Russians reverted to their monotonous existence on the Arctic ice.

The 3,500-mile flight took nearly nine hours of flying in an ejection seat not built for personal comfort, but rather for saving a pilot's life in an emergency. Austin and his crew didn't know that the feint they had just flown was a final rehearsal for a mission they were to fly two days later, on May 8. They also did not know that three RB-45C reconnaissance aircraft based at RAF Sculthorpe in Norfolk county, manned by British crews, had flown a night reconnaissance mission deep into the western Soviet Union only ten days earlier. The Russians, understandably, were more than slightly annoyed at their own inability to stop such overflights of their territory, and were quite ready should there be another attempt. Their will and ability were to be tested all too soon again. "In the early morning hours of May 8, Carl, Vance, and I had an ample breakfast at the officers' mess. We stopped by the in-flight kitchen on our way to the secure briefing area to pick up three box lunches and two thermos bottles filled with hot coffee. It was going to be just one more training mission, we thought. We intended to pick up our charts and then go out to the aircraft for preflight, have a short cigarette break, and get ready to launch. As we entered the secure area, we were met by our wing commander, Colonel Joe Preston. 'What does he want?' I thought. The colonel turned to me and said, 'Please follow me.' We followed Colonel Preston into a classified briefing room built for target study for bomber crews, providing security from sophisticated listening devices. Colonel Preston held the door for us as we entered the room, which was definitely out of the ordinary. He closed the door behind us and left. In the briefing room were two colonels from SAC headquarters in Omaha, Nebraska. The colonels had no smiles on their faces and immediately got down to business. One of them, a navigator, handed Heavilin a strip map. We looked it over and saw where our flight was to take us—over the Kola Peninsula past Murmansk, southeast to Archangel, then southwest before turning west across Finland and Sweden back to Fairford. We were stunned.

"'Please sit down, gentlemen,' said the second colonel. He wore pilot wings. Neither colonel wore a name tag on his blue class-A uniform. 'I will give you your mission brief, weather and intelligence. You will photograph nine airfields as annotated on your maps.' Later I learned that the purpose of the mission was to determine if the Soviets had deployed their new Bison bombers to any of those fields. 'You will launch in a stream of six aircraft, just as you did on the 6th. Three aircraft will fly the Spitsbergen route. You and two others will proceed to your turning point one hundred miles north of Murmansk. You, Captain Austin, are number three. The other two will turn back at that point. You will proceed on your preplanned mission. The entire mission from taxi to exit from the hostile area will be flown in complete radio silence—no tower calls, no reporting back when reaching altitude, no radio contact with the tankers, no radio calls if anyone has to abort. Radio silence is essential to the success of this mission.' Then the pilot colonel reviewed the weather at the altitudes we were supposed to fly, the camera turn-on points noted on the strip maps, and he briefed us on expected opposition. 'Only MiG-15s,' he said. 'They can't reach you at forty thousand feet. No contrails are expected to form in the areas you will be passing over.' That information was important to us if we didn't want to streak across the sky looking like a Times Square ad. 'You'll be flying through a clear air mass. The weather couldn't be better for this mission.' The briefing over, Heavilin started to annotate his chart. 'Don't do that,' directed the navigator colonel. 'Everything you need to know is on those charts.' The two SAC colonels measured their words carefully, only saying what needed saying. They answered no questions and offered no additional comments to us. On the way out, one of the colonels reemphasized the need for absolute security before and after we returned from our mission. We would not discuss any aspect of the mission outside a cleared area, we were given to understand. Nor with anyone not having a need to know. No talk about the mission, period. Colonel Preston met us as we exited the building and drove us to our aircraft. An air crew was already there, just finishing pre-flight. From the looks of it, they were none too happy to have been asked to do our job. As they slid down the ladder from the crew compartment, the pilot said to me, 'The aircraft is cocked'—a bomber term—and he, his copilot, and his navigator walked to their crew car without saying another word and drove off. We climbed into the aircraft and strapped into our seats. Every one of us was quiet, I recall, tending to our own thoughts."

Major Heavilin noted that his map had been annotated with radar offset points, such as lakes and other natural and manmade features that would show well on his radar scope. Austin was number six in line, last for takeoff. "I taxied after number five moved out. Number one lined up at the end of the runway, set his brakes, and ran up his engines. The other five aircraft sat in line on the taxiway, waiting to take their turn on the active. When number one received the green light from the tower, he released his brakes, and the aircraft slowly moved down the runway. The other RB-47Es launched at two-minute intervals, buffeted by the violent jet wash from the preceding aircraft. When I took the active, a trail of black smoke from the exhaust of the five pointed the way for me." Water alcohol was injected into the engines on take-off to gain an additional thousand pounds of thrust for each of the six-engines, which only generated six thousand pounds of static thrust on their own. The exhaust from a B-47 on takeoff closely resembled the black smoke of a coal-fired locomotive. With a full fuel load on a hot day, a B-47 bomber needed all the help it could get getting off the ground and could use up nearly all of the ten thousand feet of runway which was the standard runway length at most Strategic Air Command bases in the United States and overseas. Takeoff data computations were in front of Austin and Holt, strapped to their thighs. They were a team, no longer individuals. Prompts and responses were automatic. The copilot, Holt, called out the checklist. "Throttles."

"Open. All instruments checked," Austin responded. Austin slowly moved the six throttles to 100 percent. Oil pressure was within operating limits, he noted, glancing down the row of gauges on his instrument panel. Fuel flow was stabilized. He checked the EGT for all six engines at 100 percent. The EGTs were within limits. "Steering ratio selector lever," Holt continued.

"Takeoff and land," Austin responded. "Start, six lights out." Austin released the brakes of the shuddering aircraft, which began its slow roll down the concrete runway. Carl Holt quickly turned left and right and checked the engines. He saw black smoke coming from all six and reported to Austin. "Engines and wings checked." They continued their takeoff roll. When the aircraft reached seventy knots, Holt called out, "Seventy knots now." Heavilin responded, "Hack." Fourteen seconds later, their acceleration good, Heavilin called out, "S-One, now." Decision speed—their last chance to ground abort. Austin's eyes were on his EGT gauges, compass, and airspeed indicator. Temperatures looked good. Speed looked good. They continued their takeoff roll. He held the aircraft down. It wanted to climb because of ground effect before it had sufficient airspeed to sustain flight—a novice trap that had cost lives. Austin could feel the plane grasping for its element. At the 7,500-foot marker, the 180,000-pound aircraft strained to rise, and Austin let it go. "Unstick," he called out. The nose rose slightly, and the aircraft began its long climb heavenward. Climb speed was looking good, Austin noted mentally. "Landing gear," Austin called, and Holt placed the gear lever in the up position. They were at 185 knots indicated airspeed and gaining. "Flaps." Holt put the flap lever in the up position and kept his hand on it, simultaneously watching the airspeed. They were at 210 knots at 20 percent flaps, and he continued flap retraction. The aircraft's nose started to pitch down, but Hal had already cranked in nose-up trim and smoothed out the predictable perturbation.

"Climb speed," Holt called. "Climb power set." Hal set it to 375 knots indicated. They continued with their checklist as they climbed straight ahead to thirty-four thousand feet. Their mission didn't officially exist. They had filed no flight plan, which was nothing new to understanding British air traffic controllers. Holt continued to check that the HF radio was on, the APS-54 radar warning receiver was set to the nose/tail position, the chaff dispensers were on, and the IFF was on standby. He called, "Altimeters."

"Set, pilot."

"Set, nav." They reset their altimeters to 29.92 inches of mercury. When they passed over open water, Holt tested his guns. They fired. "I guess it's a go," Holt said over the intercom. Hal clicked his mike button twice on the control column in response. A little more than one hour into their flight, the navigator picked up the tankers on his radar at the briefed air-refueling orbit and gave Hal a heading and altitude. The tanker pilot saw Hal approaching from above and departed the orbit for his refueling track. At the two-mile point Hal pulled back on the throttles to decrease his rate of closure. They were five hundred feet below the tanker and slowly eased in behind the KC-97 Stratocruiser, its four engines churning at maximum power in a slight descent. Hal looked up at the tanker looming ahead and above and moved into the observation position. He watched for light direction from the boom operator—two amber, one green, two red lights on the belly of the large KC-97. He saw the forward amber light come on, urging him to move in closer. He moved in slowly. The green light illuminated, and he held in the contact position. He could see the boom operator in the tanker flying his boom toward the open refueling receptacle on the nose of the RB-47, right in front of Hal's face. The aircraft pitched in the wake of the turbulence generated by the KC-97.

"Contact," Hal muttered into his oxygen mask. Normally, he would have said it out in the open. Not this day. The green light illuminated on the air refueling panel, and Austin and Holt knew they had a good contact. The tanker transferred fuel into the empty tanks of the receiver at the rate of four thousand pounds per minute until all of the RB-47's internal fuel tanks were full, causing an automatic pressure disconnect. Hal dropped away from the tanker, saluted the boom operator, and initiated a climb to thirty-four thousand feet to rejoin his two companion aircraft. Three lone RB-47s, high above the cold Atlantic waters. Soon someone would pick them up on radar. Time passed slowly. The aircraft was on autopilot. Not much for any of them to do but listen to the static on the HF radio for a possible recall. No recall came. The three aircraft turned east toward the Barents Sea. Hal, Carl, and Vance got out their box lunches and ate their ham and turkey sandwiches and hard-boiled eggs, drank their cold milk, and put their apples aside to be eaten later, if there was time. They had coffee. They were at forty thousand feet. "How much further to the turn?" Austin asked his navigator.

"Oh, four minutes and thirty seconds, I'd say," Vance replied. They put on their oxygen masks, tight. The cabin pressure was at fourteen thousand feet. Should they get hit and lose pressurization, anything loose would be flying into their faces, so they made sure everything was tied down, buttoned, zipped, or out of the way. "On my command, turn to a heading of one-eight-zero." Hal clicked his mike button in response to the navigator's direction. "Turn now," the navigator called out to Hal. The big aircraft turned surprisingly easily toward the Kola Peninsula, the Soviet Union—bad guy country. The other two RB-47s preceding them made their 180-degree turns to the left, away from the land, and headed home. "We coasted in over the Kola Peninsula at forty thousand feet at twelve o'clock Greenwich mean time," said Hal Austin, looking at the floor. His voice was terse, his facial muscles tight. "We were about four thousand feet above our optimum altitude for our weight. Our first targets were two large airfields near Murmansk. The navigator turned on his radar cameras at the coast-in point and started the three K-17 large-area visual cameras in the bomb bay. The weather was clear as a bell. You could see forever. Perfect picture-taking weather." Carl Holt also remembered that moment well. He looked back from his position behind the pilot, and what he saw did not make his heart jump for joy. "It was a clear day as we coasted into the Soviet Union. Suddenly we started to generate contrails like six white arrows pointing to our airplane. As we passed over our first target, I could see the fighters circling up to meet us, and I knew it would only be a matter of time before they reached our altitude."

"About the time we finished photographing the second airfield near Murmansk," Hal Austin continued, "we were joined by a flight of three Soviet MiG-15s. I don't know whether or not they were armed. I don't believe they were. They kept their distance and stayed about half a mile off our wing. About twenty-five minutes later, another flight of six Migs showed up. These too were MiG-15s, appeared to be unarmed, and kept their distance. I guess they confirmed we were the bad guys. A few minutes after their arrival, another two flights of three each arrived behind us with obvious intent to try to shoot us down. By this time we had photographed five of our assigned target airfields and were turning southwest near Archangel toward our last four targets. We had been over Soviet territory for an hour. We had been briefed that the MiG-15 would not be able to do any damage to us at forty thousand feet with our airspeed at 440 knots. Well, you can imagine what we called those Intelligence weenies as the first Soviet MiG-17, not a MiG-15, made a firing pass at us from the left rear and we saw cannon tracer shells going above and below our aircraft. And the MiG was still moving out rather smartly as he passed under us in front. 'Enough of this forty thousand feet stuff,' I thought. I pushed the RB-47 over, descending a couple thousand feet and picking up about twenty knots indicated airspeed in the process."

Carl Holt remembered, "When I saw the flashes of fire from the nose of the fighters, I knew it would not be a milk run. I had trouble getting the tail guns to fire, and since I was in a reverse seat position, I could not eject in case of a direct hit. Also, the radar firing screen would not work [because the Migs stayed outside the RB-47's radar envelope], so I felt a little like Wyatt Earp, looking out the back end of the canopy and firing at will. I did not hit any of the fighters, but it kept them out of a direct rear firing pass. They could only make passes from either side at a greater than forty-five-degree angle to stay outside the area covered by our guns."

"The second MiG-17," Hal Austin said, "made his firing pass, and I don't care who knows, it was scary watching tracers go over and under our aircraft. This guy had almost come up our tailpipes. Carl Holt turned around to operate our tail guns after the first MiG shot at us. It was typical for the two remotely controlled 20mm cannons not to fire. I told Holt he'd better kick them or something, because if our guns didn't fire, the next SOB would come directly up our tailpipes. Fortunately, when the third MiG started its pass, our guns burped for a couple of seconds. General LeMay did not believe in tracers for our guns, but the Soviet pilots must have seen something, because the third guy broke off his firing pass. The next flight of six MiG-17s which joined us later stayed about thirty to forty degrees to the side, outside the effective envelope of our guns. Of course, the MiGs didn't know that our guns wouldn't fire again.

"The fourth MiG of the second group of MiG-17s finally made a lucky hit as I was in a turn, through the top of our left wing, about eight feet from the fuselage, through the retracted wing flap. The shell exploded into the fuselage in the area of the forward main fuel tank, right behind our crew compartment, knocking out our intercom. We felt a good *whap* as the shell exploded, and all three of us were a little bit anxious—scared is a better word—but we continued to do our mission as briefed, basically because of habit. I firmly believe that's what good, tough, LeMay-type SAC training did for his combat crews. Later we also discovered the shell had hit our UHF radio. It would no longer channelize, meaning it was stuck on channel 13, our command-post frequency, which we had on the set at the time."

"After we were hit in the left wing and fuselage," recalled Carl Holt, "one MiG tried to ram us by sideslipping his fighter into our aircraft. On one ramming pass, he stalled out right under our aircraft, and our vertical camera took one of the first close-up pictures of the new MiG-17."

"By then we had covered our last photo target," Austin continued, "and turned due west toward Finland to get the hell out of there. The six Migs which dogged us since Archangel must have run short of fuel. They left. Six others appeared to take their place, two of whom initiated firing passes but didn't hit anything. After those two made their unsuccessful passes, the third came up on our right side, close enough to shake hands, and sat there for two or three minutes. As we departed the area south of Helsinki, Finland, he gave us a salute and then turned back toward the Soviet Union. We proceeded to cross neutral Sweden, then Norway. Over the North Sea we headed south-southwest looking for our tanker. Our excitement for this mission was not over by any means. An airborne standby KC-97 tanker was holding for us about fifty miles from Stavanger, Norway. We really weren't sure how the damage to our left wing and fuselage would affect fuel consumption. Initially, it didn't look bad. As we came into UHF radio range of the tanker, I heard him calling in the blind on command-post common, the only frequency we had available to us on our radio. He came in garbled. His transmission was breaking up. We were running about thirty minutes behind schedule. I heard the tanker pilot say that he was leaving his orbit at the scheduled time. I tried frantically to acknowledge his call, but when I later spoke to the tanker pilot he said he never heard me. Of course they had not been briefed about our mission, but they were aware that six RB-47s went through refueling areas that morning and that only five had returned. Usually they were smart enough to figure out the situation. Not this time.

"As we coasted out of Norway, it was obvious we had fallen behind the fuel curve. I climbed to forty thousand feet and throttled back to maximum-range cruise. I thought we could get back to a base in England, not necessarily Fairford. We knew there was a tanker on strip alert at Mildenhall awaiting our call. Carl Holt had spent much of the time since the last Migs departed sitting in the aisle below me, acting as the intercom between me and the navigator. You don't realize how handy the intercom is until you don't have one. Holt was monitoring our fuel consumption and beginning to panic as we reached a point about 150 miles from the Wash. [The Wash is a shallow area of the North Sea off East Anglia.] Carl wasn't afraid for himself. He was worried about losing our film. He said to me, 'All this effort was for nothing if we have to bail out of the airplane and have no film for Intelligence to process.' He was right. At one hundred miles off the Wash, I started calling for the strip tanker from Mildenhall to launch. Jim Rigley, the tanker pilot, later said to me, 'I heard a word or two of your transmission, enough to recognize your voice.' He was one of our tanker guys from Lockbourne. We all knew each other. He attempted to get permission to launch. The tower wouldn't give permission because the RAF had an emergency of some sort working at nearby RAF Brize Norton. Rigley announced that he was launching. And he did. When he returned to base, the local American commander, a colonel, threatened him with a court-martial and British air-traffic control gave him a violation. Both situations were later fixed by General LeMay.

"In all my nine years of flying up to that time, I was never more thrilled to see another airplane in the air than I was to see that beautiful KC-97 tanker. As soon as I saw Rigley's airplane, I headed straight for him. We, as a crew, already decided to try to land at Brize Norton and were in the process of letting down when I spotted Rigley. At the same time, Holt looked at our gas gauges from the aisle below me and yelled, 'We're going to run out of gas.' The gauges were ana-log gauges and usually moved a little if there was still fuel remaining in a tank. None of the gauges moved and Holt was sure we were about to flame out. In the meantime, Rigley had his crew looking upward, searching for a glimpse of us.

They caught a glint of what they thought was our airplane rapidly descending toward them. Rigley leveled off at three thousand feet, heading south, toward land. He was positioned perfectly to allow me to use an old RB-45 refueling maneuver. Since we had no way to slow that aircraft down, other than pulling back on the throttles, we came up from behind the tanker, flew below him, and then got on his tail in a climbing turn. This bled off the airspeed in the RB-45. The old maneuver worked perfectly. When I pulled up behind the lumbering KC-97, its engines were giving all they could to keep us from stalling. The boomer skillfully flew his boom into our refueling receptacle. 'Contact,' Holt called out to me, 'we are taking on fuel. All gauges show empty.'

"Tell me when we have twelve thousand pounds, Carl. 'Now,' Holt called out at the top of his lungs, still sitting below me in the aisle. I punched the boom loose, gave the boom operator a salute, and headed for Fairford. I got down to five hundred feet and buzzed the control tower. They gave us a green light to land. When we reached the ramp and brought the aircraft to a stop, the crew chief was the first up the ladder. He saw the damage we sustained. 'What kind of seagull did you hit, sir?' he shouted at me. I smiled back at him. I couldn't give him a straight answer. Colonel Preston met us at the aircraft. We jumped into his staff car, and he took us to our quarters, where we took a quick shower and changed into class-A blues. Then he drove us to London and we met with the US ambassador to Great Britain at his home. The ambassador greeted us cordially and offered us a drink. Then he whispered, 'Let's go outside. I think my house is bugged.' The next morning my crew flew back to Lockbourne. I took another guy's airplane to get back since mine obviously needed repairs. We arrived at Lockbourne in the afternoon, and the following morning we took a B-25 base flight aircraft and flew to Offutt Air Force Base, headquarters SAC, at Omaha, Nebraska. The commander of SAC, General Curtis E. LeMay, attended our mission debriefing. We met in a room in the old Douglas aircraft plant because the new SAC headquarters was still under construction. It was a three-hour meeting. The first question the general asked was, 'How come they didn't shoot you down?'

"'I guess they didn't have the guts,' was my answer to him. There was no doubt in my mind that the MiG-17 pilots could have shot us down if they had been willing to come right up our tail pipes. General LeMay responded, 'There are probably several openings today in command positions there, since you were not shot down.'" Carl Holt also reflected on that occasion. "Having flown combat in World War II and later been recalled during the Korean War, I thought we were in a Cold War with Russia, not a hot one, since all the reconnaissance plane shoot downs had been kept secret. During our debriefing with General LeMay, I said to him innocently, 'Sir, they were trying to

Harold Austin with his girl-friend, Rosemary, soon to be his wife, at Rhein-Main Air Base, Germany, in 1949 toward the end of the Berlin airlift. Twice he smuggled Rosemary onto one of his C-54s and took her to Berlin and back.

shoot us down!' Smoking his usual long cigar, the general paused, leaned back in his chair, and said, 'What did you think they would do? Give you an ice cream cone?' His aides smiled. I was serious. I didn't smile."

Three months after the debriefing of crew S-51 (the "S" standing for select crew) at Offutt, General LeMay visited Lockbourne, where he was met by the wing commander. After the usual saluting back and forth, the general came right to the point of his visit. He wanted to meet with Captain Austin, Captain Holt, and Major Heavilin. When they arrived, he asked the wing commander to leave. General LeMay decorated each member of crew S-51 with two Distinguished Flying Crosses, in lieu of the Silver Star, for their reconnaissance flight over the Soviet Union. According to Austin, the general apologized, saying, "The award of the Silver Star has to be approved in Washington, which could cause two problems: first, they'd get the thing screwed up, and, second, I'd have to explain this mission to too damn many people who don't need to know." Hal asked if they could see their photography. The answer was "No." But to the question "How did we do?" the general answered, "You got all targets."

Colonel Austin's epic May 8, 1954, overflight of the Kola Peninsula accomplished at least two things. First and foremost, it assured the American military

The B/RB-45 was America's first jet bomber. The C-model, shown here, was the reconnaissance version and carried a sophisticated suite of cameras for day and night photography. First assigned to SAC, the aircraft were passed to USAFE once the RB-47E entered the SAC inventory.

Austin transitioned into the RB-47E photo reconnaissance aircraft based at Lockbourne AFB, Columbus, Ohio, shown here refueling from a KC-97 Stratocruiser. It was the fleet of refueling tankers, KC-97s, later jet-powered KC-135s, that gave B-47 and B-52 bombers their global reach.

and political leadership that the Soviet Union had not massed its new jet bombers at potential staging bases on the Kola Peninsula. The second, although unintended, result was to again point out reconnaissance aircraft's vulnerability to shoot down. The RB-47 could not fly high enough to escape the MiG-17's cannon fire, and even more capable Soviet aircraft would soon follow. Alternative solutions had to be found. The higher-flying U-2 reconnaissance plane was an interim solution itself, and by 1960, technology caught up with it too, when

SAMs (surface to air missiles) demonstrated that they could reach its sixty-thousand-plus-foot operating altitude. Earth orbiting satellites, as well as the remarkable high-altitude Mach 3 SR-71, eventually provided the necessary solutions. But in 1954 it took the courage of men such as Hal Austin, Carl Holt, and Vance Heavilin to fly over the Soviet Union to provide the United States the critical information needed to defend itself.

JOSEPH J. GYULAVICS

B-29/RB-47H

Destiny's Children

It's a call to arms for every man, no matter what his creed,
And it's his to answer, his to prove, the call is his to heed.
We've a job to do, a road to climb, before the trip back home.
We've a story too, to tell the world when we get back from "Rome."
—Sergeant William F. Messner, WWII MTO

"My father immigrated from a small village in Hungary, Taliandorogd, in 1912," Joe Gyulavics recalled. "He came alone to the United States to get rich. His plan was to eventually return to Hungary, buy a farm with the money he made in America, and live comfortably ever after. After years of working in coal mines in Pennsylvania, he saved enough money to buy a farm, but it was outside Buffalo, New York, not in Hungary. He sent for my mother and older brother. For several years my parents tried desperately to make the farm pay, but eventually they lost it. My father then went to work in a steel mill in Buffalo, which had a close-knit Hungarian community nearby. I was born in 1925. Everything in my life was Hungarian, including the language I spoke, until we moved to a house across from a public school and I got to play with other kids. By the time I was in the first grade, I could speak English well.

"I always wanted to fly. As a little boy, when I heard the roar of airplanes, I ran outside to watch them fly over our house. I built models out of balsa wood but could never afford to buy paint for them. There was a little airport about five miles out of town. I peddled out there on my bicycle to watch the small Taylor Cubs land and take off. I went around the back side of the field, near the runway, and hid in the tall grass so I could see the planes close up. Once one

186

Sergeant Joseph Gyulavics by accident became the lead navigator of his B-29 bomber squadron when they deployed in 1948 from Rapid City, South Dakota, to RAF Scampton, England, in support of the Berlin airlift. MSGT Gyulavic's crew is shown getting ready to leave Rapid City for Europe.

pilot saw me hiding in the grass and taxied over and chewed me out. Eventually I got a ride in an open-cockpit plane. It was a dream come true. My older brother paid the pilot three or four dollars to take me up, which was a lot of money at the time. In 1941, at age sixteen, I wanted to join the army and fly. Many of my older classmates were joining the services and going to war, but I was still too young. I went to Syracuse University for a year, but I had little money, and it was a constant struggle. As soon as I turned seventeen, I tried to join the navy. They flunked me on my physical. They said I had a heart murmur. 'I'm a healthy kid,' I thought. 'I don't have a heart murmur.' I went home and my family's doctor examined me. He found no heart murmur. I asked him to put it in writing. I intended to go back to the navy examiner with the letter in hand, but then I got a job as a draftsman at the Curtis-Wright Aircraft Company, where they built P-40s and C-46s, and I was making good money. So I waited until I turned eighteen and then tried to join the Army Air Forces before the draft board got to me. The army also flunked me on my physical, but this time it was a deviated septum. 'You can't fly with that obstruction in your nose,' the doctor said to me, 'but you can be a ground crewman.' 'What do I have to do to fly?' I asked the doctor. 'Get an operation,' he replied.

"I found a doctor who operated on my nose. He took out a couple of bones, and I paid him twenty-five dollars. The Army Air Forces accepted me in the aviation cadet program. I spent the next two years from 1943 to 1945 being bounced around as a buck private waiting for a flying-school slot to open up. None ever did. For those two years I served as assistant crew chief on a P-40 at Aloe Field, Texas; as a butcher in a mess hall in Smyrna, Tennessee; drove a fuel truck on the flight line in Stuttgart, Arkansas; and did every odd job you can think of. When the war ended, I was sitting there as a buck private and hadn't done one damn thing. 'If you want out, you can get out,' I was told. 'No,' I said, 'I haven't achieved anything yet.'

"'If you want to stay, you can go to navigator school at Ellington Field, near Houston,' the army personnel people told me. So I went to navigator school. Talk about being snake bit. On graduation from Ellington my entire class went up on the stage in the base theater and received their commissions as second lieutenants—everyone except me. Personnel lost my physical somewhere, misspelled my name on the records, and now couldn't find them. I graduated as a navigator but not as a lieutenant. My classmates went overseas while I sat at Ellington waiting for the paperwork to come through. Ten days later I got my commission, went home, and got married. I was sent to Las Vegas Army Air Field as a celestial navigation instructor. We had a nice honeymoon in the early days of Vegas. In November 1946 I was discharged. They gave me three hundred dollars mustering-out pay, and I was on my own. When I finally got back to Buffalo, it was too late to get into school. My wife was due with our first child in a few months, and I didn't have a job. Things looked bleak. I went to see the army recruiter and he told me I could enlist as a master sergeant for eighteen months, but I couldn't choose my branch of service. They put me in the signal corps, sent me to New Rochelle, New York, and put me in charge of a platoon of telephone-pole climbers. I knew nothing about the telephone business, but I was the senior NCO in charge. I wrote a letter to the adjutant general of the Army Air Forces and asked him, 'What am I doing here? I am a qualified navigator, and I should be in the air force.'

"Lo and behold, I soon got orders to go to Rapid City Army Airfield in South Dakota as a celestial navigation instructor. When I got there, they were still sweeping the wheat out of the hangars the farmers had used for storage while the base was closed. The base was being reopened for a B-29 bomber outfit coming in from Alaska. As soon as the planes hit the ramp, most of the crews said, 'We've had enough. We want out.' They got out, and the 28th Bombardment Group didn't have enough crews to fly its airplanes. I saw an opportunity and approached my squadron operations officer. 'Hey, I'm available,' I said to him. 'I'm a navigator. I know you're short. I'll be happy to fly.' 'But you're a master sergeant,' he said. His facial expression told me to get lost and leave him alone. I didn't. 'I can fly,' I said to him firmly. 'I was commissioned a second lieutenant. I have my navigator wings.' I showed him my orders. After taking a look at my orders, he said, 'OK, you're back on flying status, but only for one month at a time.' I said reluctantly, 'I've never flown in a B-29 before.' He looked at me, exasperation showing in his eyes. Then he turned to a navigator sitting at a desk nearby and said, 'Lieutenant Curtis, go and check the master sergeant out.'

"'Come along,' Lieutenant Curtis said to me in a friendly voice. We went to a B-29 parked out on the ramp and climbed in. 'This is where you sit,' he said. 'This is the airspeed indicator,' and he pointed to it, 'and this is the altimeter. There is the compass. The drift meter is over here.' That was it. A week later I was heading across the Atlantic for Germany, navigating a B-29 of the 28th Bombardment Group. I was a last-minute replacement for a crew which didn't have a navigator. On the way out to the airplane the operations officer told me, 'Oh, by the way, on your way down to MacDill, air swing the fluxgate compass.' Air swing the fluxgate compass? My God! How do I do that? I looked into my old aviation cadet textbook, which I carried with me in my navigator bag. Sure enough, there was a chapter on how to swing a fluxgate compass. It was supposed to be done on the ground on a surveyed compass rose, but we didn't have time to do that. Prior to takeoff, one of the other navigators suggested to me, 'Why don't you fly over Tallahassee. There's a good radio beacon there. Have the pilot take up a cardinal heading into the beacon while you take a sun shot with your astro compass, compare them, and then interpolate. You can work it out.'

"I said, 'Yeah, yeah,' like I knew what he was talking about. I was stunned. The rest of the squadron landed at MacDill while I had my pilot flying headings into Tallahassee radio. Even over the roar of the engines I heard the pilot, Lieutenant Gale Cummings, yell to the copilot, 'Go see what that navigator is doing back there. He's only a master sergeant. I don't even know him. I have never seen him before.' I didn't know any of them either. We landed about six o'clock that evening. Everybody went to the chow hall and ate and then went to the transient barracks for crew rest. I hadn't finished compensating the compass yet, and I was afraid to admit that to anybody. That night I went out to the airplane. I had a hard time finding it in the dark, parked on a strange airfield on a remote hard stand. When I finally found the plane, I climbed in. Of course, there was no power. I used my flashlight. It was a lot hotter in Florida than in South Dakota, and I was sweating, tired, and starting to panic. I was in my winter flying suit. I got out my old cadet manual and followed the instructions. It's a bezel ring you adjust on the fluxgate compass. I didn't have a screwdriver to make the adjustments, so I used my pocketknife. I was not too confident that the adjustments I made were correct. We took off the next afternoon for Germany via the Azores.

"I got a few drift readings over the Atlantic before it got dark. I tried a celestial fix with the old A-10 sextant. I centered the bubble on a star, made little marks on the ring covered with wax paper, and then averaged out the pencil marks I had made. Supposedly that was the altitude of the star. After shooting three stars I went into the books and calculated a line of position for each of the stars, which I then plotted on my chart. Of course, my fix was where we had been when I started the procedure an hour earlier. Come dawn the next morning, we flew in a broken overcast and undercast. No drift readings were possible. No way to shoot the sun. I was flying dead reckoning most of the time. The pilot turned around in the cockpit and yelled back at me, 'Hey, when are we supposed to hit the Azores?' Straight ahead, forty-five minutes, I yelled back at him, with as much confidence as I could muster. Pretty soon the pilot yelled, 'Hey, pretty good, pretty good, nav!' I crawled into the nose of the aircraft and there, sticking through the undercast, silhouetted against the rising sun, was Pico Alto. We were heading right for it. From then on I could do no wrong. I almost got lost going from the Azores to the coast of France. I was about fifty miles off. It didn't matter to the crew—I was golden.

"In October 1947 we finally found our way into Giebelstadt, Germany. There hadn't been much recovery. The hangars were still bombed out. The runway was in good shape, though. They had a GCA radar at Giebelstadt, but they were still practicing. We had a few hairy GCA-controlled approaches in bad weather, which I would just as soon forget. Both pilots and GCA operators needed much more practice. When we had good weather, which wasn't often, the squadron flew in formation, nine or ten aircraft, over the capitals of Europe as a show of force. It was an education for me to see places I had only read about. We flew low, at about three thousand to four thousand feet. My crew was selected to fly to Dhahran, Saudi Arabia, to demonstrate the reach of the B-29. Flying over the Arabian Desert was much like flying over the Atlantic: no landmarks, no navigational aids, nothing. We got back to Rapid City in December 1947. I was assigned to my own crew, piloted by Lieutenant J. R. Wright. Our B-29s had the letter R in a black circle painted on their tails—the same letter that was painted on the tail of the *Enola Gay* in 1945, although she didn't belong to the 28th Bomb Group. We had three squadrons in the group—the 77th, 717th, and the 718th. In the months after returning from Giebelstadt, I checked myself out on the APQ-7 radar, which was installed in our B-29s. The radar had a sixty-degree sector scan over a range of two hundred miles. I also checked myself out on the Norden bombsight. We didn't have a bombardier on the crew.

"The air force became a separate service in September of 1947, and with that the Rapid City Army Airfield became the Rapid City Air Force Base. We also changed our unit designation from 28th Bombardment Group to 28th Bombardment Wing. Names changed, but little else. We still didn't have a bombardier on the crew. One Sunday afternoon in July 1948 I got a call to report to squadron operations immediately. When I got there, everybody was filling out papers. 'We're going on TDY,' I was told. 'Go home and pack a bag for a couple of weeks and come back and you'll get briefed.' When I did, however, things didn't seem right. People were filling out powers of attorney and last wills and testaments. I packed, and when I got back to the squadron, we were briefed that we were going to Goose Bay, Labrador, and then on to an undisclosed location. The navigators got together to discuss the route. Master Sergeant Nestor Velasco and I were the only enlisted navigators—the rest were lieutenants or captains. Naturally we two didn't have much to say about the route. Takeoff was scheduled for the following day.

"The base was a flurry of activity. Engineers were running up aircraft engines, trucks full of equipment were crisscrossing the ramp. When I got to my airplane, I saw the maintenance men loading ammo in the gun turrets and filling extra ammo cans. What impressed me most was a bomb-bay kit that had been uploaded. I had never seen it before. I asked our crew chief, Master Sergeant Joe Pellerin, 'What is that stuff?' 'Flak suits,' he said, grinning knowingly. Flak suits! Well, I said goodbye to my wife and young daughter, and off we went to Goose Bay—all three squadrons, ten aircraft each. At Goose Bay, after crew rest, they briefed us that the wing was going to RAF Scampton in England. Evidently, the Russians were blockading Berlin, and we were going over in case something happened. The thing that amazed me most as a navigator was that the air force didn't have any charts for us. We were given WAC charts (world aeronautical charts) of England, nearly useless for our purposes. The whole of England was on one of these charts. The briefers gave us the coordinates of RAF Scampton, near the little town of Lincoln. There was a small circle on the chart which was the base. But there were circles all over England. The place was covered with airfields. We were advised that the best way to find the base was to fly up the River Thames until we could see the big cathedral on the hill in the center of town, then turn north for five miles, and that was RAF Scampton.

"We took off at night, flying at four thousand feet. Clouds below us, clouds above us. No stars, no drift readings possible. Nothing. We were number five. The wing commander, Colonel John B. Henry, flying ship number 6-308, was first. He was flying with the top navigator in the wing, a captain. We were flying in a bomber stream. I did a lot of dead reckoning on the way over, and a lot of praying. After several hours I cranked up the APQ-7 sector scan radar with its two-hundred-mile extended range and good land-water contrast. At about our estimated time of arrival for landfall, I picked up land. The land-water contrast was so stark I thought there were high mountains ahead of us. 'Oh my God,' was my next thought—we were heading into Norway, because I didn't know of any sizeable mountains in England. As we got closer, I realized it was just land-water contrast, not mountains. I breathed a deep sigh of relief. I tried to pick out the coastline, but with my little WAC chart, everything looked the same. There was nothing I could identify to help me determine precisely where we were. The pilots kept saying, 'Where in the hell are we, Joe?' I put them off and put them off until we came across what I thought was a distinctive bay and river just south of Scotland. 'I must have drifted north,' I thought. Authoritatively I said to the pilot, 'Turn south.' He turned south. I recognized the Wash on the radar, a prominent inlet off the coast of Norfolk, and I knew London had to be straight ahead. I picked up London. On the radar, London was a huge return. When we got to London, I told the pilot to start letting down. No clearance, no nothing. We flew at whatever altitude and wherever we wanted. We were down to about five hundred feet when we spotted a river running in the right direction and began following it. The pilot tried calling the control tower at Scampton but got no response. Sure enough, up ahead there was the cathedral. OK, turn north five miles, I told Lieutenant Wright when we got over the cathedral. 'OK,' he said, 'we're heading north. Now, which one of these fields is Scampton?'

"I looked out the nose of the aircraft, and there was one airfield after another. Well, it had to be the airfield with the B-29s on it, I told R. J. We were number five for takeoff. There should be four B-29s lined up on one of those fields. We flew all over and saw no B-29s on any of those airfields. The briefers at Goose had told us there was a signal square in front of the control tower at Scampton, a square with painted white rocks in it which spelled out the letters SA. The other fields had other letters to identify them. From our altitude we couldn't make out anything. R. J. Wright finally made contact with Scampton tower and told them we couldn't locate the field. The tower operator replied, 'You just flew over us.'

"'But there are no B-29s on the ground,' R. J. said.

"'No, no one else has arrived yet.'

"'Well, we'll wait,' R. J. replied. We circled and circled. Finally, the control tower called, 'There are important people here waiting for you. You better land.' R. J. Wright was a first lieutenant and strictly military. He wanted to do the right thing, and doing things right meant that the wing commander should be the first one to land. But he had little choice in the matter and prepared to land. He tried to make a perfect landing for the occasion; instead he slammed our bomber into the runway. He inadvertently depressed the mike button on the steering column when we hit the runway and said out loud, 'Oh shit,' a comment which was monitored by not only the tower but also the waiting guests. The tower operator made a curt remark about us using proper English while in the United Kingdom. We taxied in. There was the BBC, a big welcoming crowd, the chief air marshal of the Royal Air Force, all the big wheels had assembled for the occasion—the arrival of the first American B-29 bomber in England. Nobody else was there yet. R. J. Wright got out first. I finally got out, sweaty and dirty. I stayed out of the way while the pilot, the copilot, and the bombardier, the only three officers on the crew, gave their interviews. R. J. was making a recording for the BBC. It was broadcast every thirty minutes, I believe, on the BBC for the rest of the day, announcing, 'The Yanks are back!'

"It must have been an hour later when the next airplane came in. The wing commander, Colonel Henry, led by the wing navigator, had ended up several hundred miles too far north. Nobody mentioned anything about it. But R. J. was peeved at me because he was put in an embarrassing position by our early arrival. When Colonel Henry landed, the show was over. The brass had departed. Colonel Henry was met by the British base commander and a few low-ranking types. R. J. got all the publicity.

"No one had made provisions for our arrival, and the RAF was a bit over-whelmed by such a large group of personnel and aircraft. As a senior non-commissioned officer, NCO, I was quartered in the RAF NCO mess which had little rooms on the second floor. We crowded four of us on double bunk beds in each room. We were more fortunate than the other enlisted men who slept in dormitories or Quonset huts left over from World War II. We ate in a common mess hall and the English fare was not too great by our standards. For instance, stewed tomatoes for breakfast and meat pie for dinner. Virtually the same menu every day. There was no such thing as a base exchange or commissary on Scampton. The RAF did the best they could, but the men constantly bitched about the food. After several weeks a C-54 arrived from the States loaded with rations for us. There was fresh beef, chicken, butter, and eggs. That was great, but what really made me feel bad was that they split the mess hall down the middle and separated us from the RAF. We had our food prepared and ate on one side, while the RAF kept their standard fare. It was an awkward situation.

"Because of the sudden departure of the crews from our home base, there were a lot of problems cropping up. Wives and children had been left in Rapid City without provisions for their welfare. There was no time to make out allot-ments and now at home the bills were coming due for rent, and cash for food was running out. The morale of our troops was suffering. The problem became serious enough that one day we were all called together in a hangar and who should arrive by plane but the senator from South Dakota, the Honorable Chan Guerney, accompanied by the 15th Air Force commander Major General Leon Johnson. They gave us a pep talk and promised every effort would be made to solve our problems. They really did help. When they got back to the States, the word was put out on the base for all the wives to meet. Partial payments were made on the spot, and groups were formed in town for the wives to help each other. Then a C-54 arrived at the base for the wives to send anything they wanted to their husbands. Most of the men needed clothes. It was getting cold in England and no one had brought any winter clothing. My wife sent me a few things, but mostly cans of tuna, chicken, and candy bars.

"We flew formation missions out of England and across France and Germany, something we had never done at Rapid City. We also flew the Berlin corridors. I had never flown in such a controlled situation before. In the States we used to fly wherever we wanted, but here we had to file a flight plan and stay within the narrow corridors. It was something new to us. There were radio beacons, but we were warned that the Russians could distort and bend the beams. As a navigator I had to put all of my skills to use flying in the European environment. Our mission was to show our presence to the Russians. I remember we would fly as individual ships and enter the southern corridor to Berlin and fly out the northern. I flew two or three of those missions. We flew above the cargo planes who never knew we were there. We had a pressurized cabin and could fly higher than the heavily loaded C-54 transports. Only one time did we encounter Russian fighters. Two Yak 9s came alongside us one day and looked us over. Our gunners activated their gun turrets and swung them around. The Yaks just sat there for a few minutes and then peeled off. That was our only excitement.

"Something else scared us more than the Russian Yaks could have. We heard that someone had made the proposal, or it had actually been done, I'm not sure which, to use B-29s to deliver coal to Berlin. Just the thought of loading bags of coal in the bomb bays about drove the maintenance guys out of their minds. They had heard that in the cargo planes the fine coal dust had gotten into everything and was a mess. The rumor had it that because we couldn't land on the short runways available, we would jettison the coal bags into the Berlin Olympic Stadium. I heard the bombardiers talking about how they would use their bombsights, and worrying about the trajectory of a bag of coal. People actually came around and looked at our aircraft to see how the bomb bays could be loaded. Fortunately it never came to that.

"The morale of the enlisted men in the wing remained shaky. We had an operations clerk in our squadron named Joe Rupe. Rupe was a former B-17 pilot and flew in WW II. One night my crew chief, Joe Pellerin, a couple of flight engineers, and Joe Rupe were in the NCO club drinking beer when I accidentally walked in with my hat on. Well, you don't do that in a British mess, so they rang the bell on me. I had to buy beer for everyone. I was furious with myself that I had to spend what little money I had on beer. The four of them asked me to sit with them, they had a proposition. 'You are the only navigator we can trust,' their spokesman said. 'We want to take a B-29 and go home.'

"'Are you kidding?' I said.

"'No, we're not kidding. We are dead serious' was the response. They were not smiling. 'The crew chiefs got a plane all fueled up and ready to roll. Old Joe Rupe here is going to fly it and we need you to navigate us home.' I was stunned by their proposal. 'You guys have been drinking too much,' I said. 'You don't realize what you're saying.' They still insisted the plan would work if I would join them. But as the evening wore on and the beer and fatigue took hold, they changed their minds. Their attitude was understandable. These men and their families were not prepared for an extended TDY. You could feel the hardship. They were probably getting letters from home saying that their families were hurting. They would resort to almost anything to go home. A few weeks later we had more high-level visitors to Scampton. The secretary of the air force, Stuart Symington, accompanied by General Hoyt S. Vandenberg, came to talk to us. I was really impressed by this young, handsome four-star who had recently taken over from General Spaatz as air force chief of staff. It indicated to me that what we were doing was viewed as pretty important for the top leadership of the air force to come and speak to us. They seemed genuinely concerned. General Vandenberg called the enlisted men together and said, 'Don't worry about things back home. We're going to take care of your families. Your replacements back in the States are getting ready to relieve you. You are doing a fine job. Stick it out for a few more weeks and you'll be on your way home.'

"We were finally replaced by a B-29 outfit from Salina, Kansas. They had three months to get ready. We had less than three days. I believe we started a continuing Strategic Air Command presence in England. It was late October 1948 when we got back to Rapid City. Our short stay at RAF Scampton had lasted over three months. When we returned, the local community gave us a big welcome picnic, showing their appreciation. In 1949, I went to B-36 upgrade training. The 28th Bomb Wing got its first B-36 bomber that August, and we were checking out in it when I applied for pilot training. My pilot at the time, Captain Q. E. Steffes, a West Pointer, had encouraged me to go. It was a major decision because I had to give up my rank as master sergeant and revert back to cadet status. If it had not been for Captain Steffes's confidence in me, I probably would not have done it. As an aviation cadet I had to live on seventy-five dollars a month. I couldn't support a family on that. So my wife and daughter went to live with my mother and I began a new life—as an aviation cadet for the second time. In January 1950 I left the 28th Bomb Wing. I trained at Goodfellow and then at Reese Air Force Base, both in Texas. When I graduated as a pilot, I was commissioned as a second lieutenant in the United States Air Force—for the second time in my brief air force career."

In 1951 Second Lieutenant Joseph Gyulavics, fresh out of pilot training, found himself in the cockpit of a B-29 bomber flying out of Okinawa, carrying his bomb load up the Yalu River to strike a North Korean airfield. It was soon after an RB-45C jet reconnaissance aircraft had been shot down by Russian MiG-15s in the same area. B-29 bombers, based at Yokota Air Base, Japan, and at Kadena Air base on Okinawa, were the principal users of the important pictorial intelligence gathered by the high-flying RB-45C reconnaissance jets also based at Yokota. "Suddenly my aircraft was at the center of several Chinese communist searchlights. We were fired upon by flak from their side of the Yalu, the side we weren't allowed to bomb. I was nearly blinded by the intensity of the lights, unable to see or do anything. A strange thought passed through my mind: 'How did I get to be here?' When I passed beyond the range of the Chinese flak, the lights suddenly shifted away from my aircraft, leaving us in near total darkness. That was almost as disconcerting as the initial illumination. It took a long time for our night vision to return. We made it back to Kadena without further incident.

"Halfway through my pilot training, the Korean War broke out. The minute I graduated, I was assigned to Randolph Air Force Base near San Antonio, Texas, for B-29 combat crew training. I crewed up as a copilot with a bunch of misfits, or so I thought. A regular leper colony of flyers. An old ex-B-17 pilot, he was in his early thirties, a bombardier who was an alcoholic, and a radar navigator who had been an overweight school teacher before being recalled to active duty. Before we went to Korea, the former B-17 pilot thought we should take a shot at getting the flight surgeon to ground us or at least have him declare us unfit for combat duty. He claimed he had enough wartime experience flying in the 8th Air Force out of England in 1944. He could pop his right arm out of its socket with ease and had one of the crew do it for him. He, with arm dangling, the bombardier, and the navigator walked into the flight surgeon's office asking to be medically excused from flying combat. The flight surgeon took one look and kicked them out of his office.

"Our leper colony actually turned into a pretty good combat crew. We flew missions against North Korea out of Kadena as part of the 19th Bombardment Group. It was a long haul to Korea and back—twelve hours. We got to Kadena about the time they lost seven B-29s on one day and nine B-29s the next, shot down or damaged beyond repair. We thought, 'Oh God, here we go. World War II all over again.' Someone at headquarters wised up and we started flying our missions at night. The Koreans didn't have night fighters worth a damn, but their searchlights were good. They would pinpoint us and then the flak started working us over. We only got hit once, in the number two engine, the inboard engine on the left side. That time we landed at Fukioka, Japan, on New Year's Eve 1951. We went into the Officers' Club in our sweaty flight suits and joined the ongoing New Year's celebration. No one took notice of us. On one of our early missions we flew in a bomber stream up the Yalu River. Our target was Sinuiju Airfield, just south of the river, one of their big fighter bases. The searchlights were on the Chinese side of the Yalu River and we were not allowed to hit them. It was then that I flew my first ECM mission. On that particular flight we were getting ready to go when a staff officer held us back saying, 'No, you are not going to be part of the bomber stream. You are going to go in first, by yourselves, and then you are going to orbit south of the target. You will take this black box with you and the radar operator is going to turn it on when you get into your orbit.' He handed the navigator a black box. Unbeknownst to us our aircraft had been modified with the necessary antennas and cabling to accommodate the ECM transmitter, which was a simple noise jammer, preset to the frequency of the radar that guided the searchlights. All the radar navigator had to do was turn it on and off. The night was very dark. We pulled off into our orbit after we dropped our bombs. Then we watched the bomber stream come along behind us with the searchlights pointing right at the B-29s. On top of each tepee—the top of two, three, or more searchlights—there was a B-29. The flak was zeroing in on them. We turned on the jammer and then the searchlights fell off. Pretty soon they came back again. We turned the jammer on and off and broke the searchlights' tracking ability. We got to thinking, as we sat in our orbit, if they found out who was doing it to them, we were a sitting duck. We were scheduled to orbit until the last bomber made it through. The jammer worked. We made it home.

"When flying up there we would nearly always fly over Wonsan Harbor and turn up the peninsula to our IP, the initial point from which we began our bomb run. Well, every time we came near Wonsan Harbor our own navy would shoot at us. Our navy sat in that area with its carriers. You would think anybody in the US Navy would know that when you had a stream of bombers coming over from the south, they were ours. But their ships would fire at us every time. Fortunately nobody got hit. I guess it was an example of a lack of coordination or procedures, or maybe just a lack of common sense. We complained about it, but it didn't do any good. Every single time we flew that way our navy would fire off at least a few rounds. While I was on Okinawa, two of our squadron aircraft were shot down by flak. One we never heard from again. The other crew was captured. The pilot lived in the same Quonset hut I lived in. He was forced to make propaganda announcements over the radio about the imperialist Americans and what they were doing to the Korean and Chinese people. We couldn't believe that he would do that because he was such a gung-ho fellow. He carried a big knife and all kinds of other stuff. He told everybody he was going to go down fighting if he ever had to bail out. I don't know what they did to him. Intelligence asked me to identify his voice. Sure enough, it was him.

"The bottoms of our B-29s were painted black. They were World War II aircraft which had been pulled out of the boneyard in Arizona. That's the way they were painted when they went there in 1945. Every aircraft still bore the nose art some World War II air crew had painted on them. We also had one modified B-29 on the base, but it wasn't in our bomb group. It could carry the ten-thousand-pound blockbuster bomb. I don't know who flew that plane or what targets they attacked. We flew our mission, came home, took a shower, went to the club and ate. That was our routine. We didn't discuss our missions a lot with the other crews, so we never learned anything about that strange B-29. Our other targets, besides airfields, were mostly bridges all over North Korea. Our missions were not only long, twelve hours on average, but bone-chilling cold and mind-numbingly boring. Time over the target was brief. The rest of the eleven hours and fifty minutes we just droned on through an empty sky, trying desperately to stay awake. But the inevitable moment of stark terror every airman dreads came. We were coming home from a Yalu River mission about two or three in the morning. Everybody was sleepy. We were on autopilot, descending from our bombing altitude. When you were descending, you pulled your throttles back and you lost your heat. We were freezing and half asleep. When I glanced out the window to my right, there was another airplane, right off our wing, gliding past us like a ghost. We were nearly touching. No matter how much you try to separate the airplanes, eventually you are all heading back the same way. Had it been a midair collision, nobody would have known why it happened.

"We never flew formation. Our bombing altitude was usually twenty-five to twenty-eight thousand feet. It took a lot of fuel to get to altitude. Over South Korea we'd begin our climb. Right after the target we'd descend again. We carried forty five-hundred-pounders. With a twenty-thousand-pound bomb load it was routine for us to use up nearly every foot of the runway on takeoff. We didn't do any weight and balance calculations in those days. We'd taxi to the end of the runway, put the power up and off we went. With a good crosswind at Kadena and a wet runway we would have to use our brakes and throttles to stay on the runway and not get blown off. In order to add more power on one side, we had to pull power off on the other side. By doing that we increased our takeoff roll. At times it was pretty dicey getting airborne when we ran out of concrete. I flew twenty-five missions out of Kadena, just under three hundred hours flying time. Then we went home."

Home for Lieutenant Gyulavics turned out to be Forbes Air Force Base, near Topeka, Kansas. He, like myself ten years later in 1962, was assigned to the 343rd Strategic Reconnaissance Squadron, of the 55th Strategic Reconnaissance Wing, then flying modified RB-50 bombers on dangerous reconnaissance missions against the Soviet Union. Unprovoked attacks by Soviet fighters against such aircraft patrolling the borders of the Soviet Union were common, and all too many men were lost on these secret missions. Two years later, in 1954, the 55th Wing transitioned to the sleek, all-jet RB-47H electronic reconnaissance aircraft. Joe began his jet-flying career as a copilot and in 1956 his crew and three others from the 38th and 343rd SRS became part of a reconnaissance task force which in addition to their four RB-47H aircraft included sixteen photo-reconnaissance RB-47E jets from the 10th SRS at Lockbourne AFB, near Columbus, Ohio, and twenty-seven KC-97 air refueling tankers from squadrons at both Forbes and Lockbourne AFB. President Eisenhower had authorized the overflight of Soviet territory from the Bering Strait to the Kola Peninsula.[51] Bomber routes of the Strategic Air Command, if war came, would take them over the North Pole into Soviet territory, and it was imperative to know what capabilities the Soviets had along their northern coastline adjacent to the Arctic Ocean. The reconnaissance missions were to be flown out of Thule Air Base, Greenland, in the dead of winter. No more hostile and dangerous natural environment could have been picked for this operation than Thule Air Base, not to mention any Soviet military response that might be encountered. So, on March 21, 1956, four RB-47H jets took off from Forbes AFB and headed for Thule, better known as "the icebox of the North."[52]

At Thule the 55th SRW maintained Operating Location 5 (OL 5) to support reconnaissance flights against the Soviet Union. Each building at Thule was built like a cold-storage vault, with large icehouse-type doors and triple foot-thick walls perched on three-foot-high pillars. Some buildings had their own water supply, delivered by truck. Water used for washing was drained into an intermediate tank and then reused to flush toilets. Joe Gyulavics put it this way: "It was pretty gruesome living." Another thing that defined Thule, aside from the cold, were suddenly arising winds, frequently bringing all outdoor activity to a halt. The final hazard flying out of such a difficult location was psychological. The dark season played with men's minds, and at seventy-seven degrees north latitude darkness was a significant factor. "We had slot machines in the Officers' Club," Joe Gyulavics recalled, "which would keep people busy for hours. And there were free movies every night. But it got to where we didn't even bother to go and see a movie anymore. We adapted as best we could. A few came close to the edge under the stress of living at Thule.

"Thule-based reconnaissance flights over the Soviet Union were *long* and required tanker support. At times we took off from Thule and recovered at Eielson AFB near Fairbanks, Alaska. A few days later we would fly a mission in reverse and recover at Thule. *Long* meant that flights were over nine hours in duration. Over nine hours meant that the air crew sat in their ejection seats for that entire period of time. For reconnaissance missions flying over the polar ice cap to reach our targets in the Laptev and Kara Seas areas usually required the support of several KC-97 tankers. Refueling was critical. We would launch up to five KC-97 tankers an hour before our takeoff time to be able to take fuel off of at least three of the tankers. One tanker usually developed engine problems and had to turn around before he got to the refueling area. Sometimes two wouldn't make it. I worked out light signals with the tanker crews, since we never used our radios on these flights, so if I met one or two of them heading back prematurely, I would get behind them and take whatever fuel they could off-load. At the final refueling point, high over the polar ice cap, they could only give us ten thousand pounds of fuel each if they wanted to make it back to Thule. On the return leg of our missions we didn't refuel, so we had to have enough fuel on board to make it on our own. To rely on aerial refueling was too risky because of possible high winds at Thule or unexpected ice fogs. We loved our tanker buddies, who were always there when we needed them. They could only surmise what we were doing, but they knew after flying ten hours or more we had covered five thousand nautical miles."

Operation Homerun was flown between March 21 and May 10, 1956. The project was top secret, and not even the participating air crews were fully aware of its scope. "The unique thing about Thule," Joe Gyulavics recalled, "was landing on a snow-packed runway. At low temperatures, it really was no problem. You could practically brake on the cold snowpack like it was concrete. Of course, you had to be judicious about it. If you steered too fast, you kept on going, as if you were in a car on ice. Our antiskid brakes helped. When there was melting, it could get dicey. Getting ready to take off one time we taxied up to a little apron near the lip of the runway. There was a slight uphill grade, and two KC-97s sat on the apron before me, running their engines, melting some of the snow. When we came up the incline, it had turned to slick ice. We couldn't see the ice from the cockpit. All of a sudden the airplane started sliding backward and sideways. We had no control in the cockpit. On a tandem gear, such as that of the B-47, this was not a pleasant experience. The nose was rotating and there were snow banks all around. We hit the number one and two engines and managed to swing around, hoping we wouldn't damage the wing tips or run the tail into a snow bank. We finally managed to swing her around without doing any damage. However, when we returned from that mission, the crew chief found a sizable dent in the left wingtip. Things like that only happened at Thule. We test-fired our guns as soon as we leveled off, about thirty to forty minutes out. You'd think you are out there with nothing but snow and ice beneath you from frozen horizon to frozen horizon. Because of the total darkness, we couldn't see anything. You can imagine my surprise when after landing one day I was asked if I test-fired my guns. 'Yeah,' I answered, 'we do on every mission at the same place.' A couple of Eskimos had come in to the Danish Council carrying several 20mm shell casings. 'They fell from the sky,' the Eskimos said. Even near the North Pole, you couldn't be sure there wasn't someone down there."

During Operation Homerun, crews fought outside temperatures of forty degrees below zero Fahrenheit or lower with fur-lined parkas, bulky mittens, heavily padded flight suits, and clumsy Mukluk boots. Maintenance people

During the Korean War, 1950–53, Joe Gyulavics flew B-29s out of Okinawa against targets in North Korea. Their B-29s had been pulled out of the "boneyard" at Davis-Monthan AFB, Tucson, Arizona. Many aircraft still bore their WW II nose art, and others had their nose art updated, such as the one in the picture above—named after the famed Mission Inn in Riverside, California.

Colonel Joe Gyulavics, on the left, with his crew in front of an RB-47H reconnaissance aircraft at Forbes AFB, Topeka, Kansas, circa 1960.

A rare photo of three RB-47H aircraft in formation returning from an overseas deployment. Operational flights were in most cases flown singly, with no need to practice formation flying.

had a particularly difficult time with tasks that required them to remove their bulky arctic mittens. One man held a stopwatch with a second hand, while the other man worked. They completed tasks in stages, switching off to keep their fingers from getting frostbitten. Photo- and electronic-reconnaissance aircraft frequently operated in pairs, with an RB-47E photo aircraft teamed with an RB-47H electronic-reconnaissance aircraft. However, the planes did not fly in formation or even in sight of one another. All aircrews were briefed individually, and because of a strictly applied need-to-know security rule, no aircrew knew exactly where the others were going. The Thule missions of 1956 photo-mapped the island of Novaya Zemlya and its atomic test site. These aircraft flew behind the Ural Mountains and across Siberia and confirmed that the Soviet Union's northern regions were poorly defended against air attack. Subsequently many of the SAC bomber routes against the Soviet Union were planned to cross the top of the world. Throughout this difficult operation, not one RB-47 was lost as a result of accident or Soviet fighters. Not that the Soviets didn't try on occasion. Joe Gyulavics remembered "a bunch of fighters coming up out of Novaya Zemlya. We heard them launch. The Ravens picked up the fighter radars on their receivers. I saw the contrails of the Russian fighters, but they couldn't overtake us. An interesting time. We thought we were invincible and immortal. We never thought of any downside." Colonel Joseph Gyulavics retired from the air force after commanding squadrons and wings. His final assignment was as commander of Andersen AFB, Guam. He served in war and peace for thirty-five years as an enlisted man and officer. Joe was eighty-five years old in 2011 when he went "west," where all old flyers go. Godspeed my friend.

SAMUEL E. PIZZO

B-17/RB-47H/A-12

My Buddy

(Dedicated to Mike Shanley who died on his 6th combat mission)

They say he died in glory, what ever that may be.
If it's dying in a burst of flame, then glory's not for me.
In the briefing room this morning, he sat with clear eyes and strong heart,
Just one of many airmen determined to do his part.
My buddy had the guts alright, he sought not glory nor fame.
He knew there was a job to do, my crew all felt the same.
But death had the final word, in its log it wrote his name.
For my buddy died this afternoon in glory—in a burst of flame.
—Author unknown, StalagLuft I, WWII ETO

"I am honored to have served in World War II, and I can truly say it was something that I, along with millions of others, was glad to do," Colonel Samuel Pizzo commented when questioned about his military service. His words define the man he is, and for me, the man he always will be. Samuel E. Pizzo was born on November 22, 1922, in New Orleans, Louisiana, his heritage—Italian, Scotch, Irish, and English—typical American. In the '20s and '30s youngsters were inspired by the airplane, which made its operational debut during the First World War of 1914–1918, and by the young men and women who, after the war, flew surplus war planes in daring stunts across the country and became known as "barnstormers." Every kid with the slightest bit of gumption, Sam Pizzo among them, wanted to become a pilot. They knew their dreams would probably remain just that, dreams never to be realized, yet in their minds they put themselves at the controls of a red or yellow painted biplane to awe the world. They didn't know what the future held for them, and for many of them their dreams would, in fact, come true but not in ways they had imagined. Sam loved everything about flying, and read about the barn-stormers and their death-defying stunts in aviation magazines. He read about air races and airplanes which became bigger and more powerful as the years passed. Inspired, he built aircraft scale models out of balsa wood, silk, paper, and glue. Not satisfied with his static models he turned to rubber band–powered models. When Sam wasn't fiddling around building a new airplane, he was reading one of the many aviation magazines of the time, or taking long bus and streetcar rides to nearby airfields to watch real airplanes come in to land on grassy airstrips and watch them take off again.

With the advent of World War II, Sam Pizzo saw his opportunity, as did so many other youngsters, to get into the Army Air Corps and maybe get a chance to fly an airplane. Wow, just imagine sitting in an open cockpit, the wind tousling your hair, speeding across meadows and forests, free like a bird. It didn't get better than that for a young man. When the call went out for young men to join the Army Air Corps, they responded enthusiastically. So Sam, with many others, stood in long lines to apply for the aviation cadet program. It was mid-1942, Sam was twenty years old, and the draft board was breathing down his neck. He finally got scheduled to take the written examination for the aviation cadet program. Sam recalls that "the passing grade was 75, and that's exactly what I made on the test. I think I floated all the way home on cloud nine. Then of course I was scheduled for the inevitable physical examination. When I took the eye test, I flunked. The corporal who gave me the test looked at my papers and saw that I was already scheduled to enter the aviation cadet program. He said to me, 'Heck, I'm not going to fail you. Let somebody else do so.' So he passed me. Everyone needs a hand in life here and there, and this corporal made all the difference in my life. I never failed another eye test. Having passed my physical examination I boarded a train to Sheppard Field near Wichita Falls, Texas. The train was filled with young men like me wanting to become flyers. We sang songs and became real buddies, comrades-in-arms, or so I thought. After we arrived, we were issued military gear and uniforms and settled into barracks life. There was a lot to learn. And lots of parades as well, marching wherever we went. I had my appendix taken out not too long before I left for Sheppard Field. The wound had not totally healed by the time I arrived, and on a strenuous ten-mile march I collapsed and was hauled into the hospital. When I was released from the hospital, my newfound comrades-in-arms had helped themselves to every piece of equipment and clothing issued to me—leaving me with one pair of fatigues, the ones I wore on the march when I collapsed, a pair of socks, boots, a plastic helmet liner, and canteen.

The bombardier's position was the most exposed of all crew positions on the B-17, in the aircraft's nose section. While under attack the bombardier also served as a gunner.

I had to repurchase every item lost, which was not easy on a salary of fifty dollars a month.

"Boot camp completed, I finally reported to an Army Air Forces classification center in San Antonio, Texas. Again I took a battery of tests and I was pleased to learn that I had passed in all three categories—pilot, navigator, and bombardier. When our assignments were posted on the bulletin board, I went into shock. I had been selected for bombardier training, but I wanted to be a pilot. My world had just come crashing down. I jacked up my courage and began the process to get things back on the right track. First, I went to see the company clerk, who sent me to the first sergeant, who sent me to the company commander, a second lieutenant. The lieutenant passed me up the chain of command until I reached the big boss—a lieutenant colonel. I told him that a mistake had been made, and that I wanted to be a pilot. The colonel listened, frowned, looked at my records, then asked, 'Why do you think we made a mistake assigning you to bombardier training?' He didn't wait for my reply. 'We don't make mistakes here,' he said firmly. 'Your bombardier test scores were the highest of all, so that's where we are sending you, bombardier training.' Then he told me to get out of his office and never show my face again. I saluted smartly, made an about-face and accepted my fate.

"Several months of training followed at Ellington Field near Houston, Texas. This was just general training, no flying involved. My next stop had little to do with becoming a bombardier either, Laredo, Texas—gunnery school. We learned to field-strip .45-caliber pistols blindfolded, and the same thing with .30-caliber and .50-caliber machine guns. How all that was going to make me a good bombardier I had yet to figure out. Then we cadets got to stand up in the back of a pickup truck that careened around a figure-eight track and we were tasked to hit clay pigeons, fired from adjacent towers, with a shotgun. I don't think anyone ever hit one of those birds, but we did get the prettiest black-and-blue shoulders you can imagine from the recoil of those guns, which were difficult to hold onto in a bouncing truck. Finally we got to step into an airplane, an AT-6, to practice hitting a target towed by another AT-6. I don't think I ever hit anything except the ground, when my bullets ran out of speed and fell to the earth below. Thankfully this bizarre bit of training finally reached its end and we bombardier trainees were presented with gunners' wings. The following day we boarded a train, destination unknown. It turned out the train went straight north from Laredo to Midland, Texas, the location of the Army Air Forces bombardier school. It was pretty much a makeshift operation like gunnery school. We learned dead reckoning navigation, aircraft identification, and Morse code—having to be able to send and receive twenty-five words a minute. Then we were introduced to the very secret Norden bombsight and taught how to operate it. Before we got the chance to test our skills in a real airplane, we had to prove ourselves on a four-wheeled contraption, about twenty-nine or so feet high which had a Norden sight installed. This beast was then towed across a large hangar simulating an aircraft on a bombing run—if you didn't master this thing, you were off to infantry training. We finally got into the AT-11, a twin-engine trainer, flying day and night navigation and bombardier training missions over west Texas. The daylight missions were not too difficult, but at night, west Texas was loaded with oil fields, it was easy to get disoriented. Nearly everyone got lost at least once. On the bombing missions, like on the training missions in the large hangar, if you didn't hit your target to the satisfaction of the instructors, you were again heading for training in the infantry.

"Finally, it was all over. We received our bombardier wings, and more important, we cadets were promoted to second lieutenants in the United States Army Air Forces—officers at last. As we walked off the stage, we were handed a set of orders telling us where to report for further training in the type of aircraft we would be flying in combat. Mine said, B-26 Marauders, Tampa, Florida. My heart sank. The B-26 had a terrible reputation, coining the phrase 'One a day in Tampa Bay.' My orders, as well as the orders of several other officers heading for Tampa, were soon changed, sending us instead to Dyersburg, Tennessee, for B-17 training. En route I had just enough time to stop at home to get married. The only difference between Midland, Texas, and

Dyersburg, Tennessee, was that the latter had trees, something not very common in the western part of Texas. All the streets had English-sounding names, a local bar was called the Pub, and the bank was the Exchequer—I guess I was heading for England. Then I met my crew. At age twenty-one, I was the oldest. When I saw my first B-17 bomber, I thought I'd died and gone to heaven. What a beauty! At my position I had two .50-caliber machine guns—now I understood why I had gone through gunnery training. Our crew training at Dyersburg involved mostly formation flying. Once I got over Germany, I understood why. We picked up a brand-new B-17 in Lincoln, Nebraska, and flew it to Manchester, New Hampshire, expecting to leave for England. Not so. Our new orders directed us to head for Marrakesh, Morocco, then on to one of the many airfields near Foggia, Italy. There we lost our brand-new B-17 and were assigned to a replacement center. We stayed in a ten-man tent, the food was lousy, and the Italian flies were huge, flying directly into your mouth if you didn't watch yourself. We stayed there for thirty days, finally receiving our assignment to the 342nd Bomb Squadron, 97th Bomb Group.

"The many airfields around Foggia held every American and British aircraft imaginable. That made for real 'peachy' takeoffs and assemblies when the weather was cloudy. I think we lost as many aircraft forming up for a four- or five-hundred maximum effort mission as we did in combat. You'd see a bright orange glow in the clouds and know that there had been a midair collision. We had no radar, and all join-ups were done by timing and maintaining briefed altitudes and headings. My pilot started his combat training by flying as copilot with an experienced crew. After he had flown a couple of sorties, he was combat certified and we flew our first mission as a crew. After flying over in a brand-new B-17, I got a little nervous when I looked at the beat-up old bird we had been assigned with patches all over. We all did our preflight inspections, which in my case included checking out the bombsight and the pins on the twelve five-hundred-pound bombs we carried. I would pull the pins, arming the bombs, after takeoff at a prebriefed altitude. Then we flew with live bombs in our belly. After a couple of hours the green flare went up, engines were started, and we taxied into our takeoff position. One by one B-17s rumbled down the runway, lifted off and formed into squadrons first, then into groups, and on some very large raids into divisions which then became a very large stream of bombers heading for their targets.

"On our first mission, our climb out was without incident. I had not figured on the extreme cold at altitude. A bare hand touching metal stuck to it. Frostbite was an ever-present danger. As we entered German airspace, I understood why many of the crews had groaned when they first saw the assigned target. The groups ahead of us were almost invisible, swallowed up in the smoke and debris of exploding flak. We suffered no serious damage in spite of the heavy antiaircraft fire, and only one plane in our group was lost. There were no German fighters. I flew a few more missions with my crew, but after I checked out as a lead bombardier, I flew with whichever crew was to lead the formation, and all the aircraft following us would drop their bombs when we did. Then came the mission we all dreaded, Munich, always heavily defended. We took a pretty heavy burst of flak directly under our aircraft, but it didn't seem to do anything to us other than superficial damage. As we turned for home, we attempted to switch fuel tanks, and we realized that the flak burst had damaged the fuel transfer valve, and we were unable to switch tanks. We knew we didn't have enough fuel to make it back to Foggia. We discussed our options among the crew—bail out over Germany or Yugoslavia, head for Switzerland, or ditch in the Adriatic. There was a small island, Vis, just off the Yugoslavian coast with a small airfield on it and we agreed to try to make Vis. It was raining like heck. We were flying down on the deck knowing that if the gas didn't hold out for a few more minutes we were going to be in the water and would probably be picked up by the Germans. The other problem we had was that the island frequently changed hands between Tito's partisans and others friendly to the Germans. We were able to make radio contact with our command post and were informed that Vis was a good choice. If we could make it. Tito's guys were running the show on Vis at this time.

"We began our descent toward Vis—it was raining and the visibility was poor. We spotted what looked like a runway, a level area covered with PSP, perforated steel matting. We all knew that it would take all the skill of our pilots to bring our aircraft to a stop before running off the slippery runway. We did run off the end of the runway, doing a slow cartwheel before we came to rest. No one was injured. The minute our aircraft settled and came to a stop a large group of Yugoslav men, women, and children surrounded the plane. All wore ammunition bandoliers across their chests, weapons of all kinds and makes hanging from their belts and strapped to their backs, with very large machete-like knives or sabers at their sides. It was a scary group of people to look at. They immediately began to strip our aircraft of its machine guns and remaining ammunition. They even wanted our .45-caliber pistols, which we refused to hand over. They got very aggressive, until an American corporal showed up who settled the matter in our favor. We stayed on Vis for several days, living in a large barn with other shot-down American and British flyers. For breakfast, lunch, and dinner our 'hosts' served us baked chicken, with lots of red wine. At mealtime this very large well-armed woman showed up with a large board balancing on her head holding a bunch of baked chickens. She'd put the board on the floor, take the machete she was carrying and cut each chicken in half with a well-aimed stroke. Three times a day—the same menu—baked chicken, bread, and red wine. We were grateful for what was provided, even more so, to still be alive. One time one of the flyers asked the Yugo woman about what happened to the eggs the chickens must have laid. I thought she was going to use that machete on him. We asked no more questions while there. After several days an American C-47 transport arrived and took all of us back to Foggia and to the war that was still going on.

"My crew, minus the copilot and me, flew a mission against Vienna. The aircraft was badly shot up and they all bailed out. Luck was with them. They were soon rescued and returned to Foggia. I had flown a total of thirty combat missions when the war in Europe ended on May 8, 1945. We headed home to the United States, expecting to train in B-29s to join the war in the Pacific. Then that war ended and we were all discharged and returned to civilian life. It was an adjustment for us all. We had left for war as young men just out of high school, learned to fly airplanes and drop bombs, then suddenly we were back home again wearing civilian clothes. It was not an easy adjustment. I went to work for Delta Airlines in New Orleans, but opted to remain in the reserves at Barksdale Field, near Shreveport, flying Douglas A-26 Marauders. In the summer of 1950, with a war raging in Korea, we were about to be recalled to active duty. That's when I decided to see if I couldn't transfer from the reserves to the active air force. I was accepted and found myself assigned as a radar navigator in B-29s at Barksdale. I had some scary experiences in the B-29, and after completing radar navigator training I was reassigned to the 343rd Strategic Reconnaissance Squadron of the 55th Strategic Reconnaissance Wing in the windswept town of Topeka, Kansas. Here I would remain for nearly eight years flying in the brand-new RB-47H electronic reconnaissance aircraft."

Two thousand B-47 bombers and reconnaissance aircraft were built starting in the early '50s to equip the strategic bomber and reconnaissance squadrons of the Strategic Air Command, replacing older, conventionally powered B-29, B-50, and B-36 bombers. The B-47 with its swept-back wings was a sleek-looking aircraft which equally challenged its designers, flight and maintenance crews. Its six jet engines had barely enough power to get a fully loaded bomber off a ten-thousand-foot runway. Engine failures were not uncommon, and when they occurred on takeoff in either the number one or number six outboard engines, they frequently were catastrophic and led to the loss of aircraft and crew. Everything was new on this 600-miles-per-hour aircraft, and failures of electrical and hydraulic systems, as well as structural failures, occurred all too frequently. It was early in the jet age, and there was a lot to be learned by all involved in designing, building, maintaining, and flying these aircraft. The mission of the recently B-47 equipped 55th SRW, which Sam Pizzo joined as a young captain in the mid-fifties, was to serve as the eyes and ears of the Strategic Air Command, which meant that the missions flown by the aircrews of this unique air force wing were demanding, dangerous, and challenging, involving overflights of the Soviet Union and constant monitoring of Soviet military deployments along its periphery. Sam Pizzo flew such dangerous missions for nearly eight years, leaving the 55th SRW about the time in 1962 when I first reported to the same squadron Sam flew with, the 343rd SRS, at Forbes Air Force Base. Crews were very stable in the 55th; there was little turnover. Sam's aircraft commander was Lieutenant Colonel James Woolbright, one of the squadron's best pilots, and better known to his fellow flyers as "Pat." Sam flew with Pat for nearly five years. Sam's copilot was Major Willard Palm. The fate of these two B-47 flyers speaks to the challenges posed by the early jet technology and the dangerous missions flown by the 55th Wing.

Major Willard Palm perished on July 1, 1960, when his RB-47 jet, flying a peripheral reconnaissance mission along the northernmost part of the Soviet Union, was shot down by a Soviet fighter over the Barents Sea.[53] Sam Pizzo flew well over one hundred such dangerous missions while in the 55th Wing and frequently encountered threatening Soviet fighters, even over international waters. Pat Woolbright, Sam's aircraft commander for five years, perished on a September morning in 1962. I had reported for duty at the 343rd SRS in the summer of 1962. By September of 1962 the Cuban missile crisis was shaping up, and we new crews were rapidly getting trained to be certified as being combat ready. I had just landed at Forbes after an eight-hour night training mission. We parked our aircraft as directed by the control tower at a remote section of the base, awaiting further instructions. As we were standing around our aircraft, waiting for transportation to maintenance for a debriefing on any malfunctions encountered in flight, an RB-47K photo reconnaissance aircraft taxied by and lined up at the end of the runway. We watched as the pilot brought up the power on his engines, released the brakes, and slowly began his long takeoff roll down our ten-thousand-foot runway. The runway, nearly two miles long, crested a slight hill, and the B-47 jet disappeared from sight as it was gaining takeoff speed. Then there was a bright flash, followed by a mushroom-like black cloud rising into the blue Kansas morning sky. We, who had been watching this aircraft taking off, knew immediately what probably happened—and we were deeply saddened. The chance of anyone surviving such a crash was very remote. The pilot at the controls of that RB-47K had been Pat Woolbright, Sam Pizzo's former aircraft commander. The number one left-outboard engine on his aircraft failed just as he rotated the aircraft for liftoff. The aircraft, laden with a full load of fuel, now with asymmetrical power, veered to the right, off the runway, cartwheeled, and blew up. There were no survivors.[54]

Yet, crew morale in the three squadrons of the 55th Wing was always high while I was a member of the organization. We liked what we were doing, knowing the importance of our missions to national security. We flew from bases in England, Turkey, Japan, Greenland, Alaska, and from other locations to monitor the Soviet Union's military deployments and missile testing activities. So, it came as a surprise to Major Sam Pizzo of the 343rd SRS, and Major Augustine Puchrik of the 338th SRS, when in September 1959 they were directed to report to the Foreign Technology Division (where I served in later years from 1975 to 1978) at Wright-Patterson AFB in Dayton, Ohio. Neither Pizzo, a navigator, nor Puchrik, a pilot, knew what it was all about. There they learned that "Major Puchrik, a Sergeant Pellham, and I were assigned as an American escort crew to accompany Premier Nikita Khrushchev on a state visit to the United States, flying two Soviet Tu 104 transports, the demilitarized version of the Soviet Badger bomber, and the Tu 114, the transport version of the Bear turbo-prop bomber," recalled Sam Pizzo. "We first met the Russians in Iceland. Our job was to guide them safely through our air defense identification zones, ADIZ, and keep them away from restricted areas. We accompanied them on several missions between Washington and London, ferrying passengers and delivering dispatches. I was selected as the American navigator on Mr. K's return flight from Washington to Moscow. I don't know why they picked me, because I didn't speak a word of Russian. Major Puchrik was fluent in Russian, and his selection was understandable. I stood or sat behind the Russian navigator, and whenever it appeared that we might be violating some danger area I would tap him on the shoulder and make a motion with my hand for him to turn the aircraft. The first time I did this the Russian navigator just shrugged his shoulders, not getting what I was trying to tell him—turn now. So I tapped him on his shoulder again and made a motion with my hands and said, 'Poof.' He got the message, and the pilot sharply wracked the plane over on its side and got back on course.

"Premier Khrushchev looked to me like a regular, little old guy. He stayed busy throughout our flight to Moscow dictating messages to the leaders of countries we flew over. More people met Mr. Khrushchev when he arrived in Washington than met him upon his arrival in Moscow. He was very diligent, shook everyone's hand, careful not to miss anyone. The Russian crew was very friendly, and before leaving the Tu 114 in Moscow, their navigator presented me with a bottle of vodka, and the first pilot presented me with a small desk ornament of *Sputnik*. As the premier was leaving the aircraft, he waved at me saying, 'Thank you. Okay.' I returned to Topeka to fly the RB-47. I had several more deployments, when in 1961 my career took another turn. I had been on temporary duty, TDY, in England, and on the first Friday evening after my return I took my wife, Mary, to the Forbes AFB Officers' Club for dinner. There we ran into Colonel Robert Holbury, the former director of operations in the 55th SRW, who was now running the headquarters SAC reconnaissance center at Offutt AFB in Omaha, Nebraska. He was here to get some flying time in the B-47. He joined us for dinner and as part of our conversation asked me if I would want to come and work for him. I assumed it would be in Omaha, but when I queried him about that he said, 'I can't say.' His response remained the same 'I can't say' to every other question I had about his job offer. Putting uncertainty aside I agreed to his offer and he told me before he left us that I would hear from him soon.

"I soon received security clearance forms which I filled out and mailed back to Colonel Holbury. Shortly thereafter neighbors and friends began telling me of strangers asking a lot of questions about me: my lifestyle, drinking habits, debts, and so on. All very personal. Then I was interviewed, took lie detector tests, and in time military orders arrived for me to report to a special activities squadron in Las Vegas, Nevada. That's how I came to Area 51, the 'Ranch' as it was euphemistically called, out in the Nevada desert. My job there was chief of the mission support group for the A-12 aircraft, the CIA version of what later became the air force's SR-71. The A-12 flew at Mach 3, over three times the speed of sound, at an altitude of ninety thousand feet, as high as the well-known U-2 spy plane was able to fly, but at a much greater speed. After settling into sparse quarters at the Ranch, I and my people headed down to the Lockheed plant at Burbank, California, where we were introduced to Kelly Johnson. Kelly briefed us on the A-12's capabilities, then took us on a tour of the Skunk Works, as the Lockheed plant at Burbank is commonly referred to. To my amazement I saw an A-12 in pieces which, I was told, would be crated, then shipped to the Ranch where the aircraft would be assembled in total secrecy. I had my hands full when I got back to the Ranch preparing potential mission profiles, planning training sorties that would simulate operational missions, and coordinating with agencies that would be involved in the project from the FAA to refueling tankers. The project's code name for this fastest and highest flying of all spy planes ever built to that date was Oxcart. The Ranch, Area 51, where we lived most of the week and worked, was so secret at the time, the government didn't even acknowledge its existence until the project was declassified in 2007.

"Air refueling was to be provided by a squadron of modified KC-135 refueling tanker aircraft stationed at Beale AFB, near Sacramento, California. Tanker fuel tanks had to be modified to handle the JP-7 fuel for the A-12 instead of the standard JP-4 jet fuel used by all other air force jet aircraft. The JP-7 was specially designed for use at very high altitude and airspeeds. Its flash point was much higher than that for standard jet fuels. You could throw a lit match into the fuel and nothing would happen. We worked very close with the tanker squadron staff establishing air refueling areas throughout the United States which would not conflict with civilian air traffic, especially during

Lieutenant Samuel Pizzo manning his position as lead bombardier for his squadron en route to bomb the Blechhammer oil refinery in December 1944.

Major Sam Pizzo in front of an RB-47H reconnaissance aircraft at Forbes AFB, Topeka, Kansas, September 1958, on the occasion of his being designated SAC navigator of the year. Sam is wearing a 343SRS patch below his name tag—the same squadron I flew with from 1962 to 1967.

descent and climb to and from the air refueling area. In everything we did we involved our pilots, listened to their suggestions, and after every training flight we debriefed them thoroughly to make sure that anything that needed to be changed was implemented promptly. The age of computers had not yet arrived and our mission planning tools consisted of what every air force navigator used to plan a route—dividers for measuring distance on a chart, an E6B handheld computer, a Weems plotter, and a slide rule. Very basic tools.

"I had never seen a plane quite like this one before. Watching the A-12 take off from the Groom lakebed after sunset was a spectacular sight. It lit up the desert, lit up the night—oh God, it was such a beautiful sight. While assigned to the Oxcart program I still had to get my flying time if I wanted to retain my rating and get paid flight pay. One day, it was near the end of my tour at the Ranch, early summer of 1965, I received a call from my director of operations. He informed me that I would be flying with him the next day. Sounded good to me. Usually we flew in what was available at the time—a T-33 trainer, an F-101, or any other aircraft that was available to us. I went out to the flight line the following day looking for Colonel Doug Nelson. I couldn't find him. Then I saw him near our A-12 trainer. I figured I got my day wrong, or something

Colonel Sam Pizzo in 2005 while attending the 55th Reconnaissance Wing's annual winter ball at Offutt AFB, Omaha, Nebraska. Sam's flying career took him from lumbering B-17s to the Mach 3 A-12, the predecessor aircraft of the SR-71.

was amiss. I walked over to Colonel Nelson and learned that he was going to get me my flying time in that aircraft. My stomach tightened up. I almost got sick right then and there. Before I knew it, I was getting a quick safety briefing. We strapped in and headed out for takeoff. I remember him saying to me over the intercom, 'Hold on, Sam, here we go.' And away we went. The flight included an air refueling. I had the thrill of a lifetime. I met General Nelson some years later and thanked him again for that ride. Not many would have done so.

"The job and association with the legendary Kelly Johnson and his Lockheed people plus our own air force personnel was something you only dream of happening to you during your air force career. After four years at the Ranch I was assigned to headquarters SAC as chief of the SR-71 section, and became the project officer for Desert Queen, the SR-71 program code name. Once the SR-71 was in the operational inventory, we were the ones to plan missions to satisfy intelligence requirements. Photographic and electronic collection was the name of the game." Promoted to colonel, Sam Pizzo finished his very different and colorful air force career at headquarters United States Air Forces Europe (USAFE) in Wiesbaden, Germany. Both Sam and I were stationed in

Wiesbaden at the time. I was in operations as a junior major, Sam in intelligence as a senior officer. We never met. After his retirement in 1973, Sam and his family returned to New Orleans where it had all begun for him many years earlier. Sam went to work for a major ocean shipping company, rising to the position of assistant vice president. Fifteen years later, in 1988, he called it quits and retired to Mandeville, Louisiana—where he and his high school sweetheart, his beloved wife, Mary, lived until her recent passing. In Sam's words, "My air force career was as good as it gets. Who could have asked for anything more?"

MARION C. MIXSON

B-24/RB-45C/RB-47H/U-2

To My Mother

Can't write a thing—the censor to blame. Just say I'm well, and sign my name. Can't tell where
we sailed from, can't mention the date, not even the number of meals I ate. Can't say where we're
going, don't know where we'll land. Couldn't inform you if met by a band. Can't mention the
weather, can't say if there's rain, all military secrets must secrets remain.
Can't have a flashlight to guide me at night, can't smoke cigarettes except out of sight.
Can't keep a diary for such is a sin, can't keep the envelopes your letters come in.
Can't say for sure just what I can write, so I call this a letter, and close with "Good night."
—William S. Duncan, WWII ETO

"I was born in Charleston, South Carolina, March 20, 1918. My first encounter with airplanes and flying was in 1929. I was eleven. I got a ride in a Ford
Trimotor. That was like going to heaven. If an airplane flew over Charleston,
I'd run outside to take a look. There weren't that many airplanes then. Once a
German Dornier seaplane landed in Charleston Harbor. It was a monstrous
thing, exciting. Aviation was spread pretty thin in those days, but I always
knew I wanted to fly. I believe it was my nanny who first called me 'Hack,' and
the name stuck with me ever since. I was raised in Charleston, went to the
Porter Military Academy, and after high school attended Presbyterian College
in Clinton, South Carolina. College was a pretty uneventful four years. When
I graduated from Presbyterian in 1939, I ended up with a commission as a
second lieutenant in the infantry. My brother, Lawrence, was four years older
than I. In World War II he served in the navy in the Pacific, where both of his
destroyers, the *Osborne* and *Renshaw*, were heavily damaged in combat with
Japanese naval forces. I went to work in the family business in Charleston, the

Mixson Seed Company, selling seed and fertilizer throughout the southeastern states.

"In the fall of 1939, I soloed a little 45-horsepower Aeronca. What a thrill it was to soar above Charleston on my very own. I'll never forget that first solo flight. Fortunately, I had a friend, Robert Carroll, who owned several airplanes. The best one was a Rearwin Cloudster made at Fairfax Airport in Kansas City, Kansas. It had a 120-horsepower five-cylinder radial Ken-Royce engine—pretty powerful stuff for that day. Between 1939 and 1941, I flew several hundred hours with Robert and his brother Edwin. In July 1941 Edwin and I took off from Charleston to fly to Los Angeles. We stopped in Atlanta and got gas. Spent the night in Monroe, Louisiana. Went on to Fort Worth, Texas, and had lunch there. It was about ninety-five degrees. Then we headed to Wichita Falls, flying at three thousand feet. I was flying. All of a sudden the RPM just went down and kept on going down. I said to Edwin, 'I can't maintain altitude. I'm going to have to land.' In those days, the sectional charts showed farm and ranch houses. Edwin located the nearest farmhouse on the map, and I headed for it. We landed in a field by a rock cairn next to the house. We got out and checked everything and found nothing wrong. We cranked the engine and it ran like a breeze. So we took off again and flew on to Wichita Falls. The mechanic there couldn't find anything wrong with the plane either. Being cautious, we decided not to go on to Los Angeles and instead flew to the Ken-Royce plant at Fairfax Field in Kansas City. They modified the engine so we didn't have to manually grease the rocker boxes with a squirt gun. We met Mr. Rearwin, the owner of the plant, and his two sons, Ken and Royce, after whom he named the engine. They checked the engine themselves and declared everything was fine. We still had our doubts, though, and flew back to Charleston.

"In December 1941 I was called to active duty at Fort McClellan. I put a letter through channels to transfer to the Army Air Corps. I had over three hundred hours flying time, I wrote, and I should be in the air corps, not the infantry. I think my first letter got thrown in the trash. Then I sent a letter directly to the Army Air Corps headquarters and four days later I was at Maxwell Field, Alabama, getting a physical. Two weeks after that, I was at a small field near Fort Worth to begin training in the PT-17. I went on to the BT-13 at Randolph Field near San Antonio, and after that to Kelly Field where I flew a little twin-engine plywood plane, the AT-10. After I graduated from pilot training, I was sent to the 13th Bombardment Group at Westover, Massachusetts, a B-25 outfit. I flew convoy escort and antisubmarine patrols along the Atlantic coast. In July 1943 I was reassigned to the 461st Bomb Group which was forming in Boise, Idaho. Before I knew it, I was a B-24 flight commander. I was still a second lieutenant and less than a year out of pilot training. My crew, there were ten of us, were all experts in their fields and great guys. Sam Gilio was the engineer and waist gunner. He had been a prize fighter as well as a mechanic for American Airlines for ten years. Sol Adler, the radio operator, spent ten years at sea copying Morse code. Sol would sit looking like he was asleep but copying everything that came in over the radio. My bombardier, Howard Kadow, was a jeweler from Brooklyn, New York. Howie was brilliant. The copilot, Tom Lightbody, was an Irish cop from Pelham, New York. Hank Wilson, a lawyer, was the best navigator there ever was. And Gino Piccione, Ed Miller, Herb Newman, and Chester Kline were our gunners. The four gunners were all pretty young, eighteen or so. Ed Miller, the largest man on the crew, was the ball turret gunner. Usually the smallest man took this position. We ten trained at Fresno, California, and at Wendover range in Utah. We finished up about Christmas 1943.

"In February 1944 our group deployed from Florida to Dakar, North Africa, then to Marrakesh. We flew a couple of missions out of Tunis and then moved to our permanent field south of Foggia, Italy, Torretta #1. On April 13 I was formation leader for the 461st Bomb Group in an attack against an aircraft plant near Budapest, Hungary. Our escort fighters, P-38s, didn't show. I didn't think we would make it back from that mission. We were viciously attacked by waves of enemy fighters firing rockets, cannon, and machine guns. They came at us head-on and from all sides, flying abreast, firing their rockets into our formation. Rockets tore off the wing of one aircraft; out of control, it collided with another. Both exploded. A third aircraft went down. Of the remaining thirty-five B-24s, thirty were damaged. Damage to my aircraft was severe, we lost one engine, another was hit by flak, but continued to run at reduced power. As I led my group over the target, enemy bombers dropped bombs through our formation, others fired rockets at us from the rear. In spite of it all—we hit the target and utterly destroyed it. I was awarded the Distinguished Flying Cross for that mission. In June 1944, I was a captain, we finished our twenty-five missions. I was told by my group commander, Colonel William L. Lee, 'Bill' to us, 'If you take your crew home and come back, I'll make you a squadron commander.' I took them home about the time everybody else landed in France. When we returned in September 1944, Colonel Lee, who in the meantime had been promoted to brigadier general, gave me the 764th Bomb Squadron.

"On December 17, 1944, we were going to destroy the last little bit of oil the Germans still had—the Odertal synthetic oil refinery in Upper Silesia, about 180 miles southwest of Warsaw, Poland. It was the longest mission ever flown by the 461st Bomb Group. I led the group, and two other B-24 groups joined us, flying at lower altitudes, the 484th and the 451st—ninety-three heavy bombers. Intelligence briefed us, 'Don't worry. You are the high group. You will be flying at twenty-six thousand feet; no one will bother you there. Keep your ball turrets up. You got plenty of fighter cover as well.' Twenty-six thousand feet was the maximum formation altitude for the B-24. Keeping our ball turrets up in the belly of the aircraft rather than extending them meant increased range on this long mission and better formation flying. Though once the decision was made, it was not easy to reverse. The ball turret gunner had to remove his chute to fit into the turret. After entering, the gunner would then lower the ball electrically. The procedure took a fair amount of time. Forty-five minutes after takeoff our formation leveled off at nine thousand feet over Bovino, Italy. We rendezvoused with the other two bomb groups and turned in wing formation over the Adriatic Sea. The 484th was the low group and led the formation, the 451st was the middle group, and my group, the 461st, trailed in the high slot. By the time we arrived over Split, Yugoslavia, my group had reached 17,500 feet and we continued our climb until we were at 26,000 feet—with our ball turrets up, the most effective gun on our ships.

"Well, we got up into Germany and didn't see our fighter escort. At that altitude it was difficult to keep the formation together. We were heavy, flying through the brilliantly blue December sky, working hard to keep the formation together. The plane was unpressurized, and the crew was on oxygen all the time, wearing bulky, heated flying gear. Finally, we saw a large group of fighters approaching. Our escort, no doubt. Wrong. They were German Me 109s, seventy-five of them. And we had our ball turrets up. The 109s jumped on my group first. Planes were exploding and going down everywhere. Seventy more German Fw 190s pounced on my group. In fifteen minutes, eight of my bombers were shot down, five more damaged. Only fifteen of an original thirty-one in my group made it to the target. Losses were lighter in the lower groups but no less tragic. *Little Joe*, piloted by First Lieutenant Charles Himmler, was attacked by six enemy fighters, burst into flames, entered a spin, and crashed. No one got out. Two other B-24s collided shortly after passing the Rally Point. On the return leg, as I was passing Vienna, a German calls me on the radio. He used our correct call sign, and in perfect, German-accented English he said, 'Where is the rest of your formation?' Then he laughed and signed off. The last aircraft we lost was that of Lieutenant Eugene Ford, attempting to reach the island of Vis in the Adriatic Sea. Ford had to ditch his damaged Liberator before reaching Vis and he and two of his crew perished. It had been a beautiful day when we took off that morning in Italy. The Luftwaffe hadn't been bothering us for weeks. We got complacent. Put our ball turrets up. That was a mistake. That ball turret was a killer, and we didn't have those guns to defend ourselves. We paid dearly for that mistake. Our escort never showed up and I still don't know why to this day.

"Not all of our missions were large formation missions. On November 3, 1944, the weather was bad and instead of launching a planned large scale 'double header' mission, aircraft were sent off on individual sorties against selected targets. We took off at eleven o'clock in the morning, four aircraft, at one-minute intervals. My target was an aircraft factory at Klagenfurt, Austria. We were in the clouds the entire way and dropped our bombs by the pathfinder method. We didn't have to worry about enemy fighters or flak because we were in the clouds the entire time—our biggest problem was icing. All four of us made it back to Toretta. The war kept on claiming its victims to the very end. On the morning of March 22, 1945, we climbed into our planes when we saw the green flare fired from the control tower. We went through our checklists, started engines, and taxied into takeoff position. Almost four hours after takeoff, we approached our target staggered between twenty-two thousand and twenty-five thousand feet. In the distance ahead of us, a group of bombers was taking heavy flak. Then there was a very large, black explosion. An antiaircraft shell must have hit one of the B-24s in the bomb bay and set off its bomb load. The sun was reflecting off aircraft parts tumbling toward the ground. Then I looked up, and there, directly over us was a formation of bombers flying on a slightly different course. I could see stack after stack of five-hundred-pound bombs in their open bomb bays. I held my breath as they cleared our group. Then we were in the flak. A B-24 from a nearby formation went into a vertical dive trailing flames and smoke—then it blew up. A bomber to my left began its death spiral downward, followed by two more. Too few parachutes blossomed. The flight home was uneventful.

"I flew thirty-five combat missions. Some missions counted double, giving me a total of fifty. Every week or so we would go up to Ploesti. Ploesti was always bad, they had a lot of flak there. Munich was bad, as was anything around Vienna. The Germans often put up a spotter plane to give their antiaircraft guns our altitude. The flak was always heavy in our target areas. That was World War II for me. After the war ended, I stayed in Italy for another year. It was one of the best years of my life. I was sitting in the replacement depot ready to go home when I got a call to work for General William L. Lee, my former boss and group commander who headed the Air Force Sub-Commission in Rome, which was part of the Allied Commission for Italy, headed by Rear Admiral Ellery Stone. After the telephone call, I'm pretty elated about this time, I chatted with a major who was heading for home, and in the course of our conversation told him that I had only minutes ago received an assignment to Rome. I had a case of bourbon whiskey with me. He said to me, 'You're going to need all that whiskey?' I said, 'Yeah, I think I do.'

"'I tell you what,' the major said, 'I got a deal for you. I have a C-47 over at Marcianise, near Naples. I commanded a service squadron. During the year I picked the wing off of one airplane, a wing off another, and I made me an airplane—my airplane. If you give me six of those bourbon bottles, I'll check you out in that plane and you can have it.' That sounded good to me, so we went over to Marcianise. It was raining lightly when we got there. We made two little runs around the field, and the major declared me checked out in his C-47. He took my six bottles of bourbon and disappeared. I then flew the airplane up to Rome. Days later I learned that at the Pomigliano depot near Naples sat thirty-nine brand-new C-47s which the Russians were going to get. They were sold to them for twenty thousand dollars apiece, three for fifty thousand dollars. The third C-47 was intended for spare parts. The planes had only ferry time on them. At the first opportunity, I jumped into my piece of flying junk and flew it over to Pomigliano where the brand-spanking-new C-47s sat. The American captain in charge of the planes was friendly and easygoing. Giving him the biggest smile I could muster, I said to him, 'Favano, I want to take this piece of junk I flew in with and put it at the end of that line and get me one of those new ones.' He laughed and agreed. We changed the serial numbers around, parked the old C-47 next to the others bound for Russia, and I flew off in my own brand-new C-47."

Now here is an American Army Air Forces officer with his personal C-47 to fly wherever he chose to go on his days off. That he had this plane at his disposal was of course known by his superiors, and tolerated. Then came a unique opportunity for Hack Mixson to put his "private" airplane to official use—flying a king to his coronation. In 1946 King Victor Emmanuel of Italy, a staunch supporter of former dictator Mussolini, was forced to abdicate. Victor Emmanuel's son Umberto was to be coronated instead to soothe the people's ill feelings against Emmanuel. On the day of the coronation, the new king's airplane was waiting for him at the Rome airport to fly him and his entourage to Naples where the coronation was to take place. A crowd had gathered at Centocele airport around the new king's airplane. Umberto, fearing sabotage, asked American authorities for help, which came in the form of a highly polished, brand-new C-47 piloted by none other than our enterprising Lieutenant Colonel Marion C. Mixson at nearby Ciampino airfield. Hack's C-47 sat idling at the end of the runway, the king's royal party drove up, and off they went to Naples where Umberto was crowned the new king of Italy. The royal family stayed in touch for many years and in appreciation for his service to the new king, Mixson was awarded the Italian Order of St. Maurice and Lazarous. "I flew that airplane for a year," Mixson recalled when I saw him last, a big smile crossing his face. "When the time came for me to go home, there was no one to turn the C-47 in to, because the airplane didn't officially exist. My boss, Admiral Stone, quickly solved my problem by giving it to the Italian air force.

"Incidentally, most B-24, B-25, and B-17 bombers based in Italy with the 15th Air Force at the end of the war were destroyed. Only a few were flown home by their crews. For a while I flew a brand-new B-25. German prisoners took the armor plating out of it, stripped the paint, and polished the airplane to a high gloss. Although I had orders to turn the plane in to be destroyed like many of the other bombers, I kept stalling for about two months. Finally, I got a message that if I didn't turn in the plane I was going to be court-martialed. So I flew it down to the Pomigliano depot. My buddy came down in 'my' C-47 to take me back. By the time we finished filing our clearance for our return flight, they had drained the gas out of that beautiful B-25, cut the engines off, cut holes in the crankcase and into the propeller blades. That airplane was completely smashed in about an hour.

"Late in 1946 I returned home to Charleston. I was a reserve officer then, not a regular officer, and was discharged from the Army Air Forces with the rank of lieutenant colonel. At twenty-eight I tried to reenter the Mixson family wholesale seed business. I was used to staying at the Plaza Athenai in Athens and the best hotels in Paris, Rome, and Cairo. I found myself traveling through South Carolina and Georgia, staying in hotel rooms with one lightbulb hanging from the ceiling. In 1948 I got a message from the air force offering me a regular commission, giving me twenty-four hours to accept or decline. Naturally, I accepted. My rank was that of a major in the regular air force. I was assigned to the 343rd Squadron of the 55th Reconnaissance Group at MacDill Air Force Base in Tampa, Florida. They were flying B-17s, C-45s, and C-47s equipped for aerial photography—a mapping outfit. Within weeks we transferred to Topeka, Kansas, and then, in October 1949, the 55th Group was disbanded. I was transferred to the 91st Reconnaissance Group at Barksdale AFB, Louisiana. I stayed there from October 1949 until June 1950, when I went to the Air Command and Staff College at Maxwell AFB, Alabama. That month the Korean War started and I was promoted once again to lieutenant colonel. When I reported back to Barksdale in December, the group had transitioned to the RB-45C, a four-engine jet aircraft, and I was given command of the 323rd Strategic Reconnaissance Squadron."

With the impetus of the Korean War, then referred to for political reasons as a police action, British Prime Minister Winston Churchill and President Harry S. Truman agreed to a combined aerial reconnaissance program for flights over the western Soviet Union. At the time, the only aircraft able to implement such a program was the RB-45C Tornado, the first American all-jet bomber. RAF Sculthorpe, hidden away among the hedgerows of rural and remote East Anglia, was home to B-45A Tornado bombers of the 47th Bombardment Wing assigned to the United States Air Force in Europe, USAFE. The reconnaissance version of the B-45 was assigned to the Strategic Air Command, SAC. Although there were organizational differences between the bomber and reconnaissance units, having the same aircraft type at one air base simplified maintenance and support functions. In all other respects, the three squadrons of B-45A bombers and the one rotational squadron of RB-45C reconnaissance aircraft remained separate. Command and control of the RB-45Cs, regardless of location, was exercised by headquarters SAC located in Omaha, Nebraska, and commanded by the legendary Curtis E. LeMay.

"Soon after I checked out in the RB-45C at Barksdale, I was sent in May 1951 to RAF Sculthorpe. Our presence at Sculthorpe consisted of the twelve aircraft of the 323rd SRS, which I commanded. By the time I arrived at Sculthorpe, RAF air crews had already joined the squadron and flown one or two joint missions. By the end of July, I returned to the United States, accompanied by three RAF air crews to continue their training at Barksdale AFB. We landed at Barksdale in a KB-29 tanker about nine o'clock in the evening. The Brits wore their heavy RAF winter uniforms. When we left England early that morning, it was chilly. When we landed at Barksdale at nine o'clock in the evening, it was ninety degrees, the humidity was 99 percent, and a thunderstorm and a tornado had just come across the end of the airfield. The RAF flyers soon got used to their new Louisiana environment and quickly made friends among the American air crews. The three RAF crews and a couple of extras were led by Squadron Leader John Crampton. Crampton was a tall, lean man with extensive World War II experience flying Whitley and Halifax heavy bombers for RAF Bomber Command. His lead radar navigator, Flight Lieutenant Rex Sanders, had similar combat experience over Germany. Only those two were privy to the real purpose of their training at Barksdale. For the others, and anyone else asking questions, the story was that the Royal Air Force was considering acquiring a number of RB-45Cs on loan and wanted to conduct air-refueling trials. B-29s had been provided to the RAF under a previous agreement, so this seemed a reasonable explanation. Each RAF crew consisted of a pilot, a radar navigator, and a flight engineer. The flight engineer sat in the seat normally occupied by an American copilot. The Brits didn't use copilots, used flight engineers instead who were not qualified to fly the airplane, although they knew the aircraft systems intimately. None of our aircraft, unlike the B-45 bombers, carried defensive armament, so there were no gunners on the crews.[55]

"As for my role in this extremely sensitive and highly classified operation, I was in charge of the planned overflights of the Soviet Union as far as SAC was concerned. To a limited degree I was involved in the mission planning and accompanied Crampton and Sanders to Bomber Command at High Wycombe near London to sit in on their briefings. There the routes were drawn up, and we met with Air Chief Marshal Sir Ralph Cochrane, Vice Chief of Air Staff, to discuss issues regarding the loan of the aircraft. I don't think SAC or anybody else on the American side had any real input into where the

Brits were going. The RAF did the planning and provided the air crews. The US Air Force provided the aircraft."

Captain Howard "Sam" Myers, a Berlin airlift veteran, was assigned to the 322nd squadron at Barksdale. Sam had his first flight in the RB-45C in May 1951. By July Sam recalled meeting RAF air crews both in the officers' club and on the flight line. He thought they were there to learn how to fly the RB-45 in case they acquired some for the RAF. He quickly struck up a casual friendship with a couple of the RAF pilots and navigators, but by August, the RAF flyers vanished. "I moved them up to Lockbourne AFB near Columbus, Ohio, the new location for the 91st SRW," recalled Hack Mixson. "A major part of the RAF air crew training took place at Lockbourne AFB, and was shared among the three squadrons of the 91st—my squadron, the 323rd, the 322nd commanded by Major Hal Connor, and the 324th SRS. The Brits cracked up one aircraft during a heavy landing, didn't hurt anybody but ruined the airplane." Recalls John Crampton, "The dramatic result of this incident was that Lockbourne's base commander along with myself and the pilot concerned were flown to Omaha, Nebraska, headquarters of the Strategic Air Command, to be interviewed personally by the commander-in-chief, General Curtis E. LeMay. The CinCSAC did not like people who destroyed his airplanes, and he left us in no doubt of that fact. His anger was directed mainly at the RAF pilot who had wrecked his RB-45C, and he departed for home from the United States soon thereafter. That pilot was immediately replaced with another RAF pilot." In September 1951 Sam Myers transferred with the rest of his squadron from Barksdale to Lockbourne and again ran into his RAF friends. In November, Sam was on his way to England as the 322nd squadron replaced the 323rd at RAF Sculthorpe for a three-month rotational, temporary duty, assignment. Soon after his arrival at Sculthorpe, that December, Sam again encountered his RAF colleagues, who by now had completed their training at Lockbourne. He began to wonder what was really going on. "During my stay at Sculthorpe," Sam recalled, "I had an RAF copilot and RAF radar navigator on several occasions. They stayed current in the aircraft by flying with us. We flew mostly along the periphery of the Soviet Union, but occasionally we flew over Soviet satellite countries, East Germany for instance. Cooperation between us and the RAF was excellent. They were great flyers."

"We rotated the three 91st Wing squadrons into Sculthorpe," Hack Mixson explained, "and because of my experience with the RAF crews and as the only one knowledgeable of the real purpose of their training, I remained behind in England when my squadron rotated home. All in all, I got to do about four three-month TDYs over there."

Meanwhile, plans were made for the first deep penetration of the Soviet Union. Four RB-45Cs at Sculthorpe were stripped of their US Air Force markings and repainted with Royal Air Force roundels on the fuselage and RAF colors on the tail fin. Aircraft numbers were omitted. On March 21, 1952, a night mission was flown into East Germany, east of Berlin, to find out how the Soviets would react to such an incursion. Their reaction wasn't sufficient to dissuade the planners from going ahead with the overflight they had planned for the night of April 17, 1952. In a 1998 letter to the Air Force Museum at Wright-Patterson Air Force Base, Dayton, Ohio, Squadron Leader John Crampton wrote, "Even though the story leaked out of the woodwork two or three years ago, I still find it strange to talk and write about it. While it was happening, it rivaled the Manhattan Project for secrecy. In fact, I think it outranked the Manhattan Project. While off base we weren't allowed to THINK about it. It was all well above top secret. It was at Sculthorpe that Hal Connor, the tough little Texan who commanded the (322nd) squadron, selected four of his airplanes (one was a spare) for our operational use." Hal Connor was the commander of the 322nd SRS, to which Sam Myers was assigned and which at the time was pulling a rotational tour of duty at Sculthorpe. Connor, however, was not aware of what the RAF was up to. Hack Mixson and a handful of highly placed military and political officials were the only Americans who knew what was in the works.

On the night of April 17, 1952, three RB-45Cs in RAF colors rose into the East Anglia sky and proceeded to their air-refueling area to the north of Denmark. The three aircraft topped off their fuel tanks from US Air Force KB-29 refueling tankers and proceeded on their individual routes, flying at thirty-six thousand feet in total radio silence into the heart of the Soviet Union. One plane photographed targets in the Baltic states of Estonia, Latvia, and Lithuania, Poland and the former German province of East Prussia. The second aircraft flew across Belorussia as far as Orel, and the third plane, piloted by Squadron Leader Crampton, with Sanders as his radar navigator, took the longest route, crossing the Ukraine and penetrating as far as Rostov on the Black Sea. Each route had frequent turning points to include a maximum number of potential targets—Soviet air bases and similar targets of strategic importance. "Timing was critical," Crampton recalls, "because our intelligence agencies would be listening for the Soviet air defense reaction to our deep penetration of their airspace. There were neither lights on the ground nor any signs of human habitation, quite unlike the rest of Europe. We continued our steady climb at mach .68 to thirty-six thousand feet and covered our briefed route taking the target photographs as planned. It was all so quiet as to be distinctly eerie. Finally, we turned for home and in due course began the letdown into Sculthorpe. We landed without incident after ten hours and twenty minutes in the air."

A month after the RAF flew its deep-penetration mission into the Soviet Union, Sam Myers prepared to return to the United States. "I went out to the flight line to preflight my aircraft for the return trip. I distinctly remember a logo painted on the nose of the aircraft—it was gone. And there was the slightest hint of an RAF roundel on the fuselage. It was clearly one of the aircraft used by the RAF for its overflights, but at the time I could only guess."

In October Hack Mixson was alerted for another possible RAF mission planned for late December. "Four aircraft were repainted at RAF Sculthorpe in RAF colors, but at the last minute the mission was canceled. It was December 18, 1952, just before Christmas, and everyone wanted to get home. I called headquarters Strategic Air Command in Omaha, and they decided to have us fly the airplanes home without first repainting them. While there were four airplanes, the RAF only had three full air crews to fly them. They were short a pilot for the fourth crew. So I flew one of them back with a British engineer in the copilot's seat and Rex Sanders as my radar navigator. It was a long and tiring flight, since the engineer couldn't help me fly the plane. Snow was blowing at Lockbourne when we arrived. There were some surprised looks by the ground crew when we taxied in, resplendent in the colors of the Royal Air Force. In January 1953 SAC began transferring our RB-45Cs to the Tactical Air Command. Between January and March 1953 I checked out in the B-47 bomber at McCoy AFB near Orlando, Florida, along with Hal Austin and many others who once flew the RB-45C Tornado. Late that year, once the 91st Wing became operational flying the new RB-47E, we deployed to Nouasseur Air Base in Morocco. While at Nouasseur I got a message to see General LeMay at Offutt—immediately. I caught a ride on a plane and headed back to Nebraska. Once at Offutt I was directed to get down to Shaw AFB at Sumter, South Carolina, and pick up four RB-45Cs, then take them to Wright-Patterson AFB for modification to their radars. And upon completion of the modifications, fly them to Sculthorpe. The aircraft had by then been taken over by the Tactical Air Command and TAC crews flew four of them to Wright-Patterson AFB, and then to Sculthorpe. The radar modification was implemented under the supervision of English radar experts, who managed to significantly improve the picture quality making it very crisp and clear, high resolution radar. When the aircraft arrived at Sculthorpe in early April 1954, Crampton and his bunch were waiting for the airplanes. They were repainted in RAF colors, and we waited for the launch date on routes nearly identical to those flown in 1952."

The date of the new mission was April 28, 1954, ten days past the two-year anniversary of the 1952 flights—and ten days before Colonel Harold Austin would make his historic flight over the Kola Peninsula in an RB-47E photo-reconnaissance aircraft. Soviet generals surely must have been enraged not only by the brazenness of British and American "spy" flights, but also by their own impotence of not being able to prevent them. That year, the Russians shot down two USAF RB-29 reconnaissance aircraft operating over the Sea of Japan off the Russian coast with heavy loss of life. Those aircraft were not overflying Soviet territory, instead were over international waters, but were easy targets for the Russians to vent their frustrations.

"Once again three RAF RB-45Cs staggered into the air from RAF Scult-horpe," recalls Crampton, "and headed for northern Denmark to refuel. After our refueling we again climbed to thirty-six thousand feet and proceeded on our individual missions. I was headed towards Kiev, when there was the sudden heart-stopping appearance of golden antiaircraft fire dead ahead, detonating at our height. My reaction was instinctive. The throttles opened wide and I hauled the airplane around on its starboard wing tip until the gyrocompass pointed west. I began a gentle hundred-foot-per-minute descent because that made us seem to go a bit faster, and since we had been observed I thought it best to change height as well as speed and direction, thus giving the gunners down below three new problems. I asked Sanders to give me a course steer to Fuerstenfeldbruck. I flew the RB-45C just on the right side of the buffet and it sort of trembled affectionately. We met up with our tankers over West Germany, but for the first time the refueling boom refused to stay connected. I thought it wiser to land at Fuerstenfeldbruck and refuel the conventional way." The April 1954 flight was the last deep penetration mission in the RB-45C flown by the RAF—but it was not to be the last time those aircraft would operate over the Soviet Union. On March 27, 1955, three RB-45Cs, led by the commander of the 19th Tactical Reconnaissance Squadron at RAF Sculthorpe, Major Anderson, flew essentially the same routes flown before by Squadron Leader Crampton and his crews. They all returned safely as well.

Colonel Marion C. Mixson, better known as Hack to his friends, continued to serve for many years in the secret world of strategic reconnaissance. In 1955 he transferred to a super-secret reconnaissance program run by the CIA, piloting Kelly Johnson's high-flying U-2. He was involved in nearly every aspect of that program, from getting the aircraft operational to hiring air crews to flying them out of various locations in Germany, Japan, Thailand, and Pakistan. After five years of constantly being on the move with the U-2 program, Mixson assumed command of the 55th SRW, in which he served as a young major in 1948 soon after being recalled to active duty. The wing had been reactivated and still operated out of Forbes AFB, Topeka, Kansas, flying RB-47H electronic-reconnaissance aircraft and RB-47K photo-reconnaissance aircraft. The 55th SRW, specifically the 343rd SRS, was my first duty assignment out of flight training, and Colonel Mixson was my wing commander and pinned my first Air Medal on my chest upon returning from a reconnaissance deployment against the Soviet Union. At the time, I had no idea what a storied career he had had. Hack Mixson retired from the air force in 1970 as commanding officer of the 100th SRW, a U-2 wing, based at

Lieutenant Colonel Mixson at RAF Sculthorpe, Norfolk, England, in 1952, posing with members of the RAF Special Duty Flight. Flight Commander John Crampton stands to Mixson's left.

A group picture of four RB-45C aircraft in Royal Air Force livery at RAF Sculthorpe. Three aircraft were flown; one was a spare.

Davis-Monthan AFB, near Tucson, Arizona. He settled in Tampa, Florida, his wife Mary's hometown, and near MacDill AFB and the occasional smell of jet fuel. In retirement Hack ran a successful real estate business in Tampa, was involved in community affairs and in helping the elderly—never considering himself as being amongst them. As with so many of Colonel Mixson's generation of flyers, it had been quite a ride, as the saying goes. He had gone from

Mixson in May 1951 at Barksdale AFB, Louisiana, in front of an RB-45C Tornado photo reconnaissance aircraft. Mixson and Austin flew in the same wing, but were assigned to different squadrons.

a tiny forty-five horsepower Aeronca to the lumbering B-24 bomber, to the sleek and fast RB-45 jet, then to the RB-47 and finally the U-2 spy plane. "I loved every minute of it, and every airplane I ever flew," Hack Mixson said to me when I last saw him.

Colonel Marion C. Mixson, who survived the carnage of World War II in the bloody skies over Germany, who then devoted much of the rest of his professional life to what we euphemistically called *strategic reconnaissance*—very dangerous missions to gain vital information about the aims and objectives of the Soviet Union—went "west" in 2010. All too few Americans know anything about men like him, about the sacrifices they made so willingly, to include laying down their lives, if that's what it took to do the job. Squadron Leader John Crampton, Royal Air Force, was Mixson's counterpart in every imaginable way. He too survived World War II over Germany, flying Halifax bombers. Anne Turner, John Crampton's daughter, wrote me when he died in June 2010, "When my father was first in the hospital back in February, and becoming more able to communicate again, I asked him which—given a choice—of all the airplanes he had ever flown he would like to have up on the wall to look at.

He replied in a faint voice, 'The RB-45C.' I went on the internet, found a picture, blew it up and posted it on the wall ahead of his bed. He had the picture beside him on the wall in the nursing home, along with his beloved model of the aircraft, when he died. What remarkable men they all were flying those brave missions. I am very proud of my papa." And so are we, Anne—and of all the valorous men who kept our lands safe.

BERNARD T. NOLAN

B-24/B-17

Voices of the Mighty Eighth

No graves no markers in the ground to show or tell their tale.
Yet I still hear them in the wind, their voices never fail.
Blown to bits and pieces, scattered in the skies.
They tell me: please do not forget, we live behind your eyes.
And yes they do, I hear their call, their voices strong and clear.
Each one is burned upon my soul forever year to year.
The debt we owe to all of them, we never can repay.
But listen—cherish peace and love and live them every day.
—An 8th Air Force Survivor, WWII ETO

"I flew thirty-three combat missions in the summer of 1944 with the 837th Bombardment Squadron of the 487th Bomb Group out of Lavenham airfield, also known as Station 137. I was twenty-one years old, a second lieutenant in the Army Air Forces, flying those aluminum death cages known as B-24s and B-17s. I didn't have time nor had the inclination to notice the beauty of the English countryside, nor the charm of Lavenham village. My prime emotion in those days was one of fear, complete with white knuckles, wet palms, and at times sheer terror. Men who have not gone into battle, risking their lives, can never wholly understand what it is like. I grew to dislike the experience intensely, yet climbed into those aluminum death cages without hesitation not wanting to let the others down. At age twenty-one I was more boy than man, but I would grow up in 1944, never again to be what I was before."

Bernard Thomas Nolan was born in 1923 in Forest Hills, New York. His mother, Eileen, died when he was only eight, and the depression drove his

Second Lieutenant Bernard Nolan, age twenty, upon graduation from pilot training. He flew both B-24 and B-17 bombers with the 487th Bombardment Group out of Lavenham, England.

family into poverty, his father into alcohol. Bernard was no stranger to hunger and cold, nor to visions of a future that seemed dark and without promise. Both of his older sisters, Eileen and Mary Jane, and he had to quit high school to put bread on the table. His family unraveled, held together by the thinnest of margins of their often woefully inadequate efforts. "I took my first full-time job in a textile printing plant at age seventeen, but I had been earning my own way in life since the age of fourteen. Although each of us would eventually find a way to escape our misery, it left deep scars in us all. My escape from a life of misery and sorrow proved to be my burning desire. The first toy I treasured was a small, cast-iron monoplane that I would maneuver by hand around the house, dreaming I was the pilot. Later I built rubber band–powered models. And I read everything I could lay my hands on that had anything to do with aviation. There were plenty of cheap magazines, such as *G8 and His Battle Aces*, which I would literally devour the minute they hit the newsstand. I can say honestly that I knew every airplane that passed overhead, knew what type it was and its performance characteristics. Anything about flying totally absorbed me, and provided a ready escape from my broken home. With the beginning of war in Europe, and especially after Pearl Harbor, I saw my chance to make my dream become a reality.

"A month or so before Pearl Harbor I tried to join the Royal Canadian Air Force. The RCAF was recruiting heavily in the US, but they were after people with some flight experience, and of course I had none. But my chance came after Pearl Harbor when the government lowered age and academic requirements for the aviation cadet program. Before Pearl Harbor you had to be twenty-one before you could be commissioned in the Army Air Corps and you needed at least two years of college. After December 1941 the age requirement dropped to eighteen and high school would do. I was nineteen, but didn't have a high school diploma. The door was slammed shut again for me. Then I learned that even if you didn't have a high school diploma you could get into the cadet program if you passed a rigorous written examination. I began to study hard to prepare myself, focusing on mathematics and English. In April 1942 I thought I was ready to give it a try. I went to the recruiting center on Whitehall Street in New York City and registered. The day of the examination I took the exam papers, studied them carefully, and then handed them back to the administrator and left. I learned that the examination focused not on math and English, but instead on American history and our political system, the structure of our government, and the names of people holding senior positions, such as the secretary of war, and so on. I refocused my study efforts and that July took the examination and passed.

"After being sworn into the US Army, I was not a cadet yet, I had to pass the physical examination. I was tall, thin, and underweight. The morning of the physical I stuffed myself with food—mostly bananas—and I passed that hurdle as well, although by a thin margin. After I passed my physical examination, I was sent home to wait to be called up. I continued to work in the textile printing plant where I had worked for the past two years—waiting for that magic letter to arrive that would change my world. That day finally came on February 3, 1943, when I boarded a train at Penn Station, filled with others like me. Our first stop was a classification center near Nashville, Tennessee. Here we changed from civilian clothes into ill-fitting army uniforms, lost our hair, learned how to stand at attention, yell 'Yes sir,' until we couldn't yell anymore, then marched wherever we went. My group of arrivals was assigned to Class 43J, the letter J denoting the tenth month of the year. We took tests to determine our aptitudes and were interviewed, then notified what we would train for: pilot, navigator, or bombardier. The fourth option, not voluntary either, was the infantry, if washed out of the program for whatever reason. March and April 1943 I spent at Maxwell Field, Montgomery, Alabama, in what was called preflight training. Preflight involved classes in meteorology, the theory of flight, communications, and whatever someone dreamed up would make us better airmen. Not to forget lots of physical exercise and oodles of discipline.

"Once I survived this phase of training, I was sent to primary training at Cape Girardeau, Missouri. Again we received lots of ground school, academics and we actually got to fly in a real airplane—the open cockpit PT-23, with tandem seats, the instructor for some strange reason sitting in the front, and his pupil in the rear. It took three cadets to start the engine—two to crank, and one in the cockpit at the ignition switch and throttle. When airborne, the PT-23 was a pussycat, very forgiving and user friendly. I loved it. We communicated with our instructors in the front seats by hand signals. There also was a funnel-shaped mouthpiece into which the instructor could yell, called a Gosport tube. But I don't ever recall understanding a single word my instructor shouted into that contraption. Flying came naturally to me. I had spent so much time building airplane models and studying the theory of flight that I knew intuitively what to do when my instructor turned the controls over to me. I learned to do stalls, spins, and forced landings. Then we went to aerobatics. It was fun. On graduation from primary training we cadets were given the opportunity to fly in the front seat of the PT-23, with the instructor in the rear. From primary we moved over to Walnut Ridge in Arkansas for basic flight training for a couple more months. Here we flew the BT-13 Vultee 'Vibrator' as it had been christened because of all the noises it made. There was another variant of the BT-13, the BT-15, that had plywood wing and fuselage sections, reflecting the demands of the war effort. We focused on formation flying, then formation takeoffs and landings. I recall on takeoff how difficult it was to maintain the lead aircraft in sight, trying to snatch glances of the runway at the same time so as not to veer off to the side. After completing night flying we moved over to Freeman Field in Seymour, Indiana, for training in the twin-engine AT-10 Beechcraft. I wanted to fly the North American AT-6, which everyone raved about, and was disappointed when I learned we would fly the AT-10. There were no solo flights in advanced training. We either flew with an instructor or another student. By now my class had been reduced to half of its former size. Those who washed out got to go either into navigator/bombardier training, or if totally unfit for flying, they wound up with a rifle in their hands in the infantry. November 3, 1943, was the day I had dreamed about—I was commissioned a second lieutenant and pinned on my silver pilot's wings. The kid from the Bronx without a high school education had come a long way I thought, never really thinking of the world I was about to enter.

"When I graduated from flight training, I thought I knew all there was to know about flying and regarded myself as a hot pilot. A rude awakening was in store for me. My orders read to report to some place in Salt Lake City, Utah, which turned out to be a converted cattle barn. I naively thought I was going into fighters—twin-engine P-38s of course. My mouth dropped open when another second lieutenant approached and asked, 'You Nolan?' Yeah, I replied suspiciously. Said the other brown-bar, 'Hi, I'm Chuck Eubank. You are my copilot. We are going to a B-24 unit.' Ours was the newly organizing 487th Bomb Group, which along with the 486th, our sister group, would comprise the 92nd Bombardment Wing, headed for the 8th Air Force in England. We headed down to Tucson, Arizona, to train on the latest version of the B-24, the

D-model. The copilot's seat became my window on the world for months to come. We were all so young. I turned twenty-one a few weeks earlier, which was about the average age of our ten-man crew. Eubank, the pilot, was the oldest at age twenty-six. The youngest, an eighteen-year-old kid named Rivers, manned the nose turret. Frank Nelson was the navigator, age twenty-two; the bombardier was Dave Wilcox, my age. Both came from Montana. Our crew would be together for less than a year—but it was to be an experience that bonded us for life.

"By March 1944 the 487th Bomb Group reached its full strength of seventy-two crews assigned to its four squadrons, mine being the 837th. Each squadron had eighteen crews and aircraft. On March 18 we received our brand-new B-24H aircraft from the Willow Run factory in Michigan. Our very own was aircraft number 42-52748—it would die on its twentieth combat mission. We left Alamogordo, New Mexico, where we had received our combat crew training, and departed for a modification center in Herrington, Kansas. Herrington had little to offer in amenities—a small Kansas town, cold, wet, with the wind never really letting up. Here our aircraft received the latest modifications. We moved on to West Palm Beach, Florida, on March 30—a very welcome departure I might add. The flight to West Palm Beach was in weather. We were cruising at sixteen thousand feet when we inadvertently entered a thunderstorm. Neither Eubank nor I had any training in how to deal with thunderstorms. The airplane nearly got away from us while we tried to maintain our altitude—precisely what we shouldn't have done. After being chewed up for too many minutes to remember, we were finally spit out into a hole allowing us to make a circling descent. Our position, it turned out, was about twenty miles off the coast near Melbourne. We had no idea how we got there. One positive aspect of this experience was that we gained a lot of respect for the structural integrity and strength of our aircraft."

Most heavy bombers going to the 8th Air Force in England were routed along the northern route to their destinations—flying from Westover in Massachusetts, then to Newfoundland, Iceland, and eventually to a base in Scotland. There the B-17s or B-24s were taken from their ferry crews and distributed to combat wings and groups in need of replacement aircraft. The crews were then assigned to a "personnel distribution center" and parceled out to whichever units had experienced sufficient crew losses requiring replacements. Ergo the term Replacement Training Unit—most trainees never knew what the initials RTU really stood for: death at its worst, imprisonment as a POW at its best. Over a period of three years the 8th Air Force lost 6,500 B-17 and B-24 heavy bombers—5,548 as a result of combat and another 952 due to accidents. The 8th Air Force attempted to maintain its bomber strength at a level of 2,000 heavy bombers. That number had to be replaced with new aircraft three times over in a period of less than three years. The bloodletting was incessant, especially in 1942 and 1943, when it seemed nearly impossible for a bomber crew to complete 25 missions. The 15th Air Force, in the Mediterranean Theater of Operations, MTO, lost another 2,755 heavy bombers in combat and 459 due to accidents for a total loss of 3,214 aircraft with ten-men crews. A total of 55,000 American airmen died in the European Theater of Operations (ETO), around 14,000 were wounded, and another 33,000 became prisoners of war.[56] British losses in Bomber Command, although over a longer period of time and flying mostly at night, were even heavier than those experienced by American bomber crews. Bomber Command aircrew killed in action or ground accidents came to 55,500. Another 9,835 became prisoners of war. Of the 125,000 aircrew who served in RAF Bomber Command, 53 percent were either killed in action or became POWs.[57] I have a British friend who retired from the Royal Air Force in the rank of Air Vice Marshall, flew Spitfires and Mustangs in World War II. On one occasion, Air Vice Marshall Harbison recalls, their commander asked his fighter pilots if any of them would like to fly as observers on a night bomber raid over Germany. There were no takers. Fighter pilots had a much better survival rate than either American or British bomber crews. The air war over Europe was a young man's war, and on both sides these teens and young twenty-year-olds died by the scores. There was nothing romantic about the air war over Germany.

The southern route for aircraft heading to the ETO started at West Palm Beach, Florida, then generally passed through Puerto Rico; Georgetown, British Guiana; Belem and Natal, Brazil, and onward to the Ascension Islands for some short-legged aircraft. Others, such as the B-24s of the 487th Bomb Group, flew direct to Dakar, in Africa. This was the shortest route to get to the Mediterranean Theater of Operations. The 487th departed Georgetown on April 5, 1944, heading for Natal, then on to Dakar across the South Atlantic, and from there to Marrakech, Morocco. On April 16 Eubank and Nolan pointed their aircraft north heading for an air base called Nutts Corner, near Belfast, Northern Ireland. "After nearly fourteen hours of utterly boring flying we finally approached Ireland above a solid deck of clouds. About a hundred miles out our navigator, Frank Nelson, gave us an estimated time of arrival for Nutts Corner, and we began our slow descent. My radio compass was solidly locked onto the signal emanating from Nutts Corner. All seemed well, going according to plan. Eubank called Nelson and told him that he would take it from here. On we went. We passed through five thousand feet, then three thousand feet—dutifully reporting our position and altitude to the Nutts Corner controller. Chuck Eubank eased back on the throttles and we began our final descent at five hundred feet per minute. We were still in the clouds, but when the radio compass needle swung 180 degrees, I noted with pride that we had just passed the transmitter site and were doing our first instrument approach to a strange field. We went through the before-landing checklist, lowered the gear, and broke through the last remaining clouds. Dead ahead was the outline of a runway. Chuck greased our B-24 onto the runway—everything went just right. A blue jeep approached with a couple of guys in strange-looking blue uniforms. The English officers politely informed us that we had landed at the wrong airfield—the American base they informed us lay three miles ahead, on the same bearing as the one we used.

"It was April 17 when we finally touched down at Nutts Corner, the American base. All of us were totally fatigued. After minimal rest we flew south on the 18th to our final destination—Lavenham, home of the 487th Bomb Group with its four squadrons of B-24 bombers, mine being the 837th. Lavenham was a typically rustic British village about ten miles south of Bury St. Edmunds. Its castle-like church and the Swan, a welcoming public house that served warm, dark beer, were the only buildings of note. For us bachelors, girl-chasing was the primary off-duty sport—unfortunately, whatever girls called Lavenham home had left long ago for more lucrative spots such as London. Ours was a typical Army Air Forces field with three intersecting runways and nearby hardstands for the seventy-two bombers of our four squadrons. Runways, taxiways, and hardstands all were made from rubble taken from bombed areas of London, covered with a layer of cement. We lived in Quonset huts, with officers and enlisted men housed separately. Life on the base, other than the essential briefings and training that took up our time, was dull beyond belief. We took every opportunity we got to get out and go to Bury, as the Brits referred to Bury St. Edmunds, then ventured further afield to Cambridge. Cambridge was surrounded by American and British air bases and on any given day sported hundreds of airmen looking for girls. It turned out that sex was a readily available commodity in the larger towns, especially London where prostitutes plied their trade day and night. A guy could get laid in a bed for two English pounds, spend the night, breakfast included. A stand-up quickie in a doorway went for only ten shillings, not even a pound, which had twelve shillings. Our transportation to Cambridge was always in the back of a six-by army truck. We bounced along over cobblestone roads at times with sore bottoms at the end of the run, but what the hell, it was free.

"On April 19, 1944, we were ordered to take our B-24H to the aircraft modification center at Warton, near Blackpool, on the west coast. Nearly all 8th Air Force bases were located on the east coast, closest to the European mainland, or down south. They installed steel plates and bullet-resistant glass for the pilots, added the Gee navigation radio system, and painted the large letter P in a white square on our tail—that was our group designator. While all this was going on, I headed into Blackpool, as did the rest of the crew, and met Irene, whose family had fled Latvia when the Russians occupied the country in 1939. After that I never saw Irene again, although we did correspond for a while. Once we returned to Lavenham, our aircraft was ready to go to war.

"The first missions we flew were practice missions to teach us how to get to altitude, join up and form a combat box. After climb out, which at times was a harrowing experience, we formed up in elements of threes, then into a squadron formation of eighteen aircraft. Our group usually fielded three squadrons for a mission—one was the lead squadron, then came a high and a low squadron, separated by five hundred feet. Once reaching the IP, Initial Point, near the target, we had to cease all evasive maneuvers and drop our bombs when the lead aircraft dropped its bombs. Then we proceeded to the Rally Point, the RP, where the group attempted to reassemble for the return flight to England. We worked our tails off flying those B-24 formations. The higher the altitude, the more difficult it became to fly the airplane. One of our most common problems was engine failure. The high power settings needed when flying in the thin air above twenty thousand feet made for a short engine life. Without superchargers we would have never been able to attain the high altitudes at which we routinely flew. Engine performance falls off markedly as the aircraft climbs and the density altitude changes—as the air gets thinner; turbo-superchargers kept the engine manifold pressures in the B-17 and B-24 engines constant, allowing us to operate above twenty thousand feet. Not that all missions were flown at those dangerous altitudes, which required fur-lined heated flying suits and constant access to aircraft oxygen. Many missions were flown at altitudes as low as ten to twelve thousand feet.

"All of us were of course interested in surviving a tour of twenty-five missions. In early 1943 the 8th Air Force loss rate was up to 8 percent—at that rate no one survived a twenty-five-mission combat tour. By the time we arrived in England, losses had diminished and a combat tour soon after our arrival was changed to thirty missions. There were many ways of dying, other than in actual combat. Midair collisions, especially on climb out, were common. You were just as dead in a midair as when you were shot down by flak or a German fighter. The chances of surviving the latter two were higher than surviving a midair collision. On July 20, 1944, two of our aircraft collided over the base during a practice exercise to check out new equipment. I witnessed another collision during formation assembly in August 1944. The orange fireball spit out large aircraft chunks, trailing smoke plumes as they plummeted to the ground below. Others 'bought the farm' doing stupid stuff. He was by far the hottest pilot in the 837th Squadron, flew as low as possible whenever he could. I was designated his copilot on a test flight. After an hour of this I was terrified. As we made our final approach, my feet were on the rudder pedals. He yelled, 'Don't you ever touch those God-damned controls when you are flying with me unless I tell you to.' I refused to fly with him again. A few days later he went on another test flight. No one would fly with him, so he got a sergeant to occupy the copilot's seat. He made one low pass too many and flew the aircraft into the trees. Aside from the flak, the fighters, and the intricacies of formation flying, there was plain old fatigue that could do you in, the bitter cold at high altitudes, and a loss of oxygen was terminal within minutes. It seemed that Chuck Eubank and I were always tired. By the time we reached altitude, fatigue was already at work. Nodding off in a formation was a sure ticket for an interview with St. Peter. Aside from the Germans, we had a multitude of ways to die.

"The 487th Group flew its first combat mission on May 7, 1944, against Liege, Belgium. Lieutenant Colonel Beirne Lay was the mission commander. Lay was a screenwriter before becoming a B-24 pilot and would later on write the screenplay for *Twelve O'Clock High* based on his own experiences. I flew my first mission on May 9 with Colonel Lay in the lead. The target was an airfield near Lyon, France. All of our aircraft recovered at Lavenham. Our mood was upbeat, like 'Hey, this ain't so bad after all.' On May 11, I wasn't on that mission, Colonel Lay was shot down in the lead aircraft over a German air base at Chateaudun." It was at Chateaudun, south of Paris, where the Germans had their long range reconnaissance operations flying four-engine Junkers 290 and Heinkel 177 aircraft. "Lay's timing was off and he flew over the heavily defended airfield at Chateaudun, losing four aircraft to flak, including his own. Lay managed to escape capture with the help of the French underground. We stood down after losing our commander until May 20. I flew my second mission on May 24 against Orly airfield near Paris. Like the first mission, it was another milk run. No more milk runs after May 24. On the 28th I flew my third mission against targets near Hannover. It was a rude awakening. I will not forget that day as long as I live. We lost a total of thirty-two aircraft.[58] As we approached the IP, my next ten minutes were filled with terror. We had to hold our altitude constant until bomb release. Eubank and I were leading the rear low element of three aircraft. The sky ahead was literally alive with flak bursts and a hailstorm of shrapnel bounced off our aircraft, or penetrated, hopefully not damaging anything critical or killing anyone. No one said a word. We were lost in our own fears. For the first time I witnessed a B-24 going down in flames. Its aft fuselage was completely gone. It burned bright white from the oxygen tanks just aft of the center wing box. A fuel fire burns yellowish-orange. That tailless B-24 fluttered downward like a falling leaf. I saw no parachutes.

"We got a three-day pass after this mission and headed for London where we tried to drown our fear in a place called the Florida Club. On May 31 we flew against targets in France and Belgium. As we crossed the English Channel at twenty-thousand feet, we could see the high clouds of a weather front ahead of us. Formation flying in clouds was terrifying. Our formation was able to hang together—I thought. When we got to the other side of the front, there was blue sky above and clouds below, B-24s were strewn all over the place. We turned around and flew back to Lavenham alone. On D-Day, June 6, and on June 7 we flew tactical support for the invasion. We went after anything that was transportation related. We lost one aircraft on June 7. It exploded over the target after taking a direct hit from flak. Three out of ten crewmen survived. On June 8, my seventh mission, half of our squadron of twelve aircraft aborted due to food poisoning. That morning we were fed a special gas-free diet. After becoming airborne both Chuck and I got diarrhea. We found some empty ammo boxes to relieve our pains. Although the lead aircraft with the Norden bombsights had all aborted, Chuck decided to press on—diarrhea or no diarrhea. Dave Wilcox, our bombardier, figured out a way for an accurate bomb release—so we pressed on. When the time came, Dave toggled the bombs. The other five aircraft which had remained with us toggled theirs when they saw our bombs coming out. Reconnaissance photos later showed that our bombs struck within the perimeter of the airfield that was our target.

"On June 20 I flew mission numbers 13 and 14. Our target was Hannover/Miesburg. I remember hearing pieces of flak rattling around in the bomb bay as they bounced off our five-hundred-pound bombs. One of our aircraft wasn't that lucky and exploded after being hit. There was only one survivor. A total of fifty bombers were lost that day out of a strike force of over 1,600 aircraft. Five hundred men didn't come home, many died.[59] On the way out of the target area I nearly had my head blown off. An antiaircraft shell exploded right off the right wingtip. I turned my head the instant I heard the sound of the shell exploding, when a piece of shrapnel penetrated the bulletproof glass to my right. Had I not turned my head. . . . The two-inch piece of shrapnel remained in the cockpit. I retrieved it and put it in my pocket. On June 23 I flew my sixteenth mission—I was halfway there, only fourteen more to go. I was on the wing of Van Dyke's aircraft. He took an 88mm shell directly in the bomb bay. There was a huge burst of orange flame, then the left and right wings slowly folded over the fireball. All I saw of the fuselage was the tail turret falling away with the gunner in his seat. The vision of that B-24 exploding lives on in my memory like an old photograph, never to be forgotten. There were no survivors. It would not be long before I would see firsthand what an aircraft funeral pyre could do to the human body.

"It was just another mission, number nineteen. My squadron was approaching the Belgian coast at sixteen thousand feet, climbing to our bomb run altitude of twenty-two thousand feet, when we were hit. There was no flak barrage, just an aimed volley, one of which went off just below the left wing, knocking out both engines. We were quickly out of the formation. Wilcox salvoed our bombs. We closed the bomb bay doors in case we had to ditch. With the six-thousand-pound bomb load gone we succeeded in reducing our rate of descent, trying like crazy to make England. When we crossed the coast, we were at five hundred feet above sea level, trying to stay airborne long enough to find some place level to put the aircraft down. I leaned across the cockpit and saw a runway dead ahead. We landed on that runway, which turned out to be an RAF base. Both landing gears were fully extended when we came down. A third engine quit just before touchdown. It was total luck finding this airstrip straight ahead of us, not requiring a turn or any maneuver that could have caused our aircraft to crash. After we got out, we saw that the flak had shredded the leading edge of the left wing between the two engines, taking out not only both engines but also destroying all the wiring in that part of the aircraft. We made the return trip to Lavenham in the back of an army truck. Nine aircraft were lost that day over enemy territory and more were written off with battle damage, including our own. That mission was the end of aircraft number 42-52748. On my next mission I would fly a brand-new B-24H which, unlike 52748, was not painted. Our leadership apparently decided that paint added lots of weight and provided little else in terms of protection. Mission number twenty-two on July 18 was my final mission in the B-24. Our group converted to the B-17, turning over our aircraft to the Second Air Division which flew only B-24 bombers. We were part of the Third Air Division, now flying only the B-17 aircraft.

"After a brief period of retraining into the B-17G my crew flew its first mission on August 1, 1944, against German airfields at Tours, France. Magdeburg followed on the 5th of August. We lost another aircraft that day. Again a direct hit in the bomb bay area. Surprisingly two of the ten-man crew survived. We continued to fly against targets in France and Germany, hitting airfields, harbor installations, and oil refineries. One thing our leaders tried to do for crews flying their last combat mission was to give them a 'milk run,' as much as that was possible. On our last mission the target could not have been more formidable—Duesseldorf in the Ruhr Valley, we called it 'happy valley.' I did not want to go to Duesseldorf. It was a place with lots of flak and enemy fighters, a place to stay away from. As we approached Duesseldorf, we could see units ahead of us being engulfed in an antiaircraft barrage. But then, as if ordained by some divine being, when it was our turn, the barrage suddenly stopped. The German fighters which usually appeared at a time like this didn't appear, and we got our 'milk run' after all. On the way home the crew exploded in joyous celebration.

"I came home from England on the *Montevideo*, a US Army troop ship, a converted passenger liner. In addition to the crew, there were sixty American

Lead crews of the 837th Squadron, 487th Bomb Group, January 1944. Nolan's crew is on the outside left, top to bottom: Charles Eubank—Pilot; Bernard Nolan—Copilot (with white scarf); Frank Nelson—Navigator; David Wilcox—Bombardier.

A B-24 of the 487th Bomb Group, 3rd Air Division, 8th Air Force, over France in 1944. The group eventually converted to B-17s, and all B-24s were reassigned to the 2nd Air Division. The square on the wing of this B-24 identifies it as a 3rd Air Division aircraft. The letter P was assigned to the 487th Bomb Group, Nolan's group. 1st Air Division aircraft had a triangle painted on their vertical stabilizer and wing, and a circle identified B-24s of the 2nd Air Division. (Art Stofko)

A B-17 of the 487th Bomb Group, Nolan's group, with its number 3 engine on fire after being hit by Me 262 cannon fire. The crew bailed out. (Ben Tepper Collection)

Out of control, a B-17 of the 487th Bomb Group enters a deadly dive after being hit by flak. The 487th Bomb Group lost a total of forty-eight aircraft to enemy action flying 185 combat missions. (James Hyland Collection)

German firefighters and children inspecting the remains of a hapless B-17 bomber from the 100th Bomb Group.

airmen aboard and five hundred German prisoners of war, all officers. The *Montevideo* arrived in New York harbor on a beautiful October day. I went home on leave, expecting to be sent into B-29 training and go off to the Pacific. I should have been ecstatic to get home in one piece. Instead, my mood was dark, I didn't feel like eating, and anxieties kept me from getting enough sleep. I was home, but nothing would ever be the same again. Although I anticipated more combat in the Far East, my combat days were actually behind me. The war went on in Europe and my old group, the 487th, lost five aircraft and crews in September 1944, two in October, six more in November, and twelve in December. The attrition continued. Death was always a random event. For my combat tour I was awarded the Distinguished Flying Cross simply because I survived.

"Once my leave was over, I was assigned to Florida, to an aerial gunnery school. Six months later I was in Lubbock, Texas, training to be an instrument instructor pilot in the AT-6, the airplane I wanted to fly, but didn't get to in pilot training. None of these assignments had any legs, until near war's end. In June 1945, I was assigned to fly the C-54, the military version of the DC-4 airliner, out of Charleston, South Carolina. In Charleston I met my future wife, Sunny. Sunny and I shared the rest of my air force career until my retirement in December 1965. Years followed working for NASA in Washington DC, where I live to this day. Wars end. Yet in my mind there are moments when I think I am still there. I see the flak bursting, the planes dying, and lives ending long before they should have."

ROBERT J. ANSPACH

P-47/Me 262/Fw 190/F-86

War

I've seen the fields where poppies grow, knelt by the crosses, row on row.
I've seen the shell-torn battlefield, where men are crushed and forced to yield.
I've seen war-mothers old and grey with bowed heads and I've heard them pray.
I've seen what once were loving sons disfigured by those murderous guns.
I've seen the toll of war and strife paid by the men who cherished life.
I've seen them as they crossed the bar—I've seen enough of bloody war.
—1st Sergeant Harry R. Chard, WWII ETO

Robert J. "Bob" Anspach was a Milwaukee boy, his mother and father of Pennsylvania Dutch descent. Bob had been exposed to airplanes early in life. "I can remember Lindbergh coming back on a cruiser from Europe and all the talk about him. He was a true American hero. When my family moved from Wisconsin to Ohio, my father took me every year to the Cleveland air races. I recall seeing Ernst Udet, Jimmy Doolittle, Roscoe Turner, and many other famous aviators. I went to the airport to watch planes taking off, and of course there were twenty-five-cent magazines, like *Battle Aces*, which I read religiously. Yet, I never thought I'd be flying an airplane myself. My family moved again, this time to Charleston, West Virginia. There I attended high school and graduated in 1940. The war was on and so was the draft. I wanted to join the paratroopers. My father took a dim view of my choice of service and suggested I take the Army Air Corps test instead. Nearly everyone in town who took the test flunked, so I didn't have high hopes of making it. 'If you don't pass,' my father promised, 'I'll sign the papers so you can join the paratroopers.' I passed.

14LS-9NOV.1944-G133-DAMAGED P47D #228955-NANCY, FRANCE-RESTRICTED

Bob Anspach flew a P-47D in combat in Europe while assigned to the 1st Tactical Air Force (Provisional), 358th FG, 365th FS—the Orange Tails. Bent props were a common occurrence on rutted airfields. Bob bellied one in after a combat mission. It was not to be his last experience of that nature.

"After graduating from flying school in class 43D I was sent to Bryan, Texas, for instrument training. From there we were sent to different flying training bases in the United States to set up instrument flying schools. I did that for a year, still flying BT-13s. That year I amassed a lot of flying time. I got the call to report to a fighter transition school for the P-47 Thunderbolt. Before I knew it, I was in Europe flying with the 365th Fighter Squadron, the Orange Tails, of the 358th Fighter Group. I was there for the Battle of the Bulge and ended the war in Sandhofen, Germany. For a fighter-bomber pilot I thought every mission was interesting, every mission different and exciting—firing my guns, dropping bombs, everything close to the ground. Once, though, I got shot up pretty badly. I was number three coming down on a target, and as I pulled out German flak nailed me. I lost one wheel, had a wing perforated, and the engine was hit. I had an escort to the bomb line where he told me to bail out. I said, 'Naw, I'll get her back.' At Toul airfield I bellied her in. The plane was ruined but it made me feel pretty good about the P-47.

"One day I was flying cover for a group of B-26s in the Lechfeld area. I was P-47 element lead, when all of a sudden, as I looked down onto the flight of bombers, there was an Me 262 jet fighter sitting right behind and a little above them, flying formation with them. The bombers didn't even know he was there, or they would have been firing their guns. We immediately broke down toward him, and the Me 262 virtually thumbed its nose at us, shoved the coals to it and disappeared in a steep climb. He didn't shoot. He obviously wasn't going to shoot anybody down. He sure could have with his four 30mm cannons. The war was nearly over. The German jets were up there just to show us the superiority of their aircraft. You can't imagine what it was like to see something like that, to see an Me 262 jet fighter in that setting. Outside of the eight or ten of us P-47 jocks, who else had seen something like that in our fighter group? We'd heard about the Me 262 from our intelligence people and we'd been told they were in our area, but no one in our squadron had ever seen one until that day. There he was, all by himself, totally superior to anything we had. To put it in perspective, imagine driving down the road in an old car at your maximum speed of forty miles an hour and have someone pass you at eighty—that's what it was like seeing the Me 262 climb away from us.

"I don't know how we were chosen, but one day during the morning briefing our operations officer mentioned that headquarters was looking for volunteers to fly captured German aircraft. The briefer didn't mention jets. I was young and had no entanglements, so I raised my hand. Fred Hillis was in my outfit too and he volunteered as well. There were several more, but only the two of us were selected. Once the selection was made, Hillis and I were flown to Lechfeld in a B-26. I don't recall talking to anybody the first day at Lechfeld. Some army troops were moving airplanes around and they pointed to an empty tent. That's where we slept. All of us arrived within a day or two of each other. We saw some planes that looked like they were ready to fly. We didn't see our boss, a Colonel Harold 'Hal' Watson, until a couple of days after we got to Lechfeld. The first person Hillis and I met was a Lieutenant Bob Strobell, who seemed to be running the operation."

Bob Anspach didn't know it yet, but he had become a member of a select group of former P-47 flyers who were to check out in captured German Me 262 jets, and eventually fly them to Cherbourg, France, for shipment to the United States. Upon their arrival, he and others were to fly them from the east coast to Wright Field, near Dayton, Ohio, where they were to be evaluated. All of them had been picked by Colonel Watson's intelligence people because of their flying record, including extensive instrument time as instructor pilots. This select group of pilots, later known as Watson's Whizzers, in addition to Hillis and Anspach included Lieutenants Roy W. Brown and James K. Holt from the 86th Fighter Group; Lieutenants William V. Haynes and Horace D. McCord from the 27th Fighter Group; and Captain Kenneth E. Dahlstrom from the 324th Fighter Group. All of these groups were assigned to the First Tactical Air Force (Provisional), a creation of General Spaatz, which was disbanded immediately upon the end of hostilities in Europe, making their pilots available to Watson. Colonel Watson, assigned to headquarters USSTAF, was personally tasked by General Spaatz, the commander of the United States

Strategic Air Forces in Europe, to bring home as many German jets as he could lay his hands on, such as the Me 262 and the Arado 234. The project's code name was Operation Lusty, kicked off by the general himself on April 25, 1945, with a terse message to his commanders: "Each Air Force of this command is hereby notified of initiation of . . . Operation Lusty, which has equal priority with operations. . . . You are therefore directed to render all possible assistance . . . to ensure successful accomplishmitt of this mission. . . . Make available all military and civilian technical personnel not engaged in critical operational duties. . . ." In other words, Colonel Harold Watson had carte blanche when it came to anything related to Operation Lusty. At one time Watson had served as the chief of maintenance for the 1st TAF, which led him to select his pilots from that organization's Thunderbolt groups. Lieutenant Bob Strobell, a P-47 pilot who had completed his combat tour earlier in the war, was assigned to the staff of the 1st TAF and gained Watson's confidence. Watson then appointed him leader of the group that was to become known as Watson's Whizzer pilots.[60]

Bob Anspach recalled that Watson "showed up briefly at Lechfeld, explained to us what we were doing and why. Otherwise he stayed pretty much out of our way. There wasn't all that much to this operation. We were there to learn to fly the airplanes, the German Me 262 jet, that was it. We were just a bunch of pilots, not a real organization—but I do think we were the first Army Air Forces operational jet pilots, and you could say that we were the first American jet fighter squadron, Watson's Whizzers, although we flew captured enemy aircraft. We even designed our own unit patch, which one of our crew chiefs came up with and painted on the nose of every Me 262, of which we had ten. We had plenty of time on our hands. There wasn't all that much to do to keep us busy. We'd eat in the mess tent Bob Strobell had the 54th Air Disarmament Squadron people set up for us. The 54th element assigned to us was there to provide whatever support we needed from jet engine maintenance to cooking our food. Occasionally some guy would go down to the Lech River and throw in some grenades, kill some very large brown trout, and we'd have a fish fry, a welcome change from powdered eggs and Spam. There were also the mundane things to tend to, like laundry. Germans would stop at the fence by the field and try to talk to us. That way we met some of the local people. They were all very contrite. Victims of circumstances, I thought. On a walk through town I saw a woman and her daughter working in their garden. I asked her if she would do my laundry. She nodded her head. I paid her in German marks, not worth much, and rations, which she was pleased to receive.

"We had two German Messerschmitt test pilots with us to check us out in the new jet—Karl Baur, who was the Messerschmitt chief test pilot at Lechfeld, and Ludwig 'Willie' Hoffmann, also a test pilot like Baur. Baur flew mostly with

Colonel Watson looking for more Me 262s and Arado 234s. Willie Hoffmann spent his time with us. He liked schnapps, and was a lot of fun to be around. I'd get a bottle of schnapps, and that got Willie started talking about this or that from his never-ending repertoire of flying stories. I remember Willie coming in one morning and saying to me, 'You know who was at my house yesterday looking for me? Lindy.' We didn't want to believe it, but Lindbergh was in the area and took the time to look up his old friend Ludwig Hoffmann. They had flown together before the war."

Bob Strobell, as the informal team leader, chose to be the first to check out in the Me 262. "When I came around and landed," Strobell recalled, "Holt and Anspach sat at the end of the runway, still in the jeep. I taxied back to the hangar and shut down the engines. They pulled right up next to me and jumped on the wing. I opened the canopy and they grabbed my shirt collars and broke the props off my Army Air Corps insignia. Bob Anspach said to me, 'You don't need the props anymore. You are a jet pilot now.' That was one of the classiest acts anyone ever did for me. From then on it became a ritual. As everyone checked out in the aircraft, off came the props."

"The next thing on the agenda," Anspach recalled, "was giving ourselves a name. Sort of an impromptu thing, just like snapping the props off our insignia. In one of our training sessions one of the fellows said, 'We should have a good time whizzing around the sky in the 262.' It struck me that obviously we pilots were Watson's Whizzers. So I proposed calling ourselves Watson's Whizzers. The name stuck. Hal Watson was as proud of that moniker as any of us."

On June 10, 1945, Watson's Whizzers, including Bob Anspach, flew nine reconditioned Me 262 jet fighters from Lechfeld to Melun-Villaroche airfield near Paris. General Carl "Tooey" Spaatz came out to Melun on June 27, inspected the German jets on display and was treated to a fly-by of three Me 262s, led by Lieutenant Strobell. That out of the way, Watson planned the transfer of the aircraft from Melun to Cherbourg, where they were to be loaded on a British escort carrier, HMS *Reaper*, for transfer to the United States. On June 30, eight of the Me 262s were to be flown in relays to Cherbourg. "We agreed to fly below ten thousand feet," Bob Strobell recalled. "Anspach decided all on his own to take her up a little higher. He flew time and distance, dead reckoning, and when he came back down through the overcast he couldn't see anything but water. Bob had overflown his destination to a considerable extent and was out over the Atlantic heading for blue water. Seeing nothing but water ahead, Anspach did a 180, and an island came into view off the nose of his aircraft—it was the British Isle of Jersey. On Jersey there was a primitive grass landing strip. Anspach didn't know where he was, but he could see that airstrip and he was running low on fuel. So he panicked a little and put her down, not knowing if the grass field was long enough to take him. He apparently did a great job putting her down, because he and the airplane survived. When he finally got in touch with me a couple of days later—the island had no modern communications and had been occupied by the Germans during the war—I got our Gooney Bird, loaded it up with a couple of fifty-gallon drums of kerosene, and sent it over to him. I thought, you got yourself into that mess, you get yourself out. And he did. I never ordered him to fly the bird out. I felt only he could make that decision. It was indeed a short runway, and grass at that."

"I took her up to fifteen thousand feet," recalled Bob Anspach, "just for once, to get the feel of that airplane at that altitude. On descent into what I thought would be the Cherbourg-Querqueville area, when I broke through the cloud deck, to my great surprise all I could see was water. I was getting low on fuel and had no real idea where I was. I have to admit that I was getting a bit frantic about this time. I did a quick 180 and saw an island in the distance. When I got over it, I could see a landing strip. Grass, not concrete. It was the Isle of Jersey, I learned after landing. Grass or no grass, I had to bring her in. It turned out I had 4,300 feet of grass strip on which to put down the Me 262, which as far as I knew needed five to six thousand feet of concrete. The strip looked very short—but I quit thinking and just began doing. I made one pass over the field—and God was with me—I got her down on the second try. I brought her to a stop near the end of the field, at the edge of a cliff looking down on the English Channel. Somebody had seen me come in for my landing and later told me that on my approach I headed straight for the steeple of their church at the approach end of the field. He thought I was going to take off the steeple. Instead, he said, 'That steeple went right between your landing gear.' So I was cutting things really close. That was my third flight in the airplane. Karl Baur and I talked about my experience a few days later and he said to me, 'If you asked me if you could put that plane down on that strip, I would have told you, no. But you did.' Baur was really amazed at what I had done.

"After landing on Jersey, I was incommunicado for forty-eight hours. I couldn't get through to the outside world. Strobell had no idea what happened to me. He must have thought I crashed somewhere and killed myself. The people on Jersey were really nice and helpful, but there was no way to communicate with anyone off the island. They put me up in their finest hotel situated on a cliff with a beautiful view of the sea. Finally, after two days, I got hooked up with Bob Strobell over radio, and he said, 'We'll get you out, Bob.' He sent a C-47 with a couple of barrels of kerosene accompanied by Lieutenant Colonel Seashore [who was in charge of loading the aircraft onto HMS *Reaper* in Cherbourg harbor]. Seashore, not a pilot, but a damn good organizer, looked at the field and shook his head. 'It's your decision, Bob,' he said to me. 'I'm not going to tell you to fly out of here. If you don't want to do it, we'll just leave her here.' Flying out became a matter of pride for me. I figured if I could get her in, I could get her out. I knew I was the one who got myself into the situation, and I didn't want it to cost us an airplane. I had that drop-off at the end of the field, and if I didn't pick up enough speed, I figured, I could drop down a little and with the help of ground-effect pick up the speed I needed to get airborne. I got into the cockpit, fired her up, and came out of there as slick as a whistle. It wasn't me who did it, it was the airplane." Upon his return to the mainland Bob was flown to Paris to pick up one more Me 262. This time Bob stayed below ten thousand feet and flew straight to Cherbourg. "Everything looked just fine to me as I made my approach," Bob recalled. "I put my gear down and concentrated on setting her down. Then, as I began my rollout, the nose dropped on me. Not another one, I thought. I slid along the concrete, starting a small fire in the nose section. The nose gear hadn't come down completely and I didn't know it, nor did the tower shoot a red flare to warn me. We had no radios. The emergency crew showed up in a hurry and put the fire out. I took our Gooney Bird with some of our maintenance people to Lechfeld, picked up a new nose section and a couple of engine nacelles, and in a couple of days the aircraft was in perfect condition again."

After the arrival, in early August, of HMS *Reaper* in New York, its aircraft were unloaded and taken to Newark Field where they were made ready for flight. "There was an Fw 190 ready to be moved, so I volunteered to fly it to Freeman Field in Indiana," recalled Bob Anspach. "On September 12, off I went heading for Pittsburgh where I intended to refuel. It was a really good-flying aircraft." Bob Anspach had not forgotten his previous two incidents flying German aircraft, and every time he took off in one he expected number three to come along. Pilots are a superstitious lot and many did believe that accidents and incidents always occurred in threes. "I was making a gradual descent over Pennsylvania heading for the greater Pittsburgh area, when I reached to make a trim adjustment. My world suddenly turned upside down. The electrically controlled horizontal trim control cycled full-up and the Fw 190 responded—its nose pitching violently up and over." Bob soon discovered that the electrical trim actuator could not be manually overridden. He pulled the power back and struggled to find a setting allowing him to make forward progress and still fly straight and level. He looked around for a place to land. He saw a small dirt strip and headed for it. It was Hollidaysburg airport, just south of Altoona. Bob's approach was rough, nose high, dragging his tail. He touched down, applied the brakes; the right brake failed immediately, pivoting the aircraft to the left, and with that movement the aircraft's landing gear collapsed. Next, the propeller dug into the soft ground and then the entire

Colonel Harold Watson surrounded by his Whizzer pilots at Paris-Melun airport, France, June 27, 1945. L–R front: Lieutenant Haynes, Captain Dahlstrom, Lieutenant Strobell. L–R back: Lieutenant Holt, Lieutenant Anspach, Colonel Watson, Captain Hillis, Lieutenant Brown.

The most famous of the ten Me 262s brought back to the United States by Colonel Watson, a combat veteran of JG 7—variously named *Dennis*, *Ginny H*, and *888* before its arrival in the United States—is now displayed at the National Air and Space Museum in Washington, DC.

Bob Anspach came up with the moniker Watson's Whizzers. After Strobell flew the first Me 262 at Lechfeld, Anspach took the AAF lapel pins off Strobell's tunic and broke off the props. A crew chief designed a unit patch. The Whizzers became, in all but name, the first American jet fighter squadron flying former enemy aircraft. Pictured are the AAF lapel pin with props broken off, belonging to Bob Anspach, and the Whizzer patch, which was painted on the nose of each Me 262.

propeller assembly spun off and away as the aircraft slid to a stop on its belly. Bob slid back the canopy as the aircraft was still moving and scampered out of the cockpit. There was no fire and he was not injured. The aircraft was later hauled away for scrap, its propeller assembly becoming an ornament in a local flying club.

The following is a record of Bob's flights in captured German aircraft:

Date	A/C Type	Time	Purpose
09 June 45	Me 262	00:10	Check out by Karl Baur Messerschmitt test pilot
10 June 45	Me 262	00:45	Lechfeld to St. Dizier
10 June 45	Me 262	00:15	St. Dizier to Paris-Melun
30 June 45	Me 262	00:45	Melun to Isle of Jersey (got lost enroute to Cherbourg)
01 July 45	Me 262B	00:45	Melun to Cherbourg (2-seat trainer/nose gear failed/fire)
08 Aug 45	Me 108	00:45	Checkout and familiarization ride
23 Aug 45	Me 108	02:25	Administrative support flight for Col Watson
26 Aug 45	Me 262	01:00	Newark to Pittsburgh (left plane to have brakes repaired)
04 Sep 45	Bu 181	04:00	Newark to Pittsburgh to Freeman Field, Indiana
12 Sep 45	Fw 190	01:00	Newark to Hollidaysburg, PA; runaway trim (A/C written off)
20 Sep 45	Bu 181	00:30	Test flight at Newark
28 Sep 45	Me 262	01:00	Newark to Pittsburgh (3 ship formation ferry flight—Anspach, Hal Watson, Jack Woolams (Bell test pilot)
28 Sep 45	Me 262	00:45	Pittsburgh to Freeman Field, Indiana
28 Sep 45	Ju 388	00:45	Freeman Field to Wright Field, Dayton, Ohio

Lieutenant Robert Anspach had more than his fair share of incidents and accidents flying captured German aircraft. Bob, like most of the other Whizzer pilots, got out of the Army Air Forces after all of the German aircraft had been delivered to either Wright Field in Ohio or Freeman Field in Indiana. He then attended college using the World War II GI Bill of Rights to pay for his education, and obtained a degree in mechanical engineering. Bob was recalled to active duty during the Korean War period, flying the F-86 Saber Jet in combat in Korea. He then decided to stay in the air force and retired in the rank of lieutenant colonel. Until his passing, Bob resided in Orlando, Florida, and as with all the other flyers of his generation, Bob's dream of wanting to fly came true, but not in a way he could ever have imagined.

LLOYD M. N. WENZEL

P-38/F-86

Lightnings in the Sky

Oh, Hedy Lamar is a beautiful gal, and Madeleine Carroll is too.
But you'll find if you'll query, a different theory among the men of a bomber crew.
For the loveliest thing of which one could sing this side of the Heavenly Gates,
Is no blonde or brunette of the Hollywood set—but an escort of P-38s.
Yes, in days that have passed, when the tables were massed with glasses of scotch or
champagne,
It's quite true that the sight was a thing to delight, intent upon feeling no pain.
But no longer the same, nowadays, in this game, when we head north from Messina Straits,
Take the sparkling wine—every time, just make mine an escort of P-38s.
Sure we're braver than hell; on the ground all is swell—in the air it's a different story:
We sweat out our track through the fighters and flak, we're willing to split up the glory.
Well they wouldn't reject us, so Heaven protect us and, until all this shooting abates,
Give us courage to fight 'em and—one other item—an escort of P-38s.
—T/Sgt Robert H. Bryson, KIA, WWII MTO

Captain Lloyd Wenzel, a P-38 fighter pilot, suddenly found himself deeply involved in a program no one wanted to explain when he was first assigned to it—he was told that he didn't have the necessary security clearance. It was this company grade officer without the necessary security clearance, a combat flyer, not a politician, who turned the final corner for Project Paperclip—the assimilation of German scientists into mainstream America. Perhaps what Captain Wenzel had going for him was that he was young and unbiased, had experienced war, and, not the least of his attributes, he was a Texan, raised in a land where one could stretch out one's arms without touching another person, a land where earth and sky merged on a distant and untrammeled horizon—and he spoke German.

"I was born on June 3, 1922, in Seguin, Texas, a small town thirty miles east of San Antonio. Seguin, named after Juan Seguin, a Mexican who sided with the Texans against General Antonio Lopez de Santa Anna, sits on the line where the black soil of the north meets the sand of the south. Germans who settled this area picked the black soil for their farms to grow cotton. Seguin had a big German community when I was a boy. Then you were either a German, or you were a 'raggedy,' that's what they called non-Germans. The Germans were very neat and kept their barns and houses painted. Other places, to them at least, looked raggedy compared to their own. My paternal grandmother was six years old when her family emigrated from Germany, shortly after Texas broke away from Mexico. They settled in the little town of Waldeck, about sixty miles from Austin. The local authorities were eager for farmers to settle the land. My grandmother's father was made a very attractive land offer, bought a farm near Waldeck, and started to grow cotton. When my grandmother was still in her teens, she married. Soon after her wedding, her fellow rode off to fight in the Civil War. The guy had one of his legs shot off and died on the way home.

"My paternal grandfather too came from Germany, but as an indentured servant. A Texas farmer paid his way over and he had to work for the man for three years to pay him back. That man's farm happened to be right next door to the farm of the young widow whose husband lost a leg in the war and died. The two married and had five sons. My uncle Albert, as the oldest, inherited the farm; Uncle Gustav and Uncle Otto became carpenters; Uncle Adolf became a blacksmith, and my dad, Robert, the youngest, wanted to go to college to become a schoolteacher. When he told the old man about his plans, his father locked him in the corncrib and told him to shuck corn until he got that foolishness out of his head. My dad had severe hay fever and nearly died shucking that corn. That night my grandmother dragged him out of the crib and saved his life. The old man finally relented, even letting my father ride his horse to school. Dad never did get a college degree, but he got enough college to teach school in Seguin for fifty years. Actually, he had retired by the time World War II came along, when the school board called on him and said, 'Robert, you've got to teach again.'

"My mother was half German, half English. Her parents too were farmers. I have a sister eleven years older than I; she taught me to speak German. Randolph Field was about fifteen miles from Seguin and my dad and I would ride out there occasionally and look at the airplanes. When they officially opened the field, General Pershing came down from Washington for the occasion. I went over to watch the ceremony. It was all very exciting for a young lad. Once an airplane made a forced landing on my grandfather's farm and we got to look at that broken-up plane. My grandmother made refreshments for the pilots until someone came to pick them up. I felt awed by the flyers. Maybe some day I could be a flyer, I thought. My best friend and I frequently rode our bicycles to Randolph Field, right into a hangar, and looked at the airplanes and kicked the tires. There were no fences or guard posts. A couple of times I sat in the lap of a sergeant when he ran up the engine. It was a BT-8, a single engine trainer. Soon I was building model airplanes, and in the Boy Scouts I went after the aviation merit badge. I sat around for hours with my friends talking flying. Airplanes became and remained an exciting part of my life.

"I spoke German like nearly everybody else. As a boy you couldn't work in a grocery or drygoods store in Seguin if you couldn't speak German. There were just too many people who only spoke German. Willie and Lena Voss were my folks' best friends. They were on the school board. Willie passed away while I was away in the war. When I came home in June 1945, my father and I went to see Mrs. Voss. My German was so rusty, I spoke in English to her. When we left, my dad said to me, 'What's the matter with you, Lloyd? Don't you have any manners? Speaking English to that old lady and putting that burden on her. You should have spoken German.'

"I attended Texas Lutheran College in Seguin with the intent of getting enough credits so I could apply for aviation cadets. You had to have two years of college to get into the program. When the war came, my mother was intent on not letting me go. When I turned twenty in June of forty-two, I applied anyway. On August 13 I went to take my test at Fort Sam Houston in San Antonio. I passed the written, but flunked the physical. I had an undescended testicle. 'If you don't have that corrected, it can become malignant,' the doctor said. I must have looked so disappointed that he said to me, 'You really want to fly, don't you?' I said, 'Yeah. I've always wanted to fly. 'Listen, boy,' said the doctor, 'I'll put your file up here,' and he stuffed my folder among some books on a shelf above his head. 'You remember where it is, because I will examine thousands before you get back. Have the thing removed and if you can get back here in two weeks I'll continue to process you. Otherwise, you'll have to start all over again.' I phoned my doctor at home from the major's office and set up surgery for the next morning and had the damn thing taken out. After I could walk again, my friends accompanied me to Fort Sam Houston and carried me up the stairs to the doctor's office so I could get sworn in. Because they cut me open in the groin, I wasn't supposed to walk up stairs and had to be carried up. I used to tell people that it cost me my right ball and sixty-five dollars to join the air corps. My fellow cadets gave me the nickname 'Stud.'

"It wasn't until February 1943 that I received a pilot training class assignment, 43K. I thought I would be going to a cadet training center in San Antonio, but they threw me instead on a train and sent me to Santa Ana in California.

L–R: Captains Schultz and White, Lieutenants Wenzel and Hilt at Y-59 Euskirchen, Germany, May 1945. The war was over and the unbelievable had happened—they had survived.

I wanted to be a B-17 pilot because my scoutmaster flew B-17s. He was highly decorated and came home on military leave from the Pacific before I went off to California. I listened to his war stories and wanted to be just like him. But once I got to California I saw the P-38 fighter and that changed everything for me. The P-38s would come in low, dive toward the end of the runway and then peel up and over, doing a complete vertical 360-degree turn, and land. In the early P-38s they had the coolers for the turbo chargers in the leading edges of the wings, and there were two little square holes near the tip of each wing allowing the air to escape. In the high humidity of California, those P-38s would pull two big streamers off each wingtip as they went up and over and came in to land. I decided, to hell with the B-17, I want to be a P-38 pilot.

"In flight training I first flew the PT-17, a beautiful Boeing biplane, and then the BT-13, known as the Vibrator for all the noises it made. Next came the AT-9, a twin-engine high-performance aircraft, and then the RP-322. The RP-322 was a twin-engine P-38 ordered by the British before the start of Lend-Lease in early 1941. Once Lend-Lease came into effect, the Brits canceled their order and those airplanes were converted to American specifications and configured as trainers. I got about ten hours in that airplane. After I was awarded my pilot wings, I was assigned to a P-38 Replacement Training Unit in California. I found the airplane to be a high-performance beast and if you didn't pay attention it would kill you quicker then the Germans could. I was lucky. The training outfit I went to had a bunch of North African campaign veterans from the 82nd Fighter Group, guys who had combat experience flying the airplane in North Africa against Rommel's Afrika Korps. I remember one of them, Captain Albert Wolfmueller, from Fredericksburg, Texas—another German. He was strafing and didn't see some high-tension lines. As he pulled up, a line caught his tail and flipped him over on his back at about ten feet off the ground. He controlled that airplane and recovered. Quite a feat. Albert was the son of the owner of the Wolfmueller bakery in Fredericksburg.

"We finished training in March 1944 and were outfitted for deployment to the Pacific. Everything was hush-hush. When we arrived in San Francisco, they had us turn in all that Pacific stuff and we drew European stuff instead. We got on a train to New York and crossed the Atlantic on the liner *Mauritania* in five days. There were only three P-38 groups remaining in England when I arrived—the 474th, the 370th, and the 367th. I was assigned to the 474th Fighter Group. We were in the IX Tactical Air Command, IX TAC, of the 9th Air Force, commanded by Lieutenant General Hoyt S. Vandenberg. [Vandenberg became the second Air Force Chief of Staff in 1948, succeeding General Carl A. Spaatz.] Major General Elwood R. Quesada commanded the IX TAC. All P-38 groups were slated to convert to P-51s or P-47s. Because of its longer range they wanted the P-38s in the Pacific. My group petitioned General Spaatz [Commander, United States Strategic Air Forces in Europe] to let us keep on flying the P-38. He approved our request. We were the only group to fly P-38s out of England onto bases in Germany.

"November of forty-four was colder than hell. I had fifty-two combat missions by then. We were in Florennes, Belgium, and experienced heavy losses. On one mission we lost eight out of twelve aircraft. Most of our losses were due to antiaircraft fire. By D-Day, the Luftwaffe was pretty much beaten down, but the ground fire was fierce. The 88mm radar-directed gun was a mean gun and could shoot you at thirty thousand feet. My squadron, the 428th, was authorized fifty-five pilots and twenty-five airplanes. We lost twenty-eight pilots in less than a year. We sustained the heaviest losses in the 474th Fighter Group. The 430th squadron had the least. Their commander had combat experience in North Africa and flew a little less aggressively than we did. Near the end of the war it was announced that a fighter tour in the IX TAC was seventy missions. We moved to Euskirchen, then to Langensalza—deep in what would become the Soviet Zone of Occupation. After I flew my seventy-second combat mission, my group commander wanted to see me. I trotted into his office and he said, 'You've got five months in grade, Wenzel. In a month I can promote you to captain, if you stick around, that is.' I said, 'No sir. I want to go home.' He said, 'No, I won't let you go home. You stay.' Well, if I stay I want to fly. He looked at me, shook his head, and said, 'Wenzel, you are through flying combat. You can run an orientation for our replacements and teach them formation flying and tactics, but your combat flying days are over.' I was kind of glad he said that. I didn't want to fly any more combat. I was sick of it.

"Once I got back to the States, in June 1945, I had orders to go to the Pacific. Two days before I was to ship out for San Francisco they dropped the atomic bomb. I was at home on leave and right near Fort Sam Houston. I reported to Fort Sam and they told me, 'Things have changed. If you want to get out you can, but you have to decide right now.' So I phoned my wife; we had married the day I got my pilot wings at Williams Field, Arizona, in 1944. We talked and agreed for me to stay in. I was ordered to Luke Field near Phoenix. All of my old friends were there. At Luke there was nothing to do but hang around. For reasons unknown to me I was selected to go to the Air Technical Service Command at McClellan Field in Sacramento overhauling B-26 Marauders. On July 29, 1946, I received orders issued by the Sacramento Air Materiel Area directing me to report at once to 'Wright Field, Dayton, Ohio, for duty with Intelligence (T-2).'

"I asked, what is Intelligence? Nobody knew. Personnel phoned Wright Field, and nobody had an answer. At that time Project Overcast, renamed Project Paperclip on September 3, was pretty well classified and no one who knew anything about it talked. So I got to Wright Field before I knew what I was going to do. I checked in with First Lieutenant Paul Robiczek. Robiczek spoke excellent German and clued me in about my job in Intelligence. Project Overcast, Robiczek said to me, was a very hush-hush operation. My place of work was a camp built in the thirties by the National Youth Administration, referred to in short as the NYA area. The camp was self-contained and included barracks, recreational facilities, and mess halls. The facility was fenced and located in an isolated part of the field. That was where the German Project Overcast scientists lived. Robiczek, a bachelor, chose to live there as well. Also, a strange Mr. Lynch lived with the Germans in the NYA area. Albert Lynch was a civilian. Nobody seemed to have requisitioned him nor knew exactly where he came from. Mr. Lynch spoke perfect German and we speculated that he must have been from counterintelligence, or something like that. Whenever I went to see Mr. Lynch, he'd insist that I join him in a vermouth *mit Zitrone*. Robiczek and Lynch spent all their time with the German scientists, twenty-four hours a day, seven days a week.

"Since I was married, I lived in town. My office was in the administration building in the NYA compound. Eventually we ended up with a little short of two hundred German scientists, not quite half of them at Wright Field; some worked in private industry, others at the School of Aviation Medicine in San Antonio. Among the first ones that came was Doktor Ingenieur Habilitatus Rudolph Hermann and his group of wind tunnel experts from Peenemuende. Dr. Hermann ran the wind tunnel tests for the V2 for Dr. Wernher von Braun, who was working with his group of missile experts at Fort Bliss, Texas. We had to treat them all as enemy aliens, which meant that there had to be restrictions. We put a sentry at the gate, not to keep the Germans in, but to keep people out. I served as administrative officer for the scientists and eventually took over the entire camp operation.

"Over the four years that I was to spend at Wright Field on Projects Overcast and Paperclip, I did just about everything that had to do with the German *Wissenschaftler* under air force control. I picked up their families at the port of New York when they began arriving and escorted them to Wright Field. I met newly arrived scientists, usually at Rome Field in New York State, and shepherded them and their baggage to Wright Field. I even became their paymaster in 1947, being designated a Class A Agent Finance Officer for purposes of making periodic payments to them. In those days we paid people in cash, and at times I carried as much as fifteen thousand dollars around with me—quite a considerable sum of money in 1947. Shiploads of scientific documentation began to arrive which had been collected under Operation Lusty by Colonel Watson and his people over in Germany. The documents were unsorted and packed in huge boxes. We had the Germans go through the piles of paper and throw out the trash and assemble what remained into a technical library. I was just a fighter pilot thrown into this thing because I spoke some German. I don't recall anymore the contractual issue that arose at about this time, but it was of a critical nature and I found myself right in the middle of the Paperclip mess."

The issue that was gumming up the works dealt with the fact that the War Department had an obligation to keep all the German scientists in military custody, pending the issuance of visas which might allow them to gain American citizenship and become productive members of American society, something that Justice and State were adamantly opposed to. Negotiations between the State and the Department of War factions dragged on. Captain Lloyd Wenzel, the fighter pilot, suddenly found himself in the awkward position of having to write a legal position, a contract, that would result in the implementation of what Paperclip, a presidentially sanctioned program, had already stipulated—to make American citizens out of enemy aliens. General Putt, the commander of the Air Materiel Command at Wright Field, had poor Wenzel up to his office and told him, "You're in charge, Wenzel. The Germans are your people. Write a contract and get it signed by the Secretary of War or his authorized representative. And I need not remind you—do it fast!"

"I was terrified," Lloyd Wenzel confessed to me when I interviewed him. "But an order was an order. I actually ended up writing a contract because nobody in the contracts section of the Air Materiel Command was cleared for Paperclip access. So I, a fighter pilot, took an old supply contract and spread it out on my living room floor. I cut and pasted and made a contract out of it, and into the contract I wrote the terms of Project Paperclip: that we would get them immigration visas, how we would go about doing that, and that we would bring their families over, and so on. Then it came time to have the contract approved in Washington. It was a personal services contract, and personal services contracts had to be approved by the Secretary of War or his designated representative, such as the Assistant Secretary of War for Air. Colonel Watson, who had brought the German jets to this country, was the executive to the Assistant Secretary of War for Air. I reviewed the contract with General Putt. He felt that what I had was 'good enough.' The general said to me, 'You have to go to Washington and get the Assistant Secretary for Air to sign this thing. If you get into trouble, which I was sure I would, call this guy,' and General Putt handed me a piece of paper with Colonel Watson's name on it, and his room number in the Pentagon.

"I put the paper in my pocket and went to Washington with my 'raggedy' contract in my briefcase. My first stop in the Pentagon was with a major in the Women's Army Corps, a WAC as they were then called. She was a contracts specialist who had been cleared for Project Paperclip and was to review my contract. She had very little compassion for my half-assed effort. She said, 'I know what you are trying to do, Captain. But what you have here doesn't even qualify as a contract. Why don't you go back to Wright Field and find somebody who knows how to write one. Now get out of my office, I don't have any more time to waste with you.' I went down the hall and got on a phone and called Colonel Watson on the number General Putt had given me. General Putt had already talked to him. Watson said to me, 'Come on down to my office right away. I'm in a hurry.' I went to his office and started telling him about my contract when he interrupted me. 'That sounds good, Captain. What do you have to have to get out of here?' I have to have the secretary's signature. 'Where?' said Watson. I opened up the contract. Right here, sir, pointing to the place where I wanted the secretary to sign. 'Come with me,' Watson muttered, and we entered the secretary's office. 'This is Captain Lloyd Wenzel from Wright Field on that German scientist program, Mr. Secretary,' Watson addressed the secretary. 'He has drawn up a contract for the Germans. It's very critical that we get them on contract so we can proceed with their employment and get them out of that enemy alien status. We need your approval, sir.' The secretary said, 'What do I need to do?' 'Sign here,' Watson said, handing the Secretary a pen and holding the signature element in front of him. The secretary signed and I returned to Wright Field. That was it.

"Without Watson we would have never moved forward on this. There were just too many people dragging their feet. All but one of the German scientists took us up on our offer and signed the contract." The State Department continued to drag its feet. "No one seemed to understand that we had to keep the Russians from getting these people. No one wanted to understand how important these people were to our national security. I had a couple of real fine young women working for me who kept track of the details and kept the immigration visas coming. Once we figured out what State wanted, we pursued things with vigor. Each scientist ended up with a dossier a foot thick. The main thing we had to prove was that they were not Nazis. Once immigration visas were issued, the scientist and his family had to leave the country to shed their enemy alien status. So we took them up to Niagara Falls, New York, drove with them across the bridge into Canada and the Canadian authorities stamped their papers. Then we turned around and had them readmitted to the United States, this time as legal immigrants. Lieutenant Robiczek was the first one to make one of those trips. I made several, as did Captain Fred McIntosh, another fighter pilot who had worked for Watson in Europe and been posted to Wright Field at the request of Colonel Watson. In 1948 the NYA camp pretty much shut down. All of the scientists had several job offers from academe or private industry. Some, like Dr. Hans von Ohain, the inventor of the Jumo 004 German jet engine, went to work for our government and in time became the chief scientist of the Wright-Patterson AFB laboratories. When I left the Paperclip project in August 1949, I remained at Wright-Patterson AFB as a student at the Air Force Institute of Technology, AFIT. The German professors who were still around tutored the hell out of me in the evenings. I graduated in 1951 with a degree in industrial administration, a degree the air force wanted for its procurement officers—my next assignment.[61]

"Before I could leave the Paperclip program to enter AFIT, I had to clear my accounts. In 1948 I had been appointed property officer for Account Number 14, German Scientists, vice First Lieutenant Paul Robiczek. Robiczek left the program to return to civilian life and I took over his account. I never gave it another thought. I should have, because I was responsible for every table, chair, spoon, towel, or bedsheet issued to the Germans. The first scientists who brought their families to the United States were moved with their families into converted barracks and I had signed for all the stuff those guys had—their furniture, linens, dishes, and so on. When it came time for me to leave the program, my replacement did an inventory, something I should have done when Robiczek left, and discovered that, among other things, I was short a thousand towels. I learned that the German women had taken the towels, dyed them, and made window drapes or throw rugs out of them. With a little understanding on the part of several officers I was able to get around my towel deficit and cleared my account without having to pay for my shortages. The remaining Germans left Wright-Patterson Air Force Base in 1950."

Colonel Lloyd Wenzel served in the United States Air Force for thirty years. He spent much of his air force career in contract management and

P-38 fighter pilots, October 1944, at A-78, Florennes, Belgium. L–R: Lieutenant Ranking (the Kid), Lieutenant Holt (the Holt), Lieutenant Wenzel (the Stud). Holt and Ranking were killed in action soon after this picture was taken.

P-38 pilots of the 428th Fighter Squadron in May 1945 posing in front of a Ju 88 night fighter and worn-out US tanks at R-2, Langensalza, a field that would soon be part of the Russian occupation zone.

"Looking back: life was simple—eat, sleep, fly, kill or be killed. Not to forget—giving each other a haircut now and then. I sure was glad when it was all over. I sure was glad." Lloyd Wenzel.

procurement, being one of the early directors for the F-15 fighter program. He retired to Palm Springs Gardens, Florida, where many of his air force friends lived, including Colonel Kenneth Chilstrom, the Wright Field test pilot, and Major General Harold Watson, who had made his name under Operation Lusty and as the first commander of the newly created Air Technical Intelligence Center at Wright-Patterson AFB, Ohio. Lloyd passed into fighter pilot heaven in July 2009—we sorely miss him.

FREDERICK B. MCINTOSH

P-47/Fw 190/TA 152/Ju 290

Gunner's Prayer

Please God I do not ask for much, just to see her eyes again and know her gentle touch.
So, keep the "ring sight" true for me and keep the "bore sight" true,
Do not let my vision fail and help me follow through.
Help me restore your "Wild Blue Wonder" back to its normal standing,
Guide our mission safely home for a "Happy Landing."
Please God, I do not ask for much, just see her eyes again and know her gentle touch.
—Corporal R. Scott Bowen, WWII ETO

Although over a thousand Me 262 jet fighters were built by the Germans, fewer than half were ever delivered to combat units. American airmen heard of these German jets, but actual encounters were infrequent, considering the thousands of American and British aircraft that roamed across German skies on a daily basis. Yet, when such encounters occurred, they were very different experiences for fighter pilots and bomber crews.

Captain Frederick B. McIntosh, a gung-ho fighter pilot if there ever was one, flew P-47s. Like many other Americans, he was of German heritage. "My stepfather's name was Heinrich Warnholz," Fred said, laughing, when I interviewed him several years ago. "I was born on June 8, 1918; don't remember when my mother married Heinrich. I was still very young. She changed her name; I kept mine. People and things in my life were pretty much German. Eleanor Vollmer, my twenty-some-year-old high school German teacher, was from Berlin. I picked up her accent. Years later in 1945 when I was retrieving captured Luftwaffe aircraft, Germans frequently asked me if I was a Berliner. After high school I went to work for the Pacific Gas & Electric Company in

Oakland. I graduated on Friday and on Monday night I was digging ditches for the gas company for fifteen cents an hour. I worked nights and went to school during the day. In college I took navy ROTC with the idea of becoming a naval aviator. When I applied for flight training, the navy recruiter told me that a junior certificate just wouldn't do. I had to have a college degree to get into naval aviation. I went across the street to the army recruiter, who didn't care what my educational pedigree was, and signed up with the Army Air Corps, Class 43C.

"I reported to Santa Ana in southern California, no more than a wheat field then and a bunch of tents. Next came Thunderbird II, again a new airfield near Phoenix with few amenities. But there at least we didn't have to sleep in tents. After graduation in March 1943 I went to Williams Field near Tempe, Arizona, where I spent a year as an instructor pilot in the P-38 Lightning. Whoever set the date for the invasion of the Continent must have foreseen the need for replacement pilots. Four hundred of us from Training Command were picked to 'volunteer.' When we arrived in Florida, we were introduced to the P-47. Hell, you could just look at that airplane and tell it wouldn't fly. We all signed up for P-38s. We got about four hours flying time in the P-47 and then were sent to New York and put on a seventy-two-ship convoy, mostly tankers, heading for Europe. Sitting on the tankers were fighter planes. We didn't see any P-38s, but we saw lots of P-47s and P-51s. When we got to England, we second lieutenants were met by several 'bird colonels,' commanders of P-38 fighter groups. Some of us thought this kind of odd and we trotted over to the intelligence section to take a look at some mission summaries for different types of combat aircraft. What fell out for me was that for every P-47 lost, they lost two P-51s, in round numbers, that is. And for every P-51 they lost two P-38s. You didn't have to be a blackjack player to figure out the way Jimmy Doolittle [who commanded the 8th Air Force] was running the air war, the first airplane to stay out of was the P-38, the second the P-51. I didn't know what they were doing with the P-47, but I decided that airplane was for me after all.

"I arrived at the 56th Fighter Group at Boxted, near Colchester, on June 5, 1944. I was assigned to the 62nd squadron. They had been in England almost a year and a half by that time. The 56th Group was the most successful fighter group in the 8th Air Force. It had more aces than any other outfit—Gaby Gabreski, Hub Zemke, Dave Schilling, Walker Mahurin, Fred Christensen, Gerald and Bob Johnson, Joe Powers, Paul Conger, Leroy Schreiber, Jimmy Steward—not the actor and bomber pilot—and many more. Zemke was our group commander through the invasion. Schilling was Zemke's deputy and my squadron commander. Schilling and I took a shine to one another. I flew twenty-five missions on his wing." Colonel David C. Schilling was the eighth highest scoring American ace in World War II, with 22½ victories. "Zemke then went to a down-and-out P-38 outfit to shape it up, the 479th Fighter Group at Wattisham, part of our wing, the 65th. They were scheduled to receive P-51s. Zemke transitioned into the P-51 and ended up bailing out over France when his aircraft iced up and spun into the ground. Zemke escaped by the skin of his teeth and ended up as a guest of the Germans at StalagLuft I, near Barth, Pomerania. Schilling took over the 56th when Zemke left. Both Zemke and Schilling were full colonels in their twenties.

"On the first of November 1944 we were escorting over three hundred B-24 bombers of the 2nd Air Division. There were nearly as many fighters escorting the bombers as there were bombers. The sky was filled with airplanes. We were on our way home, over Holland, when suddenly an Me 262 jet jumped a bunch of P-51s flying high cover. The German jet went after a straggler, and blew him out of the sky before I knew what was happening. Then the Me 262 peeled off and came down through our formation." The 56th Fighter Group history states, "The jet was at 38,000 feet and at first only its heavy brown intermittent contrail was visible. It was approaching the bombers, which were withdrawing from the target area on a course of 320 degrees. As the group turned into the jet, it went into a shallow dive of about thirty degrees and came on the tail of a P-51 above and to the rear of the bombers. The P-51 burst into flames. The Me 262 continued its dive over the bomber formation." From then on all the P-51s and P-47s were "in a mad scramble to destroy the Hun. It made a diving turn to the left in a south-westerly direction. At about 10,000 feet it made a climbing turn of 180 degrees right and headed full throttle toward the Zuider Zee in a northerly direction just above the cloud layer. At that time, if the enemy pilot had gone into the cloud undercast, he undoubtedly could have evaded our fighters. Evidently he felt that he could outrun our fighters because he kept above the clouds. As he made his last turn to the right, both P-47s and P-51s cut him off, getting strikes on the left side of the fuselage and the left wing. The *blow-job* went into a spin, and the pilot bailed out."[62]

McIntosh recalled that "Schilling went after the German pilot and killed him in his chute. When we got back, he got everybody in the debriefing room and said, 'OK, I know some of you probably think I'm an SOB because I killed a man in a chute. Did you ever think of all the mistakes that guy made?' And he enumerated them. 'And what would happen if he got back? Some of us, including you, are not going to outlast the war. It's just that simple. So think what you want, that's why I did it. Any questions, gentlemen?' Nobody said a word. Schilling was right. As he went through the German pilot's mistakes—his last was to open his chute too high, giving Schilling an opportunity to kill him." The act of shooting a jet pilot in his chute was not all that unusual, although it was distasteful to many airmen. Colonel Raymond E. Toliver describes Galland's actions to save his own life when his Me 262 was damaged on April 26, 1945, days before war's end. "His stricken Me 262 was still flying, and he did not want to risk parachuting and landing as a corpse. Jet pilots were regarded as valuable targets by the Allied commanders, although most Allied fighter pilots disagreed with the principle of shooting at parachuting enemies."[63] Chuck Yeager wrote, "Early in the war, I heard that one of the guys had seen a 109 strafe an American bomber crew in their chutes. I thought it was bad practice in every way. Both sides at least gave lip service to a gentleman's agreement not to do it. And if I had to jump for it again, I could hope the agreement was being honored that day."[64]

"The British had developed a jet of their own," continued Fred. "After our encounter with the German jet on November 1, we occasionally practiced against the British jet. Teapot, the Brits called it. We tried to devise maneuvers and tactics for the P-47 against jet fighters. Even though the British airplane was not as good as the Me 262, it became obvious to us that if the German pilot knew what he was doing, you were dead meat. I learned to love the P-47, it was a tough little airplane. I once flew one through the trees and made it home. Gaby Gabreski tried the same thing with a P-51 and ended up in StalagLuft I along with his buddy Hub Zemke. When StalagLuft I was liberated toward the end of April 1945, they brought all the POWs from Barth to Camp Lucky Strike, near Le Havre. On May 4, I got word that Zemke and Gabreski were at Camp Lucky Strike and I flew over in a Martin B-26 'Widow Maker' and flew them back to Boxted."

As the war in Europe came to its final end, Captain Fred McIntosh was called by the 65th Fighter Wing personnel section and asked if he would mind doing nine days of temporary duty, TDY, on the Continent. "Sure, why not," McIntosh replied. "The war was all but over and I didn't have a job anyway. When I picked up my orders, they didn't read nine days, but ninety days. Maybe I had misunderstood, but it was too late to do anything about it. I left RAF Boxted for Paris on May 5 on one of our B-26 Marauders. I had no trouble finding someone to fly me to Paris once they learned where I was going. I checked in at USSTAF headquarters in St. Germain. It was a beautiful location. Colonel Lloyd Pepple from the Exploitation Division welcomed me and briefly acquainted me with my new assignment—Merseburg airfield, near the heavily bombed Leuna oil refinery. I was to receive detailed instructions in the next two days, including the necessary passports to allow me to function as a member of Colonel Schilling's Air Technical Intelligence team. What a surprise. My boss, Pepple informed me, was no other than Colonel David Schilling, former commander of the 56th Fighter Group for whom I had flown wing on many missions. He had managed to get himself assigned as commander of the Merseburg Air Intelligence Exploitation Team—so he could finally fly a German Me 262. As it turned out, the 8th Air Force was slated to move to the

The Fieseler Storch was a simple, rugged liaison plane. This one flew into Regensburg to surrender. Picture was taken on May 10, 1945.

Pacific, and Schilling never got his wish to fly an Me 262. When Colonel Watson [Watson ran the part of Operation Lusty which dealt with the retrieval of German aircraft] looked for a replacement for Schilling, his engineering officer at Merseburg, Captain Edwin Maxfield, recommended me. 'McIntosh flew as Schilling's wing man,' Maxfield told Watson. That was good enough for Watson, and so I became the chief of Watson's Merseburg operation.

"I caught a ride on a courier plane to Merseburg. In Merseburg we lived in Der Alte Dessauer hotel, which we had requisitioned. It was convenient to the airfield and comfortable. The hotel had been taken over by doctors and nurses of an evacuation hospital which tended to American and British POWs being processed for release back to the US and the UK. Merseburg airfield was a dirt strip, like many German airfields, adjacent to the Junkers factory. The doctors and nurses living with us in the Alte Dessauer had put up the tents of their evacuation hospital in the middle of Merseburg airfield where the former POWs received a thorough medical examination before being shipped out for final processing and release. For some reason more former POWs arrived than the hospital folks could process and ship out. The men became restless. We had four pilots and several captured Fieseler Storch liaison planes at our disposal. We could take up a total of eight passengers at a time. The doctors ran a lottery and the winners got to fly with us over the heavily bombed Leuna oil refinery, over Leipzig and other nearby towns and villages allowing them to get a bird's-eye view of the damage the air war had done to Germany. The flights were a great success with the men, and took the edge off the situation. Soon the former POWs were all gone, and things quieted down."

The Merseburg Junkers 388L at Freeman Field, Indiana, in 1945. It was flown by McIntosh, Anspach, Watson, and others during air shows at Freeman Field.

The first airplane McIntosh's crew at Merseburg collected for eventual transfer to Wright Field for detailed evaluation was a Junkers 388L. "It was pressurized," McIntosh recalled during my interview with him, "had an ejection seat, and was intended as a high-altitude reconnaissance plane. All the records for the plane were there. It had less than ten hours' flying time on it. Watson had heard about the plane and had put it on the Wright Field want list. A note was attached to the list reading, I fly it when I get there. Signed, Watson. I didn't know who this guy Watson was, but if he ever got here, I thought, he would want some answers before he ever got into the airplane. Let's ground-check it, I suggested to Maxfield. Maxfield had devised an aircraft inspection checklist that we used to check out every airplane we intended to fly. 'I hate to fly,' I heard Maxfield mutter as we got into the aircraft—I soon learned he said that every time he got into an airplane. I started the engines on the Ju 388 and did some checking of the instrumentation to be sure I wasn't using the wrong numbers. This was the first time I had worked with instruments using the metric system. We did a taxi check. Everything seemed to handle all right. I said to Ed, Let's do at least one high-speed taxi check and see how it handles. Ed was sitting in a lower seat to one side. We taxied out. Ed said to me afterwards, 'I should have known what would happen next when you taxied clear to the back fence.' We came roaring down the field and Ed realized what I was up to. He looked up at me and yelled, 'You bastard.' We lifted off and went around the field. I did a couple of stalls, basic stuff, then landed. Watson showed up a day later. We were having breakfast together, and he was talking about what he wanted us to accomplish. Then he said, 'I understand the 388 has been ground-checked. Is that correct, Captain McIntosh?' Yes, sir, I responded. Then he said, 'How does it fly?' Everybody looked at me. I thought

I better be straight with him and said, Like a board, sir. He said, 'Good' and nodded his head. 'You and I are going to go and fly it together now.'" On May 20, 1945, Watson and McIntosh flew the Ju 388 to Kassel, a collection center for items to be sent back to the US, since Merseburg was soon to come under Russian control.[65]

"We didn't just collect aircraft for Colonel Watson, but also went after other things on the Wright Field want list such as ground support equipment for the V2 missile, submarine periscopes, radio-controlled bombs, antiaircraft fire control systems, Walther engines for the Me 163—that sort of stuff. We boxed up what we collected and sent it on to one of the collection points. We had several jeeps with trailers assigned, and teams of two to three people would go out to investigate when the disarmament people reported finding something that was on our want list. On May 30 we received a message from the Exploitation Division at St. Germain to vacate Merseburg not later than June 2 [Merseburg was located in what would become the Russian Zone of Occupation] and relocate to Munich-Neubiberg. Maxfield with the rest of my collection team drove to Neubiberg in our jeeps and trucks. I flew to Nuernberg-Roth instead where Watson had accumulated a bunch of Fw 190 fighters, and other German aircraft, including a huge Junkers 290 four-engine transport for delivery to Cherbourg." The Ju 290 had flown into Munich at war's end to surrender and Watson had retained its pilot, Hauptmann Heinz Braun, and members of the 290's crew to assist in the collection of German aircraft and to maintain the Ju 290 which Watson intended to fly back to Wright Field in Dayton, Ohio, once his aircraft collection task under Operation Lusty was completed. None of this Watson had revealed to McIntosh, who eventually would find himself as Watson's copilot in the Ju 290 on the trip back to the United States. In the meantime, McIntosh and Heinz Braun flew aircraft, such as newer models of the Fw 190, from Nuernberg to Cherbourg for eventual loading on an aircraft carrier and return to the US. "Heinz Braun spoke fairly good English and was an excellent pilot. He flew anything I told him to—the Ju 52, Fieseler Storch, Heinkel 111, and Focke Wulf and Messerschmitt fighters. There was a Heinkel 111 on the airfield, flown in and surrendered by its German crew on May 8. The 111 was a Battle of Britain vintage plane and of no technical interest to us. I asked Heinz if he knew how to fly it and he answered, 'Ja, Herr Hauptmann, I know how to fly a Heinkel 111.' I needed to get back to RAF Boxted, my old P-47 base.

"In early 1945 I was hit by German flak. Shrapnel shattered the canopy of my P-47 and shredded my parachute. I remember blood spurting from my ears. The cold air stopped the bleeding, but I couldn't hear. I pulled out of the formation, and, accompanied by another P-47, made it home to Boxted. The doctors at the hospital in Boxted took out about a third of my teeth and put a temporary plate in my mouth. The war ended and I was in Germany now, still with that temporary plate in my mouth. I received a message from the dentist at Boxted just before we were to leave Merseburg that my plate had arrived. I better come and get it quickly, the dentist added, because he was packing up to leave for home. So, Heinz Braun and I flew a Heinkel 111 over to Boxted. I chose the 111 because our airmen at Boxted had complained that they fought two and one-half years in the war and didn't even have a souvenir to show for it. I told Watson that I would fly the He 111 over so the men could field strip it for souvenirs. He thought it was a good idea. After we landed in England, I helped disconnect the batteries so the guys could begin stripping the airplane. My C-47 Gooney Bird then came over and picked up Heinz and me and flew us back to Neubiberg. It was the eighth of June, 1945, my 27th birthday.

"Heinz Braun became an indispensable member of my group. Besides teaching me to fly the Heinkel 111, he checked out Jack Woolams, the Bell test pilot, in the fun-to-fly Fieseler Storch liaison plane. Later Heinz ferried Heinkel 219 night fighters, Bf 109s, and other aircraft from British bases in the north of Germany to Cherbourg-Querqueville. Heinz Braun's most memorable experience came when Woolams, he, and I set out to ferry three nearly new Fw 190 fighters from Nuernberg-Roth to Cherbourg via St.-Dizier and Villacoublay. We took off from Nuernberg-Roth on a sunny June day, expecting to make routine refueling stops en route. Everything went fine at St.-Dizier. We landed, took on fuel, and took off again for Villacoublay, flying in a loose trail formation with Heinz in the number three position. It was late afternoon when we got into the landing pattern at Villacoublay. Braun was having problems with the setting sun. Of course, I didn't know that because without radios we couldn't talk to each other. Heinz made two unsuccessful approaches and on the third he landed. Unfortunately while concentrating on making his landing, he forgot to put down his landing gear. He bellied in and fire trucks and military police quickly appeared on the scene. Although Heinz wore an American flight suit, when the MPs got to him he was so rattled he forgot how to speak English. The MPs didn't know what to make of this German pilot in an American flying suit flying a German fighter, and before Woolams and I knew what was going on, the suspicious MPs threw Braun in jail. We wrote off the 190. As for Braun, Woolams and I decided to continue on to Cherbourg and leave Heinz behind and pick him up on our way back. While sitting in jail, Braun thought he was being punished for destroying the 190. He was relieved when we showed up the following day, although he was quite unhappy with himself—forgetting to put down the landing gear is pretty embarrassing for an experienced pilot.

"As we pulled inspections on German planes, we always looked for booby traps. We discovered that a number of the Fw 190s at Nuernberg carried explosive charges. When the pilot got out of the airplane, he simply slid his hand up the back of his seat and activated the charge by removing a safety pin. Before flying the plane he reinserted the pin to safety the charge. It was a simple procedure. Maxfield had worked out an airplane acceptance checklist, and actuating the landing gear was one of the items on the list. When we put the first 190 on jacks and actuated the gear, a wing blew off. So we went over to the POW compound and found the pilot of that airplane. That's how we learned about the wing explosives and the safety mechanism. We had a Ju 87 Stuka dive bomber on the field. It still had bombs hung on it. General Quesada, who owned the P-51 outfit on the field and who had moved his headquarters to Nuernberg-Roth, warned me that the Stuka was his airplane, he intended to fly it, and for me to stay away from it. I also wanted to fly a Stuka, at least once. When Maxfield and I looked at this thing, we decided there were just too many wires near the bombs. Mechanics from the P-51 fighter group built a wooden cradle so we could drop one of the bombs by two inches. They tied a rope to the Stuka's bomb-release handle and to a six-by-six truck. Then we all hid behind a rise in the ground as the truck drove off, and, when the bomb dropped, the Ju 87 exploded. Booby traps were not a big problem, but it was something we had to be on the alert for."

Eventually forty German aircraft were loaded on a British escort carrier, HMS *Reaper*, and shipped to the United States. Among the aircraft were ten Me 262 jet fighters, three He 219 night fighters, two Dornier 335 push-pull fighters, one TA 152, the ultimate and final version of the successful Fw 190, four Arado 234 jet reconnaissance bombers, and one Ju 388 high altitude reconnaissance aircraft which McIntosh first flew at Merseburg. In addition, packed in crates and loaded on the *Reaper* were fifteen Heinkel 162 Volksjaeger jet fighters and ten Me 163 Komet rocket-powered interceptors. All of these aircraft would eventually find their way to Wright Field, Ohio, or to Patuxent River Naval Air Station in Maryland, for test and evaluation. The TA 152 was the final version of the Fw 190 fighter series, named in honor of its designer, Professor Kurt Tank—TA standing for Tank's last name. "I am the only one of our team who flew the TA 152," McIntosh recalled with pleasure, "and it was one of the best airplanes I have ever flown. I flew it a couple of times out of Aalborg, Denmark, against a P-51 and both times I ended up on the tail of the P-51. It was a very good airplane with all the kinks of the 190 worked out of it. There was a small lake behind the British officers' club at Aalborg. I was told by my British escort that absolutely no firearms were to be discharged in the area. I noticed a fair number of ducks happily swimming around the lake. Then I remembered that we'd been living on K rations and much too much Spam for far too long. I mentioned the ducks to Jack Woolams [a Bell Aircraft Company test pilot who was flying with Watson's aircraft recovery teams]. Woolams got a hold

Watson's Ju 290, now with American markings, at Orly airfield near Paris, France, being refueled and getting ready for its transatlantic flight. It attracted a crowd wherever it landed.

of a .22-caliber rifle and shot five ducks. The Brits, of course, heard the shots, even though the .22 isn't very loud. They quickly came over to investigate. 'We told you no hunting,' the military police lectured us. The Brits became even more frustrated with us after they couldn't find any evidence of our wrongdoing. They searched every room in our quarters, including the toilet. The Brits finally left, not happy. One of our airmen had hidden the plucked ducks in the toilet water tank. Our enlisted cook cooked up all the ducks and we had a grand dinner under the wing of our C-47."

On July 20 HMS *Reaper* lifted anchor at Cherbourg and set sail for Newark, New Jersey, loaded with captured German aircraft and accompanied by several of Watson's Whizzer pilots. Fred McIntosh and Heinz Braun, on July 19, had flown the four-engine Ju 290 from a repair depot at Le Culot to Paris-Orly. At Le Culot they had installed American radios and a navigation compass and added survival kits for a crew of ten. "Maxfield checked the engine screens after we landed," recalled McIntosh, "and found metal shavings in the one engine we didn't change in Nuernberg-Roth. Maxfield grabbed a truck and Braun's three mechanics and drove from Paris to the Bayrische Motorenwerke in Munich to find another engine. Maxfield and his three helpers rolled the engine on the six-by-six and drove all the way back to Paris. After an engine change I took her up with Heinz Braun. It was the 26th of July and high time for us to get out of there if we wanted to arrive in the ZI before HMS *Reaper* got there. The airplane tested fine, its engines ran smoothly. I also swung the newly installed navigation compass. A rail line ran from Paris straight south for a stretch. I used the railroad track to verify the accuracy of our compass. Once I had done that, I felt we were ready to go. When I told Watson that we were finally ready to leave, he replied, 'Let's get this show on the road and get my ass back to New York.'" On July 28, 1945, his task under Operation Lusty complete, Watson's Ju 290 roared down the runway at Paris-Orly and headed for the Azores, his first stop, on the way to Wright Field. McIntosh was his copilot, and Captain Maxfield the aircraft's engineering officer. From the Azores they continued on to Bermuda, then Dayton, their final destination. "Flying with Watson was a delight," McIntosh recalled. "We sat side by side, he on the left, me on the right. Maxfield was flying the engineer's position monitoring engine instruments on takeoff and in flight and controlling the flaps. We had to hand-fly it all the way because somebody stole the autopilot control back in Paris. We landed at Patterson Field, adjacent to Wright Field, on July 31. We flew her to Freeman Field in Indiana, on August 1, our final destination."

The Dornier 335, named Pfeil (arrow) by the Germans, was a heavy push-pull fighter with one engine in the front and one in the rear. It was still in development when the war ended and saw no combat. At 470 miles per hour it was the fastest piston-driven aircraft in the world. The Arrow was equipped with an ejection seat. Prior to ejection, however, the pilot had to push three buttons—one would jettison the rear propeller, the second would blow off the upper vertical tail surfaces, and the third armed the seat. A complex procedure in an emergency requiring ejection. On the 17th of June, Hans Padell, a senior Dornier 335 test pilot, and another, were to fly two Dornier 335s from Nuernberg-Roth to Cherbourg for loading on HMS *Reaper*. They would be accompanied by P-51 fighters. "I had made arrangements with the P-51 outfit across the field to escort the two 335s from Nuernberg to Cherbourg," McIntosh related to me. "I was at Cherbourg awaiting their arrival. After the 335s landed, I looked up and saw the 51s coming over the field. They dipped their wings, we waved at them, and they went home. The 335s and the 51s never got together. Hans Padell later explained to me that they shut down one engine and cruised on the power of the remaining engine to give the P-51s a chance to catch up, but they never did.

"I hooked up with the airplane again when we got them ashore in Newark, after they were degunked [a protective film applied to aircraft when exposed to salt air to prevent corrosion] and cleaned up. One of our maintenance men working on one of the aircraft set off part of the ejection mechanism. The lower fin of the airplane blew off as well as the rear propeller assembly. Jack Woolams, our Bell test pilot, and I worked on the other aircraft to make it flyable. I personally greased the wheels and did all the cockpit checks. No decision had been made as to who was going to fly the airplane. When the day came, I proposed to Jack that we match coins to see who would take the thing up. I wasn't too wild about flying this machine. I won the flip. I said to Jack, I won, you fly. Something told me to stay out of that airplane. Watson called and

A shrapnel-riddled Dornier 335 at Neubiberg, near Munich, in May 1945. Willie Hoffmann, the Messerschmitt test pilot who worked for Colonel Watson, is shown climbing into the cockpit. A German officer, also a test pilot who briefly worked for Colonel Watson, is standing behind Hoffmann. The only surviving Do 335 is displayed at the Udvar Hazy Center of the NASM.

told me to get a bird out to Freeman Field in Indiana. 'Stop in Pittsburgh to refuel if you have to,' Watson added. Woolams taxied out to the end of the runway. He got a red flare from the tower. He sat there for a while, until finally the tower gave him the green light. His rear engine began to run hot, and when he accelerated, just at the point of rotation, he lost that engine and he had to feather the prop. I saw the gear coming up. He came around and I noticed his nose was a little high. He sideslipped the aircraft down to the runway and just before touchdown popped the gear. You had to be a test pilot and have nerves of steel to do that. The aircraft banged down on the concrete, he threw out the flaps and went down the runway with the fire trucks chasing him. As soon as he slowed down enough, he went over the side. What happened? A screen had been installed backwards and the rear engine overheated. After that debacle Watson told us to ship the aircraft by truck or rail. I don't know if I could have done as well as Jack, probably not. Letting him fly the airplane most likely saved my life."

Fred McIntosh was released from active duty in 1946, and like so many of his fellow World War II flyers, he was recalled in March 1951, after North Korea invaded South Korea. Colonel Watson, who at this time was heading the Air Technical Intelligence Center at Wright-Patterson Air Force Base, got a hold of McIntosh and put him to work setting up a school for technical analysts, turning a group of air force reservists, engineers, photographers, and Russian linguists into old-fashioned intelligence specialists. In July 1951 a joint

Fred McIntosh standing in the doorway of his C-47. Major General James P. Hodges on the left, AAF Intelligence, and Colonel Harold Watson on the right, next to a picture of the former German leader that once decorated the Schleswig officers' mess, June 1945.

Among the German aircraft returned to the United States were three Heinkel 219 night fighters. McIntosh flew one of the three from Grove, now Karup airfield, Denmark, to Cherbourg, where they were loaded on HMS *Reaper*. The only surviving He 219 is displayed, partially assembled, at the Udvar Hazy Center of the National Air and Space Museum.

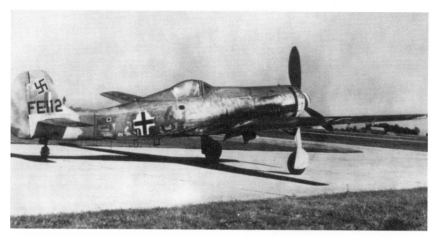

This was the only TA-152H returned on HMS *Reaper* to the United States. McIntosh flew it several times against a P-51, besting the P-51 every time. Shown here at Freeman Field, Indiana, with crudely reapplied German markings.

British-American operation recovered the better part of an MiG 15 from the mud of the Ch'ongch'on River estuary. "I was running our technical analyst school," McIntosh recalled, "when the MiG parts arrived at Wright-Pat. Watson told me and my people to put the MiG back together again. We slept in the hangar, worked twenty-four hour days. When we had the airplane put back together, we found that it had a wing-flutter problem. The Russians had solved it simply by putting a cast-iron slug in the tip of each wing. A single man could hardly carry the weight, it was that heavy. When the engineers had done their preliminary analysis, and our girls had typed up the report, Watson flew to Washington to present his report on the MiG to the air force chief of staff. Watson took a cast-iron counterweight along and put it on General Vandenberg's desk. This act of bravado was typical Watson. He had a knack for the dramatic, and it always worked for him. When the guys with the slide rules finished their analysis and came up with their final report, their findings were within 5 percent of the actual performance of the MiG 15."

Fred McIntosh separated from the air force in 1961 with the rank of lieutenant colonel and accepted a position as vice president of the National Business Aircraft Association. Fred flew 104 combat missions in the P-47 Thunderbolt in Europe. He said, "Flying German airplanes for Watson was one of my life's highlights. A time I'll never forget." Fred has joined the Whizzer pilots who preceded him out west—to fighter pilot heaven.

ROY W. BROWN

P-47/Me 262

Little Black Flowers That Grow in the Sky

I don't mind a dive in a 25 till the bombs that I'm carrying smack,
But those little black flowers that grow in the sky—oh, my achin back.
Skimming a ridge to plaster a bridge makes you feel as goofy as wine.
And your heart takes a jolt when your Thunderbolt tangles with an Me 109.
It's like shooting ducks when you come across trucks, and I don't mind the rifles that crack.
But those little black flowers that grow in the sky—oh, my achin back.
—57th Fighter Group ballad, WWII MTO

Roy Brown was born in March 1921 in the small river town of Spring Valley, Illinois. Roy was different from the rest of his fighter pilot friends in two respects. First, he was a college graduate, a rarity among fighter pilots at the time. Second, he was married. "I grew up in a house in the country. We were not farmers, but we had some cows. I did well in school, was pushed ahead by my teachers and graduated in 1935 from high school when I was fourteen. I went to a junior college because MIT at the time wouldn't accept anyone under the age of sixteen. So I entered the Massachusetts Institute of Technology as a sophomore. I graduated in 1940 at age nineteen with a degree in chemical engineering and went to work for Goodyear. While at MIT I completed army ROTC, but I couldn't be commissioned until I was twenty-one. I turned twenty-one in March 1942 and was commissioned a second lieutenant in the coast artillery. When called to active duty I reported to an antiaircraft artillery unit at Camp Haan, near Riverside, California, right across the highway from March Field. Every day I watched the planes take off and land, and I

Roy Brown's P-47 Thunderbolt, *Pick*, short for Pickrell, his wife's maiden name. Roy flew with the 86th Fighter Bomber Group, first in Italy, later in France, ending up at R-25 Schweinfurt, where the group deactivated.

decided that I would rather fly airplanes than shoot at them. I was young and foolish and craved some action. I wanted a piece of the war.

"I did my flight training in the Western Training Command and graduated in class 43I. All my training was in Arizona. I went through the usual primary, basic, and advanced phases, flying the Ryan PT-22, BT-13, and the AT-6. After graduation I was sent through instructor pilot training at Randolph Field near San Antonio, Texas, and upon completion of the course was sent back to Marana, a basic training field near Tucson. I instructed two classes in the BT-13, and once the students moved into the advanced phase I instructed them in aerobatics in the AT-6. While still in pilot training at Ryan Field, I met a coed, Frances Pickrell, who attended the University of Arizona in Tucson. Frances and I got to know each other pretty well and I talked her into marrying me while I was an instructor at Marana. We were planning our wedding when I got orders to report to a P-47 Replacement Training Unit, an RTU, near Baton Rouge, Louisiana. Fran and I moved our wedding up by a month, got married, and took off for Baton Rouge. It all ended too soon and Fran and I had to say good-bye to each other. I crossed the Atlantic to Naples, Italy, in a ninety-six-ship convoy. In Pisa we were quartered in a famous old school where Enrico Fermi received his advanced degree. Of course we all went up on the leaning tower.

"I was assigned an aircraft and named it *Pick*. My wife's maiden name was Pickrell. We called her Pick. I flew mostly close air support in the Po Valley.

But there was one mission which was quite different from the rest. It was over San Remo. We were going after ships in the harbor. We sank a couple. Then, I don't know what happened, but suddenly my cockpit was filled with hydraulic fluid which coated everything including the windshield. There was no way to wipe it off. I had nothing to wipe with anyway. I was coated by the stuff as well. I opened the canopy a little so I could look out the side for a landing. Fortunately, I had gained a little experience landing that way when I was in the RTU at Harding Field. That was my first time landing, looking out the side of the canopy. It had been good training for the real thing when it happened to me in Italy. But this stuff was on the inside of the windshield which made it even worse. I managed to land without incident."

Lieutenant Roy Brown flew close air support for the ground troops when that was called for, but principally his missions took him deep behind enemy lines looking for trucks and trains to bomb and strafe, rail lines to interdict, and bridges and tunnels to destroy. All of his work, if you could call it that, was at low level, exposing him and his fellow P-47 flyers to enemy antiaircraft fire of all calibers. Those little black flowers, as they referred to the explosions of German 88mm antiaircraft shells, were deadly, and took down all too many of his squadron mates. Roy flew with the 526th Fighter Bomber Squadron of the 86th Fighter Bomber Group. The squadron history provides a look at the day-to-day life of a P-47 flyer:

October 4, 1944 (Grossetto Air Base, Italy)
The chemical warfare people were most enthusiastic about a 110 gallon incendiary tank they devised from wing tanks. We dropped them on strong points with questionable results. Lieutenant Master did not return from a mission. His plane crashed in friendly territory and he was killed. World Series first game has brought out a few 1,000 Lira notes with most everyone liking the "Browns." General Chidlaw is scheduled to be here for presentation of awards. Twelve beers issued as a ration.

October 19, 1944
Three missions today in bad weather, two with fuel tank incendiaries (napalm). Pilots are interested to learn about the effectiveness of these weapons. They are difficult to drop accurately and must be carried rather low. Lieutenant Kritz and Captain Lucas transferred to the States after completing 100 missions.

October 23, 1944
Bad weather today. Major Benedict and Lieutenant Mabry flew a non-scheduled mission destroying five motor transports, seven locomotives and damaged 45 railroad cars. The advance echelon left today for Pisa.

October 24, 1944 (Pisa, Italy)

Major Benedict again led a mission which paid off in a big way. He led his flight on the deck in the face of accurate enemy anti-aircraft fire to destroy eight moving locomotives, one stationary locomotive and 44 railway cars, 40 of which were loaded with ammunition. A large percentage of between 200 and 300 enemy troops were killed or injured as they attempted to escape from an 11-car passenger train which was strafed thoroughly. Locomotives seem to be his specialty this month, his flight destroying nine on this mission alone.- Enlisted men's barracks at Pisa are in a technical institute named after Leonardo de Vinci, immediately in the rear of the leaning tower. The officers will occupy another school in the same area.

Major Benedict's reputation as a locomotive killer and enemy aircraft scrounger caught the attention of a reporter on the *Stars & Stripes* who wrote a piece about Benedict and his antics, entitled: "Red Haired Pilot 'Terry' of the Mediterranean Army Air Forces." "Tactical Air Force Headquarters, October 10—The Mediterranean theater's champion super scrounger is a giant red-haired Thunderbolt pilot who looks and acts like one of the hip characters in 'Terry and the Pirates.' His name is Bill Benedict. Somewhere along the line, from the time he joined the RCAF in 1941 to his present job as a squadron leader, a general made him a Major—but he is honestly a doughboy at heart. Anyone who's been shot down three times, bailed out once and gone down one way or another 14 more times must love the earth. Benedict is the daring gent who started the technique called 'tunnel busting' in northern Italy. 'The first time I spotted a tunnel was in Italy because mostly I had been with the RAF in the desert,' he said. 'I sent a 1,000 pound bomb through one, and it lobbed in so deep that the explosion seemed bigger on the other side.' He holds a half-dozen decorations from three countries, has a dozen stories to tell about each one, and shows no false modesty about his 200 missions, or the six Messerschmitts and Stukas to his credit. The fact that he's flown every Italian, German, British and American single-engine plane, that's where the scrounging championship title comes in. He admits that the pickings are not too hot these days. At one time or another he's 'owned' seven Messerschmitts, two Focke Wulf 190s, 1 Savoie-Marchette, a Paggio 108, one Fieseler Storch and a Stuka. In his own words the 26 year old flyer is not one of these 'Get your 50 missions, pick up an air medal, go home, marry, and become an instructor pilot' kind of guy. . . . The big red-headed major has vast admiration for the RAF and the air discipline it practices. He credits a great deal of his own skill to his RAF training and has an abiding love for the Spitfire. 'You can't beat that girl,' he boasted. Some correspondents call Benedict the most colorful man in the Army Air Forces."

November 5, 1944

Major Benedict flew an unscheduled four-ship mission: eight locomotives were destroyed and one damaged. Lt Huff failed to return. He called on R/T that he was on fire and would bail out. Lt Setencich, who was following him, did not see him jump. Aircraft was seen to go in and explode.

November 8, 1944

Stand-down today, bad weather. A dance is set for Saturday night. V.D. is reported high, resulting in the usual talks by the squadron surgeon.

November 10, 1944

Lt Lepry cracked up on take-off and one incendiary bomb exploded which gave him a bad time. The plane burned completely, he escaped with serious injuries. Seven aircraft attacked town of and guns at Setti Fondi, in close support of ground forces. Six fuel-tank incendiary bombs hit in target area leaving the town in flames and silencing the guns. Intense 20mm flak was encountered and silenced by both bombing and strafing. Official commendation from the Fifth Army read: "Ground support excellent. Congratulations! The Doughboys stood up in their foxholes and cheered the Setti Fondi deal."

November 11, 1944

Sixteen P-38s jumped our flight. Jettisoned wing tanks and turned into the P-38s. The P-38s finally broke off. Officers' dance this night successful. A number of hangovers—wonder how the nurses feel?

November 18, 1944

Lt Hutchins failed to return. This loss will be keenly felt and all are of the opinion that Hutchins will make it if he got out. Setencich's plane was badly shot-up by 20mm flak and set afire. He started to bail out several times but made it home—how, he doesn't know. On the same mission Lt Lender had a narrow escape. Flak entered the canopy, took the fur out of his jacket collar, creased his neck, hit the armor plate in back of him and ricochet out. Lt Hailes says he propositioned every girl in town without one "Yes," and feels further reconnaissance futile. Morale in the squadron doesn't seem all that it should be. The movie wasn't well attended last night.

November 23–27, 1944

Stand-down due to weather.

November 28, 1944

Lt Anderson, on his first combat mission, was caught in his own bomb blast. He nursed the plane back up to 3,000 feet when the engine failed and he had to bail out. He was seen to land in enemy territory.

November 30, 1944
Flew four missions today, all routine stuff with no outstanding results. Payday. We were briefed on how to brush our teeth. What next?

December 4, 1944
Lt Leader was shot up on a close support mission and bailed out safely in friendly territory.

December 10, 1944
Flew five missions today and lost two pilots. Lt Charles Williams was seen to go in with his plane. Lt Lawrence bailed out over the front lines. Word was received that Lt Anderson who went down on his initial flight was in Florence.

December 14, 1944
Returning from a mission after having his plane hit by flak, Lt Sewell was unable to lower his left landing gear or raise the right one and chose to bail out. He was picked up immediately by a boat and suffered no ill effects.

December 16, 1944
Major Richard Taylor assumed command of the squadron (526th Fighter Squadron), replacing Major William Benedict, who was transferred to the 86th Fighter Group headquarters.

December 17, 1944
Lt Arthur James failed to return from a mission, was seen to bail out of his plane and land safely in enemy territory. Lieutenant Raymond Huff was awarded the Silver Star; Major William Benedict, the 2nd Oak Leaf Cluster to the Distinguished Flying Cross.

December 20, 1944
PX supplies were issued—no beer. The USO show at our theater was very good. Delighted once again to see some American women which seem much more beautiful than the women over here. Lt Klemme who bailed out some time ago was safe in partisan hands.

December 23, 1944
An order was published by the 12th Air Force confirming the General Court Martial sentence requiring Major Benedict, our former squadron commander, to pay

a fine of $150 per month for ten months on charges of stealing an easy chair and two matching stools from a native Italian.

December 25, 1944

Christmas day. Turkey with all the trimmings, as much as you wanted. Some of the men gave out candy and food that they received from home to the children of Pisa and their cries of "grazia" could be heard all over town.

January 1945

Captain Chambers hit a high tension wire while strafing and crashed and burned on January 1. On January 6, Lt Bostad's plane was hit by flak and he was forced to bail out over water. His disposition is unknown. The Germans of late have displayed an amazing talent for repairing bombed rail lines as fast as we cut them. Lt Wiessner attempted to take off with one of our newest airplanes, and for some reason it would not get off the ground. He ran off the end of the runway and completely demolished the plane. He was lucky, the bombs he was carrying did not explode. On January 15 Lt Eastburn had a runaway propeller after coming off the target, his plane for some reason caught on fire. He bailed out at about 2,000 feet, but no chute was seen because of smoke. Good flying weather on the 21st— Lt Fields provided some excitement when just as his plane gained flying speed the left bomb fell off and bounced down the runway. The bomb did not go off, and Lt Fields dropped the other bomb over the water and landed. *Lt Roy Brown scored his first victory of a plane on the ground. Returning from a mission he spied an Me 109 sitting on a field just south of Ghedi airdrome. Diving down he gave it a short burst and the enemy plane exploded.*

February/March 1945 (Tantonville Air Base, France)

The 86th Fighter Bomber Group transferred to Tantonville Air Base in France in February, and was reassigned to the 1st Tactical Air Force (Provisional). Everyone wondered "How much longer can Germany hold out? Pilots returning from missions over Germany report seeing flight after flight of Allied aircraft bombing Germany. They report that they have never seen so many aircraft in the air at one time." Yet the war continued to claim lives on all sides. Five 526 Fighter Squadron pilots died in March. Both the squadron and the group dropped the word "Bomber" from their designation.

April 2, 1945

Weather was not good today, but one mission succeeded in getting to its target. Four planes strafed an airfield at Halle, of the four, three were hit by flak. They damaged three Me 262s and two Me 210s. One Me 262 was just preparing to take off. None of them burned, but they were seriously damaged. The price of planes came high today. Six of our planes were damaged. One pilot hit trees while straf-ing. How he brought the plane back will never be known. About the only good thing left on the plane was the rudder. The pilots have all the faith in the world in these planes and somehow they bring them back.

April 12, 1945
Lieutenant Roy Brown flew as flight leader of a formation of eleven fighter bombers. In the town of Brettach enemy troops were holding up the advance of our troops. In spite of small arms fire the flight made a perfect bombing run. The next day a report was received from the 100th Infantry Division stating that the attack was very suc-cessful and enemy fire ceased after the attack.

April 21, 1945 (Gross Gerau, Germany)
We moved to Gross Gerau on April 17. Lieutenant Shenk crashed on the field after returning from a mission and attempting to land. The cause of his crash is unknown.

April 27, 1945
Lieutenant Dornstadter failed to return from a mission. The formation was jumped by 12 Fw 190s and in the ensuing air battle Lt Dornstadter was shot down. No parachute was seen as the plane crashed and burned.

"When the war ended, we were flying out of Gross Gerau, a field located between Frankfurt and Darmstadt," Roy Brown recalls. "I flew a total of eighty-four combat missions. On only one did I engage German fighters. That was very near the end of the war, on April 27. We were flying in two flights of four, and two of us were flying rover, making a total of ten. As rovers we flew behind the two flights covering their rear. We were trying out a new leader. My wing man called me when he saw a group of Fw 190s approaching, about ten or twelve. We warned the others, aborted our planned mission, and turned into the approaching enemy fighters. By the time the 190s got to us there were ten P-47s facing them head-on. The long-nosed 190s came through us and shot down our new leader. It was a head-on shot. I happened to look down and saw him spin into the ground. I went after one of the 190s and got some strikes on him, but about that time one of our planes went by me with a 190 on his tail. I broke off the engagement and went after him. It was an interesting experience. The 190s were good planes, I knew that, and I didn't expect to be able to turn inside of one. But when the German pilot turned sharply to the left, I noticed that he stalled and snapped back to the right, which broke his turn a little bit. When I was overtaking him, he did that twice, which allowed me to turn inside of him and shoot him down. The pilot bailed out."

Colonel "Hub" Zemke, the commander of the 56th Fighter Group, better known as the Wolf Pack, wrote in *Zemke's Wolf Pack*, his autobiography, about a similar encounter he had with a Fw 190 fighter on June 7, 1944. "We came across blue-nosed Mustangs of the 352nd Fighter Group strafing a parked ammunition convoy. We joined the party which was later interrupted by some Fw 190s. Two Mustangs were seen to go down. As we climbed our P-47s to gain advantage, I saw a single Fw 190 trying to sneak up on one of our lower elements. Turning right and down to attack him, he saw me coming, changed his mind and fled to the west. Because of my superior altitude I rapidly overtook him in the dive. The Focke Wulf pilot then broke right to engage me and as I came in behind him he tightened his turn, suddenly losing control and spinning down straight into the ground. I never fired a shot."[66] As good as the Fw 190 was as a fighter aircraft, it had its drawbacks, one of which was witnessed by both Zemke and Brown. A tight turn could quickly turn fatal for its pilot if he allowed himself to get involved in a horizontal dogfight. The 190's strength lay in the vertical plane. Kenneth O. Chilstrom, a retired air force colonel and test pilot, tested the Fw 190 in the summer of 1944 at Wright Field, in Dayton, Ohio. "The Fw 190 was an airplane all fighter pilots wanted to fly. Two captured 190s were delivered to Wright Field in early 1944. I was flying as a test pilot in the fighter Operations Section after a combat tour in Europe. I was given the assignment to evaluate the 190's performance and handling characteristics. On the 26th of July, 1944, I flew both aircraft extensively and quickly discovered that the 190's rapid rate of roll was better than that of any other fighter I had flown, including the P-38, P-47, P-51 and the British Spitfire. In the vertical plane the aircraft was nearly unbeatable: a pilot's airplane. However, in a horizontal turning engagement the 190 had a tendency to stall and opposite snap, allowing a Spitfire or P-47 to get inside its turn, a truly deadly situation for the 190 pilot."[67] This was exactly the situation Roy Brown took advantage of when he shot down the 190 in April 1945. Another fatal flaw of the 190, so to speak, was its electrical trim switch, which had a tendency to short-out, trimming the aircraft into an either full up or full down position, a condition that could not be manually overridden—killing many a pilot, German and American. Flying captured Fw 190s, Chilstrom and Anspach, whose stories are included in this book, both survived such situations; Lieutenant Richard Haynes, one of Watson's Whizzer pilots, didn't. He crashed coming in for a landing when he was too low to respond and was killed instantly.

In that final engagement on April 27, 1945, in which Roy Brown downed one Fw 190 and damaged another, Lt. Moody shot down a second Fw 190. But the month wasn't over yet, nor was the war.

April 30, 1945

On Roy Brown's 77th combat mission, his last, against targets near Crailsheim,
one member of his flight, Lt Jette, was hit and had to bail out. Late that night Jette
returned to Gross Gerau and had an interesting story to tell. After bailing out of
his stricken Thunderbolt he was captured by Hitler Youths who turned him over
to the SS. The SS troopers were strictly in favor of hanging him, but he managed
to talk them out of it. He was then turned over to ordinary German soldiers,
whose commander asked Jette how they should go about surrendering to the
Allies. When American troops arrived, Jette turned them over—three German
officers and 35 soldiers.[68]

For all practical purposes, the war in Europe was over. There was to be
no more combat flying after April 30, according to the 526th Fighter Squadron history. Yet, on May 1, 1945, the 86th Fighter Group was tasked to put up
thirty-six planes for a special mission. Roy Brown remembers the occasion
well. Everyone was quite excited about it. Their group was supposed to fly to
the Munich area where they were to meet "some enemy fighters and escort
them back to the field, where the enemy planes would land. Some arrangements had been made with the enemy," the squadron's history notes, "but the
weather prevented the show from taking place." The aircraft in question were
no ordinary planes, but Me 262s, the new German jet fighter. Adolf Galland,
the one-time leader of Germany's fighter command, who had been fired by
Fieldmarschall Goering, fought his last aerial battle on April 26, 1945, as the
commander of JV-44, a jet fighter unit of his creation manned by some of
Germany's best pilots. In that last engagement Galland was shot down and
barely escaped with his life. He ended up in a Luftwaffe hospital at Tegernsee,
Bavaria. The war was over for him. He knew that. What he wanted to do was
save his squadron, its aircraft and men, JV-44, and transfer them as a unit to
the Americans. With the help of a pair of trusted officers Galland secretly
managed to propose his intentions to the US Army. The surrender scenario
proposed by Galland came to naught because of American bureaucracy finding it difficult to deal with such a proposal, and the weather. Instead, nearly all
of the German jets ended up being destroyed, except for one, which became
a part of Colonel Watson's Me 262 collection, which would in time be sent to
the United States for evaluation.[69]

"On the eighth of May, VE Day," Roy Brown recalled, "I was asked if I was
interested in a unique assignment. My group staff would set up an interview
for me in Frankfurt with some intelligence folks from General Spaatz's staff.
We had nothing to do, so I volunteered. In Frankfurt I was questioned about
my experience as an instructor pilot, and the interviewers wanted to know if

I knew anything about jet engines. Of course I didn't know anything about jet engines. At Gross Gerau we did little flying in those immediate postwar days. Life was boring and I was looking for something to do. Lots of celebrating was going on, of course, especially in the enlisted area." Notes the 526th Fighter Squadron history, "Celebrations in the enlisted men's area are a nightly occurrence and continue well into the wee hours of the morning. Shortly after arriving at this base (Gross Gerau) someone discovered a large winery close to Worms that seemed to have an unlimited stock of wine and champagne. For several days the men kept hauling it in until nearly everyone had at least one case of wine and champagne. White wine and champagne seemed to be the favorite, but a large quantity of red champagne and wine was also found. Regardless of color, the wine and champagne produced the desired effect complete with hangovers. Poker and drinking are the only diversions for the men. Their area resembles a cooperative farm in many respects. Some of the men have pigs, chicken and geese, and the savory odor of roast fowl and barbecued pork fills the air every evening. The pilots are already starting to bitch about so little flying."[70]

"I don't really know how and why I was picked for the 262 program," Roy mused, "but one day in early June I received orders to report to Lechfeld. Jim Holt, another pilot in my group, had also volunteered for the assignment and was selected. My squadron flew me down to Lechfeld in a B-25. Bob Strobell, our team leader, was already there. Holt got there a day after I did. Not only had I never flown a jet, I had never flown a twin-engine aircraft or one with a tricycle landing gear—all that was part of the Me 262 jet fighter and new to me. When I first arrived at Lechfeld, we were pretty much on our own, spent our time in the cockpits of airplanes learning where the instruments and controls were located and what the functions of the controls were. Strobell had an Me 262 tethered near the hangar and we all sat in that aircraft, ran up the power and practiced our procedures. That was helpful. But it wasn't flying. For the final checkout in the tethered aircraft we closed our eyes, a blindfold check, locating every lever, button, and cockpit control from memory. In an emergency there is no time to think, and reactions need to be automatic. That is the way we trained in flight training, concentrating on developing conditioned responses. If I am flying along and something goes suddenly wrong, I don't always have time to think about the emergency. I may have to react instinctively and that requires training yourself to do the correct thing. Our blindfold checks served that purpose.

"I sort of sat back and listened when the others talked about engine problems due to abrupt flight maneuvers, or nose gear and braking problems. The aircraft had leading edge slats, something new to me. On the ground they were out. Around 150 miles per hour they retracted automatically. The slats improved the airflow over the wing, lowering the aircraft's stall speed. The cockpit in the airplane was not crowded. At least I didn't find it to be that. The one thing I remember Karl Baur mentioning [Baur was one of two German Messerschmitt test pilots, the other being Willie Hoffmann, who taught them how to fly the Me 262] to us several times, 'When coming in for a landing keep the throttles forward a bit. Keep the turbines turning over at a pretty good speed. If you let the engines slow down to idle and you need power for a go-around, it takes a while for the jets to regain their power.' It's not like a prop job where the response is instantaneous, and all of us were used to flying that kind of airplane. I remember on my check flight with Karl, I came in a little bit hot on landing, playing it safe. Once I came near the runway, I pulled back on the stick a little to keep the nose gear off the runway, and once I touched down, I dropped the nose slowly. I don't believe Baur ever touched the controls during my initial flight. For our subsequent ferry flight—after all, that was what we were training for—Baur reminded us that the auxiliary fuel tank was right behind the cockpit. Not long after takeoff you had to start transferring that fuel from the aft tank into the main forward tank in front of the cockpit. If you waited too long, it was too late. The engines used more fuel than the pump could transfer.

"It is surprising that we had no problems checking out. Maybe it was because most of us had been instructor pilots, which made us more comfortable flying in a different plane. I think you learn a lot about flying when you instruct and it becomes easier to transition. Among the many nice things in the Me 262 was a true airspeed indicator. I was used to having to convert indicated airspeed, based on altitude, to true airspeed. True airspeed was the speed you were flying at, not indicated. I liked flying the Me 262. I thought it was an easy plane to fly, a very nice plane to fly—not noisy, not a lot of vibrations. The sort of thing I was used to in the Thunderbolt. As for Colonel Watson? I thought he was quite a person. He was something like a Steve Canyon type, the character in the comic strip. He was good-looking and certainly we all knew that he was a very good pilot. He was articulate. I remember one time sitting in the cockpit of one of the 262s in the hangar familiarizing myself with the layout when he came up with a compass in front of the airplane and told me to tell him what the compass reading was. He was checking the compasses on all the airplanes. Like everyone else, he was out there helping out wherever he could.

"Sabotage was one of the things we were concerned about. There were precautions taken. When the German mechanics got an airplane ready for flight, Lieutenant Strobell or Colonel Watson, whoever was there at the time, wouldn't let anybody know who was going to fly it for the first time. It could be Baur or Hoffmann or one of us. The Germans didn't know who they were getting the plane ready for. But I am not aware of any incidents which would have indicated that there was a problem." Sabotage, according to Colonel Watson, never became an issue. The German pilots and mechanics hired in support of Operation Lusty appeared anxious to save as many of the aircraft as possible to ensure that the technology embodied in this airplane was not lost. Said Willy Messerschmitt, the designer of the Me 262, when interviewed in May 1945, "This airplane is something unique and different from any other, and not of Hitler's making. It represents the very best of German engineering under truly adverse circumstances." Of that achievement, the Germans were justifiably proud.

Both Roy Brown and Bob Anspach spent most of their time with Karl Baur and Willie Hoffmann, and their views of the two German test pilots were shaped less by suspicion and more by the level of intimacy that developed between them as a natural by-product of their airplane talk. "Baur and Hoffmann both were friendly," Roy Brown remembered. "Baur was more reserved than Hoffmann, more serious. He didn't really enter into conversation freely, while Willie was more outgoing and loved to tell flying stories. Willie had been a famous sailplane pilot before the war. He talked to us about flying inverted in a sailplane at one meter above the ground and doing a loop at one hundred meters. Willie told us about flying the *Natter* rocket plane, which was launched from a rail, vertically. It had a nose cone with twenty-four rockets as armament. The idea was, according to Willie, to fly toward a formation of enemy bombers and shoot all the rockets. Then the pilot bailed out. The plane came down by parachute and was later recovered and reused, or that was the plan. Willie said that when he bailed out a metal fitting at the back of the chute hit his head and knocked him unconscious. Fortunately for him he regained consciousness before hitting the ground. Willie told a lot of flying stories like that and therefore we perceived him as being friendlier than Baur. Not that Baur was unfriendly, he just didn't mingle with the rest of us. And remained reserved at all times."

During the first week of June 1945, Baur and Hoffmann gave flight checks in the Me 262 to Holt, Hillis, Dahlstrom, Brown, and Anspach, all former P-47 pilots who were to fly nine reconditioned Me 262s to Paris. Colonel Watson had settled on June 10, a Sunday, as the day when they would move the aircraft out of Lechfeld. Both Baur and Hoffmann were to fly an aircraft, since there were only seven American pilots, including Watson and Strobell, and nine airplanes to be moved—Watson had already flown one airplane to Paris, for a total of ten, to test out the route of flight and an intermediate airfield where all were to land and refuel. At Lechfeld the airplanes were fueled with J-2 jet fuel. Truck diesel fuel worked just as well. June 10 was a bright sunny day filled with sounds of distant church bells. Nine Me 262 jet fighters lined up nose to tail on the Lechfeld runway for the first leg of their trip to Paris. All aircraft, except for Roy Brown's, were to land at St.-Dizier to refuel. Roy Brown was an engineer and in doing his meticulous flight planning determined that he had sufficient fuel to fly directly to Melun Villaroche airport, near Paris, without an intermediate stop. Brown and Watson were the only engineers amongst the American pilots. As long as Roy got up to ten thousand feet cruising altitude immediately after takeoff and began his fuel transfer from the auxiliary tank promptly after level off, he was good to go. After listening to Roy's proposed flight plan, neither Bob Strobell nor Watson had any objections and gave their approval.

The flight from Lechfeld to Melun was a special occasion for everyone, Americans and Germans alike. Was it not the first American jet squadron to take to the air, even if it was composed of former enemy aircraft and flown by both American and German pilots? Although Watson's Whizzers were not carried on any official table of organization, for a brief moment in time they were a de facto Army Air Forces flying unit with its own name and squadron patch—designed by one of the enlisted maintenance men. "When I took off from Lechfeld," recalled Roy Brown, "I was concentrating on seeing where I was. The speed of the plane was more than I was used to. I was impressed with my progress over the ground and had to change from one map to the next very soon. They were very good maps, even the shapes of wooded areas were shown accurately. I have to admit, I knew pretty well where I was most of the time because I had flown in this area in the war. But the last half hour or so I wasn't quite sure. It was new terrain. I found myself looking for landmarks. Finally I saw Melun coming up on my left and I breathed a sigh of relief. I flew over the field, lined up with the runway to check for signals from the tower, then circled back to the left for a gradual descend and landing. I touched down gently, leaving plenty of runway ahead of me to minimize the use of brakes. Normally when I landed a P-47 I came in hot and low, peeled up to the left in a steep climb and circled back around, using the brakes frequently after landing to steer the Thunderbolt. I did nothing fancy in the Me 262. I didn't know enough about this airplane, and Watson had impressed on us the importance of getting the Me 262s to the United States in a flyable condition. We were conscious of this at all times. At least I was. A 'follow-me' jeep met me at the end of the runway and led me to my parking place. Then I learned that I was the first aircraft to arrive at Melun."

On June 27, 1945, General "Tooey" Spaatz, the commander of the United States Strategic Air Forces in Europe, USSTAF, flew out to Melun airport to view what Colonel Watson and his crew of P-47 pilots had assembled for him. Included among the display of advanced German aircraft were ten Me 262 jet fighters and four Arado 234 jet reconnaissance aircraft. On July 17, Watson

June 10, 1945, Lechfeld. Their Me 262s are lined up, ready to go. Roy Brown is squatting on the far right. The two pilots in civilian attire are German test pilots Willie Hoffmann, left, and Karl Baur.

Roy Brown's Me 262, named *Connie the Sharp Article* by Sergeant Freiburger at Lechfeld, was renamed *Pick II* by Roy once they arrived at Paris Melun. It would become *444* when General Spaatz came to Melun to inspect Watson's fleet of German aircraft on June 27, 1945.

and his Whizzer pilots were summoned to USSTAF headquarters in St. Germain, near Paris, and recognized for their achievement. Watson received the Distinguished Flying Cross; all others received the Air Medal, pinned on their chests by the new commander of USSTAF, Lieutenant General J. K. Cannon. The aircraft were then quickly flown to Cherbourg, where they were loaded onto the British escort carrier HMS *Reaper*. The Whizzer pilots, Roy Brown among them, sailed on the *Reaper* for New York City, arriving on July 31. The

Roy Brown with Lieutenant Colonel Charles W. Samuel at Wright-Patterson AFB, Ohio, in 2004. Charles, with over 3,500 flying hours in the A-10, was honored to have the opportunity to show Roy the features of the A-10 Thunderbolt II. Charles was then serving with the 118th Fighter Squadron, Connecticut Air National Guard, Bradley IAP, Connecticut.

German aircraft were transported to Newark Field, New Jersey, where they were "degunked" and then flown to either Wright Field in Dayton, Ohio, or to Freeman Field, Indiana, which was serving as an aircraft overflow base for Wright Field. With the dropping of two atomic bombs on Japan, August 6 on Hiroshima and August 9 on the city of Nagasaki, the war in the Pacific finally came to an end.

Roy Brown had enough points to get out of the Army Air Forces when HMS *Reaper* dropped anchor at the Brooklyn Navy Yard. He was soon reunited with his young bride, Frances, and went to work as a chemical engineer for Goodyear Tire and Rubber Company in Akron, Ohio. There Roy was in charge of developing de-icing systems for airplane propellers, wing and tail leading edge surfaces, helicopter rotor blades, and engine inlets. Then he transferred to the uranium enrichment plant in Piketon, Ohio, from where he retired in 1983 as manager of the technical division. Roy and Fran now live in Chillicothe, Ohio. He is an avid jogger and tennis enthusiast, and supports his alma mater by interviewing bright youngsters, as he once was, for admission to the Massachusetts Institute of Technology.

ALBERT S. TUCKER

P-38/F-80/Gloster Meteor

POW StalagLuft I, Barth, Germany

High Flight

Oh! I have slipped the surly bonds of earth and danced the skies on laughter silver wings;
Sunward I've climbed, and joined the tumbling mirth of sun-split clouds—and done a hundred
things you have not dreamed of—wheeled and soared and swung high in the sunlit silence.
Hov'ring there I've chased the shouting wind along, and flung my eager craft
through footless halls of air.
Up, up the long delirious, burning blue, I've topped the windswept heights with easy grace
Where never lark, or even eagle flew—and, while with silent lifting mind I've trod
The high untrespassed sanctity of space, put out my hand and touched the face of God.
—Pilot Officer Gillespie Magee, No 412 Squadron, RCAF. Killed 11 December 1941, WWII ETO

"My father was an army officer. His home was Lexington, Virginia. He was born and raised there, and I feel like I grew up in Lexington because my father would send my mother and us children to Lexington for the summer each year. As a consequence I thought I grew up as a Virginian; although I was born in 1921 in Lexington, Kentucky. Of course my father, being an army officer, was stationed all around the various army posts in the country. I got my fascination for aviation at Fort Benning, Georgia, which for years, going way back, was the location of the army's infantry school. Each military specialty had a particular post which specialized in a particular arm—such as infantry, armor, artillery, and so on. That would have been back in the early thirties when I was there as a young boy, about eleven, twelve years old. The infantry school had to have some aviation, so they had a flight of O-25 observation biplanes. To my amazement I saw lots of airplanes while I was there, fighting planes as well,

which demonstrated to the infantry what they could do. I was absorbed with
the spectacle of watching these planes fly, I loved it, and decided right then
and there that I was going to fly some day. My dad's response was, 'You can fly
if you want, that's your business. But you have to graduate from college first.'
Well, I agreed with that. And since I had to go to college, that was the rule, I
decided I may as well go to the army college, at West Point, and then I would
be able to join the people I was going to fly with. I did that. Got into West Point
after going to a prep school and passing a slew of tests. I entered the Point in
1940, which would have been the class of 1944. But Pearl Harbor happened
in December 1941, and two days later Germany declared war on the United
States. The war was on, so the army decided that we would graduate in three
years rather than four. By the way, my father was not a West Pointer. He graduated from the University of Virginia.

"While at West Point it was also decided that those of us who wanted to go
into aviation would get our flight training while we were there. So, I got all my
flight training before I graduated from West Point. I received my wings a day
before I was commissioned in the United States Army as a second lieutenant.
There was a small field at Newburgh, New York, where we trained. A civilian
field had been taken over and they lengthened the runways, built hangars and
buildings, all the stuff that goes with a regular airfield operation. As a result of
me being a qualified aviator, I did not have to march in my graduation parade.
Instead I, along with several other classmates, flew over it. The day I got my
wings General 'Hap' Arnold, the commanding general of the Army Air Forces,
pinned my wings on. And then the next day, since I now was a pilot, I flew
over my graduation parade with my first passenger, the crew chief of my AT-10
volunteered to fly with me. It was a tremendous formation of AT-10 and AT-6
aircraft that did a fly-by that day, about sixty to eighty aircraft. After the parade
flyover we landed back at Newburgh and were driven back to West Point. That
afternoon they had the graduation ceremony. But the president of West Point
got sick and couldn't come. At the last minute they got General George Marshall, from VMI, to do the honors, and he shook my hand that afternoon. So, I
am quite proud of the fact that two very important people had shaken my hand
within the span of two days—Generals Arnold and Marshall. Also, I want to
mention that during my third year at West Point we got about twice as much
flying time as the average pilot trainee. So we were well prepared for what lay
ahead. Those in the flying cadet program barely got two hundred hours flying
time spread over six months—while I got a little over three hundred hours,
including instrument training. You could hardly fly through the bad winter
weather without such training. The average trainee got little or none of such
training. As a result, the losses in training and later in combat as a result of a
lack of instrument training were colossal.

ALBERT SIDNEY JOHNSTON TUCKER, JR.

CONGRESSIONAL, 7TH, TEXAS

"*Al*"

Cadet Al Tucker, West Point class of 1943. Robin Olds was Al's classmate and good friend. They flew P-38s together in combat, but Robin didn't get shot down like his friend Al did. Robin would become an ace in World War II, downing twelve enemy aircraft and four more over North Vietnam.

"Twelve of us were lucky enough to be sent to P-38 training. I think half my class of flyers volunteered for P-38s, but only twelve out of about two hundred applicants were picked. Among the people who went to P-38s was the great Robin Olds. We were buddies at the Point, and all the way through flight training and P-38 training. As a matter of fact, because we were regular officers [vice reserve officers which most of the flyers in the Army Air Forces were] we went through P-38 training about two or three times. As regular officers, the rules stipulated, we couldn't be sent to duty anywhere in a capacity less than flight leader. Wisely the squadron commanders overseas wouldn't accept us new guys as flight leaders without combat experience. So we had to find a way to get over into the war. Robin and I found a sergeant who prepared for us a request for orders. The sergeant gave the request to his lieutenant, who gave the request to his captain, and the captain took it to the colonel—who said OK. Not only for Robin and me, but the other ten as well. We walked out of the place with orders in hand, sending us to Europe—not as flight leaders, but as regular pilots. They made it legal by sending us to one final fighter group that was forming up in the United States. It was the last to go as an organized fighter group rather than just replacement pilots going to existing groups. We joined that last group—the 479th Fighter Group forming up in the United

States. All of us were at the same level—amateurs without any combat experience. I became a flight leader. The group commander didn't mind, because he hadn't been a flight leader either. We were all amateurs—and that was a mistake. We got a few drills how we were supposed to behave over there in England, how we were supposed to fly, and how to find our home base among hundreds. There weren't many aids to navigation in those days.

"Once we arrived in England, we had to get used to talking on the radio. We would call for a 'steer.' And we had a homer. The homer was the radio in the tower that steered you. I am sure it was all great fun for the British, because this whole radio bearing scheme was RAF designed. We had to fit into it, get used to their way of doing things. Most of the voices we heard would be hard to read British/Scotch brogues. We must have messed them up a little bit with our Yankee talk. At least I hope so. When I called for a steer, at least three other stations remote from each other would listen and draw a bead on you, draw a line on their charts, and then, by telephone, pass those bearings to whoever was acting as the coordinator. Where the lines crossed, that's where you were. They would call back and say something like, 'Yank, who asked for a steer. I say old chap, I see right where you are.' He'd then give you a heading to get you to your airfield. That was the only radio aid we had to navigation. Then we had to get used to what the countryside looked like. It was beautiful and navigable, when you could see it. But you had to get used to flying very low. We weren't restricted to any particular altitude in those days. We flew at any height. I have to marvel, with all the air activity over there, I don't understand why there weren't just volumes of collisions, especially for the bombers. When the bombers would takeoff in the morning, starting about four o'clock, it would take them a couple of hours just to join up. And it might be overcast. And I don't know how they got away with it. We would hear them drone overhead for hours before we even got out of bed.

"We were assigned to RAF Station Wattisham, in County Suffolk, near Ipswich, near the mouth of the Thames River. We were about as close to the English Channel as you could get. Close to the other side as well, a very short flight across the Channel. A major from another group came over to brief and lead us on our first combat mission. A good thing, since we were all amateurs. The major took us around in a couple of big formations over England to get us used to flying in England. Then he led us over the Continent a little bit, not far, but just far enough to get shot at so we knew what flak looked like. Then we were turned loose. I flew twenty-two combat missions—and was shot down on my twenty-second. One of those was a tremendously exciting mission. It was on the 5th of June, 1944. Late afternoon before D-Day. We knew something big was going to happen because we were ordered quite suddenly to go down to the flight line for briefings. As we approached the flight line, we could see our airplanes being painted with big white and black stripes over the wings. We ended up flying top cover on D-Day, the 6th of June 1944. It was raining. The visibility was poor. An ugly day to be starting a battle. I was just aghast at the spectacle below me. I saw so many boats in the water—it seemed like there were thousands. And they were all getting in line. It looked like rivers of boats heading for the Channel, one behind the other, like marching in a parade. These streams of boats then joined up into a great mass. I thought, 'Oh, my God, I wouldn't want to be on the other side, with that coming at me.' On the other hand, what a target they were. We just orbited over the Channel; didn't go over land. Our orders were to shoot down anything that was at our flight level or below us. The Luftwaffe never showed. We flew several of those missions that day and the following day. They used P-38s for this task because everyone knew what a P-38 looked like. And the other side had nothing like it. As we were circling at four thousand feet, I watched battleships hurl their gigantic shells against the enemy. The shells came past us fairly close. I could clearly see them traveling through the air.

"Then I flew several escort missions to Berlin. On one of those missions I finally got to see an enemy airplane, but we were not permitted to leave the bombers. I learned the Luftwaffe had a policy at the time, to avoid a lot of losses unnecessarily, not to attack bombers with a fighter escort. Instead they chose another bomb group without escort. So we didn't experience any air-to-air combat. Robin and I just had a ball flying the P-38. I flew a total of twenty-two combat missions, the twenty-second being my last. It was a day that we didn't have a mission assigned, the 22nd of June, just a few days after the D-Day landings. We were playing volleyball when a sergeant in a carry-all drove up and told us to go down to the airfield right away for a briefing. 'They have some kind of a mission for you all.' We quickly got into our flight gear and headed down to the briefing room. There we learned that 9th Air Force wanted us to take out a railroad bridge just north of Paris. We were assigned to the 8th Air Force. Our mission was fighter escort for the bombers, the reason we were assigned to the 8th. The 9th was responsible for supporting the ground forces. On this day the 9th didn't have enough resources to do it on their own, so they asked the 8th Air Force to help out. I wished I had dropped a bomb in the P-38 before, that was going to be our mission, but none of us ever had. I had seen it done on newsreels. I didn't know why I couldn't do it. At the briefing we learned that my squadron was to fly top cover for the other two squadrons of our group. Each of their airplanes would carry a thousand-pound bomb under each wing. In addition, the group commander, accompanied by three other pilots from his staff, was coming along as well.

"A combat squadron consisted of four flights of four. But our lead squadron this time would have five flights of four because the group commander and his staff were coming on this mission as well. Added up, that came to a total of seventy-two thousand pounds of bombs carried by thirty-six aircraft. My squadron shouldn't have carried any bombs, but someone higher up decided that we could carry a couple of hundred pounders under each wing and still be able to provide top cover. And if some Messerschmitts should show up, we'd pickle them and be ready to defend our friends down below. As soon as we destroyed the bridge, the idea was, every flight was to hit the deck and return home on a preassigned heading. And strafe any targets of opportunity that we came across on the way back. Off we went. As I remember, it took us about an hour and a half to get there. The whole group went into orbit over the target to get a good look at it. Then the number one squadron went down, five flights in trail, led by the group commander. I looked down. Bombs were going off all over the place. Most landed on dry land throwing up huge geysers of earth. The fuses had been set with an eleven-second delay, which explained why so much dirt was thrown up into the air obscuring the target itself. The bomb probably dug itself deep into the ground and when it went off it threw up a huge geyser of dirt. Some of the bombs hit the water—that was spectacular to watch. Pretty soon all the bombs had been dropped—and it looked to me like the bridge hadn't been hit. It was an open girder railroad bridge, so there really wasn't any floor to the bridge. Even if a bomb hit the bridge, it would have gone right through, or skipped over that girder and blown up somewhere else, with that fourteen-second delay set into the fuse. To me, the bridge looked perfectly fine after dropping seventy-two thousand pounds of bombs.

"My squadron leader, Major Keller, called over the radio, 'Hey, group, this is Keller.' By the way, we weren't supposed to be talking. 'That bridge looks like it's still standing. You want us to go down and have a crack at it?' With little hesitation the group commander responded, 'Yea, Keller, you might as well have a crack at it too.' So, Keller over the radio calls, 'OK, Blue Cross Gang,' that's us, 'it's going to be flights in trail. Follow me. Here we go.' Keller had the flight in front of me. Robin Olds had the flight behind me. And he had the fourth flight behind him. As soon as Keller got going down, and as soon as I got going down, I began to see what I would describe as golf balls coming up at us. That's what 40mm antiaircraft fire looked like—I had never seen a golf ball coming up at me before. Once I got to the POW camp, I learned from more experienced flyers that the 40mm round had a glow behind the back side of the shell. And it causes a halo to appear around the shell which can be seen when the shell is in your line of sight—meaning the shells were coming straight up at us. We were looking right down the barrels of the guns shooting at us—seeing golf balls coming up at us. Everything happened very fast. I didn't respond to the first one. The next shell hit my right engine right on the spinner of the propeller, knocking the spinner off. The airplane shook violently as the shell penetrated through the engine longitudinally. The engine stopped running, throwing fire back into the airstream. I knew I was hit bad, but here I was in a dive, and I figured I might as well finish the dive. Everybody went down the same chute, one right after the other. On the way down, in addition to seeing the golf balls, I saw two airplanes going in—one blew up in the air. The other one blew up when he hit the ground. Robin saw this too, and he saw me getting hit. Robin was the only one in our squadron who used his head. He pulled his flight out to the right under a lot of fire and then he approached from a different heading and dropped his bombs. His guys survived. When I got out of the POW camp and I met up with Robin, he said to me, 'Tucker, you did what you were told. I didn't.' Ours was an example of how not to fly a combat mission. Everything we did was wrong, from the bomb fusing to the way we attacked that bridge. Why was it allowed to happen? Our training was terrible. That's how I got shot down."

Robin Olds, in his book *Fighter Pilot*, reflects on those grim days. The 479th Fighter Group took some heavy losses soon after the D-Day landings. "Our losses were dispiriting yet not devastating. Lieutenants Kuentzel and Grdenich failed to return from a mission. They'd been trapped atop an overcast topping out near twenty-eight thousand feet. When last seen, both aircraft were in a steep spiral headed for the ground near Rouen. Just three days later more bad news. This time four were lost, including my pal Al Tucker. He was hit by flak while returning home on one engine. Canella, Ilsley, and Lutz went down too, lost forever, but it turned out that 'Tuck's Luck' held, and Al survived to sit out the rest of the war in StalagLuft I. Those of us who survived those days went on to fly and fight with an appreciation of life that can be known only by those who have been in combat. Laughter was as profound as sadness. Friendships deepened. Every moment of each day felt exactly right, and the edges of time seemed tinged by light."[71]

"After I got rid of my bombs," Al Tucker recalls, "I peeled off to the right and headed home. No time to be scared, just doing what I could to stay up in the air. I flew on the deck. My wingman stayed with me until we got to Reims where he saw me get shot down. We were flying at treetop level. I recall clipping the tops of trees. My good engine went through them with no problem. Beyond the forest there was a ridge line. I thought I saw some fence posts running along the top of the distant ridge. As I approached, I realized the fence posts were changing elevation because I was going higher too. They weren't fence posts, but gun barrels. I had trouble climbing. The props on the dead engine were bent forward. I couldn't feather them. They dragged me down. The most speed I could get out of my good engine was about 190 knots. But if I did any climbing I lost airspeed rapidly. I was slowing down as I approached the AAA guns on the ridge line. I was now under 150 knots. The airplane wouldn't steer between the guns, but dragged me right over a gunpit. I could see three men behind each of the guns. They were Oerlikon, 20mm guns, with two barrels each, firing alternately. They hit my wing fuel tank. The airplane was on fire and all I could do was belly it in. I could see and feel the flames. I pulled the power back. The P-38 settled down nicely and held together until I jumped out. I ran for my life. The ammunition in the nose was exploding as the aircraft burned. Very quickly a platoon of infantry arrived. What appeared to be a sergeant came up to me and said, 'For you ze var is over.' He spoke very good English, of course with a heavy German accent. I had landed right in the middle of a V-1 launch site.

"A car appeared and they took me to their headquarters. From then on I was in the hands of the Luftwaffe. The Luftwaffe fired the V-1s, but apparently the security guards were Wehrmacht—army. They first took me to a jail in Lille. There I got a little bit of an interrogation by a sergeant. Whoever he was, he was a commanding presence. He towered over me by about a foot, and I am over six feet tall. I objected to him taking my class ring. 'You can take my watch, things off my uniform, but not my class ring,' I protested. I don't speak German, but I understood every one of the expletives he uttered very loudly into my face. The following day I, along with other POWs, was put on an old-fashioned passenger car from the turn of the century which was hooked onto a freight train. The car was full. People were sitting on the floor, laying in the overhead baggage racks. For some reason I got to sit by the window. I thought that was nice. I opened the window to breathe in the fresh air. A woman in a railroad uniform sat opposite from me. She was a good-looking gal, probably in her thirties. She looked very serious. She had a bag of cherries, it was the season, and she began to eat the cherries one by one, very slowly, deliberately. I was hungry and salivating. Oh, those cherries looked so good. I thought she was expressing contempt when she looked at me. It got me irritated. I began to resent her, thought it was pretty nasty of her to be sitting there eating those cherries in front of my face, knowing that I was hungry. Then, without changing her facial expression, she rose to leave—and handed me the bag of cherries. There was a lesson for me to learn from this experience—not to judge people too quickly. A couple of times the train stopped and we had to get out, but we were lucky and didn't get attacked by our own fighters. It took about a day and a half to get from the jail in Lille to Frankfurt. In Frankfurt we got off the train and were loaded on a bus which took us to the Luftwaffe interrogation center at Oberursel.

"Our briefings had been very accurate at what to expect if we were captured and sent to Oberursel. They knew much about us, but we also knew their interrogators by name. I was interrogated by one of their very best—Herr Scharff. His winning ways were charm and gentleness. He was so helpful and encouraging that it was easy to 'spill the beans.' I was there for about thirty days. One of my West Point classmates who had been shot down the day before me was confined with me for the last ten days. We quickly determined that they probably expected us to talk to each other, so we didn't, only whispered. We looked all over for the 'bug' that we knew had to be somewhere, but never found it. In later years I learned that the bug was indeed there, concealed in the overhead light fixture, which wasn't reachable by us. Every cell was wired to a central listening point, so anything said was recorded. During the interrogations I stuck to the name, rank, and serial number response. I tried to show no surprise when Scharff mentioned something that I thought was a guarded secret. I tried to control my body language as well. Eventually both my friend and I were shipped to an intermediate POW camp before we were sent to StalagLuft I at Barth. Barth was a resort town on the Baltic Sea between Rostock and Stralsund, about a hundred miles north of Berlin. "But on the eve of our leaving Oberursel the German interrogators put on a going away party for us—hard to believe, but they did. They were all smiles, had hot tea for us, were very gracious. And then they gave us a briefing of what they knew about us. It was quite dramatic how much they knew about our organization and us individually. Information they shouldn't have had. Where did they get it? I have no idea.

"Three months after my capture I finally arrived at StalagLuft I. I received a letter from the sergeant who had taken my West Point class ring during my initial interrogation. The letter read, 'Dear Lieutenant Tucker, I am sorry that this process of interrogation took so long. I want to return to you the enclosed personal items. I hope they reach you in good health.' I got my ring back. Some of my fellow POWs received similar letters and had personal items returned to them. There was a level of civility practiced by Luftwaffe personnel—not the case with the Gestapo and the SS. The SS would inspect our camp about once a month. When they came, the Luftwaffe guys were more afraid of them than we were. The SS officers looked like something out of a Hollywood movie. Pompous peacocks, running around looking as mean as they could. Once I was on a Red Cross detail, allowing me to go from compound to compound, distributing Red Cross parcels among the prisoners—a credit to how well the Luftwaffe tried to treat its American and British prisoners. They did everything according to the rules. They exhibited no meanness or animosity. As the war came close to its end, we were in the last piece of territory still controlled by the Germans. There was a small airfield right next to our camp. What was left of the Luftwaffe flew out of this little field against the Russians. We watched them take off and land, and were cheering for them. Every day there would be fewer and fewer of them. They could have flown fifteen minutes north, to freedom in Sweden—but they didn't. They'd take off to the north, then turn around and go southeast toward the Russian lines. We could hear the artillery. Some didn't make it back; others crashed when they attempted to land their damaged aircraft. It was for us a tremendous spectacle to witness the principle of 'duty, honor, country,' as practiced by German fighter pilots. I admired their discipline and what they did in a totally hopeless situation.

"All the Luftwaffe camp guards were wounded on the eastern front. Many of our aces were in my camp at Barth. Gaby Gabreski and Hub Zemke. Zemke was a hero to us. He spoke both Russian and German. It came in handy when the Russians finally arrived. Hub also managed to work out arrangements with the German camp commander—how they should manage their final days, which were obviously coming. Hub apparently promised them to put in a good word for them when the time came. In return, he expected them to reciprocate by leaving the lights on for us and to keep the water running once they left. Gaby Gabreski became the informal commander of an adjacent compound. I was in compound North 2, and the last one that was set up was North 3, where Gaby was. We had no overall American camp commander— we were in command of ourselves and the Germans respected that. As for food, the Germans shared their food with us to the extent that they were required to, which was augmented by the Red Cross parcels. They could have easily stolen those parcels, because they had control over the parcels before they were delivered to us. But to their credit, they played by the rules and did not take any of the parcels. We in fact ate better than our German guards. The food they fed us was what they ate—horsemeat, beef from animals killed by shrapnel. The bread *Kriegsbrot* was durable stuff. They stacked it outside like bricks. A German sergeant received a quarter of a loaf of bread a day, a little bit of margarine, and a quarter of a length of blood sausage. That was his ration for the better part of a day. He received a cooked meal, soup, once a day. To some extent we ate better than the guards did. I didn't smoke, so I traded my cigarettes for candy bars.

"We had a pilot from Wright Field, Gus Lundquist, he was a test pilot. Gus was designated to get one of those Fw 190s at the airfield next to our camp ready once the Germans left. Bob Hoover, however, who arrived in the camp toward the end of the war, got impatient and decided he couldn't wait. Bob managed to get to that airfield, found a German crew chief and got him to start a Fw 190 for him. He flew west and was home free. He was the first out of our camp."

The story of how Gus Lundquist, who retired from the air force in the rank of brigadier general, ended up in StalagLuft I is quite interesting in itself. "During 1943 we received several captured German and Japanese aircraft at Wright Field, including the Me 109G, the Fw 190G, the Junkers Ju 88, and the Japanese Zero and Betty, all of which I was able to fly and evaluate. I did a great deal of flying in the Fw 190 in late 1943 and early 1944. Although not quite in the class with our P-51, I found the Fw 190 to be a first-class fighter plane. Like the P-51 it was a pilot's airplane, with an excellent cockpit layout, good visibility, excellent control response and maneuverability. Another interesting program was testing the modified Spitfire IX, then flying it across the Atlantic. It took a few stops, to prove that the Wright Field engineers had given it a bomber escort range. They had indeed accomplished this mission but in doing so had turned a beautiful flying machine into an absolute clunker. While at Boscombe Down I flew most of the RAF operational and experimental aircraft they had, including the Typhoon II, the Spitfire XXI, the Tempest, the Whirlwind, the Defiant, several training and bomber aircraft and a captured German Me 210 and Heinkel 111." Boscombe Down was the British counterpart to Wright Field. The British allowed Gus to fly any aircraft he wanted to fly, but what Gus really wanted to do was fly a few combat missions. His hosts agreed to his request. Inexperienced as Gus was flying combat, he was shot down on his third mission, ending up at Barth along with Hub Zemke and Gaby Gabreski. While at Barth, and with little else to do, Gus Lundquist talked about flying the Fw 190. Bob Hoover took advantage of that opportunity, gaining a level of familiarity with the 190's cockpit layout. Once Hoover managed to get into one of the abandoned German airplanes, he wasn't a total stranger to the situation.[72]

"Although Bob Hoover was the first to fly out of Barth, mind you, in a most unusual way, we soon followed," Al Tucker recalled. "The 8th Air Force came for us in a massive armada of B-17 bombers. A small party had arrived earlier in a couple of C-47s and set up an approach control system, tower, and so on at the German airfield. When they were ready, here came the B-17s. It was the most beautiful demonstration of formation flying with four-engine airplanes I'd ever seen. They did a beautiful job. Combat group after combat group came in. They used an inactive runway where they stopped and we got on. Twenty of us were loaded on each B-17. Now the B-17 had a crew of ten. They were all on board. Every crewman of course insisted on making this flight—because this time there would be no flak. So the rest of us had to squeeze onto that airplane. It was the most crowded flight I've ever had, but also one of the most enjoyable flights I've ever made. Our pilot took us over Essen, to allow us to see what their bombing had done to a German city. It looked like the end of the world. I couldn't figure how Germany could ever survive that. We didn't go back to England, but instead were flown to Camp Lucky Strike in France, near Cherbourg. My reaction to Lucky Strike was, 'Holy mackerel, I just got out of a prison camp, now I am back in a prison camp.' Ugly, ugly, ugly. I managed to get out of there the third day I was there.

"There was a second lieutenant in charge of this tent city. He required us to hold inspections every morning to insure our bunks were properly made up, and so on. Then we had to go to lectures and listen to how sorry they were that we were all undernourished, and all the suffering we had to go through. We got pretty sick of all this, including the dear Red Cross ladies who were constantly expressing how sorry they were that we had been treated so badly. We survived. Didn't need to listen to all that stuff. We just wanted to go home. The ladies clung to us, walking around with pitchers of eggnog, wanting us to drink that stuff. I hate eggnog, even with bourbon in it. They didn't have any bourbon of course. On the third day a C-47 landed. My tent happened to be quite close to the airstrip. Sure enough, the pilot was a member of my former P-38 squadron. He immediately recognized me. We shook hands. He had come to Lucky Strike to pick up someone. I said to him, 'You got to get me out of here. This place is terrible.'

"'Sure, I will,' he said. 'But first I need to talk to this major to pick up someone else.' So, I hung around the airplane. When he returned by himself, with a serious look on his face, he said he had bad news for me. He was in the class ahead of me at the Point, and duty, honor, country, and never tell a lie was chiseled into all of us. So he told me what he thought he had to tell me, but he didn't tell me what I had to do about it. So, he told me what the major said to him: 'No, sir' the major had said, 'he can't go.' Then he walked away. I knew what he really was telling me. Nobody was watching, so I just got on the airplane. In back I removed an access panel and hid in the area behind it. There were wires running through the area which operated the rudder and the elevators. But I fit into the space. Soon I heard voices. The airplane took off. Once we leveled off, I got out and introduced myself and got a big hero's welcome. I was still a first lieutenant, but my friend was a major by now. He was a lieutenant like me when I saw him last. We landed at RAF Honington, a former P-38 base that had converted to P-51s. There was somebody there that I knew, Sam Phillips, who met me as I arrived. He went on to become a full general and commanded the Air Force Systems Command in the seventies. Sam was a major, had a staff car, and was a squadron commander. I wore prison garb. They took the rags off of us at Camp Lucky Strike and gave us something clean to wear in the meantime, but not uniforms. At least it was sanitary, but I still felt I was wearing prison garb—and looked like a prisoner. Sam said to me, 'We got to get you some clothes to wear before we do anything else.' Sam took me somewhere and got me a uniform to wear.

"Then Sam drove over to where his squadron's airplanes were lined up in front of a hangar. Shiny new Mustangs. They were no longer in revetments; the war was over. Sam asked, 'Would you like to see mine?' Sure. So he stopped in front of his airplane. He got up on the right wing. Sam's crew chief came over to see what was going on. He got up on the left wing. I was as happy as a clam sitting in this Mustang. This was really nice. Sam says, 'You want to fly it?'

Hell, yes. They strapped me in. I hadn't been flying for a year, but no problem. The cockpit was similar to the AT-6, built by the same people. I was right at home. Wow, it flew nice. I guess I flew for about an hour and a half. I looked around for somebody to joust with, a fighter pilot compulsion, but couldn't find anyone. When I looked down, I saw all those haystacks on a meadow. Great big beautiful haystacks. So I made a simulated strafing run on one of those stacks. I turned on the gunsight, I didn't have to pull the trigger, but I did. After all, I was a combat pilot. Holy mackerel, all six guns fired. I didn't know the plane was armed. The tracers set the haystack on fire. I hurried back and landed. Sam wasn't there, but the crew chief was. He saw I fired the guns. The guns were taped over, and without me saying a word he knew I had fired them. When I taxied in, he saw immediately what had happened. He said, 'Lieutenant, I see you fired the guns. Here is what I am going to do. I am going to rearm those guns and clean them myself and nobody in Ordnance is going to know those guns were fired.' I was sure grateful to that sergeant. I was afraid I was going to get court-martialed. The next day they ferried me back to my old base, and I was back with Robin Olds again.

"What happened next was weird. They couldn't pay me because I didn't exist as far as the paymaster was concerned. They didn't have any orders on me. The finance officer said, 'Don't worry about it. Any time you need money just come over and I'll give you partial pay.' This way I could purchase a new uniform. I became civilized again, formally got checked out in the Mustang, but never mentioning my experience over at Honington and setting that haystack on fire. We were training to go to the Pacific in either a long range P-51 or P-47, but the decision had not yet been made which aircraft we would eventually fly. We flew P-51s and P-47s, and practiced gunnery and dive bombing. We had a young pilot. He was an ace. He and another were in disagreement if it was better to dive straight down at a target or approach at an angle. He chose to demonstrate diving down vertically and flew right into the target. A very sad experience. I didn't fly with Robin Olds as much now. He was the squadron commander and I was just a flyboy. We also had a B-26 and I loved flying it. I hadn't flown for a whole year while a POW, and I tried to do all the flying I could. All this fun flying came to an end when the atom bombs were dropped on Japan and the war in the Pacific ended. We then received orders to deliver all the remaining fighters in the UK to RAF Burtonwood where they were smashed, destroyed. I did three or four flights a day. Since they were going to get smashed up at Burtonwood, we flew them with the throttles wide open. No worry fouling the spark plugs or what have you. No one else volunteered to fly the P-38s. I did, and flew every one I could. Well, we jousted with each other on our way to Burtonwood and I bested the P-51 in the P-38 every time.

"After returning home I did a short tour of duty in our first jet, the P-80, at March Field, near Riverside, California, with my classmate and friend Robin Olds again. While I was there, a British officer joined our squadron—Peter West. Surprisingly, soon after Peter West arrived in California, I received orders to go to England. It was October 1948. I was assigned to Peter West's squadron, part of 12 Group, at Horsham St. Faith. Robin Olds was assigned to Number 1 Squadron, in 11 Group, at Tangmere, and became its squadron commander. That was quite a distinction. At Horsham I met a British flying officer by the name of 'Paddy' Harbison. Paddy and I became close friends." Paddy, as he was called by friends, retired as an Air Vice Marshall in the Royal Air Force, a three star general officer equivalent. He married an American TWA stewardess while he was assigned to March Air Force Base as an exchange officer, and eventually made his home in Arlington, Virginia. Paddy Harbison is a member of a group of retired flying officers that refers to itself as the Old Bold Pilots Group which meets most Fridays for lunch at the Army Navy Country Club in Arlington, Virginia. It was my great pleasure to bring these two fine officers, Al Tucker and Paddy Harbison, back together again at an OBP luncheon in 2013, after they had lost touch with each other over the years.

"At Horsham I flew the Gloster Meteor jet—first the Meteor III, then the Meteor IV. My flight leader and I discovered that it was a great airplane to fly formation aerobatics. We developed a two-ship routine. Our squadron leader saw us doing it and insisted that we fly a three-ship formation—with him as the lead. Well, he was too ham-fisted. So, what to do? I was selected to give him the bad news. Surprisingly, the squadron leader took it rather well. He was an old-fashioned Englishman—tough, set in his ways, a jolly good fellow at the bar with the loudest laugh in the room—and he agreed to fly wing instead of lead. We became really good at what we were doing. The group commander saw us, and he called the air marshal commanding. Air Marshal Trail came down to see us. He liked what he saw and designated us the Royal Air Force Meteor demonstration team. So I did little work for the rest of my exchange tour, other than practicing and flying demonstrations, including a performance for the king and queen of England. Paddy Harbison left about half way through my tour of duty and went over to the US to fly the F-80, later the F-86, with the First Fighter Wing at March Air Force Base." When the air force gained its independence from the US Army in September 1947, all former airfields were renamed as air force bases—ergo March Field became March Air Force Base. "When I finished my tour of duty in England in 1949, there was Paddy welcoming me back to March Air Force Base.

"I stayed with the First Fighter Wing. The wing moved to Palmdale for a couple of months, then we moved to Griffith Air Force Base in New York State. Robin Olds, my old friend and classmate, and I were in the 71st squadron and made the move together. Robin was my squadron commander for the second time around. It was a great friendship we had, going back to our days at West Point, then P-38 training at Williams Field in Arizona. At Willie we trained in the P-38 together. It wasn't really a P-38 we were flying then, but something called the P-322." Robin Olds in his book *Fighter Pilot* wrote, "There were some major differences between the two, although they looked alike. For one thing, the props on the 322 rotated in the same direction, as opposed to the counter-rotating engines on the P-38. The oil and coolant flaps were manually controlled. You flew with one eye on the temperature gauges, constantly adjusting settings for every phase of flight by sliding levers back and forth to keep the values in the green. The P-322 lacked the turbo-superchargers of the 38, and its performance at altitude was pathetic. These particular aircraft had been built for the Brits, who wisely refused to accept them."[73] Al Tucker recalls, "Robin and I flew formation in the 322, doing aerobatic maneuvers as a two ship. Unfortunately we were seen doing it and were turned in, resulting in a severe reprimand for the two of us. But I think it was really an expression of admiration for the flying the colonels saw us do." Robin Olds, Al's West Point classmate, saw that occasion a little differently. "Al Tucker, Lou Nesselbush, Charlie Waller, Hank Rosness, Buck Coursey, Don McClure, and Bob Orr went through fighter training with me." They had advanced to the P-322, when "within a short time, the reality of this business hit our group of eight. Bob Orr was flying solo, crashed and died. It stunned us, but it was reality in the life of a pilot. We would often dogfight among ourselves. It wasn't exactly against regulations, but it couldn't be ignored when two of us jumped a stray P-322 which turned out to be our squadron CO. That afternoon seven of us were lined up before the desk of a very livid major. We received a royal chewing out and wondered if this was the end of our fledgling careers. Finally, the major said he knew the 'ambush' had been carried out by one of us and asked who had done it. He was astounded when Al Tucker and I stepped forward and confessed. He didn't know quite what to say. I guess he had never heard of the honor code. We had learned that officers do not lie, cheat, or steal, or tolerate those who do. We simply did what we had been conditioned to do. He sputtered a bit, and I think he admonished us not to do it again."[74]

"After the war it was natural for us to team up whenever we could. Robin had gotten me out of a terrible supply job I had been assigned to right after my return to the States, and got me to fly the P-80, which was so much easier to fly than a piston airplane. So there were Robin and I doing our usual stunts of old, but now in a jet airplane at March Field. The colonel saw us doing it. Before long, the group commander was watching our routine. Then the general came over to take a look at us. Then we got another classmate, Ted Carnes, to fly with us. Now we were a threesome. The general liked what we were doing, and before long we found ourselves being sent to the Cleveland Air Races in the fall of 1946. Robin Olds, Ted Carnes, and I flew out to Cleveland in our P-80s. The airplanes had been lightened, the guns removed, and tuned to a fine pitch. Ted came close to winning the race."

Robin Olds and Ted Carnes were flying for the 1st Fighter Group; Captains Kenneth Chilstrom and Gustav Lundquist were in the race from the Wright Field flight test division. Gus Lundquist and Al Tucker had served time together at StalagLuft I at Barth—here they met again. Lundquist was going to win the race, flying Ken Chilstrom's P-80. This is how Ken Chilstrom described events to me: "I had been prepping three of our new P-80s for at least a month for the Cleveland races. Jack Sullivan, Gus Lundquist, and I were going to fly in the race. The 1st Fighter Group at March Field also sent three guys, headed by Robin Olds. When the time came, Gus looked at our three airplanes and said to me, 'Ken, I think I'll take that one,' and he pointed at my airplane. Gus outranked me, so I flew his airplane instead. As we raced down the track, we were wing tip to wing tip. Going into the third turn, I was indicating about 515 miles per hour, right on the deck, full throttle to 101 and ½ percent when the boost goes out on me. I couldn't move the stick, and I'm in a turn. All I could do was pull back and I was out of the race. Gus won the race. Robin Olds, who was a fierce competitor, had turned off his engine regulators on his planes and flew his engines at 109 percent. Olds was right on Gus's wing. It was like they were flying formation, but Lundquist won the race—in my airplane. Not one of the engines that came from the 1st Fighter Group could fly back home. They over-temped their engines and ruined the blades. When Robin landed his P-80, he flamed out immediately after touchdown."

"In addition to the race," Al Tucker continued, "we did loops, and rolls and barrel rolls for the spectators. Then, just to break things up a bit, we had a drill where Ted and Robin went up in a two-ship and crisscrossed each other, while I dove from higher up down toward the runway from the north while they were flying east west. I then pulled straight up. There was a bit of an overcast. I disappeared from view going through the cloud deck. When I popped out at the top, I just pulled the power back, flipped over and came straight back down through that same hole. The people loved it I was told. We formed up and landed. So, somehow, Robin and I probably contributed to getting the Thunderbirds off the ground as our premier air force demonstration team. That evening there was a big party attended by Group Captain Sir Frank Whittle, the inventor of the Whittle jet engine. He gave a talk. When I was in the restroom, several people entered. I heard a British voice saying, 'I certainly would like to meet that young chap Tucker.' I dried my hands and introduced myself to Frank Whittle. 'I'm Tucker, sir.'"

Lieutenant Tucker at Wattisham airbase, England, being strapped into his P-38 fighter by his crew chief.

At Camp Lucky Strike in France, former American POWs from StalagLuft I sport German rifles and souvenir pistols. Al Tucker is the tallest one in the picture.

Home at last in Virginia, surrounded by family. Al, center, in uniform, is flanked by his proud father and mother and surrounded by siblings, aunts, and uncles.

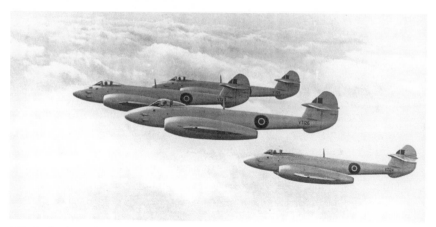

Al Tucker leading a four-ship formation of RAF Meteors. His buddy Robin Olds was on a similar exchange tour at RAF Tangmere.

After retirement, Al Tucker did a lot of sailing, as did many other flyers, finding a great similarity between flying and sailing. "My wife didn't know it when she married me," said Al, with a smile crossing his face. "She didn't only marry a flyer, but a sailor as well." Colonel Tucker resides in Harrisonburg, Virginia, in the same house he came to visit every summer as a young boy with his mother and where he grew up.

ROBERT A. HOOVER

Spitfire/Fw 190/Test Pilot/Barnstormer

POW StalagLuft I, Barth, Germany

Pilots

So many boys want to fly, but never really seem to try
Once they learn they could die, they soon seek other things to try.
It's sad that they'll never know those thrills—as pilots our stories grow.
They may sound as though they grew, but we all know that they are all true.
—Author Unknown

Aerial combat in World War II was unremitting and bloody. Airmen, whether German, British, or American, and those of many other nationalities who flew for one side or the other, died by the thousands rivaling the casualties experienced on land or at sea. For Allied airmen it was a given—if they flew into combat often enough they would either join the hundred thousand plus British and American airmen who perished with their planes, or become prisoners of war. Aerial skill might prolong the outcome, but in time there always came the moment when one was in the wrong place at the wrong time. Too many things could go wrong. StalagLuft I, near the resort town of Barth, on the Baltic Sea, was one of two major Luftwaffe-administered prisoner-of-war camps holding thousands of British and American flying officers. Of all the camps it probably held more American aces than any other, Hubert "Hub" Zemke, Gerald "Gerry" Johnson, and Francis "Gaby" Gabreski being three of the more prominent guests of the Fuehrer at StalagLuft I. And soon another was to join them, "Bob Hoover, the greatest stick-and-rudder pilot who ever lived," according to General James Doolittle.[75] Bob Hoover's story, though, as one might expect, is as unique as the flyer that he was, one of the greatest airmen America ever produced.

Robert A. Hoover was born on January 24, 1922, in Nashville, Tennessee, the youngest of three children born to Leroy and Bessie Hoover. As Bob grew up, his imagination was soon captured by an evolving twentieth-century innovation—the airplane. Like so many other youngsters of his generation Bob was infatuated by Charles Lindbergh's transatlantic flight in 1927. Here was a man, a risk taker, who flew alone across the Atlantic Ocean in a single-engine airplane without any navigation aids other than the careful tracking of his airspeed and calculation of his position from point to point—what we call dead reckoning—and who arrived within three miles of his planned landfall in Ireland. That was one incredible and inspirational achievement that fired up the imagination of youngsters not only in the United States, but in Europe as well. Like so many other boys who wanted to fly someday, Bob built models of his favorite airplanes and imagined what it would be like to be flying a Spad or an SE-5. He read everything he could lay his hands on about airplanes. There were plenty of aviation magazines to choose from. Bob idolized the "men of the air" who accomplished the near unimaginable, such as the colorful Roscoe Turner, who had a lion for a pet, and Eddy Rick-enbacker and Jimmy Doolittle, who flew those incredible flying machines as if they owned the skies. The movie *Those Magnificent Men in Their Flying Machines*, a comic version of the 1910 London-to-Paris air race, captures the spirit of wonder and excitement of the period. All too many boys, including Bob Hoover, set their sights on becoming one of those magnificent men in one of those magic flying machines.

"Berry Field was only fifteen miles from my home in Nashville, and I would ride my bicycle over there just to see the airplanes—see them take off and land. I saw the great Roscoe Turner perform at Berry Field. He was the closest thing I had to a hero. After meeting him, the only thing I ever wanted to do was fly. After school I worked at a grocery store. My pay came to two dollars a week, which I spent at Berry Field taking flying lessons. Lessons cost eight dollars an hour, so my two dollars only gave me fifteen minutes' worth of lessons a week. I soon ran into a real problem while flying the Piper Cub—I got airsick. My instructor had little confidence that I would ever amount to anything as far as flying an airplane was concerned. It took almost a year for me to build up the eight hours in the air I needed to solo. After that, once I got up in the air on my own, I pushed myself to the limit by doing wingovers, stalls, and spins. Once I could handle one maneuver, I went on to the next until I conquered my motion sickness. Each time it got easier. Finally I could perform all of my routines without getting sick. Every time I went up on my own I flew out of sight of the airport and practiced loops, spins, and different maneuvers I read about and memorized. I was eighteen years old when I graduated from high school in 1940. I didn't want to go to college. All I wanted to do was fly,

Like so many others, Bob Hoover began his military flying career in the PT-17 Stearman. It was the primary trainer at the time, with an open cockpit, single engine, fixed prop and landing gear. The instructor sat in front and could talk to the student; the student couldn't talk to the instructor. The student's instrument panel had an altimeter, magnetic compass, tachometer, and a needle and ball—no air speed indicator nor stall warning horn, probably explaining many of the crashes that were to follow. You learned to fly by "the seat of your pants."

and the Tennessee Air National Guard provided me that opportunity. I signed on to become a tail gunner in the Douglas O-38, a biplane they were flying at the time. Three months later my Guard unit was called to active duty and we transferred to Columbia, South Carolina. I was in the army now, wearing a uniform, and applied for flight training at the first opportunity. I passed the written test. My spirits were high. Then my flying career seemed to come crashing down around my ears before it even got started. I couldn't read the eye chart when my eyes were dilated.

"The flight surgeon knew I was a good flyer and took pity on me. 'Bob,' he said, 'I need to go and check on something. I'll be right back,' and he left the room. I studied the chart and memorized the letters. When the doctor returned, I passed. Captain Bob Patterson, my flight surgeon, saved my career as a flyer and gave me some good advice before I left the room. 'When you have an eye test and someone wants to dilate your eyes,' he said with a smile on his face, 'tell them that you are allergic to the eye drops. You won't have any more problems.' There was another little problem to be solved if I wanted to be a fighter pilot. In the 1940s the Army Air Corps had a policy of sending the shorter pilots to fighter training, and taller guys like me, I was six feet two inches, to train in bombers or transports. Twenty dollars of good ol' Kentucky bourbon solved that problem for me. I had a short friend who was to go into fighter training who much preferred to become a bomber or transport pilot. He agreed to switch with me. Then I gave twenty dollars' worth of bourbon to a friendly sergeant in personnel to swap our orders. It wasn't that I hated bombers or transports. My gosh, I would fly an old Dodge truck if they put wings on the sides. But my dream was to fly fighters, something I could wheel around the sky the way the barnstormers did.

"Off I went into flight training at Helena, Arkansas, where we flew the PT-17 Stearman. The washout rate was high. Only four out of ten cadets made it." By this time young Bob Hoover had so much flying experience that primary training was a proverbial "piece of cake." His instructor quickly recognized Hoover's flying skills and advanced him to the aerobatic maneuver phase of training. His commanding officer personally gave Bob his forty-hour check ride and wrote, "Sergeant Robert A. Hoover graded higher than any cadet I've ever checked." On the day of their graduation it was Bob Hoover who put on a thirty-minute flying demonstration for the cadets, including an eight-point slow-roll he had perfected by this time.

"I reported to Greenville, Mississippi, for basic training. There I learned to fly instruments. It was at first difficult for me because I was used to guiding myself using visual references. Our airplane at Greenville was the BT-13, the Vultee Vibrator everyone called it, because of all the noises it made in flight. After basic I moved a few miles over to Columbus, Mississippi, for advanced twin-engine training, and upon receiving my wings I was sent to the 20th Fighter Group at Drew Field in Tampa, Florida. I was the only pilot to report without having flown the AT-6 trainer. We had P-40s and P-39s assigned and I flew both. One day I was going out to take up a P-40 when I passed a P-39—a single-seat fighter that had a reputation as a widow-maker. In fact there was a song about the plane, it went like this: 'Oh, don't give me a P-39, because the engine is mounted behind. She'll spin, crash, and burn. So don't give me a P-39.' The Airacobra had its engine mounted behind the pilot with a drive shaft to the propeller running underneath the pilot. Pilots felt the P-39 was susceptible to tumbling and flat spins when dogfighting. I saw a crew chief working on this P-39 as I walked past and on the spur of the moment asked him, 'Do you know how to start the engine?' He did. A few minutes later I was airborne. I fell in love with the power of that plane and I put it through a series of loops, rolls, and spins. At ten thousand feet I pulled up the nose, cut the power, and the plane went into a flat spin—bad news. I panicked. To regain control, there was little else I could do, I lowered the gear and put down the flaps. The airplane recovered. I couldn't wait to land and share the experience with the other pilots. My commanding officer asked me to perform the recovery maneuver for all the pilots to see. The entire squadron stood in the blazing sun at Pinellas County Airport as I put the P-39 through its paces, including inducing a flat spin and coming out of it by lowering the gear and extending the flaps. I flew the P-39 whenever I could.

"One sunny day as I was climbing out of the traffic pattern over Tampa, the plane suddenly overheated. The tower called, 'Mad Dog 3, you're on fire. Get the hell out of there.' Fire is not a word a pilot wants to hear. I opened the side window. The rush of air sucked smoke into the cockpit rather than pull it out. My visibility was poor, I was coughing, breathing smoke. I shut the engine switches off and managed to make a dead-stick landing. When I came to a stop, the flames were licking up the side of the aircraft. I knew the fuel tank could explode at any moment. I jumped out and ran as fast as I could. When the fire trucks finished their job, there was little left of the airplane. That experience was scary and I knew I was fortunate to have escaped unhurt. The incident made me study and rehearse my emergency procedures—procedures you follow to stay alive when all is coming apart around you and you are in a high state of anxiety. Before leaving for the war in Europe, I was to have one more experience to remember. We were practicing gunnery over Mullet Key Bay, firing at a dye-slick in the water, when suddenly without warning, my P-40K Kitty Hawk began to shake, smoke and fire cascaded from underneath the engine cowling. I was too low to parachute and had to ditch in the bay. Everyone assumed engine trouble was the cause of the crash, because the P-40 had a history of engine trouble. They used a floating crane to retrieve my aircraft, and to everyone's surprise found it riddled with more than fifty bullet holes. A plane behind me apparently had shot me down. With the camouflage paint on our planes blending in with the color of the water it was an understandable mistake. Shortly after that incident I received orders transferring me to the European theater of war. I was twenty years old, loved flying, and was prepared to take on the whole German air force, or so I thought at the time. My secret orders put me in charge of sixty fighter pilots, most of them officers. I was a sergeant, but with more flying experience than all of them put together. I still have the orders to prove it.

"Before we left the United States, the army issued us backpacks, standard infantry uniforms, and old World War I 'doughboy' helmets and rifles. Marching down Fifth Avenue in New York City in full regalia caused quite a stir. Thousands lined the streets and supported us with their cheers. We had not fired a shot but already felt like heroes. An hour later we boarded the *Queen Elizabeth*," one of the two queens of the Cunard Line, the other being the *Queen Mary*, both of which had been converted to troop ships. The "Queens" could outrun any German submarine and as a result of their high speed traveled alone and had no need to join a convoy, which only moved as fast as the slowest ship among them. "On board the *Queen Elizabeth*, the other enlisted pilots and I ran into the same discrimination that we had witnessed earlier in fighter training. We were forced to ride in what had been the gymnasium, with the infantry, while the officers occupied the luxury suites." They docked five days later in the little town of Greenock, Scotland, in the Firth of Clyde, then boarded trains to a processing center near Shrewsbury in England where they learned the basics of staying alive in the air war raging over Europe—aircraft identification, how to handle an interrogation (only name, rank, and serial number, which was more easily said than done), and how the underground worked in different countries. They didn't do much flying while in England, with the English winter weather being what it was—rain, snow, and more rain. If not rain then heavy cloud layers and morning fog obscured the countryside. "When a pilot was vectored in over an airfield, ground control would shoot up a green flare to let him know he was over the field. Then pilots would circle down slowly until they broke out of the clouds to land. That kind of flying alone was scary enough, but there was a hill near the runway, and if the pilot's circles were too wide, he crashed into the hillside. We were still enlisted pilots. Finally, on December 20, 1942, in a brief ceremony we were promoted to the rank of flight officer. A flight officer was equivalent to the rank of warrant officer and received comparable pay. We were still not commissioned officers, but we received the same privileges of a commissioned officer of similar rank. Allied armies invaded North Africa in November 1942, and in January 1943 we were loaded onto trains returning us to where we had come from—Greenock, Scotland. There we boarded a ship for Oran, French Morocco. Once there, we were flown on DC-3s to an air base near Casablanca where sixty-seven of us were 'parked' as replacement pilots."

Bob Hoover's reputation as a hotshot pilot had preceded him and instead of being assigned to a fighter unit, he found himself assigned to a depot near Oran, flight testing newly assembled P-40s, P-39s, Spitfires and Hurricanes which had arrived aboard ships packed in crates. "Checking out planes from dawn to dusk kept me out of trouble for the most part, but not entirely. One of my first close calls came when an Aeracobra suffered an impeller explosion shortly after takeoff. To save the aircraft, I executed a sharp 180 degree turn, very risky at low altitude. The engine was engulfed in flames but I managed to land downwind and the fire crew saved the airplane. Another time I couldn't get the gear down on an A-20 Havoc, and had to belly it in. My most serious misadventure testing aircraft occurred in an A-31 Vultee Vengeance. It was a two-seater and I had an aircraft mechanic along. When it came time to land, I reduced the throttle to idle, and we experienced a huge explosion. I saw both of the bomb-bay doors blow away and we were completely engulfed in flames.

The sergeant tried to bail out, but his parachute harness got caught up on a machine gun mount. I turned the aircraft upside down and shook him loose. By this time it was too late for me to jump and I turned the aircraft right side up again, added full power, climbed, and shut off the fuel to the engine. Then managed to dead stick the burning aircraft into the airfield. I ran as fast as I could to get away from the aircraft once it stopped. I had carved out a reputation as a good test pilot flying many different types of aircraft and my very skills as a flyer kept me pigeonholed in what I was doing. Every chance I got I requested a combat tour—and each time my request was turned down."

During his brief stay in England Bob had met a Major Melvin McNickle. Much to his delight one day he thought he spied him in the operations office at Oran. Bob walked over to him, slapped him on the back announcing who he was—the response he expected didn't come. It actually was the major's twin brother, Marvin. Marvin McNickle had earned the British Distinguished Flying Cross flying protective cover in a Spitfire in 1942 during the ill-fated Dieppe raid. He was on his way to take over the 52nd Fighter Group at Palermo, Sicily, again flying Spitfires. Bob made his pitch wanting to join a fighting outfit. McNickle promised to do what he could. So, when Bob was reassigned to the 12th Air Corps headquarters in Algiers he thought he was on his way to a combat assignment. Not so. His new boss, Colonel Eppwright, knew of Bob's flying skills, and had requested him to check out new pilots in airplanes they had never flown before, such as the B-25 Mitchell bomber. Combat flying was not what the colonel had in mind for Bob Hoover. Then one day a corporal Bob had befriended in the colonel's office came running over to him and told him that the colonel had been sitting on a set of orders transferring him to the 52nd Fighter Group, the outfit Marvin McNickle commanded. Bob confronted his boss, Colonel Eppwright, and asked about those orders. The outcome of that confrontation was of course predictable. The colonel had no intention of letting Bob go, and didn't give Bob the orders he had come for, transferring him to the 52nd Fighter Group. "The next day I was scheduled on a B-25 training flight to check out two pilots. My corporal friend came racing up to me just before I got into the cockpit and handed me several copies of the orders transferring me to the 52nd Group. Off I went, and I didn't look back." Bob Hoover joined the 52nd Fighter Group in September 1943 flying with the 4th Fighter Squadron out of Boca de Falco airfield near Palermo, Sicily, then Calvi, Corsica, once that island was captured. Yet even there his scheduled missions did not involve air-to-air combat, but consisted mostly of escorting Allied supply ships across the Mediterranean. His reputation as a test pilot was about to catch up with him again.

A B-26 Martin Marauder, severely damaged in combat, had bellied in on a very short stretch of beach on the Straits of Messina, Sicily. The plane had been repaired but no one dared take it out. Who could possibly do such a thing? Colonel Blair, Hoover's boss when he was at Casablanca testing airplanes, called Colonel McNickle, Bob's new commander at the 52nd Fighter Group. "Marvin," he said, "see if Bob will give it a try and save that B-26. We need it." Bob Hoover was promised a Distinguished Flying Cross if he could get that beast back up in the air. Bob went to work. After looking at the plane and where it sat, he brought in a crew of maintenance men and ripped out everything that was not absolutely essential to get that airplane airborne again. Copilot seat—out. Guns—out. Everything not essential was stripped out of the aircraft. The effort to get the airplane ready took more than a month. Then it was time to do the impossible—fly that B-26 bomber out of its predicament in front of an expectant crowd which was betting heavily that he couldn't do it. Reporters from the *Stars & Stripes* military newspaper were there as well. "I ran up the R-2800 engines, dropped my quarter flaps, and off I went. The B-26 accelerated quickly, as light as it was with a minimum fuel load. Down the makeshift pierced steel planking, PSP, runway we went. I had a total of about 1,100 feet to play with. It was all or nothing. There was only four feet of clearance on each side, so I had to steer dead center to make it. Not only that, but what went for a runway was not only narrow but ran up an incline—no wonder no one thought I could make it out of there. I watched the airspeed as it climbed to twenty, then thirty, then fifty knots. At that point I had only about four hundred feet of pierced steel planking left in front of me. The end of the beach was quickly approaching and the nose still wasn't up. Over those last four hundred feet I gained fifty more knots and the Marauder lifted its nose and pitched skyward as we came to the end of the PSP. Wow, what a beautiful day that was." I might note at this point in Bob Hoover's story that many years later, from 1969 to 1973, I flew with the 52nd Tactical Fighter Wing, then based at Spangdahlem Air Base, Germany. It was the same 52nd Fighter Group Bob flew with in World War II. Only now it was called a fighter wing. In the mid-nineties my son Charles flew A-10s out of Spangdahlem Air Base with the 52nd Tactical Fighter Wing as well—it seems flying with the 52nd Tactical Fighter Wing had become a tradition with the Samuel family.

"On New Year's Eve 1943 I had three flyers with me who had completed their fifty missions and were on their way home. We sat in the bar talking. They kept telling me how slim my survival chances were. They then went on describing the fate of their many friends who were either dead or captured. I realized, perhaps for the first time, that there was a chance that I wouldn't make it out of here. But I was confident that no German pilot could shoot me out of the sky." Although confidence in one's flying ability is a great asset to a fighter pilot, yet every engagement has its moments, and sometimes it doesn't turn out well, no matter what your flying skills. "Off the northern tip of Corsica there was a small island still occupied by Germans. The island was supplied by barges and we received orders to stop the flow of men and supplies. We scrambled our squadron the next time the Germans made a supply run. We swooped down with guns blazing. The hundred or so men on board the barge tried to fight us off with their rifles but that was an uneven match. Before long, we could see no movement. The Germans were either dead or had jumped overboard. That ghastly mission bothered me more than I could have imagined. The piles of bodies haunted me, and recurring nightmares of the carnage plagued me at night, making sleep difficult for weeks. That incident still troubles me to this day, whenever I think of it.

"I wanted to be an ace more than anything else in the world." To be an ace meant that Bob would have to have at least five confirmed kills of whatever enemy aircraft came across his gun sight. "My chance seemed to come in September 1943. My friend Tom Watts and I were sitting alert in the cockpits of our Spitfires at Palermo, Sicily, ready for immediate takeoff. Then the much-hoped-for event happened. A green flare went up and we started our engines and took off. We were advised that more than a hundred enemy aircraft were heading south toward Palermo. With a clenched jaw I focused on the sky in front of me looking for specs on the distant horizon. I saw one, then another, and then a sky full of airplanes. The sheer number was staggering. They were Italians. Tom and I climbed, aiming to come in from behind and high. I clicked on my gun switch, focused on my first target—when ground control called, 'The Italians are surrendering. You are to escort their planes to base. Do you read?' My heart dropped to the basement. I acknowledged the call. Instead of becoming an ace, I became a guide for the surrendering Italians. I moved ahead of the lead aircraft and took them to Boca de Falco airfield at Palermo."

Bob Hoover and his friend Tom Watts returned to their base at Calvi, Corsica, a bit disillusioned, having just missed the air battle of their lives. Bob notes in his book *Forever Flying* that "there sat a battle damaged B-17 Flying Fortress at Calvi that had made an emergency landing." By sheer coincidence I had interviewed the navigator of that damaged B-17 bomber years earlier, retired air force Colonel Frederic Leiby. Leiby, then a flight officer like Bob, was assigned to the 347th Bomb Squadron of the 99th Bombardment Group flying out of a base near Foggia, Italy. "On a mission to Toulon," Leiby recalled, "to bomb submarine pens, we got hit by flak, were losing gas, and couldn't make it back to Foggia. So we decided to go as far as we could, rather than land in Spain, a neutral country. When we got to Corsica, running low on fuel, we saw an airstrip down below and decided to land. The runway was very short. We ended up going through a barbed-wire fence and into a field. That airstrip was used by Americans flying Spitfires. It took four days for our plane to get repaired. Then we flew it back to Foggia."

"The night before my 59th combat mission," Bob recalled, "a group of us pilots sat around our quarters, including my roommate, 'Monty' Montgomery, who had been shot down a few month earlier and spent three days in a life raft before being rescued. Another was 'Andy' Anderson. The two usually flew the dawn patrol. I still wanted a dogfight with the Germans, and tried to convince one of them to let me fly in his place. 'Why should I let you go up there?' Andy asked. 'I can handle them,' I replied. 'My buddy and I have had lots of simulated dogfights.' The disgusted look on Anderson's face let me know I had struck a nerve. I had no air-to-air combat experience as far as he was concerned, and talk was cheap, that's what he was trying to say. The next morning Monty and Andy took off and headed out over the Mediterranean. The engines on both aircraft quit. Monty managed to turn and make a dead stick landing. Andy didn't, and died. Investigators found salt water in Andy's engine. Sabotage, or someone trying to settle a grudge? Who knows. There are many ways to die in war. By this time, even though I personally hadn't encountered any air-to-air combat, the casualties in my squadron were high. There had been thirty-four pilots when I arrived. Now there were thirteen. On January 24, 1944, on my twenty-second birthday, my friend Tom Watts was shot down near the coast of Calvi, Corsica. He successfully bailed out of his Spitfire, but winds dragged him into a reef. I flew over the spot and could see his chute and body in the crystal-clear waters. Tom had been such a part of my life that I thought I could feel the impact of the reef on his body. Losing him really hurt. As I flew away, my grief only deepened. Losing a friend is hard, although I knew Tom had died doing what he loved most—being a fighter pilot.

"On February 9 I was leading a formation of four Spitfires off the Italian and French coast covering an area from Cannes to Genoa. We found a small German convoy near Nice and attacked. As I came out of my dive trying to rejoin with the rest of the flight, I spotted four Fw 190 fighters. I quickly called out their position over the radio at 12 o'clock high. Besides the P-51 and the Spitfire, I felt the Fw 190 was the best airplane in the sky during the war. One Fw 190 glued itself on Monty's tail. I called out for him to break. My adrenalin was pumping hard. This was real combat, not a practice dogfight with friends. I pulled the tank release to get rid of my external fuel tank—the handle came off in my hand. I realized that the superior turning ability of my Spitfire now was my only defense. I headed straight for one of the Germans, spitting out a burst of .50-caliber gunfire. My mind raced as I tried to hit the weaving Fw 190. Then I saw billows of smoke streaming through the sky and I knew I hit his engine. It was my first kill. No time to celebrate. Monty had been hit. The shock of seeing him struggle to save his doomed plane knocked the breath right out of me. I watched his plane as it burst into flames and spiraled toward the Mediterranean below. I doubted he had a chance to get out. Two 190s were after me. I dove left to escape, hoping that one or the other of my two remaining fighter buddies would be there to help. I saw them just as they veered off, leaving me on my own. The German fighters struck like copperheads. The external fuel tank that wouldn't jettison made my Spitfire so slow that the 190s overshot and missed me. Two more turned in toward me. I was able to turn inside them, hitting one. I thought I was out of it, when I heard shells hitting the engine cowling from underneath. A 190 pilot had hit me with a high-angle deflection shot that I had discounted as impossible. A split second later severe pain shot through my legs. My engine exploded next, and the entire nose of my plane was a ball of flames. Fear gripped me as I tried to react to the explosion. I tried to think of all my options—there was only one. Get out before the plane explodes. I opened the cockpit, released my shoulder and seat straps, rolled the aircraft upside down and dropped away from the fire.

"The unthinkable had happened. I'd been shot out of the sky by a German fighter pilot on my first encounter. As I was falling toward the waters of the Mediterranean Sea, I saw the flames trailing behind my stricken plane. Like a comet it plunged into the sea. When I opened my parachute, it turned into a streamer, didn't open properly. Then suddenly the chute blossomed, and I had just enough time to inflate my Mae West when I hit the water. The impact stunned me. I was not prepared for that. As I regained my composure, I tried to inflate my life raft. It was riddled with shrapnel. All I could do was float in the cold water and wait to be rescued. My hopes of rescue were heightened when I saw a flight of four Spitfires approaching. I waved and splashed as hard as I could. Then I saw a flight of Fw 190s swooping down on them. One of the Spits went down, the others got away. Time went by slowly. I had been shot down at three o'clock in the afternoon. It was a little after seven when I heard faint sounds in the distance. My rescuers, I thought. The vessel came closer and I realized it was a German ship. One of the sailors reached out and pulled me from the water. I was cold, wet, and wounded. I was now Flight Officer Robert A. Hoover, prisoner of war.

"I was strip-searched on the German corvette, then given dry clothes. When I was offered coffee, I refused. I learned that the ship had been searching for two German pilots when they saw me. The captain was a seasoned military man who was surprisingly cordial. He had served in World War I and seemed to have some compassion for my plight. The ship docked in Nice a little after sunset. I could see a damaged freighter. Was that damage the result of my squadron's efforts? Were the covered bodies laid out on the dock the result of our attack? Guards escorted me to a waiting car and I was taken to a jail. The steel door of the tiny cell made a thunderous clank behind me. I was more frightened than I had ever been in my life. A short time later the door opened and I was taken to the Hotel Continental in Cannes. The interrogating officer became frustrated when all I continued to give him was my name, rank, and serial number. I was strapped to a marble column in the lobby of the hotel, was cursed, spit on, and slapped in the face. The degradation continued for two days when I was transported to Marseilles. My cell had a straw mattress and an old metal chair. Two windows with metal bars provided light. When I moved the chair over to a window and looked out, I saw a six-foot-high barbed-wire fence and two sentries with mean-looking dogs by their sides. When I grabbed one of the metal bars, it came loose. I used it to chip away at the cement and loosened another bar. Then I waited for darkness. When it was dark, I removed the obstructing bars and squeezed through the narrow opening. Looking down I saw it was about a ten-foot drop to the ground. That I had not anticipated. But there was no turning back now. I let go of the window ledge and landed with a loud thud. Instantly the guard dogs came to life. My heart was racing as I ran across the yard toward the barbed-wire fence. Just as I got to the fence, a search light illuminated me and the first dog clamped his jaws around my leg. Two more German shepherds joined the first. I am sure they would have torn me to shreds if the guards had not pulled them off. My punishment was a dark basement cell. The night was filled with fear for my life and fresh pain from the dog bites. That night seemed to last forever."

The next day Bob found himself on a train headed for Germany. He attempted to escape again, was quickly recaptured, and this time shackled to his seat. Several days later he found himself at Oberursel, near Frankfurt, the Luftwaffe interrogation center. Bob didn't cooperate, and his German interrogators reciprocated by keeping him in isolation. His wounds had not been tended to, nor did he ask for medical attention. It was a standoff between Bob and the Germans, who controlled his life but got nowhere in their interrogation attempts. Even the threat of imminent execution didn't work, yet it was a terrifying experience for him. "With a wry smile on his face the captain began the countdown. At 'Ready,' the soldiers brought their rifles to their shoulders. 'Aim,' the soldiers cocked their rifles. Seconds passed as if they were hours. Then the captain turned and walked away. The soldiers lowered their guns and returned me to my cell. I sat there trembling, more frightened than I could possibly describe." But that experience, although terrifying, didn't keep Bob Hoover from trying to escape again. He did, and was caught almost immediately. The beating he received as a result of his latest escape attempt resulted in painful head and facial injuries. A week later Bob was taken to one of Frankfurt's train stations and loaded into a boxcar already filled with other prisoners. They survived a British bombing raid that night and eventually arrived in the town of Barth near the Baltic Sea as prisoners of war at StalagLuft I. As Bob Hoover and his fellow prisoners were marched into the camp, someone yelled out, "Damn, they got Hoover." "In some way I felt like a celebrity, but at the same time embarrassed and diminished for having been shot down and captured."

Flight Officer Robert A. Hoover, at times terrified by his experiences but undaunted in his efforts to escape, joined fellow POWs in their attempts to tunnel their way out of the camp. "We were making so much progress that we were sure we'd be able to escape. We hadn't counted on seismographic equipment the Germans used to detect our underground noises. Even though they were aware of what we were doing, they permitted prisoners to proceed, and just before completion of a tunnel, guards would storm the barracks. One night our tunneling efforts came to an end when the ceiling collapsed. Without coats and jackets we were ordered outside into the freezing cold for a long time. Despite our failure, I soon came up with another plan." Bob Hoover was not one to ever give up. This time around he had his fellow POWs bury him in a heap of coal in the coal shed. That night, when he wiggled himself out from under the coal, he climbed over a fence, then ran smack-dab into a startled guard. "Two weeks in the cooler was my punishment."

When Bob first arrived at StalagLuft I, there were just over a thousand prisoners in the camp. Fourteen months later, in April 1945, the prison population had grown to over ten thousand. It was obvious, even to the POWs at the camp, that the war was in its final days. Yet, Bob Hoover kept trying to escape. He could have just waited it out like the rest of his fellow POWs, but he chose not to. This time around he would succeed. A fellow flyer from the 52nd Fighter Group and a Canadian airman named George joined up to give it another try. "While other prisoners staged a fight to divert the guards, the three of us broke out of the compound. We ran from that prison until our lungs ached. We collapsed on the shoreline of the Baltic Sea. Our courage faltered when we realized that we would have to swim from the peninsula we were on to the mainland—without freezing to death. We fashioned a crude raft to hold one of us. Then George and I undressed, gave our clothes to Jerry Ennis, and slipped nude into the icy water. It was a shock. When we got to the opposite shore, we quickly dressed and continued to run. We had heard of the Russians being nearby, but no one wanted to be caught by them because of their reputation for extreme brutality. At a deserted farm house we slept in a barn. The next morning we ate raw turnips and potatoes we managed to scrounge and later that day stole three bicycles leaning against a wall of a house in a small village. George, our Canadian friend, decided to try it alone. We never saw him again. Jerry and I headed west, hoping to run into American or British troops. Instead we ran into Russians whom we had tried to avoid. Jerry spoke French and tried to communicate to one of the Russian soldiers that we were not POWs, but simply American soldiers evading the Germans. The Russians considered POWs as collaborators and either shot them on the spot or sent them off to one of their gulags. Jerry prevailed in his argument and the Russians offered us shelter and food.

"I was excited, until the food arrived. It was a large chunk of raw beef, about three inches thick, with the blood running around the plate. I did take the bread they offered, but couldn't deal with the meat. The next morning we pedaled away and soon ran into another group of Russians. They were drunk, but friendly. They took us into a darkened church filled with German women and children huddled together in fear for their lives. Jerry figured out why they had taken us into that church. 'They want us to choose a woman and rape her,' Jerry whispered to me. 'What do we do?' I asked Jerry. Jerry walked toward a group of women, acting as if we were making our selection. He found a woman who spoke French. 'I'll tell her we are going to fake it,' he told me. The tiny woman understood. We went over into a dark corner where no one could see, lay on the women and moaned and groaned enough to make our sexual attack seem real. All the while the Russian soldiers were hooting and hollering. They shone a flashlight over toward us just to make sure we were raping the women. Our performance was convincing and they invited us to spend the night with them in a small house. We left the next day as soon as we could. When we arrived in a nearby village, a woman in her fifties approached. She had a bloody cloth wrapped around her hand. 'Are you Americans?' she asked. The woman unwrapped her hand and I saw that one finger was cut off. 'They wanted my wedding band. It wouldn't come off, so they cut off my finger.' I was still staring at her hand in horror when she turned and said, 'You must come with me. I want you to remember this forever.' She took us into an abandoned department store. All the people who worked in the store had their throats slit. Every one of them the same way. We followed her to a ravine that was two blocks out of town. She said, 'You cannot believe me without seeing this.' I looked down. There were hundreds of bodies, all slaughtered and thrown like kitchen scraps into the open grave. Seeing the pile of bodies made me almost throw up. The senseless brutality made me ashamed that I was somehow allied with the Russians. Before we left the village, Jerry and I went into a house looking for food. Several Russian soldiers were squatting near the base of the toilet. It was the type where the water bowl is at the top of the wall and a chain is pulled to flush. One of the soldiers would pull the chain and then they all watched the water. They'd never seen a flush toilet before. Under other circumstances the scene would have been comical, but somehow the humor was absent in the presence of the display of cruelty we had witnessed."

Jerry and Bob kept on going, witnessing more unimaginable brutality. They came across a group of French forced laborers and Germans for whom the French had worked. "One woman gave us a small pistol which would come in handy later on. The people were generous, providing us with food and shelter.

Suddenly Russian tanks arrived. We could hear screams and gunshots as the Russians rampaged through the village. Jerry and I stood with our backs against a wall with our hands up as the soldiers roamed around. Suddenly one of them slit a pregnant woman's throat. She was full term and ready to give birth. We could see the woman was dead. Soldiers lined up, then raped her, one after another. We could do nothing, or we would have been killed on the spot. Several of the soldiers who had finished their part in this dreadful scene pulled us away. Jerry's voice cracked when he asked whether anybody spoke French or English. When no one responded, I pointed to their uniforms. One of the Russians wore an American jacket and another had shoes and pants from the USA. We tried to show them that we were wearing the same clothing, hoping they would understand that we were Americans. They finally let us go. Jerry and I walked away from what once had been a peaceful family farm. We had seen the unbelievable. It was an unspeakable horror. As we moved on, Jerry and I came upon an abandoned Luftwaffe fighter base. A few ground crew were still around. Thirty or so Fw 190 fighters sat in revetments scattered about the airfield. I had some knowledge of the plane because a fellow POW at StalagLuft I, Gus Lundquist, a Wright Field test pilot, had flown the plane and shared his knowledge with me. Hour after hour I had listened as Gus told me what he'd learned about the Fw 190 and other German aircraft.

"Jerry and I found a Fw 190 that looked to be in fairly good shape. It had a few holes in the wings and tail, but otherwise wasn't damaged and appeared airworthy. Best of all, the plane had full fuel tanks. Using the .25-caliber pistol we had been given by the French woman, Jerry 'convinced' a ground crew-man to assist our efforts to get a 190 started. Jerry held the gun on the agitated crewman, who reached into the cockpit and yanked up the landing gear handle, retracting the tail wheel. That took a few hours to fix, but eventually I was taxiing out of the revetment onto the grassy runway and took off. Jerry had decided not to join me on this flight. We would meet again in the States. I was flying away from prison, isolation, and torture, near-starvation, humiliation, and cabbage soup. The Fw 190 performed well, and I headed west along the tree line, knowing that if any American or British fighters saw me, they'd blast me out of the sky. I flew just below an overcast at four thousand feet, allowing me to escape into the clouds should I come up against some of our fighters. I followed the coastline to the Zuider Zee in Holland, then chose an open field for my landing. I figured any ex-German airfield was probably mined, my reason for choosing the less-than-perfect landing site. I ground looped the plane, wiping out the landing gear. That maneuver stopped me short of a ditch. Darkness was approaching. I climbed out of the Fw 190 and tried to figure out what to do next. Just as I started to walk in the direction of a small village, a group of Dutch farmers armed with pitchforks came running toward me. I waved my arms frantically, trying to convince them that I should not be pitchforked. Since I landed in a German plane, they thought I was an enemy deserter. Despite their strong reservations, believing I was a German, they escorted me into a small town where they turned me over to the British. I convinced the British officials of my identity. They showed me which way to go to find the Americans. I was a free man for the first time in almost a year and a half. I had spent nearly two and a half years overseas. It was an experience I'll never forget. I had seen the extremes of bravery and brutality, of kindness and cruelty, of loyalty and cowardliness. Above all, I knew more than ever what it meant for one to lose that precious gift of freedom."

Bob Hoover returned to the United States and ended up at Wright Field in Dayton, Ohio—the Army Air Forces flight test center. Here he became a member of that fabled team of test pilots headed up by Major Kenneth O. Chilstrom, including Frank Everest, Richard Johnson, Chuck Yeager, and Walter McAuley, among others. They were the best of the best in a very dangerous profession which cost all too many of them their lives. Bob flew the way he always had—at the edge of the envelope, pushing a plane to its very limits. He tested the P-59 Aircomet, the first American jet fighter, the P-80 Shooting Star, and the P-84 Thunderjet. He became the backup pilot for Chuck Yeager, who on October 14, 1947, broke the sound barrier flying at Mach 1.07, more than seven hundred miles per hour in the Bell XS-1, which is prominently displayed in the foyer of the Smithsonian's National Air and Space Museum in Washington, DC. That sharp double crack as the X-1 went through the sound barrier triggered the dawn of the space age. Hoover did not get to fly the X-1, something he greatly regretted. But it was the subsonic P-84, renamed the F-84 in September 1947 when the Army Air Forces became the United States Air Force, which nearly took his life. Bob was testing an F-84 Thunderjet over the Antelope Valley, near Muroc Field, later renamed Edwards Air Force Base, when his F-84 experienced a catastrophic engine failure. "The aircraft was diving out of control. I pulled what we called the 'next of kin handles' on the ejection seat. The seat didn't fire. I unfastened my harness and oxygen hose, jettisoned the canopy, and was sucked out of the cockpit, at over five hundred mph, my legs slamming into the F-84's tail, breaking both legs at the knee joints. Once on the ground, I could see airplanes circling and a column of smoke from the burning wreckage. The condition of my legs was frightening. I was sure I would lose them both. I lay there on the desert sand, waiting. Just before dark a ranch hand in an old pickup truck drove up. He had seen the burning plane and my chute, and it had taken him the rest of the day to find me. The cowboy lifted me into his truck and drove me to the Antelope Valley hospital. The hospital staff wouldn't treat me. They were afraid they wouldn't get paid because I was military. I lay in an isolation ward. The pain

I experienced was so intense that a nurse finally relented and gave me a shot of morphine. The morphine gave me no relief. An ambulance finally arrived from Muroc. The trip was excruciating. Every little bump in the road sent searing pain up both of my legs. It finally turned out only one leg was broken. I was in a cast when Pancho Barnes came by to visit me. 'How are you feeling, you dumb SOB?' she asked [Pancho Barnes was a Muroc Field/Edwards AFB legend with the test pilot community, a free spirit who was known for not mincing words]. Pretty damn miserable, I responded. She reached into her coat pocket and pulled out a bottle of whiskey and thrust it into my hands. 'The g-- d--- doctors don't know how to relieve pain,' she whispered, 'take a slug of that.' We passed the bottle around the room and it soon was empty and my pain was a thing of the past."

Bob didn't lose his legs, and six weeks later was back on flying status at Wright-Patterson Air Force Base. Bob's near fatal F-84 experience as a Wright Field test pilot was not his only close encounter with death. Earlier he had been doing tests on the P-80 to see if a jet could be flown using gasoline instead of kerosene. After much ground testing it seemed that gasoline was indeed a possible alternative to kerosene. Gasoline was available at all airfields, while kerosene was stocked only at a few fields, requiring careful mission planning before takeoff. "So the airplane was finally made ready for flight. As it happened, I was scheduled to fly on the assigned date in an air show at Wright Field. Since I had no trouble with the P-80 fuel test, I did not hesitate to use gasoline instead of kerosene. Upon completing my aerobatic demonstration, I climbed to ten thousand feet. But right at the top of my climb the engine flamed out. I tried an air start, but without success. I slowed the P-80 down and tried to position myself into a 360-degree overhead landing pattern. I pushed the gear handle down, but the warning light came on instead. My only option was to manually pump the gear down. While pumping I loosened up my pattern to gain more time to get the gear down, but I didn't allow for the wind. Suddenly I realized that without power I was not going to make the runway at the low altitude I found myself and with the airspeed I was at. There were hundreds of cars parked on either side of the highway watching the air show. It seemed to me that I had the choice of diving the airplane into the ground, without much chance of survival, or trying to stretch the glide across the highway. I banked the airplane about 45 degrees and in this position squeezed the left wingtip between two parked cars. But I caught a main gear wheel on the front of one car, while the nose wheel just barely dented its top and the wingtip dragged on the highway. The gear struts were driven right through the wings and torn off when I touched down. The entire aircraft was severely damaged. My immediate fear was fire, considering all the apprehensions we had with the ground runs using gasoline. And here I was stuck in the cockpit with the canopy jammed, the hot engine still attached to the airplane and the fuel tanks burst open. It seemed like thirty minutes, but in reality was only five minutes before the fire crew arrived and chopped the canopy open. There was no fire because the dead engine had probably cooled down sufficiently before the accident. I wasn't banged up much—got a cut lip, a cut nose, and my back was a bit sore. Yes, we decided, there was some risk using gasoline as a jet fuel." And that was the end of that experiment.

Bob continued to test planes and in the process met a spate of aviation personalities including Jimmy Doolittle, Jackie Cochran, Charles Lindbergh, Neil Armstrong, General Johannes 'Mackie' Steinhoff, the German fighter pilot ace Erich Hartmann, Willy Messerschmitt, and many others. Then Bob decided to leave the air force and briefly went to work as a test pilot for the Allison Division of General Motors. That didn't last long. Instead he took a position as test pilot with North American Aviation, the builders of the F-86 Sabre Jet. "The F-86," Bob recalled with pride, "would achieve great fame in the Korean war. Its kill ratio of planes shot down versus planes lost was an unbelievable 14:1 against the Russian MiG-15. Astronaut Wally Schirra, who flew the F-86 during the Korean war, said it was a plane that a pilot 'strapped on,' as compared to being 'strapped in,' that's how easy that airplane was to fly." However, before the F-86 became that easy-to-fly airplane, the plane that pilots "strapped on," men like Bob Hoover worked out the kinks at the risk of their lives. It was the Sabre Jet that would take Bob for the ride of his life.

"I tested an F-86D that had the horizontal tail located on the bottom of the fuselage, a test bed for the future F-100 Super Sabre. As soon as I became airborne, the yaw damper failed, causing full rudder deflection. At the same time, the fire warning light came on. I was concerned about landing with the nose of the plane yawed to the right because of the failed rudder. As I came in for a landing at Los Angeles International Airport, another test pilot, Dan Darnell, sitting in an F-86 nearby, yelled, 'Bob, get your canopy off. You just lost a wheel.' I knew I hit hard, but I couldn't believe one of the wheels had been torn off. Then the wheel bounced right up in front of me. The strut ran along the concrete. I slid off the runway." Bob got out safely, but the airplane was a total loss. That episode was only the beginning of several more experiences that would test Bob's flying and survival skills to the utmost. It was November 1950. The plane Bob was to test had a new flight control system installed. Up he went. "As soon as the landing gear came up, the nose of the aircraft pitched straight up. The airplane was out of control. I pushed forward on the stick with all my strength, but couldn't move it fore or aft. The F-86 then stalled, started to spin, and headed straight down. I managed to stop the spin using the rudder, which was mechanical, barely missing the ground. The plane climbed right back up, and the whole process started all over again. For the next forty minutes it was

Bob Hoover in 1945 at StalagLuft I biding his time as a POW with nearly eight thousand other American aviators—among them Hub Zemke, Gabi Gabreski, Gerry Johnson, and the well-known Wright Field test pilot Gus Lundquist. Bob is sitting front row, fourth from right.

Bob Hoover with Erich Hartmann, the top ace of World War II with 352 victories. After the war Bob's stunt flying gained him celebrity status, and he was sought out by nearly every prominent politician and aviator.

Bob with Johannes "Macky" Steinhoff who was credited with 176 victories in World War II. Steinhoff, a member of Galland's JV 44 Me 262 jet squadron, was badly burned when his Me 262 crashed on takeoff. In later years Steinhoff led the newly formed German Bundesluftwaffe.

Hoover and Brigadier General Chuck Yeager—old friends who loved to fly. Said Bob on one occasion, "I would fly an old Dodge truck if they put wings on the sides."

A prized picture presented to Bob Hoover by Jimmy Doolittle. The inscription reads, "To Bob Hoover. Pilot extraordinary and friend exemplary. Sincerely, J. H. Doolittle."

stark terror." Bob chose not to eject, but managed to bring the plane in on the dry lake bed at Edwards AFB. "Later, after some further inspection, I found that I couldn't have ejected even if I had wanted to. The ground crew had not pulled the safety pins on the ejection seat. People have asked me over the years what's the most terrifying ride I've ever had. There have been many, but none scarier than the one in that F-86."[76]

Bob continued test flying the F-86, then the supersonic F-100, which gave him and fellow test pilots more than their share of problems until it became the mainstay of the tactical air forces for many years. The air force demonstration team, the Thunderbirds, flew the F-100 for thirteen years, thrilling crowds around the country and overseas. My young son and I, Charles was two years old then, saw the Thunderbirds perform in their brand-new F-100s in 1964 at Forbes Air Force Base in Topeka, Kansas. We saw them again performing their magic at Wiesbaden Air Base, Germany, in 1970, after I returned from a combat tour in Southeast Asia. Charles was eight years old then. The thunder of those jets captured the young boy's imagination, and at age twenty-three, the boy who was inspired by the Thunderbirds was piloting his own air force jet, in time acquiring over 3,500 flying hours in the A-10 Thunderbolt II.

Bob Hoover in his iconic yellow Mustang at Burke Lakefront Airport, near Cleveland, in 1972.

Although Bob Hoover continued flying for North American Aviation, later North American Rockwell, for many years, he is best remembered for his air show performances, flight demonstrations, and the air races he participated in. If there was anything happening at Reno, Oshkosh, Pittsburgh, Daytona Beach, or too many other places to mention, you could bet Bob Hoover was going to be there. It always was a thrill to see him perform the many maneuvers he had mastered with consummate skill and apparent ease. Bob would be the first to tell you that nothing was really easy, just years and years of practice and concentration made it appear that way—the sign of the master aviator. The "roll after takeoff" at an air show was almost a given if Bob was performing. But for me it was his "four-, eight-, and sixteen point hesitation rolls" that demonstrated the kind of flyer that he was. If you had a chance to see Bob Hoover fly, you most likely will never see anything like it again. Bob Hoover's aviation career spanned a period from just before World War II into the early years of the twenty-first century—seventy years of flying and surviving. Robert A. Hoover is right up there with all the great aviators this country has ever produced. Bob chose to settle in California, where he did much of his flight testing, a place where many of his test pilot friends chose to settle as well.

FREDERICK LEIBY

B-17

POW StalagLuft III, Sagan, Germany

The Fate We Share as Prisoners

The fate we share as prisoners is drab and often grim.
Existing on such scanty fare as Reich-bread, spuds and klim.
Beds and books and little else to fill time's flapping sail.
She makes or loses headway all depending on the mail.
Oh! Drab the days and slow to pass within this barbed-wire fence,
When all the joys of living are still in the future tense.
So here's to happy days ahead when you and I are free,
To look back on this interlude and call it history.
—Joe Boyle, POW StalagLuft III, WWII ETO

"We were going into northern Italy, our target was a munitions plant at Varese, just south of the Swiss border. We flew up the Adriatic aiming to cross the coast near Bologna. German fighters hit us. An Me 109 made a head-on attack and set our number three engine ablaze. We left the formation, got rid of our bombs, and put the aircraft on autopilot. The pilot was supposed to ring an emergency bell and announce over the intercom for us to bail out. The bombardier, Johnny Moore, and I were in the nose of the aircraft and didn't hear anything. Nor could we see that the number three engine was on fire because the flames streamed backward. So I was trying to get someone on the intercom. There was no response. In the B-17G there is an astrodome in the nose of the airplane which I used for shooting stars and the sun. I could see the pilots' seats when I got up and looked through the astrodome—there were no pilots up there. So I said to Johnny over the intercom, 'Hey, there's nobody here but us.'"

The bombardier and navigator, in a B-17, sat on the lower deck, far forward of the pilots' compartment, which was on the upper deck, explaining how Fred and his navigator found themselves alone in a still-flying but ultimately doomed aircraft. The astrodome Fred Leiby refers to from which he could look up at the pilots' compartment is clearly visible just behind the radio antenna on the nose of this B-17 aircraft. This B-17 has been restored as the famous *Nine-o-Nine* of the 91st Bomb Group, which flew 140 combat missions, more than any other B-17 in the ETO.

Fred Leiby was born in York, Pennsylvania, on July 23, 1923, the older of two boys. By the time he was eight the family moved to Bridgeport, Connecticut, where Fred graduated from high school in 1941. He went to work in a nearby defense plant for a year. It was dirty work and Fred was looking for something else to do when in August 1942 he saw a poster proclaiming: "Wear Silver Wings—Join the Army Air Forces Cadet Program." "I was tired of the grease and grime at the defense plant where I was working and I put in my application. I was called up in January 1943, and took tests which were to determine if I would become a pilot, navigator, or bombardier. A major, a little older than I, said, 'Son, you qualify very, very well for navigation training. And you just about qualify for pilot training. You owe it to yourself and your country to become a navigator. What do you want to do?' 'I want to be a navigator, sir,' I responded." Fred entered navigator training and got his wings in September 1943. "At that time they assigned rank by age. The younger ones in my class, that included me, were made flight officers; the older cadets were promoted to second lieutenants.

"I was assigned to a provisional B-17 crew of ten, in a provisional B-17 group, at Grand Island, Nebraska. There we trained in a brand-new B-17G bomber to become replacements for combat units overseas. We named our airplane

The Jerry Killer, with a German helmet and tombstone painted on the nose of the aircraft. Once our training was complete, we flew from Grand Island to Florida, then on to Trinidad, Brazil, Dakar in Africa, with our final destination Casablanca, Morocco. *Jerry Killer* was deemed too provocative by the folks at Casablanca and we renamed our airplane *Geronimo* and painted an American Indian character on the nose of the aircraft instead of the German helmet and tombstone. In early January 1944 we joined the 347th Bomb Squadron of the 99th Bombardment Group at Foggia, Italy. On my first combat mission on January 16, 1944, I was assigned as navigator to an experienced crew. We were going up the Adriatic Sea where it was the practice for the gunners to fire a few rounds to make sure their .50-caliber machine guns were in working order. A ball turret gunner in another airplane shot off part of our tail, so we had to abort the mission. At the time we were required to fly fifty combat missions before going home. We received double credit for longer missions like Ploesti, when we didn't have any fighter escort. So, while I received credit for thirty-nine missions before being shot down, I actually completed only thirty-three missions. I was shot down on my thirty-ninth combat mission. Our targets ranged from southern France to Romania and included marshalling yards, submarine pens, airfields, depots, and so on. We usually carried a load of twelve five-hundred-pound bombs, but once in a while we carried two thousand pounders.

"Opposition to our raids varied. The heaviest flak we encountered was on a raid against the oil refineries at Ploesti, Rumania. On that mission the astrodome in the nose of the aircraft near me was shattered by shrapnel. My hand was scratched by debris from the shattered astrodome. When we landed, I went to see our doc to see if I qualified for a Purple Heart. At that time, if you got wounded and were awarded the Purple Heart you also received five hundred dollars. The doctor looked at my hand and said, 'That's not a deep enough wound to merit a Purple Heart.' That was that. On a mission to Toulon we were hit by ground fire and began losing fuel. We made it to Corsica, landing on a small fighter strip occupied by American-piloted Spitfires of the 52nd Fighter Group. The runway was so short we ended up going through a fence into a field. Four days later when our B-17 was repaired we resumed our flight back to Foggia. My crew got two weeks leave when we completed twenty-five missions. My bombardier and I went to the Island of Capri." Capri, the famed isle and tourist attraction, had been a German rest and recreation center before that. Once Italy changed sides and the island was captured, the same rest center was used for R&R purposes by the American military.

"It was on my thirty-third mission, thirty-ninth by the mission-counting system they used, against a munitions plant at Varese, Italy, when I was shot down. A German fighter flamed our number three engine. My bombardier and I did not hear a bail-out call nor the emergency bell, and we couldn't see the engine fire. Our pilots had put the aircraft on autopilot, and along with the rest of the crew bailed out. When I looked up, the pilot seats were empty. Johnny Moore had a backpack chute and was the first out of the aircraft. I had a chest-type chute and it took me a while to retrieve it and buckle it on. Once on the catwalk between the bomb bays I looked up at the pilots' seats and thought to myself, 'Gee, if I flew this airplane back, I could be a hero.' But I knew I couldn't have landed the airplane—so I jumped. When I hit the ground, I landed in a field. A couple Italian kids came up on bicycles. I tried to get up and run toward them but couldn't, I had broken a bone in my ankle when I hit the ground. The kids were helping me onto one of the bicycles when a German soldier appeared, pointing a submachine gun at me. The kids acted as if they were holding me for him. An Italian soldier then appeared on a motorcycle with a sidecar attached. My bombardier, Johnny Moore, was sitting in the sidecar. I joined Johnny. We were driven up to a large cave apparently used as an air raid shelter. All the people came out looking us over. A great big albino type of guy said, 'Are you Americans?' I thought I had found a friend. I replied, 'Yes. We are Americans.' He replied, 'God curse you!' An Italian soldier then approached and spit in my face. 'Don't be mad at him,' someone said in good English, 'he lost three members of his family last week to American bombs.' I understood why these people were bitter. Flying at twenty thousand feet altitude we had no idea what was happening below us when we dropped our bombs. From the shelter we were taken to an office building in Bologna. A German officer, with monocle and swagger stick, met us there. He sat behind his desk and took out a cigarette. As he was lighting the cigarette, my bombardier asked if he could have one as well. 'Suck your thumb,' replied the German, 'you filthy American pig.' From there we were taken to a jail and put in solitary confinement.

"All of my crew got down safely. There were eleven of us. We carried an extra cameraman along on this occasion who was supposed to take pictures of the target after we dropped our bombs. My interrogator had been a school-teacher in the United States, and returned to Germany during the Depression and got caught up in the war. He had a list of all the airplanes of my squadron [347th Bomb Squadron] and all our pilots. He got that information from Italian contacts who had access to our briefing rooms where all that information was posted. He showed me a picture of a B-24 bomber. The crew thought they landed in Switzerland. Instead, they had landed just south of the border on a small airstrip. After several days we were put on a train with two German guards and transported to StalagLuft III, near Sagan [about ninety miles southeast of Berlin]. It was a camp for Allied air force officers, but they used our enlisted people as kitchen help and for other assorted duties. Once there, we were put in the West Compound." The camp, opened in 1942, eventually had five compounds for Allied POWs—the original Center and East Compounds, later augmented by the North, South, and West Compounds. The Center and East Compounds, in what was called the Vorlager, also housed Russian POWs who were used for various camp-related work details. The camp would eventually hold over ten thousand Allied air force officers shot down over Germany or occupied countries. "We were shot down on April 30, 1944, and it had taken about a week or so for us to get to the prison camp. We were put in barracks-like buildings, with eight people to a room initially, twelve later on as the number of POWs in the camp continued to increase. The German food consisted of black bread with wood shavings in it, lots of kohlrabi and rutabaga. We also had pea soup with bugs in every other pea. We essentially survived on the Red Cross parcels. Late one night in January 1945—it was after midnight—we were ordered out of the camp. The Russians were getting close. We marched all night. It was really cold, and I picked up some frostbite. The first night we slept in a church, a barn the next, then a pottery factory. The factory was warm and we stayed there a couple of nights.

"We moved on to a town called Spremberg where we were loaded into boxcars. Sixty POWs to a boxcar and one guard. The guards were older, or very young. We had a young guard in our boxcar. He was scared being with us. We were in that boxcar for about two days. When we could, we would get out of the car to relieve ourselves. One time I had to go and I tapped the guard on the shoulder. He turned around and knocked me to the floor with the butt of his gun. There was a major sitting there and he said to me, 'You should have never touched him.' I replied, 'No kidding.' Then we went on to Nuremberg and we were placed in a prison camp that had been occupied by Italian soldiers. The place was a mess. We were put in barracks. Mine was the fourth bunk up. I awoke the next morning with one eye swollen shut from bedbug bites. The next morning my other eye suffered the same fate. The Americans and British were bombing the railroad marshalling yards about a mile from the camp. One night the British were bombing. Everyone got down on the floor. I stayed in my bunk. One of the bombs hit nearby blowing out windows and doors in our barracks. I got down on the floor real fast with everyone else. We were there for about six weeks when we were again put on the road heading for Moosburg near Munich. When we were marching, there were two guards in front with dogs, about a hundred POWs, then another two guards with dogs behind. On this particular night, I knew the American lines were only about thirty miles away, I ducked into the woods with another POW. We were crossing a farm the next morning when the farmer came out with a big dog and a shotgun. 'American POWs,' he said in German. I replied, 'No, Hungarian soldiers.' He didn't buy it and marched us into the next village and turned us over to the village mayor who was also the local police chief. The mayor called someone and they sent a guard on a bicycle to escort us back to our group.

"The same night that I made my escape, two of my gunners, Joe McGilligan and Jack Patzki, and one of our pilots ducked into the woods. We were all in the same woods but none of us knew that. They got up to a river and thought the Americans were on the other side of the river. My two gunners could swim; the pilot couldn't. So these two kids took off their clothes and swam across the river. When they emerged on the other side, a German soldier mowed them down. At a POW reunion many years later, I met a couple of men who were in the bushes when these two kids swam across the river and were killed. They confirmed the story. Once we got to Moosburg, we were put into another camp, where we remained until April 29 when General Patton came through with his tanks and we were liberated. The next day I went into town to a wine cellar where I met an English soldier who told me that he was living with a German family. Apparently former Russian, Polish, and other eastern European prisoners were breaking into houses, robbing the families, and raping the women. The German families wanted Americans or British to stay in their homes to protect them. I told the Brit I'd like to do that rather than sleep on the ground. I met the Englishman the following morning and he introduced me to a German family. It was an old man, his wife, three daughters, and grandchildren. The three daughters were all married to men who had been drafted into the army. One was on the Russian front and had not been heard from for some time; another was somewhere here in the west, and the third was a POW in the United States. I got pretty friendly with the family. I stayed with them for about three weeks, picked up some American food and shared it with them. Some of those people who had been coming to rob and rape came twice to the house while I was there. They left when they saw me.

"On 8 May the old man, who sat by the radio constantly and listened, said to me, '*Krieg ist fertig*,' the war is over. I said, '*Nein, nein.*' He replied, 'The radio said so.' It got me to understand how Hitler grabbed these people through the radio. Most of the people I met were just like you and me."

Fred Leiby, along with thousands of other former POWs, was flown to Camp Lucky Strike, near LeHavre, France, where they were processed for return to the United States. He shipped out on the USNS *Henry Baldwin*, a liberty ship, which took two weeks to make it back to the US. After some home leave Fred entered pilot training, but washed out. He ended up at Westover Field in Massachusetts in the military police. Postwar reductions forced his hand and he attended college and graduated with a degree in business and public administration. Fred remained in the air force reserve as an intelligence officer, eventually retiring after age sixty in the rank of colonel. He spent his civilian career principally in the Foreign Service and with USIA, the

United States Information Agency, in assignments which took him to Europe, South America, and Asia. Fred, like so many of his fellow air crew members, was just a teenager when he entered the Army Air Forces, turning twenty-one in a prisoner-of-war camp near Sagan, Germany, near which I lived as a young boy. Fred and I finally met ten years ago. I interviewed him at his home in Air Force Village West in Riverside, California, adjacent to March Air Reserve Base, the home of many fellow flyers whose stories are part of this book: Art Exon, Byron Dobbs, Charles Schreffler, Hal Austin, and others. Like Fred, most have departed on their last flight west, as the poem by an unknown author puts it so succinctly: "to a quaint little place, kind of dark, full of smoke, where they like to sing loud and love a good joke. Where you'd see all the fellows who flown west before and they call out your name as you come through the door."

Since many thousands of American airmen spent their time as prisoners of war at StalagLuft III at Sagan, and any single individual's experience will only provide a partial picture, the following is included to assist the reader in gaining an accurate and comprehensive picture of life, and death, at this particular POW camp. The information was collected by the Military Intelligence Service of the War Department and is based on former POW interviews and information provided by the Red Cross. By July of 1944, StalagLuft III was composed of six compounds, three of which were occupied by a total of 3,363 American officers. That number was to grow substantially in the following weeks and months. Three other compounds were occupied by Royal Air Force officers. Compounds were divided into fifteen buildings or blocks housing 80 to 110 men. The barracks were one-story wooden structures resembling old Conservation Corps barracks in the United States. Beds were double-decker bunks. The food was described as being adequate only because of the regular arrival of Red Cross parcels. The German rations provided to the POWs had an estimated caloric value of 1,928 calories. A conservative estimate of the caloric requirement of a person sleeping nine hours a day and doing very little exercise was 2,150 calories. German rations fell below the minimum requirement for healthy nutrition. Additional food came from four other sources: Red Cross parcels, private parcels, occasional canteen purchases, and gardens maintained by the prisoners. The Red Cross parcels (40 percent American, 25 percent British, 25 percent Canadian, 10 percent miscellaneous such as from New Zealand) constituted the greater part of the additional food supplied. The parcels were apportioned at the rate of one parcel per man per week during periods of normal supply. However, transportation difficulties in September 1944 reduced the Red Cross parcel distribution to one-half parcel per man. An American parcel included 113 ounces of Spam, corned beef, salmon, cheese, dried fruit, biscuits, klim (powdered milk), margarine, orange powder, liver paste, and chocolate. A British parcel only held ninety-eight ounces of what is referred to as meal roll, stew, cheese, dried fruit, biscuit, condensed milk, margarine, tea, cocoa, jam, powdered eggs, chocolate, and dried vegetables. Since the camp kitchens were limited to ten boilers and two ovens per compound, almost all food was prepared in the various room messes. These barracks kitchens obtained from the larger compound kitchens hot water, and four times a week, hot soup. That was it. There was no other support. With few exceptions, each barracks room cooked for itself. Food was pooled and prepared by volunteer cooks.

Despite confinement, crowding, a lack of medical supplies and poor sanitary facilities the health of the POWs was reported as astonishingly good. For trivial ailments the compounds maintained a first aid room. More serious cases were sent to sick quarters within the camp. Sick quarters for the South Compound originally consisted of twenty-four beds and a staff of three POW doctors and some POW orderlies. The Center Compound had its own dispensary. In June 1944 all compound sick quarters were consolidated into a building with sixty beds. Dental care was provided by a British dentist and an American dental student. In fourteen months they gave 1,400 treatments to 308 POWs from the South Compound alone. The Germans provided few medical supplies. Nearly all supplies were provided by the Red Cross, including much-needed sulfa drugs. Sanitation was generally poor. Although POWs received a quick delousing upon first arrival, they were plagued by bedbugs and parasites.

As for clothing, it was a mixed bag of captured Allied uniforms provided by the camp authorities in the early days of the camp. Later, as such uniform supplies ran out, they were augmented by American enlisted men's uniforms provided by the Red Cross, which proved extremely durable. As for work details—officers were never required to work. However, they did assume duties on a voluntary basis such as food distribution, cleaning their own rooms, and general repair work on their barracks. Other chores were carried out by a group of a hundred American enlisted orderlies whose existence American officers tried to make as comfortable as possible under the circumstances. There was a monthly pay scale which varied from 72 Reichsmark for a flight officer or second lieutenant to 150 Marks for a colonel. Americans adhered to the financial policy originated by the British that no money was handled by individual officers but was instead placed by the "accounts officer" in individual accounts after deductions had been made for laundry, airmail postage, entertainment, escape damages, and funds transmitted monthly to the NCO camp, which received no pay until July 1944. Mail from home or a sweetheart was the lifeblood of a POW. Incoming mail was normally received six days a week, without limit as to number of letters or length. The Germans only objected to V-mail forms. All Luftwaffe-held POW mail was censored in Sagan by a staff of German civilian men and women. Outgoing mail was limited to three letters or cards per month. Time for letters or cards to reach their destination varied between four and twelve weeks.

Morale in the camp was exceptionally high. POWs never allowed themselves to doubt the eventual Allied victory and their spirits soared at the news of the European invasion. Cases of demoralization were individual, caused for the most part by reports of infidelities among wives or sweethearts, lack of mail, or letters from home by people who failed to comprehend a prisoner's predicament. As for recreation, reading was the greatest single activity of prisoners. The fiction lending library of each compound was enlarged by books received from the YMCA until it totaled more than two thousand volumes. Athletics were second only to reading—cricket, rugby, softball, touch football, badminton, and volleyball. The "Luftbandsters" of StalagLuft III, playing on YMCA provided instruments, could hold their own with any name band in the USA according to those who heard them give numerous performances.

On April 14, 1942, Lieutenant(j.g.) John E. Dunn, United States Navy, was shot down by the Germans and became the first American flyer to be confined in StalagLuft III, then solely a POW camp for Royal Air Force officers. By June 15, 1944, American Army Air Forces officers held in the camp numbered 3,242, a number which grew to 6,844 by January of 1945, according to the International Red Cross. StalagLuft III was the largest American officers' camp in Germany. Lieutenant Colonel Albert P. Clark, Jr., captured on July 26, 1942, became the first senior American officer, a position he held until the arrival of Colonel Charles G. Goodrich two months later. The enforced seclusion of individual compounds necessitated the organization of each compound as a separate POW camp. At the time of the evacuation of the camp in January 1945 camp leaders were as follows:

Senior Allied Officer—Brigadier General Arthur W. Vanaman
SAO South Compound—Colonel Charles G. Goodrich
SAO Center Compound—Colonel Delmar T. Spivey
SAO West Compound—Colonel Darryl H. Alkire
SAO North Compound—Lt/Colonel Edwin A. Bland

How Colonel, later Major General, Delmar Spivey got himself into StalagLuft III is a story in itself. Briefly, however, he was assigned to the Army Air Forces Training Command. In 1942 and the first months of 1943, 8th Air Force losses were very high. It was felt that if our gunners were better trained, the bombers would have a much better chance of survival. "The air situation in Europe became so frantic," wrote General Spivey, "we needed to take a trip to the war theater to see our gunners in action, to determine what we were doing well in our schools in order to eliminate what was worthless. . . . All of us arrived in England in July of 1943 and found the stories about Piccadilly to be quite true. My West Point classmate, Major General Fred Anderson, was commanding the 8th Air Force Bomber Command. He announced at a staff meeting, in the presence of his division commanders—Hodges, LeMay, Armstrong, and Williams—that their gunnery troubles were over now that my mission had arrived. Had he known the troubles and grief to be the fate of most of us he would have not been that reassuring. I was finally airborne on a milk-run mission over the Ruhr—target Gelsenkirchen. Our group was attacked three times. Each time my little pilot, Captain Wiley, tried to make a pursuit plane out of the old B-17. I had a mind to give him hell when we got home for disturbing the gunners' sighting in such a violent manner. The fighters were concentrating on the lower formations. I saw several of our bombers going down, streaming black smoke. We got some of their fighters. I am sure that one of them had a dead pilot for he flew right through the formation of bombers without firing a shot while our trigger-happy gunners were deluging him with a stream of fire and incidentally, shooting up one another. We were near the target when flak appeared in quantity. A burst of flak racked the whole plane. The cowling of the two inboard engines flew off. Both engines stopped and the right one caught fire. There we were at 30,000 feet, shot-up and all our friends disappearing in the distance. But our good pilot Wiley was a veteran of many missions, he stuck the nose straight down and we headed for earth. I grabbed the microphone and asked Wiley what he was going to do. 'Make the thin strata of low clouds before the fighters get us,' he responded. Then the tail gunner asked for permission to bail out, he was badly wounded. Wiley told him to jump. He went out at 20,000 feet. I had some thoughts of my own as we went down. Why in hell doesn't the Air Corps do something about keeping windshields clear of frost and condensation? I couldn't see a thing out of the nose of the B-17. I also wondered why the crew had to watch that right wing burn off without some means of extinguishing the blaze. We were no more than 1,000 feet high. The plane broke through telephone wires and crashed to the ground."[77] So ended Colonel Spivey's trip to see his gunners in action. In time he arrived at StalagLuft III to become Senior Allied Officer for the Center Compound. Everyone in the camp had a story, but Spivey was the only visiting senior staff officer from the United States to become a POW.

Because of their status as officers and the fact that their guards were Luftwaffe personnel, the men at StalagLuft III were accorded treatment better than that granted other POWs in Germany. Generally the Germans adhered to the tenets of the Geneva Convention. However, friction between captor and captives was constant and inevitable. For example, on March 27, 1944, the

Germans instituted an extra *Appell*, or roll call, to occur any time between the regular morning and evening formations. Annoyed, the POWs fought the measure with passive resistance. They milled about, smoked, failed to stand at attention, and made it impossible for the camp officer to take an accurate count. Later in the day another formation was called. This time the area was lined with soldiers holding rifles and manning machine guns in readiness to fire. The POWs acquiesced; however, a few days later the unwanted extra formation was discontinued.

Other than the murder of fifty RAF flyers who had escaped, were recaptured, and then executed by the Gestapo (Geheime Staatspolizei/secret police), acts of mistreatment by the regular StalagLuft III guards involved two incidents. On December 29, 1943, a guard fired a number of shots into one barrack without provocation. One bullet passed through a window, seriously wounding Lieutenant Colonel John D. Stevenson in the left leg. Then, on April 9, 1944, during an air raid warning, Corporal Cline C. Miles was standing in the cookhouse doorway, facing the interior. Without warning a guard fired. The bullet entered the right shoulder of Corporal Miles and came out through his mouth, killing him instantly. This is the way Flight Officer Robert M. Slane, whose own story is included in this book, described the experience: "An air raid warning sounded shortly after noon on Easter Sunday, April 9, 1944. Some prisoners had just returned from a church service. The murder of the British prisoners was still the main topic of discussion. I had been walking the perimeter circuit when the siren sounded. I scurried back to Block 136. The German guards wanted us inside a building anytime there was indication of an air attack. I had just entered the building and was in the corridor when someone shouted, 'Look out for a goon with a gun.' The warning was in reference to a perimeter guard. The guard had his rifle resting on the outside perimeter fence and was aiming at someone or something within the compound. I darted into our washroom and looked out the window. There he was, calmly sighting his rifle at something within the compound. I looked in the direction it appeared he was aiming, and saw a man leaning against the doorjamb of the cookhouse. I heard a shot and watched in shock as the man in the doorway suddenly grabbed his throat, stumbled forward, taking two steps, and fell on his face. When the all-clear sounded, I was one of the first to reach the dead soldier. I didn't know his name, but recognized him as one of the enlisted POWs who had volunteered to work in the communal kitchen. Later I learned his name. Corporal Miles was an infantry soldier. Had been captured by Arabs in North Africa and turned over to the Germans in February of 1943. He was buried in the POW cemetery at Sagan. I will never forget the way he died."

An actual air raid, not just a warning, occurred two days later on April 11. It was one of many raids that day by the 8th Air Force, losing sixty-four B-17 and B-24 bombers and sixteen fighters in the process—one of the heaviest single-day losses of the war. Colonel Travis led the 2nd Air Division's 41st Combat Wing which bombed the Fw 190 assembly plant at Sorau, a few miles north of Sagan. As the formation of 108 B-17 bombers approached the target, passing the StalagLuft III POW camp at an altitude of eleven thousand feet, they photographed the camp, then went on to drop their bombs. I had just turned nine that February, living only a few kilometers from StalagLuft III. On that sunny April day the air raid sirens sounded, then a huge formation of bombers approached. I remember how fascinated I was by the sight of those planes. I wanted to fly one of those bombers one day, I thought. I wanted to be with those unknown men high up in the sky, forgetting that they had come to bomb my country. Many years later I would in fact fly with some of the men of the 8th Air Force whose airplanes I had seen that April day passing overhead.

As for the Germans at StalagLuft III, Oberst (Colonel) von Lindeiner, an old school aristocrat, was the original camp commandant, assuming command in May 1942. Then sixty-one years old, he had a distinguished military record in World War I and had been wounded severely, making him unfit for regular military service. He had opposed the Nazi party, and instead of being sent to a concentration camp he ended up on Field Marshall Goering's personal staff.[78] Courteous and considerate at first sight, he reportedly was inclined to fits of uncontrolled rage. In spite of that, he was more receptive to POW requests than any other commandant. After the British mass escape of March 1944, Oberst Lindeiner was replaced by Oberstleutnant (Lt/Colonel) Cordes, who had been a POW himself in World War I. He, for reasons unknown, quickly was replaced by a Colonel Braune, who was stricter than his predecessors, but business-like and direct. Most disliked by the prisoners were the security officers—Captain Breuli and his successor, Major Kircher. The Luftwaffe guards were fourth-rate troops, either too old for combat duty or wounded soldiers convalescing. They had nearly no contact with the POWs. In addition "ferrets" hid under barracks listening to conversations and looking for tunnels; they were considered obnoxious and were intensely disliked by the prisoners. The total number of guards and administrators was about eight hundred.

The evacuation of StalagLuft III began at 2100 hours on 27 January 1945. The various compounds were ordered to move out within thirty minutes. The Russian army had by that time come within twenty miles of the camp. In barracks bags, knotted trousers, and on makeshift sleds they packed a minimum of clothing and a maximum of food. Each man abandoned his personal items and took his overcoat and one blanket. By midnight about ten thousand British and American POWs marched off into the bitter cold in a column of threes. About two hundred men, too weak to walk, were left behind. They marched all night, taking ten-minute breaks every hour. The exodus was harrowing to POWs of all compounds, but especially to those of the South Compound, who made the fifty-five kilometers from Sagan to Muskau in twenty-seven hours with only four hours of sleep. Rations consisted of bread and margarine carried on a horse-drawn wagon. Guards and prisoners ate the same food. At Muskau, on the verge of exhaustion, they were housed in a building with a blast furnace which provided warmth, and in an old abandoned heating plant, which was cold. They remained there for thirty hours. Some sixty men, incapable of marching further, were left behind. The twenty-five kilometers from Muskau to Spremberg they walked on the 31st of January. The South Compound, plus two hundred men from the West Compound, entrained in boxcars, fifty men to a car, and two days later, arrived at Stalag 7A at Moosburg, near Munich. The men of the Center Compound arrived soon thereafter. The North Compound joined the remaining men of the West Compound at Spremberg on February 2, 1945, and entrained on boxcars for Stalag 13D at Nuernberg. They arrived there two days later. Throughout the march the guards drew rations identical to what was provided to the prisoners, treated their charges with sympathy, and complained of the harshness they all had to endure. German civilians encountered during the trek were generally considerate, bartering with the POWs and sometimes providing them water.

The conditions at Stalag 13D, where the prisoners were housed for the following two months, were deplorable. The barracks originally built to house delegates to Nazi party gatherings at Nuernberg had recently been inhabited by Italian prisoners, who left them filthy. There was no room to exercise, no supplies, no eating utensils or bowls to eat out of, and no Red Cross parcels. The German rations were meager, consisting of the usual dark bread, dehydrated vegetables, potatoes, and some margarine. Not enough for a man to survive on. After three weeks of starvation an emergency shipment of four thousand Red Cross food parcels arrived from another POW camp at Wetzlar. Throughout this period large numbers of American prisoners kept pouring into the camp from other camps threatened with capture by either Russian or American forces. Sanitation was lamentable. The camp was infested with lice, fleas, and bedbugs. Morale dropped to its lowest.

At 1700 hours on 3 April 1945, the Americans received notice that they were to evacuate the Nuernberg camp and march to Stalag 7A at Moosburg. At this point the prisoners of war took over the organization of the march. They submitted to the German commander plans stipulating that in return for preserving order they were to have full control of the column and to march no more than twenty kilometers a day. The Germans accepted. On 4 April, with each POW in possession of a food parcel, ten thousand Allied POWs began the march. While the column was passing a marshalling yard near the highway, P-47s dive-bombed the yard. Two Americans and one Briton were killed and three men seriously wounded. On the following day the column laid out a large replica of an American air corps insignia on the road with an arrow pointing in the direction of the march. Thereafter, the column was never strafed again. It proceeded to Neumarkt, then Bersheim, where 4,500 Red Cross parcels were delivered by truck, then to Muelhausen, where more parcels were delivered. On 9 April the column reached the Danube, which Colonel Alkire, the West Compound SAO, refused to cross since it meant exceeding the twenty kilometer a day limit. With his refusal the Germans completely lost control of the march and POWs began to drop out of the column at will. The guards, intimidated by the rapid advance of the American army, made no serious attempt to stop the disintegration. The main body of the column reached Stalag 7A on 20 April 1945. Patton's tanks arrived on April 29, and their ordeal finally ended. The war in Europe ended just over a week later on May 8.[79]

Over the years, the former POWs of StalagLuft III held several annual reunions in the spring of each year to commemorate their liberation. I spoke in early 2012 at their reunion in Arlington, Virginia, attended by the few still remaining. Their most notable reunion, however, "took place in Dayton, Ohio, in 1965, when the prisoners created a nationwide stir by inviting four of their former German captors: Gustav Simoleit, camp adjutant; Hermann Glemnitz, chief ferret; Wilhelm Stranghoner, chief NCO in Center Compound; and Dr. Helmut Haubold. General Spivey saw nothing strange about hosting the Germans on an all-expense-paid trip to America. 'We cannot help but give the German Luftwaffe credit for the fairly good treatment we received,' he said. Most of the prisoners from StalagLuft III agreed. . . . General Spivey was not ignorant of the suffering of prisoners held by the German army. In fact, precisely because he and the other prisoners in StalagLuft III were aware of the inhumane treatment given almost everyone but air force personnel, the men attending the reunion concluded that members of the Luftwaffe should receive commendation. . . . Directing the German prisoner of war system as a whole was a complex and nebulous command structure that permitted diversity in administering the camps. Under these circumstances, an influential man like Goering could not only secure control of virtually all the Allied airmen but also determine which provisions of the Geneva Convention would be observed in the camps. His decision to abide rather closely by the convention benefitted the captured fliers, if only by making it possible for lower-echelon Luftwaffe personnel to run the camps in accordance with their own sense of duty and their professional standards and without undue outside interference."[80]

In the wars that followed—Korea and Vietnam—American prisoners of war would be subjected to torture and deprivation rarely experienced by the flyers who became prisoners of the Luftwaffe in World War II. To show humanity towards your enemy, in my opinion, is a key aspect of civilization. Unfortunately it is all too often ignored, with torture and deprivation being the rule rather than the exception.

ARTHUR E. EXON

P-40/P-47

POW StalagLuft III, Sagan, Germany

Skies Above

Day in, day out, that same routine, we dream of home, of those we love.
We dream of food, of drink and song, we dream of flights in skies above.
Someday, someday we will return to all those things we're dreaming of,
To all those things so dear to us and frequent flights in skies above.
Day in, day out that same routine, a man's dreams and tho'ts of love.
There'll be no flak or fighters up when we fly again in skies above.
—John R. Johnson, StalagLuft I, WWII ETO

Fred Leiby and Art Exon both ended up as prisoners of war at StalagLuft III in Sagan. Yet neither knew the other, being in different compounds. Leiby and Exon went on that terrible trek in January 1945, which by that April had taken them to a hellhole called Moosburg, or Stalag 7A, as it was referred to by their German captors. They were survivors, but barely. Never once in fifty years did their paths knowingly cross—not until 1995, when both, accompanied by their wives, found themselves on a trip to Sagan, along with many of their onetime fellow POWs, to commemorate the fiftieth anniversary of their liberation. Not until then did Leiby and Exon meet. Fred was a retired air force colonel; Art, a retired air force brigadier general. Sagan and StalagLuft III, that experience, bound the two men together like only hardship can. Sagan no longer was a German town when they arrived in 1995, but Polish, the borders altered by the outcome of the war. Nothing remained of the compounds or the barracks or anything at all they had known, only a large concrete slab where the water storage tanks once stood, a small monument with a plaque commemorating

351

the death of Corporal Miles, and another simple monument in tribute to the British officers who had been massacred by the Gestapo. Said Fred, "We went right from where we started our trek as POWs in January 1945 and followed our trail all the way to Moosburg." This time they didn't walk, but rode in the comfort of a tourist bus accompanied by their wives. "Our group was well received by every town we visited in Germany. There was little evidence of the destruction and carnage we had seen fifty years earlier."

I interviewed Arthur Ernest Exon, better known as Art to his friends, the same time I interviewed Fred Leiby at Air Force Village West in Riverside, California, a retirement community for former air force officers and their families adjacent to March Air Reserve Base. Art grew up on a homestead his family settled in South Dakota in the late 1800s. He attended high school in nearby Fairfax, and in 1935, upon graduation, moved over to the nearby Southern States Teachers College in Springfield, South Dakota. By the time he received his college degree Art had never once left the confines of his home state of South Dakota. All that was about to change for him. Jobs were not that easy to find in those prewar days, so he accepted a teaching position in a one-room schoolhouse out on the prairie, teaching young children from first through tenth grade. When a position opened at the Fairfax Junior High School, he eagerly accepted. By 1941 he had risen to the position of school principal. But there was a war going on in Europe, and young men were being drafted into the US Army if they didn't choose to volunteer before that letter arrived which notified them that Uncle Sam wanted them. Art waited a bit too long and in January 1942 became a private in the US Army. He was put to work in a woodworking shop, not a very soldierly occupation, he thought, and he looked for a way out. There were those recruiting posters all over his post encouraging young men to JOIN THE ARMY AIR CORPS—LEARN TO FLY. So he volunteered to become an Army Air Corps pilot. He passed his written exams and flight physical and in March 1942 he formally entered the aviation cadet program. By then he was twenty-six years old, considerably older than most cadets who were still in their teens. He was "the old man" among teenagers who soon would be fighting America's air war in Europe and the Pacific. Art went through the usual phases of flight training in the trainers common at the time—the PT-17 Stearman, the BT-13 Vultee Vibrator, and the thrilling-to-fly AT-6 Texan. On November 10, 1942, Art received his silver pilot wings and was commissioned a second lieutenant in the Army Air Corps. If that wasn't good enough news, he was ecstatic when he learned that he was to enter training as a fighter pilot. Off he went to train in the P-40 at Sarasota, Florida. The various versions of the P-40 fighter were known as either Warhawk, Kittyhawk, or Tomahawk. The names did not resonate with the pilots who flew them and they simply referred to this airplane as the P-40.

The P-40 Warhawk was made famous by the Flying Tigers and saw extensive use in North Africa and the MTO.

"Once I completed training in the P-40, I received secret orders sending me to Cairo, Egypt, as a replacement P-40 pilot. Once there I was assigned to the 64th Fighter Squadron of the 57th Fighter Group." The 57th was formed in 1941 at Bradley Field, adjacent to East Granby, Connecticut. Its three squadrons—the 64th, 65th, and 66th—were equipped with the P-40 Warhawk. The P-40 was dated and not on the same level with the P-51 or P-47 which would in time replace it, but if flown competently it could hold its own in the air against an Me 109 or Fw 190. On July 1, 1942, aircraft and pilots of the 57th embarked on the USS *Ranger*, and two and one half weeks later the three squadrons of seventy-two aircraft, off the east coast of Africa, launched off the *Ranger* and headed for airfields near Cairo, Egypt. The fields had no names, just numbers such as Landing Ground 174, then LG 172 and LG 75. The group's first significant combat operation was in support of the crucial battle at El Alamein. Then, after the German Afrika Korps was in retreat, the 57th followed the Germans across North Africa until they surrendered in May of 1943. The 57th Group and its three squadrons then participated in every combat operation in the Mediterranean Theater of Operations, the MTO. They followed the US and British armies into Sicily within hours after the capture of former German and Italian airfields. They moved on to Corsica, then took the air war to the German army and air force in Italy until their surrender on May 2, 1945, six days before the formal surrender of the German armed forces and the final end of the war in Europe. Art Exon got into the fight in early 1943 as a replacement pilot while his squadron was operating against German and Italian forces west of Cairo.

"I got checked out quickly not only in how to fight, but also how to cope with intense dust storms which at times made air operations impossible. On February 11, I think it was, we experienced an intense storm for two days that put us out of operations for a week. But it was April 18, 1943, which I will never forget. It wasn't an air battle, but a massacre. We called it the Palm Sunday Massacre, others called it the Goose Shoot. We were a part of the British Desert Air Force at the time, based on a landing strip in Tunisia near El Djem. I have to spell it for you, hard to pronounce. It was late Sunday afternoon, off Cape Bon, where the Germans were making their last stand when this unequal air battle began. The Germans were running out of supplies of all kinds. Supply ships were sunk by us or the British as soon as they were sighted. So the Germans were forced to supply their troops by air, or surrender. We had been looking for their transports for some time, but without success. Then, on April 18, 1943, Palm Sunday, we caught up with them." Art Exon was part of an element of nine Warhawks of the 64th Fighter Squadron, the Black Scorpions, making a final sweep off the coast near Cape Bon, just before sundown. The other two squadrons, the 65th, the Fighting Cocks, and the 66th, the Exterminators, put up twelve aircraft each. Each of the squadrons had their own patrol area off the coast, making sweeps between Cape Bon and Tunis, looking for the elusive German transports that kept the Afrika Korps alive. "The sun was low on the horizon, a beautiful afternoon," Art recalled, "when in the distance down low, at around three to four thousand feet altitude, a thin line emerged, which quickly revealed itself as a line of German transports heading for Cape Bon.

"Here we were, thirty-three P-40s, maybe a few more, which took off after we called in our sighting, and some British Spitfires flying high cover, facing a very large formation of Ju 52 trimotor transports, escorted by a fair number of Me 109 and Me 110 fighters. This engagement was to be the equivalent of the Marianas Turkey Shoot in the Pacific. They were flying in three perfect V-formations, like Canada geese. We were flying at a higher altitude than the transports and came down on them like avenging angels. We ignored their fighter escort and just went after the transports. I managed to down one of their escort fighters, an Me 109, and probably a second. We only paid attention to them when they became a threat to us, otherwise we focused on the Ju 52s. So many Ju 52s were landing on the beach to escape our guns that I began to strafe them. They were blowing up or catching fire all over the place. It was a massacre." There is a painting by the famous aviation artist Keith Ferris hanging in the New England Air Museum which accurately depicts the engagement. After it was all over, the 57th Fighter Group claimed to have destroyed seventy-four enemy aircraft, mostly Junkers 52 trimotors. German records show that twenty-four Ju 52s went down at sea while thirty-five crash-landed on shore at Cape Bon, out of a total of sixty-five Ju 52 aircraft. Some of the escorting fighters were lost as well, including fourteen Me 109s and Me 110s. In addition to the loss of fourteen giant Me 323 Gigant six-engine transports to RAF Spitfires and South African P-40 Kittyhawks four days later, on April 22, the Palm Sunday Massacre, by the fighter crews referred to as the Goose Shoot, broke the back of the German airlift capability in the Mediterranean, dooming the Afrika Korps, which surrendered on May 12, 1943.

The German Luftwaffe's effort to provide desperately needed supplies to the doomed Afrika Korps was reminiscent of what happened in a similar effort to relieve the trapped 6th Army the winter before at Stalingrad. The Germans lacked two things in both cases: sufficient airlift capacity and the necessary air superiority to protect their vulnerable transports. Without at least local air superiority it was indeed foolhardy to send a large number of slow transport planes into an area swarming with American and British fighters. That any of them survived is indeed a miracle. The Junkers 52 trimotors by 1943 represented a very slow flying and dated design. The American C-47 Skytrain, better known to its flyers as Gooney Bird, based on the highly successful prewar Douglas DC-3, was far superior to the Ju 52, but would have shared the same fate as its German counterpart had it been put in a similar situation. If the Ju 52s were doomed, the giant Me 323s, the largest aircraft of World War II, were even more vulnerable when carrying barrels of fuel. Built largely of plywood, fabric, and metal tubes, this giant, appropriately so named, could in fact carry a load up to twelve tons at a maximum speed of around 130 miles per hour at sea level, the speed dropping with increased altitude. The aircraft did yeoman service in the more benign environment over the Soviet Union but was the proverbial sitting duck on relief missions to the Afrika Korps.

After the Goose Shoot the 57th Group morale was understandably high. The next target they took on was the small Italian island of Pantelleria, bombing it into submission. The group launched its first raids on May 18, supported by every other Allied bomber and fighter unit in the MTO. The battered Italians surrendered on June 11. The *Stars & Stripes*, the US Army's official newspaper in Europe, described the operation this way: "The much discussed, secret, underground hangars in the Pantelleria aerodrome were described today by Sergeant Love, who flies newspapers to Allied troops in Pantelleria. He said the hangars are built underneath the sides of the aerodrome, big enough to hold at least 100 planes. They open up toward the airfield by two sliding doors. Some 12,000 Italian soldiers took shelter in these hangars during the air raids. . . . About 90 wrecked Axis planes were found on the airfield when the Allied troops landed on the island." After completion of the Pantelleria operation the 57th Fighter Group moved from Tunisia to Malta, flying missions in support of Patton's and Montgomery's landings in Sicily in July of 1943. "Our job during the landings was to fly cover for the fleet,"

Art Exon recalled. "We flew at about four thousand feet altitude. There were no enemy fighters, so we had time to watch C-47s coming in pulling gliders behind them. Strong winds and poor visibility resulted in many of the gliders crashing at sea. Unfortunately, a couple nights later our fleet lying offshore opened fire on a large formation of C-47 transports loaded with paratroopers from the 82nd Airborne Division intended to capture German airfields near Catania. The navy, thinking they were German bombers, shot down a bunch of them. Hard to figure how this happened since they approached from the south. But it happened. Too many of our paratroopers died that night from friendly fire."

Writes General Matthew B. Ridgeway in *Soldier*, his memoir, "That drop developed into one of the tragic errors of World War II. The planes bearing the 504th came in over the invasion fleet just as a German air attack was ending. The guns of our fleet turned on the slow, low-flying aircraft, and the shore batteries took up the fire. We lost twenty-three planes that night and ninety-seven men, though many men jumped and saved themselves as the planes went down.[81]

"By mid July we moved from Malta to Sicily, near Catania, and flew out of there until the middle of September. On August 17, I had been promoted to captain in the mean time, I became commander of the 64th Fighter Squadron, the Black Scorpions. Nothing really changed, we just kept on doing what we had been doing—strafing and bombing and getting into the occasional dog fight. The Italians surrendered early in September. We then settled down on former German airfields near Foggia. There were so many fields there filled with bombers and fighters, American and British, that you had to pay attention not to fly into anyone when taking off or returning from a mission. From there we also started flying missions into Yugoslavia and against shipping in the Adriatic. General Cannon, the 12th Air Force commander, called our group commander, Colonel Archie Knight, one day and asked for volunteers to go after some German ships heading into Split harbor. That was sometime in September 1943. I volunteered my squadron and led a formation of four P-40s against four ships. We each carried four 250 pound bombs. I hit my target and turned for home. The ship sank. General Montgomery later called and promised Colonel Knight that he would make sure that when he returned to England he would put me in for a British DFC. The general kept his word, and after the war was over I was awarded the British Distinguished Flying Cross for sinking that German supply ship.

"We kept on bombing bridges, ammunition dumps, and anything that moved on the roads during daylight hours. On October 22 I was leading my squadron, four flights of four, against road and rail targets in the Ancona area. Ancona is a coastal town on the east coast of Italy, about halfway up the Italian boot." For that mission Major Exon was awarded the Distinguished Flying Cross. According to the DFC citation, the 64th Fighter Squadron that day, under the leadership of Major Exon, destroyed a railway station at Ancona and a train with fifty freight cars, and in the face of heavy antiaircraft fire Major Exon then reformed his squadron and attacked an approaching motor convoy, destroying several vehicles. It was a good day for the Black Scorpions, although they lost one aircraft in the process. "Then, in January 1944, we had to part with our trusty P-40 Warhawks. They were replaced with P-47 Thunderbolts. We immediately put them to good use sinking a German submarine anchored in Trager harbor, Yugoslavia. At this point in time we were frequently tasked to attack targets in Yugoslavia, just across the Adriatic Sea. The day before my Ancona mission, for instance, on the 21st of October, our sister squadron, the Exterminators, caught a flight of Ju 87 Stuka dive bombers unawares. They shot down all five. Until now I had lived a relatively charmed life, collecting a few holes here and there, but nothing serious. Then, on a mission on March 16, 1944, I was caught by German 20mm antiaircraft fire on a strafing run. The plane was badly shot up, but I managed to bring it back to our base. We were losing planes and pilots like everyone else who was flying down low. Still, I loved what I was doing—flying fighters. I was twenty-six years old, commanded my own squadron, the 64th Fighter Squadron of the 57th Fighter Group, one 'helluva' good outfit, by the way, and in just over two years I had gone from a brown bar second lieutenant to the rank of major. War or no war, I felt good about myself. I felt even better when two weeks later, on March 29, we got into a scrap with some Me 109s. I managed to get one of them, giving me a total of two kills. Three more to go to become an ace. Let me mention at this point that our group constantly moved from one landing ground to another, some better than others. We started in North Africa, then moved to a couple of different fields on Malta to support the invasion of Sicily. Once Sicily was secured, we flew out of there for a while from a couple of different fields, before moving onto the Italian mainland. There we bounced from Rocco Bernardo to a couple of fields near Foggia, then to Amendola and Arcola, before shifting over to Corsica off the west coast of Italy in support of Operation Strangle. We were flying out of Alto, Corsica, when I was blown out of the sky during a strafing run by an exploding ammunition dump that April [1944].

"It was on April 20, 1944. I was leading a flight of Thunderbolts, P-47Ds, out of Alto, Corsica, to hit an ammunition dump near Florence. It was a bunch of strange-looking buildings I remember, easy to identify. We approached the Italian coast at about eight thousand feet. I carried one incendiary and one general-purpose bomb. My wingman, Captain Bill Nuding, carried two incendiary bombs. We came in at around two hundred feet above ground level, made a left turn, southeast to northwest. My incendiary bomb dropped short

The P-47D was probably the best close air support aircraft of WWII—unfortunately Art Exon decided to strafe an ammo dump. Not even the sturdy Thunderbolt could handle that kind of punishment.

of the target, as did Bill's. I flew two circles around the target and decided to strafe the building. Bad decision. After all, we were at low level, two hundred feet or less, and the target was an ammo dump. I told Bill to stay well behind me as I made my strafing run. I got in a short burst and the building exploded in my face. The explosion set my Thunderbolt on fire. I started losing control. Managed to spin it around, open the canopy and drop out of the burning aircraft. Fortunately, I was in a climb at that point, at about three hundred feet, just enough altitude for my chute to open before I hit the ground. I was unhurt, if you don't count the fact that my pants had caught fire and been largely burned off, but without doing harm to me—so I thought at the time. It was a shock. It all happened in a split second. One moment I was flying, the next I was fighting for my life to get out of that burning aircraft.

"All this of course happened in broad daylight. As I was running to a spot where I thought I could hide, I could hear Bill flying overhead. He must have seen me and knew I made it. Maybe, just maybe, with a little luck, they could get me out. Then a German machine gun got my attention and I froze, raised my hands in surrender and hoped that was the end of that. Not until the Germans arrived did I suddenly discover that I had difficulty walking. I broke my ankle as I hit the ground hard. The German guards took me to their field hospital, and I must say I received prompt and good medical care. Then I discovered it wasn't only my pants I had burned off but I had also burned my thighs and legs. That hurt more than the broken ankle. They bandaged me up before I was put in a makeshift cell under guard. These were combat troops and they did little interrogation—name, rank, and serial number, that was it.

They quickly sent me off to a POW camp near Innsbruck, Austria. I didn't stay there long, but was put on another train, or trains, because my guards and I changed trains frequently, before we arrived in Danzig, the Polish city on the Baltic Sea where World War II began on September 1, 1939. South of Danzig [near Schubin, or Szubin in Polish] was OffLag 64, Offizierslager 64, run by the German army. It was a POW camp exclusively reserved for US Army officers—infantry and so on, not Army Air Forces. They had sent me to the wrong camp. I stayed there for about two months, until September 1944, and then was transferred to StalagLuft III, at Sagan.

"At StalagLuft III I was put in the North Compound with the British, although I was an American officer. They never moved me to the South Compound with the other Americans. As for the food, I remember eating lots of dehydrated vegetables. You've probably heard from others about life at that camp, surely Fred Leiby told you all about it. On the 29th of January 1945 the end was near. We could all feel it. It was a cold winter night when on short notice we were lined up outside the camp and began our march to—we didn't know where. The other compounds had already preceded us a couple of nights earlier. We were allowed to take whatever we could carry. I took one Red Cross parcel. Essentially it was those parcels which kept us going, because the food the Germans fed us had little sustenance. We marched through the night and into the greyness of the next day. The roads were clogged with German refugees trying to escape the Russian army. We finally got some rest in an old brick factory, were loaded onto trains, and once we arrived in a camp near Spremberg, received a very welcome distribution of Red Cross food packages. It took us several days to get to Nuernberg, in early February. From there we eventually walked to the infamous camp at Moosburg in Bavaria. I was in fairly good physical condition. My wounds had healed properly and I had exercised whenever I could. Patton's tanks finally arrived to liberate us on April 29, 1945. The general came by briefly two days later. What was most disappointing to us all was when he told us that he had orders from General Eisenhower to tell us to stay where we are. 'Have patience, the army will come and get you.' The living conditions at Moosburg were deplorable, but in time we all got home one way or another."

Art Exon returned to the United States in June 1945. In 1948 he was awarded a degree in industrial administration by the Air Force Institute of Technology at Wright-Patterson Air Force Base, Dayton, Ohio, then was assigned to the Air Material Command headquarters located at Wright-Patterson Air Force Base as well. His flying days were over. He served in numerous staff assignments for the next twenty years in the United States, Germany, and Japan. While chief of the ballistic missile division at headquarters United States Air Forces in Europe, USAFE, then located in the beautiful spa town of Wiesbaden, he was responsible for the installation of the Jupiter ballistic missile system for the North Atlantic Treaty Organization in Italy and Turkey. The Jupiter missile installation in Turkey became a key trade-off for the United States in settling the October 1962 Cuban missile crisis, which had brought the United States and the Soviet Union to the brink of nuclear war. Art retired from the air force in 1969 in the rank of brigadier general. The one-time schoolteacher in a one-room schoolhouse in South Dakota never thought he would travel the road he did. Art flew a total of 135 combat missions in P-40 Warhawks and P-47 Thunderbolts from landing strips in North Africa, Sicily, Corsica, and Italy for a total of 325 combat hours. In addition to receiving the British Distinguished Flying Cross, which Art was awarded at the behest of General Montgomery for sinking a German supply ship in the Adriatic Sea off Split, he was awarded sixteen Air Medals, the American Distinguished Flying Cross, the Purple Heart for the wounds he suffered when bailing out of his flaming Thunderbolt in Italy, and the Distinguished Service Cross, the second highest award for valor in combat after the Medal of Honor. Art was awarded the Distinguished Service Cross in October 1944 while he was a POW at StalagLuft III in Sagan, Germany. Brigadier General Arthur E. Exon retired from the United States Air Force on May 1, 1969.

After his retirement from a very active air force career Art managed several ranches in California producing nuts, citrus fruit, and grapes. Both of his sons, Jack and Douglas, followed in their father's footsteps, becoming air force flyers. Art "flew" west for the last time on July 23, 2005, to join the many men he served with in combat so many years ago. It is men like Art Exon who unselfishly, and at the risk of their own lives, preserved the many freedoms which we so easily take for granted.

ROBERT C. STROBELL

P-47/Me 262

I Flew

When the last checklist is run and the bagdrag is over I will reminisce of the days I once knew.

I will not remember the 3 a.m. alerts, but only that I flew.

I will not remember the crew rest in tents nor recall how cold arctic winds blew.

And I'll try not to remember the times I got sick, but only that I flew.

I will never forget when nature became angry and challenged my intrepid crew,

And I'll always remember the fear I felt and the pride in knowing I flew.

I will remember the sights my mortal eyes have seen colored by multitudes of hue,

Those beautiful lights on cold winter nights seen only by those who flew.

God was extremely good to me and let me touch his face.

He saw my crew through war and peace and blessed us with his grace.

So when I stand at Saint Peter's Gate and tell him that I'm new

I know he'll smile and welcome me because he knows I flew.

—Brad Baker

Robert Strobell was born in 1918 in Rutland, Vermont, and didn't know anything about airplanes. "When I graduated from high school in 1937, I went to work at the House Scale Company filling production orders. When the war came along, my buddy signed up for the army and ended up in the Phillippines. Then a couple of other guys got drafted into the army and the navy, and I figured they were closing in on me. I decided to join the Army Air Corps. I knew about the aviation cadet program from my hunting and fishing buddies, so I signed up and passed all the tests. I went through the South-East Training Command in Class 43H. Flew PT-17s, the Vultee Vibrator, and then went on to the AT-6 in advanced flight training. The AT-6 was a hot airplane. Then I got a couple of flights in a P-40, two more in the P-47, and I was shipped overseas. I arrived at the 353rd Fighter Group at Metfield, England, in March 1944. Later on we moved to Raydon in Suffolk county. As a new guy I went through a transition period at the base learning from the old timers how to fly the Thunderbolt properly. In a combat squadron they did things they never taught you in training. They taught me all about instrument flying and navigation before I flew my first combat mission. The Luftwaffe just wouldn't come up for me. I flew mission after mission in support of the invasion that June—got shot at by flak, escorted bombers, and beat up the ground strafing, but never saw a German plane. Then, finally, I got lucky and got a couple of victories. I was flying wing to the flight lead, Captain Emery. I could hear my buddy Rupert Tumblin screaming on the radio, 'Get this guy off my tail.' When I looked down, I saw a Fw 190 and I knew my flight leader heard the same thing I heard on the radio. He didn't do a thing—just sat there. So I said, 'Breaking right,' and went down and took that 190 off my buddy's tail. The 190 never knew I was back there when I hit him. At that point the pilots in the Luftwaffe were pretty thin on experience. A little later I got a Bf 109. That one I had to fight for. We pushed it up a couple of times. I came out on top and that was it.

"After I completed my combat tour, I was transferred to London, to the headquarters United States Strategic Air Forces, USSTAF, aircraft contingent, to fly the big shots around. One plane I had was an L-4 observation plane, another a Stinson L-5. There was an AT-6 trainer, a UC-64 and UC-78 twin-engine Bobcat, a C-46 transport, a Beech C-45, and a big twin-engine Lockheed Hudson. When I looked at this strange assortment of airplanes, I told them that the only one I had ever flown before was the AT-6. They just shook their heads and laughed. I told the crew chief who was assigned to me to get all the airplanes in top shape so I could check myself out in them. And, 'By the way,' I emphasized, 'you are going along when I take my first flight in each aircraft.'

"'That's great,' the chief said, 'I love to go flying.' The Hudson looked so old I told the chief not to bother with it. I checked out in all the other airplanes just by using the technical manuals and my crew chief. My approach to flying was to learn as much about an airplane as I could before I took it off the ground. I felt I needed to know the limitations of a plane and emergency procedures when critical functions didn't work. That's how you stay alive in the flying business. In October of '44 I transferred along with the headquarters staff to the Paris area. From there I flew people back and forth to London, and ferried a few more of my aircraft over to France. On a flight from London to Paris, late one afternoon, darkness caught up with me. I made several passes over the pitch-black field when I got there, hoping someone would turn on the lights for me. A line sergeant was smart enough to put a jeep at the end of the runway and leave the headlights on so I could see enough to land. I set the thing down and thought that was the end of it. The next day I had six officers on my neck asking me why I was flying at night into a place like this. One of those officers was a colonel by the name of Watson. I didn't know it then, but Watson and I would be spending a lot of time together."

Lieutenant Strobell's idyllic life, flying senior officers from here to there, came to a sudden end when he found himself reassigned to Vittel, France, to the headquarters of the newly created First Tactical Air Force (Provisional)—a brainchild of General Spaatz to gain control over a less than disciplined French air contingent. Provisional meant that Washington was not going to come up with additional funds or manpower spaces to support this temporary organization. General Spaatz would have to come up with the resources from within his own command. The hotel that served as the headquarters for the First TAC, as it was commonly referred to, also held the office of a colonel by the name of Harold Watson. Watson was tasked by General Spaatz to locate and return to the United States as many of the new German jets and rocket planes as he could find, once the war was over. In the meantime, though, late in 1944, Watson was assigned to the 1st TAC as its chief of maintenance, with an office down the hall from Lieutenant Strobell. Strobell had impressed Watson that night when he flew into a blacked-out Villa Coublay, and he had kept his eye on him. So, one day in early 1945, "Colonel Watson came to my office and said, 'Lieutenant, we are going to pick up a B-17. I need a copilot and you are going with me.' I said, fine, but you have to understand that I have never flown a B-17 before—and I really don't care about big birds. I am a fighter pilot. Watson laughed at me and replied, 'That's all right, Lieutenant, you just do what I tell you.' So we hopped into a B-26 and flew to this 1st Tactical Air Force fighter base where the commander was screaming his head off because this great big B-17 bomber was sitting on his field and doing all sorts of awful things to his operation. The colonel, red faced, shouted at Watson and me to 'Get that big ass bird out of here.' So Watson, I can still see him vividly before my eyes, walked up to the crew chief and said, 'Will this thing fly?' The chief replied without batting an eye, 'Yeah, it's ready to go.' We did a ground check, and that's when I discovered the reason why the B-17 was on the base. It was battle damaged. It had very large holes in it. This was a sad-looking airplane. We got in and Watson took the left seat, I the right. Watson cranked her up and we took off. In flight the B-17 sounded like a wind tunnel. I couldn't get the gear up. I couldn't get the flaps up. I couldn't close the bomb bay doors. This thing was down and dirty—and Watson was flying it at five hundred feet off the ground into Nancy, a depot for dead or nearly dead birds. When I got out of that airplane, I said to him, Colonel, sir, I don't like big birds. And I sure as hell don't like this airplane. Any airplane that can flap its wings like this one does, I don't want any part of. Watson got a kick out of what I said and laughed loudly. Then he said to me, 'How about flying an Me 262 jet, would that suit you better?' I didn't know what he was talking about.

"It was mid-May 1945, I had moved to Schwetzingen from Vittel, when I got word that effective May 20 the 1st TAF would be no more. On the morning of May 27 Colonel Watson walked into my office and said to me, 'Strobell, you are going down to Lechfeld.' In his hands he held a stack of papers a foot high that said Me 262 on it. He dumped this stack of papers on my desk and said, 'Get your butt down to Lechfeld, Lieutenant, and get as many Me 262s out of there as you can. I want at least ten. Remember—ten.' By that time I knew what an Me 262 was, but I had never seen one. I had no idea why I was chosen by him, but he must have had his reasons. I arrived at Lechfeld on May 27, late in the afternoon, a bright and sunny day. As far as I could see, nobody was on the field. I got out of the airplane. The pilot who flew me there never shut down the engines and immediately took off again. I stood there with a bedroll under my arm and a little ditty bag in my hand. I thought, What the hell am I doing here? There is no place to check in, no people in sight anywhere, only lots of bomb craters and trashed buildings. It was obvious to me that this airfield had been bombed many times. I saw a big building to my left and decided to check it out. I found trashed offices—as far as I was concerned I was in enemy territory and I didn't feel very comfortable. I was particularly intimidated by the fact that everything around me was destroyed, and I had no transportation. I stepped outside that building and saw what looked like a barracks. It was getting dark rapidly, so I headed for that building to see if I could find a place to sleep. There wasn't a square inch of the building that wasn't covered with glass shards and wood splinters. Bullet holes in every wall. I went upstairs, found a room, and cleared an area to put down my bedroll. Then I booby-trapped the place, hooking up empty cans to some wire I found lying about, so if anyone came up the stairs it should wake me. I readied my .45-caliber pistol, tucked it under the bedroll and went to sleep. As soon as it got light, I was up and out of there. Lechfeld was full of junked German airplanes. The devastation spread out before my eyes was deeply depressing. I walked toward an airplane hangar on the far side of the field, and there I found three American sergeants and some Germans working on two Me 262 jets. By the first week of June everyone Watson had tapped for this operation had arrived—ten American crew chiefs, twenty-seven German Messerschmitt pilots and mechanics, and six American pilots, counting myself."

The morning of May 28, after having spent a restless night in a demolished former Luftwaffe barracks, Bob sat down for a breakfast of K rations in the Me 262 hangar with several of the newly arrived aircraft mechanics from the by-now-disbanded 1st TAF. "Is this all you guys are living on?" Bob asked, pointing at boxes of C and K rations. "'Yeah,' one of the sergeants responded. The others nodded their heads in agreement. 'But we aren't really hurtin',' Lieutenant,' one of them said. 'We've been out huntin' with Sarge Freiburger. Shootin' deer. We carve 'em up and split the meat amongst us. It really ain't bad. You should try it, Lieutenant.' I thought I had to take care of that situation quickly. So I set off and found the air disarmament people on the field, Master Sergeant Eugene Freiburger's bunch. They had full mess facilities at their end of the field. I told them to set up a mess tent at the hangar and provide our guys full meal service—morning, noon, and night. Then I met with all twenty-seven of the German mechanics and test pilots. Gerhard 'Gerd' Caroli was the test engineer, also a pilot, and he supervised the mechanics—*Monteure*. I had effectively two pilots at my disposal—Karl Baur, the Messerschmitt chief test pilot, *Chefpilot*, and Ludwig 'Willie' Hoffmann, also a test pilot, *Versuchspilot*, like Karl Baur. I didn't get many favors out of Baur because Watson stole him away all the time for his own projects. But Willie was mine exclusively and he was very helpful. Karl Baur was pure German in my book, what I call an elite, upper-crust kind of guy. Karl could work with Watson, he couldn't work with me—a mere lieutenant. I didn't really care what his social outlook was as long as he did the job I wanted him to do. On the other hand, Willie Hoffmann got along great with everyone."

Strobell fell in love with the Me 262 from the moment he laid eyes on the airplane. "There were a number of things I really liked. You could remove its nose in a few minutes and replace a fighter nose with a recce nose if you cared to do so, or if the aircraft had battle damage you could quickly exchange one nose section for another. You could also change an engine in almost nothing flat. The engines were plug-in types, which in a way made up for their short life. Pull the engine cowling off, and a mechanic could get the engine out in less than thirty minutes. How many hours could anyone put on one of those engines? Ten hours, fifteen hours maximum. Flying beyond that was liable to result in catastrophic engine failure. The process of repairing airplanes and bringing them up to readiness started before I got to Lechfeld. I went to Gerd Caroli and said to him, You got this two-seater here. I need it for training my pilots. He answered me in good English, 'I can get it out for you today.' Great, how many hours does it have on the engines? 'I don't know,' was Caroli's response. What about the rest of the airplanes? 'I don't know that either.' Where are the records? 'We don't have any records.' Then you are going to take them all back into the shop and start from scratch, I told Caroli. In the meantime I put the guys to work 'hangar flying' while I waited for the first airplane to finish inspection.

"The pilots Watson had selected were all Thunderbolt pilots from the now-defunct First Tactical Air Force. They had never flown an aircraft with a tricycle landing gear before, or used the metric system. What I decided to do was to take an Me 262 that was not restorable to flying condition and have it tethered to the ground outside the hangar. Then I asked all five of them—Anspach, Brown, Hillis, Holt, and Dahlstrom—to sit in the cockpit and go through the engine start, taxi, and takeoff routine. We'd run up the engines, and shut them down again. Then we practiced conceivable emergencies and what we might do. We could ignore the radios because we had no need for them, and we were going to fly at ten thousand feet or less, so we didn't bother with the oxygen. Everything else we had to know—cold. To make them safe pilots I knew they had to learn the idiosyncracies of the Me 262—what it did that the Thunderbolt didn't do. I decided somebody had to go first, and since we didn't have the two-seat trainer available to us I decided I was going to be the first one to fly. When the first aircraft rolled out of the hangar for flight test after the engine inspection, I told Caroli I wanted Baur to fly the aircraft. Baur fired up the engines and taxied out to the end of the runway and took off. Baur flew around for about five minutes and then came in for a landing. As he rolled down the runway, we hit the runway right behind him in a jeep and followed him all the way down to his rollout. When he came to a stop, I waved at Baur to get out. I jumped in and taxied the airplane back to the hangar, refueled and took off. I found the Me 262 to be an honest airplane. I made a couple of errors on that first flight. My first error was on takeoff. I had the mistaken impression that when flying a swept-wing airplane I had to elevate the nose on takeoff perhaps a little higher than the P-47. Halfway down the runway, looking at the airspeed indicator, I noticed that it wasn't moving. I am going maybe eighty kilometers per hour, but the airspeed indicator appeared to be dead. I put the nose back down, and up went the airspeed. I used six thousand feet of a six-thousand-foot runway to get that thing off the ground.

"Among the things I really liked about that airplane was the fact that from a combat standpoint I was looking right over the nose of the aircraft, down the bore sight of its cannons. In a P-47 with the guns in the wings the pilot had to worry about convergence at three hundred yards. Where is three hundred yards in the air without reference points? With the Me 262 I sat in the cockpit looking straight down the barrels of the guns. Visibility was excellent. The first thing I heard flying the Me 262 were the leading edge wing slats which automatically opened at reduced airspeed and retracted during high speed flight. Neither Baur nor Hoffmann had told me about the slats, so it took me by surprise when they retracted and came back out—boom-bang, boom-bang. They were intended for low speed flight only—changing the airflow over the top of the wings so it could be flown at a lower airspeed without stalling. The next thing I noticed is that I was going twice as fast as in the P-47 and there were no vibrations. By my standards this thing was just screaming across the countryside, going like the proverbial bat out of hell. I flew around for a little bit, then entered the downwind leg and pulled the throttles back to idle. I was doing nearly five hundred miles per hour, I thought, and nothing happened. When I did that in the Thunderbolt, it was like hitting a brick wall. Nothing like that in a jet. I made two passes, coming in too fast, until I finally got it right. When I taxied in, Holt and Anspach sat at the end of the runway in our jeep. I taxied into the hangar and shut down the engines. They pulled right up next to me and jumped on the wings. I opened the canopy and they grabbed my shirt collars and broke the props off my Army Air Corps insignia. Anspach said to me, 'You don't need the props anymore. You are a jet pilot now.' From then on it became a ritual. As everyone checked out in the aircraft, off came the props."

Strobell managed to get ten Me 262s back into flying condition, satisfying Watson's tasking, and on June 10, 1945, a sunny Sunday morning, they flew the jets to Melun airfield, near Paris. All the jets had been given names by Master Sergeant Freiburger—Bob Strobell's aircraft was *Beverly Anne*. Watson had them spread out their departures, so it took well over two hours before the last Me 262 left Lechfeld. The flight to Melun proved to be routine. By June 19, Bob was up at Schleswig airfield with Colonel Watson. Schleswig was in the British Zone of Occupation, and the British generously offered the Americans another Me 262 two-seat trainer and a night fighter as well, one that had most likely been flown by the German night fighter ace Oberleutnant Kurt Welter. Welter, whose last assignment was with Nachtjagdgeschwader 11, based at Schleswig, flying the Me 262B-1a two-seat night fighter version, had a total of 56 victories, shooting down three Mosquitos one night within minutes of each other in the Me 262.[82] On June 19 Strobell and Hoffmann took off from Schleswig, Hoffmann flying the Me 262 trainer. They planned to fly to Twente in Holland, refuel, and continue on to Melun. "Well, I had been briefed at Schleswig that the runway at Twente was on the short side," Bob Strobell recalled, "so I planned to put her down at the very end. That's what I did. The only trouble was, I was about a foot too low and that translated into about fifty feet from the end of the runway. There was a berm in the front of the runway, and when I hit the berm, the right wheel assembly was torn off. When I hit the runway I wiped out the right side of the airplane. There was no fire. A trip that should have taken a few hours turned into four days. I should have made a hotter approach, that's what Willie and Karl always preached to us—keep that power up, keep that power up! Willie saw what happened to me, refueled and kept on going. I made a few phone calls and had the crew chiefs from Lechfeld bring up a wing and gear assembly in a Gooney Bird, a C-47. Although such severe damage would have consigned most other aircraft to the scrap heap, the Me 262's modular construction made it a relatively simple matter to replace the damaged wing and landing gear. On the 23rd of June, a week after leaving Melun for Schleswig, I finally made it back."

On June 27 General Spaatz and his small entourage arrived at Melun in a UC-45 Beech twin-engine aircraft to view the Me 262s and Arado 234s Watson had assembled for him. When the general finished looking at the aircraft, Watson escorted him to the reviewing area right next to the runway. "Three of our airplanes were ready to go. I was the lead," Bob Strobell recalled. "Holt and Hillis were the other two pilots. The crew chiefs pulled the aircraft to the end of the runway, we got in and fired them up. There was a low overcast allowing us to get up to only two or at best three thousand feet. We flew a rat race, line abreast formation. We made several high-speed, low-level passes in front of the reviewing stand. On one of the passes Fred Hillis's gear popped out and he couldn't get it back up, so he left the formation and landed. Holt and I made a couple more passes, and then I did something stupid. After I went across the airfield on the last pass, I pulled the damn jet up and rolled it. The reason I say it was stupid, it didn't add a damn thing to the demonstration and I was risking an airplane on top of that. The Jumo 004 engine didn't like radical air-intake changes. Doing a maneuver like that could upset the air flow and have it flame out. The Me 262 was not a dog fighting airplane like the F-86 was later on. Holt and I landed after that last pass. No one ever said anything to me about my impromptu maneuver, but you know how it is—you remember your mistakes in life for ever and ever."

On June 30, three days after the air show and static display at Melun, Bob Strobell was going to move eight of the Me 262s from Melun to Cherbourg, again flying them in relays rather than in formation. Watson rightfully believed that this was a safer way of moving aircraft from place to place. If they flew in a formation and one of them crashed on the runway, closing the field, the others would quickly find themselves running out of fuel. So it was one at a time from Lechfeld to Melun, and again one at a time from Melun to Querqueville where they were to be loaded on HMS *Reaper*, a British light aircraft carrier. Bob had eleven airplanes to move, nine Me 262s and two Arado 234s, with eight jet qualified pilots. Strobell assigned Willie Hoffmann to fly *Wilma Jeanne/Happy Hunter II*, named after Colonel Watson's son Hunter, with its 50mm antitank gun prominently protruding from its nose. This was Watson's prized airplane. He didn't want anything to happen to it, the reason Strobell assigned Hoffmann to fly it. The transfer of the aircraft from Paris-Melun to the Cherbourg harbor area should have been routine; after all, it was less than an hour's flying time, straight and level. First, Bob Anspach got lost and ended up recovering on the Isle of Jersey. Then Willie Hoffmann ran into trouble. "When Willie left Melun," Bob Strobell recalled, "everything seemed to be going just fine. He got up to cruising altitude, below ten thousand feet, when he lost an engine.

According to Willie it literally shook the airplane apart. In the process of the emergency the violent vibrations put the trim on the airplane in a downward mode. You can't override the trim with a control stick on this airplane. So Willie was cruising at nearly five hundred miles per hour, loses an engine, and the nose starts going down on him. He shuts down the other engine and fights to control the airplane, but he can't get ahold of the trim-tab to pull it back. He knew he had to bail out. He opened the canopy, undid his seatbelt, and he was probably the only guy who would have done that, rolled the airplane upside down and let go of the stick. The airplane went one way, he the other. He made one grievous mistake. He thought he was close to the ground and pulled the ripcord, he was still way up high. The resulting jolt blackened and blued him from his ears to his knees. His whole body was one huge bruise.

"When Luftwaffe pilots were shot down or bailed out for some emergency, they nearly always returned with their parachutes under their arms. Apparently that was standard operating procedure in the Luftwaffe. Willie had his parachute in his room when I got to the hospital. The chute had six-foot rips on each side, and he broke six nylon shroud lines. A shroud line is unbelievably strong, but they broke when he opened that chute at too high an altitude. What happened next? People in the upper echelon of the technical intelligence program tried to court-martial me for Willie's accident. Willie was working for us, but someone in Washington was looking for a more sinister reason than just an accident, and since I ran the Me 262 operation, I was it. I went to Watson and we talked. I said to him, Colonel, anybody who wants to court-martial me, ask them one question, would you please? He said, 'Sure, Bob.' Ask them if they would have rather lost one of our American boys in that airplane, or was it all right that we lost the airplane with Willie in it? After that discussion I didn't hear another thing about a court-martial. If that engine had disintegrated on me or one of my guys, we would have never rolled the airplane upside down. We were not test pilots, like Willie was. I knew Watson wanted this airplane, so I put my best pilot in it. A year or so after the accident the American crew chief assigned to service the aircraft came forward and admitted that he didn't inspect the engines at Melun. 'I know all the rest of the guys inspected theirs,' he said, 'but I just didn't inspect those engines as I was supposed to.' Had the sergeant done his job, he would most likely have caught the crack or something strange looking on one of the blades and we wouldn't have lost the airplane. It was standard procedure to visually check every engine before flight. He just didn't do it that day." The 50mm cannon from *Happy Hunter II* was later recovered and is on display in the Museum of the United States Air Force at Wright-Patterson Air Force Base, Dayton, Ohio.

Wright Field, the Army Air Forces test center, put the Me 262 through its paces and in their final report wrote, "The overall conclusion was that T2-711,"

Lieutenant Robert Strobell in March 1944 sitting in the cockpit of a P-47 fighter at RAF Metfield, England. He flew with the 353rd Fighter Group and was credited with shooting down an Fw 190 and a Bf 109.

The Me 262 Bob flew from Lechfeld to Melun-Villaroche was an aircraft once flown by JV 44, the squadron of German "fighter experts" created and led by Adolf Galland. Sergeant Freiburger of the 54th Air Disarmament Squadron named the Me 262 *Beverly Anne*, after it was made flyable again. Bob renamed it *Screemin Meemie*, after he had flown it to Melun, near Paris, France.

the number assigned to the Me 262 at Wright Field by Technical Intelligence, "was superior to the average Lockheed P-80A in acceleration and speed, and comparable in climb performance, despite a weight penalty of 2,000 lbs. A maximum true airspeed of 568 mph was measured at a pressure altitude of 20,200 feet."[83] Bob Strobell's assessment was a bit more positive. "The final test report stated that the comparison tests were pretty close. No enormous advantage of one over the other. I don't really believe that. I think the Me 262 was superior to the P-80 across the board. I flew the 262, and that's what I believe. The Me 262 was a superior airplane, the very best of its day." Other than test pilots like Colonel Kenneth Chilstrom, the Chief of Fighter Test at Wright Field, Bob Strobell had as much time in the German jet as anyone else to form a professional opinion.

L–R: Bob Strobell, Jim Holt, Hal Watson, Willie Hoffmann, and Ken Dahlstrom at Schleswig airfield planning upcoming flights on the hood of their jeep. *What Was It?*, an additional Me 262 two-seat trainer provided by the British, sits in the background.

Ole Fruitcake, an Me 262 night fighter once flown by the German night fighter ace Kurt Welter, at Schleswig airfield. Schleswig was in the British zone of occupation, the reason for the British colors on the jet. Strobell wiped out the right side of *Ole Fruitcake* in a bad landing at Twente airfield, Holland. Spare parts were flown in from Lechfeld and the aircraft was quickly repaired.

On Tuesday, the third of July 1945, Bob Strobell flew the last of the Me 262s to Querqueville. It was *Ole Fruitcake*, the night fighter. The following morning he grabbed a P-47 assigned to Watson's group and flew it to Sandhofen airport, Y79, near Ludwigshafen. Sandhofen was the last base Bob had flown out of and he had stored some of his belongings there. "I was picking up my personal stuff from Sandhofen to take back to Cherbourg. I was scheduled to return to the States on HMS *Reaper* along with the rest of the Whizzer pilots. I poured the power to it, took off—and it promptly blew the induction manifold while I was at maximum power. The engine was filled with raw, vaporized gasoline. When that happened, you either shut the fuel switch off and got the hell out of there, or you'd try a 180 and dead-stick her into the airport. I reached up to turn the switch off, intending to take her back to Sandhofen, when she backfired. The engine blew up in front of me. I barely got out. Made about one oscillation in my chute and hit the ground. What hurt the most was that I lost about twenty rolls of film I had taken in the Me 262 program. People at the airport saw me bail out but didn't see the chute open. Scratch one American, they thought. I remained in the hospital for forty-five days. HMS *Reaper* sailed without me. When I got out of the hospital, I received orders to report to Wright Field to Building 89, the building that held all the stuff we had brought back from Germany. Watson was at Wright Field as commander of the Air Technical Intelligence Center, ATIC, which he had established. He was the one who had me transferred to Dayton to serve under him."

Watson took care of his men once he returned to the United States, and nearly all who worked for him in Germany, if they didn't get out of the military, ended up working for him again at Wright Field. Lieutenant Robert Strobell took command of Building 89 at Wright Field, after he recovered from his near-fatal aircraft accident. "I had a warehouse full of enemy aircraft," Bob recalled, "and a lot of the experimental stuff, like glide bombs, V-1s, V-2s, you name it. I had a warehouse full of tons and tons of stuff of thousands of pieces and parts. We inventoried everything and held it for further testing and evaluation. In the couple of years that I was there I don't recall anyone ever calling for one piece to be tested or evaluated. We had guided bombs, but our people were thinking of atomic bombs, not conventional precision guided bombs with their small warheads. So all that stuff just sat there getting older by the day. When I left in late 1947, people referred to Building 89 as the Museum Division of Technical Intelligence. It probably was the genesis of the present-day air force museum." Bob Strobell separated from the air force in 1949. In his subsequent career he remained close to airplanes, first working as a curator at the National Air and Space Museum in Washington, DC, in later years doing volunteer work at the historic College Park Aviation Museum in College Park, Maryland. Bob died in January 2001 at age eighty-two, nine months after I first interviewed him.

CHASTEN L. BOWEN

B-17

POW Buchenwald Concentration Camp, StalagLuft III, Sagan, Germany

Roll Call Thoughts

We've stood in the rain, the snow and the sleet,
We've stood there for hours with nothing to eat
And why have we stood there, so "Browned off" and mad?
Because Unteroffizier Noyes just couldn't add.
We've dug nice long tunnels through miles of sand.
Made fancy clothes and hid in tin cans.
But why have we failed to leave "Kriegie" land?
Because Henry the "Butcher Boy" is always on hand.
We don't like this camp, so windy, so bleak,
And the barking of watch-dogs that bother our sleep.
Oh, Major Von Mueller please give us a break;
Just call off your blood-hounds and let us escape.
—Unknown StalagLuft I POW, WWII ETO

As Allied air forces took control of the skies over Europe in the summer of 1944, Adolf Hitler ordered the immediate execution of Allied flyers designated as *Terrorflieger*. The German Foreign Office expressed concern about shooting POWs and suggested that enemy airmen suspected of certain offenses not be given the status of POWs. Such offenses apparently included the wearing of civilian clothing, using forged identity papers, and attempting to be someone other than an enemy flyer. Using this justification the Gestapo sent 168 captured airmen, including 82 Americans, to Buchenwald concentration camp.

These airmen had been shot down over France and were turned over to the German secret police by traitors in the French resistance.

Most of our boys were interrogated at DulagLuft, at Oberursel, but others were less fortunate. Those who fell into the hands of the SS and the Gestapo were treated very badly before they were turned over, if they ever were, to the custody of the Luftwaffe or the Wehrmacht. The great Fresnes prison in Paris was infamous for its treatment of POWs and political prisoners. Many of our men were able to escape after being shot down and to get into civilian clothes of one kind or another. If they were captured at a later date in civilian clothes, they were thrown into prison as spies. It usually took a long time to convince the men who ran these prisons that one was an American airman and not a spy. Nothing was too cruel for them to do to get these prisoners to talk. Some were sent to concentration camps, never to be heard from again. I recall the time when two British RAF officers who had been in Buchenwald came into our POW camp and discreetly gave the senior British officer, G. C. Kellett, the names of several USAAF officers languishing in that infamous concentration camp. Kellett gave me their names, and immediately every effort was made to get the Germans to release them. I do not know for certain that our efforts did any good, but I do know that one day these American prisoners came into our compound too frightened to talk. After they had been fed, rested, and reassured, they told us of the conditions at Buchenwald and drew us a picture of the whole establishment, including the death house and house of forced prostitution. They had been there a long time and knew about the unbelievable things that went on . . . the systematic starving and killing of tens of thousands of helpless people. . . . Some of our gallant OSS men were there waiting their turn to march to that dreadful death house which later became so well known to the world.

Major General Delmar T. Spivey, USAF, former POW at StalagLuft III, Sagan, Germany.[84]

"My name is Chasten Leroy Bowen, Chat to my friends. I was born in Nevada, Missouri, on July 12, 1924. Nevada is about a hundred miles south of Kansas City. Times were not good and we soon moved to Garden City, Kansas, where my mother found a job as a nurse. Then in 1937 we moved to Compton, California. My father got a job at a Chrysler assembly plant and my mother continued to work as a nurse. I finished high school and at age eighteen, in 1942, I registered for the draft. Then I enrolled in a local junior college. When the war broke out in December 1941, a buddy of mine and I had tried to join the Royal Canadian Air Force, but they wouldn't take us, telling us that we had to have resided in Canada for a couple of years before we could join. So we just waited around until our draft notices came a few months later. I reported to the induction center in Compton where, along with many others, I was put on a bus and sent to Fresno for basic training. They gave us draftees a battery of tests to determine our aptitude. I wanted to be an aircraft engine mechanic, having worked on cars since I was a little boy. Apparently, on the tests they gave us I did best in electronics, so they sent me to radio school at Sioux Falls, South Dakota. Then to Salt Lake City, Utah, for advanced radio communications training. After that I was assigned to the Army Air Forces. I didn't ask to be in the AAF, it just happened that way. My next assignment was to Las Vegas for gunnery training. We flew in B-17s and B-24s and fired at tow targets pulled by small trainers past our aircraft. Once they deemed me qualified to be an aerial gunner, I was sent on to Dyersburg, Tennessee, where I was assigned to a B-17 crew as radio operator and top turret gunner. We flew several simulated bombing missions over Cuba, not dropping real bombs, but little sacks filled with flour—so we could look at the ground and see where we hit. Most of our missions were to give our navigator practical experience before assignment overseas. When we left Dyersburg, we knew we were going overseas but didn't know our final destination. We flew a B-17 to Bangor, Maine. There we were put on a C-54 transport, along with a bunch of army nurses, and flown to England. After a brief stopover in Wales we arrived at our final destination—RAF Station Bassingbourne, about fifteen kilometers outside Cambridge, where my crew was assigned to the 323rd Bombardment Squadron of the 91st Bomb Group, 1st Air Division, 8th Air Force.

"The British people were very nice. We met them at the local pub. Young girls would walk right on the base and talk with us. I only had one curious incident while in England. I was on leave, on my way to London. My train compartment was filled with about six people. One was a little boy, about ten years old. I reached in my pocket and pulled out a Hershey bar and gave it to this little kid. His mother scolded me for tormenting her son. 'He's never had a candy bar in his life,' she said, 'and he will probably never have another. You should not have given it to him.' I thought I was doing the little boy a favor. When walking in Cambridge or nearby villages little kids would run up to us, even grab us by the legs, begging for candy or chewing gum. So it was almost a shock for me to be scolded by that woman for giving her son a candy bar. When I arrived in London, a V1 hit near where I was staying near Hyde Park. We flew several training missions over England and the English Channel, but never entered enemy territory. As radio operator I had to go through some additional training with the Brits. We had five letter code groups, while the British had four letter morse code groups. So our navigator and I cross trained with the British for a brief time at one of their bases. I had to learn their codes and procedures before we were allowed to fly our first combat mission. Our aircraft's name was *Take It Easy*, painted on the left side of the aircraft, just

B-17G #42-97173, *Take It Easy*, before Bowen's first combat mission in June 1944. Flight Officer Fore is second from right, front row. Sergeant Chasten L. Bowen is standing on the far left.

aft of the bombardier's compartment, along with a picture of a scantily clad young lady."

Corporal Tony Starcer was the talented artist who decorated many of the B-17 bombers assigned to the 91st Bombardment Group, including the famous *Nine O Nine*, which flew more combat missions than any other heavy bomber assigned to the 8th Air Force. The other plane of fame decorated by Tony Starcer was the *Memphis Belle*, piloted by Robert Morgan, which was the first B-17 to complete twenty-five combat missions against Nazi Germany and returned to the United States to participate in war bond drives. *Take It Easy*, aircraft number 42-97173, was a B-17G, a survivor like *Nine O Nine* and the *Memphis Belle*, giving newly arrived, untested crews, like Chat Bowen's crew, confidence that its luck would probably hold and bring them home again. "Out on the flight line I watched returning B-17s with big holes in them, even sections of wing and tail missing. It was interesting watching them come in, not frightening. Flight Officer James W. Fore was our pilot on July 8, 1944, my crew's first combat mission. Fore had already flown twenty-four combat missions; this was to be his last. It was the practice at the time to send an experienced pilot with a new crew. Our pilot, Second Lieutenant Donald Bridwell, flew as copilot, and our copilot flew on another crew to gain combat experience. Fore was the same age I was—nineteen— and had been a crop duster before he joined the Army Air Forces. We rose at four in the morning, ate breakfast, briefed, then took off and assembled as a squadron. We were still climbing crossing the English Channel, ending up at twenty-nine thousand feet. I believe it was over Calais, France, one of our aircraft must have taken a direct hit in the bomb bay, because one second he was there and the next he was gone. Our target was at Dreux, France. It was a fighter base I believe. Our squadron made a run over the target, but the bombardier didn't see the target in time, so the entire formation did a 360 degree turn and made another run at the target. It's not something you want to do. By that time the German flak had our altitude. We came across the Initial Point again when the tail gunner called over the intercom that three antiaircraft bursts had just gone off behind our plane, at our altitude. Then another flak burst hit the tail section, and a second burst took part of the left wing off, between the first and second engines. We went into a spiral. The gas tank in the left wing was on fire. I could tell that the waist gunner and tail gunner had gone—it was my responsibility to check on them. As I started to bail out, I noticed that the ball turret was spinning around and around and around. I stepped back. It was sort of hard to walk around in the aircraft at this time, and banged on the top of the ball turret. I guess the gunner was disoriented. Once he heard me, he pointed the guns down, jumped out of the turret and I handed him his chute. He buckled it on, and we both jumped. I had been told to delay pulling the rip cord as long as possible. When I pulled the ripcord, I could almost see the leaves on the trees."

It was the kind of mission that official record keepers described as a milk run, unless you happened to have been in the wrong airplane. Notes the historian of the 323rd Bomb Squadron in his daily report: "On the 8th targets in France were attacked at Crepieul and Etaples. All returned safely except one ship, #7173; it disappeared. It is not known how it became lost unless it was the ship that was seen to 'Blow Up' in mid-air. Missing in action are Flight Officer James W. Fore, pilot; 2/Lt Donald F. Bridwell, copilot; 2/Lt Robert W. Ward, navigator; 2/Lt Milton Castwirth, bombardier; SSgt Robert N. Phelps, engineer; Sgt Bernhard F. Scharf, flexible gunner; Sgt Chasten L. Bowen, radio operator; Sgt George Sherman, ball turret gunner, and Sgt James F. Zeiser, tail gunner. With the exception of F/O Fore this crew was on its first mission. All appeared to be well qualified and trained. It is another instance of the fact that losses will occur. This was the 25th mission for Flight Officer Fore." As far as the 323rd Bomb Squadron was concerned, it was just another loss: unfortunate, yes, but as the report so casually stated, "losses will occur." After all, it's war.[85]

"When I landed, I saw a little boy and a woman. The boy ran toward me. I retrieved a small English/French pamphlet from my escape kit. He pointed at the word Boche in the book, then said 'hide.' He and the woman left. I hid my parachute under some bushes, then entered a small forest. When I came to a clearing, I could hear German soldiers in the distance. They carried a metal gasmask cannister which made a clanking noise when they were running. I stayed out of that clearing and hid under some bushes. A German soldier came so close to me, I could have reached out and touched his pants. He was looking out ahead, not down at his feet, so he didn't see me. He remained right there for about an hour. After he left, I walked for what seemed like hours, but actually it wasn't quite that long. Part of my survival kit was an area map printed on silk. It was very detailed—showing curves in the road, paths in the forest. I knew where I was. I continued walking through the forest. When I came to a road, I heard this big racket coming toward me. It was a four-lane divided highway with grass and trees growing in the center strip. I dove into the high grass. Soon tanks and armored cars passed me. I dug deeper. Then I came to a small farm and hid in a barn. It was getting dark and I felt pretty safe. It had been raining and my coveralls were soaked. I wore coveralls over my flight suit. I took them off and hung them up on some nails to dry. Then I lay down on some straw and went to sleep. I still had my .45. I don't remember when, but early the next morning I heard some sticks cracking outside and I got up, grabbed my .45, and took a peek outside through a crack in the barn door. There was an old man out there, he was about forty I thought. I was only nineteen, so everyone that age was an old man to me. I opened the barn door and stepped outside, not quite knowing what I was going to do: shoot the guy with my .45 because he knows I am here? But that would make a lot of noise and everyone would know where I am. The stranger solved my dilemma, holding a finger to his mouth, cautioning me to be quiet. He indicated for me to stay where I was, then he left. About fifteen minutes later he returned and motioned for me to come with him. I left my .45 behind and reluctantly followed. We set off through the forest. Eventually we came to a farmhouse and we went inside. I don't know if it was his house or not, but they fed me and took care of me, and I began to understand that they were part of the French underground, there to help American flyers escape capture. I had two dollars in my escape kit, chocolate bars, and a few other things which I gave them. They made me hot chocolate, gave me breakfast in the mornings, lunch, and dinner. A young girl, their daughter I figured, would bring me my food. This family treated me real well and gave me a real bed to sleep in. I stayed with them for about three days. Then some German soldiers came around, looking for people. I hid out in back of the house in a pig sty. After the Germans left, a man came by on a bicycle, he had another one for me. They gave me civilian clothes to put on, then he and I pedaled off to somewhere.

"We arrived at a very nice house, it had a stone wall around it and a nice garden. I was received by Madam Marie Duvall, a very nice lady. It was here where I met my pilot, Jim Fore. We stayed with Madam Duvall for two or three days. She had a radio in the basement where we listened to the BBC, and I learned a little bit of what was going on in the war. Madam Duvall made arrangements for us to be transferred to yet another place. Fore and I sat next to the driver of a two-wheeled horse-drawn cart, in civilian clothes of course. We looked like ordinary Frenchmen. It was a bumpy ride. We came through a small town and I could see German tanks parked alongside the road, and troops. It was a scary experience. They didn't pay any attention to us, but of course Fore and I knew who we were. We were let off at another house, which turned out to be a French resistance interrogation center. One of the men who interrogated me lived before the war in Long Beach, California. He started asking me where I was from. I replied, Compton, California. He says, 'Where is Long Beach Boulevard?' It runs north and south from Long Beach through Compton, I replied. 'Where is Rainbow Pier?' It's a large ocean terminal in Long Beach. I answered all of his questions. He didn't ask any personal questions, only questions about the area I claimed to be from. My pilot and I apparently passed the test and we were transferred to another farmhouse a couple of miles away. There we were greeted by a man and a woman. I was very thirsty. There was a well in the yard and I headed over there to get a drink. 'No, no,' they shouted. They gave me to understand that the water was bad. Then they brought wine for me to drink. I wanted water, but wine was all there was.

"A man arrived in an old Citroen car, it looked like a '37 Ford. The French driver wore a broad-brimmed hat that was much too big for him, and in the passenger seat next to him sat a red-headed woman with a little boy on her lap. Fore and I got in the back seat. The driver said he would take us to a place near Paris. From there we would be taken to a landing site where an A-20 from England was scheduled that night to pick us up. We stopped at another house to pick up a young English airman whose Wellington bomber had been shot down over France. When we got to Versailles, the driver stopped the car and the red-headed woman and the little boy got out. Then the driver, his name was Jacques, drove us into Paris, right to the front door of Gestapo headquarters. We quickly were surrounded by German armed guards who marched us into a prison. In later years I learned that the driver was a French-speaking Belgian who worked for the Gestapo and was paid handsomely for every Allied airman he delivered to the Germans. Apparently, about eight years after the war, Jacques was sentenced to death by a French court. Just before he was shot, so the story goes, he shouted, 'Heil Hitler.'

"Jim Fore and I were separated, and before long I found myself being interrogated again. While my French interrogator wanted to make sure that I wasn't an infiltrator planted by the Germans—if I had been, they would have killed me—the German's intentions were to define me as a *Terrorflieger*, which would eventually put me into Buchenwald concentration camp, and certain death. A woman was in the room along with the interrogator, who spoke excellent English. A pistol lay in front of him on the table as he was interrogating me. She was apparently a stenographer and wrote down every-thing that was said. I was also thoroughly searched. They took my dog tags, I had them in my shoes, and they took my wristwatch. It wasn't just an issue type of watch, but a watch given me by my mother on my graduation from high school. I had given my military watch to our navigator, who during our mission briefing told me that his watch didn't work. They put all my things into a bag. I said, 'Let me write my name on the watch.' The one who had removed my watch from my wrist replied, 'No need for that. We'll bury you in two days.' I learned later on that threat was a common comment made dur-ing interrogations. I gave my name, rank, and serial number—that was it. Not being cooperative I was put into solitary confinement for thirty-eight days in the very old Fresnes prison, with one cup of soup a day to sustain me. At the end of my confinement at Fresnes a German officer appeared with a piece of paper, pen in hand, and put it in front of me to sign. I couldn't read German, so I refused to sign. He really got upset, started kicking me, stomping around the room in his black leather boots. He called for some soldiers to come in who put me in a box about three feet square for twenty-four hours. The next day they took me out of the box, walked me into a courtyard, and lined me up against a pockmarked wall with five other POWs in front of a firing squad. It was quite apparent that they were going to shoot us. The officer started off again asking questions and I responded again with my name, rank, and serial number. He had a British accent and persisted in asking about my squadron, where we were located, how many planes we had, and so on. I just shook my head. He flailed his arms, stomped his feet, hollered. The more he did that, the more comical it all became to me. I almost laughed out loud. I figured I was already dead anyway, and cared little about what he said or did. A very strange feeling came over me while I was standing there against that pockmarked wall. I wasn't excited, I was calm, totally at peace with myself. I felt God was with me, and that changed everything for me.

"They went through all the motions, but they didn't shoot. We were taken back to our cells. My cell door was about two or three inches thick, old oak. It had a little trap door near the top so they could slide a bowl of soup in to you. In the little door there was a peephole so they could look into your cell. I had one light bulb in my cell which they could turn on and off from the outside. In one corner there was a little water spigot and a hole in the floor which served as the toilet. My bed was some straw on the stone floor. That was it. Guards would come by now and then at night and turn on the light, looking at me through the peephole. I don't know why I did this, but I took my little soup bowl and covered up their peephole. I shouldn't have done that. The guards yanked open the door and knocked me around to teach me a lesson. Then they left. The worst part of it all were the fleas. They hid in the seams of my clothes and bit me all over. I spent much of my time crunching fleas between my fingernails. Of course I knew morse code, I was a radio operator. I communicated with other prisoners by tapping against the walls. At night I could hear people screaming, gunshots all night long. Every night was like that. On the limestone prison walls were carvings done by prisoners back in the 1800s; it was an old, old prison. Then the war was coming closer to us. I could hear shelling all night long. So, one night we were taken from our cells and marched to a railroad siding where we were loaded into boxcars. In the distance I could hear the sounds of war. They shoved about 90 of us into one car. For the first time I saw how many there were of us, several hundred I thought. We were all POWs—American, English, others from throughout the British Commonwealth. Later on I learned that 168 of us POWs were on that train—one New Zealander, several Australians, 36 or so Canadians, 82 Americans, and the rest were British airmen. The cattle car we were in was so crowded that we could only stand. The toilet was a cut-off barrel in the center of the car which soon overflowed. There was no food or water. No one had any idea where we were going—probably Germany. The door of our car was yanked open when we got to the French/German border. We stumbled out into the night. We were at a railroad tunnel which had been bombed earlier that day. It was still smoking. We were led across a bridge, through a little French village. I remember people waving at us. Then, several miles later, we came to another railroad siding where we were loaded onto another train, similar to the one we had left behind, to continue our journey into Germany.

"Before we got to Frankfurt, I remember the train was going up a hill. It was moving very slowly. The men in the boxcar behind mine had torn out some floorboards. As the train slowed, some of them dropped down between the rails. The train stopped and the guards rounded them up and lined them up as if they were going to shoot them. They didn't shoot, but they were told if anyone tried to escape again, for anyone who got away, they would shoot fifteen of us. I don't know if anyone got away. High up on one end of the car there was an air vent covered with barbed wire. A French teenager was holding on to the wire to keep from falling down. A guard on the outside shot the boy right through his hand. I thought that was sort of crazy. He was already in there, couldn't go anywhere, and they shot the kid. They took him outside. His hand was bleeding badly. I was looking through a crack in the boxcar. A German officer walked him down the rail embankment into a field, then shot him right in the back. The kid fell down kicking. Another guard raised his submachine gun and killed him. They took a couple guys out of one of the cars, gave them shovels, and buried him in a shallow grave. I thought of his mother, who would never know what happened to her son. This was so callous, warning us not to try anything. Five days and five nights later we arrived at our destination—the infamous Buchenwald concentration camp. It was a shock arriving where we did. We thought we were finally being transferred to a POW camp—Buchenwald was an extermination camp.

"We were met by armed screaming guards and barking dogs, skinny prisoners could be seen in the distance in their striped uniforms. They took all of our clothes, we stood there naked. Then we were led into a shower room. I thought we would probably be gassed, but it was a real shower. After we had our shower, inmates shaved off our hair—on our heads, under our arms, all the hair on our bodies was shaved off. If they cut you, they swabbed the cut with a cloth soaked in creosote I think. It really stung, set you on fire. Then they handed out clothes for us to put on. I received a woman's silk blouse and silk slacks, something really thin—no shoes or socks. When they finished with us, they took us outside to a rock pile—that's where we lived. A few of the men spoke German, one of them was Ben Scharf, a gunner on my crew. He yelled at the guards, 'We are prisoners of war. We should be in a prisoner of war camp.' The response, if any, was, 'You are saboteurs. You will die.' While there I talked to camp inmates who spoke English—Russians, Poles, even German army troops, apparently they were deserters and were sent to Buchenwald to work and die. We were living on this rock pile when finally one day we were told that they had a barracks open for us. It turned out that the previous occupants were little Gypsy kids, ten years old, nine years old. I remember them running around our area looking for anything they could steal to eat. Then one day they were all gone. I don't know what happened to them, but you can guess. It bothered me all my life, not knowing what happened to those kids. We moved into their barracks. As for food, we received three boiled potatoes a week, and cabbage soup with a thin film of fat or something floating on top. Three times a week we would receive a slice of brown bread. It wasn't baked through totally. At the bottom it had this wet layer of dough. The bread had sawdust in it as well. But it was something to eat and you ate everything you could lay your hands on. Once, I recall, they brought in a barrel of salt herring. The herring was cured in a brine solution. We ate them like crazy.

"We associated with other prisoners. Right across from our barracks was a Polish barracks. I spoke to several who spoke English. They were part of British special operations units and had been dropped behind German lines, then were captured. There must have been thirty or forty of them. One day, I was told, seventeen were taken away, tried, and executed. Later on all the others were killed as well. I talked to some Russians who spoke a little English. Most of them were shot while I was there, shot through the backs of their heads. Every morning we had to line up for what the Germans referred to as *Appell*—my number was 78,386—to be counted. But they didn't tattoo us. The capos told us the reason we were not tattooed was because we were possible trading material; for German POWs I presume. I don't really know. *Appell* could last hours, until the 'goon' who was doing the counting was satisfied that everyone was there. Some prisoners, not any of us, were too weak to stand there for hours and would collapse. Guards would kill the unfortunate one with their rifle butts. Other prisoners then had to carry him away to the crematorium. I wondered how people could be so cruel: we are already prisoners, so why make it even worse than it had to be?"

Squadron Leader Phillip J. Lamason was a pilot in the Royal New Zealand Air Force, RNZAF, and was the senior ranking officer among the 168 prisoners of war transported from Paris to Buchenwald. Upon their arrival on August 20, 1944, Lamason assumed informal command of his group of POWs. After their first meal, near the rock pile where they lived in a subcamp of Buchenwald, Lamason is quoted as saying: "Attention. . . . Gentlemen, we have ourselves in a very fine fix indeed. The goons have completely violated the Geneva Convention and are treating us as common thieves and criminals. However, we are soldiers. From this time on, we will also conduct ourselves as our training has taught us and as our countries would expect from us. We will march as a unit to roll call and we will follow all reasonable commands as a single unit." Lamason organized his small "command" into groups by nationality and appointed commanders in each group. They lined up in a military formation each morning for *Appell*, the daily prisoner count, and marched in formation whenever directed to go anywhere, gaining the wrath of the SS guards. Buchenwald was a forced labor camp, inmates being used to work in nearby armaments factories. When they no longer could perform, they were killed. That was to be the fate of the group of 168 as well. Lamason worked feverishly with the German camp commandant to get his group recognized as POWs and transferred to a proper camp—to no avail. Hermann Pister, the commandant at the time, agreed with Lamason that it was a mistake for them to have been sent to Buchenwald, but there was nothing, Pister claimed, he could do about it. What in time would prove successful were some informal contacts Lamason initiated with other camp inmates, Russian and RAF prisoners, who worked at a nearby German airfield and were able to pass a note to German air force personnel. How their salvation was to come about was to be utterly astonishing. In the meantime, Chat Bowen and his fellow inmates tried to cope. Bowen's weight went down to eighty-nine pounds, and although none of them knew it, Lamason knew that their execution date had been set.[86]

"We were sitting on our rock pile, looking at the sky, when we saw these bombers flying overhead at about thirty thousand feet, B-17s I presumed. I could see the lead ship dropping its target markers, smoke bombs, coming right down at us. I guess they were aiming at the nearby underground factories. I was hoping they wouldn't hit us in the process. Fortunately, not one bomb dropped inside our camp, but it was a terrifying experience. The bombs coming down sounded like a freight train coming down the track—it was that close. First came explosives, then incendiary bombs, and finally leaflets. The SS started shooting at people who picked up the leaflets, but some were retrieved anyway. I saw one. It explained how Americans treated German POWs. After the bombing, having lost many inmates to the bombs, the SS came and wanted us to work in the nearby underground factories with the other camp inmates. When we refused, they told us to help with the wounded. We marched over there, and the place was largely in ruins. I didn't have any shoes. I saw this wooden shoe lying there, like a Dutch shoe. I kneeled down to pick it up, and immediately one of the guards picked up a board and began hitting me across my back. I fell down. He knocked the wind out of me. I crawled about fifteen feet to get away from him. I couldn't go any further. I thought he'd broken my back. They let me go back to the barracks, because I couldn't help with anything. I also had a wound in my upper left leg. It was either from shrapnel when my plane was hit, or I cut myself getting out. I don't know exactly how it happened. While at Buchenwald the wound got infected. The area around my knee lost all feeling, it was numb.

"After the bombing several Luftwaffe officers came by, ostensibly to look at the bomb damage. Ben Scharf, a waist gunner on my B-17, was from Minnesota and spoke perfect German. His parents had emigrated to the United States before the war. He approached one of the German officers, saluted, and told him that we were airmen and should be in a prisoner of war camp, not a concentration camp. The German officer listened. The SS guards tried to silence Ben, but the German officer pulled rank on the guards and told them to stand back. The exchange between Ben and the German officer took about five minutes or so. The German said to Ben that they didn't have good relations with the Gestapo and the SS, but that he would do what he could, and he agreed that we should be in a POW camp. About a month later a contingent of about 150 German airmen appeared. They rounded us up, loaded us onto boxcars, about twenty people to a car, and took us to StalagLuft III at Sagan. We got food, we got shoes, we got clothes—I thought it was like suddenly being in the Waldorf Astoria."

Buchenwald concentration camp, near Weimar, Thuringia, was the first concentration camp liberated by American troops on April 11, 1945. The release of American and Allied airmen from Buchenwald is generally ascribed to the efforts of Colonel Hannes Trautloft. Trautloft entered pilot training in 1931 at the age of nineteen. He, like so many American youngsters of his generation as well, had been inspired to fly by men like Lindbergh and Udet, and when the opportunity arose he jumped at it. He soon found himself involved in the Spanish civil war flying a Heinkel 51 biplane fighter, then transitioned to an early preproduction model of the Bf 109. He scored his first victories in Spain and by the time World War II ended he had a total of fifty-seven victories. In 1944 Trautloft, highly respected by his fellow fighter pilots, was inspector general for day fighters stationed at the air ministry in Berlin, on Hermann Goering's personal staff. Wikipedia, the free internet encyclopedia, as confirmed by other sources, summarizes events which led to the transfer of the 168 airmen from Buchenwald to StalagLuft III at Sagan as follows: "In late 1944 a rumor crossed Trautloft's desk that a large number of Allied airmen were being held at Buchenwald Concentration Camp. Trautloft decided to visit the camp and see for himself under the pretense of inspecting aerial bomb damage near the camp. Trautloft was about to leave the camp when captured US airman Bernard Scharf called out to him in fluent German from behind a fence. The SS guards tried to intervene but Trautloft pointed out that he out-ranked them and made them stand back. Scharf explained that he was one of more than 160 allied airmen imprisoned at the camp and begged Trautloft to rescue him and the other airmen. Trautloft's adjutant also spoke to the group's commanding officer, Phil Lamason. Trautloft returned to Berlin and began the process of having the airmen transferred out of Buchenwald. Seven days before their scheduled execution the airmen were taken by train by the Luftwaffe to StalagLuft III." Trautloft, like Galland and other well-known German aces, in early 1945 revolted against the incompetent leadership of Reichsmarschal Hermann Goering, and he, like Galland and many others, was banished to assignments that either didn't exist, jailed, or sent to the eastern front. Adolf Galland, the former chief of Germany's fighter arm, was to be executed, but was saved by Hitler's personal intervention. He then formed his own jet squadron, JV 44, and flew until shot down by an American P-47. After war's end many of these men, including Trautloft, rejoined the German Bundesluftwaffe. Trautloft retired in 1970 as deputy chief of staff in the rank of lieutenant general, the highest rank in the postwar German military. He died in 1995 at the age of eighty-two. Like so many others, Trautloft found himself serving a corrupt and despicable regime. For many of these men the only way to differentiate themselves from Hitler and his devout followers was to maintain their sense of honor, follow their conscience. As so well portrayed by Adam Makos in *A Higher Call*, Hannes Trautloft, like Franz Stigler, succeeded in a world where such concepts were generally punished by death. Saving the lives of 168 Allied airmen from execution by a barbaric regime had to be Hannes Trautloft's greatest victory in life—something, I understand, he never talked about. The story was recently made into a movie entitled *The Lost Airmen of Buchenwald*.[87]

"We became part of the American South Compound," Chasten Bowen continued his story, "where they had a hospital. By the time I got there my leg wound had gotten much worse. I had come down with gangrene, couldn't feel anything in my leg anymore, and the German doctor who looked at my wound wanted to amputate my left leg from just above my knee. Captain Daniels and one of the Doolittle Raiders, Major David Jones, pleaded, 'Can't you do something else?' The German doctor and Captain Daniels then wrapped my leg in gauze, about two inches thick. When they finished, it looked like I had a big cast on my leg. They propped up my leg at a twenty-degree angle. Then they hung a bucket filled with salt water from the ceiling, and through a very small hole in the bucket dripped salt water over my gangrenous leg wound. I was miserable just laying there, but what could I do? The gauze bandage in time turned hard as a rock with all the salt that accumulated in the gauze. About a month later Captain Daniels and the German doctor came in to see me. Captain Daniels said, 'Let's see what we got.' They cut the gauze off my leg. They then squeezed hard, and a large quantity of pus squirted out of the wound down around my ankle and over my knee. My leg, when I looked at it, looked like what you see in a sun-parched desert, all shriveled, with lots of cracks. My leg stunk like crazy. Daniels and the doctor shook their heads. 'It's doing something,' the doctor said. Then they rewrapped my leg and continued to treat me with a salt water solution for another month, cutting off the gauze each week. Surprisingly the wound began to heal and skin began to grow back. They finally sent me back to the barracks in the south compound. This strange salt-water treatment saved my leg. It was somewhat painful to walk on that leg, but it got better as time passed. I was sitting in the theater one night when all of a sudden we were told to leave the camp. The Russians were getting close. [Lieutenant] Colonel [Albert] Clark [later Lieutenant General and superintendent of the US Air Force Academy from 1970 to 1974], one of the senior American officers at the camp, came by to see me. Colonel Clark said, 'Do you want to stay here and be liberated by the Russians or go with the masses?' I replied, I'll go with the masses. They bandaged my leg; I could walk, but it hurt like the devil. It turned out that walking was good for circulation, and probably helped save my leg. It was a long and difficult journey to Moosburg, Bavaria, about halfway between Landshut and Munich. I don't recall how long it took to get there. I recall sleeping in a brick factory one night, it was warm; in a barn another. Now and then we were given some hot soup. Moosburg was crowded with thousands of POWs. We were eventually liberated by one of General Patton's units.

"When it happened, I was right down by the gate watching American tanks going by. Captain Daniels was standing beside me. There was an SS guard standing near us. As the tanks approached, the guards ran into a shack near the exit to the camp. The one standing near us picked up a *Panzerfaust* and fired it at the tanks. The projectile didn't hit a tank, but went right into the building filled with his comrades, blowing it wide open. He killed about seventeen of his own people. Captain Daniels and I were shocked. We hit the deck. American artillery was shelling the town of Moosburg. I could see tiles flying off the roofs of houses. Then the American tanks crushed the fence line. A day or so later General Patton came through riding in a jeep. He gave a little speech and left. Down in Moosburg I saw the German flag come down and the American flag being raised. What a feeling that was. The army brought in soup kitchens. I remember eating a bean soup with corned beef in it. I ate a couple of bowlsful—and threw it all up again. I got so terribly sick from that rich soup. I wanted someone to shoot me in the head to put me out of my misery. I don't ever recall being that sick in my life. I didn't eat for a few days, just lay in my bunk until I got better. A few days later they began to move us out to Camp Lucky Strike near Le Havre, France. I didn't go to Camp Lucky Strike, but was flown to a hospital in Liege, Belgium, where I stayed for about two months. After I was discharged, I too was transferred to Camp Lucky Strike for processing home. I could walk, but with a limp. The Red Cross in the meantime had contacted my mother. So she knew where I was.

"I returned to the US on a Liberty ship. It took about twelve days to get to New York. We were met by Red Cross workers who gave us a little money and sent telegrams to our families. Then they put all of us on trains home. I went clear across the United States to San Francisco. From there I hitchhiked home. Someone picked me up in a little Plymouth coupe. He was heading to Monterey Park, just north of Compton. Once there he dropped me off. I remembered my mother's phone number. When I called, my brother answered. He had been drafted, but had a heart condition, was released from the military, and lived with my parents. He drove up and picked me up. I stayed home for a while, then reported to the military side of Los Angeles International Airport for duty. They were just coming out with GCA radar about that time, and I worked on that. Since I was a trained radio technician, I was also put to work installing radios into P-51 fighters and other aircraft. A couple months later I was discharged. I was twenty-one years old and decided to take advantage of the GI Bill of Rights to study electrical engineering. When I finished, I had a first-class radio telephone license. TV just started to come out and I went to work for a guy in the TV business. Eventually I opened my own store selling and repairing TVs. One thing led to another, I decided to sell my store, and I took a job with the Firestone Tire and Rubber Company's Guided Missile Division, working on the Corporal missile. I became proficient on the missile control and launch systems, and when the missiles were shipped to Europe, I went along teaching army operators how to use and maintain the missile control and launch system. I was stationed in Mainz, near Frankfurt, this time under much more favorable conditions than when I arrived the first time bailing out of a stricken bomber over France.

Donald R. Shearer on the left, the author, and Chasten Bowen at the StalagLuft III reunion in April 2013 in Arlington, Virginia. Both Bowen and Shearer were Buchenwald inmates, subsequently transferred to StalagLuft III at Sagan.

A tie clasp worn by Donald Shearer, a reminder of his time in Buchenwald. The former inmates formed the KLB club while in the camp in 1944—KLB standing for Konzentrationslager Buchenwald. The design depicts a naked, winged foot chained to a ball bearing the letters KLB. The ball is superimposed on a white star representing the Allied forces that freed them.

Arbeit Macht Frei (work makes you free)—the sign over the main entrance to Buchenwald concentration camp. Museum of the United States Air Force, Dayton, Ohio.

Colonel Hannes Trautloft, the German Luftwaffe officer and fighter pilot who in late 1944 saved 168 Allied airmen from certain death at Buchenwald concentration camp. In later years he served in the postwar Luftwaffe, retiring as Luftwaffe deputy chief of staff in the rank of lieutenant general.

"I talked to family and friends about my time at Buchenwald. There was a family of German ancestry living down the street from my parents' house. They asked me about my wartime experiences. When I told them about Buchenwald, they said, 'That's all lies.' I, and others, stopped talking about it. No one wanted to hear what we had to say. About fifteen years ago I went to the VA hospital in Long Beach. I went there about once a month to get a checkup. On one of those visits I heard my name called out over the loudspeaker system telling me to report to a certain office. I went there, sat down. The doctor behind the desk said to me, 'I am the psychiatrist in this hospital. I want to talk to you. I see here in your records that you claim to have been in Buchenwald concentration camp.' Then he looked at me and said, 'You are a liar. You were in a POW camp.' I said, 'Doc, I know the difference,' and got up and walked out. When things like that happened, you stopped talking about it. The only time we talked about it was when our group got together. While still in Buchenwald we had formed a club called the KLB club—for Konzentrationlager Buchenwald. We met once a year in varied locations including a visit to Buchenwald. Not until recent years was there a sudden interest in our experience— we were liars no longer. We did receive some compensation, three or four thousand dollars, for having been in Buchenwald. It was paid to us by the IMF, the International Monetary Fund. The money surely came from Germany, but it was handled in this manner. In closing I'd like to say how little history, real information, is given to our youngsters. It is scary, to me, how little our young people know about all this. It disturbs me that not only our children but also those who teach them don't know what really happened. The freedoms we have depend on it." And with that final statement Chasten L. Bowen ended his interview.

CHARLES E. MYERS JR.

B-25/F9F/Test Pilot

I Was There

I was there in forty two where the mighty B-25 airplanes flew.
The Three Forty Fifth Bomb Group was born on a cold and frosty November morn.
The crews were training both day and night, all of us youngsters were learning to fight.
We grew in number and strength every day and were ready for battle the first of May.
I was there too in forty three crossing the wide pacific, the 345th with me.
The ship grunted and groaned each day and night, to Australia we sailed, all ready to fight.
The first time foreign soil touched our feet, then north to New Guinea along the Great Reef.
We made our homes near the two airstrips and started beating hell out of those nasty Nips.
I was there also in forty four after defeating the enemy here, we went looking for more. . . .
Yes I was there with all those courageous men and there was never a doubt that we would win.
We worked and fought for very little pay and never stopped until that victorious day.
—Kenneth Gastgeb, WWII Pacific

In late 1941 war came to the United States in two ugly packages. In the far west, the Pacific, the Japanese launched a surprise attack against the American fleet anchored at Pearl Harbor, Hawaii. It was war at its ugliest and was understood by every American, young and old, that this was going to be a struggle for survival. Days later, Adolf Hitler, the leader of Nazi Germany and a devoted ally of the Empire of the Rising Sun, as a gesture of friendship and commitment to their ill-fated alliance, declared war on the United States. Within days, a reluctant America was involved in wars in both the east and the west: an ocean war in the west, and a land war in the east. Both conflicts would be defined by American air power, air power that didn't yet exist when the United States was plunged into the defining conflict of its young life. There was no dearth of

L–R standing: Major General Fred Ascani,* Colonel Karl Ousley,* Colonel Ken Chilstrom,* author, Colonel Gene Dietrich.* L–R sitting: Chuck Myers,** Air Vice Marshall RAF "Paddy" Harbison, Rear Admiral Whitey Feightner,** 2009 (*=air force test pilot/**=navy test pilot).

youngsters wanting to get involved, wanting to fight for their country. And so it was in 1942, nearly a year after the Japanese attack on Pearl Harbor, that the 345th Bombardment Group was formed in Columbia, South Carolina—the Air Apaches. The group's four squadrons were equipped with B-25 Mitchell twin-engine medium bombers, the same type of aircraft that Lieutenant Colonel Jimmy Doolittle used to terrify a surprised Japan in a totally unexpected air raid on April 18, 1942—a scant four months after the Japanese attack on Pearl Harbor. The group's four squadrons—498th through 501st—originally destined to enter war in Europe, were reallocated to the 5th Air Force in the Pacific after its commander, Major General George C. Kenney, pleaded with General Arnold for more air power. Kenney in time would command the Far East Air Forces consisting of the 5th, 7th, and 13th Air Forces. Not only were the Air Apaches reassigned from Europe to the Pacific, their mission changed from being medium-altitude bombers to low-level strafers against enemy airfields and shipping. They picked up their aircraft at Hunter Army Airfield in Savannah, Georgia, modified with extra fuel tanks to give them increased range, as well as .50-caliber machine guns in the nose section of the aircraft. They started out with a couple of .50-caliber machine guns and kept adding more guns until the final version of the B-25 flew with eight forward firing guns in its nose. At Hunter the crews picked their squadron names. The 498th became the Falcons. The 499th chose Bats out of Hell for their moniker, the name assigned to one of Jimmy Doolittle's B-25s. The 500th named themselves the Rough Raiders, and the 501st voted to be known as the Black Panthers. The squadron names were an indicator of how the aircrews viewed themselves, and how they intended to fight—like bats out of hell. From Hunter Army Airfield they flew to San Francisco, then on to Bellows Field in Hawaii, and finally arrived at Port Moresby, New Guinea, after a long and arduous journey. They learned very early on that the Pacific was a "big lake." The Japanese soon felt their presence, as no airfield or ship within range of the 345th Group's B-25s was safe. Their successes came with losses, at times high. In late 1944 a nineteen-year-old second lieutenant by the name of Charles E. "Chuck" Myers joined the Falcons of the 498th squadron as a replacement pilot. It turned out that Chuck was the youngest flying officer in the 5th Air Force.

"To a degree flying was inherited from my father," recalled Chuck Myers when I interviewed him in September 2013 on his farm in the picturesque Shenandoah Valley. "Not that my father was very interested in flying, but he was a thirty-year army veteran who had experiences all the way from chasing Pancho Villa to fighting Moros in the Philippines. In the end, in World War I, he retired from a place called Langley Field. I was born near there, in Hampton, Virginia. When I was about five years old, I remember him taking me out to Langley on occasion to visit with his old buddies. He knew the sergeants who ran the mess hall and he'd always take me by the mess hall and they'd feed me a big piece of apple pie. During these trips I remember seeing officers with tall brown boots and Sam Brown belts and sabers, huge airplanes with wire between the wings, and huge airships. For a little boy all the things I saw were huge. So I got a smattering exposure to aviation from that, as well as reading about Charles Lindbergh and other people like him. But my first real aviation experience occurred when I was about ten years old, being invited to go for a flight in a plane that belonged to neighbors—a three-place, high-wing monoplane. That kind of did it for me. I got up in the air, looking around, and that's when I decided I wanted to learn how to fly. As time passed, I had lots of other interests moving from grade school to high school. I attended Phillipsburg High School, in Phillipsburg, New Jersey. Right on the New Jersey–Pennsylvania state line, north of Philadelphia, near Scranton and Bethlehem, where we had this great melting pot that produced wonderful football teams. Football became an all-consuming passion for me. I had the good fortune to play on a team that was undefeated for three years. Not only that. In the second year of this string of victories I was the quarterback. We not only were undefeated, but the other teams didn't score any points against us. In my senior year, as I turned eighteen in March 1942, my father talked about me going to West Point. I had no idea what that meant, and he didn't push it. Then I learned that the army had changed the ground rules to become a pilot, no longer requiring a college education, because they needed bodies. I signed up with the Army Air Corps. I left high school early that spring. They eventually mailed me my diploma and I checked in at Keesler Field in Mississippi. Many of my classmates did the same, joining either the army or the navy.

"The army was interested in getting people into combat as quickly as possible. Probably one of the most dangerous periods of my career was learning to fly. You look at the statistics, the losses in training of airplanes and pilots during this period were just unbelievably high. I went through primary flight training in Helena, Arkansas, basic in northern Missouri at a field called Vance. Then they sent me to twin-engine school in the AT-10 at Stuttgart, Arkansas. I got my wings in Class 44F in April 1944. I had just turned nineteen. I went home on leave for a week or so and then reported to a distribution center where people received assignments to go to transition training in fighters or bombers. I didn't want to do that because I was worried the war was going to be over before I got into it. I discovered who the guy was who was making the assignments. He happened to use the same latrine that I did in the morning. I caught him there one morning shaving. I introduced myself and told him that I would appreciate it if I could get a direct assignment to a combat unit. A week later I was on my way to Hamilton Field, California, with a half-dozen other guys. From there we flew to Hawaii, ending up in Port Moresby, New Guinea. A few days later I was sent to Biak, a desolate coral island about 185 miles northwest of Wake. I was assigned to the 498th Bomb Squadron, flying B-25 strafers. Briefly, we went through a transition period where we flew the standard glass nose B-25. Then they removed the bombing equipment and installed a couple of .50-caliber machine guns. That package of guns kept growing until we ended up with twelve .50-caliber machine guns firing forward. The aircraft coming off the North American production lines in that configuration was called the B-25J—a very different airplane from the bomber version. It should have been renamed the A-25, because low-level attack was our mission, not medium altitude bombing.

"There I am, nineteen years old, a second lieutenant, ready to go to war in earnest. I had no idea what I was facing. We only flew low level. Flying low level is a unique skill and you have to stick with it to stay proficient. By low level I mean I never flew above a target more than fifty feet. More often I was only twenty to thirty feet off the ground. If you are going to survive that kind of flying, you have to do it constantly. You can't be flying low one day and at twelve thousand feet the next. The squadron didn't have a lot of time to train me. They gave me a few familiarization flights in the airplane in the right seat, taught me how to fly it, and then they sent me on my first combat mission as a copilot to a place I will never forget—Mamalaya in the Celebes. Our target was an airfield, the source of night raiders, Betty bombers, that would come over every couple of nights to ruin our sleep. Not that they did much damage, but digging a foxhole in a coral island wasn't easy. En route to the Celebes we flew at eight hundred to a thousand feet. As we approached our target, we got down low. I think I was in about the third wave. We flew three-ship Vs, a very appropriate formation for that kind of work. My job was to sit there with the intervalo-meter in my hand punching a button to stream out parachute fragmentation bombs set to detonate a few inches above the ground spewing out chunks of steel. Others were dropping heavier delayed action bombs. As we approached, I remember, it was very hot. We had the windows open. My pilot was firing the guns, and the gun smoke was coming into the cockpit, along with the dust and corruption from bombs dropped by aircraft ahead of us. The noise of twelve machine guns firing was deafening. We fly through all this and of course the enemy is shooting back at us. This is my first combat mission, my fifth or sixth flight in the airplane. Looking back on that mission in later years, in my mind I had a picture of myself on a very tall horse riding down a narrow valley as part of The Charge of the Light Brigade. As we pulled off the target, we were turning in an arc to the left. My pilot tapped me on the shoulder and said, 'Look behind you.' There, across the airfield, a B-25 was on fire, pulling a long trail of smoke. Then he just sort of pulled up slowly to about two hundred feet, turned on his back and dove into the airfield. My pilot nonchalantly commented, 'He always did fly a bit too high.' I, a nineteen-year-old high school dropout, pondered all this after the flight. Oh my God, I had never even heard of this kind of flying. The reality set in for me. This was serious stuff.

"We moved to Tacloban airfield on Leyte in the Philippines in December of '44. This was another wild scene. There was one runway running alongside the beach. It had been used by some navy pilots whose carrier had been sunk. There were wrecks of navy and other airplanes lining the runway, pushed aside into the surf by bulldozers. The strip itself was made of steel matting. The control tower consisted of four or five coconut palms that had been lashed together and someone built a platform up there, holding a desk and a radio. The direction of takeoff depended on which was the nearest end of the run-way. Coming back to land after a combat mission was hazardous. You could get killed a number of ways, including standing in the chow line, because the Japanese were still in the nearby jungle. Or you could get shot down by a ner-vous antiaircraft crew trying to defend all the ships in the harbor from kami-kaze attacks. Our ground support people came to the Philippines on a ship as part of the invasion force. They sat out there in the makeshift harbor and were hit by a kamikaze. We lost about 250 to 300 of our ground crew that way. We flew out of Tacloban, later on San Marcelino on Luzon. Our mission was to interdict anything that moved in preparation for the landings in the Philip-pines. From San Marcelino we flew missions as far away as Formosa/Taiwan and Hainan Island. Sometimes we attacked shipping in harbors. We always would come in from the backside of the island, approaching the harbor from land to sea. Picking out a ship that was in front of us we tried to do the best we could. We made one pass only, never turned back for a second pass—that was suicide. Off the coast, if we were lucky, about five or ten miles out, there would either be a navy submarine or a Catalina flying boat to pick up survivors if we happened to be shot down."

Floyd Jensen flew with the 498th Bomb Squadron, the Falcons, as did Chuck Myers, from February 1944 until May 1945. In Floyd's detailed recollections of his combat tour he writes: "By mid-January 1945 the squadrons had received a number of B-25Js as replacements. The Js had the new solid eight gun nose which was standard on all replacement aircraft. Although the increased firepower and pleasant handling characteristics of the new plane were welcome features, the extra weight in the nose slightly reduced airspeed and made already tricky single-engine flying almost impossible. The 345th concentrated on hitting Japanese targets on the Bataan Peninsula and the small islands in nearby Manila Bay. The Japanese position on the Philippines was crumbling, but the 345th was paying a heavy price. Sixty-one men were lost during the month and sixteen aircraft—an entire squadron—were shot down or written off during thirty combat missions. . . . In February, the 345th concentrated all its effort on Luzon, hitting Japanese transportation routes and troop positions. . . . Following a mission on the 8th, the group stood down for a week to move to San Marcelino on Luzon. From there the entire perimeter of the South China Sea was within range of the strafers, including the coast line of French Indochina, China, and Formosa." Flying long over water missions "were always terrifying for the aircrews who flew them. More than one pilot felt his courage fail as he turned back prematurely from an eight- or ten-hour over water flight, where the loss of an engine or a well-aimed flak burst spelled almost certain death. The range of the aircraft was stretched to the limits almost daily and the perfect functioning of this noisy, sometimes balky machine for ten and sometimes even eleven hours determined whether a man lived or died. The airmen were briefed that no 5th Air Force crew had ever returned after losing an engine over the mainland of Asia. The group would soon break that jinx, but the cost would be fearsome. The loss rate would be the highest of any period in the group's history. Within weeks an entire squadron of planes and aircrews would be lost in areas where there were almost no chances of survival. Each man, whether openly or in the depth of his heart, wondered if the next dawn would bring his death in the depths of the China Sea or on some alien oriental shore. Worse yet, considering the danger of the missions, the targets were slim, the weather was bad, and it was a 'big' ocean and the Japanese were moving under the cover of darkness."[88]

"The navy was patrolling the expanse of ocean between the Philippines and China," Chuck Myers recalled, "particularly the South China Sea area with an aircraft called the PB4Y-2, a B-24 with a single tail built to navy specifications. It was an electronic intelligence collection aircraft that would locate the radar and radio signals of Japanese ships, pass the word to 5th Air Force, which would pass the targets to us for action. On April 5, 1945, we were alerted by 5th Air Force of Japanese ships off the China coast, about five hundred statute miles from our base at San Marcelino. Off we went. Captain Albin 'Johnny' Johnson was the lead. I flew off his right wing, Neal off his left. Smith, Ranger and Manners followed, flying a V-formation behind us. When we arrived in the target area, the weather was marginal—1,500 feet overcast, light rain, visibility four to seven miles, and a rough sea surface, not great for ditching. When we sighted the ships, they were at about our three o'clock position, a mile apart, heading southwest. I am flying in close formation on Johnny's right wing when he hand signals me to take the lead and attack. His guns were not working. Here I am, a nineteen-year-old kid, and for the first time I am the lead. Wow. I broke right, heading for the nearest ship, assuming the rest of the flight would follow, which was not the case. I don't know why no one followed me, because there is no one left to ask, but here I was all alone going in for the attack. As I am lining up for the attack, I see B-25s coming in from the opposite direction. A split-second passing thought: perhaps this will confuse the enemy gunners. As for me, I was committed and opened fire as I closed on the ship. I focused my twelve .50-caliber guns on the ship's bridge and its main battery of antiaircraft guns. As I closed, my copilot, Flight Officer Blase, opened the bomb bay doors and released a bomb as we passed over the ship at masthead level. As I pulled up, Blase tapped me on the right arm and pointed to the right wing. The number two engine was streaming black smoke—not a good sign, considering where we were and how far we had to go to get home. I reduced power and feathered the right propeller, then shut down the engine. I initiated a gentle left-hand turn into the good engine, heading east. Although I had memorized the flight manual for the B-25, this was my first experience at flying on one engine.

"I was very worried at this point of making it home. No one from my group who lost an engine had ever done it. Nor did I have any prior training flying on one engine. They had told me what to do if I lost an engine, but I had no actual hands-on training. I did the best I could. A few minutes later, Lieutenant Bronson from the 499th Squadron pulled up onto my right wing. We were still at low level. Using hand signals, we rarely used our radios and only in safe areas, he gave me to understand that he would stay with me and that we should head for an emergency airstrip. He took the lead. Bronson had a navigator on board, I didn't. Most of us were flying without navigators. I ordered my crew to dismantle all equipment not needed, such as our guns, ammunition, and whatever else was not welded to the airframe, and throw it overboard to reduce weight. I jettisoned our remaining bombs and began firing out our .50-caliber guns. I did this in short bursts to minimize the loss of airspeed from the recoil of the guns. While this was going on, I slowly climbed to 1,500 feet, trying to gain enough altitude so the crew would be able to bail out should that be necessary. Ditching was not an option because of the rough sea. The damage to the right engine, I later learned, was caused by a 25mm round which entered the oil cooler inlet duct above the engine where it exploded, causing the black smoke. From the looks of things, my fellow flyers probably thought I had gone in. Captain Johnny Johnson and the rest of my flight, I later learned, had flown on and picked another target. They attacked the heavily armed destroyer *Amatsuki*. I have no idea why Johnny led that attack against that destroyer without his forward firing nose guns working. He and another aircraft from the 500th Squadron were shot down. There were no survivors. Three and a half tense hours later we arrived at Laoag, northern Luzon. It was a short, emergency landing strip, with a ditch running just beyond the far end. I didn't want to overshoot nor do a go-around on one engine. There were lots of stories in our group about guys going around on one engine and not making it. As I flared the aircraft, I noticed I was a bit high, floating down the runway. I recalled a trick one of my instructors in pilot training had taught me during a similar situation in a twin-engine AT-10. I pulled up the flaps, and we fell out of the air onto the runway like a rock. When I came to a stop, we had used every bit of available runway and burned up our brakes. Bronson came in next. The six of us abandoned our stripped-down B-25 and boarded Bronson's aircraft and flew with him back to Marcelino. That was without a doubt the most exciting and stressful combat mission of my brief flying career. They put me in for a Distinguished Flying Cross, and the rest of my crew for the Air Medal, but none of us ever received either. Who knows what happened to the paperwork.

"There was another mission I flew just before I had my engine shot out. It was against targets on Hainan island, just off Indochina. I was flying as a fill-in with another group. After we hit our target, I saw a ship a couple miles away. I broke away from our formation and went after it on my own. A foolish thing to do. As I pulled up after strafing the ship, I saw my copilot holding his hands over his head with his head down. We were under attack by a Japanese Frank fighter [Ki-84 Hayate]. I was so focused on strafing my target that I hadn't noticed it. I never did see that fighter. All I could hear was some strange noises, which were his shells hitting our airplane. Of course, I went to full power and got out of there as fast as I could. I managed to catch up with a group of *friendlies*, which turned out to be my own group which I wasn't flying with on this day. I was very careful closing on them, fearing that their tail gunners might shoot me down. Once we got back to San Marcelino, I had no idea how much damage the Japanese fighter had done to the airplane. Everything seemed to be working all right, and none of my crew was wounded. As I touched down, I lost partial control of the aircraft. One of the rounds had hit the tire on the right wheel and forced me off the runway and into the boondocks. There we sat—a smoking, dusty hulk. Fire engines and ambulances rushed out. There was no fire. It turned out the airplane had about three hundred holes in it and never flew again. It became a source of spare parts.

"Our crew composition varied somewhat depending on the mission. Always a pilot and a copilot, of course, but we didn't have enough navigators assigned to provide one for every aircraft. They would fly in the lead ships, usually with the senior crews which had the most experience, not necessarily those with the highest rank. The crew chief also acted as engineer and top turret gunner, while the radio operator who sat right behind the bomb bay would man the outboard waist guns. Finally, there was the tail gunner. That was a typical B-25 crew. One thing I took away from my B-25 experience—it made me a believer in the merits of low altitude attack. I remember a picture of one of our guys holding up a small Japanese flag: a flag he took away from the mast of a Japanese destroyer he was attacking. His propeller went through the mast and the flag ended up in the engine cowling of his B-25. That was low-level flying—not one hundred or two hundred feet above sea level, that's where you get killed. I had about forty or fifty missions. I didn't keep a log. Few of us did. I was reassigned in late April 1945 to the Combat Replacement Training Center in Nadzab, New Guinea, to train new arrivals. My job was to give the new guys a feel for the types of missions they were going to fly, something that I didn't get, which would have been of great help to me. As I was getting ready to return to the States, I ran into Colonel 'Jock' Henebry, a man with extensive combat experience in the Pacific Theater of Operations in both the A-20 and the B-25. He said to me, 'Why are you going home, Myers? The war isn't over yet.' I responded, Colonel. Sir, I am going home to train in the A-26 and will return for the 'real' war. He knew what I meant. The real war was yet to come, the invasion of Japan. We used to joke about it and had a little ditty: Golden Gate in '48. We thought it would take that long to take down the Japanese. Of course, it all ended with the dropping of two atomic bombs in August 1945.

"I got home on leave, and before I knew it the war was over. I reported to an army replacement center somewhere in North Carolina. Did a lot of sitting around, chasing girls, drinking—wondering what they were going to do with us. Someone mentioned that there was a new thing available to us called the 'GI Bill.' We learned that we would be able to go to college for free—it would pay for our tuition and books and a little spending money on the side to live off of. My buddies and I talked it over and we decided that would be the option to take rather than hang on and wait for the next war. My home was in New Jersey and the nearest college was across the river: Lafayette College. I chose to sign up at Lafayette because it was only about five miles from my parents' house. I was in the first group of GI Bill veterans at Lafayette, still on terminal leave from the army, wearing my Australian flying boots and wash khakis. The Australian flying boots were treasured by us B-25 flyers. We never wore them on combat missions. Left them under our bunks to pass on to someone else if we didn't come back. That was what I wore to class at Lafayette. I was one of half a dozen other veterans on the GI Bill taking engineering—one was a former B-17 pilot, another a P-47 pilot, a B-24 pilot, and a P-38 pilot. We were all taking about the same classes together. The college tailored its freshman year curriculum to help us get reacclimated to studying. Our heads were still in the war we had just left behind.

"While attending school I was reassigned to the reserves. Now and then I had to go to Newark airport to fly in a BT-13 trainer. All they had there at the time were castoffs. I struggled through four years of engineering. In my fourth year I had to seriously think about getting a job as an engineer, a profession which didn't really appeal to me. In reality I was just passing my time, reading *Terry and the Pirates* and waiting for the next war. I began writing letters, looking for a job as I had to make a living somehow. In the meantime, the air force had gained its independence from the army. When I wrote the air force that I was willing to come back and fly, anything at all, they turned me down. They were looking for guys with four-engine time to go into bombers of the newly created Strategic Air Command. I decided to go to Washington to see if I could get my congressman to get me into the air force. I met with Tad Walters, the congressman from where Lafayette College was located. I told him what I wanted to do and wondered if he could help me. He was quite nice, listened to me politely, then said, 'I don't know anything about this new air force, not many people do. Besides, I am an ex-naval officer. How would you like to fly for the navy?' I had never thought about that as an option. When I replied, That's a wonderful idea, he picked up the phone and called someone, took some notes, then ripped a piece of paper off his pad, handing it to me and said, 'Go to this building and this room number' [the Navy Annex near the Pentagon], pointing at the piece of paper I was holding in my hand. 'See this captain,' and he pointed at a name he had scribbled down on that paper, 'and here is his phone number. He may have something for you.' I headed over to that navy building and met with this captain, and he said, 'Well, we didn't really anticipate anyone like you walking in the door. However, we are in need of aviators and have an approved program which will provide you a regular commission as an ensign in the United States Navy, a step below what you are now as a first lieutenant in the air force, and integrate you with the class of 1949 from the naval academy.' The catch was, I had to go through navy flight training. It didn't matter that I was already a pilot with combat experience. If I wanted to fly for the navy, I had to go through their pilot training program. 'This is your opportunity,' he said. 'You have to pass a written test and a flight physical, of course. If you pass all that, which shouldn't be any trouble for you, you are in. Good luck!'

"I grabbed the chance to go back to flying. Passed the physical and the written exams and waited for the navy to call me to active duty. In the meantime I had gotten married to an army nurse I met when I had an emergency appendectomy at a Veterans Administration Hospital when I was a junior in college. On graduation in 1949 I had a BS degree in mechanical engineering, was married, was twenty-four years old, and I was broke. I kept myself above water doing odd jobs until my navy orders arrived ordering me to report to Pensacola Naval Air Station in Florida. It turned out several other former Army Air Forces flyers were there going through the program with me. They were in different flights, so I don't know how they made out. I went through the entire training program as if I had never flown an airplane before. One interesting fact was that the second time around I not only learned how to fly the navy way, but I truly understood what I was doing. At Whiting Field in New York I went through initial carrier training in the AT-6. Then on to Corpus Christie, Texas, for advanced training in the F8F Bearcat, one of the greatest airplanes I've ever flown. I returned to Pensacola for carrier qualification to get ready to go aboard ship. Doing carrier landing practice is dangerous stuff. One day after the debriefing I remember the LSO [landing signal officer] saying, 'Myers, you are very good, but you need to slow it down a bit.' Being young and overeager I wanted to do the right thing. That afternoon we took off again. But the weather had changed and the wind was blowing, and it was turbulent. I am coming around for a landing, and I am going to slow it down a few knots as I had been told to do by the LSO. All of a sudden I lost complete control of the airplane. It flipped to the left. I remember jamming in full right rudder and full power. Made a partial recovery, then crashed almost wings level. The airplane was burning when it came to a stop and I scrambled to get out. I wasn't hurt, but that experience shook me up. I thought I was doing so good and suddenly I was in the dirt. It really shook up the other five guys in my flight as well. They didn't slow down for anything after that. It was a turning point for me in my career as an aviator. What I learned was that relying on airspeed alone to make my decisions was very dangerous, but that's what we were taught at the time. More important, for me at least, was to understand the concept of angle of attack and all that flowed from that, such as stall speed, a function of angle of attack. Add turbulence to that and you are really vulnerable if you are focusing on air speed alone, which I did, and which nearly killed me.

"Off we went onto a carrier in the Atlantic to complete our training. As if carrier flying wasn't stressful enough during daytime operations, a catapult shot into the dark of night was the ultimate scary experience. There are no lights out there, everything is pitch black, except for a couple of red lights on the masts of a nearby destroyer. Add to it that the view forward from the cockpit of an F8F Bearcat is really limited and you begin to understand that night flying can be really terrifying. We would launch into the dark, fly a pattern on instruments for a specified period of time, then try to recover on the carrier. In the landing pattern I could see a red light on the carrier and another on the mast of a destroyer, knowing their relative positions to each other was all I had as far as external visual references were concerned. There was no horizon. It was pitch black out there every which way. As I turn onto the base leg, I fly a curved path toward the carrier, trying to pick up the LSO who is standing there on the carrier island, all lit up looking like the specter of death. His suit has luminescent panels which show his body outline, arms, and paddles. I pick him up and watch him. I do whatever he tells me to do, based on the position of his arms and the paddles in his hands. I am in a slight turn to be able to see him, almost until I hit the deck. At that point I level out, he gives me a 'cut,' a gesture with his hand across his throat. I cut my power and settle on the deck at a pretty rapid rate of descent, more like a controlled crash. That is and was some of the most exciting flying I've ever done, including my test pilot experience at Pax River in years to come. The navy eventually changed to a mirror landing system which was much easier to follow and allowed us to make a straight-in approach. Flying jets was different in a number of ways. The principal difference was that as you hit the deck you went to full power, in case you didn't catch the arresting wire you were ready to go around and try again. You did just the opposite when flying a conventionally powered aircraft such as the Bearcat.

"I finally got my wings in April 1951. I was sent immediately to all-weather flight training at Corpus Christie. Then back to Pensacola for training in the F9F-2 Panther. Flying a jet airplane was different in several ways, the greatest difference for me was the rate at which the jet burned fuel. Suddenly the focus is to go and do my job and get home before I run low on fuel. The navy finally decided I was ready for assignment to a fighter squadron, VF72, the Falcons, in Air Group 7, at Quonset Point, Rhode Island. What an amazing coincidence. When I was flying B-25s in the Pacific in World War II, my squadron, the 498s, was also called the Falcons. How did that happen? We flew F9F-2s, then they started to phase them out and gave us F9F-5s. The F-5s began having engine problems. We switched back to F-2s and got ready to go to Korea. We flew to

Jacksonville, then on to Dallas and finally arrived in San Diego where we met up with our carrier, CV-31, the USS *Bon Homme Richard*, which we referred to as the *Bonnie Dick*." The original *Bon Homme Richard* was a French merchant ship provided to John Paul Jones by the king of France in 1779. It was originally named *Duc de Duras*, and Jones, in honor of Benjamin Franklin, renamed the ship *Bon Homme Richard*. CV-31 was an Essex-class aircraft carrier decommissioned shortly after World War II and recommissioned in 1950 for service in the Korean and Vietnam wars. The ship was scrapped in 1992.

"We went off to Hawaii. While there we ran some training exercises before departing for Sasebo, Japan. Before I knew it, I was flying combat again, interdicting North Korean supply lines—rail, road, what have you. We would fly in flights of four, up the roads through the mountains looking for anything that moved. One of our targets on occasion was the Saen Dok lead mines. We never figured out why we were hitting that target. They had a lot of guns there, so there must have been something there we knew nothing about. We didn't fly into areas where we could run into MiGs, because we would have been hard-pressed to deal with them with an F9. Most of the missions were pretty routine, except for the takeoffs and landings, which usually were the most exciting part. But there was one mission that I won't forget. We were looking for stuff to shoot at when I saw this building in an open area near a road. We were carrying five-inch HVARs [high velocity aerial rockets]. I remember attacking that building with one of those HVARs which to my amazement actually hit the building. As I passed over, there was this huge explosion and I suddenly lost control of the airplane. It did a 360 degree roll. I slammed the stick over to the right as far as I could and managed to right the airplane and regain control. To stay level, I discovered, I had to put in right aileron. Strange. One thing I knew immediately, I wasn't going back aboard ship with a control problem that I didn't know the source of. I looked out at my left wing and my problem became apparent. We carried tip tanks. The routine was to burn the tip tank fuel on the way into the 'beach,' as we referred to the coast of North Korea. And when I crossed the beach, and before I engaged in any combat activity, I was supposed to hit the vent button and clear out any residual gasses in the tip tanks. I forgot to do that. When I flew over that exploding building, something hit my right tip tank, causing it to explode. Pieces of the tip tank were wrapped around the right aileron, which forced me into a left roll. I couldn't go back to the carrier. I didn't want to eject, we were pretty far north, and the weather was poor to the south. What to do? I headed for K18 [Kangnung—an ROK air base]. My wingman stayed with me, as well as the other two members of my flight. I didn't quite know how to find K18, hoping it had a radio direction finder. I slid into the clouds, got momentarily disoriented, and unintentionally turned into my wingman. He and the other two decided to get

Lieutenant Chuck Myers in 1944 when he was assigned to the 498th Bomb Squadron, the Falcons, of the 345th Bomb Group, flying B-25J "strafers" against Japanese shipping.

Myers in his F9F Panther over North Korea, 1952.

out of my way and fly ahead. I heard them calling the ship and telling them what we were doing. I had my hands full trying to hold the airplane level. They landed at K18. When they heard an airplane overhead, they fired some flares. I saw the flares, turned to the left, and managed to get on the ground. A crew from the ship arrived within a couple of days, took off the tip tanks, and I returned to the *Bonne Homme Richard*. It's an example of how little things can have serious consequences.

"When our tour was over, my air group returned to Quonset Point, Rhode Island. The navy routine was when returning from deployment we would get a couple of weeks leave. Then we would begin another training cycle before

Charles E. Myers Jr.

Chuck Myers in 1956 testing
the XF-V1 Pogo Stick VTOL
fighter in a test rig at Brown
Field, California. This was his
first test pilot assignment after
leaving the US Navy.

Myers as OSD's Director for Air Warfare shaking hands with "Ace" Colonel Andy Anderson, USAF
(Retired), after an orientation flight in the F-15 at Edwards AFB, California, summer 1974.

Chuck Myers in the cockpit of an F-106 Delta Dart at Edwards Air Force Base, California, upon his return from a high altitude probe to eighty-four thousand feet in 1959.

deployment or go off to a new assignment. I was interested in going to test pilot school at NAS Patuxent River—Pax River for short. I applied, and was accepted in Class 12 in the spring of 1954. In my class was Jim Stockdale, John Glenn and the first guy from test pilot school ever to become CNO [chief of naval operations], Tom Hayward. After I finished, I was initially assigned to 'armed test,' then to the Naval Special Weapons Facility at Kirtland Air Force Base, New Mexico. After completing my nuclear training, my little group was tasked to create the loft bomb tables for delivering tactical nuclear weapons from various fighter/attack aircraft. Which, from a flying standpoint, meant going out on an instrumented range, flying as fast as I could at about fifty feet off the ground, lobbing a shape that simulated a nuclear bomb onto a target. We had one or two of every aircraft capable of delivering a nuclear weapon. I got to fly all of these airplanes. The F7U Cutlass was a challenge. It had this very long nosewheel strut. On takeoff, when I retracted the front gear, it changed the center of gravity of the aircraft. It never worked out to be what the navy envisioned—a medium to high altitude air-to-air fighter—but for our work it was a pretty nifty airplane. Lieutenant Commander Brown was the Cutlass project officer. On a test flight he got a fire warning light, shut down the afterburners, and headed for Kirtland, low level. He didn't get more than halfway there when the aircraft exploded. We lost him. A couple weeks later the Cutlass became my project. I am at low level, running the same test Commander Brown had flown, and sure enough I get a great big fire warning light on the starboard engine. When it happens, the fire warning light looks about the size of a basketball. I decided not to stay low and turn toward Kirtland. Instead, I quickly shut off the fuel to the bad engine and began a climb as high as I could from a zoom. I was doing about four hundred and some knots when it happened. That at least gave me a chance to eject if I needed to. Brown never could because he stayed at low level. I zoomed up to about ten thousand feet AGL [above ground level] and then headed for the base. I declared an emergency. The tower responded, 'You are cleared for a straight in approach to runway....' I said, 'No. Send someone up to take a look at my airplane and tell me what he sees.' They sent up an F-86. He flew under me and said, 'Well, you sure as hell had a fire. Because everything is black back there.' Nothing was burning. No smoke. I spiraled down and landed. It turned out that some fitting had come loose and was poring fuel between the afterburner and the engine shroud.

"About that time my family experienced some significant medical problems. My wife came down with rheumatoid arthritis, and my youngest daughter, who was born at Pax River in Maryland, had a congenital dislocated hip. It is something that should be caught soon after birth, but it wasn't, which made it much more difficult for her to recover. She was nearly two at that time. I knew that I would need expert and expensive medical care for my family. It was obvious that I would not be able to pursue a normal navy career, which is in and out of port, away from my family. So I went to look for a job in the civilian world as a test pilot."

Chuck Myers reluctantly resigned from the navy. He then became an engineering test pilot for Convair to refine the flight technique for the Pogo Stick VTOL [vertical takeoff and land] navy fighter. The Pogo Stick was supposed to be deployed on navy combat ships, a concept fraught with many problems. Pogo Stick never completed its test phase before being terminated. Myers then joined the fighter-interceptor test team at Edwards Air Force Base, the air force flight test center. During five years at Edwards, Chuck Myers became president of the Society of Experimental Test Pilots as well as chief test pilot on the air force F-106 fighter program. In that capacity he flew speed envelope extension tests which eventually led the air force to capture the world speed record from Russia in 1959 at the speed of 1,544 miles per hour. From 1973 until 1978 he served as the Director for Air Warfare in the Office of the Secretary of Defense during which time he launched Project Harvey, later known as the stealth program. And he was involved in the development of the A-10, F-14, F-15, F-16, F-18, and the F-117. In December 1999, Chuck was inducted into the Virginia Aeronautical Historical Society's Hall of Fame for his contributions to aeronautical progress during the previous fifty years.

JAMES F. SETCHELL

Mosquito/F-5

There's a Mission Today

There's a mission today you're scheduled to fly.
So you wait by the ship and look at the sky.
It's cloudy up there and the wind starts to blow.
But the mission ain't scrubbed—get in and go.
Your nerves are on edge, you cuss and you sweat.
If this damned ship flies you lose your bet.
But the ship takes off and you settle down
and cast a long glance at the lovely ground.
This story goes on, it has no end.
You lose a ship and you lose a friend.
Maybe some day you won't come back.
And they'll chalk it up to fighters and flak.
—Sergeant Edward A. Greenlaw, POW StalagLuft I

Dec 7, 1943
North Africa

Dear Hag,

This is a very important letter as it is being carried on the private airplane of the President of the United States on his return trip from the famous conference in the Middle East with Churchill and Stalin. For the first time I can tell you that president Roosevelt personally inspected my Group at our Airport and also very closely looked over *The Spook*. Tonight the few officers that live with Elliott

R[oosevelt] are having the honor of supper with the President. I think it is something swell to attend this supper and I look forward to having pictures to show you covering the evening. There will be several other high Government officials on hand tonight so your Old Man will really be mingling with the "big shots."

Love to Bill and the Folks

Jim

PS: This letter is being personally delivered to the President by Elliot.

The letter was hurriedly written by then Lieutenant Colonel James "Jim" Setchell to his young wife, Dorothy, in Ennis, Texas, near Dallas, her hometown, where she lived with their one-year-old son, Bill, awaiting her husband's return from war. Jim at the time was the commander of the 3rd Photographic Group of the 90th Photographic Wing commanded by President Roosevelt's son Colonel Elliott Roosevelt. Elliott and Jim shared a tent at the La Marsa airstrip in Tunisia. When Elliott learned of his father's plans to stop over at La Marsa, he invited his tentmate Jim to join him, the president, and his generals, for supper. Before leaving for the war in Europe Jim and Dorothy had decided on code names for each other to be used in their correspondence. He became "Hero," Dorothy would be referred to as "Hag," and young Bill Setchell, just a newborn, became "Spook." A curious collection of names, but it worked for the Setchells. The aircraft Jim Setchell flew at the time was a De Havilland F-8 Mosquito which he named *The Spook*, after his young son. *The Spook* would not survive the war; Jim would—but just barely.

James Frederick Setchell was born on August 9, 1913, in Chicago, Illinois, not far from present-day O'Hare International Airport, which didn't come about until the early '40s. Jim was one of four children, a typical American family trying to make ends meet in difficult economic times. Like so many youngsters of his generation Jim was inspired by all the hoopla that surrounded the airplane between the wars. Barnstormers, flying surplus army biplanes, performing daring stunts, inspired young and old at county fairs or wherever there was a level landing field with people willing to pay five dollars for "the ride of their lives." The hero status accorded men like Charles A. Lindbergh, the conqueror of the Atlantic Ocean, flying *The Spirit of St. Louis* in one daring swoop from Garden City Airport, Long Island, to Le Bourget Field in Paris, France, on May 20 to 21, 1927, was the equivalent of the Mercury astronauts taking the world into space with John Glenn's first orbit around the world on February 20, 1962. The overused word "awesome" was indeed appropriate in both cases. President Coolidge awarded Lindbergh the Distinguished Flying

Cross which had been authorized by Congress only the year before—another indication of how flying influenced even the politicians of the day to do something that would show how inspired they were as a group by "those magnificent men in their flying machines." Well, young Setchell knew what he wanted to do when he grew up—fly airplanes.

In 1938 Jim entered the Army Air Corps, receiving his pilot wings in 1939 at Kelly Field, San Antonio, Texas. War was on the horizon and the buildup had begun. He was sent to the photographic school at Lowry Field, Colorado, and subsequently assigned as commander of Headquarters Squadron of the 1st Photo Mapping Group at Bolling Field, Washington, DC. He quickly assumed the position of Group Operations Officer until transferring to Peterson Field in Colorado Springs, in the same position, but this time as operations officer of an F-5 combat replacement training unit. The F-5 was the photo-reconnaissance version of the P-38 fighter. It is interesting to note how fate brings people together. When Captain Setchell served as operations officer at Peterson Field, Barney Dobbs and his friend Al Blum, whose stories I told in an earlier chapter, were there as well getting their training in the F-5 before deploying to the Pacific. Jim Setchell was slated to head in the opposite direction—to North Africa and Europe. While at Peterson Field a curious thing happened to Jim and his young bride, Dorothy (they married in January 1942 just before Jim was transferred to Colorado Springs). As a junior captain Jim was assigned many additional duties, as is still customary in the air force to this day. And one of those duties was as unit mortuary officer. He never gave it much thought, just another job title behind his name. But then one day one of his planes went down in the mountains west of Colorado Springs, and off he went in his own car, of course, to the accident site. The pilot of the unlucky F-5 had died in the crash, and not giving it a second thought, the accident investigation team put the pilot's body in the trunk of Jim's car for return to Peterson Field. On the way back Jim stopped by his home to change his uniform. Dorothy thought it was an opportune time to make a quick run to the grocery store—they only had one car—not knowing what was in the car's trunk. Fortunately she put the groceries in the back seat. Jim was frantic when he looked outside and saw that the car was gone. Dorothy soon returned and Jim quickly drove off to deliver his unusual cargo. I have no idea if Jim ever told Dorothy what was in the trunk of their car. Those were simpler times and things were done a little differently from how they are today.

In mid-1943—Jim had by then been promoted to major—the long expected orders arrived for him to go to war. He and his navigator, Captain Jerome Alexander, went off to Toronto, Canada, and picked up a brand-new F-8 Mosquito photo-reconnaissance aircraft. They flew it to Wright Field in Dayton, Ohio, for some modification work, then set off for La Marsa, Tunisia, where they had been assigned to the 3rd Reconnaissance Group. Jim named the aircraft *The Spook*—the name prominently painted on the nose of his Mosquito. The route to their final destination was long and taxing for both man and machine. The particular route that Setchell and Alexander were to fly across the Atlantic was referred to as the North Atlantic Ferry Route, one of four such routes developed just a year earlier to allow the routine transfer of aircraft from the United States to the ETO. The North Atlantic route, coincidentally, was surveyed and established in early 1941 by then Captain Elliott Roosevelt, President Roosevelt's son, who by that time had achieved the rank of colonel and was to be Setchell's and Alexander's wing commander at La Marsa. They took off from Wright Field on September 24, arriving at Goose Bay, Labrador, the same day. Here Jim Setchell and Jerome Alexander were stuck waiting for the weather over the North Atlantic to clear sufficiently to allow them to proceed to Bluie 1, a newly constructed airfield in Greenland. On the 30th of September Jim and Jerome were still stuck at Goose Bay, so they took *The Spook* up for a forty-five-minute test flight. They encountered no problems with the aircraft, refueled it, and continued their wait for clearance to proceed. Four days later, on the 3rd of October, the weather finally cleared sufficiently for them to proceed. They were married up with a B-24 Liberator bomber with better navigation capabilities than their own and took off at 12:50 local time, following in the trail of the B-24 with the curious name of *Big Cow* painted on its snout. Bluie 1 was only 776 miles from Goose Bay, but it took them over four hours to get there. Greenland was anything but green—windswept and cold.

With full fuel tanks they took off the following morning, again behind *Big Cow*, which continued to be their lead, this time heading for Meeks Airport in Iceland. Iceland appeared green compared to Greenland. They sat for another three days at Meeks before heading on October 6 southeast to Prestwick Airport in Scotland. Here they parted with their B-24 lead to proceed on their own. They didn't know why it took so long, but they did not receive clearance for another nine days to proceed to their next staging base, St. Mawgan in Cornwall, England. The turn-around at St. Mawgan was fairly quick, and two days after their arrival, on the 17th, they departed for Casablanca, Morocco, a nearly six-hour flight, mostly over water. The following morning they took off from Casablanca, the last leg of their long journey, for a four-and-a-half-hour flight across North Africa, landing at La Marsa airfield, near Carthage, at twenty minutes after three o'clock in the afternoon. La Marsa was a typical, dusty desert airstrip, which at one time had been used by the Germans. Destroyed and damaged German aircraft littered the field. A lone Bf 109 fighter, apparently undergoing routine maintenance, had been left behind when the Germans had to hurriedly flee the airfield. Jim settled in to his new assignment and found himself appointed commander of the 3rd

Photo Reconnaissance Group. New and eager, he aimed to set an example for his men and started flying operational missions soon after taking command. The 3rd Photo Group was part of the 90th Photographic Wing (Reconnaissance) which in addition to the 3rd Photo Group had four additional groups equipped with a variety of aircraft modified for photographic work including the F-8 Mosquito, F-5 Lightning, B-17s, and B-25 bombers. Jim Setchell's group only flew the Mosquito and eventually transitioned to the F-5 Lightning, which he had trained in at Peterson Field.

The commander of the 90th Wing was Colonel Elliott Roosevelt. Roosevelt was rated a bombardier/navigator, not a pilot, because of poor eyesight. Although he flew numerous combat missions, it was always in the capacity of a navigator. In his diary Jim Setchell recalls a mission he flew with his boss to Algiers: "Flew *Spook* to Algiers November 10, 1943, with FDR Jr. Stayed all night at Hotel Argo. Went to night club that closed at 8:30. Dancing strictly prohibited. Terrible champagne for 225 Francs per bottle." As the old saying goes, "War is hell." Then on December 7 Jim, being Elliott's tentmate, found himself in select company. Reads his diary: "Attended supper with President, Harry Hopkins, Generals Eisenhower, Spaatz, Curtis, Smith and Norstad, Colonel MacDonald [Spaatz's intelligence chief], Colonel Karl 'Pop' Polifka" and others. Such diversions were indeed a rarity. Jim was there to fight in a bloody war. As a matter of fact he understood his role all too well and would fly the most dangerous missions assigned to his group himself, instead of sending his young and less experienced lieutenants.

In January 1944 the 90th Wing, Reconnaissance, including its 3rd Group, moved from Tunisia to San Severo, Italy. As part of the wing's move Colonel Karl "Pop" Polifka assumed command of the wing, relieving Colonel Elliott Roosevelt. San Severo was one of the many airfields near Foggia from where the 15th Air Force launched its B-17 and B-24 raids against targets in southern Germany, Austria, and Romania. Jim writes in his diary: "At the 5th Army Headquarters & front: Jan 15 and 16—lived in tent with Colonel Fogelsang and Pop [Polifka]. Jan 17—*Spook* hit by flak over Formia. Kept piece of flak from wing as souvenir. Jan 22—Flew *Spook* on mission over invasion fleet off Anzio harbor."

The target areas to be photographed that Jim briefly referred to in his diary entries were heavily defended by German AAA of all calibers. For the missions he flew on January 16, 17, and 22 he was awarded the Distinguished Flying Cross. The citation accompanying the award of the DFC reads, "A major tactical problem was the location of well-camouflaged guns that were taking a costly toll of Allied troops. Faced with the urgent need to find the locations of the German guns so they could be knocked out and many lives saved, Lieutenant Colonel Setchell, as commanding officer of the 3rd Photo Group, proposed to fly missions to locate the guns at 10,000 to 12,000 feet—less than half the normal operational altitude and well within range of all enemy anti-aircraft guns. Three missions were flown on January 16, 17 and 22 in an obsolete Mark IV Mosquito, the only aircraft available with camera equipment suitable for the task. The flak was intense and accurate. Lieutenant Colonel Setchell, knowing full well the importance of his mission, flew faultless flight-lines straight through the thickest of enemy defenses over Formia and Gaeta, Italy. The next day, 17 January, a similar mission was planned, and again Colonel Setchell took the assignment. This time his aircraft was hit repeatedly over the battle lines near Cassino and the Volturo River. Colonel Setchell completed the mission before limping back to base with gaping holes in his aircraft. Then, on 22 January, a similar mission was flown over Anzio harbor and the airdrome at Nettuna. The pictures obtained on these three missions were of vital importance to the Fifth Army and resulted in the saving of many lives, as well as contributing substantially to the advance of our armies. For cool courage and daring, superior airmanship and devotion to duty far beyond the call of duty, these sorties rank high in leadership, gallantry and devotion to duty. . . ." Jim Setchell was lucky to have survived. It was the time when American and British forces landed at Anzio, a drive that soon stalled, turning into a bloody battle, pounded by some of Germany's heaviest guns, guns which Jim had been tasked to locate so they could be destroyed.

In the months to come Jim Setchell flew his share of combat missions, including two missions to Cairo, photographing German dispositions on the island of Crete, and two missions into the Soviet Union, photographing targets en route and on the way back. By September 10, 1944, Jim had transitioned to the F-5, the unarmed photo-reconnaissance version of the P-38 Lightning. His group still flew the Mosquito, but as for *The Spook*, it had met its end on August 19, 1944, when the aircraft was destroyed in a crash landing after returning from a combat mission. Jim's diary tells the story of what happened next:

Sept 10, 1944: Departed from San Severo in F-5 #123. Landed at Bari and had fuel topped off. Made proper clearance and departed at 1045. Flew on the deck, weather clear and hazy, but could see island of Corfu for good check point. Approached my first target on the deck over water, dropping tanks 4 minutes off shore. Passed over harbor of Piraeus, pulled up to 300' as I crossed the coast and started my cameras. The target for a planned airborne drop was easily visible. I crossed directly over it with front and right oblique cameras operating. Noted about 40 large seaplane transports in the harbor and several active transports on Kalamika airdrome. Saw no light or heavy flak or gun flashes, but after passing Kalamika the plane lurched violently to the right while passing over a target.

Trimmed to the left and noticed a large hole in the right rear tail-boom, probably made by 20mm flak. The right rudder must have sustained some damage as well, causing the plane to swing to the right. The lower cockpit window was smashed, inflicting several cuts on my right hand. After trimming to the left, the plane operated OK. Apparently neither engine had been hit. I skirted hills and proceeded to my second target. Again I approached from over water on the deck and pulled up to 300' as I crossed the coast, starting my cameras. Many people were on the beach. After passing Khalkis harbor the temperature on the right engine suddenly hit the peg. Looking at the engine I saw fire under the engine spreading along the entire length of the boom. The fire increased rapidly, the cockpit filling with smoke making it impossible for me to see the instrument panel. I pulled the emergency canopy release, put down the left window and at about 1350 ditched the plane. The plane landed very well, then swung sharply to the left before stopping, twisting my right shoulder. I unfastened my safety belt, picked up my dinghy and first aid kit and stepped out on the left wing. Then I pulled the Mae West cords and stepped off the wing into the water as the plane sank nose first. I was about 50 yards off shore. Salt water made cuts on my arm and hand very painful. I floated fine in the Mae West survival jacket and chose not to inflate the dinghy. I noticed people on shore and waved to them. Finally a boat approached with two men in it, stopping about 50 feet from where I was. I shouted 'Americano. Americano.' One of the men fingered a mean looking gun, but they finally came toward me and pulled me into the boat. They were Greek fishermen. Thank God! We then pulled in my dinghy and parachute, which was floating nearby. We reached shore and several people put their arms around me, smiled, saying 'Americano.' By using the phrase book I carried they assured me that they would keep me safely away from the Germans. Three or four young men had old rifles with gun belts across their chests. They escorted me up a winding trail to a church, announcing proudly that they were partisans. In the priest's bedroom I removed my wet clothes while the priest bandaged my arm and hand. They gave me native clothes to wear, and I ate a good meal—goat, potatoes, brown bread and raisin wine. After an hour's rest in the priest's bed, complete with clean sheets, I awoke from pain in my shoulder and hand. The priest brought in my clothes, which had been dried and pressed. About dark, a doctor arrived and told me in English that I was to spend the night in his house. He rebandaged my arm and hand and massaged my shoulder which hurt intensely. I slept that night in a comfortable bed and fully realizing how fortunate I was. I had asked the doctor about contacting English or American forces, and while he claimed he had no knowledge of their whereabouts, he assured me that the partisans would see to it that I was taken care of properly.

Sept 11: Spent the morning talking to two Greeks from nearby towns who had lived in America. They emphatically assured me that I was safe and would not be turned over to the Germans. In the afternoon I talked to the doctor who was remembering more and more of his English. He had been a political prisoner of the Germans for two months during which time 40 or 50 prisoners from his camp were shot daily. He had studied medicine in Vienna for seven years, and his former professor, who was now in Athens in an official capacity, had obtained his release. A few days before my arrival, the Germans had come and taken most of his furniture, silver, and things he was not able to hide before fleeing into the mountains with the rest of the villagers. I walked around his property noting that he had an old Ford truck (no petrol) and Ford tractor. I watched the operation of his olive oil press. He informed me that we were leaving early in the morning.

Sept 12: At 0400 we, the doctor and two partisans, started along a narrow rocky road. After about a mile we met up with a two wheeled cart which carried us over a very rough road to Ata. We rested for an hour, sitting at a small sidewalk café. A large crowd formed to have a look at the American. Pictures were taken with the partisan chief who sported a full beard, 3 gun belts, 4 knives, a rifle with a bayonet, binoculars, big tassels on his shoes, and a funny little round hat. He said that the uniform and most equipment had been taken from Germans he had killed. He seemed a comic figure until the doctor told me that his brother and two sisters had all been killed by the Germans. I gave the partisan chief an American dollar bill as a souvenir and he gave me some German money he had taken from one of his victims. We continued on a motorcycle which had been left behind by the English. When we arrived at Lev, people lined the streets, clapping their hands, and gave me flowers and fruit. I sat in the town square drinking ouzo with three men who had lived in America. People crowded around wanting to know when the American and British armies would arrive. Small children marched by with wooden guns singing partisan songs. Being stared at by the multitude was getting tiresome and I was glad when the doctor told me that we were leaving for another town for lunch. After about an hour's ride on the motorcycle we arrived in the small town of Akos. Here I watched a parade. More flowers and fruit, and I was prodded to make a speech from a little balcony with a Greek interpreter by my side. That evening we had a wonderful dinner of fish, macaroni, chicken, potatoes, salad, wine, fruit and olive oil cake. The cake took all my democratic spirit and stomach to get it down. But I was informed that the girls of the town had made it especially for the American— so down it went. I asked where the Germans were and was told that none had been reported in the area for days. I walked around the town. Saw the damage that had been done by German naval ships when they shelled the town after a fight between the Germans and partisans. After a short motorcycle ride and a three hour mule trip up a mountain trail we arrived at the small village of Ka. The doctor and I stayed in a simple peasant's home, ate some kind of stew from a common pot. No plates. We slept on the floor with plenty beautifully colored blankets.

Sept 13: Breakfast of black bread and goat cheese. The doctor informed me that we had come to this village as he had been told that there was some sort of Allied military mission nearby. We learned the mission had recently been attacked by the Germans and moved, so we returned to the doctors home in Mel by motorcycle, arriving after dark."

As for Dorothy, Jim's wife, being told of her husband being shot down, that didn't happen. The familiar Western Union telegram was sent instead to Jim's father in early October 1944 stating, "THE SECRETARY OF WAR DESIRES ME TO EXPRESS HIS DEEP REGRET THAT YOUR SON LIEUTENANT COLONEL JAMES F SETCHELL HAS BEEN REPORTED MISSING IN ACTION SINCE SEPTEMBER ELEVEN OVER GREECE. IF FURTHER DETAILS OR OTHER INFORMATION ARE RECEIVED YOU WILL BE PROMPTLY NOTIFIED. J A ULIO ADJUTANT GENERAL." Jim's father had Western Union resend the telegram to Dorothy, informing her of what happened. Times were different then. But one thing has not changed—no one wants to receive a telegram, or communication of whatever kind, like this.

Sept 14: In the morning I helped the doctor make a cast for a partisan who had been shot through the thigh. In the afternoon I watched him remove the eye of a Russian partisan who had been wounded in a fire fight. I couldn't last out the operation and got out of the room just prior to passing out. I spent a couple of hours listening to the rantings of a communist who spoke very poor English—but he helped kill time. In the evening I watched the doctor dress the arm of a villager. He had removed the man's shattered hand in the woods at night by lantern light while the Germans were in the village. Had a good supper of chicken. Saw pathfinder flares from planes probably bombing Athens. The doctor advised me we were leaving again early in the morning. A motorcycle driver arrived claiming that many Dakota planes had landed at the mission site. I went to sleep with high hopes of soon being on my way back to Italy.

Sept 15: Departed at 0500 for the mission. Passed through several villages. Partisans on horseback directed us down roads and across fields to avoid German troops. We rode along a railroad track while a train loaded with German troops passed. After a three hour mule trip we arrived at the mission. There I was met by a British major, an Australian captain and interpreters. Had an excellent supper cooked by an American chef. Sent a radio message to the 90th that I was safe. Pleasant evening of ouzo, radio, English conversation and bed. During the morning saw 60 B-24s passing overhead.

Sept 16: The doctor returned home this morning. I walked part way down the trail with him, very sorry to part company. A sincere friendship had sprung up between us and I feel a great indebtedness toward him for the aid he has given me at great risk to himself. Had a conversation with the British major. His current job was sabotage, distributing air dropped guns, ammunition and supplies, and keeping his station one jump ahead of the Germans. A sergeant gave me fresh clothes and toilet articles. What a privilege to properly clean my teeth. He also bandaged my arm and hand which were healing nicely.

Sept 17: Have been sleeping on a pine bow bed. Very cold at night, but have plenty of blankets. Food has been excellent, cooked American style without olive oil. Sent another radio message to Cairo regarding evacuation point for me.

Sept 20: Drank our last ouzo and we are out of sugar. Waiting for next plane to arrive, and a messenger who had been sent to Athens for supplies. Athens is the best supplied city in Europe. Plenty of whiskey, chocolate, cigars. Members of the station often put on civilian clothes and spend several days in Athens mingling with the Germans. Forged passes are prepared and the only real danger is of being picked up when the Germans decide to gather up a few hostages. What a strange war.

Sept 21: An F-5 flew directly overhead making slight vapor trails. So near and yet so far. About 2000 a Dakota dropped three men and supplies from Italy.

Sept 22: Two hour hike to drop area. Helped round up chutes and supplies. Partisans and goat herders trying to steal everything. The major announced that the mission would be moving tomorrow and I will be in the advance party.

Sept 23: Up at 0600 for a four hour hike down the mountain to a fishing village. Got in a fishing boat and after about four hours rowing the fishermen decided the wind was too bad and turned around. Had a fish supper and slept on the floor of an old shack. Rats running around and over me all night. Very little sleep.

Sept 25: The British major arrived with no news. He is very friendly and says if I want to take a boat to Turkey he will accompany me to the coast.

Sept 26: Was told by the major that all boats heading for the coast of Turkey had been captured by the Germans.

Sept 27: Up at 0630, but the mules were not ready until 1000. The major gave me 10 gold sovereigns for which I gave him useless American paper money from my escape kit. I also had a parachute for bartering purposes. Walked about one mile out of the village when a charcoal burning bus picked us up and delivered us to Yer. An old woman on the bus gave me some green olives and cheese. The bus trip was uneventful—all downhill. At the coast the sea was too rough and we had to wait.

Sept 28: Spent two hours picking up shells along the beach to keep from going slap happy. Supper of bread and cheese. Tired of people standing around and staring at me.

Sept 29: Boarded a fishing schooner. Our schooner passed close to a town occupied by the Germans. Everyone was on the alert looking for German boats. We finally reached Galax. Went to the home of a lady who was the Greek wife of an Englishman, and had lived in India. I'm in heaven. Tea with maple sugar and grapes as soon as we arrive. Someone to talk to in English. Wonderful supper. Then listened to Victrola music before going to bed in an elegant bedroom. Paid one gold sovereign and parachute panels.

Sept 30: Twelve hours of walking and mule riding. Passed through Levireki. Every house destroyed and burned. Spent the night in priest's house in Lefkadeti and collected an army of fleas. Paid with parachute panels.

Oct 3: Arrived at English mission headquarters. Had tea and cakes. Wonderful to sleep on real bed, fleas exterminated. Paid for mules with one gold sovereign. Waiting for a plane to arrive.

Oct 8: Four weeks in Greece. Even Italy will look good. No plane.

On October 8, 1944, Colonel Polifka, Jim Setchell's boss, wrote a brief letter of encouragement to Jim's wife. "Dear Dottie, I am sorry I was unable to write to you these details before, but I was unable to do so because of the necessary time lapse which we must allow for and beside I was hoping that by allowing a little time I would not have to write you. Jim's last mission was a low level mission in the Athens area in making final preparation for the recent invasion of Greece by two British divisions. The only opposition anticipated was a heavy concentration of forty and eighty-eight millimeter anti aircraft on one of the coves. Here the heavy assault landing was to be made. I believe that Jim probably received a crippling hit on this run and hope that he was forced to crash land in the vicinity. I fully expect to send him home to you on thirty days leave before Easter as we have been fortunate in having every one of our people who have crash landed in this particular operational area return to us within four or five months time. I will not offer you condolences as I feel positive that Jim is okay. Sincerely, Karl."

Oct 10: Weather rainy and cold. American captain arrived with 3 American enlisted men to be evacuated. Also 3 Americans (OSS), two with fever and one with a broken leg. No plane.

Oct 12: Weather very good but informed there would be no plane tonight. Evacuation tomorrow night. So at least I have something to look forward to. After supper there was much shooting and hand grenades being set off to announce the liberation of Athens after almost four years occupation. All English and Americans went to the local café where we sat with the villagers drinking great quantities of ouzo. Listened to many good Greek songs—You Are My Sunshine, Down By the Old Mill Stream and Show Me The Way To Go Home.

Oct 13: Weather wonderful—no airplane.

Oct 14: Four Me 109s flying east in wide formation at 500'. At 1300 a Halifax circles several times, but didn't land. Another message sent to Cairo requesting plane immediately for commando with broken leg and myself.

Oct 16: American commandos and I had a long discussion on proceeding to Athens and getting a plane from there to Italy. However, the highway is in German hands. No plane.

On October 23 Jim Setchell finally managed to get a ride on a Red Cross truck from Karditsa south to Lamia, escorting the American with the broken leg. The roads were terrible, bridges were blown requiring detours through rough mountain country. Finally, on the morning of October 25 he reached Athens. The American with the broken leg was cared for at a Red Cross hospital, and Jim found luxury accommodations in the Grand Britain Hotel. Life in Athens seemed normal to him, as if there was no war going on. The following day he got a ride to Kalamika Airdrome and caught a ride to Bari, Italy, just across the Ionian Sea from Greece, accompanied by wounded British paratroopers on stretchers and four war correspondents. His odyssey, which never took him further than a hundred miles from Athens, ended practically where his plane had crashed six weeks earlier.

In a letter to Dorothy, on November 4, 1944, after returning to his unit, Jim writes, "Darling Hag, Pop [Colonel Polifka] returned yesterday from his trip to the States, and what a celebration we had last night. He brought three bottles of bourbon, which we consumed with the greatest of ease. Since my return I have been busy with physical checkups and interrogations from various headquarters regarding my experiences. For security reasons I have been taken off combat flying, so now must do my flying over friendly territory. No

The Spook and Major Jim Setchell at Prestwick, Scotland, on his way to La Marsa, Tunisia, 1943.

Luftwaffe remnants littered La Marsa, 1943.

more flak or fighters, and of course goodbye to most of the thrills and fun. All I can tell you now of my trip is that my plane was hit by flak, caught fire, and I landed it in the water. I had the laugh on lots of the boys when I got back because most of them swore it was impossible to successfully land a P-38 in the water without it immediately going to the bottom. I got out of it before it went down. My several weeks of wanderings in the mountains, and how I finally got back to Italy are, of course, secret. But you'll know the whole story after the war."

Anzio Annie (Leopold), a giant railway gun, along with another (Robert), was used effectively against the Allies at Anzio. Jim Setchell flew several missions to locate these guns so they could be destroyed. They never were, but were captured in June 1944 and brought to the US. Anzio Annie is on display at the Army Ordinance Museum, Fort Lee, Virginia.

Lieutenant Colonel James F. Setchell survived the war and returned to his wife and young son after nearly two years of combat, decorated with the Silver Star, the Distinguished Flying Cross, four awards of the Air Medal, and the Purple Heart. Most of all he was happy to have survived. Before war's end Jim was promoted to colonel and continued to serve as operations officer of the 90th Reconnaissance Wing in Italy. For the next thirteen years he and his family moved around the country, he filling various reconnaissance and intelligence related positions. In 1958 he was assigned to attend the Industrial College of the Armed Forces, ICAF, at Fort McNair, Washington, DC. Years later, I myself would attend the National War College at Fort McNair, located adjacent to the ICAF building. While an ICAF student, Jim became seriously ill. A brain tumor terminated his attendance at ICAF. He underwent two surgeries, was taken off flying status, and subsequently retired from his beloved United States Air Force—a heartbreaking experience for this dedicated officer. He died in 1960 to join the many flyers who had gone west before him. Jim, The Hero, and Dorothy, The Hag, who died in 1975, are buried at Arlington National Cemetery.

La Marsa, Tunisia, December 7, 1943: Lt/Colonel James Setchell is sitting at the far end of the table. To President Roosevelt's right sits General Dwight D. Eisenhower. On the President's left sits Lt/General Carl "Tooey" Spaatz, then the commander of the 12th Air Force and the Northwest African Air Forces (NAAF). Major General Walter Bedell Smith, Eisenhower's Chief of Staff, is sitting next to General Spaatz. Major General Lauris Norstad, then Assistant Chief of Staff of the NAAF sits next to General Smith. Colonel Roosevelt sits across from his father, and to his left in civilian clothes, sits the ever present Harry Hopkins, President Roosevelt's trusted advisor. This picture was taken just after the second Cairo conference (4–6 December 1943), where Roosevelt and Churchill met with President Ismet Inonu of Turkey. The President was homeward bound, stopping at La Marsa for the evening, an opportunity to meet with his generals and his son. General Spaatz would become the first Chief of Staff of the newly created US Air Force in 1947; General Norstad would end his career as Supreme Allied Commander Europe (SACEUR), and Commander in Chief US European Command.

THOUGHTS ABOUT SACRIFICE AND A TERRIBLE WAR— THE COST OF VICTORY

Flying West

I hope there's a place, way up in the sky,
where pilots can go, when they have to die.
A place where a guy can buy a cold beer
for a friend and a comrade, whose memory is dear.
A place where no doctor or lawyer can tread,
nor a management type would ere be caught dead.
Just a quaint little place, kind of dark, full of smoke,
where they like to sing loud, and love a good joke.
The kind of a place where a lady could go
and feel safe and protected, by the men she would know.
There must be a place where old pilots go
when their paining is finished, and their airspeed gets low.
Where the whiskey is old, and the women are young,
and songs about flying and dying are sung.
Where you'd see all the fellows who'd flown west before,
and they'd call out your name, as you came through the door.
Who would buy you a drink, if your thirst should be bad,
and relate to the others, "He was quite a good lad!"
And then through the mist, you'd spot an old guy
you had not seen in years, though he taught you to fly.
He'd nod his old head, and grin ear to ear; and say,
"Welcome, my son, I'm pleased that you're here.
For this is the place where true flyers come,
when their journey is over, and the war has been won.
They've come here at last to be safe and alone

423

from the government clerks and the management clone,
politicians and lawyers, the Feds and the noise,
where all hours are happy, and these good ole boys
can relax with a cool one, and a well deserved rest.
This is heaven, my son, you've passed your last test."
—Author unknown

There is an old canard among sophisticated strategists: battles, even wars, are won and lost before the first shell is fired. There is a lot of truth to that old saying, and there are plenty of examples to be found in World War II to validate the concept. Yet, not until the battles are fought, until men meet in deadly combat, does that truth prevail. To put it simply, you can make all the plans you want; in the end men have to go out and die to put them into action. Applying even rudimentary common sense it would seem that an attack by the Empire of the Rising Sun on the United States was doomed to failure from its beginning—they didn't have the manpower, the natural resources, nor the technologies and industrial capacity to prevail in a conflict against an adversary such as the United States. Yet, twisted logic and emotion ruled the day, and on December 7, 1941, there was no turning back—the war that could not be won was begun in a manner that could only end with total defeat for Japan—as it did. Men had to die by the hundreds of thousands to prove that Japan's form of empire building was no longer a viable concept. Hitler's ascent to power was a political anomaly, yet it happened in a unique post–World War I environment that provided rich opportunities for demagogues to rise to power—not only in Germany, but in Italy, Spain, and Russia as well. Hitler's Third Reich could probably have survived for years, like Stalin's Soviet Union, through pure terror and repression. Yet it was war that Hitler chose in the briefest amount of time after coming to power, not only against Great Britain, France, and Stalin's Russia, but when the time came, he added to his foes a sleeping industrial giant—the United States of America. Before long Germany was fighting a three-front war—in the Mediterranean, Russia, and the west. But before the predictable outcome arrived in May 1945, not tens of thousands, but tens of millions of men, women, and children had to die to prove a schoolyard truism—to prevail in conflict you have to make more friends than enemies. Both Japan and Germany did exactly the opposite. World War II was not a schoolyard scenario, and the outcome was a devastated Europe and Asia, the dislocation of millions of people, not to mention the loss of human life for which there is no accurate count, only approximations which run well beyond fifty million dead.

As the war expanded after September 1, 1939, and came into full bloom on December 7, 1941, the United States military establishment seemed ill equipped and undersized for the task at hand. The Army Air Corps possessed 1,700 aircraft, many of them obsolete, and it had an officer corps of 1,600.[89] By the time war ended in 1945, sixteen million Americans had worn the uniforms of America's military services, and its once-dated army and air corps had grown in size and quality, defeating its adversaries in battles of a magnitude and ferocity probably never to be fought again. As Richard H. Kohn, the chief of the Office of Air Force History put it in a letter on April 13, 1982, to Lieutenant General Jerome F. O'Malley (AF/XO): "[I]t took until 1944 to produce the aircraft and crews in the numbers necessary to accomplish the job. AWPD-1 called for a total of 61,799 operational aircraft and 1,164,916 military personnel. As of June 1944, the AAF possessed 78,757 planes of every conceivable type and 2,372,292 military personnel."[90]

That brings me to the men who fought the battles. They were individuals from all walks of life, mostly young, very young, in their teens and early twenties, who formed bomber crews, squadrons, groups, wings, and air forces, and then assembled in the sky to fly into the unknown—into combat against a battle-tested enemy. Good training can prepare a young man to fly an airplane, but there is no real way to teach young men how to die. The scope of conflict may be worldwide, but in the end combat is an individual thing—one man flying against another, a bomber crew never turning back in spite of brutal opposition. Doing it again, and again, and again after searing losses. The Bloody 100th, as the men of the 100th Bombardment Group referred to themselves, flying their B-17 bombers out of Thorpe Abbots, England, in 306 missions, lost 177 of their bombers.[91] Each B-17 carried a crew of ten—meaning that 1,770 airmen died, went missing in action, or became prisoners of war. More were wounded or perished in training or crashed into each other while assembling in poor weather over their air bases. It all gets very personal for the men fighting a war—it is me against him, us against them, all for one, one for all. It was deemed a remarkable achievement in early 1943 when a B-17F, the *Memphis Belle*, piloted by Robert Morgan of the 91st Bombardment Group, completed twenty-five combat missions on May 17 over German-held territory without losing any of its crew. Twenty-five combat missions were implemented as an operational tour of duty to give aircrews a 50 percent chance of survival in the 8th Air Force. Later in 1944 with the introduction of long-range escort fighters, principally P-51s, and a general decline of the German fighter force, a tour of duty was lengthened to thirty and then thirty-five combat missions. For air crews assigned to the 15th Air Force in Italy the number of combat missions required varied, but was higher than that required of 8th Air Force air crews.

War is a collection of searing stories of individual sacrifice, courage, endurance, suffering, and in the end prevailing—if you are on the winning side. The stories I presented in this book are of young men, boys in many cases, flying their fighters and bombers over North Africa, Europe, and the vastness of the Pacific. Those who survived were changed men, not boys anymore, and never again would view the world through the young and naive eyes of yesterday. Doesn't everybody know how awful war really is? No, they don't. Most only read about it. Even if in uniform, only a small fraction of men, and today women as well, are directly involved in life or death situations, facing the enemy, risking their lives. The great uniformed majority is, so to speak, "passing the ammunition." That is not meant to be pejorative; it is a fact of warfare—if you run out of supplies, you are going to lose. Hitler and Napoleon never learned that lesson when invading Russia, both invasions failing miserably not because of lack of courage on the part of their men, but because they ran out of the necessities to sustain life and combat. The Japanese, never expecting the American fleet to move as fast as it did, quickly lost the initiative and found themselves on the defensive within months of starting a war they could not win. Admiral William "Bull" Halsey and his staff quickly figured out that if they wanted to take the fight to the enemy they needed the necessary supplies, especially fuel, to keep the fleet moving forward and fighting. So the admiral prepositioned tankers at forward locations, and had others meet the fleet en route, refueling his ships as they were heading into battle. Halsey's slogan, "Hit hard, hit fast, hit often," worked—because he had the means to do so.

As time passes, the experiences of those who prevailed in combat are largely forgotten and replaced by the global aspects of conflict—dates, places, and numbers. It is a depersonalizing process that occurs over time and as the participants of a war fade from the scene. No longer do we remember the heroic deeds of individual men, their courage, struggles, failures, and triumphs, but rather we tend to focus on dates, places, and numbers—it is an inevitable, and yes, depersonalizing process, which we refer to as *history*. James D. Hornfisher, the author of *The Last Stand of the Tin Can Sailors*, in a *Wall Street Journal* article entitled "The Passing of the World War II Generation," put it this way: "For those of us who have never served in uniform, it's easy to see World War II as a grand, sweeping drama, featuring actors large and small driven by a sense of overriding mission, all sins and failings vindicated by victory. Yet for the veterans I meet, the war is often about something else entirely. Any talk of it brings them back to a single, pervasive memory sequence. . . when through their action or inaction, they believe, a comrade paid the eternal price. . . . They can't talk about the war without revealing how it changed them."[92] For the direct participants in war, those who shoot and are shot at, it is a very personal and life-changing experience—it was for me as a young child, and I never was the same again after that. In the preceding stories I've attempted to present the personal aspects of war through the eyes of the men who fought our battles. They are the stories of survivors—the dead can't talk. So I think it is worthwhile to provide some context, to look at some of the dates, places, and numbers which defined the environment of the World War II airmen, and of those who continued flying for their country into the Cold War years.

War came on September 1, 1939, when Hitler's armies invaded Poland, which provided the incentive for the War Plans Division of the War Department General Staff to get serious about planning for war. In July of 1941 President Franklin D. Roosevelt asked for an estimate of "over-all production requirements to defeat our potential enemies," the potential enemies at the time being Germany and Italy. The US was still at peace then, yet actively planned for a war that seemed inevitable. The blueprint that evolved became known as AWPD-1. Air War Plans Division plan number 1 "emphasized precision bombing of specified targets designed to wreck the military, industrial, and economic structure of Germany. The major targets were electrical power, transportation and POL. The German Air Force was labeled an intermediate objective." The plan's success depended on the AAF's bombers being able to penetrate deep into Germany, and concluded that this could be done by day from high altitude—a strategic concept that had been advocated by such air power visionaries as Giulio Douhet and William "Billy" Mitchell. Just in case the Flying Fortress proved not as invincible as its name suggested, a long-range escort fighter was proposed as well. The plan was approved, noting that an air offensive could be started as early as mid-1942; however, an all-out offensive would not be possible until April 1944, depending on the production and delivery of aircraft. Amazingly, this general plan proved to be quite accurate and served as a blueprint for the buildup of the Army Air Forces. At war's end in Europe in May 1945 the AAF possessed a total of 69,089 aircraft worldwide, 17,061 of which were part of the United States Strategic Air Forces based on 152 air bases in Europe, serviced and flown by 450,000 airmen.[93]

War came to the United States on December 7, 1941, not totally unexpectedly, but very suddenly. The Japanese attack on Pearl Harbor, Hawaii, was quickly followed by a declaration of war against the United States by Adolf Hitler, who believed that it was his duty to stand by his Japanese ally. By January 1942, only a month after Hitler's irrational declaration of war against the United States, the 8th Air Force was stood up at Savannah Field, Georgia, today the army's Hunter Army Airfield. Colonel Asa A. Duncan assumed command of the 8th on January 28. Once he moved the headquarters to Bushy Park, a leafy London suburb, Major General Carl "Tooey" Spaatz assumed command. Many years later, in 1955, I myself was stationed at Bushy Park as a young airman, working in the same barracks which once housed not only the 8th AAF headquarters, but also General Eisenhower's headquarters. General Spaatz relinquished command of the 8th to Lieutenant General Ira C. Eaker on December 1, 1942, and thirteen months later returned from the MTO to take command of the United States Strategic Air Forces in Europe, including the 8th Air Force, for the remainder of the war in Europe. In addition, the 15th Air Force was stood up on November 1, 1943, in the MTO, with the aim of operating against German targets when the 8th Air Force in England was unable to do so because of weather. The 15th, commanded by Major General Doolittle, began life in Tunis, Tunisia, with six heavy bomb groups of B-17 and B-24 bombers. By November 1943 Major General Nathan F. Twining, a future USAF chief of staff, assumed command of the 15th, and General Doolittle took over the reigns of the 8th Air Force from General Eaker. By that time the 15th had grown to its full strength of twenty-one bomb groups. The 8th and the 15th were the major strategic air forces to take the war to the German heartland, supported by the 9th and 12th Tactical Air Forces and eventually the 1st Tactical Air Force (Provisional), a creation of General Spaatz, all of which flew medium bombers and fighters.

The 8th Air Force based in England consisted of three air divisions. The 1st and 3rd air divisions were mostly equipped with B-17 bombers, while the 2nd Air Division flew B-24s. The 2nd and 3rd air divisions were composed of fourteen bombardment groups; the first had twelve groups for a total of forty bomb groups. Each bomb group had four bombardment squadrons with twelve aircraft nominally assigned. A steady stream of replacement aircraft and crews kept the 8th Air Force at a two thousand bomber level, which it reached for the first time on June 6, 1944, the day of the Normandy landings, and maintained thereafter. The 8th flew its first combat mission on July 4, 1942. It was a combined British/American raid against four German airfields in the Netherlands. Three of four A-20 Boston bombers, belonging to the Royal Air Force, flown by American crews, were shot down. One aircraft, although damaged, flown by the squadron's commander, Captain Charles C. Kegelman, managed to return to its home base of Swanton Morley. The mission set the tone in terms of losses of what was to come in daylight bombing raids against German-occupied Europe.[94] By August 17, 1942, the 8th launched its first heavy bomber raid against a target in France with twelve B-17s from the 97th Bomb Group. All aircraft returned with only superficial damage. One of the pilots was Major Paul W. Tibbets, who in August 1945 would end the war in the Pacific flying a B-29 named *Enola Gay*, dropping one of two atomic bombs dropped on Japan—the *Enola Gay* is displayed at the Udvar Hazy center of the National Air and Space Museum near Dulles International Airport in Virginia. Of the 111 men who flew on that first B-17 mission, 31 would soon be killed or go missing. They never came close to completing twenty-five combat missions.[95]

The 8th Air Force would take some horrendous losses in the next 33 months. Focusing on "specific targets designed to wreck the military, industrial and

The remains of 42-230725, a B-17F from the Bloody 100th, downed on October 10, 1943, near Muenster. The 100th lost twelve aircraft that day—120 men.

economic structure of Germany," as prescribed by AWPD-1, the 8th set to work to wreck the German ball bearing industry. In a raid on August 17, 1943, against Schweinfurt and Regensburg, 60 aircraft were shot down, 4 more returned home but were no longer flyable, and 168 B-17s were damaged. Suddenly there were 600 empty bunk beds, and daylight raids were quickly throttled back. A raid on September 6 of that year against ball bearing plants around Stuttgart lost another 45 aircraft, 10 more returned home but never flew again, and another 116 were damaged. The 8th returned to Schweinfurt on October 14. It was deja vu—60 Fortresses shot down, 7 damaged beyond repair, and another 138 with some kind of battle damage. Even after the introduction of long-range escort fighters the carnage continued. A raid on January 11, 1944, against Oschersleben and Brunswick cost another 60 aircraft, and on a raid on the Big B, Berlin, on March 6, 1944, 51 aircraft were shot down. The commanding general of the Army Air Forces, General Henry "Hap" Arnold, put immense pressure on the commander of the 8th Air Force, Lt/General Ira C. Eaker, to intensify his raids, no matter the losses. When Eaker didn't move fast enough for Arnold, he was replaced by Lieutenant General James H. Doolittle, then a lieutenant colonel, who led the early 1942 B-25 raid against Japan.[96]

Air Chief Marshal Sir Arthur Harris, who became better known as "Bomber Harris," and RAF Bomber Command had flown its first thousand bomber raid on May 30, 1942. What was keeping the 8th Air Force from doing the same? A simple fact. Eaker was losing aircraft and crews faster than he could replace them, much less assemble a force of a thousand bombers. When Lt/ General Spaatz returned to take over the United States Strategic Air Forces headquartered at Bushy Park, Arnold took the opportunity to replace Eaker with Major General Doolittle, who until then had commanded the 15th AAF in the Mediterranean. The first 8th Air Force thousand bomber raid didn't come until February 3, 1945, in a raid on Berlin. I had just turned ten the day before. I will never forget that raid. My family was spared, but it was close. Just over two thousand old men, women, and children died in the raid, variously reported as over twenty thousand, which is incorrect. Yet, two thousand deaths is nearly four times the number of civilians who died when the Luftwaffe raided Coventry in 1940.[97]

The United States Strategic Bombing Survey conducted immediately after the war lists the operational loss of 5,945 heavy bombers, B-24s and B-17s, by the 8th Air Force. That does not include those who made it home and crashed, those lost forming up for a bombing raid, and others lost in training which came to an additional 607 bombers. The 15th Air Force, according to the *USS Bombing Survey*, in less than a year lost another 2,380 B-17s and B-24s. The total losses of aircraft in the European Theater (a curious term) of Operations in combat, not including other losses, came to nearly 10,000 heavy bombers over a period of less than four years, and 8,420 fighters, for a total of 18,369 aircraft lost in combat. The actual losses, including various other accidents not involving combat, took that total to well over 20,000 aircraft.[98] Aircraft were made of aluminum, easily replaced. The air crews were flesh and blood, young men and boys—their lives were not replaceable.

No World War II set of numbers is ever totally correct, but the following put out by the US Air Force are about as close as I could come. In the ETO 94,565 airmen were listed as combat casualties. Of those, 30,099 were identified as killed in action, 13,660 were wounded and evacuated. The remaining 51,106 are listed as MIAs, POWs, evaders, and internees, the latter being a very small number. When the 26,000 Army Air Corps POWs are subtracted from that number, left are 25,000 MIAs (PL 490, 1946, formally declared all MIAs as KIA, allowing next of kin to be paid money due by the US Government. However, statistics of war casualties retain the MIA classification). That would bring the total death toll to nearly 55,000 men.[99] When I reviewed listings of numbers of AAF POWs held at various German camps, I came up with an AAF POW total of 33,035 men. Subtracting that number from the total MIAs still leaves an MIA count of 18,071. Adding that to the official count of 30,099 KIA would bring the number of airmen who perished in combat in the ETO to 48,170.[100] Another source estimates the total number of KIA by the AAF in the ETO at 55,000. The higher number reflects a POW estimate of only 26,000 men.[101] The *US Strategic Bombing Survey* lists a loss of 79,265 airmen in the ETO killed and missing in action. Using that number as a baseline and subtracting 33,035 (my estimate of the number of AAF POWs held by the Germans) brings the number of who actually perished in combat to 46,230. Maybe the closest we can come to the truth is found on the 8th Air Force Memorial in Arlington National Cemetery, which reads, "In memory of the 350,000 airmen who served and in memory of the 47,742 combat crewmen killed or missing who paid the supreme sacrifice." Numbers being what they are, the death toll of American airmen in the air war against Germany was close to the losses experienced by RAF Bomber Command.

RAF Bomber Command kept meticulous records of aircraft and personnel losses. The authoritative *Bomber Command War Diaries* lists the loss of 10,321 aircraft due to enemy action and operational crashes, very close to the total loss of bombers by the 8th/15th Air Forces in the ETO, although over a longer period of time, 1939–1945. The number of men killed in action, accidents, or dying as POWs came to 55,500, again close to AAF losses. That number does not include 1,479 ground crew and 91 women serving with the RAF. The number which does not parallel Army Air Forces losses is the number of Royal Air Force Bomber Command POWs, that being a mere 9,838 airmen and 52 ground crew.[102] By far the greatest number of operational sorties in Bomber Command were flown by Avro Lancaster bombers of which a total of 3,677 were lost. The highest loss was experienced on the night of March 30, 1944, when 96 of 795 attacking bombers were lost on a raid against Nuernberg—a loss rate of 11.8 percent.[103] The total number of airmen who died in the air war against Germany—American and British airmen, including many from throughout the Commonwealth countries—came to over 100,000. Stephen Ambrose, the noted author and dear friend who died all too young, puts the casualty count this way: "[T]wice as many AAF officers died in battle than in all the rest of the Army. On average, almost 4 percent of the bomber force were killed or missing in action on each mission. The mean number of missions completed for the Eighth Air Force was 14.72, meaning more than half its crews never got much past the halfway point in compiling the twenty-five missions required to go home. . . . [A]t least by late 1943 they had the satisfaction of a declining loss rate as they gained experience."[104]

Not included in most tallies are the men who died in flying training accidents in the United States. "The AAF lost 439 lives in the *primary* flight schools during the war. In *basic* flight schools there were 1,175 fatalities, while in *advanced* training—flying bigger, faster airplanes, with more complicated training—there were 1,888 deaths," according to Stephen Ambrose. But a far greater number of deaths among AAF flyers occurred when they got into their primary aircraft—fighter, medium, or heavy bombers. "In 1943 alone," wrote Ambrose, "850 airmen died in 298 B-24 accidents training in the States, leaving the survivors scared to death of their airplanes. . . . Once while fly-ing in formation, [George] McGovern's squadron was practicing warding off an attack. A two-engine B-25 dove on the B-24s. The B-24 pilots expected the B-25 to go under their formation, but instead the plane kept coming and collided head-on with a Liberator. There was an explosion that took out two other B-24s. Four bombers were just gone. Fortunately they did not have full crews in them—only the gunners and the pilots—but twenty-four men were dead."[105] Bob Hoover's early flying career is another good example. Before deploying to Europe, Hoover barely escaped a flaming P-39 fighter, and was shot down in a P-40 by a fellow flyer during target practice. Only a country like the United States, with a prolific production capacity and endowed richly with natural resources, could take such horrific losses in men and aircraft and end the war in Europe with an aircraft inventory of over 17,000. A total of 12,731 B-17s were built; another 18,482 B-24s in various versions joined the war effort against Germany and Japan. Tens of thousands of single- and twin-engine aircraft were produced, leading to a total production run for the year 1944 of over 92,000 aircraft—exceeding the aircraft production of all other belligerents, friend and foe, combined. Not only was American aircraft pro-duction prolific; the crews to maintain and man them were trained as well—but at a cost, of course, because everything was done in a hurry.

The air war against Germany was a combined operation between Ameri-can air forces and Britain's RAF Bomber Command. The Pointblank directive issued at the Casablanca conference on January 21, 1943, between President Roosevelt and Mr. Churchill formalized that arrangement. Each national command, however, decided how it was going to carry out its part of that directive. Bomber Command, after experiencing heavy losses in daylight raids against German targets, decided to fight its war at night, quickly expanding its four-engine bomber force of Lancaster, Stirling, and Halifax bombers. The principal targets of RAF Bomber Command were German population centers, specifically the housing of its working class—very different from the American approach of attacking critical industrial target sets. The technique employed by Bomber Command was to drop high explosive bombs on a city to damage roofs, then drop incendiaries, phosphorus bombs, to set the exposed houses on fire. Air Chief Marshall Arthur Harris, labeled Bomber Harris in later years, took command in February 1942. Harris believed along the lines of Giulio Douhet, the Italian bomber advocate, that the bomber, if employed properly, using high explosive and phosphorous bombs against population centers could so demoralize a population as to end a war. Har-ris's aim was not only to destroy, but to intimidate, and toward that end, and as soon as possible, he launched a series of one thousand bomber raids. The target cities were Cologne, for the first raid on the night of May 30, 1942; Essen and Bremen followed that June. To raise that number of bombers Harris had to use every available Lancaster, Halifax, and Stirling at his disposal, including those from training units. It was not a sustainable operation, but it was a first, to be followed by other raids of the same nature—when more aircraft and crews became available.

That time came in late July 1943. Harris ordered a series of four raids on the city of Hamburg. For the first time radar countermeasures were employed, what the British referred to as *window*, the Americans as *chaff*—small aluminum strips cut to the wavelengths of German radars saturated their radar screens with false returns, significantly reducing the effectiveness of the German antiaircraft defenses. The second of the four raids on the 27th of July proved devastating. A firestorm of never-experienced proportions developed, sucking the oxygen out of the air. If not burned to death, those seeking shelter in basements and cellars died of carbon monoxide poisoning. The death toll was terrifyingly high—no one knows exactly how many died, but it was estimated to be around forty-six thousand. The majority of those who died were women and children. Bomber Command raids continued along the same line of what proved so successful against Hamburg until near war's end. Only one other raid came close to the horror of Hamburg—Dresden. The war was nearing its end by early February 1945, obvious to every American or British general. The Russians were resting and resupplying their forces on the other side of the Oder River, east of Berlin, getting ready for the final push. American and British forces were getting close to their first foothold across the Rhine River, having defeated Hitler's last gasp at the Battle of the Bulge. Germany's armed forces were in disarray. Industrial and commercial activities across the country were grinding to a halt. The cumulative effect of American and British air raids was taking effect. On February 13, 1945, less than three months before war's end in Europe, Air Chief Marshall Harris launched a series of raids against the city of Dresden. Dresden was a rail center. Its schools had been turned into overflowing hospitals for wounded soldiers from the Russian front; the rail yards were filled with Red Cross trains and even more trains filled with refugees. The ensuing firestorm was reminiscent of what happened in Hamburg in 1943. After the first two Bomber Command raids, the 8th Air Force joined in a daylight raid. The death toll was overwhelming, more than Hamburg's forty thousand—no one actually knows for sure how many died in the inferno.

Writes Max Hastings, "[T]he attack on Dresden by Bomber Command and the American 8th Air Force between 13 and 15 February 1945, which destroyed the city and killed a minimum of 30,000 and perhaps as many as 100,000 people, aroused a revulsion even in the dying days of the war which has not been diminished by the passing of a generation."[106] It was pure chance that kept me and my small family from being among the victims of the Dresden raid. The town of Sagan, where I lived, and where StalagLuft III was located, was formally evacuated early in February. The trains filled with Sagan refugees sat in the Dresden rail yards when the bombers struck. At the time of the raid I had just turned ten and was living with strangers in Berlin, who were kind enough to allow my mother, sister Ingrid, and me to stay with them. It was their son, a young lieutenant, who had persuaded my mother to leave Sagan on the last train for Berlin on January 25, 1945. Dresden was also a European cultural jewel, and no one expected it would be bombed. Although Prime Minister Churchill approved the raid, he quickly distanced himself from it once its enormity was realized. Neither Air Chief Marshall Sir Arthur Harris nor the truly deserving airmen of Bomber Command were recognized for their sacrifices once the war ended. They were ignored, as if their contribution to the war's end was negligible. Negligible? Over 120,000 aircrew, British and from Commonwealth countries, served in RAF Bomber Command. They lost over 10,000 aircraft in raids against the Reich. Over 55,500 air crew died flying 364,000 sorties. More were wounded or became prisoners of war.

On the German side 593,000 civilians died in bombing raids during the war years from 1939 until 1945, according to the Federal Statistical Office in Wiesbaden. The majority of destruction and deaths occurred during the last year of war when the German air defense system collapsed. The Luftwaffe, at one time a formidable adversary, by late 1944 had lost most of its experienced air crews. Between January 1941 and June 1944 the Luftwaffe lost 31,000 airmen. Between June and October 1944 alone, in less than five months, the Luftwaffe lost 13,000 airmen.[107] In all of 1944, exclusive of the Eastern Front, the Luftwaffe lost 14,060 single engine fighters, not counting any other aircraft type.[108] No air force could stand losses on that scale. Finally, in late June 2012, a monument was unveiled in London's Green Park to honor the men of Bomber Command. The queen herself, Elizabeth II, was present for the unveiling. Mr. Giles MacDonogh, a British authority on German history, said when interviewed at the unveiling of the Bomber Command memorial: "Dresden is a metaphor for all the bombing, just as Coventry is for Britain. . . . It was reprehensible the way Harris devastated the cultural heart of Europe, let alone the terrible human toll. . . . Harris gave those orders. It is right to honor the brave fliers, but whether to honor Harris—that's another matter." Even in war, when commanders are vested with great authority, responsibility is the other side of the coin, and never to be forgotten.

Admittedly Bomber Command's raids against German cities left behind a wasteland. I remember walking down ruin-lined streets in Berlin, Munich, and Hannover during the postwar years. Not a sign of life to be seen anywhere. It was depressing, knowing the terror and death that led to this state. As I was training in Hannover in 1950 to become a baker, I lived in a renovated room in such a ruin. To get into my room I had to climb over a mound of rubble, walk through the burned-out shell of the house, down wet and rat-infested corridors, until I came to my room, which had no heat, only running cold water, and no light. I am not sure if the RAF's city bombing had a measurable effect on the war's outcome. Nor do many experts on the subject. Bernard Brodie, an American strategist, writes in *Strategy in the Missile Age*, "The bombing of German cities cost the Germans much in production and more in the diversion of military resources to defense; but we must nevertheless state that no critical shortages in war commodities of any kind are traceable to it. To cause inconvenience and unhappiness to the enemy is a reasonable military aim in war, but in view of the promises made by Douhet and his followers, and in view also of the great military resources invested in it, the urban-area bombing of World War II must be set down unequivocally as a failure."[109]

In contrast, even as a little boy, I could see the effects of the AAF bombing campaign. Gasoline became a rarity for civilian uses. Civilian and even some military trucks were modified so they could be powered by gas produced by a charcoal burner mounted in the back of vehicles. The horse, a World War I transportation staple, was a poor substitute for the lack of gasoline. Yet that is where the Wehrmacht had to turn if it wanted to keep moving. My uncle Alfred, a farmer, had to surrender half of his horses to the army, and make do with what was left. The same thing happened to every other German farmer, leaving them with the very old or very young animals to accomplish what they did before with a full stable. The first bombing by 8th Air Force B-17s I witnessed was in April 1944 against an aircraft assembly plant in the small town of Sorau, just a few kilometers from where I lived in Sagan. Not only did such bombings eventually deplete the inventory of the Luftwaffe, but in the raging air battles in which the 8th Air Force lost so many heavy bombers, they depleted, then totally destroyed the German fighter force as a viable instrument of war. Command of the air is what decided the outcome of war in Europe. *Command of the Air* was the title of Giulio Douhet's insightful book about strategic bombing, written long before there were any strategic bombers to implement such a concept. Where Douhet and the RAF missed was to focus on the wrong target set—intending to demoralize a nation into surrender by destroying their homes. Fortunately people, whether British, German, or any other nationality for that matter, always are more resilient than expected and adapt, even to terrible conditions, rather than surrender. In contrast to the RAF's Bomber Command, the Army Air Forces picked the right target set for its bombing campaign to bring Nazi Germany to its knees.

As for those American, British, and Commonwealth airmen who became prisoners of war—they were of course prisoners, confined to barracks, and to camps surrounded by barbed-wire fences, but largely treated fairly and in accordance with the provisions of the Geneva Convention. Writes Major General Delmar T. Spivey, USAF, deceased, in his recollections of his time in StalagLuft III: "Practically no one knows or believes that there were over 13,000 United States Air Force [Army Air Forces] flying officers fortunate enough to live through the hazards of being shot down over enemy territory and unfortunate enough to fall into enemy hands and into prisoner-of-war camps. Nor will many believe that almost to a man all of these officers returned to America after the war was over in good mental and physical health. Great numbers were killed during combat, some were killed by the Germans during or after capture, and some escaped into friendly hands, but those who fell into prisoner-of-war channels were, almost without exception, treated with considerable decency and respect by German military personnel." General Spivey was a colonel when shot down on August 12, 1943, and became one of the highest ranking AAF officers held by the Germans. The camp he was sent to was StalagLuft III, at Sagan, then Silesia, now a part of Poland.[110]

"Fighting Boredom, Not the Nazis" is the title of an article published in the November 8, 2012, issue of the *Wall Street Journal*. Writes Mark Yost, "While some POWs were assigned to work details, many of their days were defined by interminable boredom. Add to this the fact that living conditions were harsh and rations sparse. Diets, thankfully, were supplemented by some 27 million Red Cross packages that made their way by ship from Philadelphia to Marseille and then by rail into Germany." The National World War II Museum, founded by my friend Stephen Ambrose in New Orleans, has a comprehensive exhibit on American World War II POW experiences. "Until 1944, when Allied ground forces invaded Western Europe, about 90% of the American POWs in Europe were airmen shot down on bombing raids over Germany," writes Yost. After that their numbers grew to nearly 93,000. "Only about one percent, or 1,100, of US POWs held by the Germans died in captivity. By contrast, about 40 percent of the estimated 20,000 American prisoners held by the Japanese never made it home, and roughly half of the five million Russian prisoners held by the Nazis died in captivity."[111]

Defeating Hitler's Germany was the number one priority of the Allies, and most of the AAF assets were deployed to the ETO. General George C. Kenney, the commander of the Far East Air Forces (principally US and Australian) including the 5th, 7th, and 13th Air Force, fought a supportive war in the Pacific for most of the time. He operated on a shoestring supporting the Fleet, when called to do so, and General MacArthur's strategy of island hopping. The P-38 and its reconnaissance version, the F-5, were Kenney's best fighters, supplemented by the older P-40 and P-39 Airacobra. But what he put to best use were B-25s armed with multiple .50-caliber machine guns in the nose and

My friend Byron Schlag (L), in October 1999. A tail gunner on a B-17 of the 447th Bomb Group, he was shot down near Siegen on March 23, 1945. His chute did not open, yet he survived, falling into a haystack. Byron, along with most of his fellow flyers, has gone "west."

wings which decimated Japanese shipping. Once the war in Europe ended, General Carl Spaatz took command of the 20th Air Force and the 8th, which had moved from Paris, France, to the Pacific. Major General Curtis LeMay, who cut his teeth flying B-17s in Europe, had run the B-29 war against Japan before Spaatz moved his headquarters from Europe to the Mariana Islands. LeMay opted for low-level night attacks using incendiaries—which in effect burned down the greater part of Japan's industrial cities before the dropping of the atomic bombs on Hiroshima, August 6, and on Nagasaki, August 9. "In March 1945, Major General LeMay, then commanding the XXI Bomber Command, made one of the important decisions of the war—to attack Tokyo with incendiaries at low level at night with his full force. On the night of 9 March Tokyo was attacked by 279 B-29s at a mean bombing altitude of 7,050 feet. The Tokyo attack was followed by devastating night incendiary attacks on Nagoya, Kobe, and Osaka."[112] B-29 bomber losses were significantly lower than combat losses experienced by B-17s and B-24s in Europe. XXI Bomber Command lost 359 B-29s to all causes. Total AAF losses in the Pacific in combat were just over 4,000 aircraft, a fraction of the losses experienced in the ETO.[113]

Such was the larger context in which young airmen fought their individual battles. As General Sherman is said to have philosophized, "War is hell." And so it is. War is an ugly business, yet there are times when there are no other options to right a wrong. Poems, which I have used extensively to introduce each story, are a powerful shorthand to describe love and war and everything in between—so is music. I close this summary of undaunted courage with the haunting tunes young men of the World War II generation, who so quickly are passing from the scene, longingly listened to. It was Vera Lynn of course who could and would bring tears to a flyer's eyes singing "As Time Goes By," "Among My Souvenirs," "Something to Remember You By," and "Unforgettable." For those based in England she sang "The White Cliffs of Dover," "Lili Marlene," and "There'll Always Be an England." Charlie Johnson, a young 8th Air Force navigator shot down over Germany in the waning days of the war, said to me, "'I'll Be Seeing You' was my song, it was our song, it was the song of all of us who wanted to come home and had yet to live life."

NOTES

1. Kit C. Carter and Robert Mueller, *The Army Air Forces in World War II* (Washington, DC: HQ USAF), 314. Provides a listing of 8th Air Force targets on April 11, 1944.

2. 303rd BG (H) combat mission number 134; 11 April 1944, mission summary.

3. Arthur A. Durano, *StalagLuft III—The Secret Story of "The Great Escape."* (New York: Simon & Schuster: 1988). Chapter 17 provides a detailed description of the liberation of the men held in the overcrowded Moosburg POW camp.

4. *Army Air Forces Statistical Digest, World War II*, tables 35, 159, 160. Published by Headquarters Army Air Forces, Washington, DC, 1945, and available on the internet at maxwell. af.mil.

5. Wolfgang W. E. Samuel, *I Always Wanted to Fly: America's Cold War Airmen* (Jackson, MS: University Press of Mississippi, 2001), 96–103.

6. The *25th Tactical Reconnaissance Wing*, Wikipedia, provides a detailed history of the wing's organization, commanders, and equipment flown during World War II and in the postwar years. Interesting to me is that the wing, once reactivated in 1965 at Chambley, France, flew the RB/EB-66 aircraft, which Bob Walker flew as an acceptance test pilot and later on during the Vietnam War.

7. George R. Sesler, *Aerial Intelligence of the 8th Air Force* (Dallas, TX: Taylor Publishing, 1996), 89–90.

8. Ibid., 174–78.

9. Mission report, Headquarters 25th Bombardment Group (Reconnaissance), APO 634, Subject: Navigation Report on Operation Red Stocking 3/1, dated 2 March 1945. USAF/History Office files.

10. The Joan-Eleanor system consisted of a handheld transceiver (Joan) and a transceiver carried by an aircraft overhead (Eleanor), and used in OSS-directed missions flown by the 25th Bomb Group. The only books dealing with the employment of the J-E system in some depth are *Aerial Intelligence of the 8th Air Force*, *Piercing the Reich*, and Norman Malayney, *The 25th Bomb Group in World War II* (Atglen, PA: Schiffer Military History, 2011).

11. *Aerial Intelligence of the 8th Air Force*, 25–31, describes in some detail the OSS-related missions flown by Robert Walker in both the A-26 and the B-25. Especially detailed and interesting is the story of the agent named Bobbie who operated in German-occupied Holland. Bobbie, it appears, was the most successful and prolific provider of information of all the agents dropped by Walker and others in his squadron.

12. Joseph E. Persico, *Piercing the Reich* (New York: The Viking Press, 1979) makes fascinating reading of OSS operations against Nazi Germany. Again, Walker figures prominently in this description of the Hammer mission and the J-E program: 157–83, 211–13, and 318–20.

13. Interview with Clifford Parrott, Douglas Aircraft Corporation (Ret.).

14. Wolfgang W. E. Samuel, *Glory Days* (Atglen, PA: Schiffer Military History, 2008), 210–12.

15. Roger A. Freeman, *Mighty Eighth War Diary* (London: Jane's, 1981) provides a day-by-day listing of 8th Air Force operations against German-occupied Europe. Freeman, an authority on AAF operations out of England, readily admits that "[t]he figures given may sometimes be at variance with those in other published works. Even 8th Air Force records covering the same operation often have different sets of statistics."

16. Detlef Boelk, *Kiel im Luftkrieg 1939–1945* (Kiel, Germany: Gesellschaft fuer Kieler Stadtgeschichte, 1980) provides a detailed account of one German city's suffering during the Allied air war against Germany. The experience on the ground is very different from that in the air—in one word "horrifying."

17. Peter W. Stahl, *KG 200 The True Story* (London: Jane's, 1981) includes several pictures of B-17Gs and B-24Js, one of which was shot down by German antiaircraft guns.

18. *Contrails*, the 95th Bombardment Group's book of memories, provides detailed tables of all missions flown by the Group, results, and losses of aircraft and men. The first mission flown by the 95th was against St. Omer, France, with the results classified as fair to poor, but they didn't lose any aircraft. The last missions flown were those to drop food to the Dutch and retrieve American POWs from StalagLuft I—the mission numbers went from 321-1 to 321-8, the results being described as EXCELLENT, as they should have been. On mission number 321-6 to Utrecht/Hilversum, on May 7, 1945, one B-17 was lost in the North Sea due to engine failure, costing many young men their lives. The 95th lost a total of 157 B-17s in combat according to a listing published on the internet entitled 8th Air Force Combat Losses. The 95th Bomb Group in its own listing from mission number 1 to the final combat mission flown, including number 321-6, agrees, listing a total of 157 aircraft lost as well. Its heaviest loss was experienced on June 13, 1943, on mission number 9 against Kiel, when 10 aircraft and 103 men were lost.

19. *Santa Fe New Mexican*, "Aborted Rescue Haunts Santa Fe Pilot," December 29, 1997, 1 and 4.

20. Letter from General John D. Ryan, Chief of Staff USAF, to Colonel David M. Taylor, undated.

21. *Mighty Eighth War Diary*, 432.

22. Ibid., 468. Additional information related to the shoot down of Francis Taub's aircraft was provided by the 303rd Bomb Group Association's historian Harry D. Gobrecht, Missing Aircrew Report number 13569.

23. Hubert Zemke, *Zemke's Stalag* (Washington, DC: The Smithsonian Institution), 78–79.

24. Ibid., 112–14.

25. Ibid., 110. Zemke states in his book that there were "7,725 Americans in the camp at the time of our taking over from the Luftwaffe." He also noted that at that time there were "1,458 British and Commonwealth men" in the camp, for a total of 9,183 POWs.

26. Subject: "Plane #13 in Doolittle's Raid on Tokyo." Edgar McElroy's personal story of his participation in the Doolittle raid on Japan in April 1942. Pacific Aviation Museum, Pearl Harbor, Ford Island, Hawaii. Posted on the internet April 5, 2011, www.pacificaviationmuseum.org/pearl-harbor-blog/aircraft-13-on-the-doolittle-raid.

27. Wikipedia, the free encyclopedia (edirected from James H. Doolittle), wikipedia.org/wiki/James_H._Doolittle.

28. Jim Winchester, ed., *American Military Aircraft: A Century of Innovation* (New York: Barnes & Noble Books, 2005), 96–97. The Convair B-32 Dominator was an upgraded B-24 Liberator, built as insurance in case the B-29 did not meet performance standards. Only a limited number were built, flying very few combat missions. However, on August 18, 1945, a B-32 was attacked by rebelling Japanese fighter pilots while flying reconnaissance over Tokyo. One crewman was killed—the last American to be killed in World War II.

29. Matthew B. Ridgeway, *Soldier: The Memoirs of Matthew B. Ridgeway* (Westport, CT: Greenwood Press, 1956), 191.

30. James P. Finley, *The US Military Experience in Korea 1871–1982* (HQ US Forces Korea, APO SF 96301, 1983), 94–96.

31. Ibid., 96.

32. Kenneth O. Chilstrom, *Test Flying at Old Wright Field* (Omaha, NE: Westchester House, 1993), 239.

33. *Soldier: The Memoirs of Matthew B. Ridgeway*, 73. "The planes bearing the 504th came in over the invasion fleet just as a German air attack was ending. The guns of our fleet turned on the slow, low-flying aircraft, and the shore batteries took up the fire. We lost twenty-three planes that night and 97 men." Other sources say that over two hundred men died in this tragedy.

34. For details on Operation Lusty and the various German aircraft returned to the United States by Colonel Watson, see Wolfgang W. E. Samuel, *American Raiders: The Race to Capture the Luftwaffe's Secrets* (Jackson, MS: University Press of Mississippi, 2004).

35. *Test Flying at Old Wright Field*, 264–67.

36. Ibid., 197–98.

37. *American Raiders*, 338–43 relate the experiences of Robert Anspach and Richard Haynes when flying an Fw 190 and experiencing runaway trim. Anspach managed to land his plane and walk away from it; Lieutenant Haynes crashed and died.

38. *Test Flying at Old Wright Field*, 253–54.

39. Ibid., 80–82.

40. Ibid., 82–84.

41. Ibid., 121–22.

42. Although earlier statistics put the F-86 versus MiG 15 kill ratio at 17 to 1, that was a little over the top, so to speak. Reference *Air & Space Magazine*'s January 2014 issue: "In the 1970s, an Air Force study called 'Sabre Measures Charlie' upped the Sabre losses directly attributed to MiG combat to 92, which cut the F-86 kill ratio to 7-to-1." It may in fact have been even less. The MiG 15, although not faster than the F-86, could outclimb its adversary and had greater firepower. Yet it had many shortcomings, mostly addressed in the MiG 17, which entered the Soviet fighter inventory in 1954, after the Korean armistice. States *Air & Space*, "[W]hen Americans faced Soviet pilots who flew against the Luftwaffe . . . the kill ratio flattens out to a nearly even 1.4 to 1, slightly favoring the Sabre."

43. *Test Flying at Old Wright Field*, 239.

44. Although the official designation of the Me 109 and Me 110 was Bf 109 and Bf 110, as German boys my friends and I always referred to the 109 or 110 fighters as Me 109 or Me 110,

as did German air force personnel. So, Bob Slane's reference to Me 109 fighters in my estimation is quite acceptable.

45. *Mighty Eighth War Diary*, 126.

46. Ibid., 124.

47. *The Port Arthur News Chronicle*, "Another Chapter Written in Saga of Bomber Crash, 31 Years Ago," by Doug Ferguson, *Chronicle Journal* staff, 1987

48. Chuck Yeager and Leo Janos, *Yeager: An Autobiography* (New York: Bantam Books, 1985), 130.

49. John T. Bohn, *Development of Strategic Air Command 1946–1976* (Omaha, NE: HQ SAC, 1976), 35; *I Always Wanted to Fly*, 165.

50. *I Always Wanted to Fly*, 150–51. In the secret war of strategic reconnaissance, numerous reconnaissance aircraft, navy and air force, were lost to Soviet fighters. In 1950–53 one RB-45C, one P2V, three RB-29s, and one RB-50 were shot down by Soviet fighters over Korea/Sea of Japan.

51. *MHQ The Quarterly Journal of Military History*, Spring 1997, Volume 9, Number 3, "The Truth about Overflights," 25. R. Cargill Hall, historian of the NRO, writes: "During the first half of the 1950s, before the introduction of the U-2, the United States and its allies sent military aircraft on secret reconnaissance flights over the Soviet Union. They flew over Siberia and behind the Ural Mountains, photographed cities such as Stalingrad, Murmansk, and Vladivostok, and on occasion were engaged by Soviet interceptors. Not a single plane was lost. These were never rogue operations. Between 1951 and 1956, Presidents Truman and Eisenhower and Prime Minister Churchill periodically and on a case-by-case basis authorized these military overflights of the USSR and other 'denied territory.' The risks were great, but so were the intelligence payoffs."

52. Ibid., 38. "To this day, the SAC Thule missions remain one of the most incredible demonstrations of professional aviation skill ever seen in any military organization at any time."

53. William L. White, *The Little Toy Dog* (New York: E. P. Dutton, 1962) provides the detailed story of the shoot-down of Major Willard Palm's RB-47H on July 1, 1960, over the Barents Sea. Of the crew of six only Bruce Olmstead, the copilot, and navigator John McKone survived. Olmstead and McKone were held in the infamous Lubyanka prison in Moscow and released on January 24, 1961, after President Kennedy's inauguration, as a good-will gesture by Premier Nikita S. Khrushchev. Since ours were not combat missions flown during a declared war, we did not qualify for the Purple Heart, which was to be awarded if someone was injured or killed by enemy action. Nor did we qualify for the Silver Star, only to be awarded in wartime. We usually received Air Medals or the Distinguished Flying Cross if warranted. Olmstead and McKone were awarded the Silver Star years later by an act of Congress.

54. Lieutenant Colonel James Woolbright, an experienced RB-47H instructor pilot, had a maximum of six seconds to assess the loss of engine power and apply opposite rudder to keep the aircraft aligned with the runway. The B-47 could be an unforgiving aircraft on takeoffs and landings.

55. R. Cargill Hall, the former historian of the NRO, in chapter 4 of *Eye in the Sky: The Story of the Corona Spy Satellites* (Washington, DC: Smithsonian Institution Press, 1998) notes: "Description of the training and the missions flown have appeared in the memoirs and published recollections of RAF crew members. See, for instance, Squadron Leader John Crampton,

RAF (Ret.) 'The Royal Air Force RB-45C Special Duty flight, 1951–1954,' an address to the RAF Historical Society at the RAF Staff College, Bracknell, March 22, 1996."

56. *Mighty Eighth War Diary* and *Army Air Forces Statistical Digest*, World War II tables 35, 158, 159, 160; *The United States Strategic Bombing Survey—Statistical Appendix to Over-all Report.*

57. Michael Varley, "Aspects of the Combined British and American Strategic Air Offensive against Germany 1939 to 1945," 2010, homepage.ntlworld.com/r; Martin Middlebrook and Chris Everitt, *The Bomber Command War Diaries—An Operational Reference Book 1939–1945* (Midland Publishing, 1985); *Bomber Command: Churchill's Epic Campaign.*

58. *Mighty Eighth War Diary*, 252. Thirty-two B-17/B-24 bombers were lost that day, 211 were damaged, including one beyond repair, and 274 air crew went missing, died, or became prisoners of war.

59. Ibid., 272.

60. *American Raiders*, 105–6.

61. Ibid., 371–421.

62. Albert H. Davis, Russell J. Coffin, and Robert B. Woodward, *The 56th Fighter Group in World War II* (Washington, DC, 1948), 84.

63. Raymond F. Toliver, *Fighter General: The Life of Adolf Galland* (Zephyr Cove, NV: AmPress, 1990), 289.

64. *Yeager: An Autobiography*, 63.

65. *American Raiders*, 235–36.

66. *Zemke's Wolf Pack*, 177.

67. Kenneth O. Chilstrom interview, November 28, 2001, Palm Beach Gardens, Florida.

68. *526th Fighter Bomber Squadron History*, October 1944–October 1945.

69. *Fighter General: The Life of Adolf Galland*, 289–92.

70. Ibid.; *526th Fighter Bomber Squadron History.*

71. Robin Olds, *Fighter Pilot* (New York: St Martin's Press, 2010), 57.

72. *Test Flying at Old Wright Field*, 187–90.

73. *Fighter Pilot*, 19.

74. Ibid., 20–21.

75. General James Doolittle introducing Bob Hoover at the Monterey County air show, 1988.

76. Robert A. Hoover, *Forever Flying* (New York: Pocket Books, 1996), an autobiography.

77. Delmar T. Spivey, *POW Odyssey* (Cambridge, MA: Harvard University Press, 1984), 1–6.

78. Ibid., 49.

79. Military Intelligence Service, War Department: *American Prisoners of War in Germany, StalagLuft III.*

80. *StalagLuft III*, 357–63.

81. *Soldier: The Memoirs of Matthew B. Ridgeway*, 73.

82. Gebhard Aders, *History of the German Night Fighter Force 1917–1945* (London: Jane's, 1979), 206–14.

83. *Test Flying at Old Wright Field*, 173, 266; *American Raiders*, 22–23.

84. *POW Odyssey*, 24–25.

85. From Dailies of the 323rd Squadron, 1944, 91st Bomb Group (H), transcribed by Nancy Perri.

86. "Phil Lamason," from Wikipedia, the free encyclopedia, 1–12. Squadron Leader Phillip Lamason's efforts, and probably complementary efforts initiated by the senior officers at Stalag-Luft III, reached Goering's personal staff and eventually led to the release of the Allied airmen from the Buchenwald concentration camp.

87. "Hannes Trautloft," from Wikipedia, the free encyclopedia, 1–5.

88. "Floyd R. Jensen's Southwest Pacific Tour of Duty February 1944 to May 1945," Vanderford family web site, vanderfordfamily.com.

89. Stephen E. Ambrose, *The Wild Blue* (New York: Simon & Schuster, 2001), 78.

90. Pre-World War II Air Planning, Richard H. Kohn, AF/HO letter to General O'Malley, AF/XO, HQ USAF, Washington, DC, April 13, 1982.

91. Tom Philo, "Eighth Air Force Combat Losses in World War II," personal study, Beaverton, OR, 2008, 2. The losses listed for the 100th BG in this document are corroborated by the 100th BG web page.

92. James D. Hornfisher, "The Passing of the World War II Generation," *Wall Street Journal* (May 28/29, 2011), C5–C6.

93. Martin E. James, *Historical Highlights USAFE 1945–1979*, HQ, USAFE, APO NY 09012, 1980, 4; letter Kohn to O'Malley, April 13, 1982.

94. *The Army Air Forces in World War II*, 24.

95. *Mighty Eighth War Diary*, 10. Major Paul Tibbets with Colonel, later General, Frank A. Armstrong, flew *Butcher Shop*, a B-17E, assigned to the 340th Bomb Squadron, 97th Bomb Group. The B-17Es were withdrawn from combat operations as soon as later model aircraft arrived and assigned to tow targets and perform transport duties.

96. Ibid., 34–161.

97. Max Hastings, *Bomber Command—Churchill's Epic Campaign* (New York: Simon & Schuster, 1989), 94.

98. *The United States Strategic Bombing Survey, Statistical Appendix to Overall Report (European War)*, Washington, DC, February 1947, 2.

99. *The United States Army Air Forces in WW II*, statistical digest, tables 35, 159, 160.

100. *Behind the Wire: Allied Airmen in German Captivity*, Al Zimmerman, writer/producer, produced by the Eighth Air Force Historical Society, 1996, excerpts by the US Air Force Academy: StalagLuft III—Aerial Combat. Hell's Angels—303rd Bomb Group—German POW Camps with 303rd BG(H) Prisoners.

101. *Aspects of the Combined British and American Strategic Air Offensive against Germany*, 19.

102. *The Bomber Command War Diaries*, 708–12.

103. *Bomber Command*, 267.

104. *The Wild Blue*, p 111.

105. Ibid., 100.

106. *Bomber Command*, 340.

107. Ibid., 336.

108. *The United States Strategic Bombing Survey*, Statistical Appendix (European War), 99.

109. Bernard Brodie, *Strategy in the Missile Age* (Princeton, NJ: Princeton University Press, 1965), 124.

110. *POW Odyssey*, xi–xii.

111. Mark Yost, "Fighting Boredom, Not the Nazis," *Wall Street Journal* (November 8, 2012), D7.

112. H. H. Arnold, *Third Report of the Commanding General of the Army Air Forces to the Secretary of War*, November 12, 1945, 37.

113. Ibid., 64.

INTERVIEWS AND PHOTOGRAPHS

Interviews

Robert Anspach

Harold R. Austin

Chasten L. Bowen

Chasten L. Bowen, United States Holocaust Museum interview

Roy W. Brown

Kenneth O. Chilstrom

Byron A. Dobbs

Arthur Exon

Joseph J. Gyulavics

Robert S. Hamill

Patrick Harbison

Robert A. Hoover

Charles P. Johnson

Frederick Leiby

Frederick Leiby, interview by Ann Apleton

Frederick McIntosh

Marion C. Mixson

Charles M. Myers, Jr.

Bernard T. Nolan

Samuel E. Pizzo

Herbert Schaefer

Charles E. Schreffler

James F. Setchell Jr.*

Robert C. Strobell

David M. Taylor

Albert S. J. Tucker Jr.

Robert P. Walker

Lloyd M. N. Wenzel

Russell B. Witte

*Interview was conducted with the son of Colonel James F. Setchell.

Photographs

Photographs came from the personal collection of the author and from the following individuals and organizations:

Lieutenant Colonel Robert J. Anspach, USAF (Ret.)
Colonel Harold R. Austin, USAF (Ret.)
Roy W. Brown
Colonel Kenneth O. Chilstrom, USAF (Ret.)
Lieutenant Colonel Byron A. Dobbs, USAF (Ret.)
Martin Frauenstein
Colonel Joseph J. Gyulavics, USAF (Ret.)
Colonel Robert S. Hamill, USAF (Ret.)
John Hay
Robert A. Hoover
Charles P. Johnson
Anthony Kambic
Colonel Marion C. Mixson, USAF (Ret.)
Charles E. Myers, Jr.
Lieutenant Colonel Bernard T. Nolan, USAF (Ret.)
Colonel Samuel E. Pizzo, USAF (Ret.)
Colonel Charles E. Schreffler, USAF (Ret.)
James F. Setchell
Raul Sifuente
Colonel Robert M. Slane, USAF (Ret.)
Lieutenant Colonel Robert C. Strobell, USAF (Ret.)
Colonel David M. Taylor, USAF (Ret.)
Colonel Albert S. Tucker, USAF (Ret.)
David Vuich
Mrs. Ruth Watson, the widow of Major General Harold Watson
Colonel Lloyd M. N. Wenzel, USAF (Ret.)
Russell B. Witte
The B-66 Association and its membership

BIBLIOGRAPHY

"Aborted Rescue Haunts Santa Fe Pilot," *Santa Fe New Mexican*, December 29, 1997: A1, A4.

Acheson, Dean. *Present at the Creation*. New York: Norton, 1969.

Aders, Gebhard. *History of the German Night Fighter Force 1917–1945*. London: Jane's, 1979.

Ambrose, Stephen E. *The Wild Blue: The Men and Boys Who Flew the B-24s over Germany*. New York: Simon & Schuster, 2001.

Andrews, Paul M. *We're Poor Little Lambs*. Springfield, VA: Foxfall Press, 1995.

Army Air Forces Statistical Digest, World War II, Tables 35, 159, 160. HQ Army Air Forces, Washington, DC, 1945, maxwell.af.mil.

Arnold, H. H. *Third Report of the Commanding General of the Army Air Forces to the Secretary of War*. Baltimore: Schneidereith & Sons, Baltimore, November 12, 1945.

Austin, Harold R. "A Cold War Overflight of the USSR." *Daedalus Flyer* 35 (Spring 1995): 15–18.

Bahn, Eugene, ed. *Yanks in Britain: A Book of Verse and Poetry Written by Men and Women of the U.S. Forces Who Served in the E.T.O. 1942–1945*. London, England: The Daily Mail, 1945.

Bailey, Bruce M. *We See All: A History of the 55th Strategic Reconnaissance Wing, 1947–1967.* 55th Elint Association Historian, 1982.

Berlin Airlift: A USAFE Summary 24 June 1948–30 September 1949. Headquarters USAFE, Wiesbaden, Germany, 1949.

Blum, Allen H. *War Diary of a Lieutenant Colonel, 1943–1944*. Unpublished manuscript in possession of the author.

Boelk, Detlef. *Kiel im Luftkrieg 1939–1945*. Kiel, Germany: Gesellschaft fuer Kieler Stadtgeschichte, 1980.

Bohn, John T. *Development of Strategic Air Command 1946–1976*. Headquarters SAC, Offutt AFB, Omaha, NE, 1976.

Brodie, Bernard. *Strategy in the Missile Age*. Princeton, NJ: Princeton University Press, 1965.

Carter, Kit C. and Robert Mueller. *The Army Air Forces in World War II, Combat Chronology 1941–1945*. Washington, DC: Office of Air Force History, Headquarters USAF, 1973.

Chilstrom, Kenneth O. *Test Flying at Old Wright Field*. Omaha, NE: Westchester House Publishers, 1993.

Davis, Albert H., Russell J. Coffin, and Robert B. Woodward. *The 56th Fighter Group in World War II*. Washington, DC: Infantry Journal Press, 1948.

Durano, Arthur A. *StalagLuft III: The Secret Story of "The Great Escape."* New York: Simon & Schuster, 1988.

Ferrell, Robert H., ed. *The Twentieth Century: An Almanac.* New York: World Almanac Publications, 1985.

Finley, James P. *The US Military Experience in Korea, 1871–1982.* Headquarters, US Forces Korea, APO SF 96301, 1983.

Frater, Stephen. *Hell Above Earth.* New York: St. Martin's Press, 2012.

Frederiksen, Oliver J. *The American Military Occupation of Germany, 1945–53.* HQ US Army, Europe, APO 164, 1953.

Freeman, Roger A. *Mighty Eighth War Diary.* London: Jane's, 1981.

General Marshall's Report—The Winning of the War in Europe and the Pacific, Biennial Report of the Chief of Staff of the United States Army 1943 to 1945, to the Secretary of War. Published for the War Department in cooperation with the Council on Books in Wartime, Washington, DC, Simon & Schuster, 1945.

Hall, Cargill R. *Early Cold War Overflights 1950–1956, Symposium Proceedings, Volume II: Appendixes.* Office of the Historian, National Reconnaissance Office, Washington, DC, 2003.

———. *NRO History—Early Cold War Strategic Reconnaissance.* Office of the Historian, National Reconnaissance Office, Washington, DC, 2003.

Hanak, Walter, ed. *Aces & Aerial Victories: The U.S. Air Force in Southeast Asia 1965–1973.* Washington, DC: HQ US Air Force, 1976.

Hansell, Haywood S. *The Air Plan That Defeated Hitler.* Maxwell AFB, AL: Air University, 1973.

Hastings, Max. *Bomber Command: Churchill's Epic Campaign.* New York: Touchstone, Simon & Schuster, 1989.

Henderson, David B. *The 95th Bombardment Group H United States Army Air Forces.* The 95th Group Photographic Section, US Army Air Forces, 1945.

Hoover, Robert A. *Forever Flying.* New York: Pocket Books, 1996.

Hornfisher, James D. "The Passing of the World War II Generation," *Wall Street Journal* (May 28/29): 2011.

James, Martin E. *Historical Highlights: United States Air Forces in Europe, 1945–1979.* Office of History, Headquarters USAFE, APO New York, 0i9012, 1980.

Johnson, Charles P. *Memoirs of a Navigator: WWII.* Pittsburgh: Rose Dog Books, 2003.

Kohn, Richard H. Chief, Office of Air Force History, Letter to Lt/General Jerome F. O'Malley AF/XO. Subject: Pre-World War II Air Planning, HQ USAF, Bolling AFB, DC., April 13, 1982.

Lopez, Donald S. *Fighter Pilot's Heaven: Flight Testing the Early Jets.* Washington, DC: Smithsonian Books, 1995.

———. *Into the Teeth of the Tiger.* Washington, DC: Smithsonian Books, 1997.

Makos, Adam. *A Higher Call.* New York: Penguin Group, 2012.

Mast, Burdette P. *A Special Study of Operation Vittles.* Aviation Operations, New York: Conover-Mast, 1949.

Middlebrook, Martin, and Chris Everitt. *The Bomber Command War Diaries—An Operational Reference Book 1939–1945.* Midland Publishing Ltd, 1985.

Military Intelligence Service, War Department, Captured Personnel and Materiel Branch, Special War Problems Division: *American Prisoners of War in Germany, StalagLuft III.* Washington, DC, November 1, 1945.

Mitcham, Samuel W., and Friedrich von Staufenberg. *The Battle of Sicily.* New York: Orion Books, 1991.

Neillands, Robin. *The Bomber War: The Allied Air Offensive Against Nazi Germany.* New York: Barnes & Noble, 2001.

Nolan, Bernard T. *Isaiah's Eagles Rising.* Xlibris.com, 2002.

Olds, Robin. *Fighter Pilot: The Memoirs of Legendary Ace Robin Olds.* New York: St. Martin's Press, 2010.

Persico, Joseph. *Piercing the Reich: The Penetration of Nazi Germany by American Secret Agents During World War II.* New York: The Viking Press, 1979.

Philo, Tom. "8th Air Force Combat Losses in World War II," personal study. Beaverton, OR, 2008.

Pizzo, Samuel. *As Good as It Gets.* Tommy Towery Publisher, 2008.

Ridgeway, Matthew B. *Soldier: The Memoirs of Matthew B. Ridgeway.* Westport, CT: Greenwood Press Publishers, 1956.

Samuel, Wolfgang W. E. *I Always Wanted to Fly: America's Cold War Airmen.* Jackson, MS: University Press of Mississippi, 2001.

———. *American Raiders: The Race to Capture the Luftwaffe's Secrets.* Jackson, MS: University Press of Mississippi, 2004.

———. *Glory Days: The Untold Story of the Men who Flew the B-66 Destroyer into the Face of Fear.* Atglen, PA: Schiffer Military History, 2008.

———. *Watson's Whizzers: Operation Lusty and the Race for Nazi Military Technology.* Atglen, PA: Schiffer Military History, 2010.

Sesler, George R. *An Accounting of the 25th Bomb Group (RCN, SP), 8th Air Force, WW II, Watton, England 1944–1945.* Dallas, TX: Taylor Publishing Company, 1996.

Setchell, James F. Diary of World War II operations in ETO—1943–1944; letters and notes.

Slane, Robert M. *Journey to Freedom and Beyond.* Victoria, BC, Canada: Trafford Publishing, 2004.

Spivey, Delmar T. *POW Odyssey—Recollections of Center Compound, StalagLuft III and the Secret German Peace Mission in World War II.* Cambridge, MA: Harvard University Press, 1984.

Stahl, Peter W. *KG 200, The True Story.* London: Jane's, 1981.

Stanaway, John, and Bob Rocker. *The Eight Ballers: Eyes of the Fifth Air Force.* Atglen, PA: Schiffer Military History, 1999.

The United States Army Air Forces in World War II. Washington, DC: AAF, War Department, 1945.

The United States Strategic Bombing Survey, Statistical Appendix to Over-All Report (European War), Washington, DC: Department of War, February 1947.

Toliver, Raymond F. *Fighter General: The Life of Adolf Galland.* Zephyr Cove, NV: AmPress Publishing, 1990.

United States Air Force Combat Victory Credits Southeast Asia. Washington, DC: Office of Air Force History, US Air Force, 1974.

Varley, Michael. An independent paper: "Aspects of the Combined British and American Strategic Air Offensive against Germany 1939 to 1945." homepage.ntlworld.com/r_m_g.varley/strategic_air_offensive.html, 2005, revised 2010.

White, William L. *The Little Toy Dog*. New York: E. P. Dutton & Co., 1962.

Winchester, Jim (general editor). *American Military Aircraft: A Century of Innovation*. New York: Barnes & Noble Books, 2005.

Yeager, Chuck, and Leo Janos. *Yeager: An Autobiography*. New York: Bantam Books, 1985.

Yost, Mark. "Fighting Boredom, Not the Nazis." *Wall Street Journal* (November 8, 2012), D7.

Zemke, Hubert. *Zemke's Stalag*. Washington, DC: The Smithsonian Institution, 1991.

———. *Zemke's Wolf Pack*. New York: Orion Books, 1988.

526th Fighter-Bomber Squadron, 86th Fighter-Bomber Group, history October 1944–October 1945, Headquarters, 526th Fighter Squadron, 86th Fighter Group, APO 650/374.

INDEX

Index